Sardis from
Prehistoric
to Roman Times

S A R D I S

from Prehistoric to Roman Times

GEORGE M. A. HANFMANN
assisted by W I L L I A M E. M I E R S E

with contributions by
Clive Foss, Jeffrey Spier, Andrew Ramage,
Sidney M. Goldstein, Robin U. Russin,
Louis Robert, Fikret K. Yegül,
John S. Crawford, Andrew R. Seager,
A. Thomas Kraabel, Hans Buchwald

Results of the Archaeological
Exploration of Sardis
1958–1975

H A R V A R D U N I V E R S I T Y P R E S S
Cambridge, Massachusetts
and London, England
1983

D
156
S3
A8
1983

The publication of this volume was made possible
by grants and subventions from the Samuel H.
Kress Foundation, the Loeb Classical Library
Foundation, and the George M. A. Hanfmann
Publication Fund, Harvard University; and by a
grant from the Publication Program, Division of
Research Programs, of the National Endowment
for the Humanities.

**Library of Congress Cataloging in Publication
Data**

Archaeological Exploration of Sardis (1958–   )
  Sardis from prehistoric to Roman times.

  Includes bibliographies and index.
  1. Sardis (Ancient city)--Addresses, essays,
lectures. I. Hanfmann, George Maxim Anossov,
1911– . II. Mierse, William E. III. Foss,
Clive. IV. Title.
D156.S3A8 1983   939'.2   82-9307
ISBN 0-674-78925-3   AACR2

Book design/Edith Allard, Designworks

Contents

Preface

In the history of mankind there are centers of millennial duration whose leadership remained significant over many generations and a succession of cultures. Of such centers Rome is the prime example. There are other great communities that, though of long duration, only briefly held center stage. For classical antiquity, Sardis was the paradigm of this type. The new knowledge gained by some twenty years of research at the site by the Archaeological Exploration of Sardis presents a challenge to attempt a synthesis that would make accessible to the generally interested public the archaeological results and their potential interest and to give to specialists a preview of what may be expected from the final publication.

The specific impulse to begin this attempt came in 1975 when Dr. Ronald Berman, then Chairman of the National Endowment for the Humanities, suggested that a synthesis of the first seventeen seasons might be helpful. Subsequent discussions with Dr. P. N. Marcus and Mr. Mark Kontos of the Research Grants Division of the Endowment resulted in the decision that the Archaeological Exploration of Sardis would pub-lish a one-volume work entitled *Synthesis, Summation, and Interpretation of the Major Results and Accomplishments of the Sardis Program.*

In principle the present volume encompasses only the results of the eighteen campaigns undertaken at Sardis by the Harvard-Cornell Archaeological Exploration of Sardis under the field directorship of George M. A. Hanfmann (1958–1975) and A. Henry Detweiler (1958–1970). These campaigns are designated by the Sardis Expedition as "Stage I." Fieldwork at Sardis has continued since 1976 under C. H. Greenewalt, Jr., in a series of campaigns designated as "Stage II." Annual reports of these campaigns must be consulted for the latest results.

The present study has three major aims. The first is to make known in brief and preliminary form the major results attained by the Harvard-Cornell Expedition from 1958 through 1975. The second aim is for the study to serve as a guide to scholarly and scientific work that bears on various aspects of the expedition, whether published in the Sardis Series of final publications or elsewhere. As far as the tentative conclusions of research still in progress permit, the third aim is to interpret the significance of the results for our knowledge of the cultural pattern of the various periods, especially the Lydian-Persian (ca. 1000–334 B.C.), the Hellenistic (334 B.C. to A.D. 17), and the Roman–Late Antique (ca. A.D. 17–616). We shall not, in principle, include the Byzantine and Turkish periods. They have been synthesized in a well-documented study by Clive Foss (*Sardis* M4, *Byzantine and Turkish Sardis,* 1976).

On many aspects definitive results cannot be expected until the detailed specialized researches on the various excavation areas and groups of finds have been completed. This interim summary is designed to help orient the scholars and the public about the results of one of the major American archaeological projects of our times.

From the beginning it was the principle of the Harvard-Cornell Expedition that the most important results should be reported and illustrated promptly. These reports are listed in the Bibliography. With some exceptions imposed by request of individual collaborators, the Sardis program made its results freely available to interested qualified scholars. As far as they had become known to us, the resulting articles were listed in the annual report.[1] Greek inscriptions found at Sardis or relating to Sardis were reported annually by Louis Robert and Jeanne Robert in their famous "Bulletin Épigraphique" reports, appearing in *Revue des Études Grecques* (*REG*).[2]

In 1967, after a decade of excavations, the Archaeological Exploration of Sardis proposed to Harvard University Press a plan of final publication of the results. It envisaged two series, the *Reports* and the *Monographs*. The *Reports* contain the evidence of excavation, accounts of conservation and restoration activities, and certain major categories of excavated objects. The *Monographs* include categories of objects best treated in monograph format and special subjects supplementing the *Reports.*

In addition to the publication of special categories of material, the *Monograph* series contains studies that unfold broader historical views.

Since the present attempt at summation comes in midstream of our final publication process, we shall draw not only on published volumes but also on manuscripts as yet unpublished as well as on field reports and field records. A listing of *Reports* and *Monographs* published and forthcoming will be found in the Bibliography. Other relevant publications are briefly surveyed in a Bibliographic Note that precedes the Bibliography.

The manuscript as envisaged in 1978–1979 was to include a chapter on objects. It became obvious, however, that a satisfactory treatment of objects could not be undertaken within the scope of one chapter. Because the manuscript had already exceeded the limits of financial viability and because reports on certain categories were not forthcoming, it was decided to eliminate that chapter. This omission meant grave injustice to the authors of several excellent accounts, whose names and subjects appear below. Their contributions are included in the Appendix on "Major Types of Evidence" in a longer version of this study, of which the typescript is on deposit with the Sardis Research Facility and Harvard University Library.

These scholarly contributions are as follows: "Metalwork," by J. C. Waldbaum; "Coins," by G. M. A. Hanfmann; "Pottery, Corinthian," by J. S. Schaeffer; "Pottery, Attic," by N. H. Ramage; "Pottery, Hellenistic," by A. Oliver, Jr.; "Pottery, Byzantine Glazed," by J. A. Scott; "Pottery, Glazed, of Turkish Period," by H. G. Crane; "Traditional Pottery Making in the Sardis Region," by H. G. Crane; "Multiple Analysis of Clays, Glazes, and Slips," by D. C. Kamilli; "Hellenistic Terracotta Figurines from Sardis," by R. S. Thomas; "The Sector Pactolus North: Architecture of the Turkish Period," by H. G. Crane. Interested scholars may consult these studies and the entire long version subject to the usual safeguards for unpublished material.

We have incurred many debts of gratitude in the course of preparing this work. Our first thanks must go to the National Endowment for the Humanities. Beginning in a critical moment,

---

1. Usually listed in the first footnote in *BASOR* reports from 1959 through 1973, and listed after the report in later *BASOR* issues.

2. The references for "Bulletin Épigraphique" from 1938 through 1960 are cited in *Titres et Travaux de Louis Robert* (Athens 1961; no publisher or other details). An index for the years 1938 through 1965 has been compiled by J. Pouilloux. At the time of writing (1978), the most recent "Bulletins Épigraphiques" were *REG* 90 (July–December 1977) 314–448; 91 (July–December 1978) 385–509.

the Endowment ensured the survival of the Sardis program, which has been described by one Turkish expert as "one of the major archaeological enterprises of the twentieth century." The actual grants are listed below.[3] Our special gratitude goes to the friends and foundations who enabled the project to receive the Endowment's support through their matching contributions. The Endowment also helped us to complete this book by a supplementary grant for research assistance. In accordance with the expressed wishes of the Endowment we state that nothing in this publication should be construed as representing the views of the Endowment. It may be emphatically stated, however, as the senior author's personal point of view, that the policy of long-term continuous support of major American research efforts abroad and their final publication is still an objective that has not become clearly established with United States government authorities. Such long-term investment is an absolute necessity if this nation is to play a cultural part commensurate with its general significance in the modern world.

It is because of the enlightened and generous policy toward foreign scholars of our host country, Turkey, that we had the privilege to work at Sardis. For the period under review (1957–1975), we were supervised and aided by the Department of Antiquities and Museums, until 1970 under the Ministry of National Education, then under the Ministry of the Prime Minister and Ministry of Culture (1974–1975). We pay tribute to the devoted aid of the various Directors General, Associate and Assistant Directors and their staff and to the Government Representatives attached to the expedition.

Other Ministries were ready to assist in special needs, as the Ministry of Waterworks did in the regulation of the Pactolus torrent in order to save the precinct of Artemis, and the Ministry of Mines in the dispatch of a consultant to supervise a tunneling operation in the royal mound of Gyges. It is impossible here to describe the variety and multiplicity of forms of Turkish cooperation. Our detailed official acknowledgments are

3. NEH Grants to Sardis: H67-0-56; H68-0-61; H69-0-23; RO-111-70-3966; RO-4999-71-171; RO-6435-71-264; RO-8359-73-217; RO-10405-74-319; RO-23511-76-541; RP-10050-80-0387; RO-20047-81-0230; RP-20247-81-2162.

to be found in our preliminary reports and final publications, and, in a more informal vein, in the *Letters from Sardis,* but it deserves to be noted that from the very first season Turkish students took part in our work. By the end of 1975, some seventy Turkish scholars, scientists, and students had worked with us.

On the American side, the successive Consuls, then Consuls General of the United States in Izmir, were always willing to assist to the limits of their possibilities. In this country, the grant of funds in Turkish currency by the Department of State (1962–1965) was a pioneering venture; its greatest benefit was a regular training program for Turkish student trainees, several of whom became valued colleagues in the Sardis work, notably M. C. Bolgil, F. K. Yegul, M. T. Ergene, and Teoman Yalçinkaya.

It was the matching grant from the Bollingen Foundation, given to Harvard and Cornell in 1957, that was decisive in making it possible for G. M. A. Hanfmann and A. H. Detweiler to start the Sardis operation. Subsequently, the Old Dominion Foundation, the Ford Foundation (for student fellowships only), the Loeb Classical Library Foundation, the Memorial Foundation of Jewish Culture, the Charles E. Merrill Trust, and the Billy Rose Foundation made major contributions to our work at various times. University Funds were given by Cornell University. The Corning Museum of Glass became a participant in 1960. It is, however, no exaggeration to say that it was the constant support of private individual and corporate friends of the Sardis program, known as Supporters of Sardis, that provided an unbroken thread of financial continuity and a steadying balance against the fluctuations of government and foundation funding.

Through the liberality of the present Field Director, C. H. Greenewalt, Jr., Ilse Hanfmann and G. M. A. Hanfmann were able to revisit Sardis during the season of 1981 and review the results of 1976 to 1981. Greenewalt and his staff also generously permitted the several authors of this book to mention new discoveries.

In the writing of this book, my greatest debt is to William E. Mierse. Appearing at a critical juncture, he was so much willing to make the project in a very real sense his own responsibility that he soon emerged as the logical coauthor. My other collaborators, who had agreed to contribute accounts of their Sardian specialties, deserve much credit for their cooperation in the face of new demands and long delays. My successor as Executive Director, J. A. Scott, facilitated the progress of the work in every way. Illustrations, unless otherwise credited in the captions, are reproduced courtesy of the Archaeological Exploration of Sardis.

Work on preparation of this book was carried on by W. E. Mierse under two extensions to the NEH grant RO-23511-76-541 and on Sardis Expedition funds by Amy Brauer and S. M. Darlington, who worked with much devotion in difficult times to get the book into the production stage. Elizabeth Wahle completed the final work on illustrations. Mary Whallon guided the work on proof and indexes. Gregory Crane indexed the ancient authors and inscriptions.

Because this book presents itself as a collaborative venture with a coauthor and ten contributors, it is perhaps only fair to recall that the senior author, G. M. A. Hanfmann, is responsible for the overall concept and has critically examined and edited every chapter and section. While some differences of opinion and unresolved problems remain, in general this work may be considered as representative of his overall interpretation of Sardis achievements and results for the time under review.

Howard Crosby Butler (1872–1922) and his first Sardis Expedition (1910–1914, 1922) are mentioned but not discussed anywhere in this book. I have memorialized their achievements in the first Sardis *Report,* but it seems appropriate to acknowledge that much of the present synthesis incorporates Butler's results.

In connection with the publication of this book, the senior author feels a particular obligation to J. A. Scott, D. G. Mitten, and Amy Brauer, who organized the effort on behalf of a G. M. A. Hanfmann publication fund, and to J. R. Cherry, L. T. Clay, M. M. Davis, A. H. Houghton, Jr., T. B. Lemann, F. D. Murphy, Marilyn Perry, Norbert Schimmel, Alice Tully, and two anonymous donors for their generous help.

We regret that no bibliographic references that reached us after spring 1981 could be included.

October 1982   George M. A. Hanfmann

Technical Abbreviations and Terminology

General Technical Abbreviations

ca.	circa	P.diam.	preserved diameter
cm.	centimeters	P.H.	preserved height
D.	depth	P.L.	preserved length
diam.	diameter	P.W.	preserved width
esp.	especially	r.	right
est.	estimated	sq.m.	square meters
H.	height	Th.	thickness
km.	kilometers	W.	width
L.	length	Whitmore	report on examination of marble at Museum of Fine Arts, Boston
l.	left		
m.	meters (unless noted otherwise, all dimensions are in m.)	* (preceding numeral)	level (e.g., *98.00)
max.	maximum		
mm.	millimeters		

Object Abbreviations

In addition to the General Technical Abbreviations listed above, the following abbreviations were used for object categories:

BI	Bone-ivory	NoEx	Not from the excavations
C	Coin	P	Pottery
G	Glass	S	Sculpture
IN	Inscriptions	S.	Stone sample slide number
L	Lamp	T	Terracotta
M	Metal objects	WP	Wall painting
Ms	Mosaics		

The usual method of citation is category abbreviation followed by year and running inventory number: P 58.38, or M 58.22:224.

Sector Abbreviations

For more complete sector information see *Sardis* R1 (1975) 13–16; for locations of abbreviated items see Fig. 8.

Ac	Acropolis	E	Church E at PN
AcN	N spur of Ac	EA	Church EA at PN
AcS	S spur of Ac	EB	Eski Balikhane
AcT	Top of Ac	ERd	East Road
AhT	Ahlatli Tepecik	HoB	House of Bronzes and Lydian Trench area
AT	Artemis Temple		
B	Gymnasium-Bath complex	KG	Kâgirlik Tepe Cemetery
BCH	Central hall of B	L	Building complex SW of AT
BE	Eastern area of B		
BE-A, BE-B, BE-C, BE-D, BE-E	Rooms S of BE-H and BE-S	LA	Altar of Artemis W of AT
		LNH 1–3	Long N hall N of Pa at B
BE-AA, BE-BB, BE-CC, BE-DD, BE-EE	Rooms N of BE-H and BE-N	LVC	Large vaulted chamber at PC
		M	Church M
BE-H	Hall with pool W of MC	MC	Marble Court at B
BE-N	Room N of MC	MD	Magara Deresi
BE-S	Room S of MC	MMS	Monumental mudbrick structure
BK	Başliogluköy		
Bldg. A	Roman civic center(?)	MRd	Main Avenue (Main Road)
Bldg. C	Roman basilica		
Bldg. D	Church D	MTE	Middle Terrace East, trench S of HoB
BNH	N apsidal hall of central part of B	MTW	Middle Terrace West, trench S of HoB
BS E 1–19	Byzantine Shops, E shops from E 1, S of BE-A, to E 19, S of porch E of Syn Fc	NEW	Northeast Wadi
		NSB	Stelai bases set up along N side of LA
		Pa	Palaestra E of MC at B
BS W 1–13	Byzantine Shops, W shops from W 1, at SW corner of BE-A, to W 13, S of latrines	Pa-E, Pa-W, Pa-N, Pa-S	E, W, N, S corridors of Pa
		PBr	Pactolus Bridge
		PC	Pactolus Cliff
BSH	S apsidal hall of central part of B	PHB	Hypocaust Building
		PIA	Pactolus Industrial Area
BT	Bin Tepe Cemetery	PN	Pactolus North
BW	Western area of B	PT	Peacock Tomb
BWH	Central hall of BW	R	Building R and Tetrapylon(?)
BWN Area	Northern part of BW		
BWS Area	Southern part of BW	RT	Road Trench
CG	Roman bath (formerly "City Gate")	SSB	Stelai bases set up along S side of LA
		SVC	Small vaulted chamber at PC
CW	City Wall		
DU	Duman Tepe	SWG	Southwest Gate

Syn	Synagogue	UT	Upper Terrace at HoB
Syn Fc	Forecourt of Syn	WRd	West Road
Syn MH	Main hall of Syn	* (preceding numeral)	level (e.g. *98.00)
Trench S	Trench S of AT		
TU	Tunnel in N face of Ac		

Note on Grids and Levels

Since it proved impossible to retrieve the data which had served for a Princeton survey in 1913, a new survey in a scale of 1:2000 was made in 1962 by A. Sait Tukun of the Board of Waterworks. It extended for 2.8 km. west/east and 2.2 km. north/south. It covered approximately the area shown in our site plan (Fig. 8) and did not take in a large part of the western cemeteries. It provided numerous triangulation points from which other grids could be developed. Eventually, an arbitrary so-called "B" grid was adopted based on the orientation of the Gymnasium. The southeastern point was designated as grid zero (Fig. 8); the north/south axis was established as the face of the eastern wall of Building B (Fig. 206, Halls BNH, BCH, BSH). It is not a true north/south grid. Its direction in 1958 was 26°20' east of magnetic north. This grid was extended over the entire site, except that separate local grids were adopted for Bath CG and the Acropolis. For a more detailed explanation of Sardis cartography and grids, see *Sardis* R1 (1975) 7–16.

The level system adopted was also arbitrary, with an arbitrary elevation of 100. Such separate level systems were adopted for the Gymnasium and HoB (100 = 115.11 a.s.l.); the Temple of Artemis and PC (100 = 138.38 a.s.l.); and Bath CG (100 = 99.36 a.s.l.).

Only on the Acropolis was the usual geographical system of giving altitude above sea level used (grid zero at 400.20 a.s.l.).

Local grid systems were used for the various excavations at Bin Tepe, at the Gyges Mound (BT 63.1, Fig. 106), and the prehistoric cemetery sites of Ahlatli Tepecik and Eski Balikhane (Fig. 13).

Levels in Bin Tepe were generally taken above sea level from known sea-level benchmarks, set by Turkish geocartographic survey.

Key to Initials

AR	Andrew Ramage	HB	Hans Buchwald
ARS	Andrew R. Seager	JS	Jeffrey Spier
ATK	A. Thomas Kraabel	JSC	John S. Crawford
CF	Clive Foss	RUR	Robin U. Russin
FKY	Fikret K. Yegül	SMG	Sidney M. Goldstein
GMAH	George M. A. Hanfmann	WEM	William E. Mierse

Bibliography on Sardis

This bibliography includes publications relating to Sardis and referred to in this volume. Publications drawn upon for comparative purposes are cited in the General Bibliography.

Abbreviations of periodicals are those listed in the *American Journal of Archaeology* 82 (1978) 5–10. Abbreviations of classical authors generally follow the *Oxford Classical Dictionary*, 2d rev. ed., N. G. L. Hammond and H. H. Scullard (Oxford 1970) ix–xxii.

The monographs and reports published by the Harvard-Cornell Expedition are cited under *Sardis*. Those yet unpublished are cited as follows: *Sardis* (M9) or (R5) . . . (forthcoming). The reports of the first Sardis expedition were published under the general series title of *Sardis, Publications of the American Society for the Excavation of Sardis*. Seventeen volumes were planned by H. C. Butler, Director of Excavations (*Sardis* I [1922] viii); of these nine were actually published and are cited here under *Sardis*.

Reports of the Harvard-Cornell Expedition for the period 1958–1975 have appeared regularly in the *Bulletin of the American Schools of Oriental Research* (*BASOR*) 154 (1959)–228 (1977), usually with a complete Sardis bibliography for the year, and in *Türk Arkeoloji Dergisi* (*TürkArkDerg*) of the Turkish Department of Antiquities, 9:1 (1959)–24:1 (1977).

Thomas, *Interim Bibliography*, Category 4c, lists preliminary reports including *TürkArkDerg, Anatolian Studies*, and *Illustrated London News*. A select bibliography of preliminary reports in *BASOR* and *TürkArkDerg* from 1958 through 1972 appears in Hanfmann, *Letters*, 345–349. Because of their importance for this book we list them through the 1976 campaign.

BASOR: 154 (1959) 5–35; 157, 8–43; 162, 8–49; 166, 1–57; 170, 1–65; 174, 3–58, 177, 2–37; 182, 2–54; 186, 17–52; 187, 9–62; 191, 2–41; 199, 7–58; 203, 5–22; 206, 9–39; 211, 14–36; 215, 31–60; 228, 47–59; 229 (1976) 57–73.

TürkArkDerg: 9:1 (1959) 3–8; 10:1 (1960) 3–20; 11:1 (1962) 18–22; 11:2 (1962) 40–45; 12:1 (1964) 26–33; 12:2 (1965) 8–23; 13:2 (1965) 58–63; 14:1 (1965) 151–154; 15:1 (1966) 75–78; 16:2 (1967) 77–84; 18:1 (1969) 61–64; 19:1 (1970) 99–119; 20:1 (1973) 89–105; 21:2 (1974) 59–77; 22:1 (1975) 17–36; 23:1 (1976) 55–64; 24:1 (1977) 115–24.

Other annual reports have appeared in M. J. Mellink's "Archaeology in Asia Minor," *American Journal of Archaeology, Anatolian Studies* (biannually) and *Fasti Archeologici*, published by the International Association of Classical Archaeology.

Other Publications of Sardis Harvard-Cornell Expedition Materials

To the Sardis series proper must be added some closely related books and monographs outside the series. G. M. A. Hanfmann's *Letters from Sardis* (Harvard University Press, 1972) presents an informal review of earlier Sardis research as well as the development of the Harvard-Cornell Expedition from 1958 through 1971.

One of the most interesting series of finds of the Lydian period has been treated by C. H. Greenewalt, Jr., in a study which combines archaeology, zoology, mythology, and ritual: C. H. Greenewalt, Jr., *Ritual Dinners in Early Historic Sardis* (University of California Publications of Classical Studies, 17, Berkeley, 1978).

Louis Robert's *Nouvelles Inscriptions de Sardes* (*NIS*) (A. Maisonneuve, Paris, 1972) with a workable select bibliography through 1971, is basic for the understanding of the Synagogue inscriptions and many other matters.

Andrew R. Seager has given a masterly summary of the Sardis Synagogue results in *Archaeology at the Ancient Synagogue of Sardis, Turkey; Judaism in a Major Roman City*, Ball State University, Faculty Lecture Series, Muncie, Ind., 1974.

In a similar but more detailed monographic account, Hans Buchwald has published "Sardis, Church E, Preliminary Report," *Jahrbuch der Österreichischen Byzantinischen Gesellschaft*, Vienna (1977) 265–299.

Certain consecutive serial discussions have appeared in periodicals. These include the anthropological articles by Enver Bostanci, "An Examination of Some Human Skeletal Remains from Sardis Excavation, 1963," in *Antropoloji* 1 (1968); "Morphological and Biometrical Examination of Some Skulls from the Sardis Excavations," *Belleten* 31 (1967) 1–48; *Study of the Skulls from the Excavations at Sardis and the Relation with the Ancient Anatolians* (Ankara 1969).

The articles on Eastern Greek and Lydian pottery by C. H. Greenewalt, Jr., *California Studies in Classical Antiquities* (*CSCA*) 1, 1968; 3, 1970; 4, 1971; 5, 1972 are another example of serially published research, as are the studies devoted to the discussion of soils by G. W. Olson.

General Literature on Sardis

The 1973 *Interim Bibliography of Sardis* by R. S. Thomas lists some forty general articles on studies on Sardis. A few retain some usefulness because of literary references and older sources, but most have been superseded. Thus, for a brief history one should now turn to J. G. Pedley, *Sardis in the Age of Croesus* (Centers of Civilization Series, Norman, Oklahoma 1968), while the fundamental sources are given by Pedley in *Sardis* M2 for "Mythical Age through A.D. 284," and by C. Foss in M4 for A.D. 284 to the present time. The most up-to-date, short archaeological summary without illustrations is J. A. Scott and G. M. A. Hanfmann, "Sardis," *Princeton Encyclopedia of Classical Sites* (PECS), Princeton (1976), 808–810, with a recent bibliography.

A brief illustrated guide to the site by G. Yügrüm appeared in 1973 in Turkish and English. Reasonably updated guidance will also be found in the most recent edition of E. Akurgal's *Ancient Civilizations and Ruins of Turkey* (1978). Prior to the appearance of the present volume, H. B. Butler's introduction in *Sardis* I (1922) and our *Report* 1 (1975) were the most comprehensive accounts of the topography of Sardis. The *Letters from Sardis* (1972) has the most extensive collection of recent illustrations.

Integration into Wider Perspectives

Sardis has been increasingly considered in general histories of ancient cultures and arts; some of them are listed in *Letters,* 345–346. Among the surveys of Anatolian cultures, the pre-excavation accounts by H. Th. Bossert, K. Bittel, A. Götze, and C. Roebuck and the recent treatments of Lydian arts by E. Akurgal and by G. M. A. Hanfmann in K. Schefold may be mentioned.

An attempt to integrate our results at Sardis into the general framework of the development of Western Anatolia in ancient times was made in G. M. A. Hanfmann's *From Croesus to Constantine* (University of Michigan Press, 1975). A similar objective was served by the inclusion in the *Proceedings of the Tenth International Congress of Classical Archaeology* (An-

kara-Izmir 1973, published Ankara 1978) of several papers on Sardis, including G. M. A. Hanfmann, "Lydian Relations with Ionia and Persia"; C. H. Greenewalt, Jr., "Lydian Elements in the Material Culture of Sardis"; A. Ramage, "Gold Refining at the Time of the Lydian Kings of Sardis." Aspects of Lydian urbanism and Lydian textiles are considered by Hanfmann and Greenewalt in Keith DeVries, ed., *From Athens to Gordion: The Papers of a Memorial Symposium for Rodney S. Young, University Museum Papers 1* (Philadelphia 1980), "On Lydian Sardis," "Lydian Textiles."

Akurgal, E. *Ancient Civilizations and Ruins of Turkey,* 3d ed. (Istanbul 1973).

——— *Die Kunst Anatoliens von Homer bis Alexander dem Grossen* (Berlin 1961).

Amandry, P. "Statue de Taureau en Argent," *BCH* Supp. 4 (1977) 273–293.

Ambraseys, N. N. "Value of Historical Records of Earthquakes." *Nature* 232:5310 (August 6, 1971) 375–379.

American Schools of Oriental Research, *Annual.* Cited as AASOR.

——— *Bulletin.* Cited as *BASOR.*

Arias, P. E., and Hirmer, M. (revised by B. Shefton). *A History of 1000 Years of Greek Painting* (New York 1962).

Arundell, F. V. J. *Discoveries in Asia Minor* (London 1834).

——— *A Visit to the Seven Churches of Asia* (London 1828).

Asemakopoulou-Atzaka, P. *The Technique of Opus Sectile in Wall Decoration, Byzantine Monuments* 4 (Thessalonike 1980).

Atkinson, K. T. C. "A Hellenistic Land Conveyance," *Historia* 21 (1972) 45–74.

Balmuth, M. S. "Remarks on the Appearance of the Earliest Coinage," in Hanfmann, *Studies,* 3–7.

Bammer, A. *Die Architektur des jüngeren Artemision von Ephesos* (Wiesbaden 1972).

Bammer, A., Brein, F., and Wolff, P. "Das Tieropfer am Artemisaltar von Ephesos," *Studien zur Religion und Kultur Kleinasiens, Festschrift für Friedrich Karl Dörner,* ed. S. Şahin, E. Schwertheim, and J. Wagner (Leiden 1978) 107–157.

Bammer, A., Fleischer, R., and Knibbe, D. *Führer durch das Archäologische Museum in Selçuk-Ephesos* (Vienna 1974).

Barnett, R. D. "Early Greek Ivories," *JHS* 68 (1948) 1–25.

Bean, G. *Aegean Turkey* (New York 1966).

Bengston, H. *Die Strategie in der hellenistischen Zeit* (Munich 1944).

Berve, H., and Gruben, G. *Greek Temples, Theaters and Shrines* (New York 1963).

Bikerman, E. *Institutions des Seleucides* (Paris 1938).

Birgi, S. "Sart (Salihli) Civarindaki Altin Zuhurlari" (Occurrences of Gold in the Sardis [Salihli] Region), Mineral Research and Exploration Institute of Turkey (Ankara 1944).

Bittel, K. *Grundzüge der Vor und Frühgeschichte Kleinasiens* (Tübingen 1950).

Boardman, J. "Pyramidal Stamp Seals in the Persian Empire," *Iran* 8 (1970) 19–45.

Bolgil, M. C. "Marble Court Reconstruction" in *Sardis* (R3) *Gymnasium* (forthcoming).

Bolin, S. *State and Currency in the Roman Empire to 300 A.D.* (Stockholm 1958).

Bossert, H. Th. *Altanatolien* (Berlin 1942).

—— *Asia* (Istanbul 1946).

Bostanci, E. "An Examination of Some Human Skeletal Remains from the Sardis Excavations," *Antropoloji* 1 (1963) 121–131.

——— "Morphological and Biometrical Examination of Some Skulls from the Sardis Excavations," *Belletin* 31 (1967) 17–22.

——— "Study of the Skulls from the Excavation at Sardis and the Relation with the Ancient Anatolians," *Ankara Üniversitesi Dil ve Tarih-Cografya Fakültesi* 185, Paleoantropoloji Kürsüsü Seri III (Ankara 1969).

Bowersock, G. W. *Greek Sophists in the Roman Empire* (Oxford 1969).

Brein, F. "Geometrisch Dekorierte Keramik aus Ephesos," in *Proceedings of the Tenth International Congress of Classical Archaeology,* ed. E. Akurgal, Ankara-Izmir 23–30/ix/1973, 3 vols. (Ankara 1978) 721–728.

Brill, R. H. "The Record of Time in Weathered Glass," *Archaeology* 14:1 (1961) 18–21.

Brill, R. H., and Hood, H. P. "A New Method for Dating Ancient Glass," Nature 189:4758 (1961) 12–14.

Brill, R. H., and Shields, W. R. "Lead Isotopes in Ancient Coins," *Methods of Chemical and Metallurgical Investigation of Ancient Coinage,* ed. E. T. Hall and D. M. Metcalf, Royal Numismatic Society, *Special Publication* 8 (1972) 279–304.

Buchwald, H. "Lascarid Architecture," *JÖBG* 28 (1979) 261–296.

——— "Sardis Church E—A Preliminary Report," *JÖBG* 26 (1977) 265–299.

Buckler, W. H. "Lydian Records," *JHS* 37 (1917) 88–115.

Buckler, W. H., and Robinson, D. M. "Greek Inscriptions from Sardes," *AJA* 16 (1912) 11–82. Cited as Buckler-Robinson.

——— "Greek Inscriptions from Sardes III," *AJA* 17 (1913) 353–370.

Buerchner, L., Deeters, G., and Keil, J. "Lydia," *RE* 13 (1927) 2122–2202.

Burrell, B. "Neokoroi: Greek Cities of the Roman East" (Ph.D. dissertation, Harvard University, 1980).

Butler, H. C. "Fifth Preliminary Report on the American Excavations at Sardes in Asia Minor," *AJA* 18 (1914) 427–430.

Cahn, H. "Die Löwen des Apollon," *Kleine Schriften zur Münzkunde und Archäologie* (Basel 1975) 17–32.

Calder, W. M., and Bean, G. E. "A Classical Map of Asia Minor," British Institute of Archaeology at Ankara (London 1958).

Carruba, O. "Lydisch und Lyder," *Mitteilungen des Instituts für Orientforschung* 8:3 (1963) 383–408.

Cavaignac, E. *Population et capital dans le monde méditerréen antique* (Strasbourg 1923).

Chandler, R. *Travels in Asia Minor* (Oxford 1775).

Charanis, P. "A Note on the Byzantine Coin Finds in Sardis and Their Historical Significance," *Epet* 39–40 (1972–73) 175–180.

Chase, G. H. "Two Vases from Sardis," *AJA* 25 (1921) 111–117.

Choisy, A. "Note sur les tombeaux Lydiens de Sardes," *RA* 32 (1876) 73–81.

Claude, D. *Die byzantinische Stadt im 6. Jahrhundert* (Munich 1969).

Collignon, M. "Note sur des bijoux d'or de Sardes," *CRAI* 7 (1899) 188–191.

Cook, A. B. *Zeus: A Study in Ancient Religion* (New York 1964).

Corpus Inscriptionum Graecarum. Cited as *CIG.*

Crawford, J. S. "Roman Commercial Buildings of Asia Minor" (Ph.D. dissertation, Harvard University, 1969).

Crawford, J. S., and Greaves, J. "A Brass Lamp from Sardis," *AJA* 78 (1974) 291–294.

Cumont, F. *Recherches sur le symbolisme funéraire des Romains,* Bibliothèque Archéologique et Historique 35 (Paris 1942).

Daux, G. "Note sur la liste Delphique des Théarodoques," *BCH* 89 (1965) 658–660.

Delehaye, E., ed. *Synaxarium Ecclesiae Constantinopolitanae* (Brussels 1902).

Demus-Quatember, M. *Etruskische Grabarchitektur* = Walser, G., ed., *Deutsche Beiträge zur Altertumswissenschaft* 11 (Baden Baden 1958).

Dennis, G. *Cities and Cemeteries of Etruria* (original edition 1848; London 1907).

Desborough, V. *The Last Mycenaeans and Their Successors* (Oxford 1964).

Dittenberger, W. *Orientis Graeci Inscriptiones Selectae* 1–3 (Leipzig 1903–1905). Cited as *OGIS.*

——— *Sylloge Inscriptionum Graecarum* (3d ed., Leipzig 1915–1924). Cited as *Syll.*

Doguer, S., Deniz, E., Çalislar, R., and Özguden, T. "Osteological Investigations of the Animal Remains Recovered from the Excavations of Ancient Sardis," *Anatolia* 8 (1964) 49–65.

Donner, H., and Röllig, W. *Kanaanäische und aramäische Inschriften II* (Wiesbaden 1964).

Dussaud, R. *La Lydie et ses voisins aux hautes époques* (Paris 1930).

EGF, see Kinkel.

Englemann, H. "Eine Prägung des ionischen Bundes," *Zeitschrift fur Papyrologie und Epigraphik* 9 (1972) 190–191.

Finkel, D. J. *The Dynamics of Middle Eastern Skeletal Populations* (Ph.D. dissertation, University of Oregon, 1974).

Fleischer, R. *Artemis von Ephesos und verwandte Kultstatuen aus Anatolien und Syrien* (Leiden 1973). Cited as Fleischer.

———— "Artemis von Ephesos und verwandte Kultstatuen aus Anatolien und Syrien, Supplement," in *Studien zur Religion und Kultur Kleinasiens,* ed. S. Şahin, E. Schwertheim, and J. Wagner (Leiden 1978) 324–358.

———— "Marsyas und Achaios," *JOAI* 50 (1972–1973) 105–122.

Foss, C. "Aleipterion," *GRBS* 16:2 (Summer 1975) 217–226.

———— "Atticus Philippus and the Walls of Side," *ZPE* 26 (1977) 175–177.

———— "Byzantine Cities of Western Asia Minor " (Ph.D. dissertation, Harvard University, 1972).

———— *Ephesus after Antiquity: A Late Antique, Byzantine and Turkish City* (Cambridge 1979).

———— "Explorations in Mount Tmolus," *CSCA* 11 (1979) 21–61.

———— "The Fall of Sardis in 616 and the Value of the Evidence," *JOB* 24 (1975) 11–22.

Franke, P. R. "Inschriftliche und numismatische Zeugnisse für die Chronologie des Artemis Tempels zu Sardis." *AthMitt* 76 (1961) 197–208.

Frankel, S. H. *Money and Liberty* (Oxford 1980).

Gabelmann, H. *Studien zum frühgriechischen Löwenbild* (Berlin 1965).

Gall, H. von, "Felsgräber der Perserzeit im pontischen Kleinasien," *AA* 82:4 (1967) 585–595.

Gentner, W., Müller, O., Wagner, G. A., and Gale, N. H. "Silver Sources of Archaic Greek Coinage," *Naturwissenschaften* 65 (1978) 273–284.

Goldman, H. "Sandon and Herakles," *Hesperia* Suppl. 8 (1949) 164–174.

———— *Tarsus III: The Iron Age* (Princeton 1963). Cited as Goldman, *Tarsus.*

Goodenough, E. R. *Jewish Symbols in the Greco-Roman Period,* 13 vols. (New York 1953–1968).

Götze, A. "Die Lyder" in "Kleinasien," *Kulturgeschichte des alten Orients, Handbuch der Altertumswissenschaft,* 2d ed., 3:1:3 (Munich 1957) 206–209.

Greenewalt, C. H., Jr. "Campaign of 1978" (forthcoming in *BASOR*).

———— "Ephesian Ware," *CSCA* 6 (1973) 91–122.

———— "An Exhibitionist from Sardis," in Hanfmann, *Studies,* 29–46.

———— "Fikellura and 'Early Fikellura' Pottery from Sardis," *CSCA* 4 (1971) 153–180.

———— "Lydian Elements in the Material Culture of Sardis," in *Proceedings of the Tenth International Congress of Classical Archaeology,* ed. E. Akurgal (Ankara 1978) 37–45, pls. 13–20.

———— "Orientalizing Pottery from Sardis: The Wild Goat Style," *CSCA* 3 (1970) 53–89.

———— *Ritual Dinners in Early Historic Sardis,* University of California Publications Classical Studies 17 (Berkeley 1976).

———— "Sardis," in "Archaeology in Asia Minor," ed. M. J. Mellink, *AJA* 81:3 (1977) 308–310, fig. 19.

———— "The Twentieth Campaign at Sardis, 1977," *RdA* 1:1–2 (1977) 105–108.

———— "Two Lydian Graves at Sardis," *CSCA* 5 (1972) 113–145.

Greenewalt, C. H., Jr., and Majewski, L. J. "Lydian Textiles," in *From Athens to Gordion: The Papers at a Memorial Symposium for Rodney S. Young,* ed. K. DeVries and E. Kohler (Philadelphia 1980) 133–148.

Greenewalt, D., "An Electrical Search May Aid Archaeologists," *Technology Review,* Massachusetts Institute of Technology, 64:2 (December 1961) 27.

Groag, E., and Stein, A., eds. *Prosopographia Imperii Romani,* 2d ed. (Lipsiae 1933). Cited as *PIR.*

Gruben, G. "Beobachtungen zum Artemis Tempel von Sardis," *AthMitt* 76 (1961) 155–196.

———— *Die Tempel der Griechen* (Munich 1966).

Gusmani, R. "Der lydische Name du Kybele," *Kadmos* 8:2 (1969) 158–161.

———— "Die lydische Sprache," *JRAS* 2 (1975) 134–142.

———— *Lydisches Wörterbuch* (Heidelberg 1964). Cited as Gusmani, *LW.*

———— *Lydisches Wörterbuch: Ergänzungsband Lieferung 1* (Heidelberg 1980). Cited as Gusmani, *LW 1.*

———— "Neue Inschriften aus Lydien," *Indogermanische Forschungen* 69 (1964) 130–138.

———— "Onomastica iranica nei testi epicorici Lidi," *Umanità e storia, Studi in onore di Adelchi Attisani* (Naples 1972) 3–10.

Habicht, C. "New Evidence on the Province of Asia," *JRS* 65 (1975) 64–91.

Hamilton, W. J. *Researches in Asia Minor* (London 1842).

Hammond, M., and Bartson, L. J. *The City in the Ancient World,* Harvard Studies in Urban History (Cambridge, Mass. 1972).

Hanfmann, G. M. A. "Ahlatli Tepecik," in M. J. Mellink, "Archaeology in Asia Minor," *AJA* 73 (1969) 203–227:209.

——— "The Ancient Synagogue of Sardis," Fourth World Congress of Jewish Studies, *Papers* 1 (Jerusalem 1967) 37–42.

——— "Archaeology and the Origins of Greek Culture: Notes on Recent Work in Asia Minor," *Antioch Review* 25:1 (1965) 41–59.

——— "Archaeology in Homeric Asia Minor," *AJA* 52 (1948) 135–155.

——— "The Central Marker" (unpublished ms., 1975).

——— "The Crucified Donkey Man: Achaios and Jesus," in *Studies in Honor of H. P. von Blanckenhagen,* ed. G. Kopcke (Locust Valley 1979) 233–235.

——— "Forerunners of Pasargadae at Sardis" (unpublished ms., Oxford 1972), for Sixth International Congress of Iranian Art and Archaeology.

——— *From Croesus to Constantine* (Ann Arbor 1975).

——— "Horsemen from Sardis," *AJA* 49 (1945) 570–581.

——— *Letters From Sardis* (Cambridge, Mass. 1972).

——— "Lydiaka," *Studies in Honor of Werner Jaeger,* HSCP 63 (1958) 65–88.

——— "Lydian Relations with Ionia and Persia," in *Proceedings of the Tenth International Congress of Classical Archaeology,* ed. E. Akurgal, Ankara-Izmir 23–30/IX/1973, 3 vols. (Ankara 1978) 25–35.

——— "Lydische Kunst," in Schefold, *Die Griechen,* 282–284.

——— "On the Gods of Lydian Sardis," *Festschrift für K. Bittel* (forthcoming).

——— "On Late Roman and Early Byzantine Portraits from Sardis," *Hommages à Marcel Renard III, Latomus* 103 (Brussels 1969) 288–295.

——— "On Lydian and Eastern Greek Anthemion Stelai," *RA* (1976) 35–44.

——— "On Lydian Sardis," in *From Athens to Gordion: The Papers of a Memorial Symposium for Rodney S. Young, University Museum Papers 1,* ed. K. DeVries and E. Kohler (Philadelphia 1980) 99–132.

——— "On the Palace of Croesus," in *Festschrift für Frank Brommer,* ed. U. Höckmann and A. Krug (Mainz 1977).

——— "A Painter in the Imperial Arms Factory at Sardis," *AJA* 85 (1981) 87–88.

——— "A Pediment of the Persian Era from Sardis," *Mélanges Mansel* (Ankara 1974) 289–302, pls. 99–104.

——— "Prehistoric Sardis," in *Studies Presented to D. M. Robinson* I, ed. G. Mylonas (St. Louis 1951) 160–183.

——— "A Preliminary Note on the Glass Found at Sardis in 1958," *JGS* 1 (1959) 51–54.

——— *Roman Art* (Greenwich, Conn. 1964).

——— *Sardis und Lydien,* Akademie der Wissenschaften und Literatur, Mainz, Abhandlungen der Geistes und sozialwissenschaftlichen Klasse 6 (1960) 499–536.

——— "Sepulchral Markers—Phallic?" (unpublished ms., 1975).

——— *Studies,* see Mitten, D. G., Pedley, J. G.

Hanfmann, G. M. A., and Balmuth, M. "The Image of an Anatolian Goddess at Sardis," *Anadolu Araştirmalari Helmuth Theodor Bossert in Hatirasina Armagan* (Istanbul 1965) 261–269.

Hanfmann, G. M. A., and Detweiler, A. H. "From the Heights of Sardis," *Archaeology* 14 (1961) 3–12.

——— "Sardis-Lydian, Hellenistic and Byzantine: Excavations into 2,000 Years of the City's History," *ILN* (April 1962) 542–544.

Hanfmann, G. M. A., and Erhart, P. "Pedimental Reliefs from a Mausoleum of the Persian Era at Sardis: A Funerary Meal," *Studies in Honor of Dows Dunham* (Boston 1981) 82–90.

Hanfmann, G. M. A., and Masson, O. "Carian Inscriptions from Sardis and Stratonikeia," *Kadmos* 6:2 (1967) 123–134.

Hanfmann, G. M. A., and Mitten, D. G. "Sardis–Eski Balikhane," in M. J. Mellink, "Archaeology in Asia Minor," *AJA* 74 (1970) 157–178:163.

Hanfmann, G. M. A., Polatkan, K. Z., and Robert, L. "A Sepulchral Stele from Sardis," *AJA* 64 (1960) 45–56.

Hanfmann, G. M. A., and Waldbaum, J. C. "Kybele and Artemis: Two Anatolian Goddesses at Sardis," *Archaeology* 22:4 (1969) 264–269.

——— "New Excavations at Sardis and Some Problems of Western Anatolian Archaeology," in *Near Eastern Archaeology in the Twentieth Century: Essays in Honor of Nelson Glueck,* ed. J. A. Sanders (Garden City, N.Y. 1970) 307–326.

Hansen, D. P. Report on Grant No. 269, 1959, "Late Roman–Early Christian Bronzes from the 'House of Bronzes' in Sardis, Turkey," *Year Book of the American Philosophical Society* (1960) 587–589.

——— "L'antica Sardi cristiana," *Bibbia e Oriente* 4 (1962) 169–174.

Hansen, E. V. *The Attalids of Pergamon,* 2d ed. (Ithaca, N.Y. 1971).

Hayes, J. W. *Late Roman Pottery* (London 1972).

Head, B. V. *Catalogue of the Greek Coins of Lydia: A Catalogue of the Greek Coins in the British Museum* 22 (London 1901). Cited as Head, *BMC, Lydia.*

——— *Historia Nummorum* (London 1911). Cited as Head, *HN.*

Henrichs, A. "Despoina Kybele," *HSCP* 80 (1976) 435–503.

Herter, H. "Lydische Adelskämpfe," *Wege zur Buchwissenschaft* 14 (Bonn 1966) 31–60.

Heubeck, A. *Lydiaka, Untersuchungen zu Schrift,*

Sprache und Götternamen der Lyder (Erlangen 1959).

——— "Überlegungen zur Entstehung der lydischen Schrift," *Kadmos* 17:1 (1978) 55–66.

Hirschland, N. L. "The Head-Capitals from Sardis," *PBSR* 35, n.s. 22 (1967) 12–22, pls. 5–36.

Hogarth, D. G. "Lydia and Ionia, The Central Anatolian Powers: Phrygia and Sardes," in *The Cambridge Ancient History* 3 (Cambridge 1925).

Hostetter, E. "The Tiles of Ancient Sardis," *Archaeology* 34:3 (1981) 56–59, 7 figs.

Hutton, C. A. "The Travels of 'Palmyra' Wood in 1750–51," *JHS* 47 (1927) 102–109.

Huxley, G. L. *Achaeans and Hittites* (Oxford 1960).

——— *The Early Ionians* (New York 1966).

Illustrated London News (9 July 1960) 61–63. Cited as *ILN*.

——— (1 April 1961) 536–538.

Jesus, P. S. de. *The Development of Prehistoric Mining and Metallurgy in Anatolia* (London 1980).

Johnson, S. E. "A Sabazios Inscription from Sardis," *Religions in Antiquity: Essays in Memory of Erwin R. Goodenough,* ed. J. Neusner (Leider 1968).

Jones, C. P. "Toward a Chronology of Plutarch's Works," *JRS* 56 (1969) 72.

Jongkees, J. H. "Gottesnamen in lydischen Inschriften," *Mnemosyne* 3:6 (1938) 355–367.

Kaletsch, H. "Zur lydischen Chronologie," *Historia* 7 (1958) 1–47.

Kamilli, D. "Mineral Analysis of the Clay Bodies," in A. Ramage, *Sardis* M5 (1978) 12–14.

Karo, G. "Vetuloneser Nachlese," *St.Etr.* 8 (1934) 49–57.

Kasper, S., "Belevi Grabtumulus," *ÖJh* 47 (1964–1965) 12. Cited as Kasper, "Belevi[1]."

——— "Der Tumulus von Belevi (Grabungsbericht)," *ÖJh* 51, *Beiblatt* (1976–77) 129–179.

Kawerau, G., and Rehm, A. *Milet, Ergebnisse der Ausgrabungen und Untersuchungen* I:3, *Das Delphinion in Milet* (Berlin 1914).

Keil, J. "Die Kulte Lydiens," *Anatolian Studies Presented to Sir William Mitchell Ramsay* (Manchester 1923) 239–266.

Kenna, V. E. G. *Cretan Seals: With a Catalogue of the Minoan Gems in the Ashmolean Museum* (Oxford 1960).

Kinkel, G. *Epicorum Graecorum Fragmenta* (Lipsiae 1877). Cited as *EGF.*

Kleiner, F. S., and Noe, S. P. *The Early Cistophoric Coinage, ANSNS* (New York 1977).

Knibbe, D. "Ein religiöser Frevel und seine Sühne: Ein Todesurteil hellenistischer Zeit aus Ephesos," *ÖJh* (1961–1963) 175–182.

Knudsen, A. "From a Sardis Tomb: A Lydian Pottery Imitation of a Phrygian Metal Bowl?" *Berytus* 15 (1964) 59–69.

Koubetsos, K. "Hoi Chryselephantinoi Thesauroi," *Tachydromos* 26 (29 June 1978) 36–41.

Köy Işleri Bakanligi. Topraksu Genel Müdürlügü, *Gediz Ovasi Topraklari Raporu* (Village Works Ministry, Soil and Water Conservation Directorate, *Report on the Soils of the Gediz Plain;* Ankara 1968).

Kraabel, A. T. *Anatolian Judaism* (forthcoming).

——— "The Diaspora Synagogue: Archaeological and Epigraphic Evidence since Sukenik," in *Aufstieg und Niedergang der römischen Welt,* ed. W. Haase (Berlin, forthcoming).

——— "*Hypsistos* and the Synagogue at Sardis," *GRBSA* 10 (1969) 81–93.

——— "Melito, the Bishop and the Synagogue at Sardis: Text and Context," in Hanfmann, *Studies* 77–85.

——— "Paganism and Judaism—the Sardis Evidence," *Mélanges offerts à Marcel Simon: Paganisme, Judaisme, Christianisme, Influences et affrontements dans le monde antique* (Paris 1978).

Kraft, K. *Das System der kaiserzeitlichen Münzpragung in Kleinasien* (Berlin 1972).

Lane, E. *Corpus Monumentorum Religionis Dei Menis,* 1–3 (Leiden 1971–1976). Cited as Lane, *CMRDM.*

Lawrence, A. W. *Greek Architecture* (Baltimore 1957).

Lidell, H. G., Scott, R., and Jones, H. S. *A Greek-English Lexicon,* with Supplement (Oxford 1968). Cited as *LSJ* Suppl. (1938).

Lloyd, S., Muller, H. W., and Martin, R. *Ancient Architecture: Mesopotamia, Egypt, Crete, Greece* (New York 1974).

LSJ Suppl. (1938), see Lidell, H. G.

Lucas, P. *Voyage du Sieur Paul Lucas fait par ordre du roy dans la Grèce, l'Asie Mineure, la Macedoine et l'Afrique,* 2 vols. (Paris 1712).

Luschey, H. *Die Phiale* (Bleicherode am Harz 1939).

Magie, D. *Roman Rule in Asia Minor to the End of the Third Century after Christ,* 3 vols. (Princeton 1950).

Majewski, L. J. "Conservation at Sardis," paper presented at the Meeting of the Archaeological Institute of America, 79th Meeting, Atlanta (1977).

——— "The Conservation of Archaeological Materials at Sardis, Turkey," *Bulletin of the American Institute for Conservation of Historic and Artistic Works,* 13:2 (Kansas City 1973) 99–104; figs. 1–10.

——— "Restoration and Conservation of Sardis Monuments," paper presented at the *Tenth International Congress of Classical Archaeology,* Ankara 1973: *Abstracts* 3–4.

Mallowan, M. "Cyrus the Great," *Iran* 10 (1972) 1–17.

Manisa Il Yilligi 1967 (Yearbook of the Vilayet Manisa; Izmir 1968).

Masson, O. *Les Fragments du poète Hipponax* (Paris 1962).

Masson, O. "Un nom pseudo-Lydien à Sardes: Beletras," *Studi in Onore di Piero Meriggi, Athenaeum*, Nuova Series 47, Fascicles 1–4 (1969) 193–196.

Mee, C. "Aegean Trade and Settlement in Anatolia in the Second Millennium B.C.," *AnatSt* 28 (1978) 121–156.

Mellaart, J. "Anatolian Trade with Europe and Anatolian Geography and Culture Provinces in the Late Bronze Age," *AnatSt* 18 (1968) 187–202.

Mellink, M. J. "Archaeology in Asia Minor," *AJA* 70 (1968), 140; 73 (1969) 209; 74 (1970) 163; 77 (1973) 175; 81 (1977).

——— Review of E. Akurgal's *Phrygische Kunst* in *AJA* (1957) 392–395.

Metraux, G. P. R. "A New Head of Zeus from Sardis," *AJA* 75 (1971) 156–159.

Miller, M. "The Herodotean Croesus," *Klio* 41 (1963) 58–94.

Milne, J. G. "Herodotus I.94; ΝΟΜΙΣΜΑ," *CR* 63:3–4 (1949) 85–87.

Mitten, D. G. *The Ancient Synagogue of Sardis* (New York 1965).

——— "A New Look at Ancient Sardis," *Bibl. Arch.* 29 (1966) 38–68.

Mitten, D. G., Pedley, J. G., and Scott, J. A., eds. *Studies Presented to George M. A. Hanfmann,* Fogg Art Museum Monographs in Art and Archaeology 2 (Cambridge, Mass./Mainz 1971). Cited as Hanfmann, *Studies.*

Mitten, D. G., and Yügrüm, G. "Ahlatli Tepecik beside the Gygean Lake," *Archaeology* 27 (1974) 22–29.

——— "The Gygean Lake, 1969; Eski Balikhane, Preliminary Report," *HSCP* 75 (1971) 191–195.

Mørkholm, O. "Some Seleucid Coins from the Mint of Sardes," *Nordisk Numismatisk Arsskrift* (1969) 5–20.

Müller-Wiener, W. "Die Stadtbefestigungen von Izmir, Sigacik und Çandarli," *IstMitt* 12 (1962) 59–114. Cited as Müller-Wiener.

——— Review of *Sardis* R1, *Erasmus* 32 (April 10, 1979) 237–240.

Muscarella, O. W. "Phrygian or Lydian?" *JNES* 30:1 (1971) 49–63.

——— "The Tumuli at Se Girdan: A Preliminary Report," *Metropolitan Museum Journal* 2 (1969) 5–25.

Neumann, G. "Der lydische Name der Athena (Neulesung der lydischen Inschrift Nr. 40)," *Kadmos* 6 (1967) 80–87.

——— "Ein weiteres Fragment der Synagogeninschrift aus Sardeis," *Kadmos* 7 (1968) 1:94–95.

——— *Untersuchungen zum Weiterleben hethitischen und luwischen Sprachgutes in hellenistischer und römischer Zeit* (Wiesbaden 1961).

Newell, E. T. *The Coinage of the Western Seleucid Mints* (New York 1941; reprinted with summary of recent scholarship by O. Mørkholm, 1977). Cited as Newell-Mørkholm, *WSM.*

Noe, S. P. "The Beginnings of Cistophoric Coinage," *ANS* (American Numismatic Society) *Museum Notes* 4 (1950).

Nylander, C. *Ionians in Pasargadae* (Uppsala 1970).

OGIS, see Dittenberger, W.

Okar, S., and Aydin, A. "Sart Hafriyatinda Bulunan Altin Numunelerinin Nötron Aktivasyon Analizi" (Neutron Activation Analysis of Gold Samples Found at Sardis) Çekmece Nükleer Araştirma Merkezi, Istanbul (CNAEM) (Nuclear Research Center Istanbul, *Communications*) 65 (1969) 1–11; figs. 1–13.

Olfers, J. F. M. von. "Uber die Lydischen Königsgräber bei Sardes und den Grabhügel des Alyattes nach dem Bericht des Kaiserlichen General-Consuls Spiegelthal zu Smyrna," *AbhBerl* (1858) 539–556.

Oliver, A. "A Bronze Mirror from Sardis," in Hanfmann, *Studies,* 113–120.

——— "Hellenistic Pottery," in *Sardis* (R5) *Pottery* (forthcoming).

——— "Lydia," *Metropolitan Museum of Art Bulletin* 25:5 (1968) 197–199.

Olmstead, A. T. *History of the Persian Empire* (Chicago 1948).

Olson, G. W. "Ancient Cities of the Dead—Victims of Ecological Suicide," *Science Digest* 71:3 (March 1972) 39–44.

——— "Descriptions, Notes, Maps, and Data on Soils of Sardis, Turkey," Cornell University, *Agronomy Mimeo* 71-1 (1971).

——— "Field Report on Soils of Sardis, Turkey: A Description of Fieldwork and Research Orientation in a Study of Soils Environment around the Ancient Lydian Greek, Roman and Byzantine Ruins," Cornell University, *Agronomy Mimeo* 70-8 (1970).

——— "Landslides at Sardis in Western Turkey," *Geological Society of America, Reviews in Engineering Geology,* 3 (1977) 255–272.

Olson, G. W., and Hanfmann, G. M. A. "Some Implications of Soils for Civilizations," *New York Food and Life Sciences Quarterly* 4:4 (1971) 11–14.

Overbeck, J. *Die antiken Schriftquellen* (Leipzig 1868).

Pászthory, E. "Investigations of the Early Electrum Coins of the Alyattes Type," *Metallurgy in Numismatics* 1, ed. D. M. Metcalf and W. A. Oddy (Oxford 1980) 152–156.

Paton, W. R. "Sites in East Caria and South Lydia," *JHS* 20 (1900) 65–73.

PECS, see Stillwell, R., ed.

Pedley, J. G. "Carians in Sardis," *JHS* 94 (1974) 94–99.

——— *Sardis in the Age of Croesus* (Norman, Oklahoma 1968).

Penella, R. J. "An Unpublished Letter of Apollonius of Tyana," *HSCP* 79 (1975) 308–311.

Perrot, G., and Chipiez, C. *History of the Art of Phrygia, Lydia, Caria and Lycia* (London 1892).

Peyssonel, C. de. *Observations historiques et géographiques sur les peuples barbares; . . . suivies d'un voyage fait à Magnésie, à Thyatire, à Sardes, etc.* (Paris 1965).

Pfuhl, E., and Möbius, H. *Die ostgriechischen Grabreliefs* (Mainz 1977).

Philippson, A. *Reisen und Forschungen im westlichen Kleinasien* (1910–1915).

Picard, C. *Manuel d'archéologie grecque: La sculpture I–IV* (Paris 1934–1963).

PIR², see Groag, E.

Polanyi, K. "On the Comparative Treatment of Economic Institutions in Antiquity," in *City Invincible*, ed. C. H. Kraeling and R. M. Adams (Chicago 1960) 329–350.

Polanyi, K., Arensberg, C. M., and Pearson, H. W. *Trade and Market in the Early Empires* (Glencoe, Ill. 1957). Cited as Polanyi.

Pouilloux, J. "Décret Delphique pour Matrophanes de Sardes," *BCH* 98 (1974) 159–169.

Price, M. J., and Trell, B. L. *Coins and Their Cities: Architecture on the Ancient Coins of Greece, Rome and Palestine* (Detroit 1976).

Pryce, F. N. *Catalogue of Sculpture in the British Museum* 1:1 (Oxford 1928).

Radet, G. *Cybébé: Étude sur les transformations plastiques d'un type divin,* Bibliothèque des Universités du Midi 13 (Bordeaux, Paris 1909).

——— *La Lydie et le monde grèc au temps des Mermnades, 687-546,* Bibliothèque des Écoles françaises d'Athènes et de Rome (reprint of Paris 1893 edition) Fascicle 63:1 (Rome 1967).

Ramage, A. "Gold Refining in the Time of the Lydian Kings at Sardis," in *Proceedings of the Tenth International Congress of Classical Archaeology 23-30/IX/1973,* ed. E. Akurgal (Ankara, Izmir 1973) 730–735.

——— "Studies in Lydian Domestic and Commercial Architecture at Sardis" (Ph.D. dissertation, Harvard University, 1969).

Ramage, A., and Ramage, N. "The Siting of Lydian Burial Mounds," in Hanfmann, *Studies,* 143–160.

Ramage, N. H. "Draped Herm from Sardis," *HSCP* 78 (1974) 253–256.

——— "A Lydian Funerary Banquet," *AnatSt* 18:1 (1979) 77–99.

Robert, L. "Documents d'Asie Mineure, Séismes en Asie Mineure," *BCH* 1978:1, 395–543.

——— "Épigraphie et antiquités grecques," *L'Annuaire du College de France* (1973).

——— "Une fête à Sardes," *RN* 18 (1976) 49–56.

——— *Les gladiateurs dans l'Orient grec* (Paris 1940).

——— *Hellenica, Recueil d'épigraphie, de numismatique et d'antiquités grecques,* 12 vols. (1940–1961).

——— "Inscriptions grecques de Sardes," *RA* (1936) I, 233–240.

——— "Inscriptions grecques de Sidè en Pamphylie (époque impériale et bas empire)" *Rev. Phil.* 32 (1958) 15–53. Cited as Robert, "Inscriptions grecques."

——— "Une nouvelle inscription grecque de Sardes: Règlement de l'autorité perse relatif à un culte de Zeus," *CRAI* (April-June 1975) 306–330.

——— *Nouvelles inscriptions de Sardes,* Fascicule 1 (Paris 1964). Cited as Robert, *NIS.*

——— "Recherches épigraphiques VIII. Alcée de Sardes," *REA* 62 (1960) 344–346.

——— "Reliefs votifs et cultes d'Anatolie. I. Dedicace à Heracles et aux Nymphes. II. Inscriptions de Lydie," *Anatolia* 3 (1958) 103–136.

——— "Un rhéteur judaisant," *CRAI* (1978) 249.

——— "Un tribu de Sardes," Études anatoliennes, Institut Français d'Istanbul, *Études Orientales* 5 (1937).

——— "Types monétaires à Hypaipa de Lydie," *RN* 19 (1976) 25–48.

Robert, L., and Robert, J. "Bulletin épigraphique," *REG* 61 (1958)–88 (1975). Cited as Robert, *Bull.*

Roebuck, C. *Ionian Trade and Colonization* (New York 1959).

Rostovtzeff, M. *The Social and Economic History of the Hellenistic World,* 3 vols. (Oxford 1941).

Rumpf, A. "Lydische Salbgefaesse," *AthMitt* 45 (1920) 163–170.

Şahin, S., Schwertheim, E., and Wagner, J., eds. *Studien zur Religion und Kultur Kleinasiens, Festschrift für Friedrich Karl Dörner* (Leiden 1978).

Sardis I: H. C. Butler, *The Excavations,* Part 1: 1910–1914 (Leiden 1922).

Sardis II: H. C. Butler, *Architecture,* Part 1: *The Temple of Artemis* (text and atlas of plates, Leiden 1925).

Sardis VI.1: E. Littmann, *Lydian Inscriptions,* Part 1 (Leiden 1916).

Sardis VI.2: W. H. Buckler, *Lydian Inscriptions,* Part 2 (Leiden 1924).

Sardis VII.1: W. H. Buckler and D. M. Robinson, *Greek and Latin Inscriptions,* Part 1 (Leiden 1932).

Sardis X: T. L. Shear, *Terra-cottas,* Part 1: *Architectural Terra-cottas* (Cambridge, England 1926).

Sardis XI: H. W. Bell, *Coins,* Part 1: *1910–1914* (Leiden 1916).

Sardis XIII: C. D. Curtis, *Jewelry and Gold Work,* Part 1: 1910–1914 (Rome 1925).

Sardis M1: G. E. Bates, *Byzantine Coins* (Cambridge, Mass. 1971).

Sardis M2: J. G. Pedley, *Ancient Literary Sources on Sardis* (Cambridge, Mass. 1972).

Sardis M3: R. Gusmani, *Neue epichorische Schriftzeugnisse aus Sardis* (1958–1971) (Cambridge, Mass. 1975).

Sardis M4: C. Foss, *Byzantine and Turkish Sardis* (Cambridge, Mass. 1976).

Sardis M5: A. Ramage, *Lydian Houses and Architectural Terracottas* (Cambridge, Mass. 1978).

Sardis M6: A. von Saldern, *Ancient and Byzantine Glass from Sardis* (Cambridge, Mass. 1980).

Sardis M7: A. E. M. Johnston, T. V. Buttrey, and K. MacKenzie, *Coins: Lydian, Greek, Roman, Islamic* (Cambridge, Mass. 1981).

Sardis (M8): J. C. Waldbaum, *Metalwork from Sardis: The Finds from 1958–1974* (forthcoming).

Sardis (M9): J. S. Crawford, *Byzantine Shops* (forthcoming).

Sardis (M10): R. Thomas, *Small Finds and Terracotta Sculpture from Sardis* (forthcoming).

Sardis (M11): R. Thomas, J. C. Waldbaum, M. Balmuth, G. M. A. Hanfmann, and P. Neville, *Bibliography of Lydia and Sardis* (forthcoming).

Sardis (M12): J. A. Scott, *Oil Lamps from Sardis* (forthcoming).

Sardis (M14): J. A. Scott and R. L. Vann, *Early Travelers' Accounts of Sardis and Unexcavated Buildings* (forthcoming).

Sardis (M15): L. Robert and J. Robert, *Greek and Latin Inscriptions* (forthcoming).

Sardis R1: G. M. A. Hanfmann and J. C. Waldbaum, *A Survey of Sardis and the Major Monuments outside the City Walls* (Cambridge, Mass. 1975).

Sardis R2: G. M. A. Hanfmann and N. Ramage, *Sculpture from Sardis: The Finds through 1975* (Cambridge, Mass. 1978).

Sardis (R3): F. K. Yegul and M. C. Bolgil, *The Gymnasium Complex and the Marble Court* (forthcoming).

Sardis (R4): A. R. Seager, I. Rabinowitz, J. H. Kroll, and A. T. Kraabel, *The Synagogue and Its Setting* (forthcoming).

Sardis (R5): D. G. Mitten, C. H. Greenewalt, Jr., J. A. Schaeffer, N. H. Ramage, A. Oliver, Jr., I. Hanfmann, G. M. A. Hanfmann, J. Wrabetz, J. A. Scott, and H. Crane, *Pottery, Prehistoric to Turkish* (forthcoming).

Sardis (R7): A. Ramage and S. M. Goldstein, *The Excavation Areas of the Pactolus and the Lydian Gold Refineries* (forthcoming).

Sardis (R9): L. J. Majewski, *Mosaics and Wall Painting* (forthcoming).

Sayce, A. H. *Reminiscences* (London 1923).

Saydamer, M. "Turgutlu-Salihli arasindaki aluvyonlarin genel altin prospeksiyonu ile Sart çayi ve civarinin altin bakimindan detay etüdü hakkinda rapor (Sart Çay)" (Report on gold prospecting of the alluvium between Turgutlu and Salihli with a detailed study of gold in the area around Sart Çay), Maden Tetkik ve Arama Enstitüsü (Ankara 1963).

Schefold, K. *Die Griechen und ihre Nachbarn, Propyläen Kunstgeschichte I* (Berlin 1967).

Schmidt, J. "Aus Constantinopel und Kleinasien," *AthMitt* 6 (1881) 132–153.

Scott, J. A. "Unpublished Eighteenth-Century Drawings of Sardis by Giovanni Baptista Borra," paper presented at the Eleventh International Congress of Classical Archaeology, London 1978: *Final Program Abstracts,* 126.

Seager, A. R. *Archaeology at the Ancient Synagogue of Sardis, Turkey: Judaism in a Major Roman City,* Ball State University Faculty Lecture Series 3 (Muncie, Ind. 1974).

——— "The Architecture of the Dura and Sardis Synagogues" in *The Dura-Europos Synagogue: A Re-Evaluation (1932–1972), Religion and the Arts* I, ed. J. Gutmann, American Academy of Religion, Society of Biblical Literature (Missoula, Montana 1973) 79–116. Reprinted in Gutmann, *Synagogue,* 149–193.

——— "The Building History of The Sardis Synagogue," *AJA* 76 (1972) 425–435.

——— "The Synagogue at Sardis," *Qadmoniot* 7 (1974) 123–128.

Seyrig, H. "Monnaies Hellénistiques," I–X *RN* 6:5 (1963) 7–64.

Shanks, H. *Judaism in Stone: The Archaeology of Ancient Synagogues* (New York, Washington 1979).

Shear, T. L. "A Hoard of Staters of Croesus at Sardis," *Numismatist* 35 (1922) 349–352.

——— "Sixth Preliminary Report on the American Excavations at Sardes," *AJA* 26 (1922) 396–401.

Shiloh, Y. "Torah Scrolls and the Menorah Plaque from Sardis," *Israel Exploration Journal* 18 (1968) 54–57.

Smithsonian Institution, *Art Treasures in Turkey* (Washington, D.C. 1966).

Sokolowski, F. "TA ENPYRA: On the Mysteries in the Lydian and Phrygian Cults," *ZPE* 34 (1979) 65–69.

Spiegelthal, see von Olfers.

Stillwell, R., ed. *Princeton Encyclopedia of Classical Sites* (Princeton 1976) 360–361.

Stronach, D. *Pasargadae: A Report on the Excavations*

Conducted by the British Institute of Persian Studies from 1961–1963 (Oxford 1978).

Sutherland, C. H. V. *Gold: Its Beauty, Power and Allure* (London 1959) 61–82.

Swift, G. "The House of Bronzes Area at Midseason" (unpublished 1965).

Syll., see Dittenberger, W.

Sylloge Nummorum Graecorum. Deutschland. Sammlung v. Aulock, ed. E. Bosch and H. von Aulock, 13 vols. (Berlin, Mann 1957–1968). Cited as *SNG, Aulock* 8.

Synaxarium, see Délehaye.

Texier, C. "Asie Mineure, description graphique, historique et archéologique," *L'universe, historie et description de tous les peuples* (Paris 1862).

Thompson, M. "The Mints of Lysimachus," *Essays in Greek Coinage Presented to Stanley Robinson* (Oxford 1968) 163–182.

Thompson, M., Mørkholm, O., and Kraay, C., eds. *An Inventory of Greek Coin Hoards* (New York 1973).

Trell, B. "Prehellenic Sanctuaries on the Greco-Roman Coins of Anatolia," *Proceedings of the Tenth International Congress of Classical Archaeology* (Ankara 1978) 107–120.

Uluçay, M. Ç. *Saruhanogullari ve Eserlerine dair Vesikalar,* 2 vols. (Istanbul 1940, 1946).

Vann, R. L. *A Study of Roman Construction in Asia Minor: The Lingering Role of a Hellenistic Tradition of Ashlar Masonry* (Ph.D. dissertation, Cornell University, 1976).

Vermeule, C. C. III. "Hellenistic and Roman Cuirassed Statues: A Supplement," *Berytus* 15 (1964) 95–109.

——— *Roman Imperial Art in Greece and Asia Minor* (Cambridge, Mass. 1968).

Wainwright, G. A. "The Teresh, the Etruscans and Asia Minor," *AnatSt* 9 (1959) 197–213.

Waldbaum, J. C. *From Bronze to Iron: The Transition from the Bronze Age to the Iron Age in the Eastern Mediterranean,* Studies in Mediterranean Archaeology 54 (Gotenborg 1978).

Warfield, W. "Report on the Geology of Sardis," Appendix I in *Sardis* I (1922) 175–180.

Weidauer, L. *Die Probleme der frühen Elektronprägung,* Schweizerische Numismatische Gesellschaft, Monographien zur antiken Numismatik, *Typos* I (Fribourg 1975).

Welles, C. B. *Royal Correspondence in the Hellenistic Period: A Study in Greek Epigraphy* (New Haven 1934).

Wheeler, T. "Early Bronze Age Burial Customs in Western Anatolia," *AJA* 78 (1974) 414–425.

Whitmore, F. E., and Young, W. J. "Application of Platiniridium Inclusions in Gold," in *Applications of Science in Examination of Works of Art,* Proceedings of the seminar, 7–16 Sept. 1965, Museum of Fine Arts (Boston 1976) 88–95.

Whittlesey, J. H., "Aerial Archaeology: A Personal Account," *JFA* 1:1–2 (1974) 206–208.

——— "Balloon over Sardis," *Archaeology* 20:1 (Jan. 1967) 67–68.

——— "Bipod Camera Support: An Aluminum A-Frame Simplifies Recording for Archaeology," *Photogrammetric Engineering* (November 1966) 1005–1010.

——— "Photogrammetry for the Excavator," *Archaeology* 19:4 (October 1966) 273–276.

——— "Tethered Balloon for Archaeological Photos," *Photogrammetric Engineering* (Feb.-Mar. 1970) 181–186; fig. 1.

Will, E. *Histoire politique du monde hellénistique, 323–30 ar. J.C.* (Nancy 1966–1967).

Wischnitzer, R. *The Architecture of the European Synagogue* (Philadelphia 1964).

Wrabetz, J. "A New Serenus Stamping from Sardis and the Origins of the Eastern Sigillata B Ware," *HSCP* 80 (1976) 195–198.

Yarden, L. *The Tree of Light* (Ithaca 1971).

Yegul, F. K. "Early Byzantine Capitals from Sardis: A Study in the Ionic Type," *DO Papers* 28 (1974) 256–274.

——— "The Marble Court of Sardis and Historical Reconstruction," *Journal of Field Archaeology* 3:2 (1976) 169–194.

Young, W. J. "The Fabulous Gold of the Pactolus Valley," *BMFA* 70 (1972) 5–13.

General Bibliography

Abdul-Hak, S., and Abdul-Hak, A. *Catalogue illustré du Département des Antiquités Greco-romaines au Musée de Damas* (Damas 1951).

Akurgal, E. *The Art of the Hittites* (New York 1962).

—— *Bayrakli, Erster Vorlaufiger Bericht uber die Ausgrabungen in Alt-Smyrna,* Universität Ankara, Philosophische Fakultat, *Zeitschrift* VIII, no. 1 (Ankara 1950).

—— *Die Kunst Anatoliens von Homer bis Alexander dem Grossen* (Berlin 1961).

—— *Die Kunst der Hethiter* (Munich 1961).

—— "Smyrna," in *Princeton Encyclopedia of Classical Sites,* ed. R. Stillwell, W. L. MacDonald, and M. H. McAllister (Princeton 1976) 847–848.

Alpan, S. *Türkiye Mermer Envanteri* (Ankara 1966).

Angel, L. "Appendix: Early Bronze Karataş People and Their Cemeteries," *AJA* 80 (1976) 385–391.

Archaeological Calendar 1980 (Mainz 1980).

Arik, R. O. *Les fouilles d'Alaca Höyük 1935* (Ankara 1937).

Avi-Yonah, M. "Ancient Synagogues," *Ariel* (Jerusalem) 32 (1973) 29–43. Reprinted in Gutmann, *Synagogue,* 95–109.

—— *The Jews of Palestine* (Oxford 1976).

—— "Synagogue Architecture in the Classical Period," in *Jewish Art, An Illustrated History,* ed. C. Roth (New York 1961) cols. 155–190.

Babylonian Talmud, *Megillah* (Soncino edition) 144–145.

Ballance, M. H., and Brogan, O. "Roman Marble— A Link between Asia Minor and Libya," in Campbell, 33–38.

Balty, J. Ch. *Colloque Apamée de Syrie* (Brussels 1972).

Bammer, A. "Amazonen und das Artemision von Ephesos," *RA* 1:1976, 91–102.

Barnett, R. D. *A Catalogue of the Nimrud Ivories in the British Museum* (London 1957).

—— "Mopsos," *JHS* 73 (1953) 140–143.

—— "A New Inscribed Lydian Seal," *Studi in Onore di Piero Meriggi, Athenaeum,* Nouva Series 47, Fascicles 1–4 (1969) 21–24.

—— "Oriental Influences in Archaic Greece," in *The Aegean and the Near East, Studies Presented to Hetty Goldman,* ed. S. S. Weinberg (Locust Valley 1956) 212–238.

—— "Phrygia and the Peoples of Anatolia in the Iron Age, *Cambridge Ancient History,* 2d ed., vol. 2, fascicle 56 (Cambridge 1967).

Beazley, J. D. *Attic Black-figure Vase-painters* (Oxford 1956).

—— *Attic Red-figure Vase-painters,* 2d ed. (Oxford 1963).

—— "Hydria-Fragments in Corinth," *Hesperia* 24 (1955) 305–319.

Beazley, J. D., and Ashmole, B. *Greek Sculpture and Painting: To the end of the Hellenistic Period* (Cambridge 1932).

Bellinger, A. R. "Electrum Coins from Gordion," in *Essays in Greek Coinage Presented to Stanley Robinson,* ed. G. K. Jenkins and C. M. Kraay (Oxford 1968) 10–15.

Berchem, D. van. "Trois cas de'asylie archaique, I Éphèse," *Museum Helveticum* 17 (1960).

Bieber, M. *The Sculpture of the Hellenistic Age* (New York 1961).

Biringuccio, V. *The Pirotechnia,* trans. C. S. Smith and M. T. Grudi (New York 1942).

Bittel, K. *Bogazköy die Kleinfunde der Grabungen 1906–1912* (Osnabrück 1967) = *WVDOG* 60 (1967).

—— *Bogazköy III,* Deutsche Orient-Gesellschaft und das Deutsche Archäologische Institut (Berlin 1957).

—— *Die hethitischen Grabfunde von Osmankayasi* (Berlin 1958) = *WVDOG* 71 (1958).

—— "Ein Gräberfeld der Yortankultur bei Babaköy," *AOF* 13 (1939–1941) 1–28.

—— "Karabel," *AOF* 13 (1940) 188.

—— "Osman-Kayasi, eine hethitische Grabstätte," *MDOG* 86 (1953) 37–47.

Blake, M. E. *Ancient Roman Construction in Italy from the Prehistoric Period to Augustus* (Washington 1947).

Blegen, C. W. *Troy and the Trojans* (London 1963).

—— *Troy III* (Princeton 1953).

—— *Troy IV* (Princeton 1958).

Blinkenberg, C. *Fibules Grecques et Orientales* (Copenhagen 1926).

Boardman, J. *Greek Gems and Finger Rings* (London 1970, New York 1972).

Boethius, A. *Etruscan Culture, Land and People* (New York 1962).

Boethius, A., and Ward-Perkins, J. B. *Etruscan and Roman Architecture* (Baltimore 1970). Cited as *ERA.*

Borchhardt, J. *Die Bauskulptur des Heroons von Limyra: Das Grabmal des Lykischen Königs Perikles* (Berlin 1976).

—— "Epichorische gräko-persisch beeinflusste Reliefs in Kilikien," *IstMitt* 18 (1968) 161–211.

Bossert, H. Th. "Santas und Kupapa," *Mitteilungen der Altorientalischen Gesellschaft* 6:3 (1932).

Bowersock, G. *Augustus and the Greek World* (Oxford 1965).

Boyce, M. "On the Zoroastrian Temple Cult of Fire," *Journal of the American Oriental Society* 95.3 (1975).

Boysal, Y. "New Excavations in Caria," *Anatolia* 11 (1967) 31–56.

Brendel, O. J. *Etruscan Art* (New York 1978).

Brill, R. "Notes and News: Beth She'arim," *IEJ* 15 (1965) 261–262.

Brinkmann, R. "The Geology of Western Anatolia," in Campbell, 171–190.

Broneer, O. *Corinth* 4:2, *Terracotta Lamps* (Cambridge, Mass. 1930).

Brown, P. R. L. *The World of Late Antiquity* (London 1971).

Brown, W. L. "Pheidon's Alleged Aeginetan Coinage," *NC* 10:3–4 (1950) 177–204.

Bruno, V. J. "Antecedents of the Pompeian First Style," *AJA* 73 (1969) 305–317.

Buchwald, H. *The Church of the Archangels in Sige near Mudania* (Vienna 1969).

Buresch, K. *Aus Lydien* (Leipzig 1898).

Burn, A. R. *Persia and the Greeks, The Defense of the West, c. 546–478 B.C.* (London 1962).

Cahn, H. A. *Knidos, die Münzen des sechsten und des fünften Jahrhunderts vor Christ*, Deutsches Archäologisches Institut, Antike Münzen und geschnittene Steine 4 (Berlin 1970).

Caley, E., and Richards, J. *Theophrastus on Stones*, Ohio State University Graduate School Monographs, Contributions in Physical Sciences I (Columbus, Ohio 1956).

Cameron, A. *Circus Factions* (Oxford 1976).

Campbell, A. S., ed. *Geology and History of Turkey* (Tripoli 1971).

Canet, J., and Jaoul, P. *Géologie de la région de Manisa-Gördes* (Bölgesi Jeolojisi Hakkinda Rapor, typescript, 1946), Maps 1:100,000.

Cardascia, G. *Les Archives des Murasu, une famille d'hommes d'affaires babyloniens à l'époque Perse (455–403)* (Paris 1951).

Carruba, O. "A Lydian Inscription from Aphrodisias in Caria," *JHS* 90 (1970) 195—196, pl. 3:2.

—— "Zur Grammatik des Lydischen," *Studi in Onore di Piero Meriggi, Athenaeum*, Nuova Serie 47, Fascicles 1–4 (1969) 39–83.

Charbonneaux, J., Martin, R., and Villard, F. *Hellenistic Art* (London 1972).

Codex Theodosianus, ed. T. Mommsen and P. Meyer (Berlin 1905). Trans. C. Pharr (Princeton 1952).

Cohen, N. "Rabbi Meir, A Descendant of Anatolian Proselytes," *JJS* 23 (1972) 51–59.

Coldstream, J. N. *Greek Geometric Pottery* (London 1968).

Collignon, M. "Note sur les fouilles de M. Paul Gaudin dans la Necropole de Yortan en Mysie," *CRAI* (1901) 810–817.

Comnena, A. *Alexiade*, trans. B. Leib (in French), 4 vols. (Paris 1943–1976).

Compendia Rerum Iudaicarum ad Novum Testamentum I.1, 2 editions, ed. S. Safrai and M. Stern (Assen 1974, 1976).

Conant, K. J. *Carolingian and Romanesque Architecture, 800–1200* (Harmondsworth 1959).

Cook, J. M. *The Greeks in Ionia and the East* (New York, Washington 1963).

—— "Old Smyrna, 1948–1951; the Site and Its Environs; the History of Old Smyrna," *BSA* 53–54 (1958–1959) 1–34.

—— "Old Smyrna: Ionic Black Figure and Other Sixth-Century Figured Ware," *BSA* 60 (1965) 114–142.

Cook, R. M. *Clazomenian Sarcophagi*, ed. J. Boardman and H. Cahn, *Kerameus* 3 (Mainz 1980).

—— "Speculations on the Origins of Coinage," *Historia* 7 (1958) 257–262.

Corpus Inscriptionum Iudaicarum, ed. J. B. Frey (Rome 1936, 1952). Cited as *CII*.

Coulton, J. J. *Ancient Architects at Work: Problems of Structure and Design* (Ithaca 1977).

Coupel, P., and Demargne, P. *Fouilles de Xanthos III, Le Monument des Néréides, L'Architecture*, 2 vols. (Paris 1969).

Crema, L. *L'architettura romana*, in *Enciclopedia Classica III*, 12.1 (Turin 1959).

Cross, F. M., Jr. "An Aramaic Inscription from Daskyleion," *BASOR* 184 (1966) 7–13.

Curtius, L. *Die Wandmalerei Pompejis* (Koln 1929, reprinted 1960).

Daniel, J. L. "Anti-Semitism in the Hellenistic-Roman Period," *JBL* 98 (1979) 45–65.

Deichmann, F. W. "Frühchristliche Kirchen in antiken Heiligtümern," *JdI* 54 (1939) 107.

Deiss, J. *Herculaneum* (New York 1966).

Delorme, J. *Gymnasion* (Paris 1960).

Dentzer, J. M. "Aux origines de l'iconographie du banquet couché," *RA* (1971) 215–258. Cited as Dentzer, "Banquet."

—— "Reliefs en banquet dans l'Asie Mineure du Ve siècle avant J.-C.," *RA* (1969) 195–224.

Desborough, V. *The Greek Dark Ages* (London 1972).

Dessenne, A. *Le Sphinxe, Étude iconographique* (Paris 1957).

Deubner, O. "Expolitio, Inkrustation und Wandmalerei," *RömMitt* 54 (1939) 14–41.

Deutsche Heereskarte Türkei, Ausgabe Nr. 3, Blatt-Nr. GIII, Manisa, No. F-3 (1941) 1:200,000.

DeVries, K. "Greeks and Phrygians in the Early Iron

Age," in *From Athens to Gordion: The Papers of a Memorial Symposium for Rodney S. Young,* University Museum Papers 1 (Philadelphia 1980) 33–50.

Dewdney, J. C. "Physical, Human and Economic Geography of Turkey," in Campbell, 83–110.

Diller, H. "Zwei Erzahlungen des Lyders Xanthos," *Navicula Chiloniensis, Studia philologa Felici Jacoby* (Leiden 1956) 66–78.

Dinsmoor, W. B. *Architecture of Ancient Greece: An Account of Its Historical Development* (London 1950).

Dominian, L. "History and Geology of Ancient Gold-Fields in Turkey," *Transactions of the American Institute of Mining Engineers* 42 (New York 1912) 569–589.

Dorigo, W. *Late Roman Painting* (New York 1971).

Downey, G. *Ancient Antioch* (Princeton 1963).

—— *A History of Antioch in Syria from Seleucus to the Arab Conquest* (Princeton 1961).

Drees, L. *Olympia; Gods, Artists, and Athletes,* trans. G. Onn (New York 1968).

Drew-Bear, T. "An Act of Foundation at Hypaipa," *Chiron* 10 (1980) 509–536, pls. 24–26.

Driehaus, J. "Prähistorische Siedlungsfunde in der unteren Kaikosebene und an dem Golfe von Çandarli," *IstMitt* 7 (1957) 76–101.

Dunbabin, T. J. *The Greeks and Their Eastern Neighbors, Studies in the Relations between Greece and the Countries of the Near East in the Eighth and Seventh Centuries B.C.,* The Society for the Promotion of Hellenic Studies, Suppl. 8 (London 1957).

Duru, R. "West Anatolian Jewelry," *Belleten* 142 (1972) 123–135.

Easton, D. F. "Towards a Chronology for the Anatolian Early Bronze Age," *AnatSt* 26 (1976) 145–173.

Eddy, S. "The Gold in the Athenian Parthenos," *AJA* 81 (1977) 107–112.

Eichler, F. *Das Heroon von Gjölbaschi-Trysa* (Vienna 1950).

—— "Die österreichischen Ausgrabungen in Ephesos im Jahre 1961," *AnzWien* 99 (1962) 50–52.

ERA, see Boethius, A.

Erinç, S. "The Gediz Earthquake of 1970," in Campbell, 443–542.

Evans, G. "The Recent Sedimentation of Turkey and the Adjacent Mediterranean and Black Seas: A Review," in Campbell, 385–406.

Fasolo, F. "L'Architettura Romana di Efeso," *Bollettino del Centro di Studi dell'Architettura* 18 (1962) 1–92.

Finley, M. I. *The World of Odysseus* (New York 1972).

Firatli, N. "Hypogaeum," in *Mélanges Mansel,* ed. E. Akurgal and U. B. Alkim (Ankara 1974) 924–929, figs. 130–131.

Fowden, G. "Bishops and Temples in the Eastern Roman Empire A.D. 320–435," *JTS* 29 (1978) 53–78.

Francovich, G. de. "Problems of Achaemenid Architecture," *East and West* 16:3–4 (1966) 201–260.

Fränkel, M. *Die Inschriften von Pergamon* (Berlin 1890) no. 248.

Frankfort, H. *Kingship and the Gods: A Study of Ancient Near Eastern Religion as the Integration of Society and Nature* (Chicago 1948).

Frantz, A. "From Paganism to Christianity in the Temples of Athens," *DO Papers* 19 (1965) 187–188.

French, D. H. "Prehistoric Sites in Northwest Anatolia II: The Balikesir and Akhisar-Manisa Areas," *AnatSt* 19 (1969) 41–98.

Freyer-Schauenburg, B. *Elfenbeine aus dem samischen Heraion* (Hamburg 1966).

Furtwängler, A. *Antike Gemmen,* 3 vols. (Leipzig, Berlin 1900).

Gall, H. von. *Die Paphlagonischen Felsgräber, Eine Studie zur Kleinasiatischen Kunstgeschichte* (Tübingen 1966) = *IstMitt-BH* 1 (1966).

Garbrecht, G. "Fragen der Wasserwirtschaft Pergamons," in *Pergamenische Forschungen* 1, ed. E. Boehringer (Berlin 1972) 43–48.

Garbrecht, G., and Fahl, H. "Die Kaikos-Leitung," *Mitteilungshefte des Leichtweiss-Instituts für Wasserbau der Technischen Universität Braunschweig* 44 (1975).

Garbrecht, G., and Holtorff, G. "Die Madradag-Leitung," *Mitteilungshefte des Leichtweiss-Instituts für Wasserbau der Technischen Universität Braunschweig* 37 (1973).

Gardiner, E. A. *Naukratis,* vol. 2 (London 1888). Cited as *Naukratis,* 2.

Gerkan, A. von, and Krischen, F. *Thermen und Palaestren,* Milet 1:9 (Berlin 1928).

Ghirshman, R. "Invasions des nomades sur le Plateau Iranien aux premiers siecles du Ier millénaire avant J.-C.," in Mellink, *Dark Ages,* 3–8.

Giglioli, E. Q. *L'arte etrusca* (Milan 1934).

Gimbutas, M. *The Prehistory of Eastern Europe,* The American School of Prehistoric Research Bulletin 20 (Cambridge, Mass. 1956).

Goldman, H. *Tarsus I, The Hellenistic and Roman Periods* (Princeton 1950).

—— *Tarsus II, From the Neolithic through the Bronze Age* (Princeton 1956).

Greifenhagen, A. *Antike Kunstwerke,* 2d ed. (Berlin 1966).

Gültekin, H., and Baran, M. "The Mycenaean Grave Found at the Hill at Ayasuluk," *TürkArkDerg* 13 (1964) 125–133.

Gurney, O. R. *The Hittites* (London 1952).

Güterbock, H. G. "New Excavations at Boghazköy, Capital of the Hittites," *Archaeology* 6 (1953) 211–216.

Gutmann, J. "A Note on the Temple Menorah," *Zeitschrift für die Neutestamentliche Wissenschaft* 60 (1969) 289–291. Reprinted in *No Graven Images: Studies in Art and the Hebrew Bible,* ed. J. Gutmann (New York 1971) 36–38.

———— ed. *The Synagogue: Studies in Origins, Archaeology and Architecture* (New York 1975).

Hall, H. R. "Mursil and Myrtilos," *JHS* 29 (1909) 19–20.

Hammer, J. "Der Feingehalt der griechischen und römischen Münzen," *ZfN* 26 (1907) 1–144.

Hanfmann, G. M. A. "A Hittite Priest from Ephesus," *AJA* 66 (1962) 1–4.

———— "Ionia, Leader or Follower?" *HSCP* 61 (1953) 1–37.

———— Review of P. J. Riis, *Hama, Les cimetières à crémation* 2:3 (Copenhagen 1948), in *JNES* 12 (1953) 230–233.

Hanfmann, G. M. A., and Waldbaum, J. C. "Two Submycenaean Vases and a Tablet from Stratonikeia in Caria," *AJA* 72 (1968) 51–56.

Harden, D. R. "The Rothchild Lycurgus Cup: Addenda and Corrigenda," *JGS* 5 (1963) 9–17.

Harrison, E. B. *The Athenian Agora XI, Archaic and Archaistic Sculpture* (Princeton 1965).

Harta Genel Müdürlügü Basimevi, T. C. Maden Tetkik ve Arama Enstitüsü Genel Direktörlügü 1946, Manisa 87: 1, 2, 4; 1:100,000 (unpublished).

Harta Genel Müdürlügü 1943, 1951, Manisa 1:200,000.

Harvey, F. D. "Sostratos of Aegina," *La Parola del Passato* 31 (1976) 206–214.

Hecht, K. "Zwei Aquedukte der Ketios-Leitung," *Mitteilungshefte des Leichtweiss-Instituts für Wasserbau der Technischen Universität Braunschweig* 45 (1975).

———— "Zwie Weitere Aquedukte der Kaikos-Leitung," *Mitteilungshefte des Leichtweiss-Instituts für Wasserbau der Technischen Universität Braunschweig* 54 (1977).

Helbig, W., and Speier, H. *Führer durch die öffentlichen Sammlungen Klassischer Altertümer in Rom,* 4th ed., 1–4 (Tübingen 1963–1972).

Herrmann, P. "Antiochos der Grosse und Teos," *Anatolia* 9 (1965) 28–159.

———— "Mên, Herr von Axiotta," *Studien zur Religion und Kultur Kleinasian, Festschrift für Friedrich Karl Dörner,* ed. S. Şahin, E. Schwertheim, and J. Wagner, 2 vols. (Leiden 1978).

Heubeck, A. "Lydisch," in *Altkleinasiatische Sprachen, Handbuch der Orientalistik* 1:2:1, 2 (Leiden, Cologne 1969) 397–427.

Hogarth, D. G. *British Museum, Excavations at Ephesus, The Archaic Artemisia,* 2 vols. (London 1908).

Hopkins, C. *The Discovery of Dura* (New Haven 1973) 242–249.

Houwink ten Cate, P. H. J. *The Records of the Early Hittite Empire* (c. 1450–1380 B.C.), Uitgaven van het Nederlands Historisch-Archaeologisch Instituut te Istanbul, XXVI (Istanbul 1970).

Huemer, F. "A Dionysiac Connection in Early Rubens," *AB* 61:4 (1979) 562–574.

Hüttenmeister, F., and Reeg, G. *Die antiken Synagogen in Israel,* 2 vols. (Wiesbaden 1977).

Ilhan, E. "Earthquakes in Turkey," in Campbell, 431–442.

Inscriptiones Graecae ad Res Romanas Pertinentes, ed. R. Gagnat and G. LaFaye, 4 vols. (Rome 1927). Cited as *IGRR.*

Iosi, E. "Ampolla," *EC* 1 (1949) 1113–1115.

Izdar, E. "Introduction to Geology and Metamorphism of the Menderes Massif of Western Turkey," in Campbell, 495–500.

———— *Petrographisch-geologische Untersuchungen am Nordwestrand des Menderes Massivs Westanatolien* (Habilitation thesis, Izmir, 1971: 1969 German version in print; Turkish version unpublished).

Jacobsthal, P. "The Date of the Ephesian Foundation-Deposit," *JHS* 71 (1951) 85–95.

Jidejian, N. *Byblos through the Ages* (Beirut 1968).

Johnson, S. "Asia Minor and Early Christianity," in *Christianity, Judaism and Other Greco-Roman Cults: Studies for Morton Smith at Sixty,* ed. J. Neusner (Leiden 1975).

Jones, A. H. M. "The Cloth Industry under the Roman Empire," *Economic History Review* 18 (1960) 183–192.

———— *The Greek City From Alexander to Justinian* (Oxford 1940).

———— *The Later Roman Empire 284–602. A Social, Economic and Administrative Survey* (Norman, Okla. 1964).

Jones, C. P. *Plutarch and Rome* (Oxford 1971).

Kadish, B. "Excavations of Prehistoric Remains at Aphrodisias, 1967," *AJA* 73 (1969) 49–65.

———— "Excavations of Prehistoric Remains at Aphrodisias, 1968–1969," *AJA* 75 (1971) 121–140.

Kamen-Kaye, M. "A Review of Depositional History and Geological Structure," in Campbell, 111–138.

Karageorghis, V. "The Relations between the Tomb Architecture of Anatolia and Cyprus in the Archaic Period," in *Proceedings of the Tenth International Congress of Classical Archaeology,* ed. E. Akurgal, Ankara-Izmir 23–30/IX/1973, 3 vols. (Ankara 1978) 361–368.

Kaspar, S. "Eine Nekropole nordwestlich von Soma," *AA* 85 (1970) 71–85.

Keil, J. "Die Lysimachische Stadt," *Ephesos: Ein Führer durch die Ruinenstätte und ihre Geschichte* (Vienna 1964).

———— *Ephesos: Ein Führer durch die Ruinenstatte und*

ihre Geschichte (Vienna 1964). Cited as Keil (1964).

——— *Führer durch Ephesos* (Vienna 1957).

——— *ÖJhBeibl* 29 (1935).

Keil, J., and Premerstein, A. von. "Bericht über eine Reise in Lydien ausgeführt," *DenkschrWien* 53:2 (1908); "Bericht über zweite Reise," 54:2 (1911); "Bericht über eine dritte Reise," 57:1 (1914).

Kienast, H. J. "Der Tunnel des Eupalinos auf Samos," *Architectura* 7.2 (1977) 97–116.

Kiepert, H. *Karte von Kleinasien* (Berlin 1911) 1:400,000.

——— "Tschihatscheff's Reisen in Kleinasian und Armenien 1847–1863," *Petermann's geographische Mitteilungen,* Suppl. 20 (Gotha 1867).

Kindler, A. "A Coin Type from Apameia in Phrygia (Asia Minor) Depicting the Narrative of Noah," Museum Haaretz, *Bulletin* 13 (1971) 24–32.

Kitzinger, E. "The Threshold of the Holy Shrine: Observations on Floor Mosaics at Antioch and Bethlehem," in *Kyriakon, Festschrift Johannes Quasten,* ed. P. Granfield and J. A. Jungmann (Münster Westfalen 1970) 639–647.

Kleeman, I. *Der Satrapensarkophag aus Sidon, Istanbuler Forschungen* 20 (Berlin 1955).

Kleiner, G. *Alt-Milet* (Wiesbaden 1966).

——— *Die Ruinen von Milet* (Berlin 1968).

Kothe, H. "Die Herkunft der kimmerischen Reiter," *Klio* 41 (1963) 1–37.

Kraabel, A. T. "Social Systems of Six Diaspora Synagogues," forthcoming in *Ancient Synagogues: The Current State of Research,* ed. J. Gutmann.

——— "Synagogues, Ancient," *New Catholic Encyclopedia,* Suppl. (Washington 1974) 436–439.

Kraay, C. M. *Archaic and Classical Greek Coins* (Berkeley 1976).

Krautheimer, R. "The Constantinian Basilica," *DO Papers* 21 (1967) 117–140.

——— *Early Christian and Byzantine Architecture* (Harmondsworth, Middlesex 1965). Cited as Krautheimer.

Krefter, F. *Persepolis Rekonstruktionen: Der Wiederaufbau des Frauenpalastes, Rekonstruktionen der Paläste, Modell von Persepolis, Teheraner Forschungen* 3 (Berlin 1971).

Kroeber, A. L. and Kluckhohn, C. *Culture: A Critical Review of Concepts and Definitions,* Papers of the Peabody Museum of American Archaeology and Ethnology 47:1 (Cambridge, Mass. 1952).

Kurtz, D. C., and Boardman, J. *Greek Burial Customs* (Ithaca, N.Y. 1971).

Kyrieleis, H. *Throne und Klinen, JdI,* Ergänzungsheft 24 (Berlin 1969).

Lähnemann, J. "Die Sieben Sendschreiben der Johannes-Apokalypse. Dokumente für die Konfrontation des frühen Christentums mit Hellenistisch-Römischer Kultur und Religion in Kleinasien,"

Studien zur Religion und Kultur Kleinasiens, Festschrift für Friedrich Karl Dörner, ed. S. Şahin, E. Schwertheim, and J. Wagner, 2 vols. (Leiden 1978) 516–539.

Lanckoronski, K., and Niemann, G. *Die Städte Pamphyliens und Pisidiens* I (Vienna 1890).

Lane, A. "Lakonian Vase-Painting," *BSA* 34 (1933–1934) 99–198, pls. 20–49.

Laroche, E. "Koubaba, déesse anatolienne et le problème des origines de Cybèle," *Éléments Orientaux dans la Religion Ancienne,* Centre d'études supérieures spécialisé d'histoire des religions de Strasbourg (Paris 1960) 113–118.

Lehmann, P. W. "Lefkadia and the Second Style," in *Studies in Classical Art and Archaeology, A Tribute to P. H. von Blanckenhagen,* ed. G. Kopcke and M. B. Moore (Locust Valley, N.Y. 1979) 225–229.

——— *Samothrace 3, The Hieron,* Bollingen Series 60 (New York 1969).

Leix, A. "Historical Cleaning," *CIBA Review* 12 (1938) 423.

Leon, H. J. *The Jews of Ancient Rome* (Philadelphia 1960).

Levi, D. *Antioch Mosaic Pavements* (Princeton 1947).

——— "Le campagne 1962–1964 a Iasos," *ASAtene* 27–28 (1965–1966) 505–546.

——— "Le due prime campagne di scavo a Iasos," *ASAtene* 23–24 (1961–1962) 555–571.

Linfert, A. *Kunstzentren hellenistischer Zeit, Studien an weiblichen Gewandfiguren* (Wiesbaden 1976).

Lloyd, S. *Beycesultan II, Middle Bronze Age Architecture and Pottery,* Occasional Publications of the British Institute of Archaeology at Ankara (London 1965).

Lloyd, S., and Mellaart, J. "Beycesultan Excavations: First Preliminary Report," *AnatSt* 5 (1955) 39–92.

——— *Beycesultan I, The Chalcolithic and Early Bronze Levels,* Occasional Publications of the British Institute of Archaeology at Ankara 6 (London 1962).

Lorimer, H. L. *Homer and the Monuments* (London 1950).

Maas, P. "Philaenis," *RE* 19:2 (1938) 2122. Cited as *RE* 19:2.

Maccanico, R. "Ginnasi romani ad Efeso," *ArchCl* 15 (1963) 32–60.

MacMullen, R. *Enemies of the Roman Order: Treason, Unrest, and Alienation in the Empire* (Cambridge, Mass. 1966).

——— "Roman Imperial Building in the Provinces," *HSCP* 64 (1959) 207–235.

Makaronas, C. L., and Miller, S. G. "The Tomb of Lyson and Kallikles," *Archaeology* 27 (1974) 248–259.

MAMA VI, see *Monumenta Asiae Minoris Antiqua VI.*

Manisa Vilayeti (Manisa 1932).

Mansel, A. *Die Ruinen von Side* (Berlin 1963).

Marinus, *Vita Procli, Graece et Latine recensuit adnotationesque et indices addidit*, ed. I. F. Boissonade (Leipzig 1814).

Martin, R. *Manuel d'archéologie grecque I, Matériaux et techniques* (Paris 1965).

—— *Recherches sur l'agora grecque*, Étude d'histoire et d'architecture urbaines, Bibliothèque des Écoles françaises d'Athènes et de Rome, Fascicle 174 (Paris 1951).

—— *L'Urbanisme dans la Grèce antique* (Paris 1956).

Masson, O. *Les écritures de l'Anatolie antique* (Pisa 1977).

Matz, F. *Die dionysischen Sarkophage, Die antiken Sarkophagreliefs* 4:1, Deutsches Archäologisches Institut (Berlin 1968).

Mazar, B. "The Archaeological Excavations near the Temple Mount," in *Jerusalem Revealed: Archaeology in the Holy City 1968–1974*, ed. Y. Yadin (Jerusalem 1975) 25–40. Cited as Mazar, "Excavations."

—— *Beth She'arim I* (Jerusalem 1973).

—— *The Excavations in the Old City of Jerusalem: Preliminary Report of the First Season, 1968* (Jerusalem 1969). Cited as Mazar, *Jerusalem*.

—— *The Excavations in the Old City of Jerusalem Near the Temple Mount: Preliminary Report of the Second and Third Season, 1969–1970* (Jerusalem 1971). Cited as Mazar, *Temple Mount*.

McCredie, J. R. "Hippodamos of Miletos," in *Studies Presented to George M. A. Hanfmann*, ed. D. G. Mitten, J. G. Pedley, and J. A. Scott, Fogg Art Museum Monographs in Art and Archaeology 2 (Cambridge, Mass. 1970).

McDonald, W., and Rapp, G. *The Minnesota Messenia Expedition, Reconstructing a Bronze Age Environment* (Minneapolis 1972).

Meiggs, R. *Roman Ostia*, 2d ed. (Oxford 1973).

Mellaart, J. *The Chalcolithic and Early Bronze Ages in the Near East and Anatolia* (Beirut 1966).

—— "Iron Age Pottery from Southern Anatolia," *Belleten* 19 (1955) 74.

—— "Western Anatolia, Beycesultan and the Hittites," *Mélanges Mansel I*, ed. E. Akurgal and U. B. Alkim (Ankara 1974) 493–526.

Mellink, M. J. "Anatolian Chronology," in *Chronologies in Old World Archaeology*, ed. R. W. Ehrich (Chicago 1965) 101–131.

—— "Archaeology in Asia Minor," *AJA* 71 (1967) 155–174.

—— "Archaeology in Asia Minor," *AJA* 81 (1977) 289–321. Cited as Mellink, "Archaeology."

—— ed. *Dark Ages and Nomads c. 1000 B.C.*, Studies in Iranian and Anatolian Archaeology, Nederlands Historisch-Archäologisch Instituut 18 (Istanbul 1964) 3–8.

—— "Excavations at Karataş—Semayük and El-mali, Lycia, 1968," *AJA* 73 (1969) 319–331, pls. 71–78.

—— "Excavations at Karataş—Semayük and Elmali, Lycia, 1972," *AJA* 77 (1973) 293–303, pls. 41–46.

—— *A Hittite Cemetery at Gordion* (Philadelphia 1956).

Mengarelli, R. "Caere e le recenti scoperte," *StEtr* 1 (1927) 145–147.

—— "La Necropoli di Caere Nuove Osservazioni su speciali usi e riti funerari," *StEtr* 11 (1937) 77–93.

Meriggi, P. "Der indogermanische Charakter des Lydischen," *Festschrift für Herman Hirt* 2 (Heidelberg 1936) 283–290.

Meyers, E. "Synagogue, Architecture," *The Interpreters Dictionary of the Bible*, Suppl. (Nashville 1976) 842–844.

Miltner, F. *Ephesos, Stadt der Artemis und des Johannes* (Vienna 1958).

Minns, E. H. *Scythians and Greeks: A Survey of Ancient History and Archaeology on the Northeast Coast of the Euxine from the Danube to the Caucasus* (Cambridge 1913).

Monumenta Asiae Minoris Antiqua VI, Monuments and Documents from Phrygia and Caria, ed. W. H. Buckler and W. M. Calder (Manchester 1939). Cited as *MAMA VI*.

Moore, C. B., ed. *Reconstruction of Complex Societies*, BASOR Suppl. 20 (1974).

Moretti, L. *Iscrizioni agonistiche greche*, Studi pubblicati dall'Istituto italiano per la storia antica, fasc. 12 (Roma 1953).

Mørkholm, O. "Some Reflections on Cistophoroi," *ANSMN* 24 (1979) 47–61.

Müller, K. O. *Die Etrusker*, 2 vols. (Stuttgart 1877).

Muscarella, O. W. *Phrygian Fibulae from Gordion*, Colt Archaeological Institute, Monograph 4 (London 1967).

MythLex, see Roscher, W. H.

Nash, E. *A Pictorial Dictionary of Ancient Rome*, 2 vols. (London, Zwemmer 1961, 1962).

National Geographic Society. "Classical Lands of the Mediterranean" (1949) 1:2,750,000.

Naukratis, 1, see Petrie, W. M. F.

Naukratis, 2, see Gardiner, E. A.

Naumann, R. *Architektur Kleinasiens*, 2d ed. (Tübingen 1971).

Nayir, K. "Excavations of Mounds at Alahidir, 1979," *Anatolian Researches* 7 (1979) 115–120, pls. 1–9. In Turkish.

Neumann, O. "Lydisch-hethitische Verknüpfungen," *Studi in Onore di Piero Meriggi, Athenaeum*, Nuova Series 47, Fascicles 1–4 (1969) 217–225.

Neusner, J. *Early Rabbinic Judaism*, Studies in Judaism in Late Antiquity 13 (Leiden 1975).

———— A History of the Jews in Babylonia, 5 vols., Studia Post-Biblica 9 (Leiden 1965–1970).

Nilsson, M. P. Die Hellenistische Schule (Munich 1955).

Noble, J. "The Technique of Egyptian Faience," AJA 73 (1969) 435.

Noe, S. P. Bibliography of Greek Coin Hoards, Numismatic Notes and Monograph 78 (New York 1937).

Nylander, C. "Clamps and Chronology," Irania Antiqua 6 (1966) 130–146.

Oberleitner, W., ed., Gschwantler, K., Bernhard-Walcher, A., and Bammer, A. Funde aus Ephesos und Samothrake, Kunsthistorisches Museum, Wien, Katalog der Antikensammlung 2 (Vienna 1978).

Ogilvie, R. E. "Application of the Solid State X-ray Detector to the Study of Art Objects," in Examination of Works of Art, ed. W. J. Young (Boston 1970).

Ögün, B. "Die urartäischen Bestattungsbräuche," in Studien zur Religion und Kultur Kleinasiens, Festschrift für Friedrich Karl Dörner, ed. S. Şahin, E. Schwertheim, and J. Wagner, 2 vols. (Leiden 1978) 639–678.

Oppenheim, A. L. "The Golden Garments of the Gods," JNES 8 (1949) 172–193.

Orthmann, W. "Keramik der Yortankultur in den Berliner Museum," IstMitt 16 (1966) 1–16.

Otten, H. "Ein Totenritual hethitischer Könige," MDOG 78 (1940) 3–11.

———— "Sprachliche Stellung und Datierung des Madduwatta-Textes," Studien zu den Bogazköy-Texten, Heft 11 (Wiesbaden 1969).

The Oxford Classical Dictionary, ed. N. G. L. Hammond and H. H. Scullard, 2d ed. (Oxford 1970). Cited as OCD.

The Oxford Dictionary of the Christian Church, ed. F. L. Cross (London 1966). Cited as ODCC.

Oxyrhynchus Papyri, ed. B. P. Grenfell and A. S. Hunt (1898–1927). Cited as P.Oxy.

Özgüç, T. Ausgrabungen in Kültepe. Bericht—1948 (Ankara 1950). Cited as Özgüç, Ausgrabungen in Kültepe.

———— Ausgrabungen in Kültepe—1949 (Ankara 1953).

———— Die Besttatungsbräuche im vorgeschichtlichen Anatolien (Ankara 1948).

P.Oxy., see Oxyrhynchus Papyri.

Pace, B., Ricci, G., Vighi, R., and Moretti, M. "Scavi di Raniero Mengarelli," MonAnt 42 (1955).

Pallottino, M. The Necropolis of Cervetri (Rome 1960).

Pamir, H. N., and Erentöz, C., eds. Explanatory Text of the Geological Map of Turkey: Izmir, MTAE Yayinlarindan (Ankara 1973).

Parkes, J. The Conflict of the Church and the Synagogue (Cleveland, New York, Philadelphia 1961, 1934).

Pearson, L. Early Ionian Historians (Oxford 1939).

Pembroke, S. "Women in Charge: The Function of Alternatives in Early Greek Tradition and the Ancient Idea of Matriarchy," JWarb 30 (1967) 1–35.

Petrie, W. M. F. Naukratis, vol. 1 (London 1886). Cited as Naukratis, 1.

Pfuhl, E. Malerei und Zeichnung der Griechen, 3 vols. (Munich 1923). Cited as Pfuhl, MuZ.

Pharr, C. The Theodosian Code and Novels and the Sirmondian Constitutions: A Translation with Commentary, Glossary, and Bibliography (New York 1952).

Philippson, A. Topographische Karte des westlichen Kleinasien (Gotha 1910) Blätter 3, 4; 1:100,000.

Podzuweit, C. Trojanische Gefässformen der Frühbronzezeit in Anatolien, der Ägäis und angrenzenden Gebieten, Heidelberger Akademie der Wissenschaften, Monographien Bd. 1 (Mainz 1979).

Pollitt, J. J., ed. The Art of Greece, 1400–31 B.C.; Sources and Documents (Englewood Cliffs, N.J. 1965).

Porada, E. The Art of Iran (New York 1962) 90–103.

Prayon, F. "Zur Datierung der drei frühetruskischen Sitzstatuetten aus Cerveteri," RömMitt 82 (1975) 165–179.

Preger, A., ed. Scriptores originum Constantinopolitarum, 2 (Leipzig 1907).

Price, E. R. "Pottery from Naucratis," JHS 44 (1924) 180–222.

Price, M., and Waggoner, N. Archaic Greek Coinage: The Asyut Hoard (London 1975).

Radt, W. Pergamon, Archäologischer Führer (Istanbul 1978).

Ravndal, G. Turkey, A Commercial and Industrial Handbook (Washington, D.C. 1926).

RE 19:2, see Maas, P.

Rehm, A. Delphinion: Ergebnisse der Ausgrabungen und Untersuchungen seit dem Jahre 1899 I:3, ed. T. Wiegand (Berlin 1906).

Restle, M. Byzantine Wall Painting in Asia Minor (Greenwich, Conn. 1967).

Reusch, W. Der historische Wert der Caracalla Vita, Klio, Suppl. 24 (1931).

Richter, G. M. A. The Furniture of the Greeks, Etruscans and Romans (London 1966).

———— Korai: Archaic Greek Maidens (London 1968).

———— Kouroi: Archaic Greek Youths (London 1960).

———— The Portraits of the Greeks, 3 vols. (London 1965).

Robert, L. "Malédictions funéraires grecques," CRAI (1978) 241–289.

———— Noms indigènes dans l'Asie Mineure Gréco-Romaine (Paris 1963).

Robertson, D. S. Greek and Roman Architecture (Cambridge 1969).

Robinson, E. G. S. "The Coins of the Ephesian Artemision Reconsidered," JHS 71 (1951) 156–167.

Robinson, S. *A History of Dyed Textiles* (Cambridge, Mass. 1969).

Röder, J. "Marmor Phrygium—Die antiken Marmorbrüche von Isçehisar in Westanatolien," *JdI* 86 (1971) 253–312.

Roebuck, C. "The Organization of Naukratis," *CP* 46 (1951) 212–220.

Roscher, W. H. *Ausführliches Lexikon der griechischen und römischen Mythologie* (Leipzig 1889–1924).

Rostovtzeff, M. "Ancient Decorative Wall-Painting," *JHS* 39 (1919) 144–145.

—— "Notes on the Economic Policy of the Pergamene Kings," in *Anatolian Studies Presented to Sir William Mitchell Ramsey,* ed. W. H. Buckler and W. M. Calder (Manchester 1923) 359–390.

—— *Social and Economic History of the Roman Empire* I (Oxford 1957).

Ryan, C. W. *A Guide to the Known Minerals of Turkey,* Mineral Research and Exploration Institute of Turkey (Ankara 1960).

Safrai, S. "Was There a Women's Gallery in the Synagogue of Antiquity?" *Tarbiz* 22 (1963) 329–338.

Saller, S. *Second Revised Catalogue of the Ancient Synagogues of the Holy Land* (Jerusalem 1972).

Saxl, F. *Mithras; typengeschichtliche Untersuchungen* (Berlin 1931).

Schafer, J. *Hellenistische Keramik aus Pergamon, Pergamenische Forschungen* 2, Deutsches Archäologisches Institut (Berlin 1968).

Schauenburg, K. "Die Cameliden im Altertum," *BonnJbb* 155–156 (1955–1956) 59–94.

Schmidt, E. F. "The Alishar Hüyük; Seasons of 1928 and 1929," *OIP* 20 (Chicago 1933).

—— *Persepolis III: The Royal Tombs and Other Monuments,* University of Chicago, Oriental Institute Publications (Chicago 1953–1957).

Sevoroskin, V. V. *Lidiyskiy Yazik* (Moscow 1967).

Smallwood, M. *The Jews under Roman Rule,* Studies on Judaism in Late Antiquity 20 (Leiden 1975).

Smith, C. "The Ivory Statuettes" and "Other Ivory and Bone Objects," in Hogarth, *Ephesus,* 155–198.

Snodgrass, A. M. *The Dark Ages of Greece* (Edinburgh 1971).

Sokolowski, F. "A New Testimony on the Cult of Artemis of Ephesos," *HThR* 58 (1965) 427–431.

Sommer, F., and Kahle, P. "Die lydisch-aramäische Bilingue," in *Kleinasiatische Forschungen* 1, ed. F. Sommer and H. Ehelolf (1927).

Spinazzola, V. *Pompei alla luce degli scavi nuovi di Via dell'Abbondanza anni 1910–1923* I (Rome 1953).

Strocka, A. M. *Die Wandmalerei der Hanghäuser in Ephesos,* Forschungen in Ephesos 8:1 (Vienna 1977).

Stronach, D. B. "The Development and Diffusion of Metal Types in Early Bronze Age Anatolia," *AnatSt* 7 (1957) 89–125.

Sukenik, D. *The Ancient Synagogue of Beth Alpha* (Jerusalem 1932).

—— *Ancient Synagogues, Palestine and Greece,* Schweich Lectures on Biblical Archaeology 1930 (London 1934).

Swindler, M. H. *Ancient Painting, from Earliest Times to the Period of Christian Art* (New Haven 1929).

Takaz, H. "28.12.1973/26.1.1974 Amasya Kulistepe Nekropol Kazisi On Raporu, *TürkArkDerg* 22:1 (1975) 109–111, plans 1–4, figs. 1–6.

Täschner, F. *Das anatolische Wegenetz nach osmanischen Quellen* (Leipzig 1924–1936).

Tertullian, *De resurrectione carnis,* ed. E. Evans (London 1960).

Thomas, E. *Mythos und Geschichte* (Köln 1976).

Thompson, H. A., and Wycherley, R. E. *The Athenian Agora XIV, The Agora of Athens, The History, Shape and Uses of an Ancient City Center* (Princeton 1972).

Torelli, M. "Vulci," in *Princeton Encyclopedia of Classical Sites,* ed. R. Stillwell (Princeton 1967) 991.

Travlos, J. *Pictorial Dictionary of Ancient Athens* (New York 1971).

—— *Poleodomike Exelixis ton Athenon* (Athens 1960).

Tuchelt, K. "Bemerkungen zu den Capito-Thermen in Milet," *Mélanges Mansel* I (Istanbul 1974) 147–164.

Türkdogan, O. *Salihli'de Türkistan Göçmenlerinin Yerlişmeleri* (Erzurum 1969).

Tylecote, R. F. *Metallurgy in Archaeology* (London 1962).

Van der Kaaden, G. "Basement Rocks," in Campbell, 191–210.

Verdelis, N. "Tiryns' Water Supply," *Archaeology* 16 (1963) 129–130.

Vereschagin, N. K. *The Mammals of the Caucasus: A History of the Evolution of the Fauna* (Jerusalem 1967).

Vermaseren, M. J. *Corpus Cultus Cybelae Attidisque (CCCA), III: Italia-Latium* (Leiden 1977).

—— *The Legend of Attis in Greek and Roman Art* (Leiden 1966).

Vermeule, C. *The Goddess Roma in the Art of the Roman Empire* (London 1974).

Vermeule, E. T. *Greece in the Bronze Age* (Chicago 1964).

Vetters, H. "Zum Stockwerkbau in Ephesus," *Mélanges Mansel,* ed. E. Akurgal and U. B. Alkim, 1 (Ankara 1974) 69–92.

Wace, A. J. B. *Mycenae* (Princeton 1949).

Wainwright, G. A. "Meneptah's Aid to the Hittites," *JEA* 46 (1960) 24–28.

Ward-Perkins, J. B. *Cities of Ancient Greece and Italy: Planning in Classical Antiquity* (New York 1974).

Wegner, M. *Das Musikleben der Griechen* (Berlin 1949).

Weickert, C. "Die Ausgrabung am Athena-Tempel in Milet 1955," *IstMitt* 7 (1957) 102–145.

——— "Westabschnitt," in W. Schiering, P. Hommel, C. Weickert, A. Mallwitz, and A. Kleiner, "Die Ausgrabung beim Athena-Temel in Milet 1957," *IstMitt* 9–10 (1959–1960) 1–86; 63–66.

Weidner, E. F. "Jojachin, König von Juda," *Mélanges Syriens, offerts à René Dussaud,* Institut Français d'Archéologie de Beyrouth, Bibliothèque Archéologique et Historique 30 (1939).

Weinberg, G. D., and Weinberg, S. S. "Arachne of Lydia at Corinth," *The Aegean and the Near East, Studies Presented to Hetty Goldman,* ed. G. D. Weinberg (New York 1956) 261–267.

Weinberg, S. S. "Excavations at Prehistoric Elateia, 1959," *Hesperia* 31 (1962) 158–209.

Weitzmann, K. *Ancient Book Illumination,* Martin Classical Lectures 16 (Cambridge, Mass. 1959).

——— *Illustrations in Roll and Codex,* 2d ed. (Princeton 1970).

Wiegand, T., and Schrader, H., eds. *Priene, Ergebnisse der Ausgrabungen und Untersuchungen in den Jahren 1895–1898* (Berlin 1904).

Wilamowitz-Möllendorff, U. von. "Apollon," *Hermes* 38 (1903) 575–586.

——— *Euripides' Herakles,* 3 vols. (Bad Homburg von der Höhe 1959).

Wilberg, W., Benndorf, O., Niemann, G., Heberdey, R., Schindler, A., and Kukula, R. C. *Forschungen in Ephesos I* (Vienna 1906).

Winnington-Ingram, R. P. *Mode in Ancient Greek Music* (Cambridge 1936).

Winter, F. E. *Greek Fortifications* (Toronto 1971).

Woolley, C. "Excavations at Al Mina, Suedia, I, II," *JHS* 58 (1938) 1–30; 133–170.

Yassıhüyük: A Village Study, Middle East Technical University (Ankara 1965).

Young, R. S. "Early Mosaics at Gordion," *Expedition* 7 (Spring 1965) 4–13.

——— *From the City of Midas: Phrygian Art,* Catalogue of a Loan Exhibition from the Turkish Government (Philadelphia 1958–1959).

——— "Gordion, A Preliminary Report 1953," *AJA* 59 (1955) 1–18.

——— "Gordion 1956: Preliminary Report," *AJA* 61:4 (1957) 319–331.

——— "The Gordion Campaign of 1959: Preliminary Report," *AJA* 64 (1960) 227–244.

——— "The 1961 Campaign in Gordion," *AJA* 66 (1962) 153–168.

——— "The Gordion Campaign of 1965," *AJA* 70 (1966) 267–278.

——— *Gordion, A Guide to the Excavations and Museum* (Ankara 1975).

——— "Making History at Gordion," *Archaeology* 6:3 (Autumn 1953) 159–166.

——— "The Nomadic Impact: Gordion," in Mellink, *Dark Ages,* 52–57.

——— "Old Phrygian Inscriptions from Gordion: Toward a History of the Phrygian Alphabet," *Hesperia* 38 (1969) 270–275.

——— "The Phrygian Contribution," in *Proceedings of the Tenth International Congress of Classical Archaeology,* ed. E. Akurgal (Ankara 1978) 9–24.

Zahle, J. "Archaic Tumulus Tombs in Central Lykia (Phellos)," *ActaA* (1975) 77–94.

Zahn, R. "Thongeschirr," in Wiegand-Schrader, *Priene.*

Ziegenaus, O. "Hallenstrasse," in E. Boehringer, "Neue Ausgrabungsarbeiten zu Pergamon in Jahre 1965," *AA* 30 (1966).

Ziegenhaus, O., and De Luca, G. *Pergamon XI.2 Das Asklepieion, 2.Teil,* Deutsches Archäologisches Institut (Berlin 1975).

Sardis from
Prehistoric
to Roman Times

I

The City and Its Environment

GEORGE M. A. HANFMANN

CLIVE FOSS

General Topography and Ecology

Nowadays (1980), the landscape of Sardis (Figs. 1–5)[1] appears as a riverine plain of the Gediz Çay, the ancient Hermus River, verdant with cotton, orchards, and vineyards. On its northern side, wheat, sesame, and poppy fields have begun to spread among the mounds of the Royal Cemetery of Bin Tepe (Figs. 2, 5–7, 97–99, 104) toward the Mermere Gölü, the ancient Gygean Lake. The natural fertility of the plain, praised already by the ancients (Strabo, 13.4.5), has been increased by an elaborate system of irrigation canals linked to the lake and the river and controlled from the great dam and artificial lake at Demir Köprü dam, 45 km. upstream on the Gediz Çay.[2] Two eroded conglomerate peaks, the spreading Acropolis with its funny little knob on top and the precipitous Necropolis Hill, flank the narrow Sart Çay, the ancient Pactolus valley, and stand guard like two red towers over the great west-east Izmir-Ankara highway (TC 68). Behind them rises the mighty Bozdag (ancient Tmolus) range, part of the great Maeander massif (Figs. 4, 6, 7).[3]

Spreading over some 800 sq. km., the Sardian Plain is rimmed on the north by a low neogene limestone ridge which on the northeast and southwest of the Gygean Lake turns into higher hills (Figs. 11, 12). On the west, one first overlooks the plain and the Bin Tepe ridge from a low rise at Derbent (about 14 km. west of Sardis). C. Foss assumes that in Roman times, administratively, the Sardian territory might have reached to Gökkaya (Aureliopolis)[4] some 15 km. west along the highway and northeast ca. 20 km. toward Adala (ancient Satala). On the east, the confluence of the Gediz (Hermus) and Alaşehir Çay (ancient Cogamus) constitutes a natural parting of ways. Foss would allow some 30 km. in this direction.

Built in 1873, the railway keeps to the trough of the valley. It was responsible for the growth of the village of Sart Mahmut,[5] which is now a town. Keeping above the floodline, closer to southern foothills, the new highway from Izmir to Ankara, which replaced the old medieval cobble road, was built and surfaced from 1952 to 1960. It has already pulled and is still pulling population toward it; small new houses have covered since 1969 the presumed center of ancient Lydian Sardis.[6] Other new highways include a road going diagonally across Bin Tepe toward the road to Akhisar (ancient Thyateira) and a road running from the Pactolus bridge across the Tmolus range to Ödemiş (near ancient Hypaipa).[7]

If we want to reconstitute the ancient landscape, we must not only eliminate the present courses of railway and highways; we must also allow for complex changes by earthquakes and landslides. Because of violent winter rains and the character of soils the valley was subject to floods, and the trough of the valley, prior to modern flood control and irrigation canals, consisted of a much larger marshy area; even with the flood control in effect, the Bin Tepe area was cut off by floods in 1966.[8] These swamps would have provided more pastures for the famous Lydian horses and for water buffaloes. Among the crops, there would have been neither cotton nor tobacco, but wheat and vine are likely to have led then as they do today.[9]

Unmistakably, then as now, the landscape of Sardis presented itself as combining two worlds —the world of the plain and the world of the mountain.

Cartography

The site of ancient Sardis lies south of the present-day railway station of Sart Mahmut, which is at latitude N 38°29′55″, longitude E 28°02′32″. "The altitude varies from ca. 95 m. a.s.l. at Bath 'CG' to over 410 m. a.s.l. on the Acropolis."[10] Official Turkish geological maps are on the scale of 1:500,000, and Manisa 87-2 is 1:100,000 (officially unpublished). A useful addition to the scant cartographic coverage available in Turkey is the automobile maps issued by the Highway Department on the scale of 1:850,000. A good geological sketch map and profile was published by E. Izdar (Fig. 3).[11] A new geological map of the site has been prepared by D. F. Belknap.

The Harvard-Cornell Expedition used a new partial survey by Turkish surveyors known as SAS which covers only part of the site, and for some purposes the "first expedition" survey of 1913 which takes in more territory (cf. Fig. 8).[12] As explained by S. L. Carter, *Sardis* R1 (1975) 7–8, the survey made by Turkish surveyors for the Harvard-Cornell Expedition in 1962 covers an area of only 2.8 km. east/west and 2.2 km. north/south, corresponding to Fig. 8 in this volume. It omits everything west of the Pactolus torrent and south of the Artemis Temple, and is incomplete as to contours and roads north of the gymnasium complex. It follows an arbitrary orientation, derived from Roman orientation of the gymnasium complex, rather than true north/south orientation. The scale is 1:2,000.

The survey made by L. J. Emery for the "first" Sardis expedition and published as plate I in *Sardis* I (1922) and in *Sardis* R1 (1975) 7, fig. 3, goes nearly 6 km. south of the railway line up to the marble quarries in the Bozdag (Tmolus) and

takes in over 2 km. of the precipitous terrain in the Necropolis Hill as well as all of the Acropolis area east of the Pactolus. Its scale, however, is only 1:16,000.

According to the ancient authors,[13] Sardis was 540 stades (ca. 105 km.) or three (walking) days' journey distant from the Aegean coast at Ephesus. The highway distance from Izmir is ca. 90 km. The present automobile driving time is slightly over an hour.

Although we are not certain of the exact course within Sardis of the old east-west road, the so-called Royal Road from the Aegean to Iran,[14] it is clear that the growth of Sardis as a capital was due to the intersection of this major intercontinental highway with an important traffic artery toward the northwest, via Thyateira, to Pergamon and the Troad (Figs. 2, 10) at a highly defensible spot. Sardis lay also near the juncture of the second branch of the Royal Road which came via Laodicea and Philadelphia (Alaşehir) as well as of secondary southward roads across the Tmolus to Hypaepa and Ephesus.[15]

Geology

Part of the Alpine orogenic system, the area of Sardis belongs to the "Aegean Coastlands" and is distinguished by a number of well-defined east-west fractures resulting in a sequence of mountain blocks and east-west *grabens* filled with alluvial (waterborne) and colluvial (landslide) materials. Through the valleys above the *grabens* flow the rivers Gediz (Tmolus), Küçük Menderes (Cayster), and Büyük Menderes (Maeander). Among the geological factors affecting Sardis is the contrast of the newly formed plain and the older mountain formations. Sardis lies at the foot of the Bozdag—the ancient Tmolus. This is the southern part of the Maeander Massif, one of the three geologically oldest massifs of Turkey.[16] Rising to 2,159 m., the Bozdag has on its north, the Sardis side (Fig. 3), a series of marble limestones, ca. 1000–2000 m. thick, with a front of biotite and marble. The marble is, in fact, an enclave; within it, in the gorge of Magara Deresi, lie the quarries of marble which were examined for the Harvard-Cornell Expedition by D. Monna and analyzed by F. H. Whetmore as "calcite marbles with a low percentage of dolomite."[17] As seen in Izdar's section (Fig. 3), the oldest geological formations, the *Augengneisses,* are closer to the surface on the south, the Küçük Menderes (Cayster) Valley side of the massif, than on the Sardis side.

A second geological factor affecting Sardis is the recent neogene formations, sandstone and conglomerate, and limestone, which are water-deposited and susceptible to erosion and landslides. Several of these younger sedimentary rocks were tested. The red sandstone favored by the Lydians in archaic times is, according to Izdar, a mica-bearing sandstone of the Upper Miocene.[18] Limestone used in the construction of the Bath CG has been identified as lithocarenite, possibly from lower ranges of the Bozdag.[19] Neogene limestone quarried locally was used in Bin Tepe crepides and chamber tombs. Quarrying platforms may be seen at several mounds, and attempts to quarry limestone from the north side of Alyattes mound were still made in the 1970s. This limestone of Bin Tepe was tested for magnetic conductivity and resistivity by D. Greenewalt (1961–1963).[20]

G. Olson (1977) describes the Acropolis of Sardis (Figs. 4, 6, 7) as composed entirely of crumbling Tertiary conglomerate. Its pebbles are of schist and gneiss cemented with lime. He remarks that the outcroppings of Quarternary and Tertiary as well as Cretacean Age lithologies along with the effect of landslides (and earthquakes) make the Sardis geomorphology very complex.

The third factor is the surface soils, the subject of pedology or soils science. In 1970, Olson made a thorough study based on 55 sites and 105 samples determining the saturation, field capacity, and silting, as well as the percentages of organic matter, silt and clay texture, and chemical composition. In their texture, the majority emerge as sandy loams or loam. Most samples are high in sand and low in clay. Many display a plate formation and are prone to sliding. These geological propensities toward landslides have been increased by overgrazing and deforestation.[21]

In an attempt to determine the possible local character of clays used for pottery, lamps, and terracottas, D. C. Kamilli, in cooperation with J. A. Scott, has analyzed a series of such artifacts. The results indicate considerable probability of local deposits, since the ingredients are consistent with local geological components. "The mineral assemblage of all ten Lydian architectural terracotta samples strongly resembles that of the standard Sardis ceramic mineralogy and is characterized by the presence of quartz, untwinned feldspar, traces of Na plagioclase, biotite, muscovite, hematite (both as grains and staining), and varying amounts of chert. Several samples also contain traces of microcline, chlorite, magnetite, epidote, and schist fragments." Kamilli points out that these materials are found partly in the older Palaeozoic low to intermediate grade metamorphic schist and partly in the Mesozoic unmetamorphosed younger sandstone, conglomerate, and arkose of the regions.[22]

Olson deals with much waterlaid (alluvial) as well as windblown material. Rapid formation of both of these is characteristic of the Sardis landscape, which also favors formation of torrents with wide alluvial fans where they issue into the plain.[23] Mineral occurrences in the alluvia of the entire Bozdag range have been the object of studies commissioned by Maaden Tetkik ve Arama Enstitüsü, those on Sardis being undertaken by Mustafa Saydamer (1968).[24] Cengiz Saran of the Ministry of Waterworks also contributed helpful observations on the formation of alluvial gravel which ran through the Lydian Market area.[25]

Instability and Seismicity
Olson gives for the immediate urban area of Sardis the dramatic estimate that 1,000,000 cubic m. had been involved in landslides.[26] Not all of these, by far, were caused by water saturation. The fourth important geological factor in the makeup of the area of Sardis is its seismicity. The region is an intensely faulted and deformed geological area. According to E. Ilhan, the Aegean zone comprises a system of east/west trending *grabens* intersected by faults trending more or less north/south, and its current activity is related to the subsidence of the Aegean basin. The Gediz (Hermus) valley is a *graben* ca. 120 km. long with currently active faults at its boundaries.[27] In A.D. 17 Sardis had a major earthquake for which we have literary and inscriptional evidence.[28] Ilhan states that 350 earthquakes are reported for the area from the eleventh century A.D. on. As late as 1969, purely local tremors compelled partial evacuation of Salihli. They were said to have been connected with steam pressure building up under a nearby part of Boz-

dag. Near Sardis, there are also found hot sulphur springs with temperatures up to 70°F.[29] In 1970, one of the most intensive earthquakes of recent times struck the town of Gediz east of Sardis. As is characteristic of other earthquakes of the region, it was distinguished by relatively shallow location of its focus.[30]

No systematic detailed seismological investigation of the area of Sardis has yet been undertaken. Eventually, as in the case of the landslides investigated by Olson, closer correlation of datable archaeological findings with verified seismological data may become possible; thus Butler's and our observations in the Artemis precinct, in the gymnasium (Marble Court), and in the Pactolus North areas have not only brought together much material on the effects of the earthquake of A.D. 17[31] but also have indicated possible consequences of earthquakes in the seventh (Artemis Temple, overthrow of Marble Court of the gymnasium), the twelfth (effects in gymnasium area), and the sixteenth or the seventeenth centuries.[32] Additional dates can be secured from archaeological study of the landslides and erosive wadis.[33]

One lesson to be drawn for archaeology is that the complex twisting and superposition of the Sardis landscape by natural forces has often resulted in upsetting the depositional stratigraphy that is normally formed by habitation sites in the plain. For example, Lydian remains may be found deeply buried or close to the surface or even carried out of their original position by erosion, landslides, or earthquakes.[34]

Climate and Hydrology
Climatically, Sardis belongs to the Aegean coastlands of the Mediterranean climate, with mild winters (7–9°C in January) and hot summers (above 25°C in July-August). An annual precipitation of 513 mm. places Sardis into the "subhumid" range (400–600 mm.) with a marked rainy season. Days with more than 100 mm. rain have been recorded. Because the Bozdag (while it has no perennial snowline) yet retains some snow into July and August and has substantial runoff, the Sardian plain is a well-watered region.[35] The great contrast between flooding in winter and dryness in summer and early fall makes water conservation important. Overabundance of water and attendant flooding can result in droughts when coupled with hot and dry cli-

matic conditions, as the authors of the report by the *Köy Işleri Bakanligi* have noted. This has been the case in various parts of the Gediz (Hermus) Plain.[36] A notice in Strabo seems to indicate that the Lydians had dug the Gygean Lake "to contain the floods."[37] They may have employed it as a reservoir. For urban use, there are signs of systematic well building and channeling in both Lydian and Persian Sardis. Systematic research for a history of hydrology, water use, and irrigation, such as the studies done for Pergamon by G. Garbrecht and his associates,[38] remains to be done for Sardis. There are still extant data from epigraphic sources (such as a list of public fountains)[39] and the archaeological evidence of wells, cisterns, and a long Roman aqueduct built ca. A.D. 53–54. A very elaborate Roman water distribution system seems to have reached its greatest expansion in the fourth century A.D. This evidence is described in detail according to the periods from Lydian to Byzantine in *Sardis* R1 and will not be repeated here.[40] As we have been able to prove in the case of Bath CG, this system had also controlled individual brooks and springs; its decay led to the decline of irrigation, isolating the villages and turning the plain into malarial marshes.[41]

GMAH

Agriculture, Pastoralism, Hunting, Forestry

Agriculture

Geological and pedological investigations show that in general the soils of the Sardian plain are fertile, except in certain spots "where salinity is a problem."[1] A description and maps of the soils as they are today have been compiled for the Ministry of Villages under the title "The Soils of the Gediz Plain."[2] This survey treats the Hermus Plain from Muradiye to Alaşehir, an area of ca. 100,000 sq. hectares that corresponds to the heartland of ancient Lydia (Figs. 2, 10).

As we have already indicated, the percentual distribution of crops must have differed in antiquity from that of modern times. In the absence of systematic excavations and analysis of rural settlements and of cultivated and uncultivated areas and the lack of systematic pollen analysis data, we are reduced to inferences from ancient sources backed up by some archaeological facts.

But we may at least ask some questions. Supposing that following modern procedure, we should like to establish percentages of land use given over to (1) urban settlement, (2) agriculture, (3) pasture, (4) forests, (5) industry, and (6) nonproductive use. Comparing modern statistics, we could only say that the forests have definitely decreased and the grazing land increased from antiquity until very recent times (ca. 1960).[3] Otherwise, unless one tried such methods as those in Messenia,[4] where land usage for agriculture was estimated on the basis of size and population density of modern villages, we have no effective way of estimating the ancient percentages of land use. The modern percentages for all of Turkey as of 1950 are as follows: cultivated land: 39.3%; grazing (pasture) land: 48.5%; forests: 13.4%; other (waste): 17.3%. For the Vilayet Manisa, however, as much as 45% was counted as "forests."[5] The land percentages assigned to major crops (omitting the modern crops of cotton and tobacco) in the Salihli region in 1963–1964 are as follows:[6]

	Hectares	Acres	Percentage
Wheat	91,588	228,970	45.5
Barley	65,621	164,052	32.6
Grapes	42,310	105,775	21
Olives	1,491	3,727.5	0.9
Total	201,010	502,524.5	100.0

The percentage of olives was probably higher in antiquity than now, and the statistics do not include orchards and vegetable gardens for the many delicious kinds of fruit (peaches, melons, cherries, apples), vegetables, and condiments grown today around Sardis, which probably occupied considerable acreage immediately adjacent to Lydian settlements. Lydian cuisine was famous, and the basic ingredients wheat, milk, and honey, as well as herbs and spices, were readily available.[7]

On the vital question whether Lydia was self-supporting in grains, the evidence is somewhat contradictory. The story that one part of the Lydian population was forced to emigrate to Etruria because of a famine in the Late Bronze or Early Iron Age is perhaps more plausibly ex-plained as due to upheavals of agricultural organization by military action than to drought or other natural causes.[8] There are no later reports of famines in Lydia. Some historians have thought that Lydia was capable of exporting wheat. They have interpreted the Lydian policy under the Mermnad Kings of periodically destroying crops in the territory of Miletus as an attempt to create an export market for Lydian crops.[9]

The literary traditions and Greek archaeological material suggest a great expansion of the cult of the Lydian wine god (Baki-Dionysus) in the late seventh and early sixth centuries B.C. This may in turn have promoted both cultivation and export of Lydian wines. The large number of specialized wine-drinking vessels found in Lydian dwellings and graves supports the notion of a very wide use of wine.[10]

A certain kind of large terracotta tray has been tentatively interpreted as a "bread tray." According to A. Ramage, it was very probably used to bake bread. It was found in virtually every Lydian house and would attest abundant daily use.[11] At any rate, the Lydians took baking very seriously and enjoyed special fame as bakers. The baking woman was a key figure in providing royal food; Croesus' baker refused to poison Croesus.[12] One may surmise that bread was the main staple food of the Lydian diet.

Population

There is no certain answer to the size of the population which Lydia could support. In *Sardis* R1 we gave a guess of 40,000–80,000 for the Sardis region during the Lydian-Persian period (ca. 680–334 B.C.) and well over 100,000 for the late Roman Empire (ca. A.D. 200–400).[13] This compares with a minimum estimate of 50,000 for the fertile region of Messenia in mainland Greece during the prosperous Mycenaean Age, as estimated by McDonald. His may, however, be a low figure, as the population figures for the sixteenth to eighteenth centuries in Messenia ran between 60,000 and 80,000.[14] For the Roman period, a good comparison is provided by Pergamon, which, according to the physician Galen, had 120,000 people in the second century A.D.; the figure counts women and slaves and may include all the *polis,* the entire territory, rather than only the city.[15]

Animals

It is clear from the abundant finds of the bones of sheep, pigs, and cattle, which display signs of butchering, that the consumption of meat in ancient times was presumably no smaller than in nineteenth or early twentieth century rural Turkey. These animals were bred in considerable numbers.[16] The statistics of bones found in the excavations from 1958 through 1963 show the following percentages for all periods of antiquity: sheep and goats, ca. 50%; cattle, ca. 25%; pigs, ca. 8%; horses, ca. 16%.[17]

Animals eaten included dogs, or, at any rate, puppies. C. H. Greenewalt, Jr., has surveyed the curious evidence of the strange finds made by the Harvard-Cornell Expedition. They are the so-called puppy burials—burial caches which included three pottery vessels, an iron knife, and "the skeletal remains of an immature canid" contained in a jug (Figs. 145, 146). These were probably ritual meals. In his discussion, Greenewalt has provided much information on Lydian diet and cuisine generally.[18]

The Lydians also bred war dogs; King Alyattes is said to have used them against the Kimmerians. The bones examined did not provide very specific indications of the breeds, but representations of war dogs and hunting dogs are found on Lydian terracotta friezes and painted vases.[19]

The history of equids begins at Sardis (for the time being) with a skeleton found in the Submycenaean-Protogeometric level. In the time of the Lydian kingdom, horse breeding was a Lydian speciality, and Herodotus considers the Lydians to be horsemen *par excellence*. When Mimnermus speaks of the phalanxes of Lydian cavalry,[20] he implies that there were hundreds of Lydian mounted knights in the seventh century B.C. Such elite cavalry suggests the existence of a horse-riding aristocracy.[21] The actual Lydian breed of horses has not been determined.[22]

As to the beasts of burden, the count of animal bones through 1963 indicated that 15% were horses and less than 1% were donkeys.[23] It is quite possible, though, that some of the equids counted as horses in the analysis of bones were actually donkeys.

The Lydians probably used camels as beasts of burden. Herodotus, to be sure, tells the famous story that the Lydian cavalry horses ran away from the Persian camel corps of Harpagos during the battle for Sardis (547 B.C.), "because horses cannot stand the smell of camels"; but since we have found camel bones and representation of camel legs from a terracotta statuette in Lydian levels, the story cannot mean that Lydians were unacquainted with camels.[24] The use of the camel as a beast of burden continued through the Roman period.[25]

The animal and vegetable dietary resources were supplemented by hunting, which is mentioned in history and myths but was not very important in the general diet, to judge by the small number of bones of wild animals found in the domestic areas.[26] The Gygean Lake was and still is famous for its fish and fowl, and delicious trout is still caught in the Hermus further upstream. Fishing may have been particularly important in the Bronze Age, and fish hooks of bronze have been found. One would like to think that the lovingly drawn fish on the local goblets of ca. 600 B.C. from the Indere tomb reflects a local species (Fig. 119).[27]

Among the wild animals, the lion is enormously prominent in Lydian art and on Lydian coins as a royal symbol; he is the sacred animal of the goddess Cybele. Yet his zoological identification among the felines of Lydia, and indeed his very existence in Lydia in historical times, is still controversial.[28] So far no lion bones have been found at Sardis.

The boar, the animal which was hunted by the son of Croesus, is still hunted in the mountains. We ourselves have seen boars dashing across the highway in the Sipylos mountains. In the Lydian finds of the Harvard-Cornell Expedition, the boar is represented on a fine Lydian plate, in a bronze relief (Fig. 81), in a terracotta frieze, and, together with a lion, on the so-called Cybele monument (Fig. 160).[29]

Forestry

As to forests in Turkey generally, the area of good forest has much declined as a result of uncontrolled grazing by sheep and goats and widespread cutting for fuel and building materials. Over wide areas the forest has degenerated to low scrub. Nevertheless, Lydia contains some of the major timber sources. The north side of the Tmolus ridge is still wooded, though the timber, principally pine, does not seem of good quality.

Previously, cedar and oak also grew in the area. Reforestation has been initiated in the Sardis region near Salihli and on the Sipylus.[30]

In antiquity, timber of good quality was available and probably more abundant. This is implied by the story that in order to defeat the Ionians, Croesus began to build a fleet.[31] We should note the existence of royal forests attested at least in Hellenistic times; during the reconstruction of Sardis in 213 B.C., citizens were permitted to obtain timber from the royal woods at Tarantzoi, according to an unpublished letter of Antiochus III.

Ancient wood does not survive very well at Sardis. The largest and best-studied example from the Harvard-Cornell Excavations is the piece of a couch from the tomb BT 63.2 at Bin Tepe.[32] Some wooden ornaments have also been found. Traces of horizontal timbers have been reported from the Lydian (city?) wall (MMS) discovered in 1976–1977.[33] About 1966, there was also a tantalizing report, never substantiated by actual remains, of a wooden boat allegedly having been found in another tomb at Bin Tepe. A terracotta model of such a boat was discovered by Butler in a tomb of the Necropolis Hill at Sardis.[34] Traces and remnants of wooden knife handles and a sheath of the Lydian period are known.[35] According to Butler, "ordinarily the dead were carried in upon wooden biers or stretchers which were laid on the couches; remains of these have been found in bits of rotten wood, and in bronze details such as rings of carrying poles."[36] Finally, the wooden ashes over the roof of the Tomb of Alyattes (ca. 560 B.C.) were tentatively identified by the local foresters as oak.[37]

Timber was indispensable in the construction of Lydian buildings decorated with terracotta revetments, but the actual wooden supports have not survived.[38] And in vernacular architecture, wood rather than thatch was used in the mountain villages for roofing.

Even allowing for the poor survival of wood at Sardis, it seems that both the amounts of wood available and the spread of its usage were less extensive in Lydian Sardis than they were in Phrygian Gordion, where the huge chamber of the Royal Tomb and some other chamber graves were constructed of timber, and where a distinctive wood carving style of ornamentation was developed for furniture.[39] In Lydia, stone and mudbrick rather than wood were the monumental materials.

GMAH

Mineral Resources

Already rich in agricultural and pastural products, Lydia had unusual mineral resources which eventually raised her for a brief time to the leading role on the world stage of economic and social history. The immediate vicinity of Sardis and the larger ambient of Lydia were rich in these useful material deposits; gold, iron, silver, copper, arsenic, antimony, cinnabar, yellow ochre, and sulphur compose the list that can be drawn up from ancient sources and actual field explorations. Some of them were utilized for specialized purposes in medicine, manufacturing cosmetics, dyeing of cloth, and silvering of mirrors.[1]

Gold played a crucial part in transforming Lydia from an agricultural and pastoral economy into a commercial, industrial, and trading country. Our greatest discoveries at Sardis pertain to the Lydian technology of mining and working of gold; they will be treated in detail in Chapter III, "Lydian Excavation Sectors." Here it must be sufficient to note that gold both in stratified formations and in the alluvia of the Sardian torrents must have been available at Sardis since earliest Prehistoric times, having been formed thousands of years earlier.

Reports concerning the occurrence of gold in the Pactolus torrent and its probable origin in the Tmolus mountain are cited in *Sardis* R1 and in J. C. Waldbaum's introduction to her volume on metal objects from Sardis.[2] Unfortunately, the earlier reports by M. Collignon and L. Dominian on mining in the Tmolus and by H. C. Butler on the pits he dug are not precise enough to permit identification of their location.[3] Philippson has discussed the type of geological formations in which gold might be found,[4] which he observed near Salihli.

More precise, but unfortunately largely unpublished, scientific information about the occurrence of gold in the Sardis area and in Lydia has come from surveys conducted by the Mineral Researches Institute of Ankara (MTAE).[5] The unpublished reports by S. Birgi (1944) and

M. Saydamer (with whom the Harvard-Cornell Expedition collaborated) are particularly important.[6] Further work was done west of the Pactolus in 1976. The Harvard-Cornell Expedition did not undertake independent work in quest of gold or gold-workings, but at least one location upstream of the Pactolus was thought by Clarence A. Wendel, Minerals Attaché to the U.S. Embassy, Ankara, to show possible traces of workings.[7] Saydamer conclusively proved the presence of gold in alluvium of the Pactolus, and Birgi studied it in conglomerate strata. He also looked at what he believed were ancient pits around the Acropolis. We are not aware, however, of any mines in the Tmolus definitely identified as Lydian by archaeological finds.

We have found gold "earplugs," as well as silver and copper objects (Figs. 16, 18) in Early Bronze burials on the Gygean Lake (ca. 2500 B.C.). There is no certainty that the gold is local, but J. C. Waldbaum remarks that the silver percentages and presence of copper are consistent with later Sardian gold.

It must have been some special event, some strong effort combining large-scale labor organization with better technology, which made Lydia under Gyges (680–645 B.C.) the leading producer of gold. Together with the invention of coinage, it resulted in an economic constellation totally new in world history. The fame of Lydian gold is attested by Gyges' contemporary, the Greek poet Archilochus, who has a craftsman say, "I do not care for Gyges' gold!"[8] Archilochus' adopted home, the island of Thasos, was a gold mining area. If he was impressed by Gyges' gold, the production of Lydia must have been substantial. That Gyges, who showed himself a very active organizer in politics and warfare, would have organized the gold production on a larger scale is very plausible; it is also likely that not only the alluvial gold was the subject of a large-scale effort. Prospecting and mining may have begun either at the same time or very shortly thereafter. Mining gold was well known in the ancient world,[9] and, according to Herodotus, it was practiced by Phoenicians on Thasos at the time of Gyges or a little earlier (ca. 700 B.C.).[10]

While we have not securely identified any ancient gold mining Lydian pits, mining is attested for the Persian period. It has been rightly observed by the mining engineer L. Dominian and others that tracing the goldbearing veins cannot conceivably have been neglected by Lydian kings.[11]

Plutarch tells a story of the famous Lydian millionaire Pythes/Pythios, which, however fantastic its plot, shows that the gold industry required a very substantial labor force. Pythios (ca. 500–480 B.C.) supposedly forced his fellow citizens to spend all their time digging gold *in his mines,* carting it off, and washing it so that they could do no other work, and their regular agricultural means of living were lost.[12] We catch a glimpse of the social and economic dislocation caused by the gold industry and the new economy.

Later, much of this gold was exported as tribute to Persia.[13] Nonetheless, the samples of Achaemenian gold jewelry found at Sardis suggest that gold was in good supply at Sardis under the Persians.[14]

Silver was probably another source of Lydian wealth. There were deposits at Sart Çamur Hamamlar (sulphur baths) in the Salihli district; Balya in the Balikesir area and even Astyra in the Troad were within Lydian territory.[15] The most immediate source, however, may have been silver extracted from the electrum of the Pactolus and the Tmolus. The process of parting gold and silver will be described in connection with the description of the goldworking plant in Chapter III, "Lydian Excavation Sectors." It should be noted that analyses of worked gold (electrum?) samples with silver content up to 25–30% are known. A sample of native gold analyzed at MTAE had 14.5% silver. A sample from the Pactolus analyzed at the Turkish Nuclear Research Center, Çekmece, had 24.9%.[16] Another analysis of natural electrum from the Pactolus is expected from W. Gentner's group in Heidelberg, who are investigating the major sources of silver used in ancient Greek coinages. They also suggest on the basis of lead isotope analysis of Lydian coins probably made in Sardis that Lydian silver may have been used in mints in and about the Greek mainland, especially in the famous coinage of Aegina.[17] The close resemblance of Persian silver sigloi, one of which was found by the Harvard-Cornell Expedition in 1962 (Fig. 162), to "Croeseid" silver coins[18] argues that the same silver supplies continued to be available under the Persians. Although they begin with the Early Bronze Age (silver ram, Fig. 18), the number of silver objects found in excavations is small.[19]

The immediate sources of Lydian iron are not known with certainty. J. C. Waldbaum has listed a number of rich iron ore sources which would have been within Lydian territory.[20] However, Sardis can boast relatively early examples for the use of iron: fragments of knives, a sickle (Fig. 30), and a heavy iron adze from stratified sub-Mycenaean-Protogeometric contexts of the "Lydian Market" (HoB) area, which the excavators date from the twelfth to eleventh centuries B.C. and Waldbaum to the tenth century B.C.,[21] demonstrate the transition to agricultural tools, presumably made from local sources. Used since the Early Bronze Age (see Fig. 16), the resources of copper in the immediate vicinity of Sardis were apparently insignificant, and the metal was imported from elsewhere, possibly Eastern Anatolia.[22]

Considerable quantities of lead were available at Sardis. Waldbaum emphasizes the importance of the Balya mine in the Balikesir region, which is known to have been exploited in antiquity and where lead is associated with silver, and she notes occurrences closer to Sardis in the Alaşehir, Salihli, and Manisa regions.[23] Whether or not zinc was obtained in the Tmolus range seems to be controversial, but a number of sources were within reach.[24]

In addition to metals, the area around Sardis contained deposits of such useful minerals as cinnabar (mercury), yellow ochre (pigment), and sulphur used for softening wool.[25]

Stones

The occurrence of marbles in the Tmolus range and near the Gygean Lake has been mentioned above. The studies and analyses made by the expedition are reported in greater detail in *Sardis R2*. The distinctive Tmolus quarry marble is light white in color and apt to have coarse crystals and occasional gray banding. These are calcite marbles with low percentages of dolomite.[26] Ancient sources attribute to Mt. Tmolus the touchstone, a kind of slate used to test gold, and the semiprecious "sard."[27] Archaeological finds make it likely that other semiprecious quartzes as well as rock crystal were available nearby.[28]

Rock crystal was worked at Pactolus North (PN).

Clays

Finally, we must not overlook the clays suitable for production of both utilitarian pieces, such as rooftiles and waterpipes, and molded objects, such as decorative architectural reliefs, lamps, and Hellenistic relief-decorated wares. From the Early Bronze Age on, through at least the eighteenth century, large quantities of domestic pottery were produced. Claybeds suitable for tiles and architectural terracottas have been located in connection with the program of restoring a building decorated with Lydian terracottas.[29] Molds for making Hellenistic pottery and Roman lamps support the idea of local production from local materials.[30] Lamps were being made at the Pactolus. A much destroyed Lydian potter's kiln and a Byzantine kiln for firing pipes have also been found.[31]

GMAH

Industry

The making of useful artifacts at the Sardis settlement and in the Sardis area extended over four or five thousand years. Naturally, the industrial situation changed substantially with social and economic changes in each major period. The industrial situation of Lydian-Persian Sardis was quite different from that of the Roman-Early Byzantine city, which was part of the large economic system of the Roman empire. Fundamental surveys of literary evidence have been given by Roebuck, and an excellent survey of major Lydian industries from archaeological data has been brought together on the basis of Harvard-Cornell Excavation data and other finds by Greenewalt. The industries of the late Roman, the Byzantine, and the Turkish periods have been discussed by C. Foss.[1]

In this introductory section, we shall briefly survey only such industries as Sardis was famous for and emphasize the earlier periods, although several basic industries continued through the ages. We must caution again that the intensive collaborative study of archaeologists, technologists, and economic historians on the primary material from the excavations is still in progress. Only the detailed studies, reports, and monographs of the final publication series can adequately present the industrial materials, methods, and output and treat the role of import and export of industrial materials on a firm basis.

Stone

A microlithic blade (Fig. 20) may be the earliest evidence of a stone industry in Prehistoric Sardis. This and other finds of Neolithic and Bronze Age celts are of uncertain location, as is a Neolithic stone head (Fig. 21).[2] With a Protogeometric seal from the Submycenaean-Protogeometric strata of the "Lydian Market" area,[3] there begins a series of seals, gems, and ringstones, some inscribed in Lydian, which assumes the dimensions of a considerable industry.[4] The height of its activity occurred from ca. 600 (620?) to ca. 300 B.C., and it may have received its main patronage first from the Lydian royal entourage, then from the Persian satrapal court. Because of the use of stones in jewelry, gem cutting was closely allied to metalwork.[5]

The cutting of rock crystal may have been a specialty at Sardis. We have a rock crystal lion and fragments of worked rock crystal of the sixth century B.C.[6] Finds of Hellenistic, Roman, and Byzantine gems suggest that this local industry continued, and R. S. Thomas (in her monograph on *Small Objects*) cites an inscription of the second century A.D. which mentions a young *daktylokoiloglyphos* from Sardis, an "engraver of gems."[7] It is quite likely that Sardis retained some gem cutters' and jewelers' workshops of local significance through Early Byzantine times. It is less likely, but not impossible, that pieces like the horseman rock crystal gem were cut at Sardis as late as the twelfth century A.D.[8]

Metalwork

The subject of metalwork is surveyed in detail by J. C. Waldbaum's treatment of some 900 metal objects in her forthcoming volume, *Metalwork from Sardis: 1958–1973*.[9] It will be sufficient here to anticipate the major points. Gold, silver, and copper were already found in use in the Early Bronze period.[10] Already toward the end of the second millennium B.C., iron was used in Sardis routinely for agricultural and carpenter's tools.[11] Assyrian annals emphasize that Gyges sent Kimmerian captives to Assurbanipal in manacles and shackles of iron (644–636 B.C.). The arsenal of offensive arms which Croesus (560–547 B.C.) had confiscated when told that his son would come to grief from an iron lance–inflicted wound[12] was obviously all of iron. This developed iron industry may have provided the foundation for the establishment of an Imperial arms factory under Diocletian, as Waldbaum suggests.[13]

The iron industry of Sardis, though not by any means the largest of the ancient world, was important but not unique. On the other hand, the treatment of gold (electrum) and silver and the connection of this bimetallic technology with the invention of coinage in general, and bimetallic (gold/silver) coinage in particular, were events of epochal significance, which changed the course of the economic history of the world. By the discovery of the industrial workshop on the Pactolus with its probable evidence for the processes of cupellation and cementation, the Harvard-Cornell Excavation has contributed decisively toward our knowledge of the technology on which the riches of Alyattes and Croesus (and probably already Gyges) rested.[14]

It is worth recalling in this survey section that the Lydians and the Persians at Sardis must have used stupendous amounts of gold during this period. The seemingly exaggerated testimonials of the ancient writers[15] are backed up by archaeological finds. The life-size gold and silver bull (found in Delphi) was possibly one of Croesus' presents—as were perhaps the chryselephantine images found with the bull.[16] The incompletely plundered graves found by the first Sardis expedition have given proof that the Lydians wore every kind of jewelry including earrings and that their garments were covered with stitched-on gold plaques. Molds for making jewelry supply archaeological proof for local production.[17]

Although the substantial placers and deposits may have been worked out by the time of Alexander, a trickle of gold objects continued to be made at Sardis to Middle Byzantine times. As with gem-carving, there is epigraphic evidence that goldsmiths thrived at Sardis from the late Classical era through to the later Roman Empire.[18] They are mentioned in the inscriptions of donors to the Synagogue.[19]

Reinforced by some samples from recent finds, the great variety of techniques used by Sardian goldsmiths through the ages has yet to be studied systematically. Examples from recent finds are the fine granulated bead from Indere (Fig. 121) and the gold leaf rosettes found by researchers from the Museum of Manisa at Bin Tepe in 1976.[20]

Although silver was used plentifully in Croesan coinage, few objects have been found in the excavations at Sardis, just enough to suggest what has been lost. A silver hawk was found in an Indere grave (Fig. 120); a silver bowl and a silver phiale mesomphalos of the Persian era were excavated by the first Sardis expedition.[21]

Both the Harvard-Cornell and the first Sardis expeditions found more evidence for bronze objects and also some indication of processing of bronze for the Hellenistic period. It is possible that under the Persians, Sardis had an "Achaemenid" workshop specializing in Persian-influenced types of mirrors and horsetrappings. There was a sizable and interesting production in Roman and Early Byzantine times.[22]

For over two centuries (680–500 B.C.) Sardis had the world leadership in technology and production of gold. Thereafter, its metallurgical industries were of local importance. We must not forget, however, that an Imperial *fabrica* of arms was a large enterprise employing probably several hundred people, and the marked wealth of Early Byzantine Sardis in metal objects may have derived in part from the presence of many skilled metalworkers. The "Hardware Shop" (E9–11) with its 126 iron locks and a variety of other iron finds graphically illustrates how abundant and available metal goods were at Sardis even under the East Roman Empire.[23]

Textiles

From times immemorial until today, the Lydian region of Sardis and neighboring Hypaipa had produced textiles using wool and goats' hair (mohair). The legendary Arachne (Spider) was credited with the invention of linen and nets and her son "Closter" with the introduction of the spindle in wool working. The art of dyeing was supposed to have been invented in Sardis. The red Sardian "phoenix" dye was famous in antiquity. Carpets, coverlets, couch covers, cushions, blankets, embroidery, hats, and chitons are

among the Sardian products mentioned by ancient authors and inscriptions from Samos. They are cited in detail by Greenewalt and Majewski,[24] who have given a detailed description and analyses of the Lydian textiles and weaves and have indicated the great range of colors used in chitons and selvages. It suffices to note the gold-woven chitons of the Lydian period and the famous carpets of the Persian era, presumably part of the Lydian tribute, upon which the King of Kings alone could tread.[25]

According to the information furnished by Greek authors, the Lydians used "fabrics of wool, linen and gold thread; and colors taken to be flesh-colour, woad, 'hyacinthine;' sea-purple; and blood red."[26] The descriptions of the ancient authors have been made more concrete by the discovery of imprints of textiles on iron plates from a Lydian couch in tomb BT 63.2 at Bin Tepe.[27] The fabric (in BT 63.2), which lay tightly against the iron plates of the couch, may have been a shroud or coverlet or garment. Imprints on iron show at least four different kinds of woven fabrics (flat weaves) and a possible tassel or fringe. The closest weave has 22–23 yarns per centimeter (55 per inch).[28]

The scant original textile samples preserved from Sardis material do not measure up to the "breath-taking image of early Anatolian textile art provided by the Gordion finds with their muted colors and fine spun closely woven yarns of linen, wool, and mohair."[29] But the gorgeousness of Royal Lydian and Persian satrapal splendor of Sardian textiles is illustrated by the crimson-purple robe of a Lydian of the time of Croesus[30] with an embroidered border of meanders and by the white, red, and black colored garments of Persian type (sleeved cloak, leggings, and a shirt-like garment perhaps of cloth-of-gold) worn by a man whose terracotta likeness was fashioned into a trick vase; perhaps he was a Lydian of the Persian era (Figs. 142, 143).[31]

Leather, Ivory, and Bone

Leatherwork is attested in literary sources.[32] A famous Homeric passage has led scholars to assume that carving and dyeing of ivory also may have been practiced in Lydia: "As when some Maionian woman or Carian with purple colors ivory to make a cheek piece for a horse; it lies away in an inner room and many a rider longs to have it, but it is laid up to be a king's treasure."[33] Apart from the clearly imported disks of Scythian-like animal style, the finds from our own excavations include only few and unspectacular ornamental Lydian ivory pieces: ivory foot amulets and pendants. Mirror handles of ivory are mentioned among the finds of the first Sardis expedition.[34]

Nothing comparable to the great ivory finds at the archaic Artemision of Ephesus has been found at Sardis.[35] A much reproduced ivory— and gold—head is marked with a crescent brand of the moon god.[36] G. M. A. Hanfmann considers the piece to be of Phoenician import or else Lydian imitation of Phoenician work. Yet the haunting possibility remains that great gold and ivory statues were made at Sardis. P. Amandry has proffered the exciting speculation that the beautiful archaic gold and ivory heads found in Delphi (in 1939 and restored by 1978) are Lydian presents and may include the portrait of Croesus himself![37] The matter is not capable of proof, but the pieces suggest vividly what Lydian –Eastern Greek chryselephantine sculpture of highest quality was like at Croesus' time.

These were mostly luxury arts. The production of oils, ointments, and perfumes had started at Sardis under the Lydians and is mentioned by ancient authors. It fits into the same concept of *tryphe* which helped create the image of luxury-loving Lydians.[38] It has been suggested that the *lydion,* the most original Lydian archaic vase shape, was a container for oil or perfume.

The indispensable crafts of blacksmiths, coppersmiths, masons, woodcutters, carpenters, and the purveyors of daily necessities such as the potters flourished through the history of the city and will be mentioned under the different periods of Sardis. Here we may cite only some highlights and sidelights in the development of building activities. Wattle and daub technique was used in the hut of the Middle or Late Bronze Age. The houses which burned in the conflagration of 499 B.C. (Herodotus 5.101) were of reeds, and even those which were of brick had reed roofs.[39] The very comprehensive measures for the restoration of Sardis after the siege of 213 B.C. included permission to cut timber in the royal woods at Tarantzoi.[40] Another vast expansion of building trades must have occurred

when the decision to rebuild the city after the great earthquake of A.D. 17 was made by an Imperial Commission. Toward the very end of the Early Byzantine City, the famous "Union" inscription of A.D. 459 attests both a strong organization of builders and technicians and substantial building or rebuilding activities.[41]

The enormous organization for the procurement of building materials under the Romans (ca. A.D. 17–270) can only be discussed in conjunction with the actual structures, as can be the associated industries of brick making, marble cutting and trade, mosaic production, wall painting, and many other trades associated with building.

In these industries, Sardis was probably no more than the equal of other great Roman cities of Asia Minor such as Ephesus and Pergamon.[42] There is, however, one industry which is less common, the glass industry, for which Sardis appears to have become a center in late Roman times. With the cooperation of the Corning Museum of Glass, glass found at Sardis has been carefully studied by A. von Saldern, P. Perrot, and R. Brill (*Sardis* M6 [1980]). Glass of more or less luxury wares was imported to Sardis in the Lydian-Persian (sixth to fifth centuries B.C.) and the Hellenistic periods. Some simple types of the Roman Imperial period (first to fourth centuries A.D.) are also represented. The total is about 300 pieces. Then around A.D. 400, when many glass factories of the ancient world ceased to operate, at least one and possibly two factories were founded at Sardis, perhaps by glass makers from Syria. Fragments of some 4,000 vessels and some 1,000 windowpanes were discovered by the Harvard-Cornell Excavations. According to von Saldern, "astonishingly large quantities of ordinary ware, flat plate, and tesserae were produced until the fall of the city in A.D. 616." The Sardian glassmakers used only about three dozen basic forms—principally goblets, bottles, and lamps. These may, however, "provide a link between the better known late Roman and early Islamic glass."[43] Two spectacular finds deserve mention: a bit of the rare "dichroic" glass, which looks green in direct and red in transmitted light, and a piece dated by its decomposition layers to A.D. 378.[44]

Like metalwork, the glass industry had a modest postlude in the Middle Byzantine period (tenth to twelfth centuries), when bracelets and probably windowpanes of colored glass were made.[45]

The destruction of Sardis in A.D. 616 brought about the plunge from flourishing industrial urban center, whose gross product must have been very considerable, to domestic and village shop production. It is only in simple glazed wares and in utilitarian objects for village life that craft production continued into the Turkish period.[46] But one destructive industry lasted from late Roman times into the nineteenth century—the burning of ancient marble buildings for lime. Limekilns were operated in the Artemis Temple before A.D. 616; they were observed in the gymnasium as late as the 1880s.[47]

GMAH

Regional Settlement Pattern: Prehistoric to Twentieth Century

Prehistoric, Lydian, and Hellenistic Periods

Although a systematic survey has yet to be made, the two soundings carried out at Ahlatli Tepecik and Eski Balikhane and observations of a number of other sites suggest that already during the third millennium B.C. parts of the Sardian plain were quite densely populated.[1] Individual units may have been small hamlets and villages, often not more than a mile apart; very probably, they resembled in size other villages of Yortan-type culture known to the north and east.[2] We have almost no evidence for the second millennium B.C., the Middle and Late Bronze Age. Sardis was inhabited not much later than 1500 B.C., and there may be some Late Bronze Age material from Ahlatli Tepecik. The nearest safely datable place is Gavur Tepe at Philadelphia, where Mycenaean sherds have been found.[3] There is more to go on for the period of Lydian culture, from ca. 1100/1000 to 547 B.C., and for the Persian period, 547–334 B.C.

Villages in Anatolia tend to keep their positions through the ages because they are usually situated in places where water is readily available, and unless earthquakes and other catastrophes intervene, this remains an overriding consideration. If we accept the hypothesis that the country was divided into areas ruled by landowning aristocratic families, then more indications of the location of Lydian settlements may be derived from the distribution of groups of mounds in the vicinity of Sardis. This hypothesis is made attractive by the striking regularity with which groups of such mounds appear along the modern Turgutlu-Salihli highway. They have been plotted by A. and N. Ramage, whose discussion should be consulted for more detailed information.[4]

The first group of mounds occurs some 12–14 km. from Sardis at Ahmetli. Southward there are cemeteries in the Pactolus Valley which for 1 km. or so may still belong to Sardis, even though they include isolated mounds. The discovery in 1971 of a group of at least five mounds at the hamlet of Keskinler in the district of Başlioglu Köy[5] ca. 4.5 km. southwest of the Artemis Temple seems to indicate a separate settlement. To the east, the pattern is less clear. The first large tumuli occur on the road to Alaşehir (Philadelphia) ca. 36 km. from Sardis and on the northeast road up the Hermes to Demir Köprü, ca. 20 km. east of Sardis (Durasalli Group).

We know very little about the actual settlement forms in Lydian times. Presumably, the wealthy aristocracy owned much of the land, but we do not know what relation they had to the farming population. Plutarch's passage about Pythios[6] suggests that some landowning families became owners of gold mines (and hence possibly bankers and traders) and that they had the power to compel the farmers to leave the land and work in the mines. It is probable that for the farmers, informally organized cluster or ribbon-plan villages served as nuclei in the plain. A. Ramage has suggested that a rather substantial structure, partially excavated at Ahlatli Tepecik on the Gygean Lake (Fig. 13), might have been a Lydian farmhouse.[7] Scattered walls on the nearby beach and inland showed that it was part of a settlement.

It is not unlikely that the great Hellenistic estate of Mnesimachus perpetuated features of large Lydian and Persian estates. According to the Mnesimachus inscription of the third century B.C., this estate contained "the village (kome) of Tobalmoura in the Sardian plain on the hill of Ilos . . . villages of Tandos and Kombdilipia . . . Periasasostra in the water of Morstas . . . Nagrioa; village of Ilos in Attoudda."[8] It had at Tobalmoura a squire's house (aule), and outside the house were houses (oikiai) of serfs (laon) and slaves, and two gardens requiring fifteen artabas of seed and slaves dwelling at that place; four slaves are named for Tobalmoura. In addition to revenues payable in gold staters, wine vessels are mentioned as revenue payable in kind.

The size of these ancient villages in the plain remains uncertain. The modern villages of the Salihli district range from 25 to 2,450 inhabitants, with forty-nine villages having populations between 200 and 1,000, nine below 200, and nineteen above 1,000.[9] The present population of the Salihli district was 28,328 in 1927, of whom 21,137 lived in the country. In 1965, it was 87,766, of whom 58,857 lived in the country. According to local informants, in July 1978 the upper village of Sart Mustafa had 1,700, the lower village of Sart Mahmut 2,300 inhabitants. With a world capital at its center, instead of merely a district capital, the Lydian population of the Sardian plain may have been of about the same size as the population in 1965. The ratio of urban to rural population in 1927 was ca. 1:3, and in 1965 ca. 1:2.[10] If we assume that ancient Sardis had between 20,000 and 50,000 people in the Lydian period, the rural population of the Sardis region may have been between 20,000 (as in 1927) and 30,000, hardly more than that without the benefits of intensive agriculture. The total for the Sardis region under Croesus may have numbered from 40,000 to 80,000.

Roman, Byzantine, and Turkish Periods

The pattern of settlement in the Sardis region is relatively well known for the Roman period. In that age, when peace and a developed network of highways provided the conditions in which trade and industry could flourish, a high standard of living prevailed. Even small towns were able to erect substantial stone buildings, and individuals could afford to set up dedicatory monuments and memorials in marble. Since many material remains of the period have survived and since the region has been relatively well ex-

plored, it is possible to gain an idea of the pattern of settlement and density of population, two aspects in which Roman and modern Lydia seem to have resembled one another.

Most of the settlements were located on the north and south sides of the Sardian plain, along the foothills of the mountains, and around the Gygean Lake (Figs. 2, 11). Remains have not been discovered in the middle of the plain, near the Hermus, for that area would have been subject to the constant danger of floods. The district immediately adjacent to Sardis and that around the lake have been explored to some extent, but other parts of the territory are less well known. There are doubtless many sites as yet undiscovered and many more which will have disappeared altogether, for remains are constantly being destroyed as the local population and the demand for building materials increases. The following discussion, therefore, does not pretend to completeness.

Central Lydia in Roman times, as at the present, contained a few cities or towns and numerous villages. Of the cities, the greatest by far was Sardis, but Magnesia and Philadelphia were also places of some size and importance. The other "cities" of the area—as defined not by their size but by the possession of a territory and municipal rights, including in most cases that of striking their own coins—were probably large market towns, roughly comparable to their modern successors Ahmetli, Mermere, and Adala. These cities, as mentioned above, were Tmolus-Aureliopolis, Daldis, Satala, and an unidentified site at Mermere.[11]

The great majority of remains which have been discovered belong to village settlements. Most of them cannot now be identified, since the ancient sources rarely have occasion to mention individual villages and since few inscriptions have been found naming them. In the immediate vicinity of Sardis there were at least five villages within an hour of the city (Fig. 2): at Mersindere on the highway to the west, Metallon in the Pactolus Valley, Üç Tepeler on the hill south of the Temple of Artemis, Çaltili on the east slopes of the Acropolis hill, and Sart Camur Hamamlari, the hot spring about an hour southeast of the Acropolis. The latter may have contained a shrine of the nymphs.[12]

Along the south side of the Sardian plain,

traces of settlements have been found in the hills to the east at Allahdiyen, where remains of Roman buildings survive; at Tatar Islamköy in the plain, where the ruins have suggested the presence of a large estate; and at Yeşilkavak in the west part of the Cogamus Valley, where a village called Mylos has been identified.[13] Several other sites stood in the plain east of Salihli, near the confluence of the Hermus and Cogamus. Numerous Lydian burial mounds around the village of Durasalli and a Lydian inscription found not far away at Hacili suggest that the Lydian town of Thymbrara was located in the neighborhood. That town is mentioned only in sources which deal with the Persian period; it apparently lost its importance in later ages and declined to a village.[14]

On the north side of the plain, a site at Çapakli has been identified as the center of a group of villages called Trikomia, while other settlements have been located between there and the lake. In one of these, Poyrazdamlari, an inscription was found which commemorated the construction of a sacred precinct. Numerous settlements occupied the fertile lands around the Gygean Lake, where fish and waterfowl as well as an abundant supply of fresh water were available. Considerable remains, dating from prehistoric times through the Byzantine period, and several inscriptions have been found all around the lake.[15]

The mountainous areas of the Sardis region also supported village life, as they continue to do. There was a sizable town at Gürice northwest of the lake and another at Lübbey Yaylasi in a valley of Mount Tmolus about five hours south of Sardis. In the same region, pottery and small artifacts have been discovered at the resort town of Bozdag below the summit of the mountain. Further exploration of these districts, which were quite likely included in the territory of Sardis, would probably reveal many more remains.[16]

Of potential importance not only for urbanization in Roman times but also for tribal and urban arrangements in earlier times is the new material on the *conventus iuridicus* of Sardis organized under the late Roman Republic. The *conventus* of Sardis included twenty-eight known and some unknown cities, towns, tribes, and demes, many of them pre-Roman. It encom-

passed, however, a much larger area than the Sardis region discussed in this book, and the histories of the individual units remain to be worked out.[17]

For the Byzantine period, not much is known of the roads or the settlement pattern, though there is at least evidence to show that the highway system remained substantially unchanged. The disasters of Persian and Arab invasions in the seventh century, which reduced Sardis from a flourishing city to a small town with a fortress, disrupted the communication system and caused widespread depopulation. The highway up the Hermus was only rebuilt forty years after the destruction of Sardis in 616, a fact which gives some idea of the wretched conditions of the times. Later, casual mentions in sources of the twelfth century show that the highway from Thyateira through Sardis to Philadelphia was in use—it was followed by the Third Crusade—and that the route along the Hermus Valley and that over the Tmolus were still functioning.[18]

In the Byzantine era the period of greatest prosperity for the Sardis region was that of the Nicene Empire (1204–1261), when the political and economic center of the state was in Lydia, at Magnesia, and the emperor's favorite residence was nearby at Nymphaeum. At this time Philadelphia was the major frontier fortress of the region, and Sardis was thus in a strategic location on the main highway of the kingdom.

The location of settlements in the Byzantine age remains uncertain, but the general pattern of a few towns and many villages seems to have been unchanged. The sources mention only a few villages, none of which has been identified with certainty, but Byzantine remains have been noted on several of the sites which were inhabited in the Roman period, in the vicinity of Sardis, at the east edge of the plain, and around the lake.[19] The Roman pattern of dense village settlement probably prevailed through late antiquity, as indicated by the remains, but a sharp decline of population followed the troubles of the seventh century. Recovery was gradual in this and other regions; old sites grew or were reoccupied in the eleventh and twelfth century, but stability did not return until the Empire of Nicaea and its successor state, the Emirate of Saruhan, were established.

Under the Turkish state of Saruhan (1313–

1410), which comprised most of Lydia and had its capital at Manisa, the main centers remained those which had been important under the Romans, with only minor changes.[20] The administrative centers of the region were at Sardis, Ilica (near Tmolos-Aureliopolis), Mermere, and Adala. Of these, Adala was the most important. In documents of the time, the names of several villages are mentioned, many of them on ancient sites. Modern village names are already mentioned, and illustrate the continuity from that time to the present.

The obscurity of the Middle Ages finally yields to more detailed knowledge after the establishment of Ottoman control in Lydia in the fifteenth century. The Ottoman government carried out surveys of the countryside for tax purposes; many of them have survived, though few have been published. Documents from the seventeenth century show that the modern pattern of dense village settlement with a few large market towns was established by then and has undergone relatively little change except that occasioned by growth of population and alteration of trade routes.[21]

The Ottoman highway system, known from records of Turkish and western travelers, clearly illustrates the diminished importance of Sardis, then hardly more than a village. The main highway from Akhisar to Alaşehir passed through Adala, not Sardis, but accounts of travelers, anxious to visit the ancient ruins of the city, show that routes from Akhisar, Gördes, and the Cayster Valley were still practicable.[22] With the growth of the caravan trade from Izmir to the interior in the seventeenth century, the Hermus highway once again assumes importance, as illustrated by the increasing number of travelers visiting Sardis by that route.[23]

The greatest changes have taken place in the last century. In 1873, the railway from Izmir to Kasaba was extended via Sardis to Alaşehir. Sardis, however, remained a village and a whistle-stop on the line, for the center of the region had become established at the nearby town of Salihli, already a place of some importance in the early eighteenth century. Salihli is now the major market town of the district and has, since the construction of the railroad, replaced Adala as the administrative center.[24] The prosperity of the whole area has been increased and the accessibility of Sardis furthered by the recent construction of the highway from Izmir to Ankara, which follows roughly the route of the Persian Royal Road and passes through the ruins of the Lydian capital.

CF

II

Prehistoric and Protohistoric Periods

J E F F R E Y   S P I E R

Early Bronze Age Sites on the Gygean Lake

Two decades of archaeological work at Sardis have enabled us to discern the lineaments of the development of the urban site from the Prehistoric through the Turkish periods. It may be useful to explain at the outset the chronological system which has emerged as appropriate for the local development at Sardis. The major periods are the Prehistoric, divided into the Neolithic and Copper Age, ca. 5000–3000, and the Bronze Age, ca. 3000–1000 B.C.; the Lydian, ca. 1000–547 B.C.; the Persian, 547–334 B.C.; the early Hellenistic (Seleucid), 334–213 B.C.; the middle and late Hellenistic and early Roman, 213 B.C.–A.D. 17; the Roman Imperial and Late Antique, A.D. 17–616; the Byzantine, 616 to ca. 1300; and the Turkish, ca. 1300 to the present day.

Early Bronze Age sites were revealed on the southern shore of the Gygean Lake (Marmara Gölü) (Fig. 2). The first, a small mound called Ahlatli Tepecik ("Wild Pear Tree Mound"), ca. 800 m. west of Tekelioglu Köy, the principal village on the south shore of the lake, was excavated in 1967 and 1968.[1] Eski Balikhane ("Old Fishery"), ca. 2 km. to the northeast of Tekelioglu Köy, was explored in 1969.[2] Several other sites along the lake were reported to have pithos burials, including Boyali Tepe (Fig. 11), where

the pithoi were of different character and contained Middle or Late Bronze Age pottery.[3]

At Ahlatli Tepecik, several trenches ("Lake Trench") were dug along the lake (Figs. 12, 13), but the largest area was on the slope of the pasture to the south of the actual mound where a cemetery ("South Cemetery") of Roman and Early Bronze Age burials was found. This area is approximately bounded by E15-W13/S45-63 with outlying trenches to the north and west. In 1968 a number of 5 m. square test pits were dug, totaling 264 sq. m., to the east of the cemetery. These uncovered a Lydian house and several more burials (Fig. 13).

Eski Balikhane is probably the principal ancient site on the lake, with remains of Ottoman, Byzantine, Roman, Hellenistic, Lydian, and Bronze Age occupation. A 10 by 5 m. trench was laid out, oriented north-south, ca. 50 m. south of the lake shore. The Early Bronze Age level lay ca. 1.0–1.2 m. below the surface and was a distinctive reddish-brown color. This level contained a large number of sherds and stone objects, such as flint blades and blade tools, and five pithos burials.

The Burials

Excavations at Ahlatli Tepecik revealed six Early Bronze Age pithos burials, five cist grave burials, and two rock-covered burials (Fig. 13). The cist graves were rectangular in shape, with schist slabs used for the sides and lids. Two of these (AT 67.8 and 67.9) were empty, containing only later pottery fragments that filtered in with the earth. A similar grave (AT 68.5), found in the Lake Trench, contained the bones of a woman over 50 in a flexed position, a posture also observed in a cist grave. The largest (AT 67.29; Fig. 15), 2.25 m. by 1.30 m., found in South Cemetery, contained a single burial with a red ware one-handled jug and two pots, one black ware and one brown ware. The other cist grave (AT 67.27) was found in the outlying northern trench and contained bone fragments and a Yortan-style black ware three-footed vase with lid and incised decoration, a red ware jug, a brown ware jug, a bronze pin, and a spindle whorl.

In 1968 two burials (AT 68.3 and AT 68.6) were found close to each other that contained the bones of two women crushed beneath large chunks of limestone. One woman was identified as being over 50 years old and the other 55–65 years old. A brown ware jug was placed by the head of the latter. According to D. Finkel, the women may have been crushed to death.

The pithos burials were all very similar. Five of the six were oriented east-west with the mouth of the jar towards the east, often closed with a schist slab. In five cases the pithoi contained bones of one individual and in one the bones of two people. One pithos (AT 68.7) was small and two-handled, oriented north-south, containing the bones of an infant and a black burnished bowl. The other pithoi were all similar, with four vertical strap handles alternating with four horn-like lugs. All the pithoi contained from one to three pieces of pottery. Pithos AT 67.10 contained two red ware jugs, a copper dagger, and a stone pendant (S 67.27:7471). AT 68.8 (Fig. 14) contained the bones of a male, 24–28 years of age, a red ware jug, a shale pendant, a copper needle, and a spindle whorl.

Of the five pithoi at Eski Balikhane, two were similar in orientation and content to those from Ahlatli Tepecik. A third (EB 69.2) was small and two-handled, containing the bones of an infant. EB 69.4 had no neck and was sealed by a schist slab at the break. It was oriented north-south and contained the bones of a woman, ca. 35 years of age. There were also a brown ware one-

handled jug, a black burnished bowl, a black burnished one-handled jug, and some mussel shells. A fifth pithos (EB 69.1) was also oriented north-south but was empty.

Pithos EB 69.5, one of the two similar pithoi, with the mouth to the east, contained the bones of a male, ca. 35 years old, and a one-handled jug, a round-bodied, three-handled vase, and a Yortan-style miniature three-footed black ware vessel (Fig. 17). EB 69.3 was particularly rich in finds. The pithos itself was different in that in addition to the four vertical strap handles, there were one or two oval clay medallions fastened onto the neck and at least two raised relief signs in the form of a T with a circle hanging from the vertical bar. The mouth was closed with an oval schist slab and limestone chips, and inside was the flexed skeleton of a man, ca. 35 years of age. With the skeleton were found two black ware one-handled jugs (P 69.36:7970 and the other crumbled), a red ware vase (P 69.37:7971), a copper dagger (M 69.5:7972), a small pendant of silver in the shape of a ram (M 69.6:7973), and two bullet-shaped gold earplugs (M 69.7:7974 and M 69.8:7975; Figs. 16, 18).

Pottery

The pottery is all handmade, almost all monochrome, red, black, and brown ware, and mostly burnished. A great amount of sherds were found, but most of the intact vessels came from the graves. The most frequent shapes were the black burnished bowls with thickened, incurved rims and wide-mouthed, one-handled jugs (Figs. 14, 16). There were also a number of fragments of tripod bowls and many lug handles. Exceptional shapes and types include a red ware one-handled jug with raised disc designs around the sides (Fig. 19), a small red ware two-handled vase, a miniature black ware three-handled vase with a cylindrical neck, and three Yortan-style thin black ware vessels: a small black thin-necked, one-handled jug with incised patterns of zigzags, dots, and circles; a three-legged pot with lid and incised zigzags and dots (P 67.93:7498); and a three-footed vase with lugs and white-filled incised decorations (P 69.42:7980; Fig. 17). There were also a number of biconical spindle whorls, some with incised decoration.

Metal Objects

The metal objects are of copper, silver, and gold. These objects include three copper daggers, two matching gold earplugs, a silver pendant in the shape of a ram, three silver finials, and several copper pins. One dagger (M 68.24:7894) was found in fill near Pithos AT 68.8. Pithos EB 69.3 yielded a dagger (M 69.5:7972; Fig. 16), the silver ram (M 69.6:7973; Fig. 18), and the gold earplugs (M 69.7:7974, M 69.8:7975; Fig. 16). The ram has a thin, elongated body, 0.027 m. in length and 0.008 m. in width, with a small, stubby tail and a head with curling horns. The right front and rear legs are missing. There is a transverse perforation, indicating that the ram was used as a pendant. The two gold earplugs or labrets are roughly bullet-shaped, with a pointed head with cross-hatched incised lines and a concave neck that flares out into a flat bottom. They are made of sheet gold around a core of dark, grainy material. Neutron activation analysis showed a high percentage of silver (ca. 6–15%) and some copper 1.6–2.7%). The silver content is consistent with later Lydian samples and suggests that the gold may have been obtained locally.[4] Three silver tubular objects were found in fill (best preserved uncatalogued—L.:0.075 m., diam.: 0.024 m.) and are thought to be finials for wooden poles, similar to the gold ones found in the royal graves at Alaca Höyük.[5]

Stone Objects

Some stone objects, including a number of flaked stone blades and tools of flint, chert jasper, and some of obsidian, were found. The earliest find, dating from before the Bronze Age, was a tiny lunate microlith of honey-colored and white chalcedony (S 68.17:7776; Fig. 20). It resembles certain Mesolithic microliths and may date to as early as 7000 or 6000 B.C. Another pre–Bronze Age find is a Neolithic stone head broken from a figurine that was found in a dry torrent bed before 1957 (Fig. 21).[6] It is 0.04 m. in height and of soft stone and dates from the fifth to fourth millennium B.C. A basalt celt (S 68.27:7808) was retrieved from an outcropping of a wall near AT 68.7.

A piece of sculpture contemporary with the Early Bronze Age burials was found at Eski Ba-likhane. This piece (S 69.7:7959) is the lower half of an idol, showing the feet and wide hips, probably of a "mother goddess."[7] It is of gray, hard schist and was found in fill near Pithos EB 69.4. A long, cylindrical stone pendant (S 67.27:7471) was found in Pithos AT 67.10. Another pendant (BI 68.6:7814), this one of bone and rectangular in shape (0.046 m. by 0.018–0.022 m.), was found in Pithos AT 68.8.

Cultural Parallels and Dating

The location of the site suggests a small community of farmers, hunters, and fishers,[8] but only the cemetery area was discovered. The burials are similar to those of many other Western Anatolian Bronze Age sites,[9] notably Karataş-Semayük,[10] Aphrodisias,[11] Yortan,[12] and Babaköy,[13] where the cemeteries are extramural and consist predominantly of pithos burials with some cist graves and inhumations. At these sites, the pithoi were usually placed in a hole dug in the ground on their sides with the mouth at a slightly higher level than the base and facing east. The flexed body was then placed in the jar on its side along with the grave gifts. Then the mouth of the jar would be sealed with a stone slab. Usually a single individual was buried, but sometimes there were successive burials, as is seen in burial AT 67.25 and at Karataş and Babaköy.

The cist graves that were found at Ahlatli Tepecik are contemporary with the pithoi, containing identical pottery. These graves are also similar to other Anatolian sites, where pithos and cist graves are mixed, and are especially comparable to those at Iasos in Lycia, on the southwest coast, where there is an extensive cist grave cemetery.[14] Cist graves were predominant in the Cyclades. T. S. Wheeler suggests interactions between the Cyclades and Western Anatolia.[15]

The pottery, although plentiful, is all very similar, with a limited number of shapes. It is most similar to Troy I types.[16] Typical Troy II types, like the depas and Schnabelkanne, are completely absent. There is also no wheelmade pottery, first introduced in the Troy II period. Found with the simple pottery were three pots evidently imported from sites of nearby Yortan culture (P 67.93:7498, P 67.100:7511, and P 69.42:7980), whose style lasted through Troy

I and Troy II.[17] According to Mellaart,[18] the destruction of Troy I caused the coastal people to flee to the Manisa-Akhisar plain. These people used Troy I pottery in the EBII–Troy II period, accounting for the large number of sites with Troy I pottery, but no Troy II pottery. J. C. Waldbaum also dates the cemetery to the EB II period.[19] Mitten sees the closest parallels in EB I and dates Ahlatli Tepecik 3000–2500 B.C.[20]

The Eski Balikhane pithos EB 69.3 was the source of most of the metal objects (Fig. 16). The earplugs found there are similar to a number found in Western and Central Anatolia, from Karataş, the Yortan-Balikesir area, Yalincak-Kocumbeli (near Ankara), Karayavşan (between Polatli and Haymana), and Alaca Höyük.[21] A comparison with Troy II jewelry is made.[22] There are no parallels to the silver ram pendant.[23] According to Waldbaum, dagger M 68.24:7894 is a type dated from before 2500 B.C. to after 2200 B.C.[24] Daggers M 67.22:7426 and M 69.5:7972, the latter found in Pithos EB 69.3, are dated after 2200 B.C.[25]

The Gygean Lake sites were apparently occupied only periodically. At the city site the microlith and the Neolithic head (Figs. 20, 21) indicate occupation as early as 7000 B.C., but are the only evidence. EB II occupation is the best attested, but no other Bronze Age evidence is found, except at nearby Boyali Tepe where there are a few pithoi possibly of Middle or Late Bronze Age date.[26] There was also one Iron Age or possibly Late Bronze Age single burial inhumation at Ahlatli Tepecik (AT 67.38).[27] This was followed by Lydian, Hellenistic, Roman, and later occupation, probably all small fishing villages.

JS

Late Bronze and Early Iron Age in the City Area

The "Lydian Trench" in the House of Bronzes area (Figs. 8:4, location; 5, 31) is contained roughly in squares W35–E20/S85–S120. The levels showed continuous occupation, interrupted by periodic flooding, from Byzantine times back through Roman, Hellenistic, Lydian, Protogeometric–late Mycenaean, and to the Late Bronze Age. The deep Prehistoric and Protohistoric levels were found in three pits dug in 1960, 1962, and 1966. The 1960 pit was measured by squares E4–14/S95–105 and in part reached a depth of ca. *92.[1] The 1962 pit measured W2–E10/S86–101 and reached the Late Bronze Age level at ca. *91 (Figs. 22, 23).[2] The 1966 pit was bordered by E5–W6/S98–109 (Fig. 22), and its lowest level, W4–E3/S103–107.5, reached to ca. *90.[3] The total excavated area of the three pits was ca. 250 sq. m.

General Stratigraphy

The physical stratigraphy of these pits consists of alternating layers of waterlaid sand and gravel and sandy clay and earth. Sometimes gravel would be mixed in with the clay. These clay levels indicate occupation and probably are largely the remains of disintegrated mudbrick buildings. Floors are frequent and close together, and sherds are plentiful and well-preserved in these levels. The sand and gravel beds were apparently laid by the flooding of the Pactolus and vary from a few centimeters to over a meter in depth. There are few sherds in these levels, and they are water-worn.

This stratigraphy presents certain problems. The levels slope slightly both from south down to north and west to east. The flood deposits also sometimes interrupt the stratigraphy. Floors are often very close together and are sometimes disrupted, and architectural features in the lower levels are scarce. The evidence retrieved from the three major pits is set forth in Table 1.

Late Bronze Age

The earliest level dates to the Late Bronze Age of the fourteenth to thirteenth centuries B.C., or possibly earlier, and is represented by the remains of a circular wattle and daub hut and a pithos cremation burial (Figs. 22–25). A few monochrome sherds were also found. All that remained of the hut (Fig. 24) was a red-burnt floor measuring ca. 2 m. in diameter. On the floor were lumps of clay bearing impressions of parallel reeds and branches, which were evidently used for the construction of the roof or walls.[4]

A little northwest and below the hut, the pithos burial was found. The pithos

Table 1. Comparative stratigraphy of 1960, 1962, and 1966 pits

1960	1962	1966
*97.65–97.49 Upper burning level (Kimmerian destruction)	*98–97.5 Upper burning level	*97.9–97.3 Dated by Protocorinthian pottery. Not as much burnt material
*96.97–96.45 Lydian level III–IV Greek and Lydian Geometric pottery	*97.5–96.3 Greek and Lydian Geometric	*97–95.8 Geometric sherds in earth and gravel, water-worn
*96.04 Lydian Geometric disappears		
to *95.68 Local gray and red ware, some Mycenaean (?) or Protogeo- metric	to *94.75 Local, gray ware, pithoi, Proto- geometric. Hearth	*95.8–94.1 (Floors at *95.5, 94.75) Local wares, pithoi, Protogeometric, Mycenaean Small stone wall, pits
ca. *95.5–95.08 (sloping top) to 94.56 Lower burning level Mycenaean sherds	*95–94 Protogeometric	
to *93.8 Mycenaean	*94–93.6 Fewer pithoi, little gray ware. Iron knife. Submycenaean or Mycenaean sherds	*94.1–89.9 Less gray ware. Mostly orange- buff ware
*93.8–92 Isolated bones and sherds	*93–92.65 Gravel	
	*92.65 Mycenaean, spindle whorl	
	*92–91.3 Late Bronze Age hut and pithos burial	*91.2 Clay level

(P 62.463:4867) is of coarse red ware with an everted rim and two small lug handles just below (Figs. 24, 25). The height is 0.52 m. and the body tapers off to a rounded base. The pithos lay on its side, with the mouth facing east. The mouth was sealed with clay and stones. Inside were found the badly preserved bones of an adult, probably female, some of which were burnt, along with a quantity of fine sandy soil and some gray material, probably disintegrated bone and ash. There were no objects.

There were relatively few sherds found in the area of the hut and pithos, and none of these were painted. The few monochrome sherds were from cooking pots, and there were also bits of yellow-red pithoi, buff ware, and a few black burnished sherds. The 1966 pit at this level yielded mostly orange buff ware of varying textures.

This intramural cremation burial of the Late Bronze Age makes Sardis one of the few sites in Bronze Age Anatolia where the change in burial customs from inhumation to cremation is found. Both intramural and extramural burials existed in the Bronze Age, and at Sardis Early Bronze Age extramural inhumation cemeteries were found along the Gygean Lake. In the Middle and Late Bronze Ages (late third to second millenium B.C.), some intramural burials were used in Alişar, Kültepe, and other sites,[5] but no cremations have been found. Cremation burials apparently developed in Anatolia in the fourteenth to thirteenth centuries B.C., although possibly earlier at Bogazköy, and are found, although rarely, in Syria, Palestine, and in Anatolia at Troy and Bogazköy.[6] They do not occur in Greece until Protogeometric and Geometric times.

At Troy, a cremation cemetery was found at level VI h, dated ca. 1325–1275 B.C. by pottery present in the pithoi, including Mycenean LHIII A and B.[7] Pithoi of various shapes were used, including some similar to that at Sardis. Blegen notes the change in burial customs and emphasizes that the settlement was no longer Mycenaean at this point. He also mentions T. Özgüç's theory of possible connections with Hittites and the East.[8]

Osmankaya, on the road to Yazilikaya near the Hittite capital Bogazköy, yielded the other Hittite cremation cemetery.[9] Here there were a large number of cremation burials, some in pithoi and some in ornamental jars, and inhumation burials dating from possibly Old Hittite Kingdom through the Empire. There were few offerings placed in the burials, but quite often a horse's head would be included. E. Akurgal states that cremation was a Hittite practice and denies that the cemetery at Gordion, where there were pithoi but no cremations, was Hittite.[10]

It is difficult to interpret the Sardis burial, since the evidence is so scant. No pottery or other objects were found in the pithos, and no other burials or huts were discovered. Only a few small monochrome sherds were found in the area. In some respects the burial is similar to the other Anatolian burials, especially those of Troy, and probably should be dated to the fourteenth to thirteenth centuries B.C. The pithos itself (Fig. 25) is similar to pithoi dating from the Middle and Late Bronze Ages found at a number of sites, including Troy, Bogazköy, Beycesultan, and Gordion.[11] The scant evidence makes it hard to say to what culture the burial belonged, or, more broadly, what culture—Greek, Hittite, or other—influenced this part of Western Anatolia. Mycenaean sherds are not found until a later level. Some extrusive sherds of a red ware Hit-

tite beaked rhyton (P 61.533:4055) were found at a high level (ca. *99). These five sherds were ribbed and red burnished, and one sherd had a white band. These, however, were almost the only sherds of Hittite type found at Sardis. One bronze arrowhead was found in mixed fill in the Road Trench. Waldbaum considers that this variant of the barbed-and-tanged type is closest to those of the Hittite Empire (ca. 1400–1200).[12] But close dating is impossible. Although different, notably in being intramural, the Sardis burial is perhaps best compared to those at Troy. The situation at Troy appears to be that of a local culture influenced by other people, both by the Hittites in the East and the Greeks in the West. Like Troy, Sardis appears to be a native culture that borrows and absorbs from Central Anatolia and Cyclades and others but retains a local character.

Other Prehistoric Finds

Two stone celts were found, and although they were both extrusive (*95.5 and *98.5), they do indicate Prehistoric habitation. S 65.6:6717 is of green stone, and S 66.11:7085 is of dark-flecked purple stone and is highly polished.

A damaged stone sculpture of a bird's head (S 64.36:6260)[13] was found in MTE upper in mixed fill. It is of grayish large-grained marble, discolored green. The height is 0.039 m. The date is unclear, but possibly as early as the third millennium B.C. (?), "either early Lydian or more likely Bronze Age."

Cretan Seals

Two seals from Sardis in the Ashmolean Museum were attributed to Minoan Crete by V. E. G. Kenna. The first, a sardonyx seal, is said to be Middle Minoan.[14] The second, of brown steatite, is called Late Minoan.[15] Boardman includes the first seal with his Middle Minoan I-II group.[16] However, Ingo Pini (correspondence with Eric Freedman) disagrees with these attributions. The former (no. 134) he believes is not Cretan, and the latter (no. 396) not even Aegean.

Mycenaean and Submycenaean Levels

Mixed in with the abundant local monochrome sherds were a number of painted sherds of late Mycenaean and Submycenaean types (LH IIIB–

IIIC:2, thirteenth to eleventh centuries B.C.).[17] Although they constituted a small percentage of the total number of sherds (2–5%), about 250 Mycenaean and Submycenaean sherds were found. Some are imported; most are of local clay. Shapes include kraters, deep bowls, and cups. In the opinion of G. M. A. Hanfmann, imported sherds may include a very few mainland pieces, and a limited number of Eastern Greek Mycenaean products from places like Miletus and Rhodes. The bulk is imitated from a diluted Mycenaean tradition. Detailed study by specialists will bring greater clarity, but as A. Ramage rightly insists, contact with Mycenaean traditions is unmistakable.[18]

In the following discussion, "Mycenaean," "Submycenaean," and "Protogeometric" are used in the broad sense of pottery displaying traits of the Mycenaean, Submycenaean, and Protogeometric ceramic traditions.

The earliest level where there is evidence of Mycenaean-style pottery is just above the *92.65 floor in the 1962 pit (Fig. 23), about 1 m. above the level with the cremation pithoi burials. Here two sherds and a spindle whorl (T 62.50) were found. One of these sherds (P 62.448:4844) was from a Mycenaean closed vessel and has painted bands and a small part of a spiral (?). The other sherd (P 62.449:4845) was part of a small carinated red ware vessel of Aegean character.

The other Mycenaean sherds were found in all three deep soundings between ca. *95.8 and *93.6, with most being found in 1966. The upper strata were marked by a burned level (Lower Burning Level), at some points up to a meter thick (ca. *95.5–94.5 in the 1960 pit and ca. *95–94 in the 1962 pit). This level contained both Mycenaean and Protogeometric sherds. The Mycenaean sherds were largely of light orange-buff ware, medium to fine texture, with a smoothed cream surface and bright orange-red paint. Cup fragment P 66.114:7159 is of red-buff clay, also local, and is decorated with wavy lines. Among these are sherds of a crater (P 66.119:7164; Fig. 26) which are Submycenaean according to C. Özgünel (1980). It is of buff clay, probably local, with orange paint, decorated with bands and wavy lines.

P 66.137:7188 is a loop handle and part of the rim from a brown on light-buff cup, probably imported. Some other possibly imported Mycenaean wares are P 60.555:3070, a jug rim and

vertical handle of beige-buff clay and red paint, and P 60.524:3037, a rim of a large cup with vertical loop handle stump, made of greenish clay and thought to be Rhodian.

Local Monochrome Wares
In the earlier levels, below the burned level (ca. *95) and corresponding to the Mycenaean-Submycenaean levels, the pottery consists mostly of red or orange-buff ware, buff cooking pots, pithoi, and some gray ware and yellow-buff ware. Orange-buff ware is found in the deepest levels of the 1966 pit; it was used in the Late Bronze Age and is also the material of some Mycenaean sherds. Some examples of buff cooking pots are P 66.139:7191, a band handle and rim, and P 66.140:7192, a cooking pot with band handle. In later levels (Protogeometric) the pithoi sherds become predominant, sometimes 50% or more, and the gray ware becomes more frequent, a tradition that lasts through Lydian times. Examples of early gray ware are P 60.547:3061, the base and body fragments of an unevenly made slipped and burnished bowl, and P 60.552:3066 (Fig. 27), the band handle and rim fragments of a jug. In the later Mycenaean and Protogeometric levels, 50% (or more) of the sherds were of pithoi; 50–60% of the rest were plain reddish-buff ware, 10–30% gray ware, 10–20% cooking pots, 5–10% fine yellow-buff ware, and 2–5% painted Mycenaean and Protogeometric.

Lower Burning Level—*94.75 Floor

A thick habitation layer of brown earth and clay, ca. *95.5–94 (varying thicknesses at different locations), with several floors was found in all three soundings. Patches of charcoal were found throughout, indicating destruction by fire. A floor at ca. *94.75 was found in all three soundings, and at this level were some of the rare architectural features. In the 1962 pit, a hearth was found on this floor (Fig. 23). It was 0.70 m. square and was constructed of two stone slabs on edge and one pithos base. In 1966 on the *94.75 floor was found a little wall of small, flat stones reaching from W5/S109 to E3/S106 (see plans HoB 69 and HoB 75; Fig. 22). Near this wall, at E1/S103 and W2/S102, were two small circular stone walls 1 m. in diameter. Just to the south of the short mass, the lower two-thirds of a sunken red ware pithos was discovered, and at W2/S106 and E2/S104.5 were two pits, about 20–30 cm. deep and about 1 m. in diameter, containing charcoal. Slightly below this level, at *94.2, E3/S104, another small row of stones 1.2 m. long was found. A little northwest of this wall was a complete skeleton of a small equid and another small pit at W1/S108. Above this level, at *95.5, was another floor, which showed signs of burning.

Protogeometric Sherds

In all three pits a floor was found at ca. *96, and below this floor and down to as low as *94, sherds of Protogeometric type were found. Although they begin and continue slightly later than the Mycenaean sherds and are generally on a slightly higher level, the Protogeometric sherds are often found with Mycenaean sherds. This may be due in part to stratigraphic disruption (such as that by the small ancient pits), but many of the Protogeometric and Mycenaean sherds may be contemporaneous. Most Protogeometric sherds were thought by G. F. Swift to be of local make. Protogeometric shapes include cups, some with high loop handles, oinochoai and other closed jars, and bowls. These are painted in dark brown and black in typical designs, such as wavy lines, bands, and concentric circles and half-circles. Among them is a fragment of a Cycladic plate identified by Hanfmann. At the *94.7 floor, two-thirds of a local cup with Protogeometric circle decoration (P 66.107:7145; Fig. 28) was found in one piece. It is of buff clay and painted with dark brown lines, bands, and concentric three-quarter circles along the rim.

Immediately following the Protogeometric level, above the ca. *96 floor, were Greek Geometric sherds and local (Lydian) copies of Geometric pottery.

Objects

Important finds from the Protogeometric levels include several iron objects: a curved sickle blade, 0.20 m. in length (Fig. 30; 1966—E3/S98 *95.5), an adze blade (1960—E10–18/S100–105 *94.8), a knife (HoB 1966—W0–3/S100–106 *95.5–94.8), and a hook (?), 0.14 m. × 0.06 m. (1966—W0–6/S103–106 *95.8–95.5).

J. Waldbaum points out that they are the earliest iron tools from Sardis.[19]

Bronze objects include an arc fibula (M 66.13:7150; Fig. 29) of Phrygian type[20] and two pins (M 66.11:7111 and 1966—W4–6/S100–108 *95.5–94.85). Perforated glass beads, possibly Phoenician, were found in all three pits.[21]

At ca. *95.4 a flat, button-shaped seal was found (Seal 66.1:7109). It is of green schist and engraved with a linear long-horned goat or other animal.[22]

Animal bones from these levels were primarily those of cattle and swine, with sheep and goat bones also present.[23]

Cultural and Historical Parallels

These discoveries at Sardis give important information regarding the pressing questions about the cultural contacts of Western Anatolia with the Greeks and the East and the cultural traits and continuity of the local inhabitants from the end of the Bronze Age through the "Dark Ages." Like many other sites, Sardis was burned (Lower Burning Level) at the end of the Bronze Age, ca. 1200 B.C., but there is a considerable evidence of continuity into the Early Iron Age.

A number of written sources may be relevant to the situation in the Sardis area.[24] Hittite records tell of the reprisal attacks of King Tudhaliyas against the rebel confederacy of Assuwa,[25] a name possibly related to that of the tribe Asias which later existed at Sardis.[26] Following Götze, Pedley also notes the linguistic similarity of Hittite and Lydian names, for example, Maduwattas and Aly-attes.[27] Hittite archives tell of the kingdom of Ahhiyawa, which led to the controversial equating of Ahhiyawa with Achaeans and the controversy over the location and chronology of the kingdom, variously believed to be in different parts of Greece, Anatolia, or the islands.[28]

Evidence for Greeks settling at some Western Anatolian sites has been much discussed. In Miletus,[29] possibly the Millawanda of Hittite texts, a fortified Mycenaean settlement was destroyed ca. 1200 B.C. At Ephesus, a fourteenth to thirteenth century tomb containing Mycenaean LH IIIA:2 vases was found under a parking lot.[30] Ephesus may be the Apasas, capital of the kingdom of Arzawa, mentioned in Hittite records.[31]

As to Lydia, Herodotus (I.7) relates that the Herakleidai settled in Sardis 505 years before the accession of Gyges (ca. 1185?), and this event may indicate the arrival of Mycenaean warriors who seized the rule of Sardis and then assimilated.[32] Another Aegean Bronze Age warrior was Moksos (Mopsos), who came to the Gygean Lake and later ruled over the Danuna in Cilicia, as is revealed in a Luvian-Phoenician bilingual text from Karatepe.[33]

Archaeological evidence for Aegean presence in Western Anatolia has been reviewed by Boysal and Mee.[34] Boysal reports the discoveries of Mycenaean sherds at Gavurtepe in Alaşehir (ancient Philadelphia in Lydia). One sherd was identified as Myc. IIIA:2 (fourteenth century), and Boysal notes a possible Late Bronze Age link with Troy and Yortan. A similar situation may have existed at Sardis. Boysal also cites Mycenaean finds from Caria and identifies Ahhiyawa as the area containing Caria, Southern Ionia, and the islands with the center at Rhodes.

The Sardis discoveries support the theory that Greek invaders came to Sardis.[35] The succession of Mycenaean, Submycenaean, and Protogeometric pottery, without interruption, constitutes only a small percentage of the total pottery, but is almost all locally made, indicating that Mycenaeans settled at Sardis. Similar events may also have occurred at Troy VII a and b,[36] Tarsus,[37] and other sites[38] where Late Mycenaean pottery of local manufacture were found.[39]

Related to the Greek contacts, another important aspect is the cultural continuity of Sardis. The Mycenaean (late thirteenth to eleventh century) and Protogeometric (eleventh to tenth century) pottery is directly followed by Greek Geometric and Lydian copies of Geometric pottery in an uninterrupted succession. The local plain ware also developed without interruption. Admiration for Greek things and the desire to copy them, a trait that becomes obvious in Geometric and later Lydian times, may go back to the Late Bronze Age.[40] In general, however, although Greeks probably did settle at Sardis, the culture of the Early Iron Age remained native Anatolian in character.

JS

III

Lydian Excavation Sectors

ANDREW RAMAGE

SIDNEY M. GOLDSTEIN

WILLIAM E. MIERSE

House of Bronzes/Lydian Market: Stratification Sequence and the Lydian Levels

That the Lydian city of Sardis is at long last taking concrete form and that the lineaments of some aspects of Lydian culture begin to emerge, we owe. to the excavations of the several sectors examined in this chapter. Among them the so-called House of Bronzes/Lydian Market area, stretching south of the modern—and probably of the ancient—east-west highway (Figs. 8:58; 31; Plan I), holds a key position. For it is here that the longest sequence of human settlements at Sardis has been discovered. An interpretation of this sequence depends on close study of the Lydian levels and Lydian finds made in the field. Table 2 illustrates the preliminary results of these observations, and the following discussion takes this table as a guide.

The Prehistoric and Protohistoric finds at HoB (Lydian Trench, W40–E5/S130; Fig. 22) fall into four main divisions, separated from one another by layers of more or less barren alluvial deposits of fine sand or heavy gravel. Chronologically, the four lowest levels encompass the Late Bronze and Early Iron Age (Table 2, nos. 1–4).

1. The lowest level reached produced, amidst much sand, some sherds in what seems to be a variety of native Anatolian monochrome, which has been compared to wares of the Hittite sites.

Table 2. Major levels at House of Bronzes, Lydian Trench

	Period	Levels	Years (B.C.)
8	Lydian I	*99–*100	600–547
7	Lydian II	*98–*99	650–600
6	Lydian III	*97.1–*98	700–650
5	Geometric Age	*95.8–*97.1	850?–700
4	Protogeometric	*95–*95.8	1000–850?
3	Submycenaean	*94–*95	1200–1000
2	Late Bronze Age	*92–*94	1400?–1200
1	Indications of habitation	Below *92	Earlier than 1400

2. Occupation of the Late Bronze Age is indicated by circular hut and pithos burial (Figs. 23–25) in this level.

3. Mycenaean connections (Fig. 26) are mingled with another Anatolian tradition in the form of gray monochrome ware (Fig. 27).

4. Just above this is a level with Mycenaean connections and pottery in the Protogeometric style (Fig. 28). These two levels seem very close in time, since substantial quantities of both kinds of sherds were found together—in one instance associated with a floor. Actual domestic remains were found *in situ* (wall, pithos, hearth, bones), and we may conclude in general that although some occupation areas were carried away by flood, we are not dealing with piles of rolled rubbish but with fragments of occupation areas which survived the rush of water and gravel.

5. The appearance of pottery with geometric designs justifies the designation of the fifth main level as "Geometric." There are several minor levels above this where painted pottery is rare and coarse pithoi and jars the rule. The place of the finer painted wares seems to be taken by monochrome pottery (usually gray, sometimes yellow, red, or black), which increases in frequency to a peak of about 50% of the whole by number of pieces. There are occasional noteworthy painted pieces using geometric motifs, generally in the black on red technique (where the red is a little brownish and the black has a purplish bloom). It is still unclear where the central inspiration for this style comes from, especially if one thinks that the color scheme is what makes it distinctive, since the syntax of the ornament is quite simple. If this is so—and the question is still open at present—we can perhaps see the potters at Sardis as mixing the native and Greek traditions in the Early Iron Age. Other pieces, less numerous and found in the upper part of this group of strata, are Greek imports whose precise place of manufacture has not yet been determined.

The three levels numbered 6, 7, and 8 in Table 2 were called by the excavator, G. F. Swift, "Lydian III, II, and I" respectively.[1] By virtue of correlation with historical sources they can be definitely considered to belong to the historical Lydians. This sequence provides invaluable clues to the development of the city in the time from the late eighth to the early to mid-sixth century B.C.

Counting from the top down, the excavator placed Lydian Level I above *99, II from *99 to *98.4, and III, *97.6 to *97.

Lydian Level III

At the lowest level of the three mentioned, structural remains are scanty and frequently interrupted. Enough remains, however, to see that the habitations were essentially the same in construction and layout as those that survive in better condition from later periods.

At about level *97–*97.6 there is a distinct stratum which can be made out all over the trench at slightly varying levels (Figs. 32, 33). This layer shows clear traces of burning, and there are suggestions of suddenness and of violence from the evidence of (1) a small girl ap-

parently smothered in her sleep (Fig. 34)[2] and (2) several disarticulated skeletons found in a rough-and-ready charnel house.[3] In addition, below the stone circle several crania but remarkably few associated long bones were found. This is all towards the northeast corner of the trench; there are no similar traces in other parts. This surface is the first Iron Age level in which there are considerable remains of structures from which we can reconstruct a dense living pattern. We cannot, however, be sure of the form of the dwellings themselves. The construction is the same as in succeeding levels and the pieces of wall that we have seem to be straight. Perhaps one might say, on the basis of these remains, that the houses were not so solid and smaller, but on the other hand perhaps they made use of lighter materials such as wattle and daub and reeds to a greater extent than their successors. Traces of light carbonized thatch were found beside the girl mentioned above and some impressions of reeds on baked clay, presumably from a roof, in the Lydian II level. Granted we have not found traces of a long series of holes to anchor the uprights for the wattle and daub, but the single lines of stones that keep turning up could be some sort of ad hoc draft excluder or attempt to anchor an otherwise rather frail wall.

The problem of the scanty wall remains has been greatly complicated by the very large number of bothroi (presumed to be storage pits but perhaps industrial installations, tanks, baths, vats; Figs. 32, 33) which have been dug into this level from above. It is clear that they were dug in from above, since in many cases they interrupt the lines of walls associated with the main floor. It is not clear, however, from which level they originate, since the only traces were found in the clayey floor layers and not in the gravel. Generally speaking the fill in these pits was not very rich or indicative, either of their origins or of the use to which they might have been put. One or two seem to have been lined with a clay plaster facing, but this is quite uncommon. One might mention that this use of holes in the ground is not common in Lydian I or in Lydian II. Is it possible that there is an intermediate phase IIa, where the use of bothroi was particularly advantageous? The idea of an accumulation of vats for a specialized purpose, not requiring any permanent structures, is intriguing.[4] We can infer that the buildings were oriented north-south from the presence of fragments of rectangular or straight-sided structures, but we cannot recreate them with any certainty.

The economic situation reflected in this level is markedly different from that of those directly below, even if it is a logical development from them. First, we come to a stage in the archaeological record where floors and portions of buildings are increasingly preserved. One might infer from this that the structures were themselves more substantial and represent a growing material prosperity and ability to put more effort into construction of dwellings rather than subsistence. Second, there is a much wider range of pottery shapes, fabric, and decoration. The change that occurs is away from the overwhelming use of pithos and coarse pottery towards a much greater reliance on thinner-walled, finer fabrics, with a growing preference for painted ware. At this point there also appears a much larger variety of imported pottery. Where Rhodian and Cycladic types had been preponderant, we now see a considerable upsurge in the frequency of Corinthian pottery to an extent that subsequent Lydian pottery shapes seem closely related to Corinthian models (whether at first or second hand is not clear). One might speculate that this growing preference for "table-wares" rather than storage vessels corresponds to a change in the economy—a development from each household's rough-and-ready self-sufficiency, as indicated by the artifacts, to a more developed urban style of life and economy, where larger-scale storage was practiced by specialized groups. This would correspond to the beginnings of two of the Lydians' traditional skills: those of being merchants and traders. Further investigation through pollen studies may suggest changes in agricultural patterns which would account for these differences. For the moment we might speculate that viticulture as well as the production of oil and cereals was increased, at the expense of pastoralism, as the urban center expanded.

This level of burning at *97–*97.6 has been associated with the attacks of the Kimmerians against Sardis in the middle of the seventh century. The question of which of two attacks (668 or 652) might have been responsible for the burning and carnage at HoB is not yet fully resolved. We must face the fact that the texts mention two successful attacks on the lower town[5] and that at HoB we have only one stratum of widespread burning with a suggestion of violence which is, in any case, beginning to look earlier than the time of Kimmerian attacks.

Whether we associate the burning directly with the Kimmerians or not, this horizon must represent the culmination of the Lydians' first move towards prosperity and domination of Western Anatolia and a purposeful looking westward in political and economic affairs.

Chronology

The dating of this level is extremely important in terms of both Lydian chronology and culture. It is interwoven with controversies of long standing over the dating of various styles of Greek pottery and their origins. The question of Greek pottery is important to us here because it offers the only way at present to suggest an actual chronological horizon for the different levels, since the Lydian pottery does not have an established chronology of its own and there are no historical materials which can be tied in without dispute.

In simplified fashion our task is to examine the levels and circumstances of the finds of imported pottery and to rely on these to give an approximate date to the main level known at present as Lydian III. This task is not yet completed, and our conclusions must remain tentative until the evidence of the different kinds of pottery has been analyzed and combined with that derived directly from the stratigraphy. A few imported sherds were found in the lower levels in the course of digging the test pits of 1960, 1962, and 1966, and a few more Lydian imitations or pieces done in a similar decorative style were found also.

The most distinctive of the painted sherds in Lydian III are decorated with geometric motifs. They are found in Lydian II also, but in company with more pieces of imported and orientalizing styles. They continue to be found sporadically in higher levels as a result of disturbances like pit or foundation digging. We can, however, distinguish two types of geometric decoration and organization in the Lydian pottery.

1. A close style of tightly arranged elements like cross-hatched triangles, hatched meanders, and butterfly patterns apparently related closely to "Rhodian" geometric (Fig. 36). The typical color scheme for this ware is black on red.

2. A much looser arrangement using a different vocabulary, where the individual patterns take up a much larger proportion of the overall design. The typical patterns here are concentric semicircles, parallel wavy lines, and concentric pendent hooks. This style is particularly common on fruit stands or dishes (Fig. 37) and on jars. The preferred color scheme is brown on buff. These elements, which have much more in common in terms of their arrangement and simplicity with Protogeometric pottery than with developed Geometric, are continued long after geometric designs, as the fundamental decorative element for pottery, had become outmoded among the Greeks except for quite "common ware."

As mentioned above, the two styles overlap, but the tight style seems to precede the looser and to die out before it. If this is so, it is very curious, since the loose style has much more in common with earlier decoration than with later. There may, however, be a continuing conservative strain in Lydian pot decoration which is missing in our sample from the ninth century or earlier, or there may be a recombination of older elements to produce these antique-looking forms. What is really at issue is how and when the East Greek Geometric style developed and how long it lasted.

This material is not well known or widely published, and much of the Greek series at present depends on stylistic analysis from grave groups rather than on stratigraphic comparisons relying on occupational contexts. With the material from three deep soundings in HoB we shall soon try to arrive at some useful associations.

There is nothing that could be termed "orientalizing" in unmixed contexts below the *97 floor, and A. Ramage thinks nothing on it later than Corinthian Late Geometric (sometimes called Protocorinthian Geometric) or Early Protocorinthian. A trefoil oinochoe (P 65.224; Fig. 38) is considered by J. Schaeffer to be late M.G. II (around 750 B.C.),[6] which suggests a date in the late eighth century for the stratum, if the pot were imported and broken fairly soon after manufacture. It seems likely that it was imported soon after its making, but there is no way of telling how long it survived. Whatever specific date we put on this piece, we must bear in mind that there is a similar piece from the same level and the same general area and other material which

is to be dated in the late eighth century. A. Ramage sees no way to avoid redating the main Lydian levels more or less in accordance with Schaeffer's tentative suggestions in her 1975 unpublished field report on Corinthian pottery.[7] Thus Lydian III falls into the late eighth century B.C.; Lydian II into the early and mid-seventh century; and Lydian I into the early to mid-sixth century (547) B.C.

Schaeffer's dating of the levels is arrived at by the grouping of datable pieces of Corinthian pottery by findspot and levels, while A. Ramage's comes from considering the prevalence of East Greek geometric pottery and its imitations. Furthermore, this solution gives a more even balance to the assignment of levels: we are not forced into unlikely compression or expansion of the stratigraphy. Neither solution would be impossible, but since the location is the same and the habits of life very conservative, the unrevised dating would be strange.

Lydian Level II

It looks as if the Kimmerian attack and the effect of the destruction represented only a temporary setback in the commercial or domestic life of the area, for we have found part of what seems to be an ambitious complex of buildings dating to the middle of the seventh century (Figs. 35, 39). There is also a rapid increase in the number and variety of Greek pots and more imitation of their style.

The better preserved Lydian buildings of the historical era in HoB are listed alphabetically; this order corresponds roughly to the order in which they were discovered. Many of them have been removed in order to reach the earlier levels, and checking dimensions and descriptions in the field is no longer possible. The stratigraphy and dating are difficult, since many of the buildings and their associated floors are islands in a sea of gravel. Several buildings, however, can be connected, either by architectural association, as here, or by the similarity of the pottery and small finds within them.

The buildings designated by letters fall into two main groups (Fig. 39). Buildings A (upper), B, D, E, F, M, and N belong to Lydian I, and Buildings G, H, J, K, and L belong to Lydian II, as do early phases of A and F. Building C (Fig. 41) is considered separately, since it seems to belong to the Hellenistic period, although there is much disturbed debris from earlier levels within its walls. Also considered separately are the buildings and fragmentary walls found below or just to the west of the actual House of Bronzes. These are known as the "Lydian Shop"[8] and the "Lydian Room" (and are so designated in Fig. 186).[9] In this area, too, three main strata were distinguished, but at lower levels than for corresponding buildings to the southwest. These levels and approximate chronological horizons are as follows: *98.6 (ca. 550 B.C.); *96.7 (ca. 625–600 B.C.); and *96 down (seventh to eighth century B.C.).

Only one secure corner of the Lydian Shop is preserved, but with its associated remains and isolated wall fragments we can reconstruct the main period of use of the shop, which seems to have been at the very end of the seventh century on the basis of the pottery found on the *96.5–*96.7 floor.[10] Substantial signs of earlier occupation were found below it in the form of gray monochrome pottery and other early Lydian sherds. Subsequent excavations slightly further to the west brought to light the "Lydian Room" (3.7 × 4.0 m.)[11] and confirmed the pattern established in 1958.

These were the first signs to the excavators of the Lydian occupation in an area which has since been enormously extended both to the south and west. The ambitious building complex mentioned above is unified by a mixture of associations already alluded to: physical connection, or close agreement in orientation of the buildings themselves, and similarities among the finds.

A strong line is established at ca. W35 where three single-roomed structures (G, H, K) are joined by a curtain wall running north-south, which itself forms one wall of the buildings, for a distance of ca. 30 m. (Figs. 35, 39, 40). There are no openings in this run of the wall, and the effect is one of enclosure. If our views about the commercial and industrial nature of the area as a whole are correct, this arrangement could represent an early version of the bazaar form; within these confines the Lydian merchants mentioned by Herodotus[12] might have conducted their business or acquired their stock. There is nothing in the finds from any of this group of buildings that indicates specialized activities inside or next door, although there is an unusual and recurrent presence of sizeable iron objects

that are not standard domestic equipment like knives. In fact the interior fittings of G, H, and K are remarkably similar (especially G and H; Figs. 40, 135), and these similarities appear to be more domestic than industrial. Three other buildings complete this group: L, O, and J. L is exactly aligned with K, and the space between them seems to form a narrow street running northeast-southwest and giving access to the quarter from outside (Fig. 39). The west wall of O is set parallel to the east wall of K, forming an even narrower alley at right angles to the street. J is nearer the center of the supposed enclosure, but if we restore O as a proper building or living space, it does not seem so isolated and its alignment could be fitted in to the rather loose pattern that is emerging.

The floors in these buildings are not all at the same level but are progressively lower from southwest to northeast. The uniformity of the finds, however, enables the units to be linked together and the main period of occupation placed a little before the middle of the seventh century. This is indicated by a trend away from gray monochrome pottery and painted pieces with strict geometric decoration towards a richer and more flamboyant decoration in patterned bichrome technique. The presence of some imported Greek wares with both patterned and figural decoration should be noted.

The construction of all these buildings is the same (Figs. 35, 39, 40), and the general description covers all Lydian structures excavated, except for tombs and other specialized categories (altars, city or palace walls). They consist of walls of fieldstone set in mud, about 0.45 m. thick (except for the enclosure portion, 0.70 m.), which were intended to support a superstructure of mudbrick. The preserved height of this socle varies from a maximum of ca. 2.0 m. to 0.30 m., but it is clear that uniformity was not required since mudbrick is preserved *in situ* on the south and east walls of K, which have only about two courses of stone to form the socle.

All the fully excavated and well-preserved structures associated with the complex share certain internal living arrangements or have comparable subsidiary structures within them. They are best preserved in G and H (Figs. 35, 40, 135), but details can sometimes be added from the other buildings.[13] In both G and H near a corner (southwest and northwest, respectively) there is a small boxlike form made of stone and divided into two roughly equal compartments (D. 0.75 m.; L. 1.0; H. 0.30; approximate). It has been suggested that they are supports for a wooden cupboard or chest. They could, however, be storage containers in themselves, either for loose material or for smaller containers such as jars or boxes; it is unlikely that they were hearths or ovens, since no ash or charcoal was observed and the mud mortar showed no signs of reddening by fire. Indeed in H there was a "hearth or small furnace" in two compartments made of clay and burnt red and hard, just beside this structure, on the south. At the south end of H, in its north-south walls, are two matching vertical grooves about 1½ m. from the south wall. The resulting line between them is more or less parallel with the south wall, which has a gentle bulge outwards. These grooves are probably provision for some kind of wooden fittings and can be matched in several other buildings. Another internal feature which is common at HoB is a clay and stone bench or platform along a wall, raised about 0.30 m. from the floor. This seems to have been used as a working and storage surface, much as a table-high counter is used in modern houses.

In Lydian II building, therefore, we see considerable uniformity both of planning and of interior arrangements. Furthermore, careful analysis of the finds within the houses and by the entrances to them is beginning to show that they belong together quite closely in time, in spite of the various levels of the floors mentioned above. What caused the demise of the Lydian II group is not clear, but a major flood seems a likely explanation if we take into account the large quantity of sand and gravel to the west of the boundary wall and the fact that it was perhaps repaired in some places and clearly broken in others.

Lydian Level I

The group of buildings assigned to Lydian Level I (Fig. 39) consists of seven freestanding structures or substantial remains (A, B, D, E, F, M, and N), either situated at more or less equivalent levels or having generally similar assemblages of pottery and small finds on or near the floor. Most of them are in the eastern part of the trench (E15–W20), although M and N (only partially exposed) seem to leapfrog the earlier

complex of buildings (G–L, W30–40) almost as if some of them had been still in existence during the later period.

Building A is situated at ca. E0–4/S100.5–104 and measures ca. 3.5 × 3.0 m., with poorly built walls about 0.40 m. thick, preserved to a height of 0.20 m. Floors were found at *99.45 and *98.90, and many pieces of terracotta rooftile were found within the building. That the final phase of the structure dates to the late sixth century is indicated by the finding of a late Attic black-figure sherd at the upper level (if it really belongs), but its original occupation should be placed considerably earlier. The basis for this is the Lydian pottery found on the lower floor. Thus the structure should be included in Lydian II also, in its original form.

Building B (W2.5–6.0/S97–100) is a similar structure measuring about 4.75 m. × 4.0 m. Its east wall was partially disrupted by a stone deposit. Its shape and dimensions correspond closely to those of the Lydian Room (Fig. 186:24) and Building A in that both seem to have had door openings at one of the corners. Building A is not shown with a doorway in the plans, but the excavator suggested one in the north side in the fieldbook. The walls of the Lydian Room are broken away, but since there is intentional thickening of the north end of the west wall of B, one might be justified in restoring an opening here even if not a door proper. The floor of B is at *99.2, which is comparable to the upper floor in A, 3 m. away to the southwest. There is a considerable amount of domestic pottery compatible with an early to middle sixth century date.

Between ca. W10–20/S97–107, and running obliquely to the lines of our grid, are the remains of a rectangular building dating to the early sixth century on the basis of finds from a floor at *99.4. Building D was at least 10 × 4 m. and had remains of built-in internal features, including two hearths, whose layout suggests that the building was at one stage divided into two rooms, since the small three-sided rectangles found elsewhere back onto a wall. "The west wall of D disappears at the north under a much heavier wall of a structure excavated in 1961,"[14] which was itself under—or among—the foundations of Building C. Although the overall features of this earlier building to the north of D are vague, it is unusual because of its probable

L-shape, which is in contrast to the pattern of simple structures so far observed. All these buildings seem to focus on the remains of industrial activity, which was particularly marked in the areas W15–30/S90–110 between *99.3 and *99.0. This would be an earlier industrial center, which finds a later counterpart in the stone circle of the Hellenistic period mentioned below (at E0–10/S85–97, *99.5 approximate; Fig. 41).

Building E is a round structure, with external diameter ca. 2.25 m. at W20–24/S110–113. Its floor was at *99.38, but no satisfactory conclusion as to its purpose was reached; a furnace or kiln was suggested but it did not seem sufficiently burnt, although considerable remains of charcoal were noted. Several used lamps were found within it (L 63.60:5849) complete and a few pieces of imported pottery, probably from the early sixth century.

Further to the south at W7–13/S109–117 is Building F, a simple rectangular structure about 6.5 × 5.0 m.[15] A substantial part of the northwest corner was missing. The floor sloped down from *99.49 at the southeast corner to *99.1 at the northwest corner. (It is very unusual to find so great a gradient within such a small building; we suspect that in places the top surface of fallen mudbrick may have been mistaken for floor.) Within the room were some stones indicating foundations for built-in clay furnishings and another three-sided configuration of small stones. This room is dated early in the sixth (late seventh?) century by finds from the floor (especially P 63.642 "Ephesian" plate; P 63.641 Rhodian type rosette bowl; P 63.646 Lydian bichrome krater). Attached to it by a substantial but low wall is a well which seemed to have been filled in during the fourth century but had not been cleaned out at 18 m. depth when work stopped. Aligned with F, just to the south, are some fragmentary walls of the same scale and at about the same level which were previously considered part of a Hellenistic destruction by the excavator but are now considered to be much earlier. Substantial quantities of late seventh century pottery with a high proportion of Greek imports were found in this area. The uniform space between the south wall of F and these walls suggests a narrow street or passage.

The buildings of Lydian I seem to continue the tradition of what was started in Lydian II, but they do not show the same clear spatial organiza-

tion and several of them are distinctly smaller. There is, nevertheless, a great deal of occupational debris along with Lydian and imported pottery from the early sixth century in the area, and we could posit some more elaborate Lydian structures somewhere in the vicinity. Indeed, excavations undertaken since 1976 at the sector MMS(N), some 50 m. northeast of the Lydian Trench, have begun to produce evidence for the existence of such structures (Figs. 132, 133).

Persian and Hellenistic Periods

Neither the Persian nor the Hellenistic period is well represented in the architectural record at HoB except for Building C, a large, rectangular (at least 20 × 8 m.), but poorly constructed building at ca. W6–30/S82–95 (Fig. 41). It lies over part of D and J, and its construction and use may have been responsible for the disturbance in that area. Its function is not known; no preserved floor was found, although some indication of the floor level is given by three interior supports surmounted by marble blocks placed axial in accurate alignment. Associated with it, to the east, is a roughly circular cobbled area about 10 m. in diameter which seems to have been associated with industrial activities involving fire and metalwork. This continues in a more obvious way the tradition set in the seventh century for the use of the area for pyrotechnic industry. The finds are still under investigation, but there is strong evidence for bronzeworking from different kinds of craftsmens' debris.

The main area of the Lydian Trench to the south must have lain open in Persian and Hellenistic times, as it did during most of the early Roman period. Some use was made of the northern area beside the House of Bronzes itself for tombs in Hellenistic and Imperial times: they lie alongside the modern highway[16] which is more or less parallel to the ancient Roman road at this point, but the whereabouts of an earlier road are not yet determined.

Conclusion

The results of excavations in the House of Bronzes area, summarized above, have shown a long tradition of occupation at the site and great continuity in the manner of life and use of materials. This could be said of many cultures in a similar stage of material development, but it is remarkable that the Lydians remained so conservative in their building practices and in their pottery decoration in spite of powerful and at least partly effective cultural pressure from outside. This can be seen in the very close association of Lydian and Greek sculpture,[17] which might be contrasted with the tenacious continuation of native Geometric pottery alongside popular Greek styles and their imitations.

The most important aspect of the Bronze Age finds is the fact that the pithos burial and hut (Figs. 24, 25) are within what was later the city area. We cannot tell yet, but suspect, that groups of Lydians moved from the shores of the Gygean Lake, where Early Bronze Age communities are attested (Figs. 11, 12)[18] to form the nucleus of the village later to become the city of Sardis. When this took place exactly is still a mystery, but we can be sure that there was a substantial settlement by the end of the Bronze Age because of the relatively high concentration of fine pottery found in the deep pits (Figs. 26, 28). For this purpose it matters little whether the pottery was produced locally or abroad. If it was made at Sardis then we must postulate much greater centralization than our meager exposure shows; if it came from abroad then we must postulate some mechanism for gathering local products and exchanging them for imports. Either of these situations allows us to reconstruct the necessary conditions for an ancestor to the city of Sardis. Tradition, too, has it that the city was founded at this time,[19] and perhaps the confusion with the Maeonians indicates something of the process. The recurring names of prominent Lydians[20] not only suggest baronial squabbles over acreage, but some central focus (king and city) where influence was important and apparently pursued with some vigor.

For the "Dark Ages" we can see a much lessened contact between the mass of Asia Minor and the Aegean area, but slender indications persist in the form of painted pottery that was probably imported from Greece, usually Rhodes or the Cyclades but conceivably from the mainland too. For the time being there is no profit in speculating on the reasons for the breakdown of the Bronze Age civilizations in the Eastern Mediterranean, and it is not clear whether Sardis was a grand center in that period or not, although further work near HoB may throw light on the subject. What we can say is that occupation in the area went on largely without interruption, and perhaps the people looked inland more than previously for imports or inspiration. An example of this is to be found in the frequent finding of black-polished ware which is very common at Gordion and has some claim to be regarded as Phrygian, and the attachment of the Lydians to black-on-red decoration on their pots. It is possible that the Lydians as a whole were subordinate to the Phyrgians at this time, but if so, this does not show up in the archaeological record so far exposed.

What caused the remarkable upsurge in Lydian power and their abrupt turn towards the Aegean coast for artistic inspiration is not known. In many ways there is a more natural affinity between the Hermus valley and the Aegean littoral than between the Hermus valley and the western edge of the Anatolian plateau (Figs. 1, 10), even though the traditional Lydian heartland includes a considerable area of mountainous terrain. On the other hand, the Mermnad dynasty, once established, did not hesitate to expand eastward onto the plateau, eventually as far as the river Halys. Motives or explanations do not show up among the material remains, but it is clear from both the surviving artifacts and the texts that the Lydians' commercial contacts were overwhelmingly with the Greeks during the period covered by the finds at HoB after the eighth century. The only obviously "oriental" objects are a few glass beads of Phoenician type and a piece of glazed pottery of Assyrian type. Otherwise they are self-sufficient or look to the west for decorative and useful *objets de luxe*.

While building traditions continued, the planning and growth of the Lydian Market area seem quite unusual and support the general idea of the Lydians as leaders in the development of commercial activities in the Aegean world at this time, a position frequently exemplified by their introduction or dissemination of the idea of coinage for the simplified conduct of exchange. The finds at HoB show the Lydians in their domestic and commercial activities over more than five momentous centuries.

AR

Pactolus North

Lydian Levels

The excavations on the east bank of the Pactolus (Figs. 42, 54), a sector called Pactolus North (PN; Fig. 8:10) to distinguish it from a sector a few hundred meters upstream called Pactolus Cliff (PC; Fig. 8:13), were begun in 1960. Part of an archaic kore statue was found there in 1954,[1] and there were many stubs of Roman wall visible in the scarp left by the Pactolus. In addition, many large brick and mortar fragments of a Byzantine church were visible half buried in the surface nearby.[2]

Since that time much has been uncovered and a great variety of things has been found. The range is enormous (Fig. 43), and the importance of the findings for the history of Sardis as a great center must be emphasized. For Lydian Sardis we not only have a number of houses and a semi-public complex of the sixth century B.C. (Fig. 33), but we have a gold refinery with reconstructible evidence of most of its furnishings and a sacred complex dominated by an altar to the goddess Cybele, which was probably intimately connected with the working of the refinery (Figs. 45–49, 139). For the Hellenistic and early Roman eras we do not have impressive remains, and occupation was sparse; in fact the area may have been more or less abandoned in the early Roman era. The late Roman period (Figs. 43, 288, 289) saw a resumption of activity in the area, although the density of "occupation" was by no means so great as during the Lydian period. The last occupation before the area of PN became a Common for public grazing and threshing was in the Osmanli and early Ottoman periods, when there were two distinct villages (one over the other), set directly above the Roman remains and perhaps incorporating some of them.

In the course of his description of the burning of the lower town of Sardis, Herodotus[3] mentions that the river flows through the agora. In the vicinity of PC (Fig. 63, W225–250/S600–625) the area in the valley seemed rather restricted, although Lydian remains were found, but at PN where the landscape was more open (Fig. 54), the prospect of finding the Lydian agora seemed more promising. While no impos-

ing public buildings of ashlar masonry turned up, several well-built socles for mudbrick walls were exposed, and a complex of matched apsidal buildings with a narrow pathway between them was discovered (Fig. 53; plan Fig. 44).[4] At the head of the southern apse was a well, and indeed there was another earlier well just beside it, a fact which suggested that the complex owed its existence to the need to provide water. These buildings seem to belong to the middle of the sixth century and are at present considered to date from just after the Persian sack.[5] Their use certainly continued into the Persian period, but the original design and construction may belong to the period of the Lydian empire.

In contrast to the HoB Lydian Trench sector, the Lydian remains at Pactolus North are generally of the sixth century or later. They do not give the impression of shops but rather of dwelling units, often in quite close juxtaposition and sometimes holding walls in common. There are persistent finds of chips of rock crystal (sometimes worked) in the excavation and a chance find of a goldsmith's mold as well as a few actual pieces of Lydian jewelry that suggest the possibility of a craftsman's quarter. This would be very suitable in view of the proximity of the gold refinery. There are two obvious exceptions to this: the gold refinery complex with the altar, and the community well mentioned above.

The gold refinery, described further in the next section, is included within the coordinates W260–285/S325–350, ca *86.2–*85.4, which also includes the altar and part of the supposed House of the Priest (Figs. 42, 45:XXVIII, 58).

There seem to have been two main functions for the refinery: (1) the production of a precious metal (electrum) by the vigorous heating of dust recovered from the Pactolus and other local streams; and (2) the separation of the two major components of this metal, gold and silver, so that they were available for distinct uses such as the production of a bimetallic (gold and silver) coinage, where a dependable purity was important for commercial transactions.[6]

Within the area W260–277/S340–347 there were two places which had large concentrations of small rings in the ground (Figs. 46, 55–58). On the surface immediately visible one could estimate that there were over a hundred, and it turned out that there were many more below the surface and intersecting one another. The diameter of these rings varied from ca. 0.15–0.30 m.; the average was about 0.20 m. They showed signs of intense heat in the form of dribbles of glassy slag and reddened clay. Also present was a considerable amount of ash, used as lining for the rings, and several pieces of oxidized lead which had a substantial metal content remaining. The rings themselves were the indication, on the surface, of what had been little hollows scooped in the earth and filled with bone-ash (Figs. 46, 56). These basin-like forms (called "cupels" or little cups by medieval metallurgists, who actually used separate crucibles) served them both as hearths and as collecting vessels. One should imagine at first a mixture of charcoal, gold dust, and lead being fired up in the basin and a draft created with bellows. Later, more charcoal might be heaped up and pieces of old pottery used to keep it together and increase the draft and temperature. The lead would melt first, combine with impurities, and be burnt off or removed as slaggy scum. Ultimately, after the high temperature necessary to melt gold was reached, a lens-shaped lump of precious metal would be left at the bottom. This could be used "as is" or it could be processed further, because the product of melting the gold from the Pactolus and nearby rivers is in fact a mixture of gold and silver known to the ancients as "electrum." This term is used by archaeologists to denote a mixture of between 50% and 75% gold, which was the usual form of most gold bullion and jewelry in the Aegean region until the sixth century B.C. We reconstruct the process described above both by analogy, using later accounts, and from the actual remains (Figs. 46, 56) of lead, ash, and slag as well as fragments of tuyeres (bellows nozzles), which must have been used with substantial bellows (0.03 m. airhole diameter; Fig. 57), and great quantities of large amphora and hydria sherds, many of which had been overheated to the point of surface scoriation and deformation. In addition, many sherds were found with a covering of glassy slag in which were embedded large numbers of minute globules of gold, most smaller than a pinhead and many just specks.

The second process mentioned above, that of separating the gold from the silver (known as "cementation" in later texts), took place in several sets of furnaces (Figs. 45, 47), two of which have been recovered while a third can be postulated but not proved.

To separate the two metals the Lydians seem to have taken advantage of the fact that silver is attacked by acidic substances available in the ancient world, whereas gold is not. First the metal was hammered into thin sheets to increase the surface area, then the pieces were placed in pottery vessels with a mixture of crushed brick and salt between each layer (Fig. 48). The vessels were then sealed up and heated for several days at red heat. At the end of this period the silver would have combined with the salt and the gold would be left pure if a little spongier in texture, depending on the original proportion of silver to gold. Hammering (Fig. 139) or remelting (Fig. 55) would restore the texture of the (now pure) gold.[7]

One set of furnaces ("A," W280–283/S342–346) consists of six squarish enclosures of coarse mudbrick, about 0.60 m. W. × 0.75 m. D., set side by side against a wall (Figs. 47, 55). In the center of some there was a tile or purified baked brick, presumably to act as a support. The whole ensemble was colored a dull red, indicating considerable exposure to high heat in an oxidizing atmosphere. The temperature reached in the furnaces was not so high as that in the cupels, for no sign of vitrification was found although one or two furnaces had a distinctly yellowish crust in the firing chamber. The furnaces in the second set ("B," W273–276/S325–328) were arranged differently, facing inwards around three sides of a hollow square surrounded by a low wall (Fig. 139, in the back). There were three left in all, one of which was much better preserved (B1 in Fig. 45) than any in group A (0.50 m. W. × 0.35 m. D. × 0.60 m. H.; Fig. 47). This gives more indication of the original height and the provisions for draft and stoking, since it is so well preserved and there was a small square opening (ca. 0.10 × 0.12 m.) in the bottom of the center front. There is enough room in each to take one hydria (Fig. 48) or similar wide-necked vessel (which is, incidentally, the most commonly found shape among the pottery finds) and a quantity of charcoal. It is hard to tell whether this much fuel would be enough for the whole period indicated as optimum, but since stoking from above might not be very practical, perhaps the process of cementation was carried out in several heatings.

This discovery is so far unique in the classical world; similar installations for treating silver have been discovered in Greece (Thorikos near Laurion) and in Roman Britain at Silchester, Wroxeter, and Hengistbury Head;[8] but nowhere has there been such direct evidence for retrieving gold in what could qualify as a documented historical situation. For explanation we should turn to Herodotus, an important though frequently maligned source of historic and ethnographic information. He credits the Lydians[9] with the introduction of coinage in two metals (gold and silver) in place of a previous use of electrum and makes a similar point again when he lists Croesus' donations to Apollo at Delphi, by mentioning that some of his gold bricks, which supported a statue of a lion, were of purified gold and some of electrum.[10] Pottery finds from the gold refinery, as well as sculpture from the precinct of Cybele described below, indicate that the installation was working during the time of Croesus (Fig. 139), and so we have been able to share in the excitement of the age through our finding what must have been a major scientific and economic discovery at the time.

Altar and Precinct of Cybele

The altar is the focal point of an open area W260–271/S331–341 (Figs. 42, 43, 45, 49, 54, 58); this makes a rough square (slightly oblique to our grid), bounded on the east and west by large rectangular buildings (ca. 13 × 5 and 9 × 5 m.) and on the north and south by the wall of a house and cobbled yard and a lesser wall (Fig. 58, "cobbled floor"). The boundary walls allow for an open space to the east and a bit to the north but hardly any to the south and the west, except for the priests.

The house just mentioned is interesting for itself, too; it lies just beyond the north wall of the altar precinct.[11] This is Unit XXIX on the plan (Fig. 44, ca. W258–268/S329–332), and it consists of just the southeast corner of a carefully built structure with 5 m. of a cobbled yard to the west of it and a little paving to the south. The importance of this building lies in the clear domestic indications in the yard, animal bones and pottery with dark charcoaly earth, and the fact that a more or less complete architectural terracotta was found right beside the corner of the building just above the cobbles. It is a sima of the "star and scroll" variety[12] (T 67.12:7440; cf. Fig. 66); it was found in a context with a number

of datable Greek potsherds, which will require that the dating of this kind of terracotta pattern be made one or two decades earlier than is usual at present, i.e., before 550 B.C. (perhaps ca. 575) rather than after it. It is unfortunate that so much of this house and its yard was washed away and replaced by gravel, since the disturbed fill within and around the late Roman mausoleum produced several fine pieces of archaic pottery, both Lydian and Greek.

The large building on the east side (Figs. 42, 45:XXVIII, 58); has been interpreted as (possibly but not certainly) a priests' house, on the basis of its size and regularity.[13] The finding of a small bronze hawk's head filled with lead (Fig. 51) adds some weight to this suggestion, if we remember the connection between *Kubaba* (*Kuvava*) and the hawk.[14] The house originally had three rooms in the early sixth century (N-S, 3.4 × 4 m.; 3.3 × 4 m.; 5.4 × 4 m.). Only the south crosswall remained, but a robber trench showed the position of the one to the north. Later the south room and middle room were combined to make one large unit (9.2 × 4 m.) at a higher level, and the whole structure was eventually engulfed by a layer of gravel about 1 m. thick which must have covered the whole area some time in the fifth century B.C. The other large building (Unit XXX), that to the west of the altar (Figs. 42–45), is even more enigmatic. It is hardly more than a trace, since most of the stones from the socle have been removed. Sufficient evidence remains, however, for us to be confident of the dimensions of the building, since there was a buildup of disintegrated mudbrick on all sides but particularly on the east and south, so that the building as excavated looked like a large pool with a step around the sides. The whole thing was full of barren gravel, and there was no occupational debris on the floor. We therefore have no idea of the precise function of the building and associate it with the altar precinct on architectural grounds alone. A narrow trench was cut in the floor, but nothing was found except bands of gravel and silt with occasional waterworn sherds.

The altar itself (Figs. 42–45, 49, 54, 58, 139) is ca. 3 × 2 × 1.75 m. and is built of roughly dressed gneiss put together with mud mortar. We can be sure that it is an altar both from the form and the alternating layers of ash and earth found on it as well as charred bone and horn at the very bottom. We can attribute it to Cybele (*Kubaba, Kuvava*) both because of the sculpted lions (her beast) and because of a sherd with a graffito reading *Kuvava* (Fig. 50), which is the Lydian way of writing the name.[15] A boxlike structure was built and filled with material that looks like debris from the gold refinery in the form of disintegrated burned mudbrick. There is a step on the west side, and there was a low coping surrounding a cobbled floor on which was the sacrificial fire. At each corner, there was a stone lion *couchant* probably facing east. We have confidence in this reconstruction because we found two and a half lions (Figs. 49, 52) not precisely *in situ* but carefully placed within the structure during a later rebuilding.

Stylistic considerations indicate that the lions are likely to have been made before 550 B.C., and historical circumstances may have required that the altar carry no sculptural ornament during the Persian domination of Lydia. From the evidence of both the filling of the altar and the fact that it lies over a layer containing remains of the gold refinery, we can tell that the gold refinery antedates the altar, although it is possible that the refinery continued in operation in a more restricted area after the building of the altar.

What we cannot gauge very accurately at present is just when the refinery began operations and whether both parts of the process were carried on from the very beginning. We have found one or two imported potsherds (scraps of black glazed Ionian bowls) which might go back to ca. 600 B.C., but we cannot be very precise. It is our feeling that the altar is not there by chance, that it has an intimate relationship to the refinery and may well commemorate and give thanks for a technological breakthrough in refinery technique. This would be the second part of the purifying process and would be the aspect which made Croesus' bimetallic coinage and his bricks of pure gold so noteworthy. At present we cannot tell whether the refinery went out of use at the time of the Persian conquest, but there seems to be a consensus among numismatists and historians that the Persians minted coins at Sardis and remitted gold bullion to Susa. When the refinery did finally close, some of the facilities were converted to domestic use (Units I and II, Figs. 136 and 137, and later plans) and there seems to have been a group of houses around a

well at ca. W275–300/S320–347 (Figs. 43, 44).

The pattern continues on from the area further south where several houses were found, dating from the early sixth century on (Fig. 44).[16] We cannot isolate a complete house because the remains are in a deep trough between the Roman house with the mosaic suite on the north and the subsidiary buildings of the Early Christian Church EA on the south (Fig. 43:8–11). The only explanation for the exposure of this area is that it lies below the Roman street (called by us the Street of the Pipes). We have found, however, that the quarter centers on the water supply to the extent that there is a pair of apsidal buildings, separated by a narrow alley (ca. 1.30 m. west; Figs. 43:10–11; 53), of which the southernmost has a well at its apex. Indeed the predecessor of this building also had a well just beside the later one, which is partly what leads us to think that water with all its connotations of necessity and neighborliness is the focus of this complex.

The construction of the apses is much like that of the altar, and the southern wall and north-south crosswall are preserved to a considerable height (ca. 2 m. maximum). The apses seem to be part of a major remodeling of the area around the earlier well (W255/S382) which included the provision of a new well. It is unfortunate that just at the points of the apses the remains have been carried away by the bend of the Pactolus mentioned above; otherwise we would be better able to judge how this building fitted in with its surroundings. It remains enigmatic, however, built in the same general style as its neighbors yet much more substantial and giving suggestions of organization and planning beyond what most of the evidence found up to now would justify.

AR

Goldworking Installations and Techniques: Lydian Gold Industry at Sardis[1]

The Sardis valley area possesses fertile land and ample forests, and it is in this valley through ancient Sardis that the Pactolus river makes its way (Figs. 7–9) down Mt. Tmolus to join the Hermus. It is this river, the "Golden Pactolus," that provided one of the natural bounties for the Lydians of the seventh and sixth centuries B.C. in the form of electrum, collected and mined from the bed and banks of the river. Herodotus relates an Ionian account which expresses the position succinctly: "Lydia is a fertile country, rich in gold."[2]

The agricultural wealth and unique topographical position combined to favor the early center of trade established by the citizens of Sardis. Herodutus takes us a step beyond and not only credits the Lydians with issuing coinage and later using both gold and silver currencies, but he also relates that they were the first *kapeloi*, merchants or traders.[3] Roebuck prefers to combine loosely the first two inventions of the Lydians.[4] He has suggested that the statement made by Herodotus is better interpreted as attributing the actual invention of coinage to the Lydians and not to the bimetallic coinage of Croesus to facilitate the exchange of gold and silver on a fixed ratio. It is just such a preference which should be rethought in light of the recent discoveries of the goldworking industry located at PN. Certainly, the strong doubt expressed by some scholars with regard to the importance of the Pactolus gold within the collective Mermnad wealth must be reappraised. Perrot and Chipiez in their extensive and popular history of ancient art felt the reputation of the Pactolus was inflated and that the river supplied "but a small fraction, perhaps a very small fraction indeed."[5] With more careful statements, but with some caution, current authors are still hesitant to accept the accolades of poets and historians regarding the wealth of the Pactolus.[6] Again, our evidence of at least two if not three or more industrial refining areas for gold and silver makes the prospect of a substantial gold-bearing alluvial deposit more likely. More often than not, archaeological exploration substantiates the history and mythology of antiquity. Obviously, the empire built by the Mermnad dynasty profited immensely from expansion, subsequent tribute, and regenerating state monopolies, all of which helped to fill the royal treasuries. The Greeks Archilochus, Herodotus, Xenophon, Diodorus Siculus, Dio Chrysostom, Pausanias, Lucian, Diogenes Laertius, and many others, along with the Latin writers Catullus, Propertius, Seneca, Aelian, and Lactantius, offer testimony to "Golden Sardis"[7] and continue to build the mythical and proverbial synonym for riches. We

are no closer to establishing the percentage of gold added to the Lydian fortune by the Pactolus, and we shall probably never know it. What we have learned is that the Lydians in the time of Croesus were making gold and silver in extensive industrial complexes, and their location beside the Pactolus river and in conjunction with a sacred precinct cannot have been fortuitous.[8]

A view to the northwest over the village roofs of Sart Mustafa in the foreground gives a general feeling of the location of the Pactolus North area and its setting (Fig. 54). The excavation runs along the Pactolus river, defined by the line of trees along one side with the village of Ahmetli in the distance and the vast plain beyond. A limited view gives a more intelligible picture of the industrial area and adjacent structures (Fig. 42). The major reference point, the rectangular Lydian altar of Cybele in the gold refining area, is easily recognized in this view and on the plan in grid square W265–270/S335–340 (Fig. 45).

In the preceding section, "Pactolus North," Ramage has described the installations excavated and has outlined the two major processes assumed to have been practised in the refinery. The following section will present the most important items of evidence on which the theories about the use of cupellation and cementation are based, as well as illustrations in tentative reconstructive drawings (Figs. 55, 139). After a brief review of the analytical and metallurgical investigations so far, the technological and economic problems raised by our discoveries will be briefly discussed.

Cupellation Area

Over sixty cupels (Figs. 45, 46, 58) were selected and described during excavations and research. Drawings of several representative cupels were made. Some mention should be made of the attempt to preserve the area by refilling the excavations and covering the cupellation floors in order to forestall damage by destructive winter weather and possible excavation or misuse of the area during the absence of the expedition.[9] Several cupels were selected, mounted in plaster, and removed from the floor before the area was filled in. These specimens await examination by colleagues in the field laboratory.

Two banks of small furnaces (Figs. 45, 47)

were discovered during the 1968 season which seemed to relate to the refining area (Figs. 45, 58).[10] These installations were not intensely fired, and it was suggested that gold foil was purified by the cementation process in these units.[11] Fig. 55 shows a reconstruction drawing of what the cementation installations may have looked like in operation.

A considerable amount of material related to the cupellation and cementation of gold was unearthed around, on, and beneath the cupellation floors and in the areas immediately before the furnaces in Unit II. The map indicating findspots and concentrations of gold material (Fig. 58) will be considered here.

Catalogue of Selected Finds

1   (Sample 1; also A)
    Description: Deep gold foil, triangular shape, extremely granular surface, no indication of dendritic structure. Several tears in sheet, long edges may have been cut, others are jagged and thin, three small burrs on edge.
    Dimension: L.: 6.5 mm. (tip folded under)
                 H.: 2.5 m.
    t. 10 mg.
    Findspot: W265.4/S344 *86.15
    FB1968, *PNI*, 123 (unpublished)

2   (Sample 2; also B)
    Description: Three pieces, dark gold foil, extremely granular surface, pitted, no cut edges, several cracks in surface, edges folded.
    Dimensions: A. 4.5 mm. × 3.5 mm.
                 B. 5 mm. × 3 mm.
    t. 10 mg.
    Findspot: W265.4/S344 *86.15
    FB1967, *PNI*, 123 (unpublished)
    Spectrographic analysis

3   (Sample 3)
    Description: Spherical bead, dark gold, porous surface with pink cast, probably indicating copper impurity.
    Dimension: Diam.: ca. 1 mm.
    t. 7 mg.
    Findspot: W265/S344 sifting at *86.00
                 Cupellation floor
    FB1968, *PNI*, 123 (unpublished)
    Spectrographic analysis. MTA

4   (Sample 4; also C)
    Description: Two pieces of foil, A. dark gold, somewhat lighter than no. 1, more compact

surface yet granular, thicker cross section, foil is curved and bent with thickened ridge along one side, thickness visible in profile, one edge has been cut, subsequently flattened. B. light gold, one surface more compact than others, slightly porous buff-colored particles adhere to surface, relatively thicker than A, possibly some tooth marks on surface.
    Dimensions: A. W.: 4.5 mm. L.: 7.5 mm.
                 B. W.: 4.5 mm. L.: 4.5 mm.
    t.: A. 30 mg.; B. 20 mg.
    Findspot: W264–265/S344.2–345 *86.15–*86.00
                 First trench through cupellation floor
    FB1968, *PNIII*, 1 (unpublished)

38 (TS 153)
    Description: Coarseware working palette or crucible fragment, medium gray exterior, consistent through cross section and interior, large quartz inclusions, mica, interior is deeply pitted and bubbly, large gold globule adheres to original surface.
    Dimensions: 3.7 cm. × 3.3 cm.; Th.: ca. 7 mm.
    Findspot: W277/S332 *85.4
    FB1969, *PN69I*, 97 (unpublished)

39 (TS 154) (Fig. 57)
    Description: Coarseware working palette or crucible fragment, medium brick red exterior continues through cross section in majority of fragment, section near large quartz pebble on the interior is gray in cross section and very friable, large quartz inclusions, mica, interior is slightly slagged with cracking and small gold globules spread over the interior.
    Dimensions: 6.7 cm. × 3.5 cm.; Th.: 9 mm.
    Findspot: S278–280/S345–347 *86.2–*85.9
    FB1969, *PNI*, 141; *PNII*, 97 (unpublished)

40 (M 68.19:7819) (Fig. 57)
    Description: Blow pipe nozzle, iron, two fragments preserve what appears to be the body of a conical nozzle which was attached to a reed or tube, heavily oxidized with sandy inclusions trapped in the corrosion product.
    Dimensions: L.: 8.3 cm.; Diam.: ca. 2.3 cm. to 0.008 m.
    Findspot: W272.3–277/S346–346.7 *86.2–*85.7
    FB1968, *PNIII*, 49; *PNIV*, 87 (unpublished)

41 (TS 139 d–g) (Fig. 57)
    Description: Tuyere or bellows nozzle, four joining fragments, light brick red matrix with gray patches in cross section, tempered with

quartz and vegetable fiber, body tapers toward tip on all four sides, where preserved, smaller end of nozzle is grossly misshapen on exterior and heavily vitrified producing a greenish black slag, air hole through interior is oval and retains linear impressions where the object was molded around a bundle of straw or possibly a twig was pulled through to smooth the interior.

Dimensions: H.: 5 cm.; W.: 5.9–6.5 cm.;
Diam. of hole: 3 cm. × 2.2 cm.
Findspot: W264–266/S345–347 *85.75–
*85.45
FB1968, *PNIII*, 101; *PNIV*, 153 (unpublished)

Analyses and Metallurgical Problems

Spectrographic analysis was first carried out by the Maden Tetkik ve Arama Enstitüsü in Ankara by arrangement with Director General Sadrettin Alpan. Dr. Nilüfer Bayçin, Director of the Technical Laboratory, reported the results of the gold analysis in 1968.[12] Since that time, we have been able to send samples for neutron activation to the Cekmece Nuclear Research Center in Istanbul. Further neutron activation analyses were run on an entire series of nondestructive rubbings made by S. M. Goldstein at Sardis and in Manisa in 1969. Through the kindness of Professor Adon Gordus, University of Michigan, Department of Chemistry, over ninety rubbings from Sardis were studied and compared with Lydian electrum and silver coinage from the Ashmolean and British Museums respectively.

Extensive spectrographic analyses were carried out on refinery materials in 1968 along with the work on the gold fragments. Supplemental analyses were kindly undertaken by Dr. Robert H. Brill, Research Scientist, Corning Museum of Glass, in 1969.[13]

The discovery of the refinery area has, at this stage, raised more questions than it has answered. The silver content of early Lydian coinage is a problem still disputed by scholars of economic history and early coinage.[14]

S. Bolin pointed out the discrepancies between the remarkably precise weights and strikingly variable fineness of the earliest series of Lydian electrum coins (gold content from 55 to 31%, silver from 45 to 69%). Bolin argued that the Lydian state cheated its customers from the beginning by deliberately raising the silver content of the electrum beyond that found in natural ore.[15]

The discovery of a coin fragment in the area has added an intriguing element in the interpretation of the fineness.[16] The fragment was identified during the reexamination of the large lump of gold (sample 15; Fig. 59) which has been cut on three sides. While the sample was being cleaned under the microscope, the underside, or the reverse as we now know it, revealed a long rectangular strip with indications of stress shearing and separation resulting from mechanical pressure. This rectangular area is the border between the incuse squares on the reverse. Furthermore, the small face of the obverse appears to retain the muzzle of the lion. E. Wahle has drawn a reconstruction of this fragment (Fig. 60) showing the preserved edge of the original coin on the top and the location of the lion protome on the obverse. The cut piece weighs 180 mg.: exactly one-tenth of a Lydian hecte, and one-sixtieth of a stater. The question yet to be answered is whether or not the sample identifies this area as a part of the Lydian mint. Perhaps the weight was used by the jewelry industry. In either case, it indicates an extremely accurate measure and suggests that cuttings and shavings of gold were melted together to form precise weights.

Finally, the question of platinum-iridium inclusions must be considered. W. J. Young, F. E. Whitmore, and R. E. Ogilvie have suggested that these inclusions represent native Pactolus gold which has been worked in the form of nuggets.[17] All of the industrial area samples as well as all of the gold objects excavated at Sardis since 1959 were examined with a binocular microscope. Not one type of gold sample from the industrial area contained traces of platinum-iridium inclusions. These samples included both dark and light foils as well as globules and irregular runs of appreciable size. Inclusions were observed on the surface of a hecte of Croesus (C 63.1; Fig. 61) and the well-known ram earring (J 67.3; Fig. 62) found at PN in 1967.[18] It is difficult to imagine that a piece of jewelry as complicated as the ram earring was worked from an unrefined nugget. Thus, the absence of platinum-iridium inclusions in the industrial materials and its presence in the ram earring will require careful consideration.

There are two additional problems which

should be considered but may not be included in the present study. The problem of gold enrichment on the surface of the foils is an often-discussed question. The foil samples from the industrial area exhibit widely divergent surfaces and colors, which suggests that they are not finished products but raw materials in various states of purification; but only thin section analyses would clarify the mystery.

Some analyses have been carried out on lead samples from Sardis. It has been suggested that a local lead mine was the source of the metal used for cupellation. R. H. Brill has analyzed samples of different leads from Sardis in order to establish a lead isotope ratio. In an attempt to identify possible geographic sources for the lead, these samples were compared with leads from other ancient sites. The tentative results suggest that the various lead samples are significantly different from each other. This strengthens the possibility that sources of lead were different during the various periods at Sardis. The problem of whether the "local" mine was discovered later is also as yet unsolved.[19]

To date only the preliminary reports by A. Ramage and S. Goldstein and discussions by G. M. A. Hanfmann and J. C. Waldbaum[20] have appeared in print. The final report on the PN material is now being readied for eventual publication in the Sardis series.[21]

SMG

Pactolus Cliff

In 1959 the collapse of a cliff along the east bank of the Pactolus brought to light another Lydian urban area (W225–242/S600–615; Fig. 8:13). Three seasons of excavation opened 200 sq. m.[1] and revealed continuous occupation from the Early Iron Age (?) (*87.1–*87.4)[2] through the Late Roman–Early Byzantine era (*92.7). A layer of heavily carbonized matter effectively sealed off the Lydian strata below from the Hellenistic above. Unfortunately, village houses above the dig made complete excavation of any unit impossible. By 1980, the excavated areas were torn away by the Pactolus floods.

The Lydian structures divide into four distinct levels (Fig. 64).[3] Stone walls and remains of pisé

and mudbrick constructions were found in each of these strata. The Early Iron Age (?) gray monochrome sherds (P 60.398:2853) found in Level IV (*87.4–*87.1) are the oldest indication of occupation from that sector; and a wall of Level IV points to the existence of structures. As A. Ramage points out, at the HoB sector gray monochrome occurs already with Mycenaean-Submycenaean types of pottery in the twelfth and eleventh century B.C., but the monochrome tradition peaks in the ninth and early eighth centuries. At PC, Level IV may go back to the ninth century, but too little is known of it. Level III may begin early in the eighth century. It had a long period of habitation destroyed by the Kimmerian invasions of the mid-seventh century B.C. A paved street 3.5 to 4 m. wide ran east from the Pactolus between two large buildings and then turned north-northeast into the scarps. Pottery recovered spans the early development of ceramic industry at Sardis, with gray ware coming from the lower layers and Greek Geometric imported pieces (P 60.159:2451) and Lydian painted wares with Protogeometric and Geometric decoration (Fig. 65) from the top ones. A pithos rim with two incised signs may represent very early writing.[4] The upper reaches of Level III are delineated by a charred layer (*89.5–*89) perhaps caused by the Kimmerian invasion of the mid-seventh century B.C. Level II (*89.7) represents a period of short duration. It contains only one clay floor from a building with plan and may indicate a period of building between the Kimmerian destruction and the destruction caused by the Treres a few years later.[5] It produced a Protocorinthian linear kotyle (P 60.67:2323), pieces of orientalizing mid- to late-seventh century pottery, a local imitation of "Ephesian" ware (P 60.66:2322), and examples of Lydian Geometric black on red ware (P 60.68:2324). Level I (*90.1–*89.1) was brought to a sudden end by fire. The level can be dated by the star-and-scroll terracotta sima (Fig. 66; T 60.2:2289) that A. Ramage now dates before 550 B.C. Hence the destruction may be that of 547 rather than 499 B.C., as was suggested in the preliminary report.

The extensive Lydian ruins at PC paint a picture of long and continuous usage of the area. Certainly the buildings were adorned in the later stages; terracotta revetments, much used in Lydian houses, have been pulled from Levels I and

II.[6] Yet the great size of the structures in Level III supports the idea of a sacral or public purpose for the area during Phase III. The obtuse angled building with walls 1 m. thick measures 6 × 6 m. in the excavated part; special libation bowls and pithoi with incised signs indicate a special function.

The PC sector is of great importance; it demonstrates that the Lydian city extended up the eastern bank of the Pactolus towards the Artemis Temple precinct. Perhaps as at Ephesus and Didyma, it lay on a "Sacred Road" linking the major urban agglomeration and the settlement at the temple.

WEM

Pyramid Tomb

High on the southern flank of a ravine on the side of the Pactolus in the shadow of the Acropolis stood the Pyramid Tomb (E10/S910; Fig. 8:14). It was first examined by H. C. Butler in 1914.[1] In its 1914 state it consisted of a squarish mound of earth covered on all four sides by limestone steps. It was preserved on its corner to a height of six steps, but in other parts most of the courses had fallen away. Butler drew a reconstruction based on the model of the stepped plinth tomb of Cyrus at Pasargadae with a chamber atop it.[2]

During the decades following the termination of the Butler excavations, the Tomb became covered with debris. In 1960 and again in 1961 the Harvard-Cornell Expedition worked to free the structure (Figs. 67, 69), and in 1968–1969 S. Kasper made a detailed analysis of it.[3] He concluded that it had always been a fully developed stepped pyramid which enclosed a chamber (Fig. 68). Early in the clearing it had been noticed that the masonry work was unusual in that it contained both finely finished blocks with drafted margins and almost unworked blocks, as well as blocks representing every stage of treatment in between (Fig. 69).[4]

Sure dating of the structure has proved impossible. Two Lydian terracotta sarcophagi (G 61.50) and two pieces of archaic pottery (P 61.511:5731 and an Ionian cup fragment) were recovered near the Tomb, but not in a datable context. The high quality of finish which some of the blocks show, with drafted margins and finely treated surfaces, would place the building of the Tomb into roughly the same era as the AcN walls, the altar LA 1, the Bin Tepe tomb chambers, and the MMS structure (Figs. 79–80, 95, 102, 116). The absence of clamping on the Pyramid Tomb may even indicate a date earlier than LA 1. Similarities in masonry exist with known Achaemenid monuments at Daskylion[5] and Pasargadae.[6] For the latter, the staircases A and B of the Tall-i-Takht (ca. 530 B.C.) display the same mixture of finished, partially finished, and unfinished masonry treatment that has been noted on the Tomb.[7] Nylander has pointed out that both the Cyrus Tomb and the Pyramid Tomb have a common metrological unit of a foot that equals 34–35 cm.[8]

These ties which the Pyramid Tomb has both with other Lydian architectural constructions and with Persian structures argue for a mid-sixth century B.C. date. Xenophon tells a romantic tale about the noble Persian Abradatas who died at Sardis, and Cyrus had a great tomb built for him.[9] G. M. A. Hanfmann has concluded that the Pyramid Tomb may well have been built for a Persian noble, perhaps one who fell in the battle for Sardis, in which case the building would date from ca. 540 B.C.[10] The Pyramid Tomb displays some striking similarities with Achaemenid masonry works at Pasargadae built for Cyrus between 547 and 530 B.C. They may be the result of importation of trained Lydian stone masons to work at Pasargadae during its first building stage. Not much later, Lydian masons worked on the palace of Darius at Susa.[11]

WEM

The Acropolis

The Acropolis of Sardis (E885–1160/S950–1140; Fig. 8: 20.1, 20.2, 20.3),[1] from the days of the earliest Lydian settlement through the final days of the city under the Ottomans and even into the twentieth century during the Turkish revolution,[2] has served as a natural stronghold, a place of refuge from the valley below. As the city of Sardis developed in the seventh to sixth century B.C., it followed a pattern common to other Anatolian river valley sites, a citadel crowning a mountain spur and overlooking an urban area beneath.[3]

Butler (1910–1914) did not excavate on the Acropolis. However, in 1922 T. L. Shear sank several test pits near the break in the Byzantine wall on the south side of AcT but ceased exploring once he determined that he had reached the Lydian stratum at 3.55 m. below ground level.[4] Between 1958 and 1975, the Harvard-Cornell Expedition excavators spent seven seasons investigating the Acropolis and exposed ca. 260 sq. m. of a total area of ca. 1470 sq. m.

The Acropolis was a vital feature of the urban landscape of Lydian Sardis. Not only have fortification walls been found—indicating that it served as a defensive bastion for the city—but also fine ashlar masonry walls of what may have been the palace of Croesus, suggesting that the Acropolis functioned as the home of the king and the center for the Lydian imperial administration.

The Acropolis is subject to earthquakes and landslides, both of which have wrought great changes in the physical appearance of the mountain and which make verifying topographic information in ancient sources all but impossible. As now preserved, the Acropolis ridge divides into three parts from north to south. Acropolis North (AcN; Figs. 8:20.2; 70, 79), E870–900/S955–980, with an area of ca. 1050 sq. m., is turned full front like a broad bastion toward the Hermus valley, with a rather wide sloping platform on top surmounted by a hillock which is in turn capped by a knob (Figs. 4, 6). A short razor-like spine flanked by sharp, steep falls links it to the central part, Acropolis Top (AcT; Figs. 8:20.1; 74), E1010–1060/S1030–1080, ca. 2500 sq. m. in area. Sheared-off sides to the east and west make access difficult, but a ravine starting from the Artemis Temple (W100–200/S1210–1260; Fig. 7) permits a more gradual approach to the Byzantine fortress gate at the south side of AcT. Due to eroding on the east, only a narrow spur topped by a Byzantine wall joins AcT to the platform which is the upper half of the Acropolis South (AcS; Figs. 8:20.3; 70), E1140–1160/S1130–1160, ca. 450 sq. m. in area. The southern limit of the citadel in late antique times is identified by the so-called "Byzantine Barracks," but earlier walls downhill (Figs. 70, 72, 73) indicate that the original area was larger. It has been estimated that up

to half of the Lydian Acropolis has fallen or slid away.

The cliffs which form the Acropolis are composed of crumbling tertiary conglomerate which consists of fine grains of kaolin, muscovite, biotite, and other ferro-magnesian minerals (Figs. 6, 7).[5] The land mass is rendered unstable during periods of great movement and shifting and during heavy rains, because of the reduced shearing resistance of the mica-rich soil with its low coefficient of friction. Combined with seismic action, this instability has resulted over the centuries in massive physical changes occurring as whole sections of the mountain slide or fall away. Just this happened in A.D. 17, when because of an earthquake the west side of the Acropolis was shaken from its foundations and fell, leaving the broad precipice that exists today (Figs. 7, 84).[6]

According to Herodotus, the Sardian Acropolis was first fortified in the eighth century B.C., at which time King Meles used magic to assure its invincibility.[7] It must have been fortified to some extent by the mid-seventh century B.C., for though there is both literary[8] and stratigraphic evidence for the Kimmerian destructions of the city—a burned layer and skeletal remains at HoB (*97.6–*97.5)[9]—there is no indication that the Acropolis suffered the Kimmerian wrath, yet there is evidence that the Acropolis was being inhabited at the time: sherds of early seventh century B.C. pottery have been found in hollows in the native conglomerate, as well as Phrygian black burnished pottery fragments and a plaque (T 60.496:2987; Fig. 71) with a Phrygian-inspired motif.[10]

In 547 B.C. Croesus fought his final campaign from the Citadel, where he successfully held out against the armies of Cyrus for fourteen days.[11] This suggests a strongly fortified mountain top in the mid-sixth century B.C.; Herodotus' implication that the Acropolis only fell through error and oversight would seem to support this view.[12] Arrowheads of a type known to be from the mid-sixth century B.C. were picked up on the AcS platform and may be witnesses of a Persian attack on the AcS walls (Figs. 70, 72, 73).[13]

Mentions of the Acropolis and its function during the Persian period, both in contemporary and later sources, continue to paint a picture of a strong, impregnable fortress called into action when the city proper had fallen to an enemy. This happened already in 547 B.C. when the

Lydian comptroller for the now Persian-ruled city revolted against the Persian garrison commander and held him trapped on the Acropolis until Persian reinforcements arrived. The destruction of the Ionian revolt of 499 B.C. is testified to by Herodotus.[14] The satrap Artaphernes and the Persian soldiers withdrew to the summit,[15] which was not scathed.

As a defensive fortification, the citadel atop the Acropolis at Sardis must have been admirable. Of the sieges recounted in the testimonia which took place between the seventh and fifth centuries B.C., only that of 547 was successful. Alexander the Great was impressed by the strength of the triple walls he saw encircling the Acropolis when he peacefully took control of the city in 334 B.C.[16] The Harvard-Cornell Expedition examined in 1973 three walls to AcS 10 m. downslope from the Byzantine Barracks which may be the remains of these great defenses on the AcS (Figs. 72, 73).[17] The wall complex stretches downhill for ca. 15 m. The lowest wall is aligned southwest-northeast and is preserved to a maximum length of ca. 7.5 m. and a maximum height of ca. 5.5 m. It has a single remaining face and is rubble-packed. The middle wall, the best preserved and largest of the three, runs in a southwest direction downhill with a maximum preserved length of ca. 16.50 m. and a maximum preserved height of ca. 7.35 m. It was constructed with two faces of roughly hewn or unhewn stones (ca. 1.20 × 0.80 m.) chinked with smaller stones. Between the faces is a core fill, 3.5 m. thick, of smaller stones set in mud cement. The upper wall is aligned northeast-southwest and is preserved to a maximum length of ca. 9.75 m. and a maximum height of ca. 6.4 m. Like the lower wall, it has one observed face and is rubble-packed. The walls are certainly pre-Hellenistic. Pottery found within the core fill of the middle wall is of the sixth and fifth centuries B.C., establishing a possible Lydian date. These powerful walls are the same type of construction as the mighty walls at Gordion.[18]

To what extent the summit was encircled by defensive curtains is impossible to determine; too much of the surface has fallen away. The remains of a monumental mudbrick structure MMS in the valley (E116.8–138.5/S51–58.5; Figs. 132, 133), first noticed in 1976 and now identified tentatively as part of the seventh and sixth century B.C. city walls,[19] pose a new question: what was the relationship between the lower city and the Acropolis fortifications? For the pre-Hellenistic period too little is left to allow even for hypotheses. All that can be noted is that in his description of the enceinte of Sardis in 213 B.C., Polybius states that a wall running across a ridge connected the lower city and Acropolis walls.[20] Such a connection may have been designed as part of the pre-Hellenistic defensive system.

On the AcT, a floor of green clay (E1030–1040/S1070–1080) was bounded by two Lydian walls of fairly large riverstones set in mud mortar (Fig. 74). Finds under and on the floor (*400.51 a.s.l.) suggest that the floor was in use from the sixth into the third century B.C.[21] The structure may have been decorated with colorful terracotta tiles such as the magnificent one with a winged horse (T 62.5:4212; Fig. 75) found in gravel fill beneath a Byzantine floor on the AcT.[22] Pottery sherds recovered from the AcT represent many types known from the lower city.[23]

The hollows cut into the native conglomerate may have served as either storage bins or cisterns, the latter being an important consideration since the Acropolis is without a natural water supply. This was underscored dramatically when in 1961 a tunnel was discovered which runs from the north side of the Acropolis 106 m. down and inside the mountain (Figs. 82, 83). Its ultimate goal remains unknown, but it may have led to a source of water.[24] The same purpose may have inspired the cutting of a tunnel on the west side, found in 1981. It led to the subterranean spring at the "Lydian Reservoir" (Plan I).

Unearthed in a water cistern, a lovely black-figure wine cup (Fig. 77) was imported from Athens just before the Persians captured the citadel. "Drink!" proclaims one of its inscriptions, a hint that some inhabitants of the fortress were no strangers to bibulous merriment.[25]

A piece of sculpture found on the AcT provides another clue to the nature of constructions atop the platform. This is a double-sided relief of a lion sejant carved from marble (Fig. 78).[26] The style would suggest a date between 580 and 560 B.C. The double-sided relief indicates its original use as part of a piece of furniture, probably the side of a throne or the leg of a table. The lion was the animal sacred to the Anatolian goddess Cybele. The legend of King Meles carrying the lion cub born of his wife around the ramparts of the Acropolis as a means of ensuring its invulnerability[27] may be a reference to the linking of the royal house of the Heraklids with the symbol of Cybele's lion, an association kept by the Mermnad dynasty.[28] A lion device appeared as obverse on the early Lydian coins (Figs. 60, 61).[29] The lion sculpture may have formed part of a throne for the goddess Cybele, or it may have had some royal connection.

That the Lydian kings may have lived at times atop the Acropolis can be in part ascertained from Arrian, who noted that Alexander chose the site of the palace of the Lydian kings as the spot upon which to erect a temple to Zeus, and he made this decision while standing atop the Acropolis and witnessing a sudden cloudburst drench the palace.[30] The Harvard-Cornell Expedition has come across three terracing walls of what may have been this palace (Figs. 79, 80) on the slope of AcN (E891–900/S955–975).[31]

The three walls sit on two scarps, one above the other, in a roughly parallel arrangement. Walls 1 and 2, exposed in 1960, ride the same ridge and form a single continuous wall with a slight jog 1.5 m. between the two parts. Wall 3, discovered in 1971, is situated on a higher cliff and is L-shaped, 2.57 m. × 9.35 m. Walls 1 and 3 are of pseudo-isodomic ashlar masonry (Fig. 80). Wall 2 is of random ashlar masonry construction. Drafted margins were applied to all the blocks. The center panels of the blocks in wall 2 and in the upper courses of wall 1 are dressed with finely punched faces; those on the lower courses of wall 1 and throughout wall 3 have a rusticated surface treatment (Fig. 79). Limestone blocks form the building material for walls 1 and 3; greenish sandstone was used for wall 2. The walls show only fragmentary preservation: wall 1 maximum height of eight courses (3 m.), wall 2 maximum height of nine courses (3 m.), and wall 3 maximum height of five courses (2 m.).

Cuttings on the lowest courses at the south end of the west face of wall 1 and projecting, broken blocks in the lowest courses of wall 2 confirm that an open staircase, descending from south to north, once joined walls 1 and 2. There may have been a landing immediately south of the south face of wall 1 (Fig. 80). This was an open and exposed staircase running up the out-

side of the structure it served; it emphasizes the nondefensive aspect of the walls, further indicating that they belong to a building complex and not to a fortification system.

When first uncovered, the walls were thought to be Hellenistic in date because of the marginal drafting.[32] Further studies revealed resemblances with the dressing of the blocks in the pre-Hellenistic walls of the tumuli at Bin Tepe, implying contemporaneous building dates for the two. Stratigraphic evidence lends support to this stylistic conclusion; mixed in with the layer of limestone chips found in front of wall 3 were Lydian sherds of the seventh to fifth century B.C. Gusmani also notes that mason's marks cut into the blocks include a sign resembling a sign on the crepis wall (cw) of the tumulus of Gyges, ca. 650 B.C.(Figs. 109, 110).[33]

Only one item has been found in conjunction with the putative palace walls—a small, attractive, archaic bronze relief of a boar (M 60.24:2367; Fig. 81). Similar ivory figures are known from Ephesus. The attachments on the back have Scythian counterparts. The piece may have been part of a horse trapping, although it was probably too heavy to have served at the crossing point for two straps and was more likely a cheek piece for a bit or a buckle for a girth strap.[34]

Parallels in masonry technique have been seen between the AcN walls and the monumental platform at Pasargadae, the Tall-i Takht.[35] The masonry in both structures shows the combination of marginally drafted blocks and centrally pecked faces. D. Stronach, the most recent excavator at Pasargadae, has written that nothing is known from an earlier context from the Iranian sphere which demonstrates such a sophisticated knowledge of masonry handling as is shown in the Tall-i Takht.[36] He argues that the novel treatment comes from Lydia, in particular Sardis, and was possibly brought to Iran by the same kind of masons who built the AcN palace walls.[37] Besides the masonry treatment, the two complexes have in common two structural features, unprotected staircases that run along the outside of walls and rusticated masonry courses on the foundation level.

During the 1974 season a large, L-shaped, limestone monolith (2.8 × 1.15 × 0.9 m.) which is situated ca. 15.50 m. downslope from the lower walls was excavated (W194/N104).[38]

The excavators laid out a trench linking the walls with the block (W179–193/N100–105). In most spots the native conglomerate was reached. Instead of the hoped-for palace wall, the excavators discerned an area of burned, homogenous matter that had been banked up to form an artificial shelf (386.02 and 389.01 m. a.s.l.). The archaic and Hellenistic artifacts retrieved from the fill, including a catapult ball, indicated a date in the third century B.C.[39] Since the stone and the burned earth platform have no structural relationship with the palace walls, it is possible that they are the remains of Antiochus III's siege operation directed against the citadel and the palace in 213 B.C.

The three walls on the AcN are too few and too fragmentary to allow for a detailed reconstruction. From Vitruvius' description,[40] it can be gathered that the palace superstructure was of mudbrick probably set on a stone foundation, which in turn rested on the ashlar masonry socles that remain. The palace complex would have been tiered, rising in terraces as do the mountain palaces represented on the Lycian reliefs from Gölbaşi-Trysa. The great expansive platform palaces such as those known from Assyria would have been out of the question.[41] The structure probably was decorated with painted terracotta revetments, such as the one found in fill downhill which shows a chariot scene.[42]

The relation of the palace on the north slope of the Acropolis to the fortification walls, of which remnants exist only on the south side is difficult to determine. Charon of Lampsacus, cited by Aristotle, says in writing of the 499 B.C. Ionian attack that the Ionian Greeks were successful in capturing the entire city "except for the fortress (teichos) of the palace."[43] This implies a protected structure, defended either by the Acropolis triple fortification walls or as a separate independent unit.

Confusion within the literary sources regarding the palace of Croesus has long been a problem in determining its possible location. The mention of such a structure by both Arrian and Vitruvius seems to assure its onetime existence. It may have been in some way altered to build Alexander's Temple to Zeus Olympios.[44] Vitruvius claims that the palace housed the gerousia after Alexander captured Sardis.[45]

Two later inscriptions refer to the gerousia. One concerns the setting up of a painted portrait on a shield in the Presbeutikon, "Hall of Elders," which may have been in the same building as the gerousia. The other, a later inscription, lists a fountain across from the "Gymnasium of the Elders" which may have been connected with the gerousia. The complexity of the issue has led to several tentative identifications of the palace with various unexcavated buildings,[46] but the present association of the palace with the three fine examples of pre-Hellenistic pseudo-ashlar masonry walls (Figs. 79, 80) is the most persuasive. They are among the best masonry walls known from a Lydian context; they have no funerary association, and they were not defensive. They are properly located to suit Arrian's topographical placement. One problem remains, however: if the palace did become the seat of the gerousia which in turn was near to or part of a "Gymnasium of the Elders," there had to have been level ground for the palaestra. There is also a possibility that what remains of the palace may well be the upper part of the palace, connected perhaps via the tunnels already mentioned (Figs. 70, 82, 83) to a lower part near the level area where today stands a Byzantine fort.[47]

The Acropolis of Sardis is such a naturally strong defensive position that it was surprising to find no Prehistoric Bronze Age pottery and artifacts, such as have been found on the citadels of neighboring Philadelphia, Aphrodisias, and Pergamon.[48] Perhaps it served only as a lookout post. For a real settlement of any size at such a height over the valley, the lack of water supply would have been a great drawback.

It seems a plausible hypothesis that this problem was solved at only a relatively late date (eighth century B.C.), when Meles built the first defenses. To dig a subterranean tunnel to a source of water and to develop at the same time an extensive system of cisterns would permit a garrison and perhaps even a royal household to remain on the citadel. It is for this reason that the incomplete tunnels which lead down from the top of AcN are likely to go back to Lydian times. Rock-cut subterranean cisterns still exist, though their date of construction is difficult to establish.[49]

Apart from T. L. Shear's passing reference to some terracotta revetments found on the slope,[50] nothing was known about the Lydian and Persian citadel prior to the Harvard-Cornell excavations. Scanty though the evidence gained may seem, it does suggest an impressive picture of development. From the mid-seventh century to the fifth century B.C., mighty mudbrick walls seated on tall stone foundations, comparable to Gordion's twenty-foot curtains, enclosed the Acropolis.[51] Its north part, with sweeping views of the Hermus valley (Figs. 4, 6, 79), was occupied by a majestic palace rising up the slope on substructures of some of the finest archaic stone masonry work known. It may have used the same combination of monumental stone dadoes with door frames of stone and walls of mudbrick as the Persian Achaemenid palaces. One might argue from the preserved corner of a Lydian structure atop the Acropolis (AcT; Fig. 74) that the central and southern portions were built up with smaller structures like those on the Athenian Acropolis during Turkish times.[52]

Details remain unknown, though it is clear that much filling and leveling took place and that a gate was probably located on the south. Because the original area of the citadel is not ascertainable and too much has fallen away, it is impossible to estimate the number of people who could regularly dwell or take refuge in emergency in the fortress. It cannot have been more than a couple of thousand, at most.

There is no literary or archaeological evidence to indicate that the Lydo-Persian fortifications and buildings underwent major changes between the conquest of Alexander in 334 B.C. and the siege of Antiochus III in 213 B.C. With the changes in military warfare techniques in the Hellenistic Age, it is likely that something was done to strengthen the fortress after the siege.[53] Later, the configuration of the citadel was radically changed by the earthquake of A.D. 17 and possibly by another in the seventh century A.D. The last stage of the Acropolis defenses, the Early Byzantine fortress, was built to take into account the drastically altered form of the landscape (Figs. 4–7, 84).

WEM

Acropolis Tunnels

In 1960 a passageway cut into the Acropolis conglomerate was noticed by G. Bakir when, because of a collapse of a rock-face of the Acropolis, three zigzag turns became exposed (Fig. 83).

The excavation of the tunnel was undertaken in 1962[1] and again in 1964. The difficult working conditions—inadequate air supply, and windings and turnings which had in parts fallen away—made a complete clearing impractical, and so the lower terminal point of the passage was not reached; but 127 m. were opened and mapped.

The tunnel entrance is situated on the north slope of the Acropolis (E900/S800) downhill from the palace walls of the AcN (Fig. 70). It descends from a height of 315 to 280 m. a.s.l. The actual passageway differs in height from 1.70 to 2.10 m. and in width from 0.70 to 1.10 m. (Fig. 82). On top is a large, roughly rectangular chamber hollowed from the conglomerate, the floor of which had been cut in three stages becoming increasingly deeper toward the west. Around the entrance were cavities and hollows suggesting sockets for jambs, a lintel, and a threshold for a door. The tunnels descend in a series of continuing windings and turnings, parts of which are quite steep. Stairs have been cut into the conglomerate to facilitate movement. No evidence for wall niches or brackets was discovered, indicating that the turns were not lit. The passage seems to have been dug from below; this explains a couple of sharp drops in windings where the angle for the turn was miscalculated.

The tunnel was filled up by a gradual silting process. The fill content was a heterogeneous mixture containing Lydian, Hellenistic, Roman, Byzantine, and Turkish articles. No reliable stratification could be made out for the upper chamber, which had suffered from a sizeable collapse at the east end and therefore had introduced into the fill artifacts from the Acropolis topsoil. The tunnel fill included pieces which had evidently filtered down from the topsoil incursion in the upper chamber into the passageway proper.

The date and the purpose of the construction have not been determined. The mixed fill and the lack of finds in a stratified context make a clear decision on a date impossible. The heterogeneous artifacts recovered would allow for more than a thousand-year building span, from the archaic (sixth century B.C.) through the Middle Byzantine (twelfth century A.D.). The amount of fill that has accumulated may possibly suggest that the construction could not have taken place later than the Middle Byzantine period.

A date in the Lydian era (sixth century B.C.) is certainly credible, especially if the tunnel had been constructed to serve as a linkage between the Acropolis and a dependable water supply.[2]

A regular water source was an important prerequisite for the full settlement of the Acropolis. After the site became a garrison fortress in the late eighth and seventh centuries B.C., it can be assumed that measures were taken to secure an adequate supply. Rock-cut tunnels leading to or conducting water are known from a sixth century B.C. context at Samos[3] and even earlier from Late Bronze Age Mycenae and Tiryns[4] and elsewhere in Asia Minor in Phrygia and settlements in Paphlagonia.[5]

WEM

The Northeast Wadi

The Northeast Wadi (NEW) is located about 100 m. uphill and northeast of the Artemis Temple Precinct (W105–130/S1110–1120) on the lower slopes of the Acropolis. This wadi is a torrent bed created by the rainwater runoff from the Acropolis (Figs. 7, 8:16, 84).[1] H. C. Butler excavated a portion of the area during 1914,[2] and later T. L. Shear explored the spot.[3] Both excavators recovered Lydian pottery fragments, and Butler claimed there were Lydian walls at a depth of not more than 6 or 8 m. beneath the surface.[4] A cache of pottery, revealed by a rainstorm, spurred the Harvard-Cornell Expedition to dig at NEW, and during 1969 and 1977 to open a trench of 78 sq. m. So much debris was carried down from the Acropolis into the wadi between 1969 and 1977 that the depth of the fill in 1977 was equal to what it had been prior to the 1969 clearing.[5]

The torrent action from the water rushing through the trench that Butler had cut in 1914 caused disruption of the stratigraphic record in the lower portions of the trench and also made preservation of the pre-Hellenistic structures unearthed impossible.[6]

Beneath a top layer of Roman remains (*113.72–*112.72–.29), the excavators encountered pre-Hellenistic constructions with some twenty walls at *111.80 to *109.86 (Fig. 84). Two occupational surfaces appear to have been contemporaneous with the walls. A gravel lense running through the western half of the trench (*111.09–*111.15) serves as the demarcation.[7] A possible threshold for a door in wall *f* (threshold *111.11, wall bottom *111.21) marks the lower stage in the eastern half of the trench, and two artifact deposits which rest on horizontal layers, *112.16 and *111.72, prove the existence of the upper stratum. There is no evidence for occupation below *109.72.

A circular wall with only an inside face probably served as an underground storage facility; other walls might have formed a trapezoidal room or courtyard (3.50–4.00 m. by 4.50 m.). A trapezoidal construction with only an inside face possibly was also an underground storage unit. There are some similarities in construction with the older pre-Hellenistic walls at PN and HoB. The socles are built of roughly hewn fieldstones laid in irregular courses with the larger stones at the bottom; mud mortar is sometimes used. Hunks of mudbrick and pisé detected in the debris imply that the superstructure may have been of mudbrick.[8]

The ceramic finds from the NEW have been among the most spectacular from Sardis (Fig. 87). Especially notable were shoulder and body fragments from a large amphora decorated with an orientalizing scene of two sphinxes *passant* (Fig. 85; P 69.71:8025)[9] and a fragment from a vase with a frieze of horsemen (P 77.41:8361), other parts of which were found by Butler (Fig. 156).[10] Within the context of stratification, the upper levels (*112.80–*112.00) produced standard Lydian types,[11] some "Rhodian" Subgeometric, and a few sherds of Wild Goat style. Between *112.00 and *111.09 the shapes of the vessels found were amphora, lydion, omphalos phiale, and column crater (Fig. 86), and the types of ware included Lydian bichrome and marbled, Wild Goat, and Chiot. Below the gravel lense at *111.04–*110.96, the Wild Goat ware disappears. A few seventh century B.C. bird bowl fragments have turned up, usually in conjunction with Lydian assemblages. The additional piece of the vase with the frieze of horsemen came from this stratum. From *110.94 down through the lowest occupation level (*110.47–*109.72), the finer wares decrease and the amounts of pithos and plain, coarse, gray ware sherds increase. Lydian skyphoi have not been seen lower than *110.94; bird bowls, however, continue to occur to *110.65.

THE ARTEMIS PRECINCT AND ALTAR   49

Lydian and Greek pottery retrieved from the Lydian strata at the NEW dates to the late seventh and early sixth centuries B.C. V. J. Harward has noted in his field report for the 1977 season that the abundance of gray and coarse wares in the lower occupation stratum may indicate that NEW was not a particularly prosperous quarter during the early seventh century B.C.[12]

The quantity and general character of the ceramic material at NEW, the number of walls and their close proximity to one another, the discovery of the bones of slaughtered flock and herd animals in the upper level (Fig. 87), and the lack of any objects arranged in sets or with a votive purpose suggest that NEW was secular and not sacred in function. The similarities with HoB and PN and the presence of storage containers argue for a domestic quarter.[13] The presence of this densely built-up habitation area near the Artemis precinct suggests that the city may have expanded very far southward in archaic times.

WEM

The Artemis Precinct and Altar in Lydian and Persian Times

Exploration of the Artemis Precinct

The Artemis Temple Precinct (Figs. 7, 8, 88, 89, 90, 284, 285; W50–250/S1110–1320), with its standing columns, has long been one of the more conspicuous elements of the Sardian landscape.[1] The Princeton expedition cleared ca. 46,000 sq. m. of the site during the four seasons 1910–1914; their attention was concentrated almost exclusively on the temple proper. The Harvard-Cornell Expedition spent nine seasons working in the precinct and opened an additional (ca.) 26,000 sq. m.[2] Explorations were made of the southern sector in 1958 and of the eastern sector in 1969. Small-scale excavations were undertaken in the temple proper during 1960, 1961, and 1972 and on the platform which stands before the temple (Artemis Altar, "LA"; Figs. 94, 95) on the west side during 1968, 1969, and 1970. Conservation and restoration work essential to the survival of the structures within the precinct was performed throughout the years of exploration and excavation.[3] Close collaboration with the Turkish Min-

istry of Waterworks resulted in the successful relocation of the Pactolus torrent channel which had threatened to erode and undermine the area of the precinct immediately to the west of the temple (Fig. 88).[4]

The Harvard-Cornell Expedition plotted and explored the precinct, determined the building history of the various sectors within the precinct, developed a detailed chronology for the building of the temple, and discovered that much of the precinct had been reordered during the Roman period following a flood in the third century A.D.[5] The Artemis Altar was examined and proved to be two separate structures, the earlier and smaller archaic or Persian one encased in the later, larger Hellenistic altar.

In an attempt to determine the earliest period of occupation at the Artemis Temple Precinct, the Harvard-Cornell excavators sunk sondages south of the temple proper (Trench S)[6] in Building "L" (three trenches), and in the temple itself (ten trenches; Fig. 89); the temple trenches were also dug in the hopes of ascertaining the building chronology of the structure and of retrieving any remains of an archaic temple, if one ever existed. Beneath Roman-Byzantine and Hellenistic levels, discontinuous pre-Hellenistic surfaces were encountered, in trench 5 under the south colonnade of the temple (*99.12–*98.75; *98.30–*98.40) and under Rooms A and B (*98.12–*98.20) of Building "L" (Fig. 88). A series of alternating clay levels—the results of occupations—and gravel bands showed up in the sounding in Room A; a Lydian spool handle (P 68.148:7850) supplies a fifth to fourth century B.C. date. From this layer came pieces of Lydian and Greek pottery. Lydian sherds from Trench S were identified as seventh to sixth century B.C. A terracotta antefix (T 72.1:8192) is similar to one pulled from a well at the PN (T 64.4:6499) which is considered to be from the fourth or fifth century B.C.[7] Three sondages terminated in a sterile stratum of river-laid deposits, indicating that the precinct had originally been a torrent bed (Trench S, *98.50). This probing of the stratigraphic record produced no evidence to support the theory of an archaic precinct in the area. The picture obtained was of an area which may have been in some type of occasional use as early as the sixth century B.C. but which did not really see occupation before ca. 400 B.C.

Description of the Precinct

In its present state, the Artemis Temple Precinct is essentially of Roman design, rearranged and ordered during the third century A.D. (Figs. 88, 94). To the south of the temple (W140–200/S1260–1310), the ruins of the precinct consist of Roman and early Byzantine vaulted tombs and graves and a large Roman structure, Building L. The function of Building L has not been determined.

The area north of the temple is divided into three large building and structural complexes, the Northwest Quarter (W190–250/S1150–1220), the North Terrace (W125–192/S1160–1190), and the Northeast Terrace (W60–140/S1120–1200).[8] The Lion-Eagle-Nannas Bakivalis Monument, located on the North Terrace, is composed of Lydian votive figures which were set into their present configuration during the Roman precinct renovation. Though not in its original form, the monument remains important for its Lydian/Greek bilingual inscription which dedicates the marble pedestal to Artemis and indicates that the Lydian name for Dionysus was *Baki*.[9] North Street, which is the main artery through the Northwest Quarter, may have been an entrance into the temple precinct; it is the oldest feature in the Northwest Quarter. The two monument bases in the Northeast Quarter, numbers 20 and 21 (W80/S1180) are of Persian or Lydian origin but were reset during the Roman era.

Monument 10, a Hellenistic construction composed of three rooms, lies to the east of the temple (W63–73/S1260–1310).[10] The area south of the Northwest Quarter and west of the temple (W196–230/S1218–1257) contains the Artemis Altar structure and the associated stelai base groupings, South Stelai Bases (SSB) and North Stelai Bases (NSB; Figs. 88, 94). With the exceptions of numbers 23 and 40, the bases are of Persian or early Hellenistic origin (as is indicated by the use of anathyrosis to join the blocks and the remains of claw-chisel marks on the blocks), but they were placed in their present positions during the third century renovation.[11]

The Problem of a Pre-Hellenistic Temple

A major problem which the Harvard-Cornell Expedition sought to solve at the Artemis Tem-ple proper (W100–200/S1210–1260) was the question of whether an earlier archaic structure had stood on the site prior to the great Hellenistic temple which the Butler excavations had largely uncovered.[12] It is this question, and the other evidence for conditions in the Artemis Precinct in Lydian and Persian times, that is considered here.

Butler claimed that the temple dated from the fifth or fourth century B.C. He cited several features which he thought had been incorporated into the structure from an earlier temple of the era of Croesus: the purple (red) sandstone blocks used in parts of the construction,[13] the east cella base under which was found a coin of Croesus,[14] and two reused columns on unfinished bases, one of which carried a Lydian inscription on its foot.[15]

Small-scale excavations were conducted at various points in the temple complex. Under the guidance of K. J. Frazer, ten trenches were laid out during the 1972 season (Fig. 89). The archaeological search by the Harvard-Cornell archaeologists for more substantial evidence of a Lydian temple produced no relevant evidence. The temple now standing can be dated to the early years of the Seleucid rule.[16] Only in Trench 5 were Lydian remains of "bread trays" and pottery fragments found in stratified context (*98.75–*98.00),[17] but there was no indication of an earlier structure. A column fragment of astragal molding (NoEx 78.15) with a Lydian inscription (IN 78.4) was found out of context in 1978 by K. J. Frazer.[18] Reinvestigation of the east cella image base (Figs. 88:17; 90, 178, 179) in 1960–1961 invalidated Butler's theory that the base was archaic. The cement layer on the lowest level of the image base is no earlier than the Hellenistic period, and though the stones used to construct the image base may have been cut during the archaic or Persian eras, the nonfunctional arrangement of the clamp cuttings suggests that the stones are not in their original positions, but rather are reset from other structures.[19]

From Ephesus has come an inscription (Inv. 1631)[20] regarding the death sentences for forty-five Sardians who attacked a sacred embassy making its way according to custom of the fathers from the Artemision in Ephesus to an Artemis precinct at Sardis. The text mentions that the cult of Artemis at Sardis was founded by the

Ephesians and is, therefore, a branch of the Ephesus institution. The date of the inscription is debated, though it was not set up before the mid-fourth century B.C. nor after the early third century B.C.[21] The earlier date does not agree with the date after 280 B.C. proposed for the erection of the Hellenistic temple in this volume (Chapter VII), but suggests that another, possibly older sanctuary of Artemis did exist at Sardis. An interesting funerary stele (Fig. 159),[22] which according to the Lydian inscription demands that transgressors of the grave who are caught pay their fines to the Artemis of Ephesus, may have been put up by a priest of that goddess; its sixth century B.C. date and its presence at Sardis again draw attention to the close ties existing between the two cult centers. Lydian inscriptions of the Persian period from the Necropolis[23] testify to the importance of Artemis as protectress of tombs and graves, for she is regularly invoked in curses against those who desecrate a sepulcher. It may have been for this older sanctuary that Alexander confirmed the right of asylum after 334 B.C.[24]

No certain images of the goddess from the Archaic and Persian eras have turned up, but a crowned head from ca. 600 B.C. (NoEx 62.8) might be that of Artemis; the presence, however, of a hawk or lion mask on the crown means that Cybele cannot be ruled out.[25] The upper torso of a female figure (S 59.10:1419) with right arm slightly raised and left arm extending sideways could be from a statue of Artemis as Huntress.[26] A relief of the late classical era seems to portray a fifth century statue of Artemis next to a statue of Cybele (Fig. 93).[27]

Moses of Chorene listed gilded bronze statues of Apollo, Artemis, and Herakles by the sculptors Dipoinos and Skyllis as taken from Croesus by Cyrus, though whether the pieces were from Sardis rather than elsewhere in what later became the province of Asia is unclear.[28] Artemis' retainers are also represented. There are two statues of priestesses to the goddess, one from the first century B.C.,[29] the other from the second century A.D.[30]

Artemis Altar (Lydian Altar: LA)

To the west of the Artemis Temple, ca. 15.57 m. from the ancient masons' setting marks for the northwest anta of the temple, stands the Artemis Altar (W200/S1220–1250; Figs. 88, 94, 95).[31] It is in actuality two structures (LA 1 and LA 2); the earlier construction (LA 1) is encased in the later monument (LA 2).

Butler, in his reconstruction, showed the structure now remaining as forming part of a grand staircase entrance to the temple,[32] though in a later elevation drawing he interpreted it as functioning as an altar.[33] During the 1969, 1970, and 1972 seasons, the Harvard-Cornell Expedition excavated the altar, and the results of their exploration led to the distinguishing of two distinct building phases. Studies concentrated on determining the building and historical chronology and on understanding the relationship of the altars to the temple proper.

LA 1 is a four-stepped structure (8.82 m. E-W by 8.14 m. N-S at its base) covered over by LA 2 (21.22 m. N-S by 10.74 m. E-W). It was constructed of well-cut but not finely finished blocks of calcareous tufa which were laid in courses. Pi clamps held the blocks in place, but no dowels were used. Originally the altar was faced, probably with marble. LA 2 was built of double-layered walls, the outer shell composed of roughly cut stone, the inner layer formed of irregularly shaped riverstones cemented to the back of the outer shell with mud mortar.

LA 1 is an archaic structure of the late sixth century B.C. The clamp types used[34] would suggest such a date. Several pieces of decorative marble features may come from the altar: a corner piece with an egg and dart pattern of archaic appearance (S 69.13:8040)[35] and a fragment of a lotus palmette ornament (S 69.12:8034) which probably dates from 525 to 500 B.C.[36] Alternately, it may have had a limestone superstructure attested by an egg and dart crown. A fragment of a double reverse scroll with a palmette found by Butler resembles decorations from the sixth century altar at Monodendri.[37]

The Artemis Precinct was formed by flood deposits. During the seventh and sixth centuries B.C. it was regularly traversed, as the pottery finds in Trench 5 show, but until the construction of LA 1 in the late sixth century there was no structure in the area. LA 1 stood alone; there is no evidence that it originally connected up with anything else.[38] Nor is there any proof to suggest that it shared the precinct with any other building when first built. It possibly was oriented towards the west to face the Necropolis, and in style it probably resembled the great altars at Samos, Ephesus, and Miletus.[39] The use of clamps to join the stones and the high quality of the stone handling place this altar on the list of Lydian masonry monuments after the Gyges Mound (650 B.C.), the AcN walls (600–550 B.C.), and the Pyramid Tomb (547 B.C.). No signs of burning were discovered during the excavations, and there is no reason to assume the altar was destroyed during the Ionian destruction in 499 B.C. The end for LA 1 came with the building of LA 2 in the fourth century, at which time the marble covering was torn off and the substructure totally buried by the larger Hellenistic altar.

That an archaic temple of the Sardian Artemis may have existed somewhere else or that an altogether different shrine may have been dedicated to the Ephesian Artemis remain distinct possibilities. The great Hellenistic temple for the Artemis of Sardis was probably begun by the Seleucids after 280 B.C. and was thoroughly replanned by the famous Ionian architect Hermogenes or his associates between 220 and 200 B.C. This structure and its subsequent vicissitudes are considered in Chapter VII, "The Hellenistic Period."

WEM

Peripheral Sectors

In 1960, a limestone relief sculpture (NoEx 60.13) was discovered by a local resident at a hillock known as Dede Mezari ("Saint's Tomb"),[1] ca. 1.5 km. west of the village of Sart Mahmut, and was brought to the attention of the Harvard-Cornell Expedition. Further exploration at the site revealed cut limestone masonry which had been incorporated into the saint's shrine, two pieces of which had mason's marks —EY and N—and piles of tiles, some stamped with designs, and one in particular showing what may be a Lydian or Hellenistic sign.[2]

The sculpture is of a kore presented standing fully frontal and framed by a shrine.[3] She wears a costume resembling those worn by the Athenian Acropolis maidens dated by G. M. A. Richter to 525–515 B.C. and by E. B. Harrison to 510–500 B.C.[4] The kore may represent a mortal, perhaps as part of a votary or funerary piece. The figure can also be compared with Phrygian Cybele representations, which often are similarly posed.[5] However, the figure lacks the proper attributes of Cybele, the crown and lion, and may instead be Aphrodite.

Dede Mezari yielded another archaic piece in 1976, an Ionic marble volute portion of a capital (NoEx 76.5).[6] Its small size (L. 0.227 m., H. 0.25 m., Th. 0.115 m.) points to a votive pedestal rather than a column from a building. The narrow proportions and the convex channel indicate a late sixth or early fifth century B.C. date. A floral form appendage on the volute's undersurface is a most unusual feature. These two sculptural discoveries suggest that a small archaic sanctuary may have existed at Dede Mezari outside the confines of the city proper.

Other areas of Sardis may offer further information about the Lydian and the Lydo-Persian settlements. A group of Lydian chamber tombs is located at Başlıoglu Köy (BK 71.1), a village some 3 km. southwest of Sardis.[7] A. Ramage believes that a large structure at Ahlatli Tepecik on the Gygean Lake might be the ruins of a Lydian farmhouse.[8] The regional survey initiated in 1976 by C. H. Greenewalt, Jr., and E. Sterud is specifically aimed at ascertaining the habitation pattern of the entire Sardis region.[9]

WEM

IV

Lydian Graves and Cemeteries

ROBIN U. RUSSIN

GEORGE M. A. HANFMANN

The Burial Mounds

The burial mounds of Sardis, particularly those at Bin Tepe, have long intrigued scholars and travelers alike. At the middle of the fifth century B.C., Herodotus remarked that "Lydia does not have many marvels worthy of note, like any other land . . . But there is one work far the greatest excepting only for those of the Egyptians and Babylonians"[1]—the mighty grave barrow of Alyattes.

The digging of the Alyattes mound by Spiegelthal in 1853[2] began the history of scientific excavation at Sardis. Discoveries from smaller tumuli were recorded by Choisy in 1876,[3] and Dennis carried on further excavations into the 1880s.[4] He was "much disappointed" with his finds and, after he discovered that probably "every one" had been robbed in ancient times,[5] did not even bother to publish them. Butler, excavating some thirty years later, felt that his own "trial campaign should rather be taken as encouraging, since it seems to show that many of these tumuli are still inviolate."[6] With the advent of World War I his investigations ceased, and the mounds remained unexcavated until the fifth Harvard-Cornell Expedition campaign in 1962,[7] when a comprehensive plan was developed for a systematic survey of the Royal Cemetery of Bin Tepe and the territory around the Gygean Lake (Figs. 2, 11) with a view to finding Prehistoric settlements (see Chapter II) and mapping, testing, and describing all mounds extant. Activities along these lines began in 1962 with geophysical testing, and excavation of a recently opened mound (BT 62.4), and recording of the mound of Alyattes (Figs. 97, 99–103). They continued (1963–1966) with the exploration and tunneling of the great central mound, Karniyarik Tepe (BT 63.1; Figs. 104–112). Intensified illicit grave digging led to excavations of six graves at Duman Tepe (1966) and follow-up study elsewhere.[8] Concomitant with the digging of the Royal mound (BT 63.1) and during the Prehistoric survey (1967–1969), much information was gathered by C. H. Greenewalt, Jr., and D. G. Mitten about this, the largest mound cemetery of Asia Minor, but the systematic descriptive survey had to be postponed.

The mounds are located primarily along the 10-km.-long limestone ridge of Bin Tepe (Figs. 2, 98) which rises ca. 10 km. northeast of the city and just south of the great Gygean Lake (Marmara Gölü). Others are found on its north and south shores, are scattered along the valleys and embankments of the Hermus and Pactolus Rivers, and lie within the city area.[9] There were always several major access roads to BT, one from a ford at Ahmetli in the west, one from the region of Salihli in the east (Figs. 2, 11, 96).[10]

The Royal Cemetery of Bin Tepe is generally acknowledged to be the vastest and most imposing mound cemetery of Asia Minor. The local name of "Bin Tepe" means "a thousand mounds," but this is an optimistic estimate. The aerial photographs and recent photogrammetric surveys show around ninety mounds; in addition, a considerable number have been worn down beyond recognition. The original number is not known but was certainly well over one hundred. Over twenty mounds have been examined by the Harvard-Cornell Expedition between 1958 and 1975; of these fourteen contained true chamber tombs and two contained cist graves.[11]

The mounds vary considerably in dimensions, owing not only to original size but also to subsequent erosion, farming, and spoliation. Other than the huge Royal Mounds, they range in height from 1 to 15 m. and in diameter from 10 to 40 m. All signs of crepides (supporting walls) have been lost, with the possible exception of the Royal Mounds; only a few displaced central markers, either phallic or bud-like in shape, give evidence of exterior adornment.[12] The mounds are composed of alternating layers of earth, clays, sand and gravel, limestone rubble, fieldstones and riverstones (Fig. 112). An occasional thin deposit of ashes seems to imply a pyre or a ritual dinner.[13]

Our observations considerably modify the generalizations made in 1876 by Choisy.[14] He asserted that "the sepulchral chamber is never in the center of the mound but always near the edge."[15] Almost all the chamber complexes excavated by the Harvard-Cornell Expedition (from the mounds where determination was possible) were located in or near the center. The exceptions were the two Royal Mounds: the Gyges mound (BT 63.1), where no chamber was located in the center at bedrock level (it may be higher; Figs. 106, 107), and the Alyattes mound, where the eccentric opened chamber is probably only one of several and is possibly ancillary to a central complex (Fig. 100). The cist burial BT 63.3 was at the edge of the mound. This does not mean that the mounds seen by Choisy were not off-center, but merely that recent excavations reveal no set rule.[16]

Similarly, where Choisy implied that all complexes are oriented north-south, opening south with the long walls of the chamber running east-west,[17] Harvard-Cornell Expedition excavations reveal five out of eleven oriented east-west, opening both east and west, and two oriented northeast-southwest, opening northeast, with

random variation in the direction of the long walls.

Sepulchers vary from one small chamber without door or dromos (BT 63.2) to a cloverleaf complex of three large chambers, antechamber, and dromos, with pitched ceilings (BT 76). Some are cut into local bedrock; others are built masonry (Figs. 102, 103, 115); one was built over habitation fill (T 77.1). All except one (BT 62.4) appear to have rubble packing. Nor are the chambers "of about the same size, no matter what size mound covers them."[18]

The amount of finish varies considerably, from rough-trimmed, uneven coursing to hairline precision in joining blocks weighing many tons, drafted edges, and white stucco dressing. Normally the material is local limestone, but the Alyattes chamber is built of white marble masonry (Fig. 102) with limestone used in the antechamber (Fig. 103). A late tomb near Kestelli (BT 1976) is also of marble. There are between two and six wall-courses and between two and five flat ceiling beams. The walls are more or less ashlar, often pseudo-isodomic or progressively diminishing, and show a curious notched interlock construction. The edges are usually better finished than the faces. The walls sometimes incline slightly outward to prevent collapse. The normal ceilings are flat; except for the late tomb (BT 76), we have found no pitched ceilings with imitation beams and rafters as seen in Soma.[19] Ceiling beams are usually rectangular, picked on the inner surface and rough-hewn outside (as is all the masonry); in a couple of instances the last block of the chamber or chamber-most block of the antechamber is triangular in section and trimmed on all faces. Iron clamps set in lead are often indicated; these are uniformly of the "double-dovetail" and "fish" variety described by Nylander.[20]

A post and lintel doorway usually leads out to the dromos or antechamber. The dromos is often closed by a single stone door-block[21] with flanged or rebatted edges to lock it into the doorway. Sometimes the bottom edge is chamfered to facilitate lifting and placement on the threshold. Occasionally there is a portal with coursed walls on the outer side of the doorway.

Antechambers vary considerably. Of those known from BT, one belongs to the unusual cloverleaf complex (BT 76?)[22] and has a pitched ceiling; one, now ruined, belonged to the Alyattes chamber (Fig. 103); Spiegelthal drew it with a barrel vault of rubble spanning one rubble and one ashlar wall.[23] The antechamber of BT 62.4 is constructed of fine ashlar similar to that of the adjoining chamber.

Dromoi are common; perhaps only three chamber tombs excavated do not have them.[24] The walls are normally built of rubble or rough trimmed stone.[25] The walls do not bond onto the chamber; this characteristic, along with the presence in at least two dromoi of a single well-finished ashlar block near the chamber, suggests that the dromos was added after the chamber was complete. As in the chamber, dromos walls occasionally incline outward. Floors are either of tamped chips and gravel or are cut into bedrock; in at least two instances there was evidence of roofing. Where full length was preserved, the dromoi were sealed off by dry rubble walls (Fig. 115). The dromoi appear to have been filled with earth and/or rubble at the time of original interment.

Excavation of the sepulchers has provided many valuable insights and comparisons concerning construction and technique. The extraordinary capacity to handle monumental masonry (both limestone and marble) is demonstrated in the Gyges and Alyattes mounds for the mid-seventh and early sixth centuries B.C.[26] The Sardian tombs contain the earliest evidence for the use of staple clamps; this technique does not seem to appear elsewhere in the Near East until later.[27] Such techniques may have been introduced into Lydia from Greece or Egypt; however, the Sardis chamber tombs seem never to have expanded into large halls as did the Egyptian-Hellenistic and Etruscan-Hellenistic burials. Originally intended for a man and perhaps his wife and children, the tombs need not represent many generations.

A number of inferences can be made from the location, placement, and size of the mounds (Figs. 96–99). The tumuli seem to form groups (Fig. 105) which, interpreted sociologically and literally, suggest that all the mound owners were of the same aristocratic class. An investigation by A. and N. Ramage into the occurrence and siting of 130 burial mounds throughout Lydia[28] tends to confirm the theory that these are burials of feudal families who owned and ruled important agricultural territories, while presumably still subject to the overlord-king of Sardis.

The earliest excavated mounds at Sardis date not before King Gyges (ruled ca. 680–645 B.C.).

They were certainly still being made in Persian times. A mound studied in 1976 (BT 76?) appears to be Hellenistic, as was the spectacularly located mound near Belevi on the road to Ephesus.[29] Reuse continued into Early Byzantine times, but at Sardis no mound appears to have been constructed in Roman times.

Many scholars have speculated on the origins of the mounds and on what cross-cultural associations their presence in Lydia suggests. The neighboring kingdom of Phrygia has been viewed as the immediate source;[30] parallels can be found from Greece through Anatolia.[31]

Perhaps the most intriguing parallel is with the mounds of Etruria. Herodotus (I.94)[32] relates that during a famine one part of the Lydian people under a king's son called Tyrsenos sailed from Smyrna to western Italy (Umbria), where they became the Tyrsenoi or Etruscans. One of the arguments in support of this alleged Lydian origin was presented by G. Dennis in his famous *Cities and Cemeteries of Etruria*,[33] unfortunately written before he had a chance to explore Bin Tepe at first hand (which he did ca. 1870–1882).[34]

Assuming that Herodotus' description implies five markers on top of the mound of Alyattes, Dennis found "a striking resemblance" to the so-called "Cucumella" in the Etruscan cemetery of Vulci[35] and to the tomb of the king Porsenna at Clusium, which supposedly had five pyramids on a square base of masonry, one at each corner and one in the center.[36] Dennis also commented on a supposed connection between Lydian mounds and a mound in the Monterozzi cemetery at Tarquinia.[37] The most obvious comparison is with the great cemetery of Banditaccia at Caere (Cervetri), where some 200 tumulus graves have been excavated and restored.[38] Many of them have crepides and rock-cut chamber tombs.

In September 1966, G. M. A. Hanfmann made a trip straight from the Gyges mound at Sardis to the tumuli at Cervetri. He noted that the mounds at Cervetri are very closely grouped and very steep-sided. (Of course, the Lydian mounds may have been steeper before erosion.) They are much smaller in diameter than most Lydian mounds. The careful rock-cut architecture of the earliest Etruscan tumuli is impressive but not in the same technical tradition as the cut masonry in the mound of Gyges (Figs. 102, 103). (The reliable tufa of Cervetri made cut masonry unnecessary.) The crepis profiles which in reproduction looked closest to Sardian examples, those of Tumulus I and Tumulus II,[39] were similar only in a general way: the rounded top element is not circular in section as in the mound of Gyges (Fig. 108); rather, it resembles a flattened cushion.

Since there are a great many varieties of Etruscan mounds, much more detailed studies and comparisons can be made.[40] The earliest Etruscan mounds, apparently dating from ca. 700 to 650 B.C.,[41] are nearly contemporary with the Gyges mound and other earlier Lydian mounds. They do not seem, however, to be the products of the same workshops, or even close in craftmanship. Rather, they are products of similar socioeconomic structures or models, expressions of royal and feudal classes anxious to show military power and wealth. There is no reason to deny that Etruscan seafaring corsairs were acquainted with the region of Smyrna, but the differences between the Lydian and Etruscan languages present obstacles for the assumption that a group of Asia Minor warriors, like the later Phocaeans, sailed away from home, gained power in Tuscany, and founded the Etruscan cities.

RUR

The Royal Mounds

The most imposing among the mounds are the three royal tombs of Alyattes, Gyges, and Tos or Tmolus, who may be Ardys, located along the Bin Tepe ridge. The largest of these mounds and clearly the one referred to by Herodotus is the Tomb of Alyattes (570–560 B.C.)[1] located at the east end of Bin Tepe ca. 3 km. south of the Gygean Lake (Koca Mutaf Tepe; Figs. 2, 96, 97, 99).[2]

Tunneled by ancient, probably Roman, tomb-robbers, the Tomb of Alyattes was first scientifically excavated in 1853 by Spiegelthal, who located the crepis and reached at least one chamber by tunneling.[3] His entrance, located on the south side, was closed by the time of Butler, who did not reopen it.[4] After being reopened by illicit diggers, it was partly explored and measured by the Harvard-Cornell Expedition beginning August 21, 1962 (Fig. 100).[5] Members of the Harvard-Cornell Expedition revisited the chamber area in 1980.

Of the five central markers on top of the mound mentioned by Herodotus,[6] only the broken remains of the largest one survived. It is made of hard karstic limestone and was still in fairly good condition in Spiegelthal's time, after which it was buried.[7] The stone was noted by Hanfmann in 1952 and 1957, but no trench was dug or exact measurements taken until 1962 when it was found dynamited into four pieces by treasure-hunters. Spiegelthal renders the shape as globular, but the preserved curvature suggests a budlike rise; the slope does not suggest a phallus as do some other Lydian markers.[8] As indicated by the worked upper surface of the base, the top may have been attached separately, while the base itself was perhaps fastened to a platform: such a platform was recorded by both Spiegelthal[9] and Hamilton;[10] only a few scattered tiles were found by the Harvard-Cornell archaeologists.

In 1962, the Harvard-Cornell Expedition mapped the tunnels (Fig. 100) but attempted no excavation. The chamber (Figs. 101, 102) was found to be located 30 m. southwest of the center of the mound, rather than almost 50 m. as Spiegelthal maintained, and is oriented north-south. Made of huge blocks of white marble, the ashlar masonry is four courses high and tied with iron clamps (Figs. 102, 103). One was found in the side of a block in the rear wall. The north wall (facing the door) may be double. The antechamber recorded by Spiegelthal was completely filled with rubble-fall in 1962. It was partly cleared by illicit diggers between 1976 and 1980. A follow-up exploration by Greenewalt revealed that the first ceiling block of the grave chamber and the sidewall block of the antechamber are not marble but limestone (Fig. 103).[11] We made no attempt to excavate the center of the mound, but there may be several more chambers or chamber-complexes; one of the tunnels led to a mighty marble beam, seemingly isolated ("Marble Block" in Fig. 100).

Because the tomb has been robbed repeatedly, few of its contents remained. Spiegelthal's finds included various Lydian and Greek potsherds, several lydia, and the upper half of a XXVI Dynasty Egyptian alabastron, now in the Ashmolean Museum.[12] In 1962 the lower parts of the two large lydia similar to those found by Spiegelthal were recovered at the exit from the chamber and 20 m. south of the mouth of the tunnel.[13] Two more sherds or lydia and a sherd of a delicately banded skyphos were found when the chamber was revisited in 1976.[14] Also discovered (first by Spiegelthal and confirmed by Carter and Hanfmann) was a pyre of oak ashes (Fig. 101), not from an open fire, on top of the chamber ceiling. This suggests the possibility of cremation, as does the legend of Croesus dying on his funeral pyre (Fig. 126).[15]

The Harvard-Cornell Expedition confirmed that the chamber was the earliest known marble masonry construction at Sardis. Comparisons of masonry techniques may indicate Egyptian and Phoenician or Ionian Greek influence. The roughened surface marble technique resembles work on the archaic marble sarcophagus from Samos,[16] while the chamber itself closely parallels in size, style, and appearance the chamber of the later tomb of Cyrus in Pasargadae. Especially notable in both is the use of an interior profile cornice running along the top course of the north and, in the Alyattes, part of the east walls.[17] Hanfmann suggests that the same masons who constructed the Alyattes chamber (ca. 570–560 B.C.) may have been employed by Cyrus when he took Lydian building crews to Pasargadae after he captured Sardis (547 B.C.).[18]

Based on a fragment of the archaic poet Hipponax,[19] the central "royal" mound, Karniyarik Tepe (BT 63.1), has been identified as that of King Gyges, founder of the Mermnad dynasty (ruled ca. 680–645 B.C.; Figs. 2, 98, 105).[20] It is located on the southern edge of a limestone ridge ca. 2 km. south of the Gygean Lake (Fig. 96). Rising majestically over the valley, it reaches a height of ca. 50 m. and measures more than 200 m. in diameter (Figs. 104, 105).[21] Gashes on the south and northeast sides show that it had been tunneled in ancient times. The mound was excavated by C. H. Greenewalt, Jr., during the 1963–1966 seasons[22] with assistance of a mining engineer and experienced miners (Fig. 112).

In 1963, D. Greenewalt used geophysical electrical resistivity techniques in the hope of locating an entrance; his observations helped to determine the ancient base of the mound (Fig. 107).[23] An oil-drilling rig generously lent by the University of Pennsylvania's Gordion expedition was operated in 1963 (Fig. 104), but all twenty-six soundings were stopped by pieces of limestone scattered throughout the mound without reaching depths greater than 14 m.[24]

Tunneling revealed that the mound was composed of alternating layers of harder red clays and softer, sandy, greenish clay earth. Limestone chips and chunks permeated the mass (Fig. 112); a layer of riverstones and rubble was encountered 23 m. in from the entrance.[25] No chamber was found, but a large number of tunnels were discovered. In all, 130 m. of the ancient tunnels were excavated or investigated (Fig. 106).[26]

An important dating find was a broken but completely restorable plain ware buff jug, probably Roman (Fig. 111; P 64.365:6480), found 63.57 m. from the entrance on the floor of niche "N" in tunnel "L" (Fig. 106, "pot"). On the basis of a color slide, R. de Vaux assigned it to the late first or early second century A.D.[27]

The most important find was the great Lydian crepis wall (Figs. 108, 109, "Lydian wall").[28] Discovered ca. 44 m. from the center of the mound, it may be a retaining wall for a smaller mound some 90 m. in diameter.[29] The unfinished wall was built of locally quarried limestone blocks.

Several signs were discovered along the course of the wall.[30] One monogram, deeply graven, appears a total of twenty-five times, with two groups of twelve each along both ashlar courses (Figs. 109, 110).[31] It may be read in a number of ways, but it is clear that the signs represent a combination of letters right side up (reading to left) and upside down; four signs are reversed. Two readings have been suggested: Hanfmann proposed two gammas and two upsilons, spelling *GuGu,* the name of Gyges in the Assyrian records. R. Gusmani tentatively accepts this,[32] but points out that in this case the letters would be Greek rather than Lydian. He suggests an alternative reading of two digammas and two epsilons, spelling *Veve,* but admits that this yields no satisfactory meaning.[33]

The signs may be masons' marks, but their size and depth of engraving set them apart from the several other signs found. These include: one upside-down alpha; what may be one Lydian "S" sign on its side; one horizontal bar theta; and two pairs of lightly sketched swastikas, one above the other, with traces of red paint.[34]

The finds from the mound were diverse. On the surface a coin of Constantine (A.D. 335–341; C 63.741) was found in the south scarp. The trench in the northeast gash produced a Lydian skyphos rim (P 66.71:7093); the east trench contained bones, plain coarse pottery, and sherds of Byzantine or Islamic "sgraffito" ware.[35] Inside the mound, the layer of riverstones and rubble contained three fragments of Lydian pottery, while the fill from tunnel "L" yielded lumps of charcoal, fragments of sheet-bronze, and tiny sherds of thin skyphoi, possibly Protocorinthian (P 64.233:6295).[36] A vein of ashy debris encountered in the eastern "Lydian wall" tunnel above the upper ashlar course contained bones and Lydian sherds, including fragments from a terracotta "bread-pan" (T 65.6:6657) and a lamp (L 65.4:6656).[37] Also found in the eastern crepis wall tunnel were fragments of a Lydian shoulder-drop oinochoe (P 65.92:6710; restored) and other sherds.[38] Sherds and fragmentary finds were scattered through the mound. The fragments seem to date from the seventh or early sixth century B.C.,[39] suggesting that the mound was enlarged at this time.

If the date of the inner mound, based on the rule of Gyges (ca. 680–645 B.C.), is correct, it is the earliest datable funerary mound construction in Lydia. C. Nylander has shown that the masonry of the Lydian crepis wall (Figs. 108, 109) has close affinities with the Tall-i Takht monument in Pasargadae;[40] yet the Gyges mound wall may be one hundred years older than any Achaemenian construction.[41]

The westernmost royal mound, Kir Mutaf Tepe (BT 63.4), is located ca. 1.2 km. south of the Gygean Lake (Fig. 2) and is the most enigmatic of the three great mounds. Nicander seems to have labeled it as the tomb of Tmolus; a very corrupt Hipponax fragment refers to a Tos; J. Pedley has proposed that the original reading may in fact have been Atys or Ardys.[42] It has not been scientifically excavated; there are unsubstantiated rumors of ancient robber tunnels running through it. Kir Mutaf Tepe seems to contain more broken limestone than the other two royal mounds and would be the most difficult to tunnel. It is the second highest of the mounds, with a photogrammetric survey marker of 209.08 m. a.s.l., and has a diameter of ca. 300 m. Some ashlar masonry bulldozed in building the road past the south side of the mound may come from the crepis.[43]

RUR

Rock-Cut Chamber Tombs

Not all the Lydian tombs were built of limestone masonry; Butler states that rock-cut chamber tombs were the commonest form of burial in Lydian Sardis. Most of these tombs were cut into the cliffs along the west side of the Pactolus River (Figs. 9, 90). After excavating more than a thousand tombs, Butler described their general types as follows.[1]

The ordinary type was entered through a dromos, open to the sky at the beginning and covered at the end next to the tomb. The doorway at the end of the dromos was covered by a large slab of stone, smaller slabs, or with crude rubble walls laid in clay.[2] On the other side of the door was a chamber hewn of solid clay with a pitched ceiling. On either side of the narrow passage through the chamber was a couch hewn out of conglomerate. At the end of this chamber was either a double couch approached by steps, or a doorway leading to a second, similar chamber. Some tombs contained terracotta sarcophagi[3] or bits of rotted wood and metal details indicating that the dead were carried on wooden biers.[4] Although only a few stelae were found, Butler thought it likely that the entrance to each tomb was marked by one or two stelai. No traces of any other architectural ornament were found in the tombs.

One variant was a single-chamber tomb, of which a good example is Butler's Tomb 813 (Fig. 113).[5] The oblong chamber contained four limestone sarcophagi, some pottery, and a few small gold items.[6] A sarcophagus embedded in the floor contained the bones of a large man with his head pierced by a pointed instrument.[7] The tomb is dated by an Attic vase of ca. 500–480 B.C.[8] One single-chamber tomb (Tomb 43) held the first important collection of Lydian pottery (Fig. 127).[9]

A very rare type of chamber tomb had an inner room reached by a flight of stairs descending from the end of the passage between the couches of the first chamber.

Many tombs of irregular plan were excavated along the bluffs of the Pactolus south of the city and in the sides of deep ravines opening onto the river valley.

The three tombs excavated by the Harvard-Cornell Expedition in July 1959 (Fig. 114:a, b) generally correspond to Butler's descriptions.[10] The tombs are located in a small valley above the vineyard of Hasan Dursun ca. 1 km. from the Artemis Temple. They lie on the side of a hollow in which the valley ends[11] and open toward the east.

Tomb 59.1 (Fig. 114) consists of a single chamber with recessed benches on either side of the central passage. Two holes, ca. 1 m. in diameter, open into Tomb 59.3 from an irregular area at the rear of the tomb. Only a few fragments of a terracotta sarcophagus (no number) were found.

Tomb 59.2 (Fig. 114), which is ca. 15 m. north of Tomb 59.1, is a double-chambered tomb with a dromos leading to a door with a recessed border designed to receive a sealing slab. There is a roughly triangular area above the door. On the right (north) side of the flat-roofed first chamber was a bench with the bottom of a terracotta sarcophagus *in situ*. A rectangular door leads to the second chamber; it had a rock-cut horseshoe bench. A tub-shaped terracotta sarcophagus with a broad rim was set into the floor. Objects: alabastron of alabaster, P 59.241:1610;[12] P 59.247:1624; fragment of a Lydian lekythos (no number).[13]

A 2-m. dromos leads into the first chamber of Tomb 59.3 (Fig. 114). It had no benches. An L-shaped corridor leads to the second chamber, which has two benches on either side of the passage. Sarcophagi of coarse red clay which broke when lifted and a vaulted lid with a pattern of lozenges in cretaceous white and crimson red and bands of black (T 59.13:1608) were found. One Lydian sherd[14] was found in the first chamber, three in the second chamber.[15]

The earth was so clean and finds so few that these tombs were probably excavated by Butler.

At Sardis, the earliest rock-cut tombs may go back to the seventh century B.C.[16] A study of the records and pottery surviving from the first Sardis expedition indicated to G. M. A. Hanfmann that the earliest imported Greek pieces from the tombs appear to be Corinthian or Eastern Greek, no earlier than 600 B.C., though some of the Lydian pots may be earlier.[17]

Apart from tombs of the Hellenistic or Roman period, the rock-cut chamber tombs seem to have been designed for inhumation. In a few unplundered examples found by Butler, the richly decorated garments, jewelry, seals, mirrors, and metal vessels, as well as large sets of pottery for food and drink, make up the standard equipment of grave goods.

The rock-cut chamber tombs first appear in Asia Minor perhaps in the eighth century B.C. and spread rapidly through the mountainous regions of the peninsula.[18] In Lydia they occur from the Mysian/Lydian frontier northwest of Soma to the edge of the highlands near Uşak (Güre).[19] None of the Lydian examples known

are earlier than the seventh century B.C.; they flourish in the Persian era and may at Sardis go down to Early Hellenistic times.[20]

GMAH

Furnishings

Of the furnishings the tombs originally contained, only the existence of couches can be directly inferred from the finds. Evidence for these has been found in at least eight of the tumulus chamber tombs at Sardis, consisting either of the couches themselves or of cuts or specially finished areas prepared in the walls and floors to receive them. Of the known couches only two were made of wood, the others being of limestone (often the same limestone as the walls); the design of the stone couches betrays derivation from wooden prototypes.[1]

Only one tomb (BT 63.2) contained sufficient remains to give some idea of the prototype. The remains of the couch consist of two boards mortised to a vertical piece; metal attachment-plates still retained fragments of the cloth presumably used for slung webbing.[2] The limestone couch from BK 71.1 provides further evidence for a design based on a wooden frame with slung cloth webbing. Raised rectangular blocks placed all along the raised border suggest original posts for securing stretched cloth. The double-volute scroll design cut into the two uprights (Figs. 116, 117) also suggests a wooden prototype.

The stone couches, with one exception, appear to have been made of three slabs: two upright "legs" and a covering "bed" slab. An exception was found in BT 66.2, where the couch was actually a platform cut into the bedrock. Many couches were found smashed, but as far as can be determined all had either a bevel-cut oval depression or a raised border around the top of the "bed" slab.[3]

The couches found by the Harvard-Cornell Expedition were usually quite plain; as noted, the one from BK 71.1 (Figs. 116, 117) has a simple scroll design, but nothing approaching the more elaborate palmette and scroll designs shown by Choisy[4] or the figured friezes with deer and horsemen found by Dennis.[5] The others are plainer; those from T 77.1 have only a simple recess cut into the "bed" slab, continuing the lines of the "legs" as decoration.

Conspicuously absent are the raised stone "pillows" mentioned by Choisy. Choisy also noticed the use of color; no traces of color were found by the Harvard-Cornell Expedition. However, a laminar organic substance consisting of a layer of resin between two other layers of indeterminate nature was discovered pressed into the depressions of the "bed" slabs in T 77.1; this may have had some funereal significance.[6]

In a Greek vase painting Croesus sits on a throne on his pyre (Fig. 126), and Pryce thought that the two Bin Tepe figured friezes found by Dennis might come from either a couch or a throne.[7] Wives taking part in "funerary meals" are shown seated on stools or couches (cf. Fig. 138); food and drink are served on little tables, and there are footstools. So far, no traces of thrones, stools, or tables have been observed in the chamber tombs.[8]

GMAH

Cist Graves

Cist graves have been found in various locations.[1] In the city area they occur among the chamber tombs in the great Necropolis cemeteries (Indere) and in the burials up the wadis of the east bank of the Pactolus (for example, against the Pyramid Tomb); sometimes they are cut into the floors of the chamber tombs. There has not so far been evidence of any Lydian or Persian cemetery which consisted of only cist graves, though there may have been some with such burials and sarcophagi surrounding only a few chamber tombs (as, perhaps, at Şeytan Dere).

The graves may just be rock-cut, or lined with slabs (usually greenish-gray schist). They may be covered with limestone, or, more comonly, schist slabs, and/or may contain sarcophagi (especially terracotta sarcophagi). There seems to be no general set orientation.

The natural assumption is that these were the graves of the less affluent people who could not afford family chamber tombs; but the silver and gold jewelry found in Indere show that they were not always paupers' burials. There may be some evidence of a cremation of humans or objects (see below, G 61.2).

While fairly common in later eras, cist burials are surprisingly scarce during the Lydian period. Reuse in later times is possible (see BT 66.5, below); some sarcophagi were certainly reused (see Haci Oglan, below).

Indere Region: G 61.1 and G 61.2

These two graves are located on a hillside below Necropolis Ridge and at 1180 m. west of the Artemis Temple (Fig. 129); they are 3–4 m. apart and buried at D.: 0.40–1.50 m. They were opened by illicit diggers in 1961; C. H. Greenewalt, Jr., conducted the follow-up excavation and published a detailed study.[2]

G 61.1 (Fig. 118:l.), oriented east–west, consists of two (perhaps originally three) schist slabs over a floor of tamped earth. Finds: two lydia (P 61.8:3143, P 61.9:3144); uncatalogued: one lekythos-jug (see n. 1).

G 61.2 (Fig. 118:r.), oriented north–south, is chest-like, with one schist slab for each wall and three for the cover; L.: 2.08 m.; W.: 0.70 m.; D.: 0.80 m.; cover slabs: L.: 1.60–1.65 m.; W.: 0.65 m.; Th.: 0.15 m. The floor of tamped earth yielded traces of fir (bits of cabonized wood), while the finds showed no evidence of burning; this may indicate a cremation. Pottery finds date the grave to ca. 575–540 B.C. according to Greenewalt, roughly contemporaneous with the Alyattes Mound. Finds:[3] The pottery includes two Lydian white-slip orientalizing skyphoi painted with birds and fish (P 61.1:3130, A & B); large Lydian marbled bowl with bolster-spool handles (P 61.5:3135);[4] a rosette bowl (P 61.6:3136); two streaked skyphoi (P 61.3:3132) (all in Fig. 119); an Ionian black-glaze banded kylix (P 61.2:3131); and a black on red jar (P 61.7:3141). Among the other objects are a stone alabastron (S 61.1:3134); a ribbed, granulated gold bead (J 61.1:3126; Fig. 121); an oblong onyx bead pendant with gold wire attachment (J 61.2:3127; Fig. 122); a silver hawk pendant (J 61.3:3128; Fig. 120); a round lead token (M 61.1:3129); uncatalogued: one lydion, one streaked skyphos, one lekythos-jug, two closed vessels, plain bluff bowl fragments, bone fragments; 156 sheep knucklebones; shells (from astragal games?); and bits of carbonized wood.

Bin Tepe: BT 63.3

This is a tumulus cist burial, located just southwest of the giant Kir Mutaf Tepe (63.4). The mound, much reduced in height, rises 4 m. above the surrounding fields to 163.48 m. a.s.l.; diameter is ca. 26 m.

D. Greenewalt tested this tumulus (along with several others) with geophysical location techniques and found promisingly high resistivity on its south flank; a shallow test-trench was dug, but it was not excavated until 1966 after the grave was opened by illicit diggers.[5]

Digging revealed layers of soil strata: loose brown earth, hard gray clay, yellow sand, and gravel with a double layer of pebbles running through the mound at grave-top level. The burial was located at ca. 2.5 m. southwest and 3.8 m. below the present center, oriented east-west.

The grave is rectangular and made of rubble packing which rises ca. 2.0 m. above the floor; it is covered with two schist slabs. L.: ca. 1.40 m.; W.: ca. 0.90 m.; D.: 1.05 m. (plus coverslabs). The back of a female protome (P 66.110:7154) of fine Samian workmanship[6] dates the grave to 575–550 B.C., contemporaneous with Indere Grave G 61.2 and the Alyattes Mound; its proximity to Kir Mutaf Tepe may indicate a family relationship. Finds: a female protome; an Ionian red and white banded cup (P 66.109:7153); a black and red aryballos (P 66.111:7155); a black on white jar (P 66.112: 7156); a white marble alabastron (S 66.15:7152).

BT 66.5: Located 1300 m. north-northeast of the Alyattes Mound in Duman Tepe Area, this rock-cut cist grave has no mound (Fig. 123); it was excavated in 1966. It is rectangular, oriented north–south, at 103.12 m. a.s.l.; L.: 1.91 m.; W.: 1.08 m.; D.: 0.51–0.54 m. The bedrock walls are trimmed with a pick or pointed chisel; the surrounding bedrock is leveled to accommodate the two heavy coverslabs (L: 1.50, 1.60; W.: 1.48, 1.04; D.: 0.35 M.). Pot finds date either the tomb or its reuse to Hellenistic times, ca. 200 B.C. or later. Three strikingly similar cist graves were found among the tumulus graves northwest of Soma.[7] Finds: Hellenistic relief ware (P 66.118:7163, A & B); two shoulder-pieces of flasks (P 66.117: 7162, A & B); indeterminate bone fragments.

Kuş Tepe: east of the Alyattes Mound and southeast of Balik Hane (Fig. 96, location) two graves, possibly cist burials, were reported by villagers; the Harvard-Cornell Expedition was unable to locate them or to find any evidence of mound or chamber construction.[8] The local informants brought in several finds: two lydia (P 66.89:7119, A & B); a Roman jug (P 66.108:7146); and a bronze bowl from a terracotta sarcophagus (M 66.12:7147).

A curious variant is a cist grave composed of reused (or unused?) architectural terracotta tiles (slabs), described by Shear as "sarcophagus." A skeleton had with it important Lydian pottery, notably two large amphorae, similar in style to the huge amphorae found in a domestic context in NEW, and datable to ca. 600–550 B.C.[9]

RUR

Sarcophagi

The Harvard-Cornell Expedition's discovery of stone and terracotta sarcophagi in some Lydian graves has contributed to better knowledge of this type of burial during the Lydian Period. While most of the sarcophagi were broken into or displaced, grave goods were recovered from a few of them. The paucity of finds appears to have been true for the Butler excavations as well; Butler states that the presence of sarcophagi is no indication of wealth and that in tombs with both couches and sarcophagi, more finds were associated with the couches than with the sarcophagi.[1]

Discovered in 1966, the Şeytan Dere Cemetery lies on top of the south side of a gorge 280 m. north of the excavation camp (W125/S760; Figs. 8:54; 129). G 66.2 was a limestone sarcophagus in situ (L.: 2.73 m. from handle to handle; H.: 1.13 m.) with a bathtub-shaped body and similarly shaped lid, a large part of which was missing. The burial was disturbed in antiquity. The principal finds were several complete Lydian vases[2] and disintegrated arm and skull fragments in situ at the south end. A large circular hole in the northwest corner of the lid suggested to the excavator that a lekythos was put into the sarcophagus through this hole. A second, later burial is indicated by the fragments of Hellenistic unguentaria.[3] In the cemetery were also found two phallic markers (NoEx 66.1 and 66.2) and a fragment of a Lydian stele (NoEx 66.14) of ca. 550–530 B.C.[4]

The continued use of Lydian bathtub sarcophagi into the Hellenistic period is substantiated by two graves located in Haci Oglan 850 m. west of PN and 490 m. south of the Salihli highway.[5] Both graves contained large "half-marble" sarcophagi with roof-shaped lids in situ (Figs. 124, 125). Both were also broken into in ancient times, although there were still some objects associated with the graves. They are discussed in Chapter VII under "Graves and Cemeteries."

Two displaced stone sarcophagi have been discovered. One-half of a Lydian-Hellenistic oval limestone sarcophagus, which K. J. Frazer believes is from a nearby tomb, was found in the Artemis Precinct.[6] An infant's sarcophagus of reddish limestone (NoEx 71.4; L.: 0.70 m.; W.: 0.345 m.; H.: 0.22 m.) was found in the vineyard directly east of the Synagogue.

Two other sarcophagi were reused in and near Church E. G 62.1[7] lies alongside the north side of the church. Islamic coins, identified by G. S. Miles as Sarukhan of 1374–1388 (C 62.186 and 62.187) and Ottoman of 1359–1390 (C 62.188), were found inside the sarcophagus. The burial may actually have been earlier than this, shortly after the construction of the church in 1220–1250.[8] Another sarcophagus was reused as a water container, probably during the fourteenth century or later.[9]

Terracotta sarcophagi were found in the chamber tombs in the vineyard of Hasan Dursun.[10] A few fragments of terracotta sarcophagi were found in T 59.1. The first chamber of T 59.2 held the bottom of a sarcophagus *in situ*. In the second chamber was a tub-shaped sarcophagus with a broad rim (L.: 1.95 m.; W.: 0.67 m.; H.: 0.37 m.). T 59.3 held sarcophagi of coarse red clay which broke when lifted. Gravegoods associated with the tombs were not from the sarcophagi.

An empty Lydian terracotta sarcophagus (L.: 1.53 m.; W.: 0.44 m.; H.: 0.21 m.) was found in a niche (GR 60) cut out of conglomerate just west of the Pyramid Tomb.[11] West and somewhat above GR 60 was part of a second terracotta sarcophagus[12] (L.: 0.58 cm.; W.: 51.2 cm.). Bone fragments were found outside the walls,[13] and Lydian lekythoi of late shape may belong here (P 61.511 and 61.573). The grave may date in the Persian era, after the construction of the Pyramid Tomb, sometime between 547 and 334 B.C.

The new sarcophagi all have a broad rim; the caskets may be rectangular or bathtub shape. Among the sarcophagi illustrated by Butler is one with a preserved tall lid which suggests a wooden chest with metal bands[14] The new sarcophagi display traces of painted patterns: crimson lozenges on white, and black and crimson bands, both perhaps imitating textiles.

Even if they were poorly fired and disintegrated from wetness, the firing of such large sarcophagi was a pretty difficult ceramic achievement. They were probably first made in the Greek cities of the coast, where Smyrna and Clazomenae had workshops producing elaborately painted sarcophagi.[15] A somewhat later group in the Cayster valley had vault-like lids and rectangular panels decorated with reliefs.[16] Neither figurative paintings nor reliefs are known in Sardis, where the use of terracotta sarcophagi seems to begin not later than the mid-sixth century B.C. and cease before the Hellenistic period.

GMAH

Lydian Burial Rites and Beliefs

To the Lydians, the dead mattered. During the time of the Lydian kingdom and in the Persian era, they made a great investment of labor, probably by corvée,[1] in pouring over one hundred large mounds at Bin Tepe and elsewhere and in cutting laboriously over a thousand graves into the cliffs of the Pactolus Valley. Despite the known risks of robbery, substantial investment of material values was carried by the dead to their graves, including much gold and silver and the finest garments. How keenly the Lydians were concerned about not being disturbed in their resting places is shown by the Lydian inscriptions, which put the graves under the protection of Artemis and other divinities and threaten the violators with divine vengeance.

Cremation and Inhumation

In the Early Iron Age, cremation spread widely through the Eastern Mediterranean and Asia Minor.[2] At Sardis, the Early Bronze Age burials had been inhumations, and the Late Bronze Age burial in the Lydian Market was a cremation burial. The evidence for any continuity of cremation is quite uncertain. The occurrence of carbonized matter, not clearly identified as human bones, cannot be taken as safe evidence for the cist grave Indere 61.2. A layer of ashes on top of the Alyattes mound chamber and the legend that Croesus burned himself on a pyre (Fig. 126) led Hanfmann to propose that the Lydian kings continued an old Hittite-Anatolian custom and were cremated; the Hittite kings were apparently cremated.[3] All other Lydian burials found by us were inhumations. Cremation did not become popular at Sardis until Hellenistic times.[4]

Physical Remains

Because all graves excavated by the Harvard-Cornell Expedition were disturbed, usually only chancy, scattered fragments of skeletal material were found, enough to prove inhumation and, in some cases, to guess at the age group. Thus in three graves of Duman Tepe (BT 66.2, 66.3, 66.6) were three young adults, one of whom was male, and one a child of 11–12 years. Two young adults, one male and one female, were in one sarcophagus at Haci Oglan (61.3; Fig. 125). Their skulls were at the north end, but other disturbed bones were heaped up in the center and at the south end. The skull of a man under 40 was in the center of the sarcophagus (Haci Oglan 61.4), definitely disturbed once or twice. The sarcophagus burial at Şeytan Dere, 66.2, had fragments of skull near the south end; other bone fragments were scattered.[5] Butler found three intact sarcophagus burials, one of which contained the skeleton of a 17-year-old girl, another "the bones of an old man," and the third, only white dust.[6] Yet another sarcophagus in Butler's Tomb 813 (ca. 500 B.C.) contained the bones of a large man, "whose head was pierced in front with an instrument, making the wound which probably caused his death." Shear reported a skeleton found in the tile grave of ca. 550 B.C., west of the Pactolus (near "H").[7] In 1882 Dennis found a skeleton lying on a bench but suspected that it represented a secondary, Roman burial.[8] The condition of the skeletal material found by the Harvard-Cornell Expedition in the graves did not permit detailed measurements and deductions; at most, one may say that a high percentage of Lydians appear to have died young.[9]

Not a regular grave, but an emergency burial in a stone-lined pit in the Lydian Market (HoB) area yielded the disarticulated skeletal remains of two men, two women, and a child, perhaps from one family. They were apparently victims of the destruction of Sardis by the Kimmerians around the middle of the seventh century B.C.[10]

Deposition, Gravegoods, and Offerings

The skulls of Şeytan Dere 66.2 and of Haci Oglan 61.3 indicate that the bodies were laid on their backs. The deepened body outlines on stone couches indicate the same position; and the skeleton found by Dennis was lying on its back.[11] Couches and biers appear to have been covered with textiles (BT 63.2). Our finds at Indere (see above, "Cist Graves," and Fig. 118) confirm that the dead were buried with all their personal gold and silver jewelry, bracelets, necklaces, earrings, finger rings, gems, and seals. They wore gorgeous dresses with gold ornaments stitched on, such as the dresses of the Persian era with Ahura Mazda, Achaemenid sphinxes, and rosettes (Fig. 163).[12] The best picture of a Lydian burial was gained by Butler in an intact terracotta sarcophagus discovered in 1913. It contained "a small skeleton flanked on either side by rows of alabastra. Above the head were gold fillets for binding the hair. Below, where the ears had been, were two gold rings like clusters of berries; upon the breast bone a necklace composed of beads of finest granular work with pendant spangles. Upon the finger bone was a fine seal ring with a lion signet cut into the gold bezel. About the feet lay gold beads and other small ornaments . . . had been sewn onto the dress." This was the 17-year-old "bride" whose skeleton was mentioned above.[13]

Mirrors of silver and bronze, toilet boxes adorned with golden lions, bronze jugs, silver drinking bowls (phiale), and ladles were among the metal objects found by Butler.[14] The remarkable find (1922) of thirty gold staters of Croesus in a small pot in the destroyed chamber tomb in the north fork of Şeytan Dere seems to be a hidden treasure rather than a personal possession; however, money was rumored to have been found in the chamber of BT 62.4. Butler's tomb with the fine Achaemenid jewelry (Fig. 163) also contained two silver sigloi of Artaxerxes I or II (465–404; 404–349 B.C.).[15]

Apart from jewelry and mirrors, few distinctive objects differentiate between men and women. An iron spearhead was found in the chamber of BT 62.4.[16]

Of ca. forty graves excavated or investigated by the Harvard-Cornell Expedition, none was undisturbed and all were filled with drift-in earth. Only the Şeytan Dere 66.2 sarcophagus and the Indere cist burial 61.2 had retained a substantial portion of gravegoods, and some reconstructible objects came from the large cist grave BT 63.2.[17] Other tombs contained at most fragments.[18] This was, in general, also the experience of Dennis, Butler, and Shear. The four undisturbed sarcophagi burials discovered by Butler have not been published in detail.[19]

Offerings deposited outside the grave are known in many parts of Greece.[20] It is possible that the four clay alabastra (for oil?) neatly laid in a row and a Hellenistic unguentarium outside the sarcophagus Haci Oglan 61.3 (Fig. 125) were deposited by the family rather than by grave robbers.[21] A secondary offering of a Lydian (perfume?) lekythos is likely for Şeytan Dere 66.2; the vessel lay under a hole in the lid, high above the drift-in earth. Finally, the charcoal observed above the chamber of Alyattes, in tumulus BK 71.1, and possibly in Indere 61.2 might be considered evidence for burning of gravegoods in a pyre for objects,[22] but no certain trace of objects was found.

The standard equipment included vessels for food and drink, and for perfumes and ointments. A modest chest grave like Indere 61.2 (Fig. 118) yielded nine drinking cups and bowls, two water bottles, one eating plate ("bowl"), as well as three oil perfume containers (lydion; lekythos, Fig. 119). The complete and incomplete vessels from the sarcophagus Şeytan Dere 66.2 add up (for the primary Lydian burial) to ten drinking cups, one pouring vase, and one perfume vase. The large plundered cist grave BT 63.2 had a water jar (hydria), two drinking cups, and three oil/perfume containers. A specialized form, the elongated alabastron of alabaster, clay, or glass, is attested from most of the graves.[23] A complete or near-complete inventory was excavated by Butler in a notable large but collapsed "cist" grave similar to BT 63.2. Thirty-six vessels included such rare forms as a side-spouted strainer (for beer? for yogurt?), a trick-vase with a ram's head, and a boat-shaped vase.[24]

Apparently, the vessels were placed next to, and in some cases, on the body. Owing to the constant reuses and disturbances, virtually nothing can be said about the disposition of the pottery in the tomb. Dennis observed some vessels standing on the floor of a chamber tomb at Bin Tepe that he thought were Roman; and Butler shows some vessels standing on a bench but does not elucidate.[25] There seems to be no reliable information about the contents of the various pottery vessels. Greek parallels suggest that both water and wine were offered.[26]

Shells of fresh-water clams (mussels) and possibly of marine oysters may represent remnants of food offerings but may also be intended as decoration; they also occur in Greek burials.[27]

Knucklebones appear to be intended for game pieces, even when found in great numbers as in Indere 61.2; again the practice is paralleled in Greece.[28]

Whether or not the living entered the chambers of the dead to offer food and drink on stated occasions (cf. Figs. 138, 146) is not known. That Pythes/Pythios, as a kind of living dead, withdrew into his chamber and had food sent there may echo a native ritual.[29]

On his pyre Croesus pours a libation to Apollo (Fig. 126);[30] and it is striking that so many wine cups, jugs, and mixing bowls (craters) are among the gravegoods. A possible libation hole was found in the ceiling of Chamber II in BT 66.1; a similar hole was observd by S. Kasper in the chamber of the tumulus at Belevi, where a bowl underneath suggested that libations were poured from above.[31] We have found no instance of objects "killed"—intentionally smashed or burned on a pyre—to make them usable for the dead.[32]

The canid skeleton in a lime puddle found in the dromos of tumulus tomb BT 62.4 might be a sacrifice of a favorite dog dispatched to join his owner, but the bones of a small dog were found in a jar in the large cist grave BT 63.2, and canid bones were scattered in the chamber of BT 66.3. This poses the question of whether the sacrifice of dogs might not have been part of a propitiatory ritual directed to "Hermes the Dog Throttler" (Candaules), the probable recipient of dogs sacrificed in the ritual meals found in the city—especially if like Hermes Psychopompos he conducted the dead.[33] Unfortunately, Sardis peasant lore is replete with stories of small modern dogs disappearing into tumuli and tombs; and so the matter must remain undecided until better evidence appears.

Given the habitual reuse of chamber tombs by shepherds, no other animal bones can be associated with safety with Lydian funerary sacrifices.[34]

Markers, Stelai, and Divine Protection

The markers over the tumuli were rounded stones, some suggestive of buds, others recalling phalli. They were suitable memorials for kings. Five crowned the mound of Alyattes, but they were also used for lesser men. It is remarkable that no stelai inscribed in Lydian, Aramaic, or Greek have been reported from Bin Tepe, although we know the Alyattes mound had inscriptions.[35] Two markers were found at the Şeytan Dere cemetery, one in the west bank of the Pactolus across from the camp. It is probable that they were used over either chamber tombs or cist graves or sarcophagi in the urban cemeteries.[36] Only the monograms and letters of the Gyges crepis survive (Figs. 109, 110). Within the city area, it must have been the stelai in front of the grave which carried the owner's name and requested divine protection of the grave, with curses against the violators and fines to be paid to the protecting divinity.[37] Butler believed that originally each group of chambers had two such stelai at the entrance to the tomb (Fig. 113) and that many had painted inscriptions, which now are gone.[38] Three fragments of inscribed funerary stelai have been found by the Harvard-Cornell Expedition; two of them have Persian regnal dates; one invokes Artemis as protectress.[39] These stelai begin around the mid-sixth century (540 B.C.); one with the important Lydian-Aramaic inscription is dated 394 B.C.; and a late example is dated 330/329 B.C. by the reign of Alexander.[40]

An archaic stele portrays the dead as a scribe, with his dog (Fig. 159); other "portraits" show the dead man and his wife feasting, as they also do on the pediment of a temple-tomb (Fig. 138).[41] Other motifs are decorative (Fig. 128), just possibly allusive to the life and revival of vegetation.[42]

Among the gods invoked, Artemis of Sardis (*sfardak*), of Koloe (*kulumśiś*, twice), of Ephesus (*ibiśiś*, five times) is far ahead; but *Qldans* (possibly a Moon god?), *Santaś*, an old Anatolian god, the less known *Marivda*, and finally *Kufavk* (*Kuvava*-Cybele) also act as protectors and avengers. It is noteworthy that in the Lydian-Aramaic text of 394 B.C. both Artemis of Koloe and Artemis of Ephesus are invoked.[43] So far, neither the Lydian Zeus (*Levs*) nor the popular Bacchus-Dionysus (*Baki*) appear.[44]

The stelai appear to give the Lydian terms for inscription (*sadmes*), stele (*anlola, mrud*) and tomb (*vana*). With better knowledge of Lydian, they will provide information on family relationships, property regulations, and status of the dead.[45]

The protection-malediction (curses) formulae are well known in Semitic religions; they may have come from Semitic areas with the Aramaic-speaking officials and traders of the Persian empire and thus would date from the Persian period. Such stelai with Persian figurative motifs and Aramaic curse inscriptions have been found at the satrapal center of Dascylion.[46]

The Cemeteries

The location of Sardian cemeteries (Fig. 129) seems to have been determined by natural features of landscape and by economic, social, and religious considerations. Bin Tepe took a vast area away from potential cultivation; probably it was still swampy and was used for grazing. As Choisy observed, the tumuli of Bin Tepe are grouped on natural ridges. The groupings of mounds, such as the so-called "Seven Brothers" standing on one ridge, may represent clans of phylai (Fig. 98). King Alyattes and many others (Fig. 104) looked south toward the city.[47] Others looked east–west, some possibly toward their overlords. In the network of dirt roads, major arteries passed the few known springs. The "plan" of the royal cemetery was spacious and informal.

The cemeteries in the cliffs of the Pactolus and its tributaries occupied another type of useless ground (Figs. 9, 129)—dry, precipitous, and stony. In striking contrast to Bin Tepe, the chamber tombs, tier after tier, were a kind of "high-rise" city of the dead, quite densely packed. Butler conjectured, probably rightly, that projecting terraces had carried zig-zag paths up to the various "stories." He distinguished a west cemetery on the west bank (Figs. 9, 90) from a south cemetery and a southwest cemetery. The south cemetery (Fig. 129) at least included tombs on the east bank. It is clear that the dead in the west cemetery were looking directly east, to Artemis, their protectress.[48] This was also the case with the Şeytan Dere sarcophagus (G 66.2), where the dead looked south toward the Artemis Precinct. One might argue that this cemetery lay alongside (east) the road from the Artemis Temple to the Agora;[49] but this area between the Artemis Temple and PN presents many problems since it appears that initial Lydian habitation was in some places followed by Lydian (Persian) chamber tombs.[50] One senses in any case that the separation of the urban settlement areas from sepulchers was not absolute; the precipitous walls of the torrent gorges (wadis) harbored the dead, and the slopes and flat areas on top of and between the gorges, the houses of the living. On the other hand, we have no evidence that there were extramural cemeteries outside the city walls, along the east–west highway, as there were in Hellenistic and Roman times.[51]

Conclusions

Early in the seventh century B.C., probably linked with the rise of the Lydian kingdom, a great expansion and transformation occurred in Lydian culture.[52] In the funerary sphere, the vast Royal Cemetery with its mounds (Figs. 96–98, 104), the rock-cut tombs around the city (Figs. 9, 90, 114), even the stone sarcophagi (Figs. 124, 125) seem to make their first appearance around this time. They have different origins and meanings. Whether inspired by Homeric heroes or Phrygian kings, the earth mound and its markers are primarily memorials to great men; they tell nothing about the fate of the dead.[53] The chamber tomb, whether built or rock-cut, is definitely "the eternal house," or even the eternal bedroom. That the dead sleep seems to be emphasized in Lydia. This does not exclude eternal feasting, but the evidence is much less explicit than in Etruscan or Lycian wall paintings. The pediment of a "satrapal" tomb (Fig. 138) and two funerary meal stelai indicate that the concept of the feasting dead might have gained ground in the Persian era.[54]

The sarcophagus may be house-shaped or shaped like a tub (Fig. 124). It is tempting to interpret the latter shape as a wine-vat. The occurrence of many wine-vessels among the grave-goods may argue that in the city where the Lydian Dionysus (Baki) was born and the use of the name "Bakivalis," "belonging to Dionysus," was frequent, there may have germinated some belief in divine Bacchic immortality. But no Lydian inscriptions provide explicit testimony.[55]

A hint of another concept may be discerned in the occurrence of boats, either of wood or of clay. In the story told by Plutarch, a boat brings food to the tomb chamber of the would-be dead Pythes/Pythios.[56] The boat might also be a symbol for the dead going west, to the Isles of the Blest, but we have only Bacchylides' story of Croesus being taken there. There seems to be no evidence for belief in an infernal river like Styx or for a Lydian Charon.[57]

Sociologically, the mound cemetery with its great expanse of land is indubitably a reflection of the ideal of land owners' vast estates. Their chamber tombs are modest in size (Figs. 115, 116); like the rock-cut chamber tombs, they are predicated on small family groups—husband and wife and children. They may be enlarged by adding one or two similar chambers, perhaps for later generations. There is no sign of special burials of slaves or servants in the antechambers or dromoi. Overall, the Royal Cemetery seems to represent the higher social groups, "lydische Adelsfamilien." The Lydian historian Xanthus and to some extent Herodotus portray the kind of competitive relationship in which various noble families and branches of families strove for kingship. It produced gradations of status and kinship that may be reflected in the various sizes and groupings of Bin Tepe mounds.[58] The rock-cut tombs seem to represent wealthy citizenry. In the Lydian-Aramaic bilingual inscription of Manes, son of Kumrulis, in the other inscriptions dated by Persian regnal years, and in the Achaemenid court-style gold jewelry and seals, we have intimations that some of them served the Persian administration.[59]

The origins of Lydian chamber tombs might connect with Anatolian traditions of Hittite and late Hittite principalities, with Phrygian burials, or with Aegean rock-cut graves.[60]

Sarcophagi (Fig. 124), especially terracotta sarcophagi, are cheaper than tumuli or rock-cut chambers; yet they were brought into the same family chamber tombs. Butler remarked, however, that their gravegoods seemed inferior, even if they held two people. As a mode of burial in open-air cemeteries, outside the tombs, they were more individual than the chamber tombs. Their origin in Egypt and their spread to Phoenicia, then Cyprus and Eastern Greece, suggest that this casket shape may have reached Lydia from the coastal areas.[61]

The real cist graves (Figs. 118, 123; BT 63.2 is really a doorless chamber) made of a few slabs of stone or terracotta or rubble should be the graves of the poorer folk. Yet BT 63.3 was dug into a "noble" tumulus at the time (ca. 550–540 B.C.) when the mound was undoubtedly in the original possession, and the Indere graves (Fig. 118) seem less like those of the poor than of "poor relations" who could not get into the family chamber tomb(s). Both had fine gravegoods. Perhaps there were no special cemeteries for the poor and the slaves; or, if there were, they have not been found.[62]

GMAH

V

Lydian Society and Culture

GEORGE M. A. HANFMANN

The Progress of Research

Modern research on Lydia begins with G. A. Radet's enthusiastic and comprehensive study, *La Lydie et le monde grec au temps des Mermnades* (Paris 1893), still valuable because of its mastery of ancient sources. The name of Gyges and of the people of Lud-du having been recognized in the Assyrian annals, Radet saw in the kingdom of Lydia "a natural transition between the decline of the great Eastern monarchies and the radiant adolescence of the Hellenic genius . . . During a century and a half (687–552 B.C.) everything starts from Sardis . . . Economic and industrial discoveries . . . money . . . long distance trade . . . lyric poetry and music . . . philosophy . . . astronomy and geography . . . orgiastic cults . . . and the progress of metallurgy and sculpture."[1]

In the next phase of research, linguistics and archaeology, represented by the published results of the first Sardis expedition, were brought together with the literary tradition. The comprehensive factual article on "Lydia" in *RE* (1927) stands at the beginning of this phase. That it was written by three authors—a topographer (L. Buerchner), a linguist (G. Deeters), and an archaeologist-epigraphist (J. Keil)[2]—was characteristic for the growing specialization of research. The important advance came from the linguistic studies, especially from P. Meriggi's

proof that Lydian was Indo-European and related to Hittite and other early Indo-European languages of Anatolia. Within the resultant concept of Anatolia as a continuous cultural entity, the Lydians increasingly appeared as inheritors of traditions going back to the times of the Hittite empire (ca. 1450–1190 B.C.).[3] Meantime, the concept of Lydia as the great mediator between the Mesopotamian and the Mediterranean worlds persisted; it was eloquently endorsed by H. C. Butler.[4] A more Western orientation and a focus on social and economic problems distinguish C. Roebuck's thorough account of Lydia (1960), which may be viewed as a conclusion of this second research phase.

Yet even in such masterly sketches as A. Götze's *Kleinasian* (1934; 1957) and H. Th. Bossert's *Altanatolien* (1942), the lack of archaeological material, especially material from settlements, was painfully evident, and this phase ended with K. Bittel's clarion call to archaeological action: "In Lydia, all decisive work is yet to be done by archaeological research!"[5]

The current phase of research, initiated by the Harvard-Cornell Expedition in 1958, is marked by the postulate of ecological objectives to be attained by multidisciplinary collaboration, which includes the natural and the social sciences, and emphasis on urbanistic, social, economic-technological, and ideological dynamics of cultural change.

GMAH

Stratigraphy and History

Previous views on the sources of Lydian culture can now be tested by the results of the Harvard-Cornell excavations. Some observations bring comfort to the "Anatolianists." Thus the fundamentally Anatolian character of the material culture from ca. 1400 B.C. (hut and urn burial, Fig. 24) is continued into the Iron Age in the prevalence of monochrome wares. There is clearly continuity of material life from the Late Bronze Age to the historical Lydian culture. On the other hand, relations to the Hittite empire are tenuous. There is very little Hittite-like pottery, only one Hittite-type arrowhead, and no Hittite seals.[1] Because writing is absent from strata earlier than the seventh century B.C., no concrete support has emerged for the linguistic tenet that Lydian descends from Anatolian–Indo-European languages of the second millennium.

As to the origins of Sardis, we now know that the city site was inhabited before the Trojan Wars, as early as 1400 B.C., a fact denied by Strabo. We have a choice of names—Hyde, Xuaris, Sardis?[2]—but we do not yet know whether Sardis was a village, a town, or a city with a palace. A. Ramage argues that there was a substantial settlement by the end of the Bronze Age (ca. 1200–1000 B.C.).

A series of new correlations between literary and archaeological evidence begins with this "Submycenaean-Protogeometric" settlement. Herodotus had said that a dynasty of "the sons of Herakles" was established at Sardis "505 years before the time of Kandaules." This, by one reckoning, works out to ca. 1200–1190 B.C.[3] The new datum is of great significance for the "Dark Ages" of the Mediterranean. Aegean-type pottery (Figs. 26, 28) appears at this point to support the interpretation that Herodotus' Heraklidai may have been Aegean warriors. Whether they claimed descent from the Greek hero Herakles or from the native hero Tylon we cannot know. There is a Greek and a Lydian side to the hero Mopsos/Moksos, who also in the Late Bronze Age was involved with a goddess at Lake Koloe.[4]

The next important historical correlation concerns the destruction of Sardis by the Iranian Kimmerians. The evidence of burning and slaughter (Fig. 34) in the HoB/Lydian Market area is unmistakable.[5] In the sector PN, excavation did not expose sufficiently large parts at the necessary depth to judge the issue.[6] In the sector PC (Pactolus Cliff), the important, violently burned Level III (Figs. 63, 64) must correspond to the major Kimmerian destruction.[7] Based on Assyrian annals, Kaletsch has proposed 668 B.C. for the first, 652 B.C. for the second, and "after 645 B.C." for the third attack. The second attack led to the death of Gyges and is the probable candidate for the great destruction. The third attack came under his successor Ardys. Because Gyges' death is not yet mentioned in the Assyrian annals for 648 B.C. but is mentioned in 644 B.C., Pedley adopted dates which are later by seven years: pre–657 B.C., 645 B.C. (death of Gyges).[8] In the third attack during Ardys' reign the lower city of Sardis was captured (635 or 645 B.C.). It is possible that Level II in Section PC was destroyed on this occasion.

Since the "Kimmerian question" bears on one of the great invasions of nomadic Eurasian peoples into the sedentary Near-Eastern Mediterranean world,[9] the synchronism has significance far beyond Lydian chronology. An important gain is a new, early fixed point for the so-called "Scythian animal style"; a bone-plaque decorated in this style was found in a level immediately following the destruction. Hitherto, the earliest datable manifestations of this style occurred in South Russian sites.[10]

The fall of Sardis to Cyrus was an epochal event, whether it came in 547, 546, or 545 B.C. The literary sources do not indicate a large-scale destruction: in Herodotus, Croesus urges Cyrus (successfully) to save the city; and the Babylonian chronicle says: "The garrison and the king remained therein" (in Sardis).[11] On the archaeological side, G. F. Swift and A. Ramage assume that Lydian buildings were destroyed or at least abandoned in 547 B.C. in the HoB/Lydian Market area and the city wall MMS partly overthrown.[12] For the PN sector, A. Ramage seems to infer that a burned layer may connect with this event.[13] At PC, the matter remains uncertain.[14]

The historical evidence is clear and definite for the Ionian attack on Sardis in 499 B.C. and the ensuing conflagration. Burning reed huts and thatched houses should have left unmistakable traces.[15] Archaeological confirmation was seen "in a continuous deposit of carbonized matter" which signaled the end of Level I at PC.[16] The heavy ash layer encountered within the two apsidal buildings at PN (Figs. 44, 53) seems at present a candidate for the destruction of 547 B.C., but with more detailed study of objects found, it may turn out to be a result of the Ionian destruction of 499 B.C.[17]

Finally, the destruction of the lower city of Sardis by Antiochus III in 213 B.C. is clearly attested in the historical record now clarified by the archaeological findings and epigraphic evidence. This documentation will be discussed in detail in Chapter VII, "The Hellenistic Period," but this correlation must be mentioned in a discussion of Lydian culture because survival of Lydian architectural and ceramic traditions can be proved from dwellings destroyed in 213 B.C.

GMAH

Urbanism and Architecture

It was always clear from the configuration of the site (Figs. 2–8) and literary sources that Sardis belonged to the "Acropolis" type of ancient cities, with a castle protecting and serving as refuge for the lower town (Plan I). Perpetuating a second-millennium tradition in Anatolia, the monarchic palace dominated the town. In times of Lydian kings, its power and wealth outweighed the importance of temple-monasteries, a social-religious form also traditional in Anatolia.[1] The growing importance of the commercial-civic-secular center of the Agora, then developing in Greece,[2] reflected the rise of a mercantile-industrial middle class. In Sardis, this development manifested itself in the Agora astride the Pactolus, the only feature of urban Sardis concretely located by ancient sources.[3] This Lydian Agora of Sardis is considered by some modern economic theorists as the first free market in the world's history.[4]

When it came to physical remains, apart from the locations of cemeteries, only two spots near the Artemis Temple were reported where the first Sardis expedition tests had reached presumed levels of Lydian habitation.[5]

The Harvard-Cornell fieldwork has for the first time put concrete substance into this largely theoretical model of a traditional palace-temple city transformed by the inventions of coinage, of aggressive traveling salesmanship, and of traveling commodities market into a novel economic system with features of open trade.

Area, Plan, and Circulation

First, let us consider the area of the city (Fig. 8; Plan I).[6] As is shown in Chapter IV, in the section on "Lydian Burial Rites and Beliefs," the city of the living was supplemented by the city of the dead (Fig. 129). Kings and nobility occupied the vast terrain of Bin Tepe north of the Hermus River. The cemetery west of the Pactolus with its terraced chamber tombs was always in view of the city, and similar cemeteries south of the city and in the gulches of the Acropolis also rose above it (Figs. 90, 129). C. H. Greenewalt has suggested calling these the "popular" cemeteries, though they had a middle-class occupancy.[7] This equilibrium and relative closeness of the dead and the living is traditional in Iron Age Anatolia.

The north-south extent of the Lydian city is approximately indicated by habitation material from a well about 650 m. north of the modern highway (E98/S650) and by Lydian traces reported by the archaeological survey of 1976 ca. 750 m. south of the Artemis Temple (Fig. 129; Plan I). The north-south distance between these two points is 2,650 m.[8]

The eastern boundary is presumably defined by the city wall MMS, ca. 440 m. from the modern Pactolus bridge (E116–138/S51–59). This may be one of the pre-Persian city walls implied by Herodotus in his tale of the capture of Sardis in 547 B.C.[9] The western boundary is unknown. Probably it was some distance west of the Pactolus. A reasonable guess for the overall east-west dimension may be 1,000 m.

Recent excavations (1980) have for the first time disclosed some surfaces of the Lydian predecessor of the main east-west road, the "Royal Road," at a bastion of the east gate at MMS/N.[10] Westward, this graveled road must have crossed the Pactolus. The course of the Pactolus may or may not have changed to the east or west. A Lydian lion was found during the construction of the modern road bridge in 1952, but cleaning of the area could not go to sufficient depth to reach Lydian strata.[11]

Excavated between 1960 and 1970, a part of

the Lydian commercial and industrial market (known as HoB/Lydian Market), apparently a walled, irregularly built up area, lay presumably alongside and south of the great east-west road (Figs. 8, 31).

Again, the "Gold Refinery" and adjacent shops at PN (Figs. 8, 42–45), the important buildings at PC (Figs. 8:13; 63, 64), the cemetery at Şeytan Dere (Figs. 8:54; 129) and eventually the Artemis Precinct, must have lain on the second great artery, the north-south road from Bin Tepe and Hermus ford along the east bank of the Pactolus to the Artemis Temple. The actual Lydian road has not been found.

A parallel north-south road, on which lay the house(s) discovered by Shear, must have run along the west bank at the foot of the cemetery; it may have had a branch going off toward the west part of the city (as shown in Plan I).[12]

Other probable major streets are a diagonal road from the gate of the east-west road past HoB to PN, and thence across the Pactolus (Fig. 8:57–58). An enigmatic construction of stones and uprights of wood at PN might be the trace of a bridge or landing.[13] This diagonal road may have continued beyond the east-west highway through a hollow along the so-called "Old Izmir Road." The ascent to the Acropolis was a long slope east of the Artemis Temple at the foot of the western cliffs of the Acropolis and then northward to the south gate of the Acropolis (Figs. 7, 8, 70).

None of these major roads are known in their Lydian form; hence we do not know the width or whether they were paved.[14] At PC, however, a corner of a paved street (Figs. 63, 64) 3½ to 4 m. wide was preserved.[15] All small piazzas and lanes excavated were not paved.

The excavated areas show a pattern of walled commercial and industrial precincts (HoB; "Refinery," PN)[16] and very densely built up dwellings, which may include combined living and working spaces in "domestic industry" shops (Figs. 31, 35, 39–42, 44, 63, 135–137). Only lanes and small piazzas around wells, reminiscent of traditional Turkish villages (Fig. 130), provide for circulation.

A. Ramage has pointed out the resemblances of Lydian houses with present-day Sardis village dwellings (Figs. 131, 134), but the continuous agglomeration along narrow lanes is perhaps closer to medieval Islamic towns.[17]

There seems to be some overall orientation in the placing of buildings within each sector, but it is clear that Lydian Sardis had no geometric grid plan of the kind that was emerging in archaic Greek cities of the seventh and sixth centuries, including Ephesus and Miletus. Unlike Old Smyrna, these alignments at Sardis vary from sector to sector.[18]

The principle of organization seems to be agglutination, with "heaped-up" dwellings aligned along major arteries and walled, more open spaces used for commercial, industrial, and probably sacred areas (temple precincts).

There is little among the domestic finds to indicate agricultural activities. It seems that unlike the present-day Sart Mustafa villagers, the Sardians of old did not have stables in their lower stories.[19]

No evidence has appeared to show whether gardens and orchards such as the great garden later laid out by Cyrus the Younger formed part of the city area. The overall impression is one of very urban congestion. This should not surprise us. As a keen student of Greek urbanism has noted, "In archaic cities a very dense and almost formless agglomerate of dwellings seems to have been the rule."[20]

Utilities

The placing of wells in small open areas (Figs. 39, 44; HoB, PN) outside the houses seems to mark these piazzas as semipublic conveniences.[21] Even more impressive evidence of organized concern would be the two apsidal structures on the Pactolus at PN (Fig. 53), if A. Ramage is right in attributing them to the Lydians.[22] They are surely fountain houses. The "Gold Refinery" seems to have had an open water supply channel as well as drains (Fig. 45). There are indications of at least one conduit for overflow from a well into a house.[23] To build stone wells to a depth of 20 m. (HoB) requires experience; and the tapping of the water vein in PN is expertly done. It would be very desirable to discover if the so-called Lydian Reservoir (Plan I),[24] an underground cave with a natural spring, was indeed regulated by the Lydians. We recall also the tunnel and the cisterns of the Acropolis and the royal project of controlling the Gygean Lake.[25] It seems likely that some sort of public organization and supervision were exercised over the water supply and water rights.

Defenses

In *Sardis* R1 we had raised the question of whether the lower city of Sardis was fortified. This question appears to be resolved by the discovery of the city wall MMS (Figs. 132, 133) and a review of the literary sources. The manner in which this newly discovered wall goes uphill along a ridge suggests that it was joining the Acropolis defenses. If MMS was the east wall of the city, then a large area east of MMS that was part of the Hellenistic and Roman City was left out (Fig. 8; Plans I–II).[26]

It is noteworthy that the MMS wall is built in a technique different from the fortress wall on the south slope of the Acropolis (Figs. 72, 73). Both used a stone base and mudbrick, but the latter with its chinky joining of irregular stones in the faces and crude rubble fill seems closer to Gordion. It is tempting to think of its structural technique as going back to the time of the semi-legendary King Meles, sometime in the late eighth century B.C. during the time of Phrygian influence.[27] The much more sophisticated, powerful MMS wall (Fig. 133), with its crossbeams and reed mats, bespeaks direct knowledge of Mesopotamian–late Hittite military architecture, perhaps promoted by the military alliance with the Assyrians under Gyges and Ardys. It calls for comparison with the huge fort built by the Lydians at Gordion and destroyed in 547 B.C. by Cyrus.[28]

Unfortunately, we cannot establish the course of the walls of either the Acropolis or the city; the latter must have crossed the Pactolus both north and south of the Agora. It may have protected the west road along the Pactolus and swung across the Pactolus south of the Artemis Temple and the road to the Acropolis (Fig. 8; Plan I).

Architecture: Construction

In his fundamental discussion of Lydian architecture, A. Ramage points out that Herodotus may not have overdramatized his Sardis of reed huts and reed roofs.[29] Essentially, Sardis excavations have revealed two types of construction—the riverstone, mud cement, pisé, and mudbrick (Figs. 40, 42, 53, 84, 134–137), especially for domestic, industrial, and commercial construction, and the cut-stone (ashlar) masonry which is preserved in the terrace walls of the Acropolis,

the late phase of the MMS wall, the crepis of the Gyges mound, and the various chamber tombs (Figs. 79, 108, 115, 116). The riverstone-pisé-mudbrick is a native combination which goes back to the Late Bronze Age, as proved by the Submycenaean wall in HoB.[30] It may have been rationalized under Mesopotamian or Greek influence (Fig. 133) in such matters as the dimensions and standardization of brick sizes. Ramage deduces from the buildings a Lydian foot of 0.295–0.296 m. The "Lydian" brick of 0.36 × 0.27 × 0.09 m. must have acquired some reputation.[31] The vernacular reed and thatch roofs may have continued to be built for some time after the conflagration of 499 B.C., but from the early sixth century on, tile roofs and fine terracotta friezes (Figs. 66, 75, 153) come increasingly into use.[32]

Monumental, expertly worked masonry appears fully developed in the Mound of Gyges (ca. 650 B.C; Fig. 108).[33] It came to include knowledge of clamping, doweling, and drafted edges. The Acropolis palace foundations (Figs. 79, 80)[34] suggest that masonry on the lower part of the wall was combined with mudbrick in the upper part, as in Mesopotamian and later in Iranian palaces.[35] Greece appears a less likely source.

On the other hand, the scanty finds of the decorative architectural members of limestone and marble (Figs. 138, 149–151) prove that archaic temples and altars were built of stone along Greek lines. The earliest preserved and datable marble structure is the chamber in the tomb of Alyattes (ca. 560 B.C.; Fig. 102), though earlier marble structures may have existed.[36] There is good reason to believe that leading Greek architects, such as the great theorist and practical inventor Theodorus of Samos, were working for the Lydian court under Croesus and possibly already under Alyattes and even Gyges.[37]

Lydian Domestic Architecture

Domestic architecture is attested by recognizable walls and units found in four sectors of the lower town (HoB/Lydian Market, PN, PC, NEW) as well as by fragmentary bits on the Acropolis[38] and a farmhouse near the Gygean Lake. The "cellular" character and undifferentiated plans of modest one- and two-room units such as PN I–II (Figs. 136, 137), and the fact that walls are continuous with other houses, make it often difficult to interpret rooms and functions, as in NEW (Fig. 84). One type is an oblong one-room unit represented on a small scale by PN Unit I–II and on a larger scale by the "model house H" at the Lydian Market (Figs. 40, 135).[39] The nucleus is a long space covered by (probably) a pitched roof. Their modest furnishings are described by Ramage[40]—a clay bench, a hearth, a cupboard, some baking trays, querns, and occasional circular bins (for storage) or pits. Like modern Turkish village houses, they may have been subdivided by screens or curtains and made resplendent by hangings and carpets. They were unquestionably well furnished not only with plain utilitarian but also with ambitious painted pottery (Figs. 85–87). There are some indications of a house-type with attached courtyard (PN, NEW), something like the ancestor of the later Priene house.[41] Unfortunately, the best instance was found incomplete (PN, Units XIX, XX; Figs. 44, 181). The porch house, so popular in modern rural Anatolia (Fig. 131), is apparently not attested.[42]

Modern Sardian village houses (Figs. 131, 134) include "animal spaces," stables and sties around the courtyard as well as in the ground floor story. This story is also often the place for storage of produce (corn, oil), wine, water in pithoi, pits, and circular bins.[43] Given the number of animal bones found in domestic refuse,[44] one would expect many houses to have had space for sheep, goats, pigs, cows, and horses, but this does not seem to be the case.

That more ambitious and carefully laid out houses existed is proved by the "House of the Priest" (Unit XXVIII) in PN, rather "megaron-like" in its tripartite division (Figs. 45, 58), and by the unfortunately incompletely excavated structures in PC (Figs. 63, 64). There, walls up to 11 m. long and 1 m. thick may indicate a second story.[45] These houses may have belonged to wealthier people than the craftsmen and small shopkeepers who lived and worked around the "Gold Refinery" and Lydian Market.

Finally, the splendid bedrooms of the built chamber tombs (Figs. 115, 116) seem to imply a house plan in which there was a separate room of this kind with fine beds, couches, and tables.[46] There must have been special dining rooms, too, for feasting as in the "Satrap Relief" (Fig. 138). These elegant apartments would have had the ivory chairs and couches and fine tables mentioned in literature (Figs. 117, 138).[47]

For the time being, the few reconstructible houses of Sardis (Figs. 135, 136) appear smaller and less differentiated not only than the citadel megarons of Phrygian Gordion but also than the cut stone-based megaron houses of archaic Greek Smyrna.[48] Unlike Smyrna, Sardis has not produced any examples of bathtubs.

Commercial and Industrial Structures

That Sardis was making history by transforming itself into a *mechanike polis* (as a Greek workman termed Minoan Gournia) is borne out by our excavation. Not counting the craftsmen-jewelers' house-shops in PN, which are not clearly identified, the "Gold Refinery" precinct at PN and the Lydian Market take up ca. 58% of the Lydian area excavated between 1958 and 1976.

The "Gold Refinery," the place where Alyattes' and Croesus' gold was made (Fig. 42), has been described in detail in Chapter III, under "Goldworking Installations and Techniques." Evidence for a similar establishment just to the north suggests that perhaps a series of such precincts lay between the PN precinct and the elusive Lydian Civic Agora. The location, layout, and economic construction of the Refinery precinct are carefully geared to the gold-processing operations. The high enclosure was necessary for security and possibly fire prevention. Some twenty workmen (Fig. 139) may have worked here.[49] As A. Ramage observes, the religious protection of the goddess *Kuvava* was important. Her altar was built in native riverstone and mud-cement technique rather than deluxe stone or marble. Under no circumstances can it have served an adjacent temple; there is no place for one nearby (Figs. 45, 58). That the "House of the Priest" and a parallel structure were built so close to the altar indicates a desire to save space; these structures did reduce the production area, especially the "cupellation" space.[50] The houses in PN around the precinct (Fig. 44) immediately adjoined the area; crystal cutters and jewelers may have worked in units east of the precinct.[51]

The HoB/Lydian Market (Lydian Trench) was also a precinct surrounded by rubble stone wall.[52] There were houses west of it. Its extent to the north is not known, but Lydian strata continue under the gymnasium.[53] A. Ramage points out that the three rather large, one-unit structures leaning against the west precinct wall (Figs.

35, 39) are of domestic type without special evidence of crafts or trade.[54]

The following evidence is relevant for the industrial and possibly commercial functions: ten unused Lydian lamps (Fig. 140) found on a floor of an otherwise lost building;[55] four molds for making jewelry from HoB;[56] unfinished pieces and other evidence of bronze working, possibly of a later period;[57] and a kiln and vases which had been repaired (Fig. 141) in the potters' shop at E5–14/S96–103, *96.[58]

For the entire HoB area the enormous amount of pottery suggests continuous storage and breakage. The area cannot be the Main Agora mentioned in Herodotus 5.101, since it was not astride the Pactolus, and it does not have a large open space where a great number of Lydians and Persians could gather. Hanfmann is inclined to consider HoB/Lydian Market a potters' quarter with repair and selling facilities. The big series of kilns would have been on the Pactolus bank.

No large-scale production or storage facilities seem to pertain to the latest level, 600–547 B.C. (or later), but the large number of vats or pits marked by fatty discoloration (Figs. 32, 33) may indicate larger production facilities (for oil?) in the preceding period (650–600 B.C.).

One fact deserves to be noted: of the pre-Hellenistic coins, only one Persian siglos (Fig. 162) and one silver pseudo-coin were found in the HoB area—a very low yield, if the trade was really shifting to payment in coin before 547 B.C.[59]

Whether the area had any religious functions is unclear. The disrupted, rather large Building D (Fig. 39) yielded some peculiar discards, such as the so-called "Exhibitionist" (Figs. 142, 143) and a demon-like terracotta head.[60] A painted dedication to the Lydian Zeus (Lefs; Fig. 144) was found. Either Lefs had a cult place nearby (not necessarily a temple, as Roman coins show him worshipped in an open precinct; Fig. 147),[61] or the Lydians may have had small domestic shrines.

A much debated issue is the relation of Carian inscriptions of the seventh and sixth centuries B.C.[62] to the "Ritual Dinners," sets of pots including puppy skeletons and iron knives buried presumably in pits as offerings to a divinity (Figs. 145, 146); six of them were found in a small area of HoB. In his detailed monograph, *Ritual Dinners in Early Historic Sardis,* C. H. Greenewalt,

Jr., opts for dates of ca. 575–525 B.C. and seeks to dissociate the "dinners" from the Carian inscriptions, even though an ancient author speaks of a dog offering as a Carian sacrifice.[63] It strains credulity to assume that Carians and dog offerings should appear by chance together. The matter will be considered later in the treatment of languages. Hanfmann's opinion is that in these mercantile surroundings at HoB, one of the buildings (D?) was a "clubhouse" or the like for Carian merchants rather than Carian mercenaries.[64]

Public Structures

Literary sources postulate a fortified palace,[65] a treasury or treasuries, and a mint.[66] A multitude of royal relatives, court servants, and presumably guards had to be accommodated. It is probable that a multilingual royal archive had existed since Gyges; it would have contained documents in Lydian, Phrygian, Assyrian, Egyptian, Aramaic, Greek, Carian, and other Anatolian languages. It is not clear whether craftsmen, jewelers, and metal and ivory workers formed part of the royal household as they had in the palatial economies of the Near East.[67] What we have of the palace is only the splendid masonry of the lowest wall of rising terraces (Figs. 79, 80). From Vitruvius we learn that they were surmounted by mudbrick walls. Because decorative terracotta friezes were found on the Acropolis, it is tempting to consider their use on the palace (Fig. 75).

The only general plausible parallel is with the fortified pitched roof palaces of Lycia. C. Nylander's ingenious suggestion that the two-towered archaic palace in "Larisa" on the Hermus imitated the palace of Croesus is pure speculation.[68]

All accounts of the siege of 547 B.C. imply that a number of Lydian warriors were housed on the Acropolis.[69] Even allowing for lost surface areas, they cannot have numbered many thousands, especially if Croesus' palace population was there. The scanty traces do not permit us to discern any plans of service buildings or barracks. The pattern of cisterns and storage bins (Fig. 74) indicates that they occupied the central and south part.[70]

Alexander's permission to the Lydians (334 B.C.) to use their own laws assumes the existence of Lydian authorities who could take over; a

Council of Elders, but no Council House, can be identified.[71] The presumed apsidal fountain houses, if their first period is Lydian, would be an illustration of an important public concern.

The imposing pre-Kimmerian structures (Figs. 63, 64) with powerful walls in sector PC may have had a public function (storage) or a sacral function (libation, rituals); it was noted that there was an unusual number of pithoi, some with incised signs, and of knobbed, so-called omphalos bowls.[72]

Religious Structures[73]

Open-air altars such as the altar of Zeus Lydios in a grove represented on coins (Fig. 147) may have been frequent in Lydia,[74] but we cannot safely locate them. The earliest altar preserved, the altar of *Kuvava* (Cybele) at PN (Figs. 42, 45, 49), is in "vernacular" riverstone technique and is decorated with limestone lions. It belonged to the Gold Refinery precinct (Fig. 139), not to a temple. The lion altar resembled the altar of gold bricks which Croesus gave to Delphi.[75] The archaic or "Persian" altar of Artemis was a stepped altar (Fig. 95) built of limestone masonry. Here the temple was added later.[76]

Representations of the images of Kore (Fig. 148), of a snake goddess (Fig. 149), and of Cybele (Fig. 150), the Lydian names for several divinities, and references to other Greek (Zeus, Apollo, Hera, Demeter) and Anatolian (Agdistis, Attis, Ma, Mên, Sabazius) deities[77] pose the question of shrines and temples. A probable site of a shrine to a goddess was identified at Dede Mezari, a mile west of Sardis, but was not excavated.[78]

No excavated building of the Lydian or Persian era has been convincingly identified as a temple or shrine. Nevertheless, we have found secure evidence that Sardis had temples of Greek type and that Lydian architects and patrons worked closely with Greek architects during the experimental stage of the Ionic order. The most important are the two reproductions of archaic shrines, one a facade with two columns, ca. 570 B.C. (Fig. 149), the other an interesting Cybele shrine with engaged half columns on the sides and a central half column on the axis of the back wall (Figs. 150–152, 160). Three zones of painted relief panels adorned the sides and the back in a unique arrangement, perhaps

influenced by Mesopotamian models. Hanfmann suggests that though the votive dates from ca. 530 B.C., the building represented may be earlier (560? B.C.); it might portray the shrine of Cybele burned by the Persians in 499 B.C.

These are achievements of the same school of architects as the gigantic temple of Artemis in Ephesus, partly endowed by Croesus.[79] Apparently postdating 499 B.C. are very fine marble fragments of an epistyle Lesbian cyma and Ionic marble capitals; they are not burned. They came from a smaller (tetrastyle?) temple.[80] The *parastades* (pilasters) of the later, Persian period temple of Cybele (Metroon) have been found in the Synagogue (Fig. 169).[81]

Since terracotta friezes probably adorned civic and domestic structures as well as religious ones, we must leave open the question of whether such early terracotta friezes as those with a goddess or god and with lions (Fig. 153), griffins, and sphinxes may have belonged to early Lydian shrines.[82] Except for a possible small Cybele shrine of the Persian period,[83] we have found no traces of domestic places of devotion.

The distribution of sacred buildings and "religious hallowing" throughout the city remains little known. Similarly, we have more questions than answers concerning the organization and functions of sacred precincts, temples, and monasteries. Priests and priestesses occur in Lydian and Greek inscriptions.[84] Two symmetrical, rectangular buildings flanking Cybele's altar in PN (Fig. 45, nos. XXVIII, XXX) are candidates for priestly dwellings.[85] No service buildings or houses have been found associated with the archaic altar (LA 1) of Artemis (Figs. 94, 95).[86] Finally, ritual functions may have taken place at one of the structures at HoB/Lydian Market in connection with ritual dinners.[87]

Development

It is probable that already around 1400 B.C. the ford across the Pactolus acted as a focus and attracted settlement.[88] Despite floods, people lived and traded in the HoB (and possibly PN/PC) areas during the Dark Ages and early Iron Age. A shift from light reed to more durable stone/pisé construction and from domestic storage to lighter consumption wares and imports is noted by A. Ramage for the time after the Kimmerian invasion. This upsurge and improvement in the standard of living are surely to be connected with the "gold rush" and the rule of Gyges. The same upsurge may account for the settling of the outlying district at NEW (ca. 640 B.C.?) and the start of the great Necropolis Cemetery west of the Pactolus (Plan I).

The Acropolis was fortified by the last Heraklidai (ca. 700 B.C.?). The evidence of the earliest pottery yet found does not invalidate the historical tradition.[89] Phrygian and possibly late Hittite and Mesopotamian influences seem reflected in the fortification of the castle. Assyrian connections may be discerned in the subsequent building under Alyattes (615–600 B.C.?) of a huge city wall around the lower city (Fig. 133). The palace may have survived from the time of the Heraklids, but it was surely rebuilt by Alyattes or Croesus. A claim to inherit the Phrygian overlordship may be surmised in the planning of colossal mounds (Figs. 97, 98, 105) and the Royal Cemetery in general.[90] The construction technique of the palace, however, suggests a long "diffusion jump" from distant Mesopotamia, where Gyges and Ardys sent their ambassadors, and where Lydian princes stayed (as hostages?) at the court of Babylon.[91]

A last, Alyattes-Croesan phase at the culmination of prosperity is reflected in the building of the Gold Refinery and rearrangement of the Lydian Market. The partial destruction of 547 B.C. and the devastating fire of 499 B.C. do not seem to have caused any fundamental changes in the character of the Lydian city.

The change under the Persians, 499–334 B.C., appears to have been gradual, especially since HoB/Lydian Market was not really abandoned. It may be that the Gold Refinery at PN was reconverted to dwellings after 547 B.C. (Figs. 136, 137). Pactolus floods rather than man seem to have destroyed the precinct. That shifts in the use of urban space may have taken place is suggested by the finding in 1978 of Lydian houses under a Lydian-type chamber tomb (T 77.1) on the northwest foothill of the Acropolis—the inhabited area had become a cemetery (Plan I and Fig. 129: T 77.1). Important Persian mausolea also appeared near the Pactolus (Fig. 138).[92]

Ramage also conjectures that the city wall MMS (Figs. 132, 133) was pulled down under the Persians; if so, they may have pushed the fortified city line eastward, to the east scarp where

Polybius' "Persian Gate" (Plan I) could have lain.[93] This shift would imply a fundamental urban relocation eastward; further excavation is needed to confirm or refute this theory. Otherwise, the Lydian city area and plan appear to have experienced little change until the destruction of 213 B.C. (Plans I, II).

So much, then, has become known about the real, concrete Sardis. It is interesting to compare it to two verbal evocations. G. Radet gave a marvelous verbal picture of Mermnad Sardis, with its towering Acropolis, its palace and bastions, its rich residential quarters, its teeming markets, bazaars, and workshops—an evocation as romantic as J. L. Gerôme's painted Pompeian vision of the palace of the Lydian kings.[94]

By contrast, our major ancient informant, Herodotus (5.100–101), seems to attest an agglomeration of rustic, thatched huts piled up in a circle around the Agora. Was Herodotus a liar? We must remember that he spoke from the vantage point of a participant in the Periclean Athens, as a man who was acquainted with the most advanced thinking about the best city or state, the most advanced geometric rational grid-planning by Hippodamos of Miletus, who had just rebuilt the Piraeus[95] and was about to plan in the most modern fashion the very place to which Herodotus went and where he possibly died—the Athenian colony of Thurii. Herodotus' remark is very much of the same kind as Thucydides' famous observation, that nobody would believe that Sparta was a great power if archaeologists dug it up,[96] so much did it resemble a poor and mean village. Herodotus overdramatized—his point is that if a traveler saw Sardis before 499 B.C., he would hardly believe it to be the richest city in the world. Taken literally, however, Herodotus is correct, as A. Ramage notes;[97] he did not say that *all* houses of Sardis had thatched roofs but that *the majority* were of reed or mudbrick and reed; and this is the picture that seems to emerge. The majority of Lydian houses were "vernacular" architecture (PN, NEW, part of HoB); but there are intimations of better, grander structures perhaps at HoB, and almost certainly in PC. Our excavations show that no verbal picture can ever match the concreteness and complexity of material realities. In this way, the spade is mightier than the word.

GMAH

Production and Trade

Production

Weighty claims are made on behalf of Sardis; they affect the fundamentals of economic history. Thus it is proposed that: (1) state-guaranteed coinage was invented at Sardis; (2) bimetallic currency was first minted at Sardis; (3) the transition from barter to a money (coinage) economy, postulated in theory by Aristotle, took place at Sardis; (4) the "free" market system, based on supply and demand, operated at Sardis for the first time in world history.

Let us look at the background. Finds of the Early Bronze Age (Figs. 16, 18) raise the possibility that gold and silver were worked at Sardis in the third millennium B.C.[1] Proof of continuity into the first millennium, however, is missing. The picture as drawn by A. Ramage for the period 1000–700 B.C. is one of a domestic, largely self-sufficient economy, with facilities for storage of staple foods and breeding of domestic animals, the early occurrence of iron being the only remarkable technology. Ramage sees a shift to a more complex (domestic?) economy sometime in the period 725–650 B.C., partly pre-Kimmerian.[2] G. M. A. Hanfmann views the discovery and exploitation of Pactolus gold as the impetus which released the great economic expansion.

To appreciate the significance of this event, one must recall that gold had become rare in the Eastern Mediterranean during and immediately after the Dark Ages. Near Eastern prospectors like the Phoenicians on Thasos were apparently looking for it. Sophisticated gold-processing techniques appear in the "Gold Refinery," and a great variety of jewelers' techniques including granulation are evident on early Lydian jewelry.[3] It seems very likely that experienced metallurgists from the Near East, where gold had been worked since Sumerian times, entered Lydian service very soon after the "strike." Phoenicians cannot be ruled out. Legends of Meles' sojourn in Babylon and possibly finds of proto-coins in Assyria[4] point toward Mesopotamia—as do the embassies of Gyges to the Assyrian court. When did the sudden expansion occur? Greek legend gives "the golden touch" to King Midas, last King of Phrygia (died 696 B.C.?) and makes him lose it in the Pactolus. One might interpret this as a sign that the first Lydian "gold strike" occurred as early as the reign of Midas. We have found no gold earlier than the reign of Gyges.

The unique "Gold Refinery" on the Pactolus got going either under Ardys or more likely under Alyattes (ca. 615?–560 B.C.). The exquisite ram earring (Fig. 62) was fashioned ca. 600 B.C., the fine sample of granulation (Indere, Fig. 121) about 600–575 B.C.

The Harvard-Cornell excavations have contributed concrete illustrations of the technology which made possible the gold-silver coinage of Croesus (Figs. 45–48, 55–61). Pieces of gold show silver content as low as 1 to 10%. This material should make it possible to check by scientific analysis objects claimed as exports made from Lydian gold, eventually perhaps also from Lydian silver. The analytical research is still in an experimental state, but claims of Lydian origin without analysis have been made by Roebuck for gold objects found at Ephesus and on Rhodes,[5] and with analysis but without data on Pactolus gold by W. J. Young for objects found in Iran and Sumer. On examination of Lydian gold coins, W. J. Young assumed that all Pactolus gold had platiniridium inclusions. Goldstein's tests showed the complexities of such research—not one of the ninety "Refinery" samples had the inclusions, but the little ram earring (Fig. 62) did! No platiniridium was observed in Lydian coins analyzed by Pászthory.[6]

Our material gives support to a highly controversial theory about early coinage. According to S. Bolin, the Lydian king Ardys, or Alyattes, who first minted gold-silver (electrum) coins, intentionally added silver to electrum. Our samples show a silver range up to 25+%; early Lydian coins have 45–69%; by adding 30% silver to coin alloy, the king gained 30% value over the natural electrum,[7] if it was traded in electrum bars. Such a procedure implies research into the gold and silver content of electrum. Another great gain from finds at Sardis: no longer need scholars cite Transylvanian gold to demonstrate silver content of Lydian gold; we have at least two analyses of Pactolus gold and a substantial body of material on gold worked in the "Gold Refinery" of Sardis.[8]

The discovery of a royal stamp (Fig. 60)

proves what Herodotus and others imply and what G. Radet had postulated—Sardis processing plants belonged to the King. This suggests at least a partial monopoly of processing. It does not necessarily mean that the King claimed ownership of all mines. The case of Pythes/Pythios is ambiguous. He operated what seem to be private mines after the fall of the Lydian kings; but he was related to the royal house and may have had a special position.

The Lydian kings had obviously organized a series of processing facilities along the Pactolus; each might employ twenty to fifty men (Fig. 139).[9] We do not know whether they were the King's craftsmen, either free men or slaves. Pythes/Pythios employed indentured citizens. Since the gold output of one "refinery" was small, there would have had to be a number of them to produce Croesus' presents to the Greek sanctuaries or the 500 talents of gold paid by Lydia as tribute to the Persians. Eventually it will be possible to make educated guesses about the monthly production of one such "refinery" and to compare the hypothetical output of refined gold from a series of such refineries to the annual production of 200–300 talents of gold claimed for Thasian gold mines and 100 talents of silver claimed for Siphnos.[10] For Lydia was indubitably the great gold supplier of mainland Greece from ca. 650 to 550 B.C. The nearly total lack of gold or silver coins in the excavated commercial-industrial areas of Sardis suggests that they were concentrated in the hands of the king and possibly wealthy merchants—the kind of person who could hide thirty gold staters of Croesus in a chamber tomb in 547 B.C. Apparently they were used for special types of transactions. Payment of mercenaries was certainly one, import transactions for luxury or bulk goods perhaps another. Payments of political subsidies are attested for ca. 600 B.C., when 2,000 (gold) staters were paid to Alcaeus' party in Lesbos.[11]

J. C. Waldbaum suggests that it was the discovery of the separation process and the establishment of refineries which led Croesus to adopt bimetallic coinage. She also points out that the discrepancy between the silver content of our "Refinery" and Pactolus samples on one hand, and the silver content of earlier coins (15–30% versus 50–60%) on the other, validates

S. Bolin's theory. As a sagacious Wall Street expert has pointed out, Croesus was striving to restore the credibility of Lydian currency because the electrum coinage had become suspect. Pure gold and pure silver coins were much more readily tested than electrum or even electrum-plated coins.[12]

Production of coins, first in electrum, then in gold and silver, was undoubtedly the most important industry and the most important export article of the Lydian Kingdom. The time and manner of invention of Lydian coinage are controversial. We have found no early electrum coins; the gold hecte (Fig. 61) from the Sart Sulphur Baths and the silver obel from apsidal buildings in PN do no more than reconfirm the use of bimetallic currency in Sardis.

A date of early seventh century B.C. for the earliest Lydian coins and the use of Babylonian standard were proposed by B. V. Head in his fundamental British Museum Catalogue of Lydia (1901) and his influential *Historia Nummorum*.[13] This dating was decisively lowered to around 600 B.C. in a classic study (1951) on proto-coins and coins of the deposit under the image base of Artemis in Ephesus in which E. G. S. Robinson examined the coins and P. Jacobsthal the archaeological material.[14] In 1975 L. Weidauer, after a systematic die-linked ordering of all early electrum coins, proposed to date a series of early lionhead coins to ca. 660–630 B.C., and the imageless coins to "early seventh century."[15] She die-linked this "four-rayed (nose) wart" lion type to two crucial series of coins inscribed in Lydian: *val-vel* and *kalil*. She conjectured that these four early electrum coins may have been issued by one Lydian mint, "most probably Sardis."[16] This would mean that the earliest imageless coins were struck under the last Heraklid kings (Meles? Candaules?) and the early lionheads and the inscribed coins already under Gyges (680–645 B.C.).

Weidauer's dating rests on stylistic comparisons with Greek pottery and minor arts, and this aspect is open to attack because of the use of high chronology and earliest possible comparisons; we cannot review it here.[17] From the entire disucssion, the following facts emerge: The weight standard of Lydian coins is derived from the Babylonian; the designations of coin values in Greek (and possibly in Lydian) are Babylonian. The nearest approximation to state currency guaranteed by the king is in late eighth century B.C. Syria and Assyria.[18] Finally, the "rays-warted" lionhead on early Lydian electrum coins may reflect Assyro-Babylonian lion types.[19]

The Lydian coin legends val-vel and kalil are not "moneyer's signs" like the (misinterpreted) legend "I am the sign of Phanes."[20] One does not put a moneyer's name on the first coins to be issued by a king. Val-lis means "belonging to Val," Kalis "belonging to Ka(l)." There are only two plausible interpretations: the first is that these are royal names. Val may still mean "Alayattes" (Seltman) and Kal his successor "Ardys," about whose Lydian name we are not well informed. It is out of order for linguists to pretend that they are certain either of the reading of the earliest experimental Lydian inscriptions or the Lydian forms of early royal names.[21] The second interpretation is the standard Near Eastern formula "of the King," "belonging to the King," used on Assyrian proto-currency.[22]

Molds for making gold jewelry have been found in PN and HoB.[23] The making and selling of gold objects by goldsmiths seems to have gone on in small private(?) shops and in at least two quarters of the city (HoB/Lydian Market; PN), rather than in workshops attached to the palace. This is already a step away from an economy controlled by king and feudal landowners.[24]

The documentation for iron working has been given in Chapter I. The level of technological competence shown by the Lydian blacksmiths is discussed in detail by J. C. Waldbaum. On the basis of a metallographic analysis by R. Maddin, she shows that a layer of uncarburized iron and carburized (low carbonated) iron were hammered together to form a blade "only just competitive with good work-hardened bronze."[25] Lydian iron workers worked later in Persepolis.[26] Unlike the "breakthrough" in the technology of gold, the development of iron—continuous in Lydian Sardis—was probably gradual as in Egypt, but only additional analyses will tell. It is obvious that under the Lydian kings, the Lydians had become skilled metallurgists.

Ivory carving, gem carving, and the textile industry also reached a high state, as did the production of leather goods.[27] Domestic production by women is still a distinctive feature of carpet and kilim making in Turkey and is a likely trait for antiquity. The simple weaves from Bin Tepe

discussed by Greenewalt and Majewski represent only the basic level of the famous Lydian textile technology described in literary sources. Ceramic loom weights found in the HoB/Lydian Market show that such weights were made by professional potters.[28]

In construction, technological capabilities and organization were required to move from the quarry limestone and marble pieces up to 15 tons, and to put them in place as walls and ceilings. It is noteworthy that while the large pieces of limestone used in Gyges' mound (ca. 650 B.C.)[29] were quarried at the site, Alyattes had his marble brought over a distance of several miles.[30] This transport required lifting devices; some blocks still show rope holes.[31] The mound of Gyges contains tons of earth and stone; presumably dozens of teams of oxen or horses were used to transport the earth, clay, and rubble. The Lydians put this experience to military use. In discussing the huge siege mound constructed by Alyattes at Smyrna, J. M. Cook remarks: "Construction [of such colossal work] came naturally to the builders of gigantic mounds at Sardis,"[32] an observation confirmed by the colossal mudbrick structure found at MMS (Fig. 133).[33]

The best observable Lydian industries of Sardis are ceramic—pottery, lamps, and terracottas, figurative and architectural. Enormous quantities of pottery have been found, especially in the HoB/Lydian Market area. As D. Kamilli has shown in her "Mineral Analysis of Clay Bodies," all of these industries use similar local materials. Continuity is so strong that Kamilli could establish a "typical Sardis ceramic mineral assemblage" compiled from analysis of over one hundred sherds—from archaic Lydian through Late Byzantine ages.[34] The basic material is so similar that it is quite possible to mistake an unglazed Byzantine or Turkish bowl for a Lydian bowl.

H. Crane has clarified the underlying technical traditions by observing the virtually unchanging "vernacular" traditions.[35] It is certain that Crane's first tradition involving the kickwheel and the closed vertical kiln was already practiced in the Late Bronze Age. The "Potter's Shop" in the HoB/Lydian Market area appears to have had a vertical kiln.[36]

Basic undecorated utilitarian products that are very similar in shape to their modern counterparts—storage jars (pithoi), water jugs (amphorae), deep basins (mortars), ring foot bowls—constitute a large and continuous output from the Bronze Age on. Crane's second vernacular tradition, involving a slow turntable (tournette), open, reducing fire, and the use of broken-up mica schist (biotite) to produce a gilt-specked surface, is also represented by stew pots and jugs of the so-called "gold dust" ware among the ancient Lydian material.[37]

In addition to the above "wet-smoothed" or "coarse" basic domestic wares, there existed a tradition of gray monochrome Anatolian wares which went back to the early Iron Age (Fig. 27) or earlier.[38] The relatively rare examples of painted wares were finer in technique, some inspired by Greek Protogeometric, others by Southwest Anatolian pottery, but also mixing both. Thus the characteristic Greek circles and half circles are used in the black-on-red technique (Fig. 65) which originated on Cyprus and spread along the south coast of Asia Minor (Cilicia, Pamphylia).[39]

In pottery, too, there was an upsurge in quantity and diversity in the period of the Lydian Kingdom, ca. 680 (or 700) to ca. 550 B.C. The technical refinement in preparation of clay, faster wheel, higher firing, and the use of slips result from the imitation of Greek vase painting techniques and motifs, including floral, animals, and Rhodian "bird cups." This is the time when the Lydians approach in quality the output of Eastern Greek potteries, as C. H. Greenewalt has shown for the "Sardis Style" group within the so-called "Wild Goat" style.[40]

Shapes are imitated from Eastern Greek (amphora, trefoil jug, dinos, "lebes," "wavy line" hydria (Fig. 141), Rhodian "bird cup," "Ionian bowl," alabastron, lekythos), Corinthian (skyphos, kotyle, crater; Figs. 86, 119, 146),[41] and only exceptionally Phrygian (side-spouted pitcher and the plate with half spool handles; Fig. 119).[42] Some shapes may be imitations of Near Eastern metalwork—as the "omphalos bowl with central knob."[43] Toward the end of the seventh century B.C., Lydian potters developed original wrinkles: the "marbling" technique, "whereby diluted glaze of iron oxide variety was distributed in simple, usually wavy patterns often over a cream colored slip" (Fig. 76), the "streaky" technique, and a much used decoration in white lines and dots on overall

dark glaze (Figs. 86, 127). Then there also emerged the one original Lydian shape—the conic-footed perfume jar known as lydion.[44] With the addition of more traditional Anatolian techniques and shapes, notably the use of bichrome and trichrome carinated bowls and high-footed "fruit stands" (Fig. 37), the Lydian potters now settled into a conservative—not to say monotonous—mass production of unambitiously decorated painted wares which lasted into the fifth or fourth century B.C. Some idea of the normal household crockery may be gained from the assemblage discarded at NEW (Fig. 87) and PN and the sets found in the graves (Figs. 119, 127).[45] Special purpose sets were made up in quantity for the "Ritual Dinner" sets (cup, plate, jug, cooking pot; Figs. 145, 146).[46] It is impossible to estimate the total production. The leftovers of several shops in HoB/Lydian Market run to many thousands of vessels.

There was some specialization. The coarse, heat-resistant cooking pots[47] required a production technique different from those of the plain and decorated wares; they were probably made by specialized potters. Chance survival has given us part of the inventory of a "Potter's Shop" at HoB of ca. 625–600 B.C.; his specialty was "wavy line hydriae," sufficiently valuable to be repaired with lead clamps (Fig. 141).[48]

From the relatively small number of imports, chiefly wine jugs (Fig. 38), cups (Fig. 77), mixing bowls (craters, deinoi), and perfume/oil flasks (aryballoi, Fig. 155; also stone alabastra), it follows that almost all requirements of the internal market were met by local production (see the section on "Trade" below).

The later stages of Sardis ceramics in the fifth and fourth centuries B.C. remain to be worked out, and fall in any case into the Persian era.[49]

Two simple saucer lamps with pinched nozzles ("Phoenician") are followed by bridged nozzle lamps corresponding to Greek types. Local production is assured by mineral analysis and illustrated by a pile of unused lamps of the mid-sixth century B.C. found in HoB/Lydian Market (Fig. 140).[50]

The production of architectural terracottas from terracotta or other molds required larger and somewhat different facilities. The workshops have not been found. The material as well as the painting pigments involved have been analyzed by D. Kamilli and found to be local.[51] The technical process has been clearly described by A. Ramage and elaborated by E. Hostetter, who has conducted an attempt to reconstruct part of a Lydian building with terracotta decoration. It involves a design, a master relief reproduced then in molds from which several copies can be taken. The casts were then slipped and painted.[52] The general inspiration was Greek, but there were close ties to Phrygian Gordion. As A. Ramage observes, "We must think in terms of a trade in designs or even in molds."[53] Involving acroterias, gutters (simas), roof tiles, and possibly wall friezes, the Sardian production lasted from ca. 600 B.C. into the fourth century B.C.; the ambitious figurative friezes (Figs. 66, 75, 153), however, fall largely into the time of the Lydian Kingdom. The decorative terracottas were used both in public buildings and small private houses. Unfortunately, since no set was found with its building and most are fragments, it is impossible to estimate the extent of production. Tiled roofs certainly came into vogue in Sardis after the fire of 499 B.C., and this technology eventually changed the appearance of the city.

The production of mold-made pre-Hellenistic terracotta figurines is surprisingly small in the Lydian period. They number only 35 of a total of 174 figurative terracottas from all periods. The strange bearded head with horse's ears from HoB/Lydian Market is the most striking Lydian piece. Archaic and early classical female heads (protomai) and a dove were found by the first Sardis expedition.[54] Among the fragments are many more animals than humans. There was, of course, constant production of utilitarian objects such as loom weights and spindle whorls, which may have been produced and sold in the HoB/Lydian Trench area, where thirty-two loom weights were found near an "industrial installation."[55]

Trade

From literary evidence we surmise for the "Homeric" period from ca. 1000 to 700 B.C. a primitive palace economy in which the products of daily life (baking, brewing, spinning, weaving) and luxury goods are prepared and stored within the royal palace.[56] In Homer, the Maeonian woman tints (and carves?) the ivory imported through barter by the king or received as a "present." There is an implication that the feudal horsemen aristocracy does not participate in the luxury trade; they envy the king (Iliad 4:141–145). This economy is superposed on a rural-pastoral economy of herders and peasants.[57] Then there is a sudden change toward a more complex urban and mercantile economy.

Achaeology supports and modifies this picture. In architecture, the "vernacular" primitive light construction yields to larger, more sophisticated buildings after the Kimmerian destruction (Figs 31, 35, 63). In pottery, the slow development of traditional monochrome wares was enriched by some painting techniques borrowed from Greece and Southwest Anatolia (tenth to eighth century B.C.). These indicate foreign contacts and some trade with neighboring states and regions—Greek cities such as Smyrna, Ephesus, Miletus, Samos, the Anatolian regions of Phrygia, Caria, and Lycia. A. Ramage rightly infers from the prevalence of pithoi as storage and a largely domestic economy that copper and tin and bronze objects (such as Phrygian-type fibulae; Fig. 29) had to be imported.[58]

Then everything changed. Lydia is the one state in the Mediterranean world for which the sudden rise of a social class of merchants and bankers—kapeloi or agoraioi—was very specifically noted and linked to the use of coinage by very ancient tradition, perhaps claimed by Lydians themselves. The term kapelos implied that these were people who traveled, kept accounts, and were motivated by profit. At Sardis this was a legally defined class, known as "People of the Market (agoraios)," liable to work and probably to pay for royal enterprises.[59]

An important addition is Xenophon's report on what he calls "Lydian Market"—its merchants traveled with Cyrus' barbarian part of the army, purchased grain, and resold it to individual soldiers. The name implies an overall organization by a company, the procedure an aggressive venture policy—willingness to take risks in foreign countries. The invention of readily portable money made it easier to take the profits home and, eventually, to arrange payments abroad.[60]

The rise of banking, individuals, and houses, known in detail in Mesopotamia, may be dimly surmised in Greece, chiefly from mention of rich, venturesome individuals. It must be inferred for Lydia.[61]

In this connection, Anatolian temples should be mentioned. For Sardis, a loan of gold pieces by Artemis is first known from the Hellenistic document of Mnesimachus; but property transactions with the temple are recognized in Lydian inscriptions of the Persian era. Indeed, the new long inscription (IN 71.1; Fig. 154) may contain mention of money.[62] The evidence is more explicit for Artemis in Ephesus, whose temple and cult had such close connections with Sardis. There, comprehensive financial operations reaching into several aspects of state economy are illustrated by an archaic inscription. The function of the temple as a "safe" is illustrated again by Xenophon, who left his funds with the Chief Priest of Artemis (401 B.C.) before departing on his campaign into Asia.[63]

Meantime, the King still retained his traditional position as chief agent of international exchange and some of the traditional barter and "presents" methods, but with vastly increased financial powers. Croesus' "dedications" to Delphi, Didyma, Ephesus, and Oropos have been interpreted as purchases of influence and means to dispose of surplus gold and silver. His alliance with Sparta certainly was purchased by a quid pro quo—a previous present of gold to the Spartans for a statue of Apollo. The interesting fact is that the Spartans were ready to *buy* the gold from the king. Apparently, he was expected to act like a merchant.[64]

Two stories of famous "presents" illustrate the survival of the high-level mechanism which served "trade by gift." They also show that the Lydian kings lacked an effective navy and control of convenient ports.[65] Finally, they are revealing instances of the kind of goods involved in this type of trade between Corinth, Sparta, and Sardis. Having overrun Corcyra, "Periander, tyrant of Corinth sent three hundred boys of the first families of Corcyra to Sardis to Alyattes for castration." The Corinthians put in at Samos (presumably thinking the Samians either neutral or friendly to the Lydians). The Samians saved the boys and returned them to Corcyra.[66] The Spartans "also made a bronze crater decorated with small figures and large enough to hold 300 amphorae. They set off to make a counter-present" (for the gold Croesus gave them for the statue of Apollo?). The Samians heard about it, "attacked the Spartans with warships, and took it off."[67] The inability of Alyattes and Croesus to cross the one mile of water between the mainland and Samos in order to intervene is telling.

Landowning nobility was by definition not includable among the official class of "People about the Agora," the "hucksters." Yet, unlike the Roman senators, Lydian aristocrats were not excluded from production and trade. Again Pythes/Pythios is the only concrete illustration. He was of royal blood; yet his dreadful intensity in exploiting his mines and his boasting and counting of his fortune "in millions" are entirely in the spirit of the "Robber Barons" of the Industrial Revolution. He had a millionaire's mentality and wanted to know exactly how much he was worth. In Plutarch's story, there is a suggestion of "overdoing it" but no statement that as a nobleman Pythes/Pythios was not permitted to pursue a merchant's job.[68]

What do our archaeological finds contribute to this picture? We have found neither royal treasuries nor archives; no bank or company offices with cuneiform accounts; no private or public large storage facilities such as the warehouses at Al Mina; no actual temple deposits.

For the king, there are the vague indications of provisions for storage from the Acropolis, especially if the large circular cuttings served not only for cisterns but also for storage bins of supplies for the garrison and court.[69]

Much more important and striking is the contrast between the "modern," highly organized royal production facilities of the "Gold Refinery" (Fig. 139) and the modest, combined shops-dwellings of individual jewelers and gem cutters suggested by units in PN and HoB/Lydian Market (Figs. 35, 39–41, 44)—shops such as still exist in the Near East, Italy, Greece, and Turkey. A step more specialized are individual shop structures preserved in HoB: a man who sold and repaired pottery, another who sold lamps (Fig. 140). These probably represent the lower, local trade level of the *agoraioi,* the "People about the Market." Among the vast ceramic output sold in HoB/Lydian Market, there were, however, imported foreign vases (Fig. 38), though no one shop can be clearly recognized as a foreign outlet. The great lesson of Sardis is that much of the merchant class consisted of small craftsmen-entrepreneurs, whose places of business spread through a considerable part of the city. Nothing we found suggests large trade corporations.

Our evidence does not suffice to decide whether craftsmen of one kind settled together as they did in medieval cities. The HoB/Lydian Market had pottery and bronze workers, but also jewelers and perhaps textile workers. PN had jewelers and gem cutters. If L. Robert's interpretation of the "Sacrilege" inscription is right,[70] then there was a place "at the Chitons" where dresses were either made or sold. There is a hint of Carian foreigners either settling or gathering in a definite area of HoB.

The mechanism by which import and export worked is known in part from literary tradition. It is not unlikely that royal enterprise spearheaded economic ventures, that trade "followed the flag." The iron shackles sent by Gyges were noted as much in Assur as the gold, silver-iron, and silver presents of Alyattes and Croesus[71] were noticed in Delphi, Corinth, and Sparta. They were the one form of long-distance effective advertising available to antiquity, for Lydia was undoubtedly a leading exporter of gold as bullion and coin.

As to Sardis finds, so far only "souvenir" types of objects, such as scaraboid seals (Seal 62.2:4636), were brought from Egypt, in fact, from that great center of international grain trade, "Ruler of Ships," Naucratis,[72] and signets and glazed vases from Babylon. Ivory may have come from either.[73]

Phrygia claimed political domination over Lydia up to 700 B.C. The number of Phrygian pots and fibulae is not impressive as evidence of trade, though copper may have come via Phrygia.[74] Again, only isolated objects came from Iran, and some may be booty from battles with Kimmerians and Scythians; but the appearance of pre-Persian types of metalwork and pottery bears out the historical indications of increasing contacts from the time of the Medes on.[75]

Ephesus and Smyrna must have been vital to the Lydians as ports for import and export; consequently, Lydian merchants may have operated in both places. The lydion used as a saving box in Smyrna and the strong representation of Lydian coins in the "Base" deposit of the Artemis temple in Ephesus back up this claim.[76]

Because they are recognizable and, unlike metals, not valuable in themselves, imported pots give an adequate picture of contacts with Greece.[77] The trickle of Protogeometric (eleventh to eighth century B.C.) and Geometric pots seems to have come only a short distance from Greek coastal cities like Smyrna, Ephesus, and Miletus.[78] Here again there is a sharp change in range and quantity between 700 and 650 B.C. as

Eastern Greek wares imported and imitated now include those from the island of Rhodes in the south and the Aeolis in the north.[79] More striking vases come now from the Greek mainland, Corinth, and Sparta. Corinth, represented by a total of 250 fragments, comes early (Fig. 38); its import peaks once under Gyges and once under Alyattes; this parallels the political alliance of Periander of Corinth and Alyattes. The majority of vessels are small flasks, probably shipped in with their contents of oil or perfume (Fig. 155).[80] Spartans, courted by Croesus, are represented by wine cups.[81] Attic deluxe deinoi, craters, wine jugs, and cups (Fig. 77) appear under Alyattes. We also recall the historical visit of the exiled Attic leader Alcmaeon and the possibly apocryphal visit of Solon to Croesus.[82] The findspots of the imported vases show that they were not concentrated in the palace or a few upperclass dwellings; they appear in lower- and middle-class shops and houses.

Nothing in our finds gives direct information on Lydian exports. They are enumerated by Roebuck, Greenewalt, and others.[83] Electrum, silver and gold bullion, and coinage were probably in the lead,[84] followed by perfumes, ointments, and luxury garments. We have no better basis for recognition of Lydian products than the characteristic lydions probably exported as containers filled with perfume or ointment. Greenewalt's study[85] indicates that these Lydian products were reaching Italy (Sicily, Etruria) as well as the Greek mainland. As he rightly suggests, the "wrapping" was imitated to indicate contents (bakkaris), just as the "Cologne 4711" made and bottled in the United States is sold with bottles and labels similar to those of the original Cologne product.

The itinerant "Lydian Agora" clearly traded in grains, but they were probably purchased locally, not from Lydia.

On one major question archaeology throws as yet no light: why, in view of such great supply in Lydia, did the prices of gold and silver remain so high? A mercenary fought for a goldpiece a month.[86] The appearance of gold in relatively modest graves indicates its downward spread. The stories of Midas and Pythes/Pythios preach that you cannot eat gold; perhaps there were times between 650 and 480 B.C. when Lydian city dwellers had gold savings yet insufficient food supplies.

A second conclusion emerged from the archaeological record of the HoB/Lydian Market area. Many, perhaps most retail transactions were still barter. Granted that gold and silver were eagerly retrieved at all times, and granted that many early denominations were minute, nonetheless, with exposures of the size of HoB and PN some coins should probably have appeared had they been circulating freely.[87]

Payments for labor, too, were largely in kind, as is so well illustrated by the Persepolis tablets,[88] in which it is only the merchants who are sent off with thirty silver shekels.

The "Pot of Gold" found by Shear may well have been hidden during an emergency (547 B.C.); its contents were more likely the trading capital of a rich Sardian merchant than a widow's lifetime savings.[89]

Sardis and Lydia were the first and prototypical example for the process of transition from an agricultural barter economy to an early commercial monetary urban economy. The archaeological record seems to indicate that the three or four generations between the invention of money (640–630 B.C.) and the fall of Croesus produced some great concentrations of wealth and probably an ever-increasing amount of large-scale monetary transactions; they did not suffice to make money an all-pervasive medium of exchange.[90]

GMAH

The Lydian Society

Who were the Lydians? To know them we should start with their physical remains. Since 1960, the skeletal remains found have been recorded by competent physical anthropologists and shipped to the Paleoanthropological Institute of the University of Ankara, at first under a voluntary agreement with the late Professor Muzaffer Şenyürek, subsequently under a compulsory clause of the excavation permits. Several studies were published by Professor Şenyürek's successor, Professor Enver Bostanci.[1] Because of their poor state of preservation, Bostanci did not analyze any Lydian remains. His general conclusions, based on the studies of crania and long bones of the Roman and Byzantine periods and comparisons with skeletal material from

other sites, were that the ancient Sardians included a strong dolichocephalic component and were of medium stature. He saw possible connections to earlier ancient Anatolian populations from the Chalcolithic through the Hittite periods.[2]

Lydian skeletal remains have been found partly in graves, partly in the urban area. Thus, the presence of at least fifteen individuals in the HoB/Lydian Market level afflicted by the Kimmerian destruction could be established;[3] to these must be added the skeletal remains of thirteen individuals reported from Lydian graves. Remains of one or more individuals were found in a "small stone-lined pit" in Unit XI, A, in PN.[4] The most remarkable find was the emergency burial in HoB, at E4/S104 *97–96, excavated and described by J. Savishinsky. The pit was bordered by a low stone wall (H. 0.60, Th. 0.20 m.) on the south (2.50 m.) and east (1.30 m.) sides. About 85–90% of the bones were human, 10–15% animal. The bones were found helter-skelter. Charred and uncharred human and animal bones were mixed. There were no gravegoods or even potsherds. The traces of burning were probably due to overlying osseous material. Savishinsky noted that at least ten male and female individuals ranging from childhood to maturity (ca. 35 years) were represented.[5] In a careful follow-up, D. J. Finkel argued that possible signs of a family relationship might be observed for five individuals.[6] Some of the people may have died in the fire, others from asphyxiation. Savishinsky saw no signs of violent death. Since Lydians normally did not cremate their dead, and since some bones were not charred, this strange mélange is best interpreted as an emergency burial, possibly undertaken some time after death—with whatever remains were still collectible. The presence of women and children makes it rather unlikely that these were invaders. Although one of her legs was missing, the most completely preserved individual was a girl, seven to eight years old (Fig. 34), who died under a collapsed hut in the same fire as the previous group.[7]

The detailed study of the Lydian skeletal remains is yet to be undertaken. Since some skeletal remains are also preserved from the Early Bronze Age burials and one Iron Age burial from the cemeteries of Ahlatli Tepecik and Eski Balikhane, it may eventually be possible to advance some suggestions about the development of the population from the third through the first millennium B.C. It remains to be seen whether the condition of the material in Ankara will permit specialized studies of bones and teeth and lead to observations on the state of health, diet, and life span of the ancient Lydians.[8]

The Social Strata (Classes)

If we begin our account of the Lydian society in the Early Iron Age (ca. 1000 B.C.), we perceive a somewhat contradictory picture for the pre-Mermnad period. Herodotus speaks in terms of royal dynasties; the Atyadai ruling until ca. 1190 B.C.; the Heraklidai (Tylonidai) ruling for twenty-two generations until 680 B.C.[9] For Homer, the Maeonian leaders who rule at the foot of Tmolus and the Gygean Lake are typical Homeric heroes, small, independent princes who come to the aid of the Trojans.[10] There is no implication that an overlord-king exists. Archaeology (A Ramage's levels 4–5)[11] attests to the existence of a settlement at Sardis. Some Submycenaean-Protogeometric connections are seen in the Late Bronze Age, and a rather rustic existence with marginal trade is observed between 1000 and 700 B.C. One may surmise that the Homeric warrior ideal dominated also in the society of Early Iron Age Lydia, the land of valiant horsemen.[12]

If Aristotle's collection of "State Constitutions" (Politeiai) contained an account of the Lydian polity, it is lost to us; no systematic account of the Lydian state survives.[13]

It is a persuasive conjecture that "Lydians" (liudva, Slavic) means "the People."[14] For Mermnad Lydia we can discern the existence within the state of several social "rungs": (1) the King (Qldaňs); (2) the aristocracy; (3) the priests and priestesses (kaveś); (4) the girls "who are working" (as whores), Herodotus' energazomenai paidiskai; (5) "the People about the Agora" (Herodotus' agoraioi—merchants); (6) the craftsmen (Herodotus' cheironaktes—"hand-workers"); (7) "free men": the Lydian word briga, according to Iobas via Hesychius, signifies a "freeman."[15] We do not know whether the status covered all urban classes as well as farmers; (8) serfs: the existence of a class who had to do the bidding of their lord is implied in the Pythes/Pythios story. He could compel "citizens" to work in mines or release them to be farmers and craftsmen. They may very well have been considered "free men"; (9) slaves: even without the dubious word nekyrtas interpreted as "slave, son of slave" in a poem of Hipponax, the existence of slaves must be assumed. Presumably they were, as in Homer, enslaved victims of warfare.[16]

The functions of the king are as follows: He acts as chief priest and mediator between the state and the gods, including gifts, sacrifices, and purifications. He leads the armies and presumably has judicial powers. As noted in the preceding section on trade, he eventually becomes the principal economic entrepreneur and part monopolist.

The kingship is in some myths tied to a double axe given finally to Zeus.[17] There are several indications that kingship may descend through the queen, and that possession of the right queen is part of the claim to royalty, as in the ascent of Gyges.[18] Old Anatolian traditions may have been followed in ritual renewals of the king's powers by a bath in the blood of a bull.[19] Another Hittite inheritance may be the enormous frequency of lions in art. On a divine or royal throne (Fig. 78), they may be both the sign of Cybele and the sign of the king. They do not appear as sepulchral guardians.[20]

Hittite survivals have been conjectured in the cremation of the king and in the cruel custom of having an army march between a body cut in two. The double axe or a magic ring are symbols of kingship.[21]

We have located the palace of the Lydian kings on the Acropolis (Figs. 79, 80; Plan I). Its fragments attest a monumental architecture in mixed stone and mudbrick construction which may be derived from Mesopotamia.[22] Detailed study may prove that it was built under Gyges or Alyattes rather than Croesus. Our investigations give some hope of finding more substructures but virtually no hope of retrieving the superstructure or finding the famous Treasury filled with gold or, more importantly, the archive, which must have contained correspondence with Egypt, Babylon, and the Greek states and sanctuaries.

There must have been at the court a considerable apparatus of royal servants and administrators, but virtually nothing is known of them, apart from Croesus' baking women and the royal messengers and heralds sent to Assyria and Greece. Special moneyers or officials in charge of the Mint have been suggested because of the inscriptions *Valvel* and *Kalil*[23] which Gusmani interprets as proper names, but which really should be royal designations.

We have found no representations of Croesus on the pyre, such as are known from Greece (Fig. 126).[24] We have found confirmation and illustrations of the meteoric expansion of royal power. We have ascertained that from Gyges on, the royal mounds surpassed all others in size (Figs. 97, 105); and that the king was able to command large corvées as Alyattes did to enlarge the mound of Gyges. He had the capability and resources to undertake monumental construction in stone, as in the crepis of the Gyges mound (Figs. 108, 109) and in the defenses of the city (Fig. 132) and the Acropolis. That the expansion of royal power was based on industrial technology and possibly monopoly of processing electrum has been revealed by the "Gold Refinery."[25] It exemplifies the industrial organization that made Croesus' bimetallic currency possible. The royal power also expanded through military technology. The Lydian engineers and sappers took Smyrna with a colossal assault mound, overturned a key tower in the defenses of Ephesus, perhaps by tunneling, and built the colossal mudbrick defenses at MMS in Sardis.[26]

As to aristocracy, quite certainly some of the tumuli with chamber tombs belong to the king's family and Sardian court aristocracy. The study of the distribution of tumuli groups on the Sardis region has suggested a "feudal" land-holding pattern.[27] In mythological projection or as typical scenes of contemporary life, we have the hunt ("Hunter's Vase"),[28] the Lydian cavalry on parade (Fig. 156), the battle, and the chariots and horsemen (Figs. 142, 143).[29] The horseman in the red cuirass and the Lydian in the purple cloak show the luxurious life of the aristocracy under Croesus.[30]

On the testimony of Aeschylus, himself a combatant at Marathon (490 B.C.),[31] Sardian chariotry with three- and four-horse chariots was an important component of the Persian army mustering in 480 B.C. It is very likely that the chariotry was part of the Lydian royal army before. In view of Herodotus' story that the Lydian cavalry fled before the camels, it is interesting to find the fragment of the terracotta statue of a camel together with a terracotta vase representing a Lydian horseman (Fig. 142).[32]

If the *Lud* of Jeremiah (Jer. 46:9) that "handle and bend the bow" are Lydians, then the kings had formed a corps of archers as part of establishing an army of mercenaries and had sent them to fight against Nebuchadnezzar in 608–605 B.C.[33]

It is not clear to what extent priests and priestesses constituted a separate class, though the Lydian word for priest or priestess, *kaveś*, is known. We have evidence from Lydian inscriptions, from the "Sacrilege" inscription of Ephesus, and Greek inscriptions that the Artemis Temple had a man as priest and (later?) a priestess.[34] We should recall, too, that Lydian girls served as priestesses or acolytes in the temple of Artemis at Ephesus.[35] Something has been said earlier about the role of priests as bankers. A herald for Artemis is mentioned in the "Sacrilege" inscription.

The new inscription of Droaphernes (Fig. 166) implies considerable cult personnel and a special group of "those who may enter" the sanctuary of Zeus.[36]

Two archaic statuettes of priestesses show that they wore special costumes,[37] and the women who approach Cybele on the archaic temple-model (Figs. 150–152) are probably also priestesses. The new Lydian inscription (IN 71.1, Fig. 154) does not seem to mention a specific priest but being a property document may emanate from priests as scribes.

A "high class" merchant might be represented on the stele of Atrastas, son of Sakardas (Fig. 159),[38] who is shown writing. Conjectural evidence of organization of foreign merchants has been offered for Carians (see the section on urbanism). Otherwise, archaeological evidence illustrates chiefly the houses and shops of the lower class of businessmen—small shops with pottery, lamps, bronze, and jewelry. In the state classification they may have been accounted craftsmen, "Men who work with their hands," *Cheironaktes*, rather than "Men about the Agora" (bankers?). Their dwellings at HoB, PN and NEW were simple but not uncomfortable, as A. Ramage has observed.[39] Their possessions may have included gold, silver, and gems. They certainly included imported wine jugs and cups. There is no indication that their owners were unfree or supervised.

Unfortunately, no inscription clarifies the status of the skilled workers in the royal Gold Refinery (Fig. 139)—free, slave, or conscripted.[40]

Nothing has been found which would clearly relate to slaves and slavery.

Of the life of the farmers, only the house excavated on the Gygean Lake provides a glimpse; it is a sizable building—and at the same time part of a hamlet, not an isolated homestead.[41]

New material has come to light about the urban (and possibly rural) division of Sardis into "tribes." It relates to the *phylai* Tmolis and Pelopis (Fig. 170). Together with the previously known tribes, Asias, Masneis, Mermnas, Alibalis, and probably the Lydian equivalent (*Bakivalis*) of the tribe Dionysias, they all refer to Lydian mythical heroes or gods.[42] It is not clear what relation these official "tribes" bore to the *tagmata,* criticized by Apollonius of Tyana for their shameless designations.[43] Because of their native Lydian names, it appears very likely that the tribal divisions (*phylai*) reflect some sort of pre-Hellenistic Lydian social organization.

Sex and the Position of Women

A number of ancient authors seem to reproach the Lydians with irregular sexual behavior and hint at a code of sexual conduct for women different from that of the Greeks. The most significant feature for the Lydian attitude toward sex is the worship of the bisexual figure of Angdistis, whose mystery cult is now specifically attested for Sardis by the inscription of 367 B.C. (Fig. 166). According to the cult legend of Pessinus in Phrygia, the semen of Zeus fell on earth and produced the hermaphroditic Angdistis. The other gods cut off his/her male member, which, however, impregnated the daughter of the river god Sangarios (her name, Nana, is Lydian). She gave birth to beautiful Attes (a double of Attis), with whom Angdistis and also the goddess Cybele fell in love. Attes, put into madness by Angdistis, castrated himself under a pine. "Zeus" made his body incorruptible. This legend overlaps with the better-known legend of Attis in which Attis is put into madness by Cybele, castrates himself, dies, and is revived each year. In a different form, the change of sexes is the theme of the Omphale-Herakles myth. Omphale ("The Navel Woman") is clearly an Earth Goddess (like Ge in Delphi, who also had an omphalos). In the Hellenized myth, she is the earliest Lydian queen, and the Greek hero Herakles becomes a transvestite serving her for seven

years. In both cases, men sacrifice their manhood to a woman; both in the Angdistis myth, where an almond tree is involved, and in the pine tree which is Attis there is an underlying suggestion that by blood or semen falling to earth, vegetation is enabled to continue.[44]

Men must fertilize and then perish. This self-destructive aspect is complemented by the assertive, even destructive aspect of women. Associated with this nature-bound complex is the god-sent madness and union with nature for the Lydian women, the Bakkhai, who follow the Lydian god of wine, *Baki* (Dionysus), to the mountains.[45] The Amazons (of whom Omphale is also the queen), Omphale, Damonno, and the wife of Candaules are all dominant figures taking the initiative.[46]

Because Gyges reaches kingship by possessing the queen, there has been speculation that the Lydians once had a matriarchal society; but the Lydian inscriptions give only the father's and grandfather's name. There are no clear indications of matrilineal descent, nor can we see any special powers given to women other than queens and priestesses.[47] Indeed, the wife and daughter of Croesus are supposed to die with him.[48]

In the framework of daily life functions, the women were undoubtedly involved in textile production, as the legend of the Lydian Arachne indicates;[49] and the tradition of women as specialized potters, observed by H. G. Crane today at Gökeyüp, probably goes back to hoary antiquity.[50]

Leaving aside for the moment the matter of girls earning dowry by prostitution and the alleged castration of women, there remains a specific statement that it was shameful not only for women but also for men to be naked—a very old taboo in the Near East. It is noteworthy that we seem to have found no archaic Lydian representations of either naked men or naked women, and apparently no nude athletes.[51]

For sexual behavior of men, there is an important ritual in the slaying of the bull and the bath of blood, in which the king's (and initiate's) virility was renewed. In the mysteries of the Cappadocian goddess Ma, again attested for Sardis in 367 B.C. (Fig. 166), "Rhea was called Ma and a bull was sacrificed for her among the Lydians."[52]

"Phallus cult is nature cult." Archaeology has brought some evidence. The painted phallus found in HoB/Lydian Market[53] (and which was, G. M. A. Hanfmann believes, erroneously attributed to the terracotta figure of a Lydian horseman),[54] may have belonged to a small cult place, domestic or public. Those of the Lydian grave markers which really resemble phalli indicate that Lydians believed in the survival of male procreative power, perhaps in a way analogous to the survival of the *genius* (procreator) in Roman beliefs.[55] The phallus from HoB would, of course, fit into an Attis-like cycle or might represent a more assertive male virility worship. We seem to have found no clear testimony for cults of female fertility.[56]

There is finally the question of homosexual behavior and the curious notices about male and female castrates.[57] Bisexual behavior is not the same as homosexual or heterosexual. Unless we assume that 300 young future castrates shipped to Croesus were to become objects in homosexual relations, it is very striking that with all the interest in the scandalous behavior of the Lydians, no ancient author specifically alleges male homosexual relations or lesbianism despite the fact that at least one of Sappho's disciples went to Sardis.[58]

From the fact that girls were sent to practise prostitution in order to earn a dowry, it is clear that the Lydians for marriage preferred experience to virginity.[59] Beyond this, there is a suggestion of a harem atmosphere for the court, and probably for the aristocracy. Unless the 300 castrates were to serve as priests of Cybele—which is a possibility—if they were to become "eunuchs" in the strict sense of the word, then Croesus was presumably going to give many of them to his courtiers and other important Lydians.[60] As to the "harem atmosphere," the evidence for more than one wife and/or mistress is clear for King Meles and Alyattes.[61] Castration of women makes sense if there was an intention to prevent conception of bastard children by second wives or mistresses.[62]

Some curious echoes of the character and behavior of Lydian women come from later ages: allegedly in the first century A.D. the miracle maker and sage Apollonius of Tyana reproached the Sardian women for being like the tribal names of Sardis and even more shameless.[63] Yet, in Rome and elsewhere, the name Lydia came often to mean an enchantress in the arts of love.[64]

Family, Interpersonal, Intergroup Relations

Our archaeological findings do little more than circumscribe some possibilities. From literary sources and inscriptions we learn that the family was the basic unit, that the father and his profession were important, that parents loved their children, and that Pythes/Pythios had five sons.[65] The dwellings we have excavated (Figs. 135–137) attest a physically close life in relatively small units. This does not necessarily signify small families. It was striking, on the other hand, that the chamber tombs seemed to have been planned just for one or two generations (Figs. 114–116) without provision for many descendants.[66]

G. M. A. Hanfmann believes that the existence of smaller, walled precincts may indicate community units smaller than the tribes, grouped on the basis of living-together rather than of a *genos,* and that such units stand between the nuclear family and the phyle; but of this we have no certainty.

GMAH

Languages and Writing, Intellectual and Musical Life

Languages and Writing

Seven languages are attested in ancient Sardis, five of them in the Lydian and Persian period. These latter are Lydian, an unknown language similar to Lydian, Carian, Greek, and Aramaic.

Lydian is an Indo-European language, probably related to Luvian, Hittite, and other tongues which appeared in Anatolia early in the second millennium.[1] While not numerous and unfortunately usually short, the new texts discovered by the Harvard-Cornell Expedition have given new impetus to linguistic studies and have enabled the linguists to make considerable progress in some respects. This is due to the close liaison maintained with leading scholars of Anatolian linguistics, especially R. Gusmani, O. Masson, G. Neumann, J. Puhvel, and V. V. Şevoroşkin, to whom texts were promptly made available. By the official count of R. Gusmani, who is numbering Lydian texts consecutively, continuing the numbering in his *Lydisches Wörterbuch* (1964), about fifty Lydian texts have been added.[2] Altogether, forty new words have been recorded. Outstanding is the long inscription, IN 71.1, M3, no. A I 4 (Fig. 154), a marble stele with nineteen lines of text preserved. According to Gusmani, it may contain an agreement among members of a family concerning property and funds (perhaps even "money").[3] Hitherto tentative, the Lydian name of Cybele KYFAFA (*Kuvava*) has been assured by a graffito (Fig. 50) found near her alter in PN. A painted dedication to the Lydian Zeus has appeared on a sherd of the mid-sixth century B.C. (Fig. 144) found at HoB/Lydian Market.[4]

The new gains have not brought a real breakthrough for the understanding of the Lydian vocabulary, but they have brought great gains for the history and the development of the Lydian script. Thanks to the dates derived from the archaeological stratigraphy, typology, and style, a much more sophisticated distribution of script and phonetic-morphological developments has become possible. Instead of a vague division into "Classical Lydian" and "Late Script," students of Lydian writing now have some forty dated texts beginning around the mid-seventh century and ending perhaps as late as the second century B.C. The earliest Lydian signs (Gyges Mound) may be three generations later than the earliest known Phrygian inscriptions.[5] In his careful discussion of the origins and affiliation of the Lydian alphabet, Gusmani rightly argues that no simple "family tree" can do justice to the complexities of the situation, and he sees both Phrygian and Greek as major contributors.[6]

Finally, it is of interest for the spread of literacy that in Lydia mason's marks and graffiti on simple pots are among the earliest examples of Lydian writing (ca. 650–600 B.C.). Here as in Greece literacy was not limited to royal and priestly circles but spread quickly to the middle and lower classes.

The findings of the Sardis Expedition have stimulated a phase of intensive research on Lydian. Three major attempts to synthesize our knowledge have appeared: R. Gusmani's *Lydisches Wörterbuch* (*LW*, 1959; 1964); V. V. Ševoroškin's *Lidiyskiy yazik* (1967); and A. Heubeck's "Lydisch" (1969). To these must be added O. Carruba's comprehensive critical review-articles and Gusmani's recent summary, "Die lydische Sprache" (1975).[7] Although Gusmani's *LW* and subsequent editions of texts have

been accepted as the factual basis for research, lively controversies have developed on such basic issues as the transliteration and transcription (at least two, possibly four signs/sounds are controversial); grammar (for instance, whether or not the feminine gender existed); and the degree to which Hittite and Luvian parallels may be constructively used. New texts are being added, but much more comprehensive material is needed before the Lydian language will really be known and understood.

Because the Carian language and writing are very poorly known and "practically not deciphered" (Gusmani), and because the texts have come in large part from the writings of Carian mercenaries in Egypt, exceptional interest attached to the appearance of six certain and five possible Carian graffiti in the HoB/Lydian Market (nine) and PN areas. They were dated by G. M. A. Hanfmann from ca. 650 to ca. 550 B.C. No translations have been attempted.[8]

The Carians, who occupied a large territory south of Lydia, had close ties with the Lydians. Lydos and Kar, eponymous ancestors, were said to be brothers. The Lydian royal double-axe wound up as an attribute of the Carian Zeus at Mylasa.[9] The Lydians often campaigned in and certainly held parts of Carian territory—thus a Lydian inscription has been found at Aphrodisias in Caria.[10] It is also thought that Gyges might have sent Carian mercenaries to Egypt, but this is not explicitly attested.[11] Much more important is the fact that the mother of Croesus was a Carian woman.[12] The inscriptions in HoB begin right after the Kimmerian invasion, ca. 640 B.C., and continue perhaps to 547 B.C., the date of the capture of Sardis by the Persians. Almost all of them were found near Building "D",[13] which had a later seventh century and a mid-sixth century phase.[14] Rather than a possible settlement of Carian mercenaries, the commercial ambient suggests Carian merchants, perhaps favored by some elements at the court. We conjecture that Building "D" might have been a "club house," a *lesche* of the Carians. The early dates of Sardis inscriptions make them important for the determination of the Anatolian form of Carian script.

A teasing puzzle was discovered in 1963 in an inscription written on a marble pillar in a hitherto unknown language. It has become known as the "Synagogue Inscription" (Fig. 157) because it had been reused in a late (fourth century A.D.) pier of the Roman period Synagogue. The original date of the finely cut marble pier is not earlier than the sixth nor later than the fourth century B.C. The marble piece may have served as a statue base (Hanfmann). It is somewhat too high (H. 0.88 m., as preserved) for an altar-table, as suggested by Gusmani.[15] The twelve lines resemble Lydian, but several letters differ. *Sfenals*, "property," is a Lydian-like word. Maeonian and Torrhebian, which stood in dialectal relationship to Lydian, have been suggested.[16] It is remarkable that a monument (votive?) of this size and quality should be inscribed in a non-Lydian, "unofficial" tongue. The strange text is a reminder that a much greater variety of tongues and scripts existed in Anatolia than was hitherto believed.

We have found no Assyrian or Babylonian cuneiform nor Egyptian or Phoenician inscriptions, even though the Lydian kings maintained relationships with these countries. Sardis had supplied to Butler the famous Lydian-Aramaic bilingual,[17] but no other text was found between 1958 and 1978 in this, the official language of the west part of the Persian empire.

We have indicated that Greek speakers may have come to Sardis in the twelfth century B.C.[18] A trickle of trade is attested by imported Greek pottery before 680 B.C. It increased to respectable proportions thereafter. We have tangible evidence of the presence of Greek writers in the form of a graffito on a native plain bowl, which dates from ca. 570 to 550 B.C.[19] The earliest inscription on stone known so far is almost a century later.[20] Greek inscriptions painted in Athens on Attic pots make their appearance with the "Merrythought Cup" found on the Acropolis (Fig. 77).[21] They were probably understood by the contemporaries of Alyattes and Croesus. How quickly the Greek language spread, we do not know. Already Xanthus (ca. 450–400 B.C.) wrote in Greek for Greeks (and Lydians?).[22]

The Droaphernes texts (Fig. 166) seem to show that by 367 B.C., official Persian documents were being translated into Greek (as well as Lydian).[23] The Lydian-Greek bilingual of *Nannas Dionysiokleos–Nannas Bakivalis* is probably of the mid-fourth century B.C.[24] The next Greek text we found is the stele of Matis, ca. 250 B.C. (Fig. 171).[25] The "Sacrilege" inscription (340–320 B.C., according to L. Robert) found in Ephesus and the inscription concerning an embassy from Sardis found in Miletus (dated around 323 B.C.)[26] give no hint of any involvement with Lydian language. After 300 B.C. all but two inscriptions[27] on stone are in Greek.

Intellectual and Musical Life

We have proved that the Lydians wrote early, ca. 650 B.C., but they did not write much. A galaxy of highly literate Greek poets, musicians, philosophers, scientists, and statesmen visited Sardis: Alcman, Hipponax, Terpander, probably Sappho, possibly Alcaeus, the artist-engineer Theodorus of Samos, Solon and Alcmaeon of Athens, and the founder of the pre-Socratic school— Thales of Miletus, who supposedly served as consultant to Croesus' armies. Finally, the historian Hellanikos, as well as Herodotus and Xanthus, wrote on the Lydians.[28]

By contrast, writing in Lydian can be only conjectured to have included royal annals, recording such events as Gyges' embassies to the Assyrians and Alyattes' campaigns against the Greek cities. There were royal rescripts and memorial inscriptions, such as Herodotus saw on the mound of Alyattes (Herodotus 1.94). However, the only "historic document" preserved in Lydian is the dedicatory inscription of Croesus on the column of the temple of Artemis in Ephesus.[29] There was apparently a "popular" mythical-folkloristic (oral?) tradition about the royal house of the Heraklidai (Tylonidai) and their doings. It may have been written down in some form before Xanthus picked it up. Otherwise, contracts, dedications, and monotonous sepulchral texts including standard curses against violators are all that we have.[30]

The Lydian inscriptions (Figs. 144, 154, 159) are thought by some scholars to include texts in "poetic" form.[31] The most famous invention of Lydia other than gold and silver coinage was the "Lydian mode" in music.[32] It must have had texts to be sung. We have found no inscriptions with musical notation nor any representations of musical insruments. Such representations are known in nearby Smyrna as early as the mid-seventh century B.C.; and Terpander, inventor of the seven-stringed kithara, "sang at the feasts of the Lydians."[33] The purchase by the Berlin Museums of an enigmatic, archaic ivory of a woman standing on a sphinx has led to an attempt to reconstruct a Lydian kithara; this must be viewed with caution.[34]

We have a charming picture of Lydian dances in a Doric chorus from a comedy by Autocrates of Athens (fourth century B.C.): " . . . as the dear virgin girls of the Lydians play lightly and clap their hands by the (Temple of) Ephesian Artemis, the Beautiful—and she (the Lydian girl) sinks down on her hips and leaps (rises) up again just like a wagtail bobs about" (after J. G. Pedley, with modification).[35] Representations of such dances may have been intended in the reliefs of the dancing girls on the temple model of Cybele (Fig. 152).[36]

Herodotus (1.94) credited the Lydians with the invention of "dice and knucklebones and ball and all other kinds of games." His claims for dice and knucklebones have now been validated by excavated material. We have found archaic Lydian dice of terracotta (Fig. 158). Though not really a Lydian invention, since earlier dice are known from Mesopotamia, they are said to include a mathematically interesting arrangement.[37] Knucklebones *en masse* (128 pieces) have been found in a tomb at Indere; C. H. Greenewalt notes that they were used in the astragal game and cites parallels from both Phrygian Gordion and a number of Greek sites. Nothing definite has been determined about the Lydian systems of numerical notation and mathematical-geometric operations. The only relevant information (other than dice) concerns the use of proportion in the "Lydian" type of brick. The use of a measuring system involving a foot of ca. 0.295–0.296 m. has been plausibly argued by A. Ramage.[38]

Apart from gold technology and reorganization of trade, the intellectual, literary, and scientific achievements of the Lydians are provincial compared to those of the Greeks. There was more power to their emotional utterances; but the ecstatic music for Bacchus and Cybele, and the soft plaint of the "effeminate" (Plato) Lydian mode, are lost to us.

GMAH

Religious Life

The complex subject of Lydian religion was clarified by J. Keil in a famous article in which he tried to stratify the cults of Lydia into Lydian-Anatolian, Persian, and Greek and Roman layers.[1] Basic to any modern interpretation of the data on mythology and religion of a historic culture like Lydia is the awareness that religious experience is a changing phenomenon bound up inextricably with the cultural changes yet following rhythms and diffusionary mechanisms quite different from those of political and economic life. Thus, we find in Lydia on the one hand pre-Lydian religious concepts that may well go back to the Early Bronze or even Late Stone Age, such as the vegetation goddess (*Kore*), the snake cult, the bull hunt and bull blood bath, the mountain mother goddess with lions ("Mother of Gods"), the thunder and rain god (Lydian Zeus) and the double-axe (and axe generally) as the sign of thunder.

On the other hand, we find in *Kupapa, Kuvava,* Cybele, an immigrant goddess whose travels from Syria across Anatolia, to Phrygia, and thence to Lydia can be traced in terms of datable epochs, and whose arrival in Lydia probably falls into historical or near historical times (eighth century B.C.). The greatest difficulty in studying Lydian religion and mythology lies in the question: when and how did Hellenization occur? The difficulty is compounded by the fact that some transfers and contacts may have occurred in the Bronze Age (Herakles, Pelops), others in Homeric times (ninth to seventh century B.C.), and others yet in archaic and classical (Persian) epochs. Finally, we cannot take it for granted that it was only the Lydians who borrowed. Both Artemis and Apollo have strong Anatolian components or even origin; and Cybele-Rhea, Mother of Gods, went from Asia to Greece.

What we can see is that in Lydian inscriptions there occur a number of gods, some of whom continue (*Artimu, Kuvava*); others are transformed into Greek equivalents ("Zeus," "Kore"); and a few disappear (*Santas, Marivdas*). Insight into this process of religious transformation is made more difficult by the survivals and fusions on very local levels, often resulting in very strange but quite specific figures—Mên Axiottenos or Apollo Pleurenos. Very old things are often attested only from Roman times. Such survivals present a particular difficulty for this section, which in principle deals only with the religious situation in the Lydian period. We shall in general not attempt reconstructions based on all available sources but shall give some references to relevant data in the Persian, Hellenistic, and Roman periods.

Gods and Myths

The Harvard-Cornell Expedition has brought material of considerable value for a number of divine figures mentioned in Lydian texts. This material comes partly from excavations in the Artemis Precinct but principally from sculptural representations, pottery, inscriptions, small objects, and coins.[2]

To take the gods mentioned in Lydian inscriptions, we have added information on Artemis, Cybele, Lydian Zeus (Levs), possibly the god Q (or P) ldans,[3] then "The Maiden" whose Lydian name is unknown, and an equivalent of Aphrodite.

Artemis

An old theory held that Artemis and Cybele (and possibly Demeter and Kore as well) were all one goddess and that Cybele, Artemis, and Kore were worshiped consecutively (as amalgamations of the same divine power) in the great Artemis Temple.[4]

As a result of the Harvard-Cornell researches, Artemis emerges as clearly the greatest divinity of Sardis in the Lydian period and as completely distinct from both Kore and Cybele (Figs. 148, 150). There were at least three distinct incarnations of Artemis worshiped in the area of Sardis during the Lydian period: the Artemis of Sardis, sfardak, Sardiane; the Artemis of Ephesus, ibimśiś; and the Artemis of Koloe, Koloene, kulumśiś. The Artemis "to the Chitons" (epi chitonas) mentioned in the "Sacrilege" inscription of Ephesus[5] must be another name for Artemis of Ephesus. This inscription, dating from ca. 340 to 320 B.C. (L. Robert), makes it quite clear that an annual procession went from "The Mother Church" of Artemis Ephesia in Ephesus to the "Branch" of the Ephesian Cult in Sardis.[6]

An important monument bearing on the Artemis problem is the votive relief of ca. 400 B.C. found reused in the Synagogue (Fig. 93). Artemis is the bigger sister; she holds a stag or hind, the animal also seen as her attribute in the Ephesian cult. Cybele is the smaller figure; she holds a lion. Shown as images, the two goddesses are clearly differentiated.[7] The problem now arises—did Artemis of Sardis and Artemis of Ephesus use the same precinct and temple? Lyd-

ian and Greek inscriptions leave no doubt that the archaic altar (Figs. 94, 95) and the Hellenistic temple (Figs. 7, 88) belonged to *the* Artemis, who can only be the Artemis of Sardis.

The stele of Atrastas, son of Sakardas, ca. 520–500 B.C. (Fig. 159), provides the earliest written evidence of Artemis of Ephesus protecting the dead buried at Sardis.[8] The establishment of the Ephesian cult at Sardis may go back to the time when Croesus gave columns to the temple of Artemis at Ephesus (ca. 550 B.C.), where Lydian girls served as priestesses in the temple. With the present evidence, we cannot decide whether Artemis of Ephesus had a separate shrine, either in the Artemis Precinct, or, as Fleischer suggests, outside in an entirely different, smaller precinct.[9]

Another symbiosis problem arises from the Lydian inscription of the priest of Artemis, Mitrataśtaś, of the Persian era. Here a temple is said to be dedicated to Artemis and Qldans (Apollo?), according to Gusmani.[10]

Iconographic problems, too, are not completely resolved. On the strength of the relief (Fig. 93), all lion-holding Sardian goddesses should or could be representations of Cybele-Kuvava. A representation of a Potnia Theron holding lions upside down is known from an early terracotta frieze (ca. 600 B.C.); a reconstructed plate of Sardian make shows a goddess or a god (Fig. 153) holding either lion-like creatures or snakes.[11] Our finds confirm Radet's opinion.[12] What remains unclear is: did Artemis of Sardis, Artemis of Ephesus, and Artemis of Koloe all have the same attributes and image types?

The Artemis of Koloe was worshiped on the Lake Koloe/Gygean Lake, perhaps already in the Bronze Age. She was compared to the Syrian Atargatis and may have had sacred fish (Fig. 119) and/or priests dressed up as fish.[13] We were unable to find her sanctuary, allegedly seen by Spiegelthal[14] at the southeast corner of the lake. Instead, we found evidence for a sanctuary of a regional goddess, a Roman dedication to the "Mother of Gods of Lydia" on the north shore of the lake, east of the village of Saz Köy.[15] It is unlikely that this Cybele-like figure had any relation to the Artemis of Koloe.[16]

Cybele-Kuvava

We have proved (above) that Cybele and Artemis (Fig. 93) are distinct entities. Another important piece of evidence for Cybele is a graffito dated ca. 600–570 B.C. (Fig. 50); it secures the hitherto not quite certain Lydian name of the goddess: *Kuvav.* It was found under "cuppellation floor A" (Figs. 45, 46) of the Gold Refinery,[17] not far from an altar (ca. 570 B.C.) adorned with four lions (Figs. 42, 49, 52, 139) which was built to protect the gold processing—thus bearing out the conjecture of Jongkees that Cybele, Mother of the Mountains, protected the metals in the mountains and the people who worked them.[18]

A small marble head of the late seventh century B.C. may be the earliest surviving image of Cybele at Sardis.[19]

Of greatest importance for our understanding of the Lydian Cybele is the archaic temple model, which probably represents the pre-499 B.C. shrine of Cybele (Figs. 150–152, 160). It shows a new aspect of Cybele: holding a lion, the goddess stands between two snakes. This relates her representation to those of other Sardian snake goddesses.[20] The meaning of snakes is usually chthonic, earth-bound. They may allude to the crops stored in the bins and thus to fertility. Sophocles (*Philoctetes* 391–401) unhesitatingly invokes Cybele as "All Nourisher, Earth of the Mountains." On the other hand, when snakes began to swarm in the suburb of Sardis before the fall of Croesus, the Telmessian prophets explained them as "children of (Sardian) earth" symbolizing the people of Sardis.[21] In its eighteen panels the temple model presents a carefully thought out program. The sides relate to the cult and ritual of the goddess; the panels on the back to Lydian myths.[22]

A link important for the history of Dionysiac religion is established between the cycle of Cybele/Atthis and Baki-Dionysus in the combination of procession to Cybele and ecstatic Dionysiac dancers—maenads and comasts carrying wine bags (Figs. 151, 152)—a relation alluded to by Euripides in *Bacchae,* 72–82.[23]

It is less easy to establish whether there is a direct relation between Cybele and the mythical subjects shown on the back of the shrine (Fig. 160). Only one panel, a sacred tree protected by eagles, seems to allude to Cybele as protectress of vegetation.[24]

Two significant conclusions emerge from our researches and finds. *Kubaba-Kuvava* was a Syro-Hittite goddess, who came across Anatolia through Phrygia to Lydia. Herotodus notwithstanding,[25] she was not the great goddess of Sardis—but then, as usual, Herodotus actually had not said what he is made to say; he only said "the native goddess Kybebe," which could as well mean "one goddess of many," "a goddess." It seems reasonably certain that she arrived in Lydia from Phrygia between 1100 and 700 B.C. and was superposed upon an earlier Anatolian Mountain *Potnia.*[26]

Kore

An early Anatolian image of Kore, "The Corn Maiden," of ca. seventh century B.C. has become known through a reproduction on a Roman capital (Fig. 148). Roman coins, too, show the board-like (*xoanon*) image in typical Anatolian dress with wheat and poppy, veil and crown. Some projections around the waist are interpreted as eggs or "breasts" by Fleischer. On the capital she wears a moon sickle.[27] This is the Kore to whom the greatest Sardian festival, "The Feast of the Golden Flowers" (*Chrysanthina*) was celebrated.[28] She was clearly a goddess of vegetation. On coins of the Roman period from Nero on, she, rather than Artemis or Cybele or Demeter, stands for Sardis.[29] An important testimony to her bounteous character and her continued popularity has been added by an inscription of A.D. 211–212, which alluded to the statues of the "Children of Kore": *Koros*— "Plenty"; *Eupo(sia)*—"Abundance"; and possibly *Euetesia*—"Prosperous Year."[30]

In their detailed discussion, Hanfmann and Balmuth have pointed out that very local ritual practices could attach to the Anatolian "Kore" (Maiden). Thus at Nysa, the youths and ephebi from the gymnasium brought a bull to the cave inhabited by "Kore"—and the bull expired.[31] A "Hattic" pre-Hittite goddess of grain, *Kait,* is mentioned in Hittite documents of the second millennium B.C.[32] She may be a manifestation of vegetative power parallel to a West Anatolian Grain Maiden, who has stalks of grain as her attributes (Fig. 148), to that "Kore" who at Sardis had an early image in the time of the Lydian kings. When Sardis was Hellenized, the native name of this goddess was turned into Greek as "Kore." This may be the correct translation of the generic Lydian term for "maiden," or again, it may be another example of the ability of the

Greeks to find the Greek divine equivalent for any native divinity, if not on the basis of name, then on the basis of function. Overshadowed by Artemis and Cybele, this goddess continued to be worshiped in rites that may have had special relevance for youth.[33] During the antiquarian renaissance of native cults in the second and third centuries A.D., this "Kore" was rediscovered or revitalized and served for a while as the tutelary deity of Sardis. Roman coins show Kore in a temple of her own, different from the temple of Artemis. Hence her archaic image cannot be an archaic image of Artemis.[34]

What is not as yet clear is the relation in Roman times of this "Kore" to Demeter, substitute and successor to the Mother of Gods, Cybele. Demeter was said by some authors to be the protecting divinity of Sardis. This aggrandizement of Demeter, however, occurs in a highly rhetorical passage,[35] and the standard Greek myth of Demeter and Kore (Persephone) would give sufficient reason to call a city of Kore a city of Demeter as well.

Levs, the "Lydian Zeus"

Already known from Lydian inscriptions, *Levs*, the Lydian Zeus, was addressed in a dipinto of ca. 550 B.C., a dedication painted on a vase and found in HoB/Lydian Market (Fig. 144).[36] The painted dedication rather suggests that a sanctuary was not far away. The Lydian Zeus is also seen bearded, in long dress, on a Roman glass stamp as he stands in front of a flaming altar. In a type which first appears on Hellenistic, then on Roman coins (Fig. 147), he sacrifices in an open-air precinct, either in the city, or, perhaps, as a rain god on top of the Tmolus.[37]

The cult of Lydian Zeus as a rain god on the Tmolus is attested by one of the earliest Greek poets, Eumelus of Corinth, perhaps of the eighth century B.C. He says that "Zeus was born in Lydia . . . on the western side of the city of Sardis, on the mountain ridge of Tmolus . . . at a place which used to be called the Birth of Rain-bringing Zeus."[38] There was undoubtedly a sanctuary on top of Mount Tmolus, where we have found a number of sherds but no inscriptions. An unusual representation of the birth of Zeus found in a small villa in the Sardian Plain may refer to the Birth of Zeus at Gonai-Deusion in the Tmolus.[39]

Other traditions seem to give the double-axe (symbol of the thunderclap) to the Lydian Zeus and link him with the Carian Zeus worshiped in Mylasa. Originally, this rain god Zeus was probably an Anatolian weather and storm god similar to the Hittite/Semitic storm gods. As Gusmani points out, *Levs* is benign in a votive from the vicinity of Tire avenging violation of the grave in a stele dated by the Alexander era. It is noteworthy that he was still invoked by his Lydian name in 329 B.C.[40]

In addition to this clearly Lydian Zeus, we have to consider three other Zeus figures: Zeus Baradates (Ahura Mazda), whose statue, temple, and cult were introduced in 367 B.C.;[41] "Zeus of the City" (Polieus), who occurs in Greek inscriptions; and Zeus Olympios, Protector of Kings, to whom Alexander the Great built a temple.[42] L. Robert thinks a continuous development from Zeus Baradates to Zeus Polieus possible[43] because of the resemblance in the nomenclature of the *neokoroi* and the *therapeutai* and of "those who may enter the *adyton*," the most holy part of the sanctuary. We know that by the end of the third century B.C., Zeus (Polieus?) had joined Artemis in her temple, and we have the fragments of his colossal, possibly seated statue (Fig. 176). Almost at the same time a standing, cloaked Zeus Lydios is shown on coins attributed to 226–223 B.C. by Seyrig. Then there is a gap until the coins of Nero. Like Kore, Zeus Lydios seems to have experienced a subsequent renaissance in the second (Fig. 202) and third (Fig. 147) centuries A.D.[44]

Baki-Dionysus

That Baki, Lydian god of wine (Bacchus), was equated with the Greek "Scion of Zeus," Dionysus, is assured by the dedication of Nannas, ca. 350 B.C., in which "Bakivalis" is translated "Famed of Dionysus."[45] The equation may be much older. For it was in the seventh and sixth centuries B.C. that the Lydian Dionysus invaded the Hellenic world, as Euripides describes in the *Bacchae*. We have not found a Lydian representation or a secure inscription of *Baki(s)*,[46] but we have found Lydian representations of his followers (Fig. 152, middle and lowest panels), and the great importance of viticulture for Sardis and wine for Lydian life has been confirmed by our study of Lydian pottery and imported wine vessels.

Santaś

A problem yet unsolved is the relation of Baki to *Santaś*/Sandon, an Anatolian god, who has a grape as attribute in the relief of Ivriz (eighth century B.C.) and who appears with *Kupapa* (*Kuvava*) in a Lydian funerary inscription. He is probably the same figure as Sandon of Tarsus, who was also burned on a pyre and was equated by the Greeks with Herakles.[47]

Pldans/Qldans-Apollo

Most linguists no longer accept the equation *Pldans* = Apollo. Gusmani transliterates *Qldans*; and Heubeck equates him with the Moon God Mên, known in Sardis under the Greek name only since Hellenistic times.[48] The existence of an Anatolian Moon God is probable for the Lydian pantheon; but an Apollo-like figure is absolutely required. Croesus' devotion to Apollo is hardly likely without some native antecedent, and as Wilamowitz rightly argued from Homeric data,[49] Apollo is an Anatolian god; the oracles of Klaros and Didyma have Anatolian background; and in Sardis itself, there is no getting around the fact that *Pldans* appears next to *Artimuk* in the Lydian inscriptions, and indeed shares a temple with Artemis, according to Gusmani. Then again, there are such later figures as Apollo Pleurenos and his mysteries.[50] H. Cahn has marshaled considerable evidence in support of the view that a god with lions, a *Potnios Theron*, was the Anatolian Apollo, possibly descended from the Hittite Sun God. Cahn also tries to make him the protector of the Lydian Royal House, but here Cybele is more likely.[51]

Two representations found by the Harvard-Cornell Expedition might qualify as this "Lydian Apollo." A terracotta frieze, ca. 550 B.C., shows a "human" in a long chiton holding a sphinx by the tail. To G. M. A. Hanfmann, this is a god rather than a goddess (Fig. 153).[52] A Lydian plate (ca. 620–590 B.C.) painted in "Sardis style" and tentatively reconstructed by C. H. Greenewalt is so incomplete that a *potnios* is as possible as a *potnia*.[53]

Candaules, "Hermes the Dog Throttler"

Known on the high authority of the Ephesian archaic poet Hipponax, the evidence for a Lydian god Candaules, "Dog Throttler" (*canis,* and *daviti*—throttle), has been scrutinized in detail by C. H. Greenewalt, who sees the analogies to

Hermes as Helper of Thieves and possibly as an underworld god (Conductor of the Dead) as two prominent aspects. O. Masson had sought in Candaules a figure analogous to Mars, and thus a god of war.[54] If the so-called ritual dinners (Figs. 145, 146) were intended for him, we have added very substantial evidence for his cult.

Aphrodite?

The archaic relief of ca. 500 B.C. from the sanctuary of Dede Mezari may represent a goddess and not a votary; she would be an Aphrodite-like figure.[55] In a society where priestesses were important and girls sold love for a dowry, there must have been a goddess concerned with the love life of women; but the only hint we have is the statement by Charon of Lampsacus that in Lydia Cybele was Aphrodite. This would bring the Lydian *Kuvava* close to the Mesopotamian Ishtar[56]—a goddess of love and war; but the statement may be only one more attempt by a Greek author to find a suitable Greek equation for a native divinity.

Atys, Atas, Attis

One important figure is conspicuous by its absence from the excavation material. The pathetic youth Attis, *thalamepolos* of Cybele, according to an early Hellenistic poet, came to Sardis from the great cult center of the Phrygian Mother of Gods (Cybele)—Pessinus. In one form of his myth, Attis brought the cult of Cybele to Sardis and the (Lydian?) Zeus sent a boar who killed him.[57] If we take the story literally, Attis would arrive with Cybele not later than 700 B.C. Some of the Lydian representations of boars may allude to the story. A mystery hall of Attis and sculptured representations belong to Roman times.[58]

Myths and Heroes: Santaś, Tylon, Herakles

We have mentioned that the god *Santaś*-Sandon was also sometimes a hero burned on a pyre.[59] However, the real Greek equivalent of Herakles appears to have been Tylon, ancestor of the Tylonid dynasty which by Greeks was called Heraklid. Tylon and his friend Masnes were important figures in non-Greek local myths, and Masnes was commemorated in a local phyle.[60] On the other hand, the legend of Herakles and Omphale may be a native legend in very old

Greek guise.[61] On the Cybele shrine (Fig. 160), Herakles appears in standard Greek type slaying the Nemean lion. It seems probable that he was understood by the Lydians as the Greek Herakles and not the Lydian Tylon. If this is so, Greek mythology was well known to Lydians by the time of Croesus.

Even more fascinating is the problem of Pelops. The Greek legends locate the ill-fated dynasty of Tantalus on the Sipylus in Lydia. It is not clear whether they are competitors of the Atyadai who ruled Lydia in the Bronze Age, if one follows Herodotus, or rulers of a different region. Tantalus' son Pelops goes to Olympia and wins the first Olympic chariot race against the king of Pisa, Oinomaos. Eventually, the entire southern Greek mainland is named "Isle of Pelops," "Peloponnesos."[62] We now know that it would have been quite possible for a Lydian prince to teach chariotry to Mycenaean princes in the fourteenth and thirteenth centuries B.C.; this is based on Hittite documents and Greek myths.[63] Sardians did invoke Pelops as ancestor in a petition to Tiberius (A.D. 23), but hitherto, no real confirmation for an authentic tradition of Pelops had come from finds at Sardis; the earliest were Roman Imperial coins of the second century A.D. We have now found the Hellenistic inscription of a Sardian tribe Pelopis (Fig. 170).[64] This might be dismissed as an attempt by the Hellenized Sardians to annex an appropriate Hellenistic myth to the greater glory of Sardis; but the charioteer on the archaic Cybele monument of ca. 530 B.C. (Fig. 160) is an excellent candidate for Pelops.[65] He would authenticate the knowledge of Pelops at Sardis for the archaic age.

Animals, Birds, and Monsters

Lions, bulls, boars, deer, goats, eagles and hawks, as well as geese, fishes, snakes, pegasoi, sphinxes, griffins, and sirens, appear in seventh and sixth century B.C. Lydian art in the same types as they appear in Greece.[66] Are any of these representations meaningful? And are the meanings the same as in Greece? If this were the case, these art types would be the earliest evidence of Hellenization of Lydian religion and mythology.

These matters are not simple, however. Lydian meanings may have attached themselves to

Greek types. Lions are clearly attributes of Cybele and signs of the royal house. It is curious to note what they are not: with some thirty lions now known from Sardis, none appears to have been found protecting a grave—as did the lions at the Kazar Tepe in Miletus and other Eastern Greek tumuli.[67] The boar, on the other hand, is apparently a symbol of evil.[68] Of the birds, both eagles and hawks are claimed for *Kuvava.*[69] One may argue whether or not vase painting representations were ever meaningful; but the big archaic marble bird of the Nannas monument and the triple bronze hawks in Oxford must have been meaningful, as may have been the bronze bird (Fig. 51) from the "House of the Priest" (Unit XXVIII in PN).[70] Here again, theophoric royal symbolism may be involved. *Gyges* is to some linguists the name of a bird, and *mermnos,* "hawk," gave his name to the royal house of Mermnads.[71] Used in a marble throne, the sphinx may have had the meaning of a royal guardian as in Egypt and Syria.[72] The siren, too, must have been meaningful; one would not have made a purely decorative archaic marble statue.[73]

It is not clear whether any Lydian amulets have been found. There are animals and other devices shown on a Protogeometric seal, on scarabs, and on seals and gems; others act as protective devices in jewelry. A few ivory pieces are known too, but their amuletic efficacy can only be determined after an overall study of Lydian minor arts has been made. The comprehensive and thorough treatment of Lydian pyramidal seals of the Persian Era by J. Boardman shows what needs to be accomplished.[74]

Cult and Ritual

The functions of the king and the evidence for a priestly class and special personnel at sanctuaries have been reviewed in their social context. We have mentioned too the sacrifices, processions, and dances.[75] Valuable additions to our knowledge of ritual have come from archaeological material, especially the discoveries of the archaic altars of Artemis (post-499 B.C.?) and Cybele (ca. 570 B.C.; Figs. 49, 95).

The Artemis altar LA 1 (Figs. 94, 95) surprised us by the indication that it was turned west toward the city of the dead, which Artemis protected. The west orientation has also been claimed for the temples of Artemis in Ephesus and Magnesia on the Meander.[76] At present it seems that at Sardis neither altar had initially an adjacent temple. This was the case for Artemis from ca. 490 to 270 B.C. There was no temple in the immediate vicinity of the Cybele altar throughout its career (570–450? B.C.). Unlike the altar of Artemis, the altar of Cybele was turned east and the four lions roared eastward. The little step for the sacrificant was on the west side (Figs. 45, 49). The altar contained traces of regular burnt sacrifices of animals.[77] There is not enough space and no other evidence for the ritual slaying of the bull which later formed an important part of the cults of Ma and Mithras.[78]

What unexpected surprises may yet appear is clear from the recovery of some twenty-six deposits of sets of four pots and iron knives—as well as bones of young dogs in cooking pots (Figs. 145, 146). Most of these were found in a small area in the HoB/Lydian Market, and a few in PN. These "Ritual Dinners" have been published in an exemplary monograph by C. H. Greenewalt, Jr., who in the end considers them as a series of ritual votives, untouched dinners presented to the god Candaules and buried in pits over a period of up to fifty years (575–525 B.C.).[79] G. M. A. Hanfmann, however, believes that these were deposited at a one-time occasion, just before the fall of Sardis in 547 B.C.; he also points out that the ancient tradition strongly insists on the Carian use of dog sacrifices and that the building around which the burials were made contained earlier Carian inscriptions. The offerings may have been made by Carian merchants.

Religious Attitudes

Were we to judge the Lydian religious experience entirely on the basis of the Herodotean Croesus, we would see the Lydians as a people whose almost frantic search to ascertain the divine will was expressed through oracles and who appeased the gods by sacrifices and votives. This is, however, Herodotean interpretation. If we look at the overall evidence, we see reflected not only the cumulative results of millennial experiences and influences from the East, South, North, and West; we can also perceive reflected the dualism of the plain and the mountain, agriculture and pastoralism.

Clearly, the Kore of Sardis with her wheat (Fig. 148) and Baki with his grapes are gods of agriculture; the Rain God (Lydian Zeus) and the Mountain Goddess (*Kuvava*) are of the world of the mountain. While there is much evidence of formal organized religion with priests, heralds, processions, and temple dances, there is in the Lydian culture a powerful element of emotion; such violent cults as those of Cybele, of Attis, of Angdistis, of Ma and the rapid expansion of mysteries speak of strong emotional responses to nature, which ultimately became best known through the spread of the Dionysiac cults and of the metragyrtai of Magna Mater.[80] It is probable that the mysteries of Angdistis, Sabazius, and Ma, first attested in 367 B.C., as well as those of Attis and those of Apollo Pleurenos,[81] first known in Roman times, had already spread into Lydia in the time of the Lydian kingdom. And next to these elemental religions, there may have flourished many very local manifestations of worship and obeisance to special local powers that seem to present themselves so strikingly in the varied phenomena and moods of the Sardian landscape.

GMAH

Cultural Perspectives

In the preceding sections we have sought, however imperfectly, to integrate the results of our excavations and researches with prior knowledge about Lydia derived from verbal and material sources. In the following we shall try to indicate the state of some major problems concerning the origin and development of Lydian culture.[1] In so doing, we must recall that the parameters of a complex, literate culture developing in a literate world can only be drawn on the basis of written sources. Archaeology can make three major contributions within this framework: it can produce more written (i.e., inscriptional) evidence; it can help decide among the possible alternative theories or models; and it can build up from architecture and artifacts a picture that is much more dense and concrete and provide information about aspects where written information is deficient and incomplete.[2]

Our literary sources show that between 680 and 547 B.C. under the Mermnad kingdom, Lydian culture entered an expansive, intensive, explosive phase. Centralization of royal power, effective organization of armed forces with innovative emphasis on cavalry, mercenaries, and siege-craft, energetic initiative in conquest of neighboring regions, bold pursuit of distant alliances with Assur, Babylon, Iran, Egypt, and mainland Greece (Corinth, Sparta), and a total transformation of economic life by the invention of money and the creation of new forms of domestic and foreign trade with a concomitant rise of a class of entrepreneurs—these are the constituent features of the Lydian culture at its height. In the ideological realm, the ideal of plutocracy or "monetocracy," of the power of coinage as money and what it can buy in terms of goods and services, is linked, as often happened with later nouveaux-riches, with an attempt to create a life of unheard-of splendor and luxury, full of the "useless Lydian softnesses" (Xenophanes).[3]

In an attempt to apply modern statistical methods of biological research on populations, and basing his study on sixteen osteometric variables of cranium and mandible, D. J. Finkel (1974) concluded that the ancient Sardians belonged to a "superpopulation," that is, a regional biological group, which included coastal Western Anatolia from Troy to Bodrum. He detected no major changes in the biological composition of this group between 2600 B.C. and A.D. 200. According to Finkel, the historically recorded or hypothetically postulated migrations were not a major dynamic factor, perhaps because the immigrants came from biologically similar stock. He specifically rejected the possibility of migration from Eurasian steppes, which envisaged the Lydians among other Indo-European speakers as arrivals between 2000 and 1700 B.C. Finkel's interpretation would mean that a biological, genetic continuity persisted from the third millennium B.C. to the time of the Lydian kingdom despite linguistic, political, and cultural changes.[4]

The problems posed by this phenomenon are innumerable. There is, first, the Lydian language, presumably a primary constituent trait of Lydian culture. We have shown that it was written by the mid-seventh century B.C. By finding the "Synagogue" inscription (Fig. 157, detail), we have shown that the linguistic situation may have been more complex and fluid than was suspected; there may have been dialectal di-

versity within the political Lydian heartland area. We have found no written material from the second millennium B.C.; we have found no rock-cut inscriptions in "Hittite Hieroglyphic" (Luvian), nor any cognate of Aegean scripts (Linear A, B) nor writing in any other second millennium tongue. The linguistically well founded hypotheses (O. Carruba, G. Neumann) which relate Lydian to Nesian or Luvian and see Lydians as Indo-European speakers arriving in Western Asia Minor about the same time as Hittites arrived in the center of the peninsula, i.e., 2000–1800 B.C., remain unsupported by direct archaeological evidence.[5]

The origins of Lydian culture presumably lie in the second millennium. Prior to our excavations it was a tenable "model" to assume that as Assuwa (H. T. Bossert) or Masa (G. M. A. Hanfmann), Sardis was one of the hypothesized "half Hittite" (R. D. Barnett) kingdoms mentioned in the Hittite archives of the fifteenth to thirteenth centuries.[6] A palace-state organization, literacy, and monumental architecture of palatial, sacral, and military constructions were speculative parts of this model. We have found a village hut, and a cremation burial of ca. 1400? B.C. We have found no Bronze Age palace or archive. Admittedly, our Bronze Age exposure was minimal; but the lack of literacy appears to be part of a larger phenomenon. For no writing has been found at the two extensively excavated West Anatolian sites which were continuously inhabited during the second millennium—Troy and Beycesultan in the Meander Valley. However warlike its inhabitants, for the moment all evidence for Western Asia Minor is of preliterate, semiagricultural traditions, with at best a very rustic version of palatial organizations (Beycesultan).[7]

Anatolian, Near Eastern (Syrian, Mesopotamian), and Aegean-Greek cultural traditions have been posited as components of the amalgam that became Lydian culture (Hanfmann).[8] Through the verification provided by archaeological material, we are in a better position to evaluate their relative importance. Going back to pre-Indo-European agricultural traditions of the third millennium B.C., the Anatolian component is a basic and massive foundation, a kind of "silent partner," whose importance is manifested in the survival of "vernacular," slow-changing or unchanging traits of rural and mountain life, in rustic and lower-class urban architecture, in pottery, and in other traits of folklore. Influenced by the imponderable predispositions of genetic continuity since the Bronze Age (cf. Finkel), this Anatolian undertow carries with it the fundamental emotional attitudes developed in man's adjustment to this particular environment. The special forms of religious life developed by Western Anatolians not only survived into the Lydian and Persian eras but spread powerfully through the Hellenistic states and the Roman empire. The Old Stone Age myth of the hunt of the bull and the life-giving power of bull's blood; the sexual analogy of fertilization, growth, and death in vegetation and in anthropomorphic gods; and the quest for *ecstasis* in Dionysiac cult —these major influences on the ancient world were formulated, institutionalized, and transmitted by "crusades" (Lydian Dionysus) and missions (Magna Mater) from the Phrygian-Lydian cultural complex. Archaeologically, however, we can discern the decline of the Anatolian element in the city in the early Hellenistic era, though it lived on in the countryside through Roman times.[9]

Our findings have served to reduce the share of Near-Eastern cultures. Material evidence for contacts is minimal—a bit of Assyrian glazed ware, a Neo-Babylonian seal[10]—no cuneiform clay tablets, no substantial imports. We must admit, however, that we are dealing here with a different type of cultural contact, a "sporadic, long-range, high (social) level contact" (Hanfmann).[11] There is historical reality behind King Meles' visit to Babylon in the late eighth century, and next we see Lydian horsemen arrive at Assurbanipal's Nineveh, where nobody can be found who understands Lydian. The immaterial things the Lydians borrowed from Mesopotamian culture are few but extremely important: the concept of state-guaranteed currency, the very exact system of "Babylonian" weights, and probably the advanced technology of processing gold and silver (the mining technology might conceivably be indebted to gold-rich regions of Iran).[12] Less certain but probable are borrowings in the ways of palace organization and in construction and transportation technology. Elements of luxury, too, such as "the golden garments of the gods"[13] can be traced to the Mesopotamians, the second highest culture of the ancient world.

What role the "late Hittite" principalities of Asia Minor and their imitator Phrygia may have played is as yet difficult to assess.[14] Preliminary observations have been made, but in the larger view, Phrygia presents a different amalgam of the three major traditions.

In Lydia, originally Aegean traditions, and then more clearly Greek traditions emerge overall as the formative power with surprising force. Our findings of Mycenaean and Submycenaean types of pottery have validated the mythical traditions of the early appearance of Greeks on the Sardian scene. And the cultural contact, growing during the period of preparation (1200–680 B.C.), is broadly based, socially pervasive, popular, and continuous.[15]

Imported Greek artifacts constantly increase, and by the mid-eighth century faraway Corinth is represented.[16] Then, in a decisive alignment, the alphabet is borrowed from an essentially Greek source, and the urbanization of Lydia begins in earnest. The most important addition that our excavations have made to our understanding of the Lydian cultural explosion is the concrete illustration of the technological breakthrough in the working of gold, which the Lydians brought to the Mediterranean world and which provided the capability for their meteoric rise.[17]

The great blocks of the Gyges crepis (Fig. 108) and of the foundations of the palace (Fig. 79) show another technological advance and recall that the Lydian kings employed the pioneering mechanical inventors of the archaic Greek world, who were devising transport and lifting facilities for 40-ton blocks and exploring the science of soils for construction: the geniuses Theodoros of Samos, Chersiphron, and Metagenes.[18]

From the point of view of a modern sociological approach to the study of complex societies and their social stratification, we have at long last revealed the urban organization and the housing and daily life of the average people of Sardis; and we have secured some data for the commercial and industrial life of the city. The methodical working up of all of these data is yet to come. One may say, however, that the rural life of the Sardis ambience during the Lydian era is yet to be explored; and that the key public buildings—the royal archive, the mint, the temples—have not been found. Even so, our knowledge of Lydian religion has already greatly profited by the new data. In a general sense, Herodotus' dictum of the Lydians being close to the Greeks in their customs is being upheld by our finds, but here, as in his contrast of "the richest city in the world" and its mean housing, the archaeological picture is more graduated, more complex and diversified. The manifestations of Greek influence and the manifestations of Lydian originality within the Greek-like framework are a theme already adumbrated, but the study is yet to be perfected by exact investigation and interpretation of all Greek-influenced types of finds.[19]

All in all, Lydia appears as a "mixo-barbarous" peripheral region of Hellenic culture. From non-literate finds and written evidence it is clear that especially in the intellectual pursuits, Mermnad Lydia could not rival contemporary Greece: Thales served Croesus, but no school of pre-Socratic philosophers developed at Sardis. When all is said and done, folk wisdom and tradition rightly saw Lydia as the model and paradigm of sudden rise of wealth—and this has given Lydian culture its immortality. Already Pindar sang prophetically: "The generous excellence of Croesus does not perish";[20] and the saying "rich as Croesus" has become proverbial in the cultural tradition of the Western world.

GMAH

VI

The Persian Period

WILLIAM E. MIERSE

The City Under the Persians

From 547 B.C., when Cyrus conquered Sardis, until 334 B.C., the date Alexander marched into the city, Sardis was a major urban center in the Persian empire, the capital of the western satrapy which included Sparda (Sardis, Lydia), Karka (Caria), and Yauna (Ionia).[1] Achaemenid-style jewelry and precious objects were among the discoveries made by the first Sardis expedition, as was also a major Persian tomb, the Pyramid Tomb. Diverse archaeological finds and detailed investigations were made by the Harvard-Cornell Expedition throughout the twenty years under review. Newly unearthed inscriptions from Sardis and Hypaipa have revealed that under Artaxerxes II's rule, an image of Ahura Mazda was erected; and they have further evidenced the strength of the Persian cult of Anahita which continued to flourish into the Roman era. S. Kasper and G. M. A. Hanfmann's analysis of the design and function of the Pyramid Tomb has shown clear connections with monuments in Cyrus the Elder's capital at Pasargadae. Excavations in the residential portions of the city provide a glimpse of the life of the ordinary citizens. And new work on the funerary stelae and the pyramidal stamp seals has proved that individuals with Lydian names occupied positions of some importance in the administrative structure. Close scrutiny of the pottery sequence and domestic objects has led to the conclusion that native Anatolian traditions survived and flourished under Persian domination, while Greek influences continued to gain as a major component in the cultural life of the city.

It is Herodotus who provides the most dramatic retelling of the fall of Croesus before the armies of Cyrus.[2] Xenophon points out the fact that Cyrus equipped Sardis with a Persian garrison before he departed, thus assuring the defense of the city and the control of the citizenry.[3] The Persian forces were called into action later that same year, when the Lydian comptroller Paktyes led an unsuccessful revolt against the Persian military commander.[4] In 499 B.C., the Athenians gave assistance to the eastern Greeks in their revolt against Darius I; together they attacked and burned Sardis.[5] It was in retaliation for this destruction, explains Herodotus, that Xerxes mustered an army at Sardis intent on marching into Greece.[6] After the defeat at Marathon, it was again to Sardis that the remnants of the great army gathered.[7] Xenophon described the battle between the armies of Agesilaus and the satrap Tissaphernes which was fought before the walls in 395 B.C. and was followed by an attack on the city.[8] In his biography of Alexander, Arrian notes that Sardis fell to the Macedonian conqueror without a fight, and thus the Persian reign was brought to an end.[9]

Some information regarding the topographical features of the ancient city can be gleaned from the literary sources. In his account of the 499 B.C. destruction, Herodotus mentions that the houses were constructed of reeds or of clay covered with reeds[10] and that the agora sat astride the Pactolus River.[11] He also says that the temple of Cybele, the native goddess, was burned, but does not indicate its location.[12]

The Persian fondness for gardens which manifested itself in the building of vast pleasure parks at Pasargadae[13] and Persepolis[14] found expression too at Sardis, where, as Xenophon tells, Cyrus the Younger built a great garden, with trees arranged in straight lines. To this he took the Spartan general Lysander.[15] Xenophon describes how, in 399 B.C., the Spartan king Agesilaus set up camp in the area west of the Pactolus River, suggesting that that portion of the city was not built up.[16] It can be determined from the details of Arrian's description of the city Alexander saw that the Acropolis was well fortified with triple fortifications.[17]

The archaeological record has verified certain of these testimonia. Burned levels at PN (Fig. 53) and HoB (Fig. 41)[18] are mute reminders of the capture of the city in 547 B.C., as are the Persian arrowheads found on the citadel (AcS).[19] In 499 B.C. the Ionian and Athenian Greeks laid waste to the lower city; the event may be reflected in the stratigraphic record at PN (*88.3– *88.1), HoB (*99.7, *99.5–*99.3) and PC (*99.1).[20] On the slope of the AcS have been unearthed the remains of the mighty curtain walls that awed Alexander.

The excavations at PN and PC have shown the domestic quarters of the city to be somewhat different from the way Herodotus described them. Instead of the reeds, the Harvard-Cornell excavators have found mudbrick pisé constructions. It is still possible that some were covered with thatch. These two sections continued to function as residential areas in the Persian city, much as they had in the Lydian city. While the area at NEW (Fig. 8:16; Plan I) was perhaps abandoned, Herodotus mentioned that the Lydians and Persians were forced to flee from the residential sectors into the agora, which may imply that the two groups lived together in the domestic quarters of PN and PC. The changes which took place in these two areas and at HoB may be the result of an influx of new tenants. The altar to Cybele (Figs. 42, 49) that stood in the goldworking portion of PN was converted

into a fire altar. Two apsidal fountain houses with wells may have been built during this time (Fig. 53). They indicate, because of their size, intentional planning and some control over a labor force. They appear to have served as public water supplies. A layer of burned fill confined to the inside of the buildings (*88.1–.3) marks either the 547 capture or the 499 B.C. raid. The two structures were important; they were rebuilt after being burned down.[21] Drains and retaining walls (W253-270/S348-355, *88.0) constructed after a flooding of the Pactolus are further evidence of urban planning.[22] The Persians appear to have abandoned the massive city wall (MMS) of the lower city, perhaps to move the defenses eastward (Figs. 132, 133; Plan I).

The HoB area continued to be used (Fig. 41). Fragments of both black-figure and red-figure (Fig. 165) vases and native Lydian wares known to have been produced through the fourth century B.C. are evidence for fifth and fourth century occupation.[23] The spot may have lost some of its former prominence. The only architectural feature which can be dated to this period is a well (W3/S113, *99.66) which reaches to a depth of more than 19 m.[24] The discovery of an unfinished bronze plaque with the figure of a reclining ibex (M 62.57:4476; Fig. 164),[25] which appears to have been intended for a horse trapping, shows that the industrial character of the quarter had not totally disappeared. Perhaps the Lydian shops built in the last phase were still being occupied.[26] The only Persian siglos recovered by the Harvard-Cornell Expedition came from HoB (C 62.25; W27/S116; *102.5; Fig. 162).[27] But, as A. Ramage has already explained, much of the southern extension of HoB must have been open rather than built up.[28]

In a very urban mode of congested living, PN was not so much comprised of individual units as it was built up of continuous and contiguous structures, usually with common walls (Fig. 44). The Persian presence did not radically alter the style of life in this quarter of the city, which remained much as it had been in the early sixth century B.C.; and even the building techniques developed in the last years of the Lydian empire were employed to put up new homes or repair older ones.[29] The houses at PN consisted for the most part of a single unit. The walls, built of mudbrick or pisé, stood atop fieldstone socles, the stones of which were laid with mud mortar

(Fig. 134; cf. 137). The corners were carefully squared, and in some cases there is an alternation of long and short sides of the stones. No traces of ashlar masonry work have been found in the area. Mud plaster could have been used to cover the walls, but only one trace of the plaster has been found *in situ*, and that in HoB. The scarcity of roof tile fragments suggests they were not common roofing material. Reed roofs were probably the rule. Molded and painted sima tiles and antefixes, an important facet of Lydian exterior decoration, continued to be produced.[30]

The interiors were kept simple. Slits noticeable along the inside faces of the walls supported lightweight room dividers made of perishable stuffs. Windows were placed in the walls at structurally sound places. A paving of schist on the floor of a Persian-period structure located in PN, just south of the Roman bath (W230-240/S365-375), represents perhaps the common manner of flooring. Though no remains of furnishings have been found, collapsible wooden beds, similar to the stone beds from the Lydian chamber tombs, probably existed, and simple stools would have rounded out the household furniture. At least for the first decades of Persian rule, Lydian-style pottery continued to be manufactured, and a household might have possessed marbled lekythoi or plain amphorae like those found in a fifth century B.C. context at PN (P 69.3:7961, P 70.36:8133).[31]

An administrative center required buildings to house its offices. A satrapal capital needed architecture to impress visitors with its wealth, power, and importance. Persian Sardis possessed both types of structures. There is no mention of a palace being built for the satrap as was done at Kelainai;[32] he may have lived in the Lydian royal palace. Bureaucratic areas must have existed somewhere in the city—such as offices for the Achaemenid bureau of land registration, the western offices of which were in Sardis.[33]

The mint at Sardis probably continued to function into the first years of the Persian domination. The new administrators, unfamiliar with the idea and workings of a monetary unit of exchange, did not see any reason to interfere with an economic system as well established and seemingly as well operated as that which existed between the Ionian Greek cities and the Lydian capital.[34] The earliest known sigloi date from probably just prior to ca. 500 B.C.;[35] from the

foundation deposits at Persepolis have come Lydian Croesan types dating to 516–511 B.C., and thus the type of bimetallic coinage introduced by Croesus continued to be minted until the early years of the reign of Darius I (521–486). The gold coin of the Persian realm, the daric, derives its name from that of Darius, indicating its late date.[36]

The post-Croesus issues of pre–Darius I coins show increasing degrees of stylization and the disappearance of fractional denominations smaller than the gold stater and the silver half-stater.[37] The stylistic and technical analyses which have been undertaken of these coins indicate that they come from a single mint, very likely Sardis. Die-links have been denoted which exist between coins of different metals, unlike denominations and various styles.[38] These coins and the imperial coinage of darics and sigloi that followed them were confined to the area of Western Anatolia. They formed part of the Greek-Aegean economic system, rather than the Iranian system, where barter and exchange were still being regularly employed.[39] Initially the new currency of silver sigloi and gold darics was struck on the same standard as the older Lydian system of Croesus.[40] That the mint at Sardis continued to operate seems only likely. As the major satrapal residence in the west, any coinage intended to be put into circulation in the eastern Greek world as an imperial coin would have come out of Sardis. Several of the other cities of Anatolia continued to mint coins, not imperial sigloi and darics but local city coinage. There were mints in Lycia at Antiphellus and Limyra,[41] and in the fourth century B.C. six mints operated in Cilicia.[42] So far only silver sigloi have been found at Sardis; two were recovered by the first Sardis expedition, and one (Fig. 162) was found by the Harvard-Cornell excavators at HoB. This may indicate that only silver was processed into coin at Sardis and that gold was remitted as tribute to Susa.

Two tombs testify to the nobility's love of display. Both tombs possess traits that tie them to architectural developments outside Lydia. The Pyramid Tomb with its fine masonry work (Figs. 67–69) certainly belongs to the tradition of Lydian stone masonry structures as developed and refined in the Bin Tepe chambers (Figs. 102, 103), the AcN walls (Fig. 79), and the altar LA 1 (Fig. 95); but its unusual treatment of the blocks' finishes[43] and its novel pyramidal form have no parallels at Sardis but rather reflect later developments in building at Pasargadae, such as the Tomb of Cyrus and the Staircase of the Tall-i Takht platform.[44] The tomb, probably built around 540 B.C. for a Persian noble who fell in the battle for Sardis, could be the result of an experiment commissioned by an Iranian patron who wanted to apply the Lydian talent for stone work to a different type of structure.

The second tomb is known from the two halves of its pedimental relief (S 69.14:8047; NoEx 78.1; Fig. 138). They indicate that this was a temple-like structure, and the funerary banquet scene with which they are decorated indicates that the building was a mausoleum.[45] It, like the Pyramid Tomb, is a unique find, and more closely resembles the famous temple-shrine tombs of Lycia—the "Nereid Monument" at Xanthos[46] and the Heroon at Limyra[47]—than any structure from Sardis. It was smaller than its southern cousins. G. M. A. Hanfmann's stylistic analysis of the relief sculptures has led to his dating them to the decades between 450 and 430 B.C.,[48] making the Sardis pediment an earlier work than the Heroon of Limyra or the "Nereid Monument."[49]

In its first cultural contact with its new overlords, Sardis may have supplied the inspiration for certain developments in architecture which took place in the Iranian homeland. The great substructure palace walls that climb the slope of the AcN (Figs. 79, 80) and the massive walls of the Gyges mound (Fig. 108) date from before the Persian capture of the city. The ashlar masonry walls and the treatment of the blocks with their applied drafted margins and mixture of finely pecked and rusticated dressages are paralleled in the construction pattern and surface treatment to the ashlar masonry of the Tall-i Takht platform at Pasargadae.[50] The Susa tablets list Lydian and Ionian masons as being imported to work on the construction of that capital.[51] Cyrus may well have made use of skilled craftsmen a generation earlier when building his monuments at Pasargadae, thus introducing the Lydian building vocabulary into Iran at an early date.

Sardis' position as nerve center for an important administrative network made its defense a concern of the satraps. Though new archaeological investigations suggest that the great lower

city wall, MMS (Fig. 133) was allowed to fall to ruin during this time, perhaps to prevent the inhabitants from thinking of rebelling and holding out behind massive city walls as the Babylonians had tried to do,[52] the great Acropolis fortifications were kept in good repair and withstood all the sieges laid to them. Even when Alexander took the city they could evoke praise.[53] Strabo described a white marble belvedere which stood on the Tmolus and formed part of the defensive system for the city.[54] It has not been found, though as recently as 1970 C. Foss made a thorough search of the Tmolus region, checking out possible sites.[55]

WEM

The Satrapal Court

The opulence of the satrapal court at Sardis must have overwhelmed the unprepared. As the capital of the western part of the Persian empire and as the home of one of the most powerful men in the eastern Mediterranean world, the city was one of the most important and cosmopolitan of its day. The contemporary Greek writers have left their impressions of the city, one which for some had become synonymous with decadence and wantonness. Athenaeus, an author of the second century A.D., borrowed heavily from earlier sources to piece together a picture of the city. He quotes the sixth century B.C. poet Anacreon when he speaks of "Lydian living" as tantamount to "soft living."[1] Taking from Clearchus of Soli, a fourth century B.C. author, he records that the Lydians planted great gardens in order to shade themselves from the sun.[2] He alleges the Lydian historian Xanthus as the source for his contention that the Lydians went so far as to sterilize women and use them in place of eunuchs.[3]

The satraps who ruled Western Anatolia were among the Iranian king's greatest weapons against the Greek world, and one of his chief sources of worry. They were powerful men, who waged war and conducted foreign policy in the name of the Achaemenid monarch.[4] They served as the royal court's eyes and ears in the west, and protected the Iranian heartland from the dangers of the Aegean. It was Darius I's brother, Artaphernes, who held court at Sardis in 499 B.C. when the Ionians attacked; and it was he who led the punitive forces against the Greek cities of the coast, destroying Miletus, in retaliation.[5] A century later, Tissaphernes served first as Darius II's satrap and later as Artaxerxes II's satrap, and as such, he pursued the complex diplomatic negotiations which played side against side in the Peloponnesian war.[6]

Such power as the satraps of Sardis exercised caused some to set themselves up as rival claimants to the king's position. Oroetes, Cyrus the Elder's satrap, removed all the threats to his security; he killed both Polycrates of Samos and Mitrobaus, the satrap of Daskylion, but was in turn assassinated at Cyrus' orders.[7] Darius II's younger son, Cyrus the Younger, who became the satrap at Sardis following the death of his father, sought to wrest the throne from his brother, Artaxerxes II, in an unsuccessful rebellion. He made use of Greek mercenaries; and it was at Sardis that he entertained the Spartan general Lysander.[8] A discovery by the Harvard-Cornell team in 1974 of an inscribed block (IN 74.1) in the cliffs above the Pactolus River has added a new name to the list of Sardis satraps—Droaphernes,[9] who is given the appellation *hyparchos* of Lydia (Fig. 166).[10]

This new inscription has revealed two aspects of Achaemenid religious policy in the fourth century B.C. The actual carving dates from the second century A.D., at which time several inscriptions were incorporated into a single image base.[11] The first part of the text, however, dates from the thirty-ninth regnal year of Artaxerxes II (405–359 B.C.) and is a dedication by Droaphernes of a statue of the god Zeus Baradates (Zeus the Lawgiver), an aspect of Ahura Mazda.[12] It has long been known that Artaxerxes promoted the worship of the fertility goddess Anahita,[13] and caused altars and statues to be set up to her throughout the empire;[14] but this inscription is the first indication that he also fostered the cult of Zeus Baradates and allowed cult images of the god to be made. On the other hand, the Lydian altar of Cybele in PN (Figs. 49, 52) was transformed into a fire altar and the lions immured at this time.[15] The popularity of the Anahita cult was strong enough to survive the disappearance of the Achaemenid empire; Pausanias in the second century A.D. witnessed fire priests enacting rituals in a language foreign to

him before fire altars[16] for "the Lydians, who called themselves Persians."[17] Two inscriptions found by the Harvard-Cornell Expedition and dating from the Roman era refer to Anahita (IN 73.5 and IN 64.58).[18] But the new inscribed block from the Pactolus (Fig. 166) contains the first evidence not only that Artaxerxes fostered the cult of Zeus Baradates, but also that he encouraged the setting up of statues of the god. The Greek Zeus Polieus, an aspect of the god known from Roman inscriptions who is recorded as having had a temple in the city,[19] may be a later manifestation of Zeus Baradates.[20] What the statue that Droaphernes erected looked like cannot be determined with any certainty. If it were heavily Greek in influence, as use of the Greek "Zeus" might imply, then it could have resembled the image of Zeus Lydios shown on coins.[21] However, if the art form chosen were more Iranian, the image may have appeared like the Ahura Mazda on the Perso-Lydian seals and gold plaques.[22]

The second part of the text is equally interesting. It suggests that some Persians participated in the indigenous Anatolian cults of Angdistis (Phrygia), Ma (Cappadocia), and Sabazius (Thrace-Phrygia) and caused the Persian authorities some consternation.[23] Artaxerxes II expressly forbids those who serve the god, Zeus Baradates, and the wardens of the temple from taking part in the mysteries of these native deities.[24] This action is an indication that at Sardis, the three native gods managed to attract foreign converts.[25] An inscription in Lydian which treats a financial contract between a priest with an Iranian name, Mithradatas, and the Artemis Temple at Sardis, indicates that an earlier, as yet undiscovered sanctuary of Artemis existed in the city; the agreement was written in a formula not unlike that developed for use in the Persian Chancery. In these inscriptions, Artemis is spoken of, but not in conjunction with Anahita, which suggests that the merger of the two goddesses took place later.[26]

As the satrapal capital, Sardis was home to many courtiers, some Iranian serving abroad, some Levantine or Semitic, some native Lydian in the Persian administration. That both native and foreign elements composed the bureaucracy is evidenced by the pyramidal stamped seals, a type of seal adopted by the Persians from the Babylonian seal. Sardis was a major center for their production in western Asia Minor.[27] Over 200 pyramidal seals were cut, many with Lydian legends,[28] some dated by regnal years of the Persian kings.[29] Most have Iranian iconography in the devices—horned griffins, crowned and bearded sphinxes—but only one carries a Persian name (Mitratas).[30] A funerary stele made for a Lydian named Manes who served the Persians has a bilingual inscription in Aramaic and Lydian and is dated by a regnal year of Artaxerxes II (394).[31] Whether these Lydian employees of the foreign bureaucracy chose to affect Persian manners is impossible to say, but their continued use of Lydian for such politically noticeable objects as seals and grave inscriptions might suggest they did not.

Sardis continued as a city of luxury, but now only as a reflection of the great wealth of the Achaemenid kings. Those courtiers who came to serve on the imperial administration brought with them their love for Iranian things and created at Sardis their own home away from home. They continued to use much of what had been the Lydian city. If the satraps dwelt in the old palace of Croesus, they made it more eastern in feeling with portable precious commodities.[32] From the tombs of the Necropolis on the west bank of the Pactolus, the first Sardis expedition retrieved gold plaques with Achaemenid motifs such as Ahura Mazda and bearded sphinxes (Fig. 163).[33] Many bead and chain pieces, some of which were made during the early Persian era, were also recovered from the tombs.[34] A bronze mirror that had been laid in Tomb 213, though probably not actually of Iranian manufacture, has Persian decorative features such as horse heads on the handle and was very likely produced in Asia Minor in an area of heavy Persian influence.[35] Silver incense burners similar to those shown carried by figures in the procession reliefs at Persepolis and a silver phialae stamped with the double figure of a bull, which also has a parallel in a piece from Persepolis, have been published from a Lydian-type chamber tomb in Ikiztepe near Güre in the upper Hermus Valley.[36] It seems likely that an Irano-Anatolian style of bronze and silver working had developed during the two centuries of Persian rule at Sardis;[37] not only have the remains of what might have been a bronze shop been unearthed at HoB, but in the same area was picked up a half-finished horse trapping in the form of a re-

clining ibex (Fig. 164), an Iranian motif.[38] It was possible to date the bronze piece by a fragment of a red-figure crater (P 62.128:4354; Fig. 165) to the second quarter of the fourth century B.C.[39]

A major component used to create the ambience of the satrapal court was cloth. Textiles played an essential role in the imperial economy; they were used as a source of collectible revenue and are entered as such on the inventory lists of the Susa archives.[40] Sardis was a prominent producer of fine fabric. Rugs were manufactured in the city for the imperial household, rugs on which only the King of Kings might tread.[41] Lydian "goldenwoven chitons" were renowned throughout the Greek world[42] and figure on the lists of garments for the statue of Hera at the Heraion at Samos, where they are cited as "Lydian chitons."[43] Even the dyes were special. Aristophanes noted the "bloody red" color[44] which Plato, the comic poet, claims was used to dye coverlets for dining couches.[45] The Harvard-Cornell Expedition found traces of the famous Sardian fabrics in a tumulus at Bin Tepe (BT 63.2). An imprint of what may have been one of Plato's couch covers was preserved on an iron plaque from a couch.[46] Some idea of the type of raiment which was considered high fashion in fifth century Sardis can be ascertained by examining a polychromed terracotta figure discovered in 1963. He wears a Persian *kandytes* that is open in front to reveal a shirt, painted a gold-like color to represent perhaps the cloth of gold for which Sardis was known.[47]

Some twenty pieces of sculpture can be assigned to the two centuries between the fall of Sardis to Cyrus and the arrival of Alexander. Most show the influences of Athens, Cyclades, and Ionian Greece. One may be by a Lydian who had worked in Iran. A few possess traits attributable to eastern sources. This latter group display decorative elements, particularly on some anthemion stelai (Fig. 128),[48] rosettes, palmettes, volutes, and lotuses, which also form part of the decorative vocabulary of Achaemenid court jewelers.[49] At least one piece is known which, while imitating Greek models in arrangement of the figure, presents a woman dressed in Persian garments known from Persian palace reliefs.[50]

Stelai from Daskylion, which have anthemia of a type similar to the Sardian stelai, also have figurative representations of cart and horsemen processions and funerary meals. A particularly close resemblance between a Daskylion stele with a frieze of horsemen and footmen and an anthemion fragment from Sardis poses the question of whether the Sardis piece, too, originally had an accompanying frieze; and if so, was it representative of a style of Persian court sculpture?[51]

Relief sculptures are known from the Lydian area which have as their subject a funerary banquet.[52] The iconography of the feasting scene is in origin Near Eastern, a victory banquet such as the relief of the banquet of Assurbanipal.[53] This became a type of funerary art under the Persians, and as such was introduced into the satrapal courts.[54] The scene is intended to honor the dead and to picture the pleasures of the coming afterlife.[55] It became in time a part of the subject matter of the Hellenized western portions of Asia Minor. The representations from the Lydian sphere are eastern in their iconography, with an emphasis on the ruler (husband), wife, and servant(s). It seems probable that the Lydians of the pre-Persian period envisaged the dead as partaking of funerary feasts; vessels, probably originally containing foodstuffs, have been uncovered in tombs. However, not until the Persian arrival did the scene take on a sculpted form.[56] It continued to be popular through the late fourth century B.C.[57] The small pediment from what was probably a sepulchral shrine was decorated with a funerary banquet scene (Fig. 138).[58] In Xanthus and Limyra, such temple-shrines are grave monuments of rulers; the banquet appears in Xanthus and on the royal "Satrap" sarcophagus of Sidon. It is tempting to assume that the mausoleum, unique in Sardis, may be that of a satrap.

WEM

The Lydian Survivals and the Greek Impact

The Native Elements

For three hundred years, Sardis was ruled from the Persian capitals in Iran. In its glory, it was a reflection of the Achaemenid wealth, prestige, and power. Yet the Persian presence never succeeded in fully ousting the older Lydian culture. A language, a tradition of house types and construction, a pottery style, and a variety of religious cults all of native origin flourished under the watchful eye of the satraps. Much of our knowledge of the Lydian language has been gleaned from inscriptions (many found by the Harvard-Cornell Expedition) which date to the centuries of Persian domination rather than to the era of the Lydian empire,[1] but no new Aramaic or Old Persian inscriptions have come to light. Lydian used on the pyramidal seals and a Lydian-Aramaic inscription[2] are reminders that Lydian speakers occupied important positions in the new administration, and they did not have to deny their heritage to attain their rank.

At HoB (0-E10/S87-97), the archaeological record has revealed to the Harvard-Cornell excavators fragments of Lydian-type ceramic vessels from fifth and fourth century B.C. contexts. The objects that were a part of the daily life changed only gradually. Native pottery became harder in texture and lighter in color.[3] To be certain, Greek and Persian influences affected the ceramic productions, but a native style, based on older tradition, survived into the third century B.C.[4]

Several pottery deposits, each consisting of four vessels and an iron knife, found at PN and HoB (Figs. 145, 146)[5] reveal in the forms of the pieces—chrytra, oinochoe, skyphos, and bowl—and in the surface decoration—marbled, streaked, and black-on-red—their Lydian origin.[6] Their purposeful placement and burial imply an intentional action;[7] buried with the pots were puppy remains, suggesting the assemblage was part of a sacred meal dedicated perhaps to the god Candaules.[8] The caches at HoB rest at levels between *99.65 and *98.80.[9] The earliest belong assuredly to the time of Lydian greatness, but the latest could possibly have been deposited as late as the last quarter of the sixth century B.C.[10] As with the mysteries cited in the decree of Artaxerxes II (IN 74.1; Fig. 166), we are in the presence of strong Anatolian religious cults surviving into the Persian reign.

In the routine activities of urban living, it may well have been the Lydian population who influenced the Persians. While some changes were made in the cityscape and new buildings were put up, no major topographical features were altered. In the most congested domestic quarter,

PN, the building techniques employed for new houses were those developed in the last years of the Lydian rule (Fig. 137).[11]

The Greek Impact

For much of its history, Sardis had been within the sphere of the larger Greek world of the Eastern Aegean (Fig. 1). Its kings had alternated between attacking Greek cities along the coast of Asia Minor[12] and endowing them with expensive gifts.[13] Lydian kings patronize Ionian artisans. For Alyattes, Glaucus the Chian created a silver bowl with a welded iron stand.[14] The Harvard-Cornell research has shown that this reciprocal flow changed somewhat during the Persian era; the Greek influences increased, and in addition to Eastern Greek objects, Attic finds turn up in the archaeological record. Eastern Greek pottery is well represented in the archaic levels,[15] and fragments of the last great Eastern Greek style, Fikellura, have been discovered by the Harvard-Cornell excavators.[16] From the Acropolis Top (AcT) came pieces of an Attic black-figure cup (Fig. 77).[17] Datable to the last years of Croesus' reign, the cup is the most notable example of a change in the ceramic imports; after the middle of the sixth century B.C., Attic black, and later, red-figure ware led the ceramic imports (Fig. 165).[18] Not only were Attic vases imported into the city, but they were a major influence on the local potters' craft. The ubiquitous "poor (red) glaze" and local black glaze, both of which were manufactured into the Hellenistic time, owe their inspiration to these imported wares.[19] It is at this time that small bowls and plates and fish plates enter the stratigraphic record.[20] These developments are best demonstrated in the later phases of the residential units at PN (Figs. 194, 195),[21] some of which were used until 213 B.C., and in the material recovered from under the Hellenistic altar LA 2.[22]

It was the Eastern Greek world that supplied many of the models for the sculpture of these centuries. The soft style, perfected in the Ionian ateliers, was favored during the early years[23] and was used even for pieces with Iranian motifs, like the funerary banquet pediment (Fig. 138).[24] Slowly, this style was forced to relinquish its dominant position as Attic and Boeotian-Cycladic influences pushed into the picture. Xerxes, as he retreated from Greece, brought with him statues from Athens, some of which were set up in Sardis.[25] From the Eastern Greek sculptors, the Sardian masters borrowed subject matter and presentation ideas for pieces such as a draped male figure,[26] sphinxes and sirens,[27] and a female figure draped in Greek garb.[28]

A fully developed Sardis style is discernible in the anthemion stele (Figs. 113, 128), a tall, shallow pillar crowned by Ionic volutes and terminating in a palmette. The treatment depends heavily on Eastern Greek types, the closest contemporary survivor being a stele from Samos.[29] All the finial elements are gathered into a tightly compacted oval unit cut in a soft, heavy manner.[30] The volutes are not allowed to extend sideways beyond the stelai's shaft.[31] Broad framing bands and volute stems growing antithetically out of the ground remained a favored decorative device even on late pieces.[32]

Two other Greek sources came to affect the style of Sardian sculpture in the fifth century B.C. Cycladic-Boeotian traits, albeit somewhat difficult to separate from the prevalent Ionian soft style, are apparent on a votive stele[33] and on sepulchral stelai.[34] More immediately noticeable are the Attic qualities which begin to show in pieces after 500 B.C. in the application of tectonic frame to the stele[35] and in the growing naturalism in the portrayal of figures and plants.[36]

WEM

Conclusion

Persian occupation did not dim the fame of Sardis. It was in his description of Xerxes' host that Aeschylus spoke of "Sardis rich in gold."[1] Its unique position as the most important urban center in the western empire, the third capital after Susa and Persepolis, assured its continued prosperity. With Cyrus' conquest, Sardis changed from capital of a kingdom to a major city in a worldwide empire. Its economy reflected the change as the Persian siglos, perhaps minted locally (Fig. 162), became the local tender. The city became a vast emporium for goods moving from west to east and from east to west. Both Greek and Iranian goods were a common sight in the city, and the local artisans could produce works in both Ionian soft style and Achaemenid court style. The city was linked to the other cities in the empire via the Royal Road (Fig. 1), and rapid communications between Sardis and the Iranian capitals were established. Up this Royal Road marched the Lydian master masons to help design and construct the Persian capitals at Pasargadae, Susa, and Persepolis—followed by such notables as Themistocles and Antalcidas.

547 B.C. does not mark the end of the Lydian native culture.[2] A strong Lydian element survived in Sardis of the fifth and fourth centuries B.C. These people used their own language and carved seals and inscriptions using it; they manufactured their old style pottery, worshiped their traditional gods, and continued to build their houses in a manner and technique which had been refined in the late Lydian era. Within this sphere, the Persian influence appears to have been minimal.

Strong as this native element may have been, and even though there were native leaders—those who had Lydian names and used the Lydian language to carve their seals and funerary inscriptions—the native population never rose in a revolt against the Persian masters as the Egyptians[3] and Babylonians did.[4] Those rebellions in which Sardis was involved were led by local satraps who were anxious to usurp the prerogative of the Great King—as was Cyrus the Younger before them. Persian rule of Sardis continued the role of the city as a great administrative center of power and fostered its prosperity; both factors made Sardis an important objective for Alexander the Great in 334 B.C.

WEM

VII

The Hellenistic Period

GEORGE M. A. HANFMANN

LOUIS ROBERT

WILLIAM E. MIERSE

Previous Research and the Harvard-Cornell Excavations

The first Sardis expedition produced considerable material for our knowledge of Hellenistic Sardis, principally from the precinct of Artemis. It revealed the essential traits of this, the fourth largest Ionic temple known, one of the finest examples of Hellenistic architecture (Figs. 7, 88, 178, 284, 285).[1] Supplemented by inscriptions previously found at Sardis, epigraphic monuments from the precinct and other locations yielded much information about the political, economic, social, and religious life of the Hellenized Greek city.[2] This information was enriched and supplemented by coins. They included two Hellenistic coin hoards, of great interest for the study of Seleucid and other mints and trade.[3] The theater and the stadium (Figs. 172, 173), already noted by earlier travelers, were surmised to be Hellenistic, but otherwise nothing concrete was learned about the extent or character of the Hellenistic city. As to objects, few of the sculptures have survived.[4] Pottery, lamps, metalwork, and glass came partly from the Artemis Precinct, partly from Hellenistic burials. Here again, most of the objects perished prior to 1922, and the records for the lamps and glass and other small objects were lost.[5]

The Harvard-Cornell excavations and surveys uncovered evidence for the Hellenistic city in the western part of the site and on the Acropolis (Figs. 8, 167; Plans II, III). In addition, small-scale digging and conservation work at the temple and precinct of Artemis (Figs. 90, 178) brought important insights into the development of the great Hellenistic sanctuary of the city. The major results were these:[6] from 334 to 213 B.C. the Lydo-Persian city continued to exist with major Hellenizing complexes and structures being added to the periphery (theater-stadium, probably gymnasium; Fig. 167; Plan II). As a result of the siege, capture, and punishment of the city by Antiochus III in 214–213 B.C., the western part of the city was abandoned as a residential quarter and turned over to industry and burial grounds (Figs. 8, 129; Plan III). The repopulation (*synoikismos*) of the city attested by new official documents was accompanied as in Ephesus by a total replanning and a shift of the city area to the east. In A.D. 17, an earthquake smashed the city. The near-total urban renewal directed by Roman authorities apparently entailed demolition and leveling of Hellenistic structures. Hence here, as in Ephesus,[7] there is a stark contrast between the impression of importance and prosperity conveyed by ancient historians and inscriptions, and the relative paucity of Hellenistic archaeological remains.

Evidence came from HoB, PN, PC, the Artemis Precinct, the Synagogue, and the area between the modern Pactolus bridge (W300) and ca. E150 (Fig. 8:2, 4, 10, 13, 17).[8] In sector

HoB, a large rectangular commercial-industrial building C, a circular area for metalwork, and some patches of earth "floors" or working surfaces succeeded the buildings of the Lydian-Persian market (Figs. 39, 41).[9] Building C and the circle may be late third century; other rubble and patches are attributed to the destruction of 213 B.C., and some "floors" can be dated to the second century B.C.[10] The Lydian-Persian well (Fig. 39) was stuffed with tiles and made unusable. A cemetery of chamber tombs (Fig. 186) lay south of the putative course of the Hellenistic main east-west road; a late Hellenistic mausoleum (Fig. 187), the so-called Hellenistic Steps, was north of it, as was another possibly Hellenistic masonry construction CP west of the gymnasium (Fig. 129).[11] Decisive evidence came from PN, where dwellings of Lydo-Persian type were in use until 213 B.C. (Figs. 44, 181). Then they were leveled, and the wells stuffed. Coins of Antiochus II (261–246 B.C.) and Antiochus III (223–187 B.C.) were found above in the destruction debris.[12] A marble mausoleum M was built on the new diagonal road (Figs. 129, 167:57).[13] One or two tile kilns were built over the altar of Cybele, and there may have been a lamp factory further down on the Pactolus.[14] The picture is that of a leveled wasteland with sporadic industrial installations.[15] Up the Pactolus Valley, at PC (Fig. 8:13), Hellenistic chamber tombs were built over the Lydian-Persian houses; one of them, the "Tomb of the Lintel" (Figs. 129, 168), is dated by A. Oliver to ca. 175 B.C.[16] Finally, in the Artemis Precinct, a destruction level found under the Roman building L is possibly connected with the events of 214–213 B.C. (Plan III, DF).[17]

Because it has been damaged by earthquakes, slides, and Byzantine builders, the storm center of the siege of 215–213 B.C.—the citadel of Sardis (Figs. 6, 7)—has yielded only scant information. Fragments of the powerful walls at the top of the north side (Figs. 70, 79) certainly stood during the siege, as witnessed by coins of Antiochus III,[18] but the walls themselves are known to be Lydian. A rock shelf on the slope below has preserved traces of burning, destruction debris, and catapult balls; associated Hellenistic pottery makes connection with the siege possible.[19] On the central part of the citadel (AcT; Fig. 74), occasional finds of Hellenistic coins and pottery were not associated with Hellenistic building remains;[20] but there may well be Hellenistic architectural pieces of fine masonry built into the Early Byzantine fortress wall.[21]

That the cemeteries of the city were pushing westward already in the early Hellenistic period is proved by the two sarcophagi found at Haci Oglan (Figs. 124, 125),[22] ca. 850 m. west of PN, and the grave stele of Matis (Fig. 171), found ca. 1000 m. west of the Pactolus bridge. A late Hellenistic vaulted chamber tomb of Augustan-Tiberian date was found just south of the railway, ca. 200 m. east of the railway station (Plan III).[23]

Important observations on the destruction by the earthquake of A.D. 17 and subsequent building procedure of the Romans were made in Sectors UT and under the gymnasium and Synagogue. Debris of destroyed Hellenistic houses was used in massive fills to build up parts of the Upper Terrace above HoB (Fig. 8:5a) and to fill the huge terracing platform for the Main Road, the Byzantine Shops, and the gymnasium complex.[24] Fragments of Hellenistic wall paintings, stucco, pottery, domestic objects, and coins characterize these fills. The absence of larger structural stone pieces must be caused by wholesale reuse of these pieces as masonry or as material for lime.

Unquestionably the single most important discovery for the Hellenistic history of Sardis was epigraphic. Built into the piers of the late Roman synagogue we found four inscribed marble blocks from the *parastades* of the temple of the Mother of Gods (Fig. 169).[25] They contained the end of a letter of Antiochus III, dated in March, 213 B.C.; a decree honoring Heliodorus, ambassador to Antiochus III; a letter from Antiochus to the city; a decree of the city honoring Queen Laodice with a cult precinct (*temenos*) and dated August, 213 B.C.; and her thank-you note dated July, 213 B.C.[26] The city has been partly destroyed and punished. Upon intercession of Laodice, Antiochus III permits a repeopling, a *synoikismos,* under the direction of his Viceroy for Hither Asia, Zeuxis.[27] A translation of these fascinating documents, generously provided by L. Robert, appears in the Appendix to this section.

Another historically important inscription is a decree of the city (IN 60.1), datable between

209 and 193 B.C. and honoring an ambassador to Zeuxis.[28]

The cult of Sabazius, already established under Persian rule, becomes now a cult of Zeus-Sabazius and enjoys (royal) patronage under the Pergamene rule.[29] The inscribed circular bases of two phylai statues have been found,[30] that of the phyle Tmolis probably dating from the Pergamene period. The lid of a marble urn which mentions the phyle Pelopis (Fig. 170) dates to before 133 (or 100 B.C.). Finally, the event which extinguished Hellenistic Sardis, the earthquake of A.D. 17, is mentioned in an inscription, which also proves the existence of a late Hellenistic temple of Hera (Fig. 177).[31] The history of Hellenistic Sardis cannot be written without the publication of all important inscriptions found by the Expedition, a task brilliantly begun by L. Robert.[32]

Equally indispensable for the future historian of Hellenistic Sardis are the coins, both royal and autonomous. The publication by H. W. Bell of the finds of the first Sardis expedition stimulated attempts to reconstruct the activity of the mint of Sardis under the Macedonian and Seleucid kings,[33] and to ascertain the situation under the Pergamene and pre-Imperial Roman rule.[34] In her publication, A. E. M. Johnston (Buttrey) has identified almost 400 Greek coin types and explored some aspects which this increase offers for our knowledge of coinage in Sardis, for circulation of currency, and for the cults of the city.[35]

As to the objects found, the great quantities of Hellenistic pottery, the lamps, and the less numerous metal objects, terracottas, glass,[36] and miscellaneous finds bring concrete indications of Sardian industrial production. For the first time, pottery found at Sardis has been categorized into several traditions: those of Lydian derivation, those following the lead of Greek Hellenistic models (pattern ware, "West Slope" imitation, "Lagynos" ware, appliqué, and molded wares), and those probably derived from Romano-Italian industry (Eastern sigillata B). Few finds came from closed loci; there are, however, important contexts such as the units in PN destroyed in 213 B.C. (Fig. 181), the graves at Haci Oglan (ca. 300 B.C.; Figs. 124, 125), the "Tomb of the Lintel" at PC (ca. 175 B.C.; Figs. 129, 168),[37] and the deposits laid down immediately after the destruction of A.D. 17. These help to distinguish an early (334–213 B.C.), middle (213–133 B.C.), and late (133 B.C–A.D. 17) phase in the development of pottery at Sardis.

GMAH

Appendix on Inscriptions of 213 B.C., by Louis Robert

The following translation into French of four important documents relating to the events of the year 213 B.C. was sent by Louis Robert in 1980 and is here printed in this language to preserve the exact meaning he had intended.

Sardes: Documents de l'An 213 avant J.-C.

IN 63.118. Lettre du roi Antiochos III en mars-avril 213, 5 Xandikos 99.

(début disparu)

. . . que vous payerez en trois ans; qu'il soit permis de couper du bois pour la reconstruction de la ville et de l'emporter des forêts [royales] de Taranza selon ce qu'aura combiné Zeuxis [qui prend le détail des mesures pratiques]. Nous vous exemptons du droit du vingtième qui avait été ajouté [je préfère ne pas traduire encore le mot suivant] et nous avons ordonné de vous rendre le gymnase dont vous aviez auparavant l'usage. Nous avons écrit sur toutes ces affaires à Zeuxis et à Ktésiklès [sur ce fonctionnaire séleucide à Sardes, voir mes *Opéra Minora*, IV, 265]. Sur toutes ces affaires vous rendront compte Métrodôros et ses collègues [ambassadeurs de Sardes auprès d'Antiochos III].

IN 63.121 A. [Décret de Sardes sur la gravure des documents suivants]

Hérakleidès fils de Sôstratès a proposé: attendu qu'il convient de transcrire sur la parastade de temple qui est dans le sanctuaire de la Méter la lettre écrite par la reine au conseil et au peuple au sujet des honneurs votés par le peuple au roi, à la reine et à leurs enfants, plaise au conseil et au peuple: que la transcription soit faite par le trésorier; qu'il verse la dépense pour cela sur les revenus qu'il manie. Au mois D'Holôios [juillet-août 213].

IN 63.121 B. [Lettre de la reine Laodice III à la ville de Sardes]

La reine Laodice au conseil et au conseil et au peuple de Sardes salut. Métrodôros, Métrophanès, Sôkratès et Hérakleidès, vos ambassadeurs, ont remis le décret d'après lequel vous avez voté de consacrer un domaine sacré de Laodice et d'y fonder un autel, de célébrer une panégyrie des Laodikeia chaque année le 15 du mois Hyperbérétaios, de célébrer une procession et un sacrifice à Zeus protecteur de la famille pour le salut de notre frère le roi Antiochos, pour le nôtre et celui des enfants. Les ambassadeurs nous ont priée [d'accepter ces honneurs] conformément à ce qui est enregistré dans le décret. Nous avons accueilli avec plaisir ces honneurs et nous approuvons le zèle du peuple. Nous avons l'intention de procurer au peuple tout le bien possible. Les ambassadeurs vous feront un rapport là-dessus. An 99, 10 du mois Panémos [juin-juillet 213].

[Le roi est appelé "notre frère," comme le roi appelle la reine "la reine soeur" par terme d'affection protocolaire. Laodice III, fille du roi du Pont Mithridate II et d'une soeur de Séleucos 1er, n'était pas la soeur d'Antiochos III, mais sa cousine.]

IN 63.121 C. Le début d'une lettre d'Antiochos III.

IN 63.120. Lettre d'Antiochos III. Date disparue; postérieure à IN 63.118 et à IN 63.121 B.

. . . vous ayant accordé tout ce qui concernait le relèvement [de votre ville]. Maintenant, ayant à coeur que vous parveniez à une meilleure situation, nous avons fait le nécessaire. Pour les jeunes gens [fréquentant le gymnase] nous avons réservé pour la fourniture d'huile, à la place de ce que vous receviez auparavant, 200 métrètes d'huile chaque année et, jusqu'à cette quantité, nous avons ordonné de réserver des revenus gagés sur hypothèque sur lesquels vous les recevrez régulièrement. Quant aux soldats cantonnés chez vous, nous accordons que, sur les maisons que vous avez, ils n'en disposent plus de la moitié, mais du tiers. Nous vous dispensons du loyer que vous payez pour les ateliers, si du

moins il n'en est pas prélevé sur les autres villes. Nous décidons que, dans les fêtes Laodikeia célébrées par la ville, vous jouissiez de l'atélie pendant trois jours. Sur tout nous avons écrit à Zeuxis.

LR

Historical Background

The history of Hellenistic Sardis cannot be written before the researches on Sardian inscriptions and coins are published. It must also be based on a prosopography of Sardians both at home and abroad. The following paragraphs seek only to recall some data relevant to the archaeology of the Hellenistic city.[1]

The transformation of Lydian Sardis, capital of the Persian satrapy of Sparda, into a Hellenized Greek city may be viewed under several aspects. Linguistically, Aramaic and Persian as official languages and Lydian as a popular tongue were replaced by Greek. Constitutionally, Sardis was transformed into a theoretically autonomous Greek *polis* and at the same time into a major royal administrative center of the Seleucid kings. In material culture, there was a transition from Lydo-Persian to a Hellenistic standard of living. Finally, there was a profound change in the style of life: the Lydian cultural habits[2] were replaced by ideological objectives of the Greek *polis,* with such characteristic traits as schools, orators, athletics, religious festivals accompanied by games, and theatrical performances.

Let us take the linguistic situation first. In 329 B.C. an ordinary Lydian grave stele of Atrastas, son of Timles, is inscribed in Lydian, including the date in the year 5 of the Alexander era.[3] Three generations later, around 250 B.C., the stele of Matis copies Attic grave stelai and carries a "banal" poem in Greek (Fig. 171).[4] Dedications of two columns for the Artemis Temple were still inscribed in Lydian, perhaps after 281 B.C.[5] Newly found graffiti on ordinary pottery take the dwindling use of Lydian into the second, at the latest early first, century B.C.[6] Otherwise it is all Greek. It is not certain whether the first Greek coins were minted already under Alexander the Great (III), Philip Arrhidaeus, and Antigonus; they were definitely minted by Lysimachus (301–291 B.C.).[7]

We still lack the data to determine exactly when Sardis became a constitutional Greek *polis*. In 334 B.C. Alexander received the surrender of Sardis, built a temple to Zeus Olympios, and permitted the Sardians "to use their ancestral laws."[8] The "Sacrilege" inscription found at Ephesus (probably datable after 323 B.C.), in which forty-five Sardians are condemned to death by judicial officers of the Artemis temple in Ephesus, does not speak of Sardis as a city and implies lack of strong protecting authority.[9] In the friendship treaty with Miletus around 323 B.C., Sardis acts like a regular Greek *polis,* but has no regular officials.[10] By 214–213 B.C., correspondence with Antiochus III and Laodice (see the Appendix to "Previous Research," above) reveals a typical *polis* with a Council (*boule*) and People (*demos*) passing standard decrees, and a Treasurer and *strategoi* implementing them.[11] A *prytaneion* is mentioned in 209–193 B.C.[12] The Council of Elders (*gerousia,* Senate) first appears in an inscription vaguely dated between 150 and 50 B.C. by the editors.[13] The eponymous office of *stephanophoros,* after whom the year was named, emerges under the Pergamene kings.[14]

It must be left to experts to reconstruct the changing constitutional position of Sardis. It is clear, however, that already under the Seleucids the city boasted the full complement of bureaucratic offices, public and private benefactors, honorary decrees, games, sacrifices, honorary wreaths and statues, free meals in the *prytaneion,*[15] and other paraphernalia of Hellenistic urban life.

Yet more than many other cities, Sardis was a Janus—one face a "free" city, the other a royal residence, a seat of the satrap and the strategos of Lydia, and a center under the Seleucids of royal power and administration with the Royal Archive and Royal Mint for all Hither Asia Minor north of the Taurus. In this ambiguous situation the city might run its daily affairs, but it was the King's word that counted.[16] With the possible exception of one short period (226–223 B.C.), Sardis struck no coins of its own and made no foreign treaties under the Seleucid and Pergamene kings (301–133 B.C.).

As to historic events, after contests with Demetrius and Antigonus (382–301 B.C.), Lysimachus of Thrace held Sardis for about twenty years (301–281 B.C.) and struck coins there.[17]

The battle at Corupedion won by Seleucus I (281 B.C.) made Sardis a major Seleucid administrative center and stronghold until the battle of Magnesia (*ad Sipylum*) in 190 B.C. It thus became part of a sprawling but shaky empire reaching from the Aegean to Afghanistan. We catch some revealing glimpses; in 276–274 B.C., Antiochus I removed his queen and court to Sardis.[18] During the strife between the half-brothers Seleucus II (265–225 B.C.) and Antiochus Hierax (263–226 B.C.), Hierax was defeated by the Pergamene king Attalus I in 229–228 near Lake Koloe. Seleucus II may have held the city for two years (228–226 B.C.). Sardis then struck autonomous coins, "Pseudo-Alexanders" with Zeus Lydios and Tyche (Fig. 201), until 222 B.C. when Achaeus took over.[19] Then came the strongest blow against the city, and it came from internecine Seleucid struggle. Having first loyally held the throne for his cousin Antiochus III (242–187 B.C.), the general Achaeus (Fig. 91) decided to grasp for the crown (220 B.C.). He was besieged in Sardis, captured by treachery, and cruelly executed (214 B.C.). The historian Polybius (ca. 200–117 B.C.), a near-contemporary who knew Sardis, gives a dramatic account of the siege and the death of Achaeus.[20]

The new inscriptions (Fig. 169; Appendix to "Previous Research," above) now show that Antiochus III heavily punished Sardis, and then upon intervention of Queen Laodice (II—daughter of Mithradates II of Pontus, wife of Antiochus III)[21] permitted a *synoikismos,* which perhaps included some Jewish veterans from Mesopotamia.[22] Throughout, Zeuxis, son of Kynagos, Viceroy for Hither Asia, was in charge of the proceedings.[23]

It may be noted here that under the Macedonian[24] and the Seleucid rules (ca. 320–190 B.C.) new elements were added to the population in the numerous Macedonian and Greek settlers, people like Mnesimachus who held a land grant from Antigonus, or the husband of Matis, Andromenes.[25] Many Persians also stayed and retained some degree of identity, especially in religious matters.[26] The landholding pattern, too, was fundamentally changed by large amounts allotted to "King's land" and numerous grants which the king made to the new settlers.[27]

In 190 or 189 B.C., the Romans defeated Antiochus III at Magnesia (Manisa). He fled from the Acropolis of Sardis, and the Roman general, Lucius Cornelius Scipio Asiaticus, entered the city. Preliminary peace terms were negotiated at Sardis.[28] Under the treaty of Apamea, Sardis was then given to the Pergamene kings. Not Sardis but Pergamon became the center of power and wealth in Asia Minor, and the site of a grandiose building program. By contrast, Sardis cannot have been completely recovered after the destruction of 213 B.C. when the Pergamenes took over in 188 B.C. Despite the wars with the Gauls, Bithynia, and the Pontus, the sixty years (ca. 188–133 B.C.) of Pergamene rule were peaceful for Sardis. The respect paid to the city by the Attalids appears from the appointment of a former Royal Treasurer, Timarchos, to serve as "Temple Warden" (*neokoros*, really "trustee") of the temple of Artemis at Sardis (ca. 150 B.C.).[29] Apparently the construction of the temple continued under the Pergamene kings.[30] Pergamene influence is very evident in sculpture and pottery, both imported and local.[31] Games for the protecting deity of Pergamon, Athena Nicephorus, and King Eumenes II were introduced and promoted by embassies abroad;[32] and a priest of Zeus Sabazius, a cult favored by the Pergamene royal house, dedicated an altar for the phyle Eumeneis to Zeus (Sabazius?) in the temple of Zeus during the Pergamene rule.[33]

As with all of Western Asia Minor, Sardis entered upon changeable and difficult times when the last Attalid king left his kingdom to the Romans in 133 B.C. The wars of Mithradates (88–63 B.C.) and the Roman civil wars (49–31 B.C.) spelled decline for the entire region. Ostensibly, Sardis became a free city and began to strike considerable autonomous issues, with major series of "Apollo/club" and "Herakles/Apollo." A number of magistrates' names are known from the coins and inscriptions.[34] As a free city Sardis concluded a treaty with Ephesus.[35] A Sardian officer commanded a detachment during the war of Aristonicus (ca. 129 B.C.).[36] He is perhaps a relative of a wealthy and important man, Alcaeus, son of Alcaeus from Sardis, who was put to death by King Mithradates (VI) for presuming to win against the king in a horse race.[37] Later, in 86 B.C., Sardis tried to bar its gates to Mithradates.

Yet the tide was going the Roman way. In Roman organization Sardis became part of the province of Asia and, between 90 and 70 B.C.,

the capital of one of the nine *conventus iuridici* (assizes).[38] The priesthood of Roma, after which the years were counted, became the major priesthood of the city. Between 133 and 100 B.C. Alexarchus still had two eponymous offices, being both *stephanophoros* and priest of Roma. Somewhat later, the revered official "First Man" of the city, Socrates Pardalas, son of Polemaeus, (active ca. 90?–50? B.C.) was priest of Roma only;[39] so was Iollas, son of Iollas, five times strategos, who "brought to happy ending many dangers" as advocate for the city and was honored with seven statues around 50 B.C.[40] It was upon such eminent, wealthy, and well-connected citizens that the cities came to rely during the turbulent decades of Roman civil wars. Sardis briefly appeared on the stage of world history when Caesar's assassins Brutus and Cassius met there in 42 B.C., and having been acclaimed by the army as Imperators marched to Philippi;[41] and during his tumultuous career in Asia Minor (43, 41–32 B.C.) Mark Antony, "Emperor" (*Autokrator*), accepted the appointment as eponymous official of Sardis.[42]

As for most cities of Western Asia Minor, recovery began with the Augustan peace. In 27 B.C. Sardis competed for but did not receive the honor of the first temple to Roma and Augustus to be granted to the province of Asia. By 5 B.C., a local temple of Augustus had come into being.[43] In the decrees in honor of Menogenes, we see the city vigorously courting imperial favor by sending special ambassadors to congratulate Augustus' grandson on his assumption of the *toga virilis* (5 B.C.).[44] Yet again, as in 214–213 B.C., the individual fate of Sardis diverged from the general political and economic development. The cataclysmic earthquake of A.D. 17 made very nearly a *tabula rasa* out of the city. The Roman reconstruction began an entirely new chapter in the history of Sardis.[45]

GMAH

Urban and Architectural Development

In the two preceding sections we have described the results of the excavations and outlined the major historical events which affected the urban development of Sardis in Hellenistic times.[1] In this section we shall present some hypotheses or models which seem best to fit the archaeological and historical information now available. We must recall that until 1976 only the Acropolis and the western part of the site (Fig. 8, W300–E120) had been fairly tested. Leaving aside the Pactolus Valley, the vast central and eastern parts of the site (Fig. 8, E120-100/S500–N400) were studied only in an architectural research project concerned with ruins still visible above ground.[2]

The Early Seleucid City (334–213 B.C.)

The first Hellenistic urban phase of Sardis lasted from 334 to 213 B.C. (Plan II). It represented essentially the Macedonian-Seleucid city. Its major components were the citadel, which belonged to the king, and the lower city, which became a *polis.*

The Royal Fortress

The kaleidoscopic power struggles among Alexander's successors called for fortified refuges where the ruler could hold out until the next swing of the wheel of fortune. Like the rock of Pergamon for the Attalids, the reputedly impregnable citadel of Sardis was the main stronghold of the Seleucid kings in Asia Minor.[3] To make the comparison is to see what is lost to us in Sardis; Pergamon has preserved the essentials of such a Hellenistic *Königsburg*—the fortress walls, the palaces, the arsenals, the barracks, and the temples.[4] All of this and more must have existed in the Seleucid castle of Sardis. Unfortunately, our excavations have shown that except in parts of the north and south slopes, the periphery of the citadel has fallen downhill, while on the central and southern peaks the desperate Early Byzantine builders rooted out every single stone and scraped down to conglomerate rock (Figs. 4, 6, 7, 84).[5]

In 334 B.C., Alexander the Great admired the triple fortifications of the citadel, of which bits have survived (Figs. 72, 73).[6] Possibly the Seleucids continued to use them, though one would expect revisions to meet the new features of Hellenistic offensive siegecraft.[7] No original stretch of Hellenistic defenses has been found, only debris swept down the north slope after the siege (Fig. 79).

If the palace of Croesus was at the top of the north peak (Fig. 80; Plan I), as we have argued,[8] and if it continued to be used by Persian satraps (547–334 B.C.), then it probably continued to be used by the permanently resident *strategoi,* and by the Seleucid kings when they were in residence.[9] The transformation of the mudbrick palace into the *gerousia* (Council of Elders) of the city, mentioned by Vitruvius, would then not have taken place until the end of the Seleucid occupation in 190–189 B.C. (Plan III). The Treasury, too, was located on the citadel when Seleucus took over in 282/1 B.C.;[10] and the Mint might logically be situated near the Treasury. Finally, the Royal Records Office (*hai basilikai graphai*), which contained documents on royal land grants, may have required special protection.[11]

It remains an open question whether Sardis had one or two palaces in the Hellenistic Age. Admittedly, unlike Antioch, Sardis was not a "parade-prestige" commercial capital, but a fortress. Yet if we remember that the King, the "King's Friends", his bodyguard, and his court personnel, as well as a permanent garrison, had to be accommodated, a lower palace at half height remains an attractive possibility; Hanfmann had considered a mid-height location near the so-called "Byzantine Fort" (Fig. 8:23; Plan III).[12]

The Lower City

The ideal "model" should account for the survival of the Lydo-Persian city combined with a large-scale construction program required for the transformation into a Greek *polis.* Although current excavations (1976 to the present) may change our thinking about the extent and defenses of the Persian city, we must at this point think of both sides of the Pactolus Valley as having been filled with the kind of simple Lydian houses described below. They extended in traditional disarray far north into the plain, and up and down the lower slopes of the Acropolis (Plan I). To the Seleucid kings, accustomed to stamping new colonial cities out of the ground, Sardis must have looked as old-fashioned as did Florence or Rothenburg (or Rome?) to early twentieth century builders.

On the other side, vast exploitation of the marble quarries above the city (Magara Deresi) had begun to serve the "progressive" urban renewal.[13] The colossal scale and highest engineering competence shown in the Artemis Temple bespeak a bold and ambitious program in design and execution. We know that temples of Mother of Gods, of Zeus Polieus, and of Zeus Olympios existed, as well as a precinct to Queen Laodice. By 213 B.C. the city had a theater and stadium, a gymnasium, a prytaneion, and must have had a council house (bouleuterion).[14]

We surmise that the Seleucid planners did not try to change the basic pattern of the main roads, which may have already included the "bent axis" in the main east-west road (Fig. 167; Plan II).[15] The example of the theater-stadium complex (Fig. 173) indicates that they did not reform the general city plan but platformed and regularized limited areas; thus the theater and stadium were "tacked on" to the periphery of the city (Plan II).

Nothing is known about the western limits of the Seleucid city. Hypothetically, there should have been a defensive line west of the Pactolus, beyond the Lydian Agora,[16] but the evidence is buried deeply below the fields and newly built village houses.

The approximate eastern limit of the Seleucid city can be determined by Polybius' account of the capture of the lower city in 214 B.C. The troops of Antiochus III climbed over the wall at a gate above the theater, and 2,000 men occupied the upper edge of the theater. Meantime, the King was assaulting "the so-called Persian Gates" in the plain.[17] The theater is still recognizable and must have been either part of the defenses or just inside the city wall (Fig. 172).[18] "The so-called Persian Gates," however, pose a problem (Plan II). If the nickname means "Gates toward Persia," then it can have originated only during the Persian era, when people and messengers were leaving daily to go up the Royal Road to its other terminal, Susa. The corollary of this proposition is surprising: the Seleucids must have used an old Persian or even Lydian line of defense. For an age of rapidly changing warfare this looks at first improbable, but if these defenses were huge mudbrick walls of the kind now being found at MMS (1976 to the present; Fig. 133),[19] they might have been more effective than masonry against battering rams and artillery. Vitruvius mentions Athens, Patras, and Arezzo as examples of functioning mudbrick defenses, perhaps as late as the second century B.C.[20] We should add that the Roman

wall of the fourth century A.D. takes a different course (Fig. 8:9a-b; Plan IV), also in the east; it shows nowhere any trace of Hellenistic foundations or of reused Hellenistic masonry.[21]

The area around the theater is so deeply buried in heavy fill and extensively cultivated with vineyards that we had to give up our initial plan of searching for the Hellenistic east wall.

The visible parts of the theater itself (Fig. 172) were carefully investigated by R. L. Vann, who dates the plan to the late fourth or early third century B.C. It features a ca. 190-degree auditorium (cavea), and the dimensions of the structure are 136 m. (east-west) by ca. 70 m. north-south. All upgoing walls (two parodoi and the east wall of the cavea) are Roman reconstruction after the earthquake of A.D. 17. Mighty Hellenistic blocks of marble and limestone up to 1.20 m. long and 0.87 m. high (thickness unknown) are reused, especially in the impressive facing of the east parodos. Vann calculates a seating capacity of 12,000 to 15,000.[22] Marble benches designated in Greek according to the quadrants of seating sectors (MA = "South East") have been found in different parts of Sardis. They and a fine late Hellenistic statue may be reused from the Hellenistic theater.[23] The unusual, tangential conjunction of theater and stadium may be Hellenistic; but the barrel-vaulted eastern slope of the stadium is of mortared rubble and post–A.D. 17 Roman construction.[24] Similar to that of the theater, large ashlar masonry in the wall of the Northeast Stoa above the Artemis Temple is also reused.[25]

Finally, concentration of limestone and marble masonry in a torrent bed next to "Byzantine Fort" indicates one of the possibilities for the temple of Zeus Olympios built by Alexander the Great (Fig. 8:23, 62). A beautiful, large Ionic column base, similar to the Hellenistic bases of the Artemis Temple, was discovered in the torrent bed in 1981.[26]

In general, evidence is emerging that the eastern quarter on the northern foothills of the Acropolis between the old Lydian city wall MMS and the theater (Plan II) was, indeed, regularized in a series of terraces, which lent dramatic accents to the urban composition. Clearly, this Seleucid phase witnessed a vigorous confrontation between the old-time archaic Lydian-Persian construction types and techniques ensconced primarily in domestic and commercial structures, and the "hypermodern" colossal limestone and masonry architecture that served the Hellenization and was used initially for public buildings.

The Synoikismos of 213 B.C. and the Late Hellenistic City

In his letter to the Sardians, Antiochus III says that Zeuxis is to direct the *synoikismos*.[27] This entailed both physical reconstruction and repopulation. The plea of a neighboring town to Antiochus[28] shows that many citizens had died, others probably fled, and new settlers were brought in. They had to be provided with land and housing. The master plan would have to emanate from the offices of Zeuxis in collaboration with the city. With their vast experience in planning new cities all over the Near and Middle East, the Seleucids had at their disposal a staff of expert city planners; and the contemporary code of the *astynomoi* (city supervisors) of Pergamon shows into what details the specifications and regulations could go.[29]

How far was Sardis replanned? Obviously, much of it still stood: according to the letter of Antiochus III, the gymnasium "can be used as before." The Metroon, on which the city inscribed this series of documents (Fig. 169), was standing. Though the precinct may have suffered, the temple of Artemis was not burned. There was urgent need for timber—whether for houses, scaffolds, or major public buildings is unknown.

Excavations show beyond doubt that the western quarter was intentionally destroyed; industry and cemeteries moved in. An even larger habitation area was abandoned farther west,[30] and, in a drastic change, the Agora was moved from its Lydian location on the Pactolus to an undetermined area in the central-eastern part of the city.[31] Our hypothetical plan (Plan III) implies that after the *synoikismos* of 213 B.C., Sardis covered a smaller area and had probably a smaller population than between 334 and 213 B.C.

The central and eastern areas of the city display at least two divergent but regular alignments (Fig. 167). Some complexes align east-west with the theater and stadium, others with an oblique east-northeast to west-southwest direction. Admittedly, virtually all directional readings have to be based on the state after the

earthquake of A.D. 17, but they seem to reflect an earlier plan.[32]

In the following we describe the ascertainable or inferable features of the plan (Plan III) which, we assume, Zeuxis and his advisers worked out in 213–212 B.C. Since there would hardly have been enough time to carry out the actual construction in the hectic years between the fall of Achaeus and the peace of Apamea (188 B.C.), work presumably continued well into the Pergamene era, as it did at the Artemis Temple.[33]

In the west (Figs. 5, 167), the old diagonal road from the Pactolus, now flanked by cemeteries (Fig. 129), was regularized as a wide street (Plan III),[34] anticipating the late Roman "Street of the Pipes" (Fig. 8:57). The Royal Road, still the major east-west artery, went from the Pactolus through cemeteries and industrial areas, possibly at a slightly different angle from its Roman successor.[35] Built in mixed masonry–mortared rubble technique, the mausolea "CP" (Fig. 129) and "Hellenistic Steps" (Fig. 187) on the north side and the mortared rubble chamber tombs on the south side (Fig. 186) belong to the late Hellenistic times (ca. 150 B.C.–A.D. 17).

The western city wall and gate to the west must have been located between E100 and 150, and the defense line must have climbed a ridge to join the defenses of the citadel, as did the later Roman wall.[36] The current excavations (1976 to the present) may determine whether or not the Hellenistic builders reused a Lydian line of defense.[37]

Somewhere between E250 and 400, the main east-west road bent northward, resulting in the so-called "bent axis" plan (Fig. 167), comparable to Side and Palmyra.[38] As the same direction is repeated by the large (Roman?) complex "A" (Fig. 8:24–38) south of the road, and by the huge church "D", the "basilica" "C" (gymnasium?), and a Roman marble-paved road under the mill north of the road (Fig. 8:29, 35, 30),[39] one envisages a series of avenues parallel to the bent highway.

Up the lower northern slopes of the Acropolis (Figs. 6, 167), we conjecture north-south uphill lanes, some perhaps with stairs as in the uphill streets of Priene.[40] These slopes were presumably already terraced and carried several major complexes of public structures (agora? gymnasium? temples?).[41]

In the plain north of the east-west avenue, the

so-called "Old Izmir Road," still functioning as a village road, seems to be a northeast prolongation of the "Street of the Pipes."[42] It may have led to a subsidiary northeast gate in the plain.[43]

The eastern defenses seem to have remained on the same line as the early Seleucid ones (Plans II, III). One may conjecture that "the so-called Persian Gates" (Polybius) were on the main east-west road.[44] We have no evidence as to how the presumed *plan régulateur* was subdivided into units. The column of one Hellenistic house was found standing at ca. E340/S240;[45] and a set of numbered Doric peristyle capitals of ca. 150–100 B.C. was found near a lime pit at HoB. They suggest that "modern" Hellenistic peristyle houses were replacing the old dwellings of the Lydian type.

Recognizable leftover architectural parts of late Hellenistic buildings are few and not *in situ;* pediments of Hellenistic *naiskoi* decorated with shield devices were reused in the Synagogue (Figs. 258, 274) and in the South West Gate.[46] They could come either from shrines or from sepulchral structures, such as are reflected in funerary stelai.[47] A large Hellenistic Doric (temple?) column was recut into a late Hellenistic relief (Fig. 184);[48] and some elegant late Hellenistic fragments were found in the Artemis Precinct.[49]

An important late Hellenistic development in construction techniques is reflected even in the scanty material at Sardis. This is the transition from ashlar masonry technique (original Theater, Fig. 172) to a technique of facing mortared rubble with ashlar masonry (mausolea "CP," "Hellenistic Steps," Fig. 187) to building complete vaulted units entirely in mortared rubble, as in the Stadium and probably already in late Hellenistic–Augustan vaulted chamber tombs (Fig. 188).[50] This development was well under way when the earthquake of A.D. 17 struck, and it led to some remarkable experiments with statics of construction, as in the rebuilding of the Theater (Fig. 172).[51]

Late Hellenistic Buildings, Undiscovered and Discovered

From ancient authors, inscriptions, and coins, we know a number of buildings located in the vanished late Hellenistic city. Around 150 B.C., the former Pergamene Royal Treasurer, Timar-

chus, Supervisor (*neokoros,* "Temple Caretaker") of the Artemis Temple, was crowned at the Dionysia in the pre-213 B.C. theater; the inscription implies a shrine or temple for Dionysus. The decree honoring Dionysius mentions the gymnasium as sacred to Hermes and Herakles, who presumably had shrines for their "mysteries" in the palaestra.[52] Favored by the royal house of Pergamon, Athena Nicephorus had a cult[53] and Zeus Sabazius had a priest and presumably a temple.[54] The pre-213 B.C. Metroon survived, possibly somewhere near the east-west highway.[55]

The pre-213 B.C. *prytaneion* is not mentioned, but the agora and the *gerousia* are functioning, with a Hall of Elders (*presbeutikon*) and a Hall of Boys (*paidikon*) attested by 5 B.C. The inscription honoring Dionysius certifies a gymnasium for the boys; there may have been one for the seniors.[56]

Again, possibly surviving from pre-213 B.C., there was an open-air precinct and altar of Zeus Lydios (Fig. 147).[57] Socrates Polemaiou Pardalas built a shrine to Hera (Fig. 177), probably between 100 and 50 B.C.[58] Apollo, Attis, and probably Mên as well as the Kore of Sardis (Fig. 148), Demeter, and Asclepius had their shrines.[59] The temple and precinct of Artemis continued to flourish in conjunction with Zeus Polieus; the inscription of Menogenes which speaks of "residents in the Sacred Precinct of Zeus Polieus and Artemis,"[60] together with the existence of a subdivided temple (Fig. 179) and the survival of a colossal Zeus image (Fig. 176), shows that this was a double-cult temple in the late Hellenistic (pre–5 B.C.) era. The fact that the wall dividing the two cellas does not bond into the long walls cannot stand up against the certainty of the above evidence. Probably not later than 100 B.C. there was a cult precinct and a temple for Roma; and a temple for Augustus (alone?) was built before 5 B.C.[61] A synagogue must have come into existence, as letters from Late Republican officials mention a place (*topos*) for Jewish worship.[62]

In the overview, it does not seem likely that Sardis was transformed into a Seleucid colonial grid-plan city; the impression is rather that of a terraced vertical composition with monumental accents (Plans II, III) in that style which Martin calls "Héllenisme monumental" and attributes to Pergamon.[63] Withal, Hellenistic Sardis remains "a shadow of a magnitude," its deep burial under its own Romano-Byzantine debris and ruins rivaled only by that of its ancient rival, Seleucid Antioch.

GMAH

Artemis Sanctuary

With its eight by twenty columns, its sweeping length of ca. 100 m., its amazingly precise workmanship and Greek refinements, and its ingenious and elegant capitals and bases,[1] the great Artemis Temple must have made a grandiose impression and still evokes enthusiastic appreciation from modern students of architecture.[2] Its development and condition, however, pose many problems of interpretation.[3]

The Temple

H. C. Butler concentrated much of his attention on the excavation of the temple and concluded that the structure now standing (Figs. 7, 178) was designed during the Persian era on the site of what had been a Lydian temple. It had undergone a substantial rebuilding during the Roman period.[4]

Seven seasons of excavation by the Harvard-Cornell Expedition have turned up no evidence for the existence of either an archaic structure or a Persian-period temple.[5] Instead, the excavators have refined their understanding of the construction history and have discovered three building phases (Fig. 179; cf. Fig. 88): the first beginning sometime shortly after 281 B.C. and ending in 222 B.C., the second lasting from 222 B.C. until A.D. 17, and the third (Fig. 180) covering the century and a half following the A.D. 17 earthquake.[6]

An exact date for the start of the initial construction phase cannot be given. The area was in use during the Persian era, and there is a dedication from the precinct which dates to the mid-fourth century.[7] Perhaps the temple was planned already under Alexander or Antigonus or Lysimachus.[8] A dedication by a woman named Stratonice, who may be the same Stratonice who later became the wife of Seleucus I, was made around 300 B.C. The offering makes no mention of any royal titles and therefore may predate her marriage.[9]

The political and economic stabilization that followed Seleucus I's assumption of control in Asia Minor in 281 B.C. makes this a more auspicious period into which to place the beginning of a major building program.[10] Skilled workmen could have come from the workshops at Ephesus.[11] By 254 B.C. the sanctuary was important enough for Antiochus II to set up a stele recording the sale of land to his former queen Laodice.[12] The temple was planned initially as a one-cella temple open to the west; the interior walls were of sufficient height perhaps around 250 B.C. for the Mnesimachus inscription to be cut on the north wall. The text would imply that the temple was secure and wealthy, able to make a loan of 2,650 gold staters.[13]

The beginning of the second building period coincides with Achaeus' reign at Sardis (Figs. 90, 91), and the changes made to the temple seem to reflect his desires. To accommodate a colossal statue of Zeus (Fig. 176), the cella was divided in two (Fig. 179) and the east image basis constructed (Figs. 90, 178). The east wall of the cella was pierced for a doorway. Foundations beneath the door are stronger than those under the door openings in the west pronaos and the west cella wall, indicating that the east cella wall had originally been planned without a door.[14] The alteration occurred suddenly and quickly. The new door did not cut through an existing wall; either the wall was dismantled or it was not finished at the time. The lower course of ashlar masonry was left intact and concealed by a set of stairs which may have been moved from the northwest end of the temple, where a remnant interferes with the north colonnade (Fig. 89).[15]

Within the vertical joins of the upper courses of stones that form the east image basis (Fig. 178) were found 127 silver and bronze coins, all but one Hellenistic. P. R. Franke, who examined them, thought the coins, and therefore the basis, to date to the years immediately after 200 B.C. E. T. Newell, H. Seyrig, and G. M. A. Hanfmann have argued that the coin hoard dates to the years of Achaeus' rule.[16] The cement layer on which the stones of the basis rested (*100.45) shows no sign of having been retreated during the Roman rebuilding and probably dates from the original construction (Fig. 90). The stones of the lowest course have clamp marks, but the present nonfunctional arrangement of clamp holes suggests that these stones were reset from an earlier monument.[17] It is assumed that there was a third and possibly a fourth course of stones, the top one perhaps of marble.

The head of the colossal Zeus (Fig. 176) found by Butler which originally stood on the east basis[18] was reexamined by G. M. A. Hanfmann. He noted the strong similarities which exist between the facial features of the Zeus and portraits of Achaeus known from the coinage that he issued (Fig. 91).[19] It was to accommodate this portrait statue that the temple plan was re-designed. The Zeus/Achaeus image was installed in the new east cella facing the Acropolis. Artemis continued to face the west, watching over the Necropolis.[20] The spacious "pseudo-dip-teral" colonnade (Fig. 179), with the width for two rows of columns but with the inner row omitted, is said by Vitruvius to be an invention of the architect Hermogenes. Hermogenes had already finished the temple of Dionysus in Teos by 200 B.C., when Antiochus III and Laodice joined the god in the temple. Thus Hermogenes may well have worked for Achaeus at Sardis between 220 and 214 and could have designed the pseudo-dipteral colonnade for the Artemis Temple; hitherto, it was usually assigned to the Pergamene period, because Hermogenes was dated to ca. 150–130 B.C.[21]

The work must have been so far along that Antiochus III after capturing and punishing the city decided to allow the alterations to be com-pleted. Work progressed under the Pergamene domination (188 to 133 B.C.), and King Eu-menes may even have dedicated a portion of the spoils won at the Battle of Magnesia in the tem-ple. Inscriptions record the gifts of marble blocks made by the priestess of Artemis, Mos-chion.[22] The continued importance of the sanc-tuary into the early Roman times is testified to by the stele erected to list the achievements of Menogenes.[23]

After A.D. 17, much of the precinct was reor-dered or rebuilt, first due to the earthquake, and later because of flooding. Eventually the double cella was turned into two imperial cult halls, per-haps originally to house images of Tiberius and Livia[24] and later for statues of Antonius Pius and the Empress Faustina (Fig. 89). The image bases were strengthened to hold the added weight.[25] A puzzling feature is the smaller fluted columns placed at this time on tall, unfinished bases and used to support the porch roof. Two are in-scribed with Lydian letters. The most probable explanation is that they belonged to the internal colonnade of the third century B.C. temple. As at Pergamon, Lydian may have still been in use in the third century B.C.[26]

Altar LA 2

Some 16 m. to the west of the temple sits a large monument (W200-210/S1225-1250). H. C. Butler had interpreted it as an archaic altar.[27] The Harvard-Cornell Expedition's investigations revealed two separate buildings (LA 1 and LA 2), one embedded in the other (Fig. 94). The smaller, older structure (LA 1) has already been discussed.[28] The enclosing later structure (LA 2) is rectangular: 21.22 m. north-south, 10.74 m. east-west. LA 1 forms the midpoint; to either side are pockets, ca. 7 m. in length, that are filled with artificially laid deposits.[29] The east wall of LA 2 meets with that of LA 1, and the west face of LA 2 was a stairway overlaying an earlier LA 1 staircase.[30]

LA 2 was constructed in one building cam-paign. There is evidence of later rebuildings and stuccoing on the inner surfaces of the west, east, and south perimeter walls, and the upper sec-tions of the walls seem to have been rebuilt at a later time with poorer quality materials (Fig. 95).[31] Two shells form the walls, an outer layer of large masonry and an inner shell of brick and rubble. An extra strengthening course of larger stones was placed at the bottom of the inner shell. A platform was laid on top of the altar with riverstones set in a clay-mud mortar. One mar-ble paving stone is all that is left of the marble that may have originally sheathed the monu-ment.[32]

The excavator (C. H. Greenewalt, Jr.) cau-tiously concluded from material recovered from trenches along the sides of the inner structure (LA 1), particularly the Achaemenid-Ionian bowl fragments, that LA 2 was erected before the destruction of 213 B.C.[33] The altar type of LA 2 belongs to the family of great stepped Hel-lenistic altars such as those put up at Ephesus,[34] Priene,[35] and Magnesia[36] all of which date from the mid-fourth century to the mid-second cen-tury B.C.

LA 2 is much closer to the temple than is usual for a large altar of this period (Figs. 179, 180). It was usual for the distance from the temple to the altar to be equal to the length of the long side of the altar.[37] LA 2 is not even a meter in distance from the first row of columns of the pteron. H. C. Butler at one point envisioned LA 2 as forming the platform to the grand staircase entrance to the temple.[38] K. J. Frazer suggested that the altar was built as a provisional accommodation to serve the needs of worshipers during the construction of the great temple. It may have been intended that the altar was to link in some fashion with the west facade. However, the latter was never finished, at least not in Hellenistic times.[39]

R. Martin believes that there was originally an altar which was to be enclosed by the temple begun in the third century.[40] Xenophon specifies that it was on an Altar of Artemis that Cyrus the Younger and Orontas swore their oath of friendship.[41] This would indicate that an altar was standing at least by 407—401 B.C.; it may have been the archaic altar LA 1 (Fig. 95). A statue of Adrastos, a Lydian who fought in the Lamian War for the Greeks, was erected in the sanctuary of the Persian Artemis, according to Pausanias. Though the battle at Lamia took place in 323/322, the act of erecting a statue to a Greek supporter of the Athenians would have been a decidedly anti-Macedonian act and probably not possible until after Lysimachus' defeat at Corupedion in 281 B.C.[42] Perhaps the building of LA 2 was undertaken to replace the older altar to Artemis Anahita[43] and to serve as a focal point for worship during the construction of the temple. The lack of adequate funds to speed the building program along may have assured the continued use of the altar and even led to later Roman-period repairs.

The Precinct

Two other monuments and a layer of burned material can be traced to the Hellenistic era. Under the floor of Roman Building L (Fig. 88, W165-195/S1300-1320), at levels *98.40-*98.15 (Room A) and *98.60-*98.20 (Room B), was a stratum of ash in which were found bits of late Lydian and Hellenistic pottery, burned bones, and pieces of fired tiles. This level may be the result of a fire and destruction in the area of the Artemis Temple following the recapture of the city by Antiochus III in 213 B.C., though there is no evidence for any damage having been sustained by the temple proper.[44]

Monument No. 10 is a large, three-roomed building with exedra that stands ca. 26 m. to the east of the temple (W63-73/S1251-1267; Fig. 88).[45] It may possibly be the remains of a late Hellenistic water clock.[46] A fragment of late Hellenistic relief ware (P 69.94:8059) and several "posthumous Alexander" coins were found on and under the stucco floors.[47] The base, which projects out from the exedra, was capped with a marble plinth, probably for a statue. It is of Hellenistic workmanship. If the monument antedates the A.D. 17 earthquake, then the east side of the Hellenistic precinct must have had a steep rise.

The red and green sandstone base known as Monument 20 sits atop the Northeast Terrace (W75-77/S1170-1210; Fig. 88).[48] Its stepped masonry recalls that of LA 1. The stones are not clamped. The platform on top has edges that are raised and rounded and border channels intended for either water or sacral liquids. Like the Monument of Nannas, Monument 20 may have been reset in Roman times.

The other features of the precinct owe their present form and alignments to the Roman rebuildings of the first, second, and third centuries A.D. (Fig. 88). Floods, earthquakes, and rearrangements and additional construction have completely obliterated the Hellenistic precinct plan. Only the isolated monuments remain.

WEM

Private Buildings

Two kinds of architecture figure in the private sectors at Sardis, domestic and commercial-industrial. Before 213 B.C. both existed side by side at HoB and PN. After the 213 B.C. rebuilding the two functions were separated, and the industrial quarters did not serve as residential areas. Where the new domestic blocks were is not known, though some were probably on the terraced slopes south of the main east-west road (Plans II, III). Industrial activities were kept outside the city walls, probably to forestall the possibility of conflagration from an industrial fire. Two major house types are evidenced: a traditional cellular design which continued the building style developed during the later years of the Lydian empire and still in use during the Persian era until 213 B.C., and the peristyle houses such as are known from Delos.

House of Bronzes Area

A large industrial complex unearthed by the Harvard-Cornell excavations in the Lydian trench at HoB (W20–E15/S85–105) shows that HoB (W20–E30/S5–120) was functioning as a manufacturing and industrial quarter during the first sixty-five years of the Seleucid rule (Fig. 41). There is evidence for a workshop and for an outdoor working space.[1] The workshop, Building C, is connected to the outside area via an extension of its south wall. Building C (W5–15/S83–91, *86–*95) is 8 m. by 20 m. The north and east walls are built of carefully laid and leveled large stones. The south wall and the upper portion of the east wall are less well built. Reused blocks from Lydian buildings, found in the interior, were bases for internal roof supports.[2] Five m. east of the workshop was a circular area 10 m. in diameter ("Industrial Circle"). Within and under the surface layer were burned deposits (*99.20–*99.78) containing the charred remains and ashes of goat, sheep, horse, and donkey bones. Pieces of a mudbrick furnace, fragments of terracotta molds—some with bits of bronze still attached—and an abundance of charcoal indicate that the spot was a bronze-working foundry.[3]

The destruction of 213 B.C. is testified to by patches of burned material which slope upward from north to south, *99.90–*100.30 (E5–W25/S97–120; Plan III:DF).[4] The industrial complex which lies below the burned level is dated to before 213 B.C. from fragments of black glazed ware found, a type of pottery which Oliver in his study of Sardis Hellenistic pottery states was not imported nor produced locally after 213 B.C.,[5] and from coins of "Alexander III or Successors" and Antiochus II (261–246 B.C.).[6]

Following the relocation of the city away from the banks of the Pactolus, HoB was no longer within the city walls. At least a portion of the site was returned to industrial activities.[7] But the appearance of late Hellenistic tombs indicates that HoB had also taken on the function of cemetery (Fig. 129).[8] The northern half of HoB seems to have been reserved for graves, while the industrial enterprises continued in the south. The HoB cemetery was used through the Roman era (Fig. 186). A cache of seven small, elegant marble Doric capitals such as were used on the col-

umns of peristyle houses has been found near Building C (W18–19/S84–85, *99.3–*99.6) along with wall painting fragments[9] and suggests that someone built a fashionable peristyle house near the southern part of HoB after 213 B.C., but these items remain the only hint of Hellenistic domestic construction in the area.

Pactolus North

Until 213 B.C. PN was a crowded, congested urban residential neighborhood (Fig. 44). Regular but uneven flooding of the Pactolus forced builders of new structures in PN to make terraces out of houses which had become filled with river gravel. In the northwest corner (W295–304/S326–330) a large domestic complex comprised of three units (XIX, XX, XXI; Fig. 181) was built. Its construction can be dated by coin finds to the late fourth or third century B.C.[10] The pottery finds (Figs. 194, 195) are datable by the inclusion of Attic black glazed pieces to the same general period.[11] The walls of the houses were constructed of mudbrick which sat atop riverstone socles. Relief terracotta tiles continued to be employed to decorate the roofs. Two of the three units may have formed a gate house with two doors. The remains of a hearth were found within the complex (unit XIX, *85.5). In the southeastern part of PN (W235–265/330–353) some wall remnants and a possible corner (*87.35; Fig. 45) testify to the presence of Hellenistic occupation.

Throughout much of the northwest part at PN was found a layer of clay, riverstones, and sima tile fragments which sloped from south to north (Fig. 44; W256–258/S331–333, *87.35; W273–278/S348–350, *87.9). The layer was an artificial surface which was created after the devastation of 213 B.C. The mudbrick walls of houses were knocked down, the stone socles dispersed, and the roof tiles placed in heaps; the whole was then spread out throughout the northwest part of PN and a new floor formed (Plan III:DF).[12] It would seem that at this time too, the PN wells were intentionally filled with house debris and rendered useless,[13] probably as punishment for the resistance against Antiochus III.

Houses were not built again at PN. The sector became in part industrial. Two kilns (one with an attached drainage system) rest atop the destruction level (W275/S321, *87.00; W266/S360,

*88.00).[14] One of the kilns was built of baked brick and appears to have been used for the manufacture of tiles.[15] A coin of Antiochus III (226–190 B.C.) affirms the post-213 B.C. date for the industrial operations.[16]

To the east at PN is a late Hellenistic monument (W220.6–223.4/S345–348, *87.7), Monument M (Fig. 129). Its lower part consists of fine marble steps numbered in Greek letters. It can be dated by the sigillata B sherds found in the base trench to the years just prior to the A.D. 17 earthquake.[17] Monument M and the chamber tomb behind it, the latter similar to tombs found in HoB and PC, show that a section of PN had also been turned into cemetery space after 213 B.C., and it was to serve in this capacity into the imperial era.

WEM

Graves and Cemeteries

Graves

The burial areas of the Hellenistic city already in the mid-third century B.C. had begun to move out towards the west along the east-west highway (Figs. 129, 186). Except for secondary burials in the Necropolis Hill, the Lydian burial grounds were not reused by Hellenistic Sardians. New cemeteries were created after 213 B.C.

The area called Haci Oglan, some 850 m. west and 490 m. south of Salihli highway (Fig. 129), yielded two sarcophagi (61.3, 61.4)[1] which contained third century B.C. burials. Two coins (C 61.22–23) were retrieved from within the sarcophagus 61.4 (Figs. 124, 125), one of which has been identified as a Macedonian silver drachm of Alexander III or of one of the Successors.[2] Along with the coins were found pottery pieces (P 61.21; P 61.22) which A. Oliver considers as continuing Lydian pottery traditions,[3] and seven tubular glass beads (G 61.3).[4] There were two occupants in 61.3; one was a young woman. An individual under fifty years of age was buried in 61.4 Four clay alabastra (P 61.23, Fig. 182) and a typical Hellenistic unguentarium had been placed outside 61.4.[5] Like other late Lydian sarcophagi, the two sarcophagi with

pitched roof lids of local "half-marble" are very large (length 2.30 and 2.40 m.). They clearly continue the local Lydian tradition. Sardis has not yielded so far any of the rare early Hellenistic figured sarcophagi represented so strikingly in the rival capital of Ephesus by the sarcophagus of Belevi, thought by some to be the resting place of Antiochus II (died 246 B.C.).[6]

A rock-cut cist burial type similar to a sarcophagus in size and covered by stone slabs fitted into a precut edge is known from Bin Tepe (Fig. 123). A fragment of Hellenistic relief ware (P 66.118) dates it after 200 B.C.[7]

Not too distant from Haci Oglan, but close to (south of) the highway and about 1 km. west of the modern Pactolus bridge, a grave stele for a woman named Matis was erected about 250 B.C. (Fig. 171). Provincial in character, the relief and its Greek epigram owe their inspiration to Late Classical Attic types.[8] The Matis stele is succeeded by a series of middle to late Hellenistic "Eastern Greek Reliefs," sepulchral stelae with standing facing figures (Fig. 183) or horsemen (Fig. 184). They differ in no way from those of other Hellenistic cities of Asia Minor.[9]

It is not yet clear to what extent Lydian masonry chamber tombs continued to be built into the Hellenistic period. A tomb investigated in 1976 is thought to be Hellenistic.[10] Oliver also considers as Hellenistic the chamber tomb Bin Tepe 66.4: another Bin Tepe chamber tomb (BT 66.3) may have had a secondary Hellenistic burial.[11]

During the second and the first centuries B.C., a Hellenistic Greek chamber tomb type, well known from Greece, Macedonia, and other Hellenistic regions,[12] came into use at Sardis. Harvard-Cornell excavation findings imply that at Sardis the change took place sometime after 213 B.C. The earliest example known, the Tomb of the Lintel at PC (Fig. 168), dates around 175 B.C. It had a stuccoed facade and apparently a flat stone ceiling.[13] Three chamber tombs at HoB (j, k, n: E0–10/S50–60; Fig. 186)[14] and a chamber tomb at PN[15] could only have been constructed after the city had moved away from the Pactolus. Another chamber tomb, possibly of Augustan age, was found far to the north, near the railway (Fig. 129).

The HoB and PN tombs have only a single square chamber. The Tomb of the Lintel (Fig. 168) has a dromos (5 m. long) in addition to the chamber. The tombs were built of mortared rubble stuccoed over. The interior walls of tomb n at HoB show traces of incisions in the plaster intended to suggest ashlar masonry as in the "First Pompeian Style."[16] Niches were cut into the south wall of the Tomb of the Lintel and the east wall of tomb k (HoB). Though the Tomb of the Lintel had a flat roof, the PN chamber tomb and the HoB tombs were probably vaulted. This chamber tomb type continued into the Roman Imperial era, and a complete impression can be gained from the early Imperial example in the Artemis Precinct, Tomb 2 (Fig. 188), though it had a brick rather than a mortared rubble vault.[17]

These chamber tombs were originally intended as inhumation burials. They are all furnished with two couches upon which would have lain the bodies of the deceased;[18] one of the couches usually has a raised head and shoulder rest. In tombs j, k, and n at HoB, the couches with this feature are all along the east wall. A "Lagynos" technique amphora from the Tomb of the Lintel with molded relief, painted decoration, and two plastic heads in Pergamene style (Fig. 185) was the most impressive find. None of the other tombs yielded such an ambitious ceramic piece, though a similar relief vase had been found by Butler in Tomb 535.[19]

A different type of burial structure, here designated as "mausoleum," probably carried a house or shrine-like superstructure. A set of three limestone steps and an adjacent platform of mortared rubble were encountered ca. 3 m. below the floor of "Jacob's Shop," and its neighbor, now designated as shop E12–13 (Fig. 187).[20] This part had been used as support for the south wall of the Roman Synagogue. Three walls forming the north continuation of the structure and an empty brick grave with schist slab cover were found under the Synagogue.[21] The steps are distinguished by beautiful workmanship with ruled guidelines and setting marks (crosses), but protective strips which were not removed and an unfinished block show that the work was never completed. A faceted Hellenistic Doric column fragment lay nearby.[22] The stepped south facade was 7.5 m. (east-west) and deviated almost 9° from the direction of the later Roman avenue (Fig. 167:55). Hellenistic appliqué and relief ware and five autonomous Sardian coins confirmed the Hellenistic date; one of the coins was at the level of the foundation, 0.40 m. below the leveling course under the steps; it was probably contemporary with the building of the mausoleum.[23] Made of rubble bordered with masonry, a structure "CP" west of the gymnasium (W108/N10–18.5; Fig. 129) is reminiscent of the "Hellenistic Steps" in construction and may have been the podium of another mausoleum.[24]

In PN, the preserved south side of Monument M aligns precisely with the later "Street of the Pipes" (W220.6–223.4/S345–348; Fig. 8:57). It consisted of two marble steps, 3.07 m. long (lower), backed by a mortared rubble core faced with marble slabs. Only the corners of the east and west side are preserved for ca. 0.60 m. This may have been a solid monument rather than a chamber tomb, but after the earthquake of A.D. 17 a late Hellenistic–early Roman mortared rubble chamber tomb was built against it into the south wall of "M." The step blocks were numbered *beta, gamma,* and *delta*. Eastern sigillate sherds from the foundation trench indicate a date between 30 B.C. and A.D. 17.[25]

Cremation

Sometime late in the Hellenistic period a change occurred from inhumation burials to cremation. According to Butler, many of the Necropolis tombs had been reopened in later times and cinerary urns deposited in them.[26] The late Hellenistic–early Roman vaulted tomb at Sart Mahmut,[27] excavated in 1975, contained no benches but had instead four wall niches and four cinerary urns.[28] The tomb itself consisted of a single chamber, 2.90 × 2.70 m., with a vault 3.65 m. from the floor. The longer walls, from which the vault springs, are of brick and mortar; the shorter walls are of mortared rubble. The floor is paved.

With the appearance of cremation, small house-shaped ash urns of marble replaced sarcophagi. Some are decorated with palmettes, like the new example from Tomb 1 in HoB (Fig. 189),[29] and have a flat lid. The majority have house-gable lids and are inscribed with the names of eponymous officials as well as the name and day of death of the deceased (Fig. 170). Several groups are known from the first Sardis expedition. One group dates by *stephanophoroi* and is presumed to date before 133 B.C.

or, at the latest, ca. 100 B.C.[30] Another dates by the Priests of Roma and begins after 133 B.C.[31] Yet another group dates by officials not specifically identified.[32]

A number of urns have been added by the Harvard-Cornell Expedition. Two groups supply important information. Five urns, all bought from a local collector, probably come from the same tomb. One of them (IN 69.8) shows parallel "double-dating" by *stephanophoros* and by the Priest of Roma, Dionysius son of Dionysius, hence around 100 B.C. The four other urns (IN 69.7, IN 69.9, IN 69.10, IN 69.11) date by officials whose title is not given. One of these is the triumvir "Mark Antony Autokrator," whose appointment as an eponymous official of Sardis probably occurred between 41 and 39 B.C.[33] Another urn may hold the ashes of the father of Socrates Polemaiou Pardalas, Priest of Roma between 98 and 94 B.C.[34]

The second group came from the vaulted tomb in Sart Mahmut near the railway station. If the official Damas on one of the four urns is the same as the magistrate on a Sardian coin of the time of Augustus, we obtain the latest date yet known in the series. The complete study and publication of these urns will greatly improve the Sardian chronology and the dating of late Hellenistic and early Roman tombs.[35]

WEM

Economy and Industry

Resources

From 281 B.C. when Seleucus I took control of Asia Minor until 188 B.C. when Antiochus III surrendered it, Sardis was the capital of Seleucid Asia Minor north of the Taurus. It was situated in one of the richest areas of Anatolia—so rich, in fact, that despite Sardis' fall from prominence when the Pergamene kings assumed power, Lydia was still considered by the Romans to be the wealthiest district in their province of Asia.[1]

The land of the Hermus Valley had always been productive.[2] Grain was probably still a major crop, and together with the Caicus valley, the Hermus may have served as a grain source for Pergamon.[3] Wine pressed from the grapes of vineyards around Sardis was as much enjoyed in Hellenistic and Roman times as it had been in

Lydian.[4] Theophrastus noted that apples and pomegranates were also cultivated on the slopes of Mt. Tmolus.[5]

The breeding of sheep for wool most likely continued during the years of the Seleucid rule.[6] Wherever the immigrant Greeks moved throughout the Hellenistic world, they took with them a preference for woolen clothing.[7]

Although by the first century B.C. Strabo could write that the Pactolus no longer flowed with gold and had not for some time, it is not clear when gold mining or panning ceased. Two new inscriptions dating around 200 B.C. (IN 60.1; 63.119) mention gold wreaths worth "ten gold staters" (200 drachms) bestowed by the city upon an anonymous benefactor and on Heliodorus, son of Diodorus.[8] Gilded statues for Iollas are mentioned about 50 B.C.[9] The Mnesimachus inscription states that the dues which the villages are to pay are to be in gold staters.[10]

Land Tenure

Surrounding the city were large estates, either gifts of the king or parcels purchased from the royal holdings which could be reclaimed under certain conditions at the whim of the ruling monarch.[11] Much the same system had been in effect under the satrapal rule. These estates, like the Persian estates which preceded them, may have been fortified.[12] Xenophon's description of the attack by the Ten Thousand at the suggestion of their hostess on the manor house and estate of a wealthy Persian neighbor of hers near Pergamon sometime around 401 B.C. bespeaks the feudal mores of the fifth century, which Rostovtzeff has suggested were also those of the Hellenistic era.[13] Included within land holdings were the villages and smaller farms on the property. The recipients of these lands formed an elite, Greek-speaking aristocracy, though possibly some of the Persian aristocrats were allowed to keep their lands.[14] The Mnesimachus inscription (around 250 B.C.) mentions several villages in the Sardis plain. A new inscription (IN 64.4), which is about the deeding of land, supplies the name of another village near the city (. . . soudda, perhaps Porsoudda).

Trade

As a cosmopolitan center, Sardis imported great numbers of items to suit the tastes of its heterogeneous population; we have some illustration of these items in the finds made by the Harvard-Cornell team. Fragments of Hellenistic glass bowls, most from HoB, decorated with cut rings, rosettes, and shoulder friezes, came from the glass-making workshops of the eastern Mediterranean and may have been intended for the wealthier citizens, though A. von Saldern has pointed out that by the third century B.C. glass was not such a rare and expensive item as to have been made expressly for an elite clientele.[15]

Black glazed pottery was imported from Athens in the fifth century and from Ionia and Athens in the fourth. The pieces are decorated with palmettes and rouletting. The great vogue for black glazed pots dates to the years immediately following the arrival of Alexander, and the ware continued to be imported until around 213 B.C. The finds come mainly from PN and HoB, indicating that the vessels were used in domestic settings. Shapes included kantharoi with molded and plain rims and some with fluted bodies, skyphoi with cima reversa profile, open bowls with both inward and outward turned rims, and fish plates.[16]

In the mid-second century B.C., appliqué relief ware (Fig. 192) was imported, probably from Pergamon where molds which match many of the relief decorations known from Sardis have been found.[17] The fondness for this ware lasted through the first century B.C. and into the Augustan age. The representations are in the style of the Pergamene baroque, though a few of the pieces show signs of an overlapping with Arretine pieces (Fig. 193).[18]

Beginning in the early years of the second century B.C. and extending through the middle of the century, Sardis shops stocked the Pergamene imitation of Attic West Slope pottery. Fluted amphoras, compote dishes, kantharoi, handleless cups, open bowls, and unguentaria were all bought in quantity to be used as household ware. A high percentage of the finds come from HoB. The vessels, though not as refined as their Attic models, are nonetheless well potted and not overly ornate.[19]

At the same time that the Pergamene appliqué ware was being imported, white-slipped "Lagynos" ware pottery (Fig. 185) was being sold in the city. The place of origin of this fabric is not known. The most popular shape at Sardis was the lagynos, a flask-like jug after which the ware is named. This ware was probably intended also for household use. The fine white-slip vase from the Tomb of the Lintel[20] may be local, according to A. Oliver. "Lagynos" ware continued to be marketed into the mid-first century B.C.[21]

Industry

The Harvard-Cornell excavations have clearly revealed that the local industries were a feature of the economic life of Sardis during the Hellenistic age.[22] For metalwork, HoB has yielded evidence for a bronze-working shop. There is the famous reference by Pausanias to the bronze statue of a Lydian warrior Adrastos, probably put up after the Seleucids came to power.[23] Inscriptions datable from the late third century through the first century B.C. include provisions for the erecting of bronze statues.[24]

Besides the gold wreath already discussed, a beautiful and finely worked Hellenistic gold earring (J 68.2), which came from the fill beneath the Synagogue, testifies to the skill and craftsmanship of the goldsmiths of Sardis.[25]

Prolific local ceramic manufacturers provided wares to compete with the foreign items. Lydian traditional pottery types continued to be made until 213 B.C. Many examples of older style vessels made from a local fabric were discovered in the ruined houses of PN below the 213 B.C. destruction layer (Figs. 194, 195). These represent painted as well as plain pottery which owed its origins both in shape and decoration to a pottery style that had reached its apogee in the sixth and fifth centuries B.C.[26]

Some forty fragments of terracotta molds are proof that Hellenistic relief ware was produced locally. These consist mostly of drinking cups. At Sardis they were probably manufactured from the late third through the late first century B.C., with the destruction levels of 213 B.C. and A.D. 17 serving as important termini post and ante *quem*.[27] The Hellenistic relief and appliqué wares, both locally produced and imported, came largely from the Hellenistic levels of HoB and the destroyed houses of the Upper Terrace, as well as from the platform that forms the foundation for the Roman gymnasium (Fig. 167:5, 59–61). Albeit mold-made pottery was common throughout the Hellenistic world, the selection of decorative types found at Sardis (Figs. 190–193) reveals some aspects of the interests and pursuits of the population. There are scenes with theater-related subjects (Fig. 191), racing charioteers, and many erotic episodes (Fig. 192), the latter theme being particularly favored. The relief wares simulated in a less costly medium the splendor of the silver, gold, and glass vessels that the wealthy so enjoyed. The elegance of these originals is captured in the fine naturalism of the ivy sprays and acanthus leaves and tendrils. The beautiful amphora (Fig. 185) from the Tomb of the Lintel not only testifies to the capabilities of the potters at Sardis but also gives some impression of the elegance of the now lost silver ware being imitated.

The red gloss pottery, the so-called Eastern sigillata A and B (Fig. 196), appears with much abundance in the late Hellenistic and early Roman levels and was probably of local manufacture. There is a strong resemblance between the fabric of the red ware and that of the earlier indigenous pottery. Many of the fragments carry potters' stamps. Represented twenty-four times among the Harvard-Cornell Expedition finds, the stamps of Mithres (MITHREOUS, genitive; Fig. 197) are not known from any other sites; presumably the workshop was local. In 1904 R. Zahn saw the Latin stamp of a well-known Italian ceramic entrepreneur, Caius Sentius (0–A.D. 30), which had come to light in Priene on a sigillata B sherd, as proof that Sentius had branched out from his Italian factory at Arezzo to establish production facilities in Asia Minor and to originate the Eastern sigillata B ware. The theory is confirmed and broadened to include another Italian factory by the find at Sardis in 1960 of a Latin stamp of SERENUS (Fig. 198), Quintus Pompeius Serenus (15 B.C.–0), whose factory was in Puteoli (Pozzuoli). These are striking illustrations of the way in which Roman businessmen expanded into the markets of Asia Minor.[28] The volume of red gloss sigillata B indicates a thriving business in the later years of the first century B.C. and the early part of the first century A.D. Perhaps as many as thirty or forty workshops were involved in the production of this ware in Asia Minor and other Greek Hellenistic regions over these years.[29]

Until the advent of Pergamene domination (188 B.C.), the Sardis textile workshops continued to manufacture quality fabric.[30] During the second century B.C. the *vestimenta Attalica,* a finely woven cloth with gold threads interlaced,

became famous throughout the Mediterranean world. Though probably produced in and exported from Pergamon, they may well have owed initial inspiration to the Sardian workshops and weavers.[31]

The urban survey team found in 1979 evidence for a luxury craft center which had flourished during the Roman era. The debris on the site (at E60–80/S295–330) contained quantities of chips of jasper, sard, yellow chert, amethyst, and fragments of fine glass and worked ivory. The first Sardis expedition found many Hellenistic gems, and the Harvard-Cornell excavations have turned up an earring (J 68.2) and a seal possibly of a "gryllos in the form of a horse-bird composed of the heads of a horse, ram, and Silenus, with a cock's (?) slender legs and plumed tail," which R. S. Thomas dates to the Hellenistic period.[32]

There is reason to believe that a school of sculpture was active in Sardis during these centuries.[33] Such an operation would have employed a certain number of skilled craftsmen and apprentices. The stone often used was a local grayish-white marble.[34]

A large employer of both skilled and unskilled labor throughout the Hellenistic period was the Artemis Temple. Its building program, especially after the destruction of 213 B.C., required a supply of stonemasons and craftsmen and a corps of unskilled men for the muscle power, and the need for marble kept the quarries at Magara Deresi busy.[35]

Economy

In Chapter VI we alluded to the probable activities of a Persian mint. A Hellenistic mint was established in the city, although it is a matter of controversy whether it was already operating under Alexander the Great or began under Lysimachus.[36] During the Seleucid era, Sardis was one of the royal mints for Asia Minor. Except possibly for one brief interlude of municipal coins (228–220 B.C.), only the royal silver coinage was issued. According to a theory proposed by A. E. M. Johnston, Sardis did not strike an autonomous coinage until the Romans took control (after 133 B.C.), after which time two major series of bronzes appear, Apollo/club and Herakles/Apollo.[37] Cistophori may have been used at Sardis during the first Pergamene period (228–

220 B.C.) as the federal coinage of the Pergamene Kingdom. They were in common use in
the city after Sardis officially passed under Pergamene hegemony with the peace of Apamea
(188 B.C.). Whether the cistophori were ever
struck at Sardis is a debated point. According to
F. S. Kleiner, the series struck at Pergamon for
Sardis extends from 166 to 128 B.C.[38] The Harvard-Cornell excavations have turned up no Pergamene coins earlier than the mid-second century B.C. The first Sardis expedition recorded
seven coins of Pergamon which could be dated
from the late third or early second century B.C.
Only one of them is silver.[39]

The analysis of the coin finds of the two Sardis
excavations has shown that there was a movement of currencies among some of the neighboring cities of Lydia: Blaundus, Caystriani, Magnesia ad Sipylum, Philadelphia, and Tralles. The
presence of coins from the Ionian centers—Colophon, Ephesus, Erythae, Smyrna, Teos, Chios,
and Halicarnassus—is evidence that the eastern
Greek cities still impacted to some extent on the
economic life of the Lydian city. The discovery
of issues from Syrian Seleucid cities of Antioch
on the Orontes and Apameia indicate that Sardis
was in contact with areas of the Seleucid empire
outside its immediate vicinity.[40]

During these centuries the Artemis Temple
served as a banking house.[41] The Mnesimachus
inscription records that the temple was wealthy
enough to extend a sizable loan of 2,650
staters,[42] and this must not have been the only
loan that the temple made. It may be an indication of its importance as a financial institution
that the Pergamene king appointed an experienced financier, the former Director of the
Royal Treasury (Timarchos), the Temple Warden (neokoros) of the Artemis Temple.[43] Little is
known about the organization of the temple or
its personnel, other than a musician and a
cook.[44] Exactly how much land belonged to the
temple is unclear, but it is possible that a portion
of the Mnesimachus estate may have been
carved out of what was originally a temple holding.[45]

Pergamene Involvement

Between 228 and 188 B.C. Sardis had four different rulers. It was attacked and destroyed, and
it was physically moved and rebuilt. By 188 B.C.,

when it passed into the possession of the kings
of Pergamon, Sardis was an exhausted city in
need of help to recover. Though the Pergamene
monarchs allowed it the right of self-govern-
ment, we do not know if they did otherwise pay
great attention to it. The local industries seem to
have been curtailed or subverted, as appears was
the case with the textile production. During this
period a great amount of pottery was imported
from Pergamon. The Sardis mint may have been
closed if indeed the cistophoric coinage for
Sardis was struck in Pergamon. Sardis' status had
changed from one of the great capitals of a huge
empire to that of a large subject city.

The general disruption of life in Asia Minor
due to the Mithradatic Wars affected Sardis,
which was involved in the revolts against Mithradates in 86 B.C.[46] Yet despite the economic
problems of the second and first centuries B.C.,
Sardis was wealthy enough by 50 B.C. to erect to
Iollas, a leading citizen, three gilded and four
other bronze portrait statues.[47] One senses the
return of security and confidence brought about
by the Augustan peace in the long series of honorary inscriptions to Menogenes, who represented Sardis in Rome at the investiture with the
toga virilis of Julius Gaius Caesar, the grandson
of Augustus. The hopes of commonwealth of
Asia and of the Sardians had turned toward
Rome.[48]

WEM

Religious Life

In the section on religious life of the Lydian period (Chapter V) we approached the decisive
problem of the Hellenization of the Lydian pantheon and pointed out that this was a long process beginning possibly as far back as the Mycenaean (Late Bronze) age. Unquestionably, the
process of Hellenization reached its greatest intensity during the Hellenistic period, which, for
Sardis, extends from 334 B.C. to A.D. 17. Yet the
changes of cults, myths, and religious attitudes
were far less simple and clear-cut than the rapid
Hellenization of language and political life. Persistence, transformation, and assimilation of divine figures pose a number of problems. Indeed,
in a notable study on the cults of Lydia published

in 1923, J. Keil argued that out of 354 Graeco-Roman inscriptions, only 117 were of "Hellenic" and the remaining 237 were of "non-Greek" cults, and he concluded that Lydian religion was far from completely hellenized even in the Roman Imperial era.[1]

The results of our excavations, including some significant epigraphic and sculptural finds and A. E. M. Johnston's careful work on over 400 autonomous coins of Sardis, have given us new material and new perspectives.[2] They have also started vigorous controversies about the identity and development of several divine figures. In the following survey we shall seek to ascertain which were the main cults of the developing Greek *polis* and what relation they bore to previously known cults of the Lydian and Persian eras. In this effort we shall rely principally on coins and inscriptions as guidelines, with the *caveat* that the epigraphic finds are spotty and the testimony of coins not unambiguous.[3]

The Gods of Sardis

Artemis
Assigned the rank of a "national" goddess for Seleucid Asia Minor, the Artemis of Sardis (Sardiane) remained the major divinity of the city during the Hellenistic and early Imperial Age down to the earthquake of A.D. 17. Her political importance in late Hellenistic times is underlined by the prayer of Moschine (ca. 35–25 B.C.): "Artemis, preserve Sardis continuously in concord."[4] As late as 2 B.C., the most honorific place for a painted portrait was in the sanctuary of Artemis.[5] The priest of the Persian era was replaced by a priestess, perhaps in conjunction with the construction of the gigantic new temple in Seleucid times.[6] The Pergamene kings appointed a *neokoros,* a trustee or financial administrator.[7]

The image of the Persian era had shown Artemis standing, veiled, with a tall crown (*polos;* Fig. 93). We are not certain of the appearance of the Hellenistic image. On autonomous coins of ca. 100 B.C., the profile head of Artemis has no veil. She wears a small *stephane* (frontlet); a bow and quiver are on her back. The style is "Classicistic Rococo" of the second century B.C.[8] A colossal head of Roman times had no *stephane* and is of a different type.[9] It seems probable that like

the colossal statue of Hellenistic Zeus in the east cella (Fig. 176), Hellenistic Artemis was colossal and acrolithic.

There was only one divinity associated with Artemis in her temple and precinct from ca. 220 B.C. on, and this was Zeus known as Polieus by late Hellenistic times.[10] No inscription found in the Artemis Precinct ever refers to Cybele, Meter, or Kore. It is no longer permissible after our archaeological, linguistic, and sculptural findings (Fig. 93)[11] to conflate Artemis with Cybele. Unfortunately, numismatists and others persist in postulating a synthetic Artemis-Kore or proposing that all through the ages Artemis was an ancient idol, which only modern scholars mistook for Kore.[12]

The difficulty arises from the fact that Artemis never represents the city of Sardis on coins of the Roman Imperial period. The city's representative (from ca. A.D. 150 on) is the ancient-looking idol of Kore (Fig. 148). Also, apparently, Artemis had no special festival or games such as the Artemisia at the neighboring Hypaipa.[13] Buckler's suggestion that the Chrysanthia, instituted ca. A.D. 150–175, were called after the epithet of Artemis Chrysanthe[14] has found no favor; they seem to have celebrated Kore.

Yet the archaeological and epigraphic evidence clearly shows that Artemis and Zeus Polieus, joined in the Imperial era by Faustina Maior and Antoninus Pius, remained in possession of precinct and temple until at least the mid-third century and probably all the way through to Christianity.[15]

Of the other Artemises known in Lydian and Persian times, Artemis of Koloe survived into Hellenistic times. Her sanctuary is mentioned by Strabo as a place of great sanctity.[16]

Artemis of Ephesus was invoked at Sardis from the late archaic times on (Fig. 159), and the "Sacrilege" inscription (340–320 B.C.?) found at Ephesus has spectacularly revealed that there was a "branch" at Sardis, to which an annual procession went from Ephesus.[17] Unless we count Callimachus' artful allusion to the Amazonian music for Artemis echoing from Ephesus to Sardis,[18] nothing is heard or seen of the Ephesian Artemis thereafter. Conceivably city rivalry, with the Sardian Artemis making a bid for pan-Anatolian leadership under the Seleucids, caused the decline.

The Persian Artemis-Anahita (Anaitis) may

have been identified with the Artemis of Sardis by the time of Xenophon's visit at the end of the fifth century B.C. Sometime after 322 B.C., in a possibly anti-Macedonian demonstration, the statue of Adrastos was put up in the sanctuary of Artemis Persike, as Pausanias specifically attests.[19] Although the Persians were certainly represented in the Sardis area in Hellenistic times,[20] Artemis Anaitis does not resurface until the mid-Imperial Roman period.[21] We are faced with the question of whether the cult continued across the ages, as it apparently did at Hypaipa and Hieracoma,[22] or lost official favor; or even lapsed and was reinstated during the Lydian-Persian revival of the second century A.D.

A connection was established during the Pergamene period (188–133 B.C.) between the Sardian Artemis and Athena Nicephorus ("Who Brings Victory"), official protectress of Pergamon. The only known Hellenistic issue of Sardis with the head of Artemis features Athena Nicephorus in full figure on the other side; so does the tetradrachm of Achaeus (Fig. 92); and a decree of the Roman Imperial period honors Apollonia, who was priestess of Artemis of Sardis as well as of Athena Nicephorus.[23] After the Panathenaia-Eumenia games were introduced ca. 166 B.C., Sardis probably had a sanctuary of this Athena.[24]

Cybele/Kuvava

Cybele/Kuvava is never called Cybele in Hellenistic inscriptions of Sardis. She is "Mother of the Gods" or *Meter Oreia* ("of the Mountain") or just *Meter* in Roman times; the last form facilitated her eventual assimilation to Demeter[25] Already in the fifth century B.C. she is called *Meter* by Sophocles and Timotheos, and for the Greeks her sanctuary was the Metroon, officially so designated in documents of 213 B.C.[26] The Metroon must have become a major sanctuary of the city, for in that year documents of vital importance for the city were inscribed on the Metroon (Fig. 169), not on the temple of Artemis and Zeus.

There is just a chance that as goddess of the mountains, Cybele was immortalized in her archaic form in the little Hellenistic shrine at the marble quarry; but the relief is poorly preserved.[27] A late Hellenistic marble statuette reflects the standard Hellenistic Cybele type of enthroned Cybele with a lion at her side, but puzzlingly Cybele is not represented on Sardian coins until Salonina (A.D. 253–268), when the same Hellenistic enthroned type appears without inscribed designation.[28] A Roman dedication to the Mother of the Gods, *Metri Theon,* shows her enthroned between two lions.[29]

Tyche

There is a possibility that in early Hellenistic times, Cybele was identified or amalgamated with the "City Goddess" or "Tyche" of Sardis. Her head with a turreted crown and a peculiar Oriental(?) veil appears on Sardian coins from 226–224 B.C. (Fig. 201:2) and after 133 B.C. The late Hellenistic coins show a fine, portrait-like, very Oriental profile (time of Mithradates VI, before 86 B.C.?).[30] A Hellenistic Tyche, Pergamene in style, is copied in a gilded Roman head of a veiled Tyche.[31] On the other hand, the goddess seated under a tree in a new fine Hellenistic relief of ca. 150–50 B.C. (Fig. 200) has no veil and a taller crown; she is probably Cybele, perhaps mourning Attis.[32]

Neither Tyche nor Cybele nor Meter are mentioned in Hellenistic Sardian inscriptions found so far, but *auxei Tyche Sardeon* occurs in a Roman inscription.[33]

After the earthquake of A.D. 17, Sardis is represented on the base at Puteoli by a veiled city goddess with turreted crown holding a cornucopia and leading a boy. Their overall appearance resembles Demeter and Triptolemus.[34]

Already for Sophocles, *Meter* was also Earth. It is possible that *Meter* began her transformation into *De-Meter* already in Hellenistic times. On a coin said to be "pre-Imperial" by B. V. Head, a standard Hellenistic Dionysus head similar to Fig. 204 has a standing, statuesque Demeter with torch on the reverse.[35] After A.D. 17, Livia appears as seated Demeter; by the Flavian period (ca. A.D. 70–100), coinage and literature refer to Sardis as "the city of Demeter."[36]

We have cited a possible early equation of the Lydian *Kuvava* with (Cyprian/Mesopotamian Ishtar?) Aphrodite.[37] In the Hellenistic period, however, it was the Hellenic Aphrodite, wringing out her hair as Apelles had painted her, who is represented by terracottas and marble statuettes at Sardis.[38] In the absence of epigraphic testimony, such private devotions prove neither temple nor official cult. A problem is posed by the appearance on Sardian coins struck under

Hadrian of the sanctuary of Aphrodite of Paphos, characterized by Oriental towers and courtyard with the explicit legend: *Paphie/Sardianon.* B. Trell argues that this "almost certainly represents a sanctuary located within the city of Sardis," but A. E. M. Johnston considers it "improbable that there should have been a replica of the Paphian temple."[39]

Kore

Though inferential, the earliest preserved written testimony for the cult of Kore is the festival Koraia/Aktia, which must go back to the time of Augustus, at least. It is followed by a dedication to the Kore of Sardis made in Rome under Lucius Verus (A.D. 161–169). The institution of the Chrysanthina festival is dated to ca. A.D. 150–175. We have found a statue base of the children of Kore dated A.D. 211–212.[40]

A curious xoanon-like image, early archaic in appearance and flanked by wheat and poppies, is first represented on coins of Sardis under Nero followed by Hadrianic representations.[41] A capital from the gymnasium (Fig. 148, ca. A.D. 150) has been discussed in detail by Balmuth and Hanfmann. Since Fleischer's theory that the xoanon represented Artemis is untenable,[42] only two alternatives remain, of which we consider the first the more likely. The first theory holds that there was at Sardis an archaic cult of a Lydian "Corn Maiden," also known in other Lydian towns. Her *bona fide* archaic image—or a copy—became after A.D. 17, in the course of the Lydian-Persian "renaissance," the official representative of the city. She clearly displaced Artemis in this capacity. This theory is attractive because it also explains how such a Maiden and a Mother Goddess (Meter-Cybele) could be assimilated into the Greek legend of Demeter and Kore. The second alternative would call for the introduction of a new purposely archaic—that is, archaistic—cult in early Imperial times.

Zeus

Zeus presents a number of problems. The one clearly documented Hellenistic cult is that of Zeus Polieus, "Zeus (protector) of the City," who became *synnaos* of Artemis. He was represented in the east cella by a colossal (seated?) image (Fig. 176).[43] In late Hellenistic times the city's year was designated for a while by the priest of Zeus Polieus, and foreign treaties

(Ephesus, 98 B.C.) were placed in his sanctuary.[44] His part of the temple was probably destroyed along with that of Artemis in A.D. 17, but in the second century A.D. he is called *megistos,* and high-placed citizens hold the priesthood.[45]

L. Robert has suggested in a persuasive argument that this "Zeus of the City" either absorbed or was amalgamated with the Persian Zeus, "Zeus, the Law Giver," known from the inscription of 367 B.C. He recognizes the same association of cult personnel in "those who enter the *adyton* and serve Zeus" in 367 B.C., those who crowned Socrates Polemaiou Pardalas, perhaps ca. 100–50 B.C., and those who are the "servants of Zeus" on an altar, perhaps also late Hellenistic or Imperial in date.[46]

The temple of Artemis was originally planned for Artemis alone. Why did Achaeus (or Antiochus III?) around 220–214 B.C. move Zeus, protector of kings, in with the greatest local goddess? Was he previously the "Lydian Zeus" with an open-air fire-altar, similar to the one in Pergamon (Fig. 147)? Or was he "Zeus Olympios," protector of kings *par excellence,* to whom Alexander the Great in 334 B.C. ordered a temple built near the palace of the Lydian kings?[47]

On "Pseudo-Alexanders" of Sardis assigned to 226–223 B.C., the reverse shows a seated Zeus Olympios (Fig. 201:2; standard for all "Pseudo-Alexander" coins) with the head of the city goddess of Sardis in front of him. This combination is suggestive but offers no proof that such a seated Zeus Olympios existed at Sardis. No author or inscription indicates that Alexander's temple was actually built. It may not have been built at all; it may have been started and abandoned; it may have been damaged; or the cult may have lapsed after Achaeus moved Zeus in with Artemis or after Sardis ceased being a royal capital.[48]

An even knottier problem is presented by the "Lydian Zeus." The real Lydian Zeus, called *Levs,* was worshiped by the Lydians from archaic (Fig. 144) through Persian times at an unknown location, and was invoked by his Lydian name as late as 329 B.C. In an inscription of the Persian era which was found in the Artemis Precinct, Artemis shares a temple not with *Levs* but with *Qldans,* whom some consider as Apollo but others as "Lord," "Ruler," "King."[49] The appearance of the Lydian Zeus is not known with certainty, but a standing, cloaked, bearded figure, which one would offhand identify as a statue of severe style (fifth century B.C.), appears on coins of Hellenistic times, first on autonomous coins of 226–223 B.C. (Fig. 201:1), then on a cistophorus dated by B. V. Head 128 B.C., and on a coin with Augustus.[50] The image appears in an open-air precinct behind a magnificent, monumental flaming altar with caryatids on coins of Elagabalus (A.D. 218–222) and Philip I (A.D. 244–249; Fig. 147).[51]

A majestic head of Zeus, rather "Hellenistic Baroque" in style, bears the label "Zeus Lydios" on a Sardian coin of Hadrian (Fig. 202).[52] Métraux recognizes the same type in an Antonine copy of a Zeus found at Sardis and proposes its eventual derivation from a third century B.C. original in the style of Bryaxis. He sees in the Antonine head a copy of the image of the Lydian Zeus at the altar, a proposal that seems to conflict with stylistic evidence.[53]

On one hypothesis, *Levs* was worshiped with Artemis in the Artemis Precinct, yielded to or was joined by the Persian Zeus Baradates in 367 B.C., and was eventually transformed into the Hellenistic Zeus Polieus. The difficulty is that the owner of the joint temple is not called *Levs* but *Pldans* (*Qldans*) in Lydian; and that the preserved colossal Hellenistic head (Fig. 176) does not seem to agree with either a "Severe Style" standing figure or with the Bryaxian "dynamic" Zeus Lydios of the Hadrianic coin (Fig. 202).

It seems preferable to assume that there was an early fifth century B.C. statue, associated with an altar (or a series of altars) for the offering of fiery sacrifices in an open-air precinct (Fig. 147), either in the city or on Mt. Tmolus. A possible location in the city is indicated in the Fountains inscription of ca A.D. 200, where a fountain flows from the mystery hall of Attis *eis to Dios* — "to the (sanctuary) of Zeus." He did undoubtedly stand for Sardis in Hellenistic and Roman times, but the emphatic assertion that this Zeus is *Lydian* may again be caused by the Lydian-Persian "renaissance" in the second century A.D.[54]

Zeus Sabazius

A very different kind of Zeus is Zeus Sabazius. Though this Thraco-Phrygian cult had mysteries in Sardis by 367 B.C., his assimilation to Zeus and promotion to official Pergamene cult was due to the efforts of Queen Stratonice of Pergamon. All we know is that Sardis had a priest of Zeus Sabazius in Hellenistic times.[55]

Apollo

If we were to go by popularity on Sardian Hellenistic coins, Apollo and Herakles would be the leading male contenders. In the two great series from autonomous coins which run partly parallel in the period 133 B.C. to A.D. 17, there are some sixty moneyers and monographs for the "Apollo (head)-club" (of Herakles) and some seventy for the "Herakles (head)-standing Apollo" series.[56] As we have seen, the evidence for Apollo at Sardis was elusive in Lydian and Persian times. His popularity in Hellenistic Sardis may have increased because he was the "patron saint" of the Seleucid dynasty. Cordial relations with Delphi are attested by the embassy of 166 B.C., when Apollo graciously acknowledged the Panhellenic claim of the Sardian Eumenia.[57] The coin type shows an Apollo of long, slender proportions, in an early Hellenistic stance, holding laurel in one hand and the prophetic crow (raven?) in the other.[58] This might reflect a statue of the third century B.C.

A most interesting document of local piety comes from the region of Sardis (Kemerdamlar; see Fig. 2 for location). The fine Hellenistic stele honors a Sardian citizen, who was the financial officer of the association of *mystai* of Apollo Pleurenos, all of them men. One wonders whether Pleurenos may not after all be related to *Pldans* (*Qldans*), probably a Lydian god.[59]

Herakles

Herakles was from olden times probably equated with the native hero Tylos/Tylon, and the legend of Herakles and the Lydian queen Omphale as well as Herakles' other deeds (Nemean lion) became known in archaic Sardis (Fig. 160).[60] In the Pergamene period around 155 B.C., he was mentioned with Hermes as a "god at the palaestra" who had mysteries, presumably for athletes. Herakles was also the mythical progenitor of the Pergamene dynasty, as he had been the ancestor of the Lydian dynasty of "the sons of Herakles." A Hellenistic Herakles herm fits the palaestra but also displays the portrait features of a possibly Pergamene king (Fig. 205).[61] The dynamic heads of Herakles and Omphale on a fine vase of ca. 175 B.C. from the "Tomb of the Lintel" betray Pergamene inspiration (Fig. 185).[62] The prototype of the beardless Herakles of the Herakles Apollo series (133 B.C.) still reflects Pergamene portraiture.[63] This "royal" aspect is possibly envisaged on a late issue where the head of Herakles with lionskin resembles Mithridates VI, shown as Herakles freeing Prometheus on a well-known relief from Pergamon.[64] The more properly Lydian Omphale, walking in the nude except for the lionskin, appears only on Roman coins.[65]

Herakles as a god who gave strength was probably prayed to by the workers at the Hellenistic shrine in the marble quarry.[66] Whether the standing "Scopasian" Herakles on a third century A.D. coin reflects a Hellenistic image is uncertain.[67] Another coin of the same period shows Herakles dragging a bull toward the flaming altar of Zeus Lydios (see Fig. 147). There is a chance that a small late Hellenistic torso might belong to a copy of this group,[68] but whether this reflects a local legend or a real cult association must remain an open question.

Hermes

Hermes, "the Dog Throttler, Candaules in Maeonian" (Hipponax), was a formidable figure in Lydian religion.[69] We have no indication that his Lydian aspects continued into Hellenistic times. Hermes appears with Herakles as a god of the palaestra.[70] His kerykeion (staff) is a good luck symbol (hermaion) on cistophoric coins and in the relief of the little chapel at the marble quarry.[71] As to images, a very archaic herm type might be reflected in a herm of Roman times.[72] The statue of Hermes carrying baby Dionysus more properly belongs to the latter period.

Dionysus

Already around 350 B.C., Nannas Bakivalis hellenized the Lydian wine god Baki(s) (Baki-Dionysus) by translating his father's name, Bakivalis, as "Dionysiokles, famed of Dionysus." Presumably the cult was hellenized quickly. Dionysus must have had a temple and image at Sardis, but apart from the vaguely Praxitelean head on autonomous coins (Fig. 204; after 133 B.C.) we have no evidence for either.[73] Around 150 B.C., the Dionysia were a well-established annual festival; and the phyle (tribe) Dionysias, first mentioned in a Roman inscription, was surely in existence in Hellenistic times.[74] The Pergamene kings worshiped Dionysus Kathegemon, and

their cistophoric coinage, including pieces minted for Sardis, featured the cista mystica alluding to the god's mysteries. The Dionysiac panther breaking a spear appeared on the cistophori of Sardis, and this triumphant motif is continued on the reverse of autonomous coins after 133 B.C. (Fig. 204), with the head of Dionysus occupying the obverse.[75] Perhaps Sardis also possessed a version of a famous statuary group of Hermes carrying the child Dionysus; this is suggested by a late Hellenistic copy of the Kephisodotean original and the appearance of Hermes and Dionysus on a coin issued by a strategos of Sardis.[76]

As in most Hellenistic cities, there are many representations of Dionysiac thiasus and symbols in sculpture and minor arts.[77] Actors' masks (Figs. 190, 191, 203) remind us that Dionysus was the patron of the theater built in early Hellenistic times (Figs. 172, 173). The association of "Artists of Dionysus," Dionysoutechnitai, was probably established soon after.[78] Public and private devotion to the god of wine continued unabated until the end of antiquity.[79]

Other Divinities

For other divinities, information for the Hellenistic Age is meager. If the temple to Hera built by the ubiquitous Socrates Polemaiou Pardalas between 100 and 50 B.C. (Fig. 177) was the first in Sardis, then she was very much of a latecomer. Hecate is attested only by Roman hekataia.[80]

Asclepius, the god of healing, so popular in Pergamon, is attested only by a statuette, two fragmentary sculptures, and a statue dedicated to the Nymphs, all of Roman times.[81]

Mên, the Moon God, Ouranios (IN 67.2), Lord of Axiotta, Askaenos, for whose cult our excavations have brought new evidence,[82] is represented in the late Hellenistic era by a relief which shows him as a horseman riding toward an altar.[83] His first official appearance at Sardis is on coins of Vespasian. His sanctuary, possibly somewhere near the east-west highway, is attested by the fountains list of ca. A.D. 200. Future finds may show when this important cult, which came to cooperate with and rival Artemis, actually arrived at Sardis. The occurrence of theophoric names such as Menophila and Menogenes can be traced back to at least middle Hellenistic times.[84]

Attis

In view of his strong Lydian roots (Atys, Atas, Atthis), the continuous absence of Attis from epigraphic and archaeological material of Hellenistic times is baffling but may be accidental. For the Hellenistic period was the very time when Attis' pathetic fate, including his journey to Sardis, was celebrated by Hellenistic poets.[85] The only reference to the mystery hall of Attis is again in the fountains list of ca. A.D. 200; the sanctuary was close to a sanctuary of Zeus Lydios(?), who plays a role in some versions of the Attis (Angdistis?) myth.[86] Apart from the very uncertain possibility that Attis appeared in a Hellenistic Cybele relief (Fig. 200), no Hellenistic representations or inscriptions referring to Attis have so far come to light.[87] This, then, is the evidence for the Hellenized and Hellenic deities of Sardis.

Roma

A totally new element, symbolic of the protecting power since 133 B.C., Roma's cult was acknowledged as the leading one by making Roma's priest the eponymous official, possibly between 125 and 100 B.C.[88] Again we do not know the Hellenistic shrine and image; Roma herself does not appear on autonomous Sardian coins until Hadrian.[89]

Ruler Cult

The worship of rulers, dead and alive, was a characteristic development of Hellenistic religion. For Sardis, the new inscription (IN 63.121) of 213 B.C. has added the precinct and altar for Laodice, wife of Antiochus III, for whom an annual festival (panegyris), Laodiceia, was also to be held. The festival does not seem to have survived the flight of Antiochus III from Sardis (190 B.C.).[90] Even before, Achaeus may have made an approach to a ruler cult by requesting that the head of the colossus of Zeus be made in his, Achaeus', likeness (ca. 220 B.C.? see Zeus, above, and Figs. 91 and 176), an approach far less explicit than the installation of the statues of Antiochus III and Laodice in the temple of Dionysus at Teos, ca. 203 B.C.[91]

Games for Eumenes II of Pergamon and Athena were instituted in 166 B.C. (Panathenaia-Eumenia) and continued until the mid-first century B.C. Eumenes after death is mentioned as a god in the Timarchus inscription of ca. 155

B.C.[92] A marble torso found in the Artemis Precinct was tentatively identified as "Antiochus III or Eumenes or one of his captains" by C. Vermeule, with reference to the Attalid dedication of trophies in the temple of Artemis; but in this case the honor was to Artemis, not to the "basileus" of the inscription.[93]

The legacy of the Hellenistic rulers was inherited by Augustus, whose temple received the image of his grandson Gaius in 2(? 5?) B.C.[94]

Heroization and Tendance of the Dead

Heroization after death, which had started with mythical heroes and important historical figures, spread into a popular custom in the Hellenistic age. The basic tenet is that the dead become immortal and capable of bestowing benefits on survivors. Timarchus, neokoros of the Artemis Temple, may have intended king Eumenes II when he dedicated a neat stele shrine to an anonymous "Heros Epiphanes" in the Artemis Precinct (ca. 150 B.C.).[95] A newly found early Hellenistic altar with a sacrificial bowl and two snakes belongs, however, to a standard type and served a much less lofty heroized mortal. Indeed, the word heros came to be used as nearly synonymous with "dead."[96] Among the funerary stelai from our excavations, the horseman type (Fig. 184) is often thought to represent the dead as a hero; and one senses a superhuman quality in the mighty, Zeus-like figure of the dead between two small servants on a monumental mid-Hellenistic stele.[97]

The material on tendance of the dead and development of sepulchers is given above in the section "Graves and Cemeteries." It suffices to say that the development at Sardis in general corresponds to the developments in other cities and regions of the Hellenistic world. Interesting for the progress and rising intellectual level of Hellenization, the epitaphs on Matis (Fig. 171), Elpis(?), and Menophila[98] echo sentiments, concepts, and beliefs known from many centers of the Hellenistic world.

Religious Situation at the End of the Hellenistic Era

If after this survey we return to Keil's thesis about the survival of non-Greek (Anatolian, Persian) elements in the religion of Lydia, we first observe that in a general sense Hellenization was complete—all of our material from Sardis is in Greek, and all forms of cult, worship, games, and sacrifices conform to Hellenic practice, including such evocative details as Iollas who "distributed remnants of sacrifices to the citizens generously both in his own house and in the Agora."[99] Keil lumped the Hellenistic and Roman Imperial evidence together; for Sardis, however, we sense that the earthquake of A.D. 17 may have made an important divide. Our observations will, therefore, concern only the Hellenistic period (334 B.C. to A.D. 17).

The major cults of the new *polis* were those of Lydian gods thoroughly hellenized: Artemis and Zeus Polieus, Cybele as Meter, and Dionysus, followed by the more purely Hellenic versions of Apollo and Herakles. Of the two clearly Lydian gods, "Zeus Lydios" was important throughout, while the Lydian "Kore" is not attested. What is striking is the submergence of a number of the traditional Anatolian and Persian cults. Of the three mystery cults named in the inscription of 367 B.C., only Sabazius as Zeus has official recognition, and that because of Pergamene royal interest. Neither the Cappadocian Ma nor the Phrygian-Lydian Angdistis is attested, and Attis is absent so far. Such an important and characteristic manifestation of Hellenistic-Anatolian piety as the migratory, self-castigating, begging priests of Magna Mater, the *metragyrtai,* is also missing.[100]

Of the Persian cults, neither Ahura Mazda as Zeus Baradates nor Artemis Anaitis nor any other Persian divinity is attested at Sardis between 300 B.C. and the second century A.D. Yet the Artemis-Anahita cult apparently continued in nearby Hypaipa.[101] The frequency of the name Mithres in Hellenistic times (Fig. 197) suggests not only survival of Persian families but a possible knowledge of the Persian god Mithras.[102]

In any event, the Anatolian and Persian elements, both in the pantheon and in the special features of religious life ("confessions," "eulogies," tomb curses) were less conspicuous than they became under the Roman Empire. There may be an explanation. Markedly Persian and markedly "nationalistic" Anatolian cults may have been regarded with disfavor during the early Hellenistic period, while the new Greek-Macedonian domination was being established.

Such a policy would be more clearly reflected in a capital, like Sardis, than in smaller places.

A second problem concerns the temporary eclipse of Artemis and Zeus Polieus and the upsurge of Demeter, the Lydian Zeus, and the Lydian Kore under the Roman Empire. One factor was undoubtedly the general movement in Greek cities of Asia to rediscover their ancient and mythical past as a source of pride and superiority toward the Romans. The Lydian-Persian "renaissance" is part of this movement[103] In Sardis, the picture is complicated by a very special cleavage in the life of the city. The earthquake of A.D. 17 shook more than the physical foundations. Survivors of the disaster saw the temple of Artemis and Zeus, and probably that of Meter, overthrown and lying in ruins for half a century, the gods unable to protect them. Not unnaturally, from gods that had failed them, they turned to the *praesens divus,* the "present god," the emperor who was the first to help them in their dire plight. And they transferred their allegiance from Artemis to Demeter, Kore, and the "Lydian Zeus."[104]

Entrance of Judaism

These sketchy notes on the religion of Hellenistic Sardis would not be complete if we failed to note the entrance of Judaism into this Anatolian-Hellenistic ambient. So far, this historic event is known only from documents cited by Josephus. His notices have been recently much discussed because of our sensational discovery of the gigantic synagogue of the Roman period at Sardis. It is still the most plausible hypothesis that Antiochus III brought a number of Jewish veterans' families from Mesopotamia to Sardis, where they participated in the resettlement of the city by Viceroy Zeuxis after the siege and capture of the city (215–213 B.C.). For, understandably, Antiochus regarded the "Lydian" Sardians as untrustworthy rebels.[105] The other documents of Roman authorities cited by Josephus refer to late Republican and Augustan time. They show the Jewish community defending successfully its special status, including the right to a place of worship, to payments of temple tax to Jerusalem, and even to cooperation of market officials (*agoranomoi*) in securing kosher food.[106] That they came from Mestopotamia rather than Palestine is in itself significant, as A. T. Kraabel has pointed out;[107] but nothing more is known so far about their place of worship or their beliefs. With them, monotheism entered Sardis; and their entrance paved the way for the early arrival of Christianity.

GMAH

Conclusions and Cultural Perspective

Hellenization is the overriding theme of the Hellenistic period.[1] If we look at other archaeological sites now being explored in western and central Asia Minor, we find that as a former capital of a non-Greek kingdom which faced radical cultural transformation, Sardis has a very special "laboratory case" value. Ephesus and Pergamon, both now nearing the century mark of archaeological work, were Greek before the Hellenistic period. Gordion, once one of the capitals of non-Greek Phrygia, was deserted by 189 B.C.[2] and did not complete the cycle of Hellenization.

The greatest contribution of Sardis to our knowledge of the process of Hellenization is the inscriptions of 213 B.C. (Fig. 169).[3] Like a flash of lightning they illumine not only the political and urbanistic but also the cultural situation. They suggest that we must envisage two major stages in the Hellenization of Lydo-Persian Sardis: first the pioneering transformation in the Macedonian-Seleucid era (334–213 B.C.) and then the spread of Hellenism into all aspects of life under the Pergamenes and the Romans (190 B.C. to the earthquake of A.D. 17).

Let us note some preliminary yet significant indications resulting from the Sardis work. For the all-important process of transition from Lydian to Greek, humble Lydian graffiti attest continued use of Lydian into the second century B.C. This bears on the celebrated question of the survival of native Anatolian languages; Lycaonian and Phrygian are known to have been spoken in the time of the Roman empire.[4]

For the fascinating phase of early Hellenistic transformation, our excavations hint at a Janus-like, two-faced aspect of the city, with domestic life persisting in Lydian ways and a program of monumental public buildings (fountains, theater, temples) being added or inserted into the agglomerate Lydian city.

Historical perspective and material culture benefit by the identification of the layer of the destruction (and demolition?) of 213 B.C. This important datum provides information not only for urbanistic questions but also for the chronology of artifacts, notably ceramics. While some burials give a limited angle on the "standard of living" (for the dead!), what is missing in our excavations are private and public complexes with their complete contents.

Economic, social, and population studies have to be worked out on the basis of epigraphic (especially prosopographic), anthropological, and artifactual material. Yet we can already discern something of the productivity, of downward and upward trends of economy, and the shifts of emphasis in production. It is possible that Sardis declined from an important position in the Seleucid economic system when it was the site of a royal Treasury and Mint. Gold had ceased being a source of income, but despite upheavals of Mithradatan and Civil wars, a city that could afford multiple gilded bronze statues for a benefactor around 50 B.C. cannot have been wholly destitute.[5] A shift from viticulture to wheat may be indicated by the rising importance of Demeter vis-à-vis Dionysus.

In plastic and visual arts, Theomnestus, a bronze sculptor who made a statue of a boy victor in Olympia, may belong to the very beginning of the Hellenistic age.[6] Bryaxis had made the statue of Apollo of Daphne for Seleucus I, probably after 300 B.C., and the stylistic tradition of Bryaxis has been discerned in the Hellenistic(?) prototype of Zeus Lydios and may be present—along with a strong Attic element—in the extant colossal head of Zeus (Fig. 176).[7] Since the great architect and renovator of the Ionic order, Hermogenes, was in contact with Antiochus III around 200 B.C., one may attribute the addition of the "pseudodipteral" porch of the Artemis Temple to him or his associates, either under Achaeus or Antiochus III or under Eumenes.[8] While local workshops of bronze casters are almost certain and marble sculptors very likely, we have no further evidence on the names or organization of Sardian sculptors in the Seleucid or Pergamene age.

Literary and Intellectual Culture

Since a gymnasium for boys is mentioned around 150 B.C.,[9] the standard Greek system of education was certainly introduced.[10] This probably included the usual schools of rhetoric. Strabo mentions two rhetors by name of Diodorus, the first Zonas, famous as pleader in the time of Mithradates (ca. 90–80 B.C.), the second a friend of Strabo, hence in the time of Augustus, a historian and poet who wrote "in ancient style."[11] Undoubtedly, such honored pleaders, attorneys, and diplomats as Iollas (ca. 50 B.C.) and Menogenes (5–2 B.C.) were trained orators, though they need not have been trained at Sardis. The only interesting preserved example of Sardian literary efforts in the Hellenistic Age is by the anonymous poet who wrote the epitaph on Menophila in "lyric Doric." Its interest derives from the fact that it appeals to an audience receptive to a possibly Neo-Pythagorean, not unduly sophisticated allegory and symbolism. Illustrated erotic books, such as Philaenis' and Elephantis' "Types of Intercourse," are reflected, though probably through more costly artistic prototypes (silver ware), in the erotic scenes of ceramic appliqué bowls (Fig. 192).[12] Yet another kind of Hellenistic literature, romantic tales detailing lovers' adventures and misadventures, may be reflected in the remarkable mold found under the Roman gymnasium (Fig. 193). Here a lovers' couple is assaulted by a sphinx-like monster in the presence of a dancing Pan.[13]

In speaking of religion, we have referred to the revival of interest in the mythical past generally and "autochthonous" Lydian past in particular. It is not by chance that "autochthonous," "sprung from own soil," became a title of honor for Greek cities under the Roman empire. Herodotean tales of Lydia were immensely popular, and the "Pan-Lydianism" of Xanthus was resurrected in the time of Augustus by Nicolaus of Damascus (ca. 64 B.C. to after 20 B.C.); to his "Universal History" we owe many dramatic and fanciful glimpses of mythical and early historical Sardis.[14]

Religious Life

Potentially, our greatest increase of knowledge may concern religion. We have learned much about gods and cults, and to some extent about the change of concepts about the dead. Clearly, the religion of Sardis had been Hellenized in form. What we lack is the concrete expression of beliefs such as an excavation of an urban and a rustic sanctuary would provide, with all its votives large and small. As it is, only the Artemis Precinct with its extra-urban and exceptional position is known for the Hellenistic period. There is some evidence for the increasing honor and worship of mortals such as benefactors and kings, preparing the buildup of the Imperial cult. It is unlikely that Sardis had remained ignorant of Mark Anthony's attempt in Ephesus to be worshiped as a New Dionysus (41 B.C.).

The changes of religious experience in Hellenistic Sardis elude us. We can guess at an acceptance of Hellenic Olympians followed by an undertow toward the Anatolian "old-time religion." Yet such truly Anatolian religious manifestation as the frantic self-mutilation and madness of Attis goaded by Cybele, emulated by his priests, the Galli, which Catullus (Poem 63) so powerfully renders, probably from first-hand observation during his stay in Asia Minor (58–57 B.C.), has no counterpart in our material. It is not until literacy spread through villages and hamlets under the Roman empire that we find clear expressions of the survival and impact of traditional Anatolian attitudes toward gods and nature.

Imaginary Sardis

More important than the sporadic and obviously provincial contribution of men of letters in Hellenistic Sardis was the emergence of an imaginary, mythical, sometimes romantic, often moralistic-paradigmatic Sardis in Hellenistic literature and poetry. It was the learned Hellenistic poets who made Sardis and its Lydian vicinity, Pactolus, Tmolus, and Hypaipa, the setting for scenes of mythical happenings of olden times, extending from hoary antiquity to Croesus. Callimachus lets the pipes of the Amazons dancing in honor of the Ephesian goddess echo across the mountains all the way to Sardis; and the laurel competes with the olive of Tmolus with Cybele and Pactolus as witnesses.[15] The Hellenistic sources of Ovid have King Midas capture Silenus in the vineyards of Tmolus, return him to Dionysus in Lydia, and wash off his "golden touch" in the Pactolus, "the stream which flows past mighty Sardian town." The mountain god Tmolus, "Tmolus looking far out to sea, with steep slopes extending one down to Sardis the other to little Hypaipa," judges the contest between Apollo and Pan;

Midas mixes in and gets his donkey's ears from Apollo.[16] Arachne contends with Athena in "little Hypaipa," and the nymphs of the vineyards on the slopes of the Tmolus and the nymph of Pactolus come to visit.[17] Herakles' service to voluptuous Omphale is painted in great detail.[18] Dioscorides shows Attis fleeing to Sardis.[19] For Alexander of Aetolia, Alcman's attachment to Sparta wins over the potential career of the poet as a gold-clad Lydian priest.[20] It is at this time, too, that a vision of regal Sardis, inhabited by Gyges and the wife of Candaules and by Croesus, the world's richest king, becomes ubiquitous. This mythical and legendary Sardis, created basically in the Hellenistic Age, then emerges as part of the classical image of the western world and is revived in medieval, Renaissance, and baroque art.[21]

GMAH

VIII

The Roman and Late Antique Period

GEORGE M. A. HANFMANN

FIKRET K. YEGÜL

JOHN S. CRAWFORD

Introduction

The major results of the work of the Harvard-Cornell Expedition relate to two periods—the Lydian and the Roman Imperial–Late Antique–Early Byzantine, which at Sardis extended for six centuries from A.D. 17 to A.D. 616. The terms "Late Antique" and "Early Byzantine" are partly overlapping. Politically, Sardis was since A.D. 395 under the Eastern Roman *alias* Byzantine empire, and for some numismatists Byzantine coinage (as distinct from "Late Roman") begins in A.D. 491; but for simplicity's sake we will use only "Roman" and "Late Antique" for description of largely cultural phenomena.[1]

The ruins of Roman and Late Antique Sardis cover the site with a mighty blanket of huge walls and heavy debris, permitting only limited exposures of earlier cities. The question at the beginning of our work was not whether to dig the Roman city but rather how to dig anything else.[2] Fortuitously, it was precisely the great sweep of Roman urban planning and the complex problems of design and construction in monumental Roman public buildings that kindled the enthusiasm of our colleagues from Cornell's College of Architecture, led by the late A. H. Detweiler (1906–1970) and the late Stephen W. Jacobs (1919–1978).[3] To excavate the entire Roman–Late Antique city, with an estimated area of 3 square miles, would require

enormous means;[4] even after a century's work, such a goal has not been reached at either Pergamon (begun in 1878) or Ephesus (begun in 1868; resumed 1895). As a compromise two major adjacent areas were selected in the western part of the city, which eventually developed into the bath-gymnasium/Synagogue/Main Avenue complex and the House of Bronzes sector[5] (Figs. 8:1, 2, 56, 58, 59, 52-b; 167; Plan IV). Other coherent complexes of the period were excavated and investigated on the east bank of the Pactolus (PN; also PC; Figs. 8:10, 11, 57; 64), in the Artemis Precinct (Fig. 8:16, 17, 18), on the Acropolis (Fig. 8:20, 21), and, far out to the northeast, at the bath CG (Fig. 8:28). Smaller soundings were made at various points throughout the site (Figs. 8:7, 31, 35, 33, 42; 70).

The digging was supplemented by architectural recording work on unexcavated buildings,[6] among which were the theater and the stadium (Fig. 8:25–26), the "Hillside Chambers" (Fig. 8:29), the huge platform "A" (Fig. 8:24), the Roman basilica "C," the colossal church "D," and the Byzantine fort (Fig. 8:30, 29, 24). This project was part of an effort to obtain data on the development of the ancient urban plan. Another aspect of this effort was the complete recording of the extant remains of the Roman city wall.

Out of the excavation and study of the great bath-gymnasium complex came the proposal, largely inspired by S. W. Jacobs, to resurrect in reality the hall of the Imperial Cult (Marble Court) with its sumptuous marble facades (Figs. 206–240) as an example of monumental Roman architectural exterior,[7] matched, after the discovery of the unique Synagogue, by partial restoration and conservation of its main hall and forecourt (Figs. 253–258) with samples of luxurious marble-revetted and mosaicked interior.[8]

Inextricably interwoven with the architectural studies was the work on decorative architectural elements and marble revetments, on mosaics and wall paintings, and on sculpture.[9] From the architectural context came the most important inscriptions, such as the three dedicatory inscriptions of the bath-gymnasium and the great array of nearly one hundred donors' inscriptions from the Synagogue.[10]

Meanwhile, the vast outpouring—especially from the Byzantine Shops—of coins, metal objects, glass, pottery, lamps, and miscellaneous finds was being worked up, in a process as yet incomplete.[11]

Significance of the Results

The novelty and importance of the results go far beyond individual buildings, complexes, or indeed the city of Sardis. The very fact that Imperial Roman–Late Antique–Early Byzantine Sardis represents an unbroken cultural continuum of six centuries across such critical divides of world history as the coming of Christianity and the partition of the Roman Empire into East and West is a finding of epochal import. It was made possible by the archaeological identification of the earthquake of A.D. 17 and, above all, of the Sassanian destruction of A.D. 616.[12] The excavation of the bath-gymnasium/Synagogue/Byzantine Shops/House of Bronzes complex brings into focus an almost incredible interplay of civic, athletic, cultural, commercial, artistic, political, and religious forces involving the interaction of Greeks, Romans, Jews, and Christians in a city famed in the Christian world as one of the Seven Churches of Asia.[13] The size, status, prosperity, and assurance of the Greek-speaking, Hebrew-professing Jewish community, who could build a synagogue for one thousand people (Fig. 207), is a revelation for the history of Judaism.[14] The planning and buildup of an entire Christianized region around the basil-

ica at the Pactolus (Figs. 43, 288) shows a phase of Constantinian activities not preserved elsewhere in Asia Minor.[15] Stopped in their life by the disaster of A.D. 616, the shopping center of Byzantine Shops (Figs. 239–243), the opulent Christian residence known as the House of Bronzes (Fig. 210), and the dwelling and bath on the Pactolus with its rich mosaics bespeak a standard of prosperity in Early Byzantine times which is only now beginning to be acknowledged by historians.[16] The reverse of the medal, too, is apparent in the repairs and reuse of ancient materials in the gymnasium, the Synagogue, and elsewhere.[17] Finally, the two contrasting efforts at defense prove most revealing: the Roman city wall (A.D. 350–400? Fig. 208) constructed quickly but in homogeneous technique with original material and careful deliberation against a probable danger that did not materialize (Germanic invasions, of ca. A.D. 400?), and the massive fortress on the Acropolis slammed together of destroyed buildings in desperate terror at an emergency—probably after the horrifying destruction of the lower town by the Persians and before the onslaughts of the Arabs.[18]

Method of Presentation

Nothing short of a whole book could do justice to the quantity and diversity of Roman and Late Antique material of the Sardis excavations, and even that book would have to await completion of researches and publication of studies now incomplete. The continuum of Sardian development divides into two phases, the Roman Imperial and the Late Antique, though one may argue about where the line should be drawn (A.D. 284, 312, 395?).[19] The gradual rebuilding of the city after the earthquake of A.D. 17 was followed by the height of its prosperity through the Severan dynasty (A.D. 235), the time of crisis (235–284), and the redintegration under Diocletian (284) and Constantine (312). This constitutes the properly Roman Imperial era. An upswing in the fourth century inaugurated culturally and artistically the Late Antique period, which in terms of material finds is the period most strongly represented in the archaeological history of Sardis.

Beginning with the accession of Diocletian (A.D. 284), C. Foss has written an admirable synthesis of the Late Antique period.[20] A.D. 284 is also the year in which J. G. Pedley terminates his collection of *Ancient Literary Sources on Sardis* (*Sardis* M2). We will allude only briefly to Foss's results for the period 284–616, and refer the readers to his detailed study.

No survey comparable to that of Foss exists for the period A.D. 17–284. A general sketch is given in the *Survey of Sardis* (*Sardis* R1).[21] Although informal, the *Letters from Sardis* present an illustrated running account of particular value for the restoration of the Marble Court and the Synagogue. Above all, the final publication of a number of complexes has appeared. The Artemis Temple and Precinct, the bath CG, and the Roman city wall can all be studied with definitive evidence in hand (*Sardis* R1). Of the relevant artifactual material, *Byzantine Coins* (*Sardis* M1), *Roman Sculpture* (*Sardis* R2), *Ancient and Byzantine Glass* (*Sardis* M6), and *Greek, Roman and Islamic Coins* (*Sardis* M7) have appeared. Studies as yet unpublished which contain Roman–Late Antique material are summarized in *Sardis* R3 through R9, and *Sardis* M9 through M15.

In view of the amount of published material and the general scope of the subject, a different method of presentation has been adopted here. In contrast to Chapters III–VII, no attempt will be made in Chapters VIII–X to list the relevant excavations or to consider systematically the major cultural aspects of the Roman–Late Antique–Early Byzantine period. Rather, a survey of historical and urbanistic development to A.D. 284 is followed by studies dealing with the most significant discoveries—the bath-gymnasium complex, the Byzantine Shops, the Synagogue, and the Christian churches. Together, they project the quintessential image of Roman and Late Antique Sardis.

The Earthquake of A.D. 17 and Rebuilding Priorities

"In the same year, twelve important cities of Asia collapsed in an earthquake that struck at night . . . It is reported that huge mountains settled, plains were uplifted, fires flashed out among the ruins . . . As the disaster fell heaviest on the Sardians, it brought them the greatest measure of charity. Caesar (Tiberius) promised ten million sesterces and remitted for five years their (tax) payments to the Public and the (private) Imperial Treasuries. It was voted to send a Senatorial Commissioner to inspect the present situation and initiate recovery measures." "An ex-praetor, Marcus Ateius, ranking just below the proconsular governor of the province, was elected."[22] Thus wrote the Roman historian Tacitus in a famous passage of his *Annals*.

We have spoken repeatedly of this earthquake;[23] with the aid of historical and epigraphic notices and archaeological data, it is possible to see how Ateius went about his job.

1. The first priority was unquestionably emergency housing. We have found nothing of it, but we suspect that shanty towns, such as were often seen during the mushroom growth of Turkish cities in the 1950s, sprang up around Sardis and may have persisted for three generations.

2. The second priority was demolition of destroyed and unsafe buildings. This went hand in hand with creating temporary dumps and beginning to reshape the site by terracing. The great number of recut and reused stone blocks in the piers of the gymnasium (masons' marks) points to stockpiling of masonry salvaged from Hellenistic buildings after the earthquake of A.D. 17. If one were to take an imaginary staggered section of the site (see the plan, Fig. 8) running south-north from the top of UT (Upper Terrace), through MT (Middle Terrace), the Lydian Market/HoB area, the Main Avenue, the Byzantine Shops, the Synagogue, and the East Palaestra, it would disclose a variety of these measures: destroyed late Hellenistic houses dumped inward on the UT;[24] a gradual buildup of a real "city dump" at the northeast outer edge of Upper Terrace,[25] resulting in an open area traversed only by water pipes in most of HoB (for public garden?); destruction fill heaped up to 3 m. above the Hellenistic level within the foundations of the Main Avenue and the Synagogue;[26] and finally a very incompletely known system of large vaulted chambers which were used to support parts of the vast gymnasium-palaestra platform. Other examples of large-scale terracing have been observed but not excavated.[27]

3. Under the new master plan, construction of traffic facilities (roads) and utilities had to go hand in hand. The roads were needed to transport material from demolition and for construction; the vast system of water pipes and drains had to be laid down alongside and under the streets as they were being constructed. From in-

scriptions[28] found by both the present and the Butler expeditions and from excavations we now know that the Main Avenue and the aqueduct were begun under Tiberius (between A.D. 17 and 37) and completed, probably almost simultaneously, under Claudius (ca. A.D. 41–54).[29] Although renewed several times, the basic design for water distribution is Julio-Claudian. Of the very intricate system of water distribution, we have only batches of earlier and later pipes and possibly traces of a water reservoir at PN.[30]

4. A final priority consideration was the development of an earthquake-proof, or at least earthquake-resistant, system. Modern engineers do not consider as very effective the technique favored by Roman architects after A.D. 17: moderately heavy (for small construction) to massive mortared rubble walls (Fig. 187) with enormously deep foundations, some reaching 30 feet; thus Building D in the Artemis Precinct, the stadium, substructures of the gymnasium, and the "Hillside Chambers" show that technique which remained standard for terraces, utilitarian buildings, and substructures until at least the sixth century A.D.[31]

Problems of repair in two buildings, both possibly damaged in A.D. 17, evoked interesting experimentation. In the Theater, a strange combination of alternating irregular masonry piers and mortared concrete was tried for renovating a typical Hellenistic masonry structure (Fig. 172).[32] The initial date of Bath CG is not known; but it is at least possible that the earthquake of A.D. 17, while causing minor damage, induced the builder to shift in midstream from the traditional Hellenistic masonry construction to rubble-concrete. The dividing line for the two goes irregularly through the circular unit HM.[33] This would also give us a date for beginning earlier than that considered in the final publication.

As elsewhere in Asia Minor, the mechanics of building during the first century A.D. were partly experimental; thus we find in the earlier west part of the gymnasium the peculiar *petit appareil* technique, a translation of brick into stone.[34] It was the architects active in Sardis and Ephesus, however, who developed in the second century A.D. a new, original, and—since many walls still stand—apparently effective method of construction which operated using a system of limestone or marble masonry piers and heavy walls of alternating mortared rubble and brick with many construction details in brick and concrete.[35]

The Master Plan

Ateius' mission was not just a first-aid job. He did apparently leave a master plan for the reconstruction of Sardis as a "modern" city. He and the city of Sardis had to assemble a staff including at least one urban planner and several experts on special assignments—road building, water supply, baths, public construction—and also surveyors and contractors. We know one of them: Tiberius Claudius Apollophanes, son of Demetrios of the Quirina Tribe, hence a Greek and a Roman citizen.[36] He was supervisor of the aqueduct construction and completed it under Claudius. Even if he was principally an administrator, he must have had an understanding of water technology, a great speciality of the Roman army engineers.[37] He may well have been trained in Rome.

Immediate contact with the Imperial Works Office in Rome must also be assumed for the city planner. His design comes right out of the Augustan pioneering phase of Imperial architecture. We must emphasize that with a Tiberian date of ca. A.D. 20,[38] the Sardis colonnaded Main Avenue becomes one of the earliest datable examples of this urbanistic device, following closely on Herod the Great's (20 B.C.?) main avenue in Antioch.[39] Even more astonishing is the plan for the bath-gymnasium (Fig. 206), if it was part of the original master plan of A.D. 20. In the creation of this type, such an early design date would give Sardis priority over the Milesian Baths of Capito dated to the reign of Claudius (A.D. 47–52) and cited by Yegul as a probable forerunner. The city plan (Plan IV) suggests close contact with the Augustan colonial building office.[40]

What else can we discern of this plan? The Hellenistic "bent-axis" plan (Plan III; Fig. 167) was retained and, indeed, emphasized.[41] At the north edge, a row of very large, buried public buildings, E100–900/N0–350, of which a circular one is clearly visible, align on this bent (eastern) part of the axis. The same alignment applies to one of the known secondary streets (Fig. 8:31). This public region may have been partly a new quarter. Definitely a new quarter was the bath-gymnasium complex (Figs. 167, 206, 207,

211; W60–E120/0–N120) which displaced only some tombs. The planners may have changed slightly the alignment of the Hellenistic main avenue. At any rate, the new colonnaded Main Avenue extended from the Pactolus almost a mile eastward (1400 m.). In the HoB sector, the area across from the gymnasium, apart from the tombs along the avenue, was left open until the fifth century. It may have been intended as a public or private garden. It is our guess that the "old" Hellenistic city quarter on the north slopes of the Acropolis (ca. E100 to 1000/0–S400; Fig. 167; Plan III) was repaired and reterraced in the manner known from the old Hellenistic theater (Figs. 172, 173). The new stadium was built in the new technique.[42] The Agora must have been on a height, for there was a *Kathodos Agoras,*[43] a "Downroad from the Agora"; but the Agora is still unidentified.

The plan moved the city westward and northward into areas abandonded after 213 B.C. (Plans III–IV). It left out the Pactolus Valley. If bath CG (Fig. 8:28) was a building of A.D. 17, its peripheral position is enigmatic. Perhaps a particularly good supply of water rather than any settlement was the reason.

We know only fragments of the progress that was made in rebuilding, but parallels from other cities show that difficulties in carrying through ambitious designs were common in cities of Asia Minor.[44] In Sardis it took ca. 30 to 40 years (A.D. 17–54) to do the main street(s?) and aqueduct. The small (?) temple of Hera (see Fig. 177) was restored rather quickly with private means (ca. A.D. 20–30?).[45] At the Artemis Precinct, while makeshift repairs may have made the cellas usable for cult purposes soon after the earthquake, "the first column to rise again" in the peristyle colonnade did not do so until the time of Trajan.[46] We surmise that the peristyle was as finished as it ever got to be for the bestowal of the second neocorate under Antoninus Pius (ca. A.D. 140?). The utilitarian Building D in the precinct was probably put up within the first century A.D., as was the stadium. For the gymnasium-bath, the beginning in the west may be placed in the second half of the first or the first half of the second century A.D.; the central part was complete by A.D. 116, the Marble Court by A.D. 211–212, the palaestra possibly as late as the mid-third century (Figs. 206, 207, 211).[47] We believe that the "emergency phase" of city

renewal was finished by the time of the accession of Nero (A.D. 54). The complete realization with addition of new projects was essentially the work of the second century and the Severan dynasty. It is on coins of Elagabalus (A.D. 218) that there are proudly shown four temples, three of them for Imperial cult.[48] An official project, apparently a basilica in the east quarter, was still being built and marble-revetted under Caracalla (A.D. 212–217), but with the possible exception of the city wall, no great public or religious structures were begun between A.D. 235 and 310.

The Riddle of the City Wall

It does not seem that the "Masterplan" of A.D. 17, conceived during *Pax Romana,* had provided for a new city wall. The wall we have investigated and published in *Sardis* R1 presents various puzzles (Figs. 8:9 a–i; 167, 208): first, it goes in the northeast far out into the plain, where we have no indication of any buildings or habitation. It uses the gymnasium as part of the defenses, follows a stretch of the east bank of the Pactolus, and then climbs uphill to join the citadel defenses.[49] It leaves out all of the Pactolus Valley, including the Christian quarter around PN built ca. 340–400[50] and many rich villas of the fourth to sixth centuries along the Pactolus. Its defensive trace and adaptation to terrain cannot be faulted. The buildings it leaves outside were never razed for defensive purposes, nor were they destroyed by enemy action until A.D. 616.

C. Foss[51] argues that the wall must have been built against the attacks of the Germans, that is, ca. A.D. 260, when they plundered the Artemision of Ephesus. He believes that if the Christian buildings in the Pactolus Valley had already been built, the wall should have taken them in. Coins and other material, however, found in the wall and against its foundation, indicate a date of A.D. 350–400. At that time, too, the Germans were threatening,[52] and indeed once (A.D. 399) were frustrated only by a flood. As Müller-Wiener has observed,[53] the wall was not built in an emergency, as was the wall on the Acropolis. The mortared-rubble technique is continuous and solid and the spoils remarkably few. In short, the wall was built speedily in one continuous operation—but against a danger that never materialized. We believe that its planners consciously intended to sacrifice outlying buildings and even churches and cemeteries to ensure greater defensibility. Conceivably, more tests might decide the dating question.

Historical Background

We last saw the Sardians erecting a statue to Gaius Caesar and sending embassies to Augustus (5 B.C.).[54] A fine head of Augustus in Copenhagen may date to this period.[55] If an impressive inscription GERMANIK[56] refers to the original Germanicus, whose head also appears on coins of Sardis, it may strengthen the case for a visit of that ill-starred prince in A.D. 17, but before the earthquake. Tiberius was Sardis' first savior, and he was celebrated not only by a colossus in Rome but also probably by statues erected by each phyle. A new find (1979) is a statue base calling him "Founder of the City."[57] The grateful city called itself Caesareia Sardianeon from at least A.D. 17 through the reign of Claudius, though she lost to Smyrna in competing for a provincial temple to Tiberius. Claudius, who completed the aqueduct, was celebrated by a family group which included the younger Drusus and Antonia (Minor).[58]

The local coins show new interests and devices from Nero's reign on—the Zeus Lydios (Fig. 202), the Kore of Sardis—but as A. E. M. Johnston observes,[59] the numismatic circulation in the early Empire is meager. Surely the cause is the semiruinous condition and the slow rebuilding of the city. Archaeologically, apart from rebuilding, we have only cemeteries of rather modest tile and occasionally brick graves along the highway at HoB (Fig. 186), above the Artemis temple at Kagirlik Tepe and out at the Royal Cemetery.[60] A few chamber tombs may date to the first century (A.D. 60; Fig. 188).[61] As for industry, only lamps, simple pottery, just possibly sigillata B (Fig. 196), and perhaps terracottas (Fig. 203) are known. Apparently industries other than building had suffered. Possibly, it was only agriculture—note the shift to Kore and the "city of Demeter"—which kept the economy going.

We had guessed that the emergency phase of reconstruction was over by ca. A.D. 55; but the subsequent Flavian period in Sardis seems to show a recession. Perhaps the work of reconstruction slowed down, though we have an inscribed block quarried in an Imperial quarry under Titus (IN 61.3, Caes Titi).

Three very different authors and an inscription combine to show in the Flavian period a Sardis rent by class struggle and anti-Roman rebellion, plagued by famine and censured for crude manners, (sexual?) vices, and general immorality. Writing after Domitian's death (A.D. 96) to Menemachus, a Sardian youth of good family who wanted to enter politics, Plutarch tells of a private feud which broke out between Pardalas, a member of a famous Sardian family, and one Tyrrhenus. Pardalas and his friends were executed by sword—from the context undoubtedly by the Romans. Buckler had thought of a Pardalas of Late Republican times, but Plutarch speaks with great immediacy ("Remember that the boots of Roman soldiers are over your head") as if of a more recent past. This Pardalas is apparently not mentioned in our historic or epigraphic material.[62] Menemachus, too, did not last; several years later (before A.D. 117) he was banned from Sardis, and Plutarch wrote him a consolatory tract.[63] It was most probably the same violent clashes that made the miracle worker and popular preacher Apollonius of Tyana—again under Domitian—upbraid the Sardians for their wild strife.[64]

Plutarch says quite forthrightly that it was the money-madness or acquisitiveness (pleonexia) of the upper class which usually caused the trouble. The rich were accused of driving up grain prices and causing shortages. Grain riots are known to have broken out at Prusa when the "sophist" Dio built colonnades instead of buying grain.[65] For Sardis we have an indirect indication: Lucius Iulius Libonianus, strategos of the city under Trajan, was honored because "when shortage came he nobly contributed towards alleviation out of private means one modius for each citizen."[66] Considering the size of citizen population of Sardis around A.D. 100, this was a big dole.

The notices about the shortages and famine in Asia Minor have been linked with the statement of the writer of the Revelation, 6.3–4: "And I heard a voice in the midst of the four beasts say: 'a choinix of wheat for a denarius and three choinikes of barley for a denarius'"—these high prices reflecting the famine represented by the third horseman on the black horse.[67] Now, it is precisely the writer of the *Revelation,* 3.1–6, who had visited the new Christian "church" at Sardis during this era. The dating to Domitian's rule, 93–96, is accepted by A. T. Kraabel.[68] It is the author of the *Revelation* who said, "thou art dead" and implied that most members had "defiled their garments." He may have been talking only of spiritual, theological matters, but Apollonius of Tyana addressed his letters to non-Christian Sardians, men and women whom he accused of shamelessness and vice. He, like the writer of *Revelation,* wrote for very specific addressees, and the exact facts remain enigmatic.

The mood changes with the second century. We have only a numismatic allusion to Trajan, but it was under him that the first Sardian, indeed, the first native of province Asia became a proconsul—Celsus Polemaeanus, who was (already ca. 82) honored as "benefactor and savior" by Sardis.[69] As a result of "social upward mobility," he joined the Roman aristocracy, as one of that great series of benefactors who completed the "Masterplan" program; some were known before, and our finds have added information on Claudius Antonius Lepidus, first administrator of the newly finished gymnasium under Lucius Verus,[70] and Claudia Antonia Sabina and Flavia Politte, who in A.D. 211–212 helped pay for the decoration of the Marble Court.[71]

As to emperors, Hadrian visited Sardis in 123–124 and 128 as a "New Dionysos" known from the resolutions of the Stage Guild of "Artists around Dionysos."[72] Yet another new inscription (IN 59.4, unpublished) seems to mention a *Hadrianeion.* This might be the first temple[73] of the Imperial Cult officially awarded to the city with the much coveted honor of being "Temple Warden" (*neokoros*).[74] Large-scale building activity continued in the gymnasium under Antoninus Pius, who certainly knew Sardis well from his prior service as governor of Asia (A.D. 133–136). The Artemis Temple was finished and made into a second temple of Imperial cult (ca. A.D. 140?); fragments of colossal images of Antoninus and Faustina Maior, who had joined Zeus and Artemis, have been found in the temple. As B. Burrell saw, a new inscription (IN 70.4) honoring Antoninus as Olympios may

identify him as the emperor to whom an altar with eagle of Zeus was dedicated; and indeed it suggests that Antoninus as Zeus Olympios joined Zeus Polieus (Fig. 176), as Trajan had joined Zeus Philios in Pergamon.[75]

The central part of the gymnasium was dedicated under Lucius Verus (A.D. 161–169), whose statue was erected in the apse of the south hall BSH (Figs. 212, 213).[76] Although in A.D. 196 Sardis stood with the pretender Clodius Albinus,[77] the city must have come into the good graces of Septimius Severus and his family; it was permitted to claim as its "kinsmen," as "members of the family" (Fig. 227), as it were, the emperors Caracalla and Geta, and the empress Julia Domna, to whom the "Marble Court" hall was dedicated in A.D. 211.[78] Caracalla is shown on a coin receiving the statue of the Kore of Sardis from the city goddess. His statue base has been found in the bath-gymnasium; perhaps the designation of the "Baths of the Emperor" was then bestowed upon the building.[79] Caracalla may have visited Sardis on his trips from Pergamon and Smyrna to Thyateira and possibly Philadelphia in A.D. 214–215.[80] Elagabalus had not visited Sardis, according to L. Robert, but the city celebrated the Elagabalia games in his god's honor (A.D. 218?). It was under Elagabalus that the city struck a coin with the stupendous array of four temples, three for Imperial cult, one for Kore,[81] a testimony for the preceding great building activity. The series of Imperial statue bases runs from Septimius to Alexander Severus (A.D. 222–235).[82] Unfortunately, none of the Imperial portraits have survived.[83]

The Severan period at Sardis is distinguished by the greatest accomplishments—probably completions—in building (palaestra, *xystos,* and an unidentified basilica, as well as the Marble Court),[84] the most effusive grandiloquence, the greatest number of games and festivals (four "worldwide"), the most *neokoriai* (three, Elagabalus), the strongest devotion to the mythical past—and possibly the greatest prosperity.[85] Sardis calls herself "metropolis of Greece, of Asia, of all Lydia"—the last with a backward glance to Croesus' kingdom. From Severus (ca. A.D. 200) to Valerian and Salonina (A.D. 253–256), veneration of the mythical past and local pride have a field day on coins. Zeus Lydios' monumental altar with caryatids (Fig. 147),

Kore, Demeter, Mên Askaenos, and Dionysus alternate with local and would-be local myths: Tylos-Triptolemos, Tylos-Herakles, Masnes, and Pelops; and even local geographic personifications like the Hermus River and the Tmolus appear, sometimes inscribed. We are on the way to Nonnus-like encyclopaedic erudition and education.[86]

Social interests were dominated by athletics, gladiatorial fights, and animal hunts. The last two activities may have taken over the theater. The most characteristic monuments of the age are the statue base inscription of the "world champion" in pancratium and boxing, Marcus Aurelius Demostratos Damas, who won practically everything everywhere in the Greek world; the gladiatorial reliefs; and the new remarkable representation of animal hunts (Fig. 209) and of a local tree-ritual.[87]

The end of autonomous coinage (ca. A.D. 256?) is symbolic for the end of an era. It was under Valerian and Gallienus (253–268) that the Goths burned down the temple of Artemis in Ephesus and attacked Didyma and Miletus, and the Sassanian Persians made their first raid into Asia Minor.[88] We have found no sign that the tumultuous years between A.D. 256 and 284 led to any devastation or destruction at Sardis. Unless the city wall (Fig. 208), like that of Nicaea, was built between 260 and 270, no major buildings or monuments are recorded, but the Jewish community may have begun the redecoration of the Synagogue;[89] and public buildings like the gymnasium continued in use. A new age started with Diocletian, who made Sardis the capital of his new province of Lydia, and Constantine, who made Sardis a Christian metropolis.[90]

Population

The general impression from combined excavations and sources is that the city reached its peak prosperity in the third century, and its greatest area extension (Plan IV) in the fourth and fifth centuries.[91] Magie has estimated the population of the three largest cities of the Roman province of Asia—Ephesus, Smyrna, Pergamon—to be ca. 200,000. Actually, we have for Pergamon a firm figure by an ancient author: Galen in the second century A.D. put the population at 120,000, including women and slaves, though

this may be the entire *polis* territory, not just the urban area. Sardis may not have been much smaller than Pergamon: between 60,000 and 100,000 for the urban area and suburbs in the fourth century may be as close as we can guess.[92]

Overview

The following description, based on a previous survey in *Report 1*, gives an impression of Sardis as it was in the fourth to sixth centuries—omitting, however, the purely Christian constructions and cemeteries.

We have already considered the main features of the city plan, with its bent-axial colonnaded street and its newly built up west quarter. It must be added that beginning around A.D. 400 many Roman villas were built up the Pactolus Valley (to the south), perhaps for a half mile beyond the Artemis Temple, and rich mausolea (such as that of Claudia Antonia Sabina, ca. A.D. 215) began just west of the new city line on the Pactolus (Figs. 8, 167; Plan IV).

As to evidence for the street pattern of the city, we have traced parts of the colonnaded Main Avenue, the perpendicular East Road (Figs. 167, 207), and the "Colonnaded Street" in HoB (Fig. 8:58). In addition, a marble-paved east-west street existed just west of the modern mill (Fig. 167:31).[93] A serpentine ancient road along which house walls are preserved to ca. 1.5 m. is said to go up to the top of the Byzantine Fort (Fig. 8:23; Plan IV).[94] Other streets and buildings are known from inscriptions. Thus the fragment of an inventory of city fountains[95] mentions the "Agora Descent Road" (*Kathodos Agoras*), the Odeum, the Confraternity (*mysterion*) Building of Attis, the Menogeneion, and the precincts of Zeus and Mên. We know the *gerousia* (Senate), *boule* (Council), Gymnasium of the Elders, Bath of the Emperor, an anonymous basilica, a city archive, and the Temple of Augustus from this and other inscriptions and from ancient authors.[96] *Platia Sardianorum* is mentioned in a late Latin inscription[97] and "Hypaipa Street" and a Tetrapylon figure in a fifth century inscription, which alludes to a replanning operation.[98]

Public buildings, the gymnasium, the baths, and the colonnades of the Main Avenue were richly supplied with marble-revetted floors (Fig. 235) and floor mosaics (Figs. 241–243). As to housing, a sophisticated urban residential culture is revealed by the imposing House of Bronzes, with basements, servants' quarters, marble-floored reception rooms (Fig. 210), and rich furnishings of marble, bronzes, and glass, or by the suite of gorgeous mosaic rooms (Fig. 298) attached to the probably private bath at Pactolus North (ca. A.D. 400–450?). These structures, large residences of important families, seem to resemble the Roman *domus* type.

We have not excavated completely any house or dwelling plan from the Late Antique era. The incomplete units found south of HoB entail rather loose sequences of terraced units and small courts going up the slope (Fig. 167 at no. 56); the site afforded the desirable north exposure (Fig. 241) and marvelous views. The continuous terraced buildup recalls the irregular but richly furnished and skillfully terraced "Slope Houses" in Ephesus with their multiple apartments.[99]

Intermediate between public and private buildings were halls and structures which housed the various civic and religious associations. Some of these complexes were in the nature of clubhouses. An interesting inscription of the second century A.D. speaks of the tribe (*phyle*) Dionysias. It built for itself, out of its own funds, the stoa and the exedra and a two-story storage unit in the adjacent garden.[100] The mention of gardens suggests that an unspecified percentage of the urban area was given over to "green plots," gardens, and possibly orchards. The strange lack of architectural remains in the HoB area between A.D. 17 and 400 may indicate that this was a "green area," left open south of the cemetery (Figs. 211, 241). Other Sardian *phylai* presumably had similar clubhouses and gardens; two anonymous "clubhouses" and a "confraternity hall of Attis" are mentioned in the fountain inscription.[101] The Menogeneion, too, named after a famous citizen of Sardis, may have been a stoa.

Commercial and industrial life flourished through the six centuries (A.D. 17–616). From literary sources and inscriptions we learn about a great Imperial arms factory located at Sardis since the time of Diocletian.[102] The creation of such an extensive shopping center as the Byzantine Shops, with its row of twenty-nine units (Figs. 206, 239–244), indicates a surprisingly centralized yet diversified economic life in the fifth and sixth centuries. Ancient writers infer

the persistence of traditional luxury goods industries—textiles and perfumes. Inscriptions from the Synagogue speak of goldsmiths.[103] The gilding of the ornaments (Figs. 226–232) of the Severan Marble Court (A.D. 200?–211), and of the Hall with Gold Ceiling mentioned in fifth century inscriptions from the Marble Court,[104] shows that something of the "Golden Sardis" tradition lived on. Debris from a worksite for production of gems was discovered in 1979. During the reconstruction all trades associated with building must have expanded—builders, stonemasons, bricklayers, carpenters, mosaic workers, and painters. The high level of activity continued into the *ananeosis* (renovation) of the fourth and fifth centuries. The famous Builders' Union inscription of A.D. 459 indirectly testifies to vigorous private and public building.[105]

Agriculture must have contributed to the commercial life; the reverence in which Demeter, the local goddess of harvests Kore, and her children Abundance and Good Growth were held through the pagan period speaks for the importance of agricultural wealth, reaffirmed by the inscription to the Children of Kore (A.D. 211) found in 1972. That the role of a regional grain-milling center, held by modern Salihli, had ancient precedent is indicated by the inscription of a watermill mechanic.[106]

As regards production and distribution, it is interesting that some of the economy was semidomestic. From the finds in the basements of the House of Bronzes (Fig. 210), it seems that olive oil was probably made and wool dyed right in the servants' quarter.[107] The Byzantine Shops appear to have been fairly specialized. There are indications of ironmongers, glass sellers, paint dealers, and possibly jewelers, as well as restaurateurs. The large quantity of dyes may have been intended for textiles. The highly sophisticated bronze products, such as the lion lamp (Fig. 245), the tripod, the incense shovel (Fig. 283), wine flagons, and samovars (*authepsae*), may have been locally made.[108]

In the area of public utilities and hygiene, we have mentioned the fundamental importance attributed to the Sardian water supply system in the layout of the city after A.D. 17. As in other Hellenistic and Roman towns, it was supplemented by an elaborate system of drains to dispose of waste water.[109] Two interesting illustrations of "health services" are known: the well-arranged double latrine with marble seats for the visitors (Fig. 215) in the Byzantine shopping center (ca. A.D. 400), and the hospital, mentioned in an inscription of Justinian (ca. A.D. 539).[110]

GMAH

The Bath-Gymnasium Complex

The imperial bath-gymnasium complex in Sardis is located in the northwest section of the ancient city, some 150 to 200 m. east of the Pactolus River and immediately north of the Izmir-Ankara highway (Figs. 8, 167, 211). It is defined by a rectangular structure, nearly 5½ acres in area and partly raised on an artificial terrace, measuring 120 m. north-south and 170 m. east-west (Figs. 206, 207).[1]

The complex is undoubtedly the most monumental public structure of Sardis known so far, occupying a central position in the busy downtown area. Its entire southern frontage is taken up by a row of shops (Figs. 239–242), opening onto a wide, colonnaded marble avenue—the Main Avenue—one of the major thoroughfares of the Roman city. Another marble-paved road joins the Main Avenue at the southeast corner of the large building and continues northward along its colonnaded east side; a public square, fronted by a number of civic structures, may have occupied the area immediately to the east.

Early Travelers and Modern Excavations

The impressive ruins of the bath-gymnasium complex have always been partly visible above ground and contributed to the identification of the site with the ancient capital of Lydia. It is difficult to judge how much of the gigantic structure could be seen during the eighteenth and nineteenth century, when the accounts of the early travelers begin. The rough outline of the bath block and portions of the south and north boundary walls, as well as some of the main pier groupings of B-W (Fig. 206), must have been possible to make out for the careful observer since most of these features were somewhat discernible as late as 1957, previous to the modern excavations (Fig. 210, in 1959). But it was particularly the part designated as "Building B" by

H. C. Butler, the director of the first Princeton excavation of Sardis (1911–1914), which attracted the attention and admiration of early travelers. This is a colossal structural group formed by three halls (a squarish central hall BCH, flanked on the north and south by long rectangular ones with apsidal ends, BNH and BSH; the group is some 18 m. in width and over 120 m. in length) with rubble and brick walls preserved as much as 6–9 m. above ground level.

Claude de Peyssonnel, who visited the site in 1750, described it as "a great building built of bricks, supported in some places by reinforcements of stone."[2] John "Palmyra" Wood, who passed through Sardis the same year, supplied the first measured sketch plan of the complex in its main lines. In the 1830s Charles Texier suggested that it could indeed be a "gymnasium"— although the inclusion of baths was probably not his understanding of a Roman gymnasium.[3] Butler considered the building to be Roman in date and recorded it as "baths" in the large contour map of the site. He cautiously commented that "nothing short of excavation can disclose the purpose and age of this building."[4]

It fell to the second American team, the Harvard-Cornell Expedition under the directorship of G. M. A. Hanfmann, to uncover the main portion of this gigantic structure and undertake extensive restorations and reconstruction. Excavation efforts have stretched over a period of sixteen years between 1958 and 1974 and involved the contribution of many archaeologists, architects, and epigraphists.

B-West and B (BSH, BCH, BNH)

The first attempts of the opening seasons of 1958 and 1959 were directed towards the uncovering of the southwest frontage of the building, where the west end of the row of "Byzantine Shops" and the Main Avenue came to light (Fig. 206).[5] Excavations continued inside BSH (B South Hall), clearing the south half of the colossal hall with apsidal ends (Fig. 212). Positioned in the middle of the south apse, over a semicircular podium, was found a statue base bearing a dedicatory inscription to Emperor Lucius Verus and mentioning the name of the dedicant as Claudius Antonius Lepidus, who, presumably, was the gymnasiarch (Fig. 213).[6] It was clear that the structure was of Roman date, and possibly a "gymnasium" of the Asiatic type. A deep sounding undertaken inside the hall established the stratigraphy down to the Lydian level at ca. *92.0; there appeared some walls and pavement of late Hellenistic or early Roman date, but nothing that suggested the existence of monumental architecture.[7]

The only archaeological work done in BNH (B North Hall), the north counterpart of BSH, consisted of a sondage in 1959 inside its north apse to confirm the existence of a semicircular podium similar to the south apse podium of BSH—but without a statue base.

The oblong hall between BSH and BNH, designated as BCH (B Central Hall), is only partially excavated. In 1972, investigations along its south and east sides revealed a central door connecting it with BSH; a similar door on the north side is a reasonably safe expectation. Both of the doors are flanked by semicircular niches which are completed to full circles at the ground level, forming pools and fountains (Fig. 214).[8] The hall communicates with BE-H (B East Hall), the frigidarium, through a wide open frontage of triple arches; the connection to the heated zone to the west, on the contrary, seems to have been maintained through a single, modest-sized door.

The part of the complex west of the BSH-BCH-BNH group (i.e., west of W18.10) is still largely unexcavated except for a number of test trenches and deep soundings. This area presumably constitutes the heated part of the baths. During the 1958 and 1959 seasons, the western boundary wall of the complex had been exposed at the southeast corner of the building and fixed at W52.10; subsequently it was explored for a distance of about 28 m., up to ca. N28.0. Adjoining the south end of the west wall and communicating with the complex through a door was a public latrine of Early Byzantine date (Fig. 215).[9] Immediately west of the latrine a north-south road joined the south Colonnade and the Main Avenue. This road might have been a service road (or replaced an earlier service road) for the anticipated row of furnaces along the heated west frontage of the baths.

General investigations along the west wall alignment, ca. N50–80, and an ambitious east-west trench across the central part (ca. N59–63), in 1961, revealed a number of large rectangular piers of marble ashlar construction whose east counterparts seemed to define the existence of a gigantic rectangular hall on the west end of

the complex. (This was also in accordance with a similar hall delineated roughly on Wood's plan.) In 1972, the discovery of the north boundary wall of the same space allowed a more precise reconstruction of the plan (Fig. 206). The hall, designated as BWH (B West Hall), is divided into three bays by eight huge projecting piers and measures ca. 24.0 m. by 38.80 m., with a clear distance of 18.10 m. between the piers; this makes it the most ambitious span of the complex and one of the largest to be negotiated by a masonry vaulting system in all Asia Minor. The east-west trench of 1961 had uncovered the ashlar voussoirs of a fallen barrel vault spanning between the two central piers of the west alignment.[10] It can be suggested that all of the piers of BWH were connected by lateral vaults (or arches), which, in turn, supported the main, east-west spanning vault of the hall.

In 1972, a 6 m. deep sondage between the two southernmost piers of the east side reached the floor at *96.70 and revealed a heated pool and walls heated by the use of hollow tiles—tubuli.[11] A service chamber with furnaces seemed to lie immediately to the east, between BWH and BSH. This discovery confirmed the identification of BSH as the *caldarium* for the bath-gymnasium complex.

B-East: The Marble Court, BE-H, BE-S, and BE-N

The second major effort of 1959 explored the area east of the BSH-BNH group ("Building B"). A trench roughly 5 m. by 10 m. was laid between N50–60/E30–35, revealing a north-south colonnade of double-engaged columns and large quantities of fallen marble architectural ornament.[12] During the succeeding years, 1960 and 1961, the excavations were extended from ca. N43–69 and E15–34, to clear a space roughly 18 m. by 36 m. in size and filled entirely by richly carved architectural ornament in marble—column shafts, capitals, bases, pieces of entablature, and vast amounts of multicolored marble wall veneer-revetment (Fig. 221). Quite appropriately, the hall was dubbed the "Marble Court." A podium, ca. 2.20 m. high, continued along most of the three sides of the room, interrupted only by large apses and passageways on the north and south sides and a larger pedimented gate on the west (Figs. 223, 224). The discovery of an imperial inscription carved on the first-story architrave (Fig. 227), dedicating the work to Septimus Severus and Julia Domna and their sons Caracalla and Geta, suggested that the true function of this space might have been an Imperial Cult Hall.[13] Halls or courts of similar design in association with bath structures have been found in Ephesus and interpreted as *Kaisersäle* by the excavators.[14] Quite apart from the probable function, the Sardis inscription provided a precise date for the Court sometime between A.D. 211 and 212, since Geta's name had been erased (Geta was assassinated in A.D. 212 and suffered *damnatio memoriae*).[15]

The large rectangular hall between the Marble Court and BCH was excavated mainly during the 1964 and 1965 seasons.[16] The floor was found to be almost entirely occupied by a long pool with semicircular ends. The east and west walls contain an alternating arrangement of rectangular and semicircular niches which housed an elaborate system of pools and fountains (Figs. 216, 217).[17] These investigations also revealed the existence of major vaulted drainage and supply lines on both sides of the pool. In 1972–1973, the last strip of earth piled high against the west wall, as well as the fill inside the pool itself, was cleared down to the level of the pavement. The floor, including that of the pool, is paved in rectangular marble slabs with watertight joints; the pattern, for the most part, was discernible only through the impressions on the pink colored mortar.

The heavy debris filling most of the space showed the clear patterns of sections of a fallen barrel vault in brick. Other finds were largely architectural, consisting of pilaster capitals and copious amounts of multicolored marble revetment, as well as some material from the Marble Court which must have been dragged into BEH sometime after the final destruction. Of particular significance were two inscribed statue bases, one carrying a dedication to Caracalla from Sardis, "the Metropolis of Asia"[18] (found in 1964), the other, possibly of the fourth century A.D., recording the reuse of a city fountain with intertwined bronze serpents by one Basiliskos, a governor of Lydia.[19]

A chance opening at the north end of the main pool led the excavators into a major network of vaulted subterranean corridors and tunnels which apparently were used for drainage and service purposes. Although the main tunnel

(1.0 m. wide and 2.60 m. high; Fig. 218) could be followed all the way to its discharge at the north end of the complex, N122.10, the many crossing branches and subsidiary canals were impossible to trace to any appreciable distance because they had been filled with debris after their roofs had caved in.[20]

The square-shaped, identical units BE-S and BE-N, flanking the Marble Court (Fig. 223), were excavated during 1964, 1965, and 1966.[21] The south unit, BE-S, revealed a marble slab paving over a mosaic one; the north has an *opus sectile* floor like the Marble Court (see Fig. 235). In both, an earlier floor of mosaic was found some 0.10–0.15 m. below the marble upper surface. The architectural elements of the east side colonnade of the north unit, including a fully preserved column shaft, were uncovered almost intact underneath the fallen brick vaulting of the room. These were specially studied in 1967 and formed the basis of the reconstruction for the east colonnade of BE-S and BE-N as well as for the "Screen Colonnade" of the Marble Court (Figs. 220, 224, 227).[22]

A number of rooms and halls which occupy the area south of BE-H and BE-S (designated as B-East S; Fig. 206) were cleared as a result of several campaigns. The two identical south-most rooms, BE-A and BE-B, were largely uncovered in 1966 with the intention of discovering their possible link with the Synagogue.[23] The mosaic floor at BE-A was found at *96.75, underneath the very clear configuration of a fallen brick barrel vault spanning the room in the east-west direction, supported by the 3 m. thick side walls. BE-B, which displays a central fountain, had been preserved in much poorer condition. Although patches of rough bedding of the mosaic were found in the southwest and northeast corners of the room, elsewhere the finished surface had been entirely ripped out and built over by crude squatters' walls of a much later period.[24] A rough and irregular cut made into the thick east wall of the room connecting it with the Synagogue must have belonged to this postdestruction period. A few lines of inscription found on the frescoed east wall of BE-A, *eulogeito(s ho laos)*, "blessed be the people,"[25] could not provide the definitive evidence for the Jewish use of the room, although it, too, had gone through a late occupation period, judged by the few industrial installations found on the east side. A late door connected the room with the Main Avenue on the south, providing also a convenient minor entrance into the baths directly from the street. It is interesting to note that neither of these rooms appear to have ever been revetted in marble, since no traces of the unmistakable clamp and pin holes are visible on the walls.

BE-A and BE-B are connected with a large, oblong hall designated as BE-C, immediately to the north (Figs. 206, 219). The south and southwest portions of BE-C had been excavated from ca. *100.0 down to the mosaic floor at *96.70–*96.60 as part of the operations of 1966. The coin evidence associated with the mosaic floor of BE-C, as well as those of BE-A and BE-B, was predominantly of the mid-fourth century A.D. Above the mosaic, in the east section of BE-C and BE-B, there was a concentration of coins from the reign of Constans II (A.D. 641–660). In 1972, the entire hall was cleared by removing large, amorphous sections of brick vaulting. In the center of the room, built over the mosaic floor, was a circular limekiln with a diameter of 4.85 m., whose operation seemed to have been stopped short by the collapse of the roof; several pieces of marble architecture in various stages of decomposition, as well as thick deposits of lime, were found around the limekiln (Fig. 219).

An important monument which seemed fortunately to have escaped the kiln's fire was a marble podium set against the middle bay of the wall (L.: 2.62 m., W.: 0.98 m., H.: 1.475 m.). The inscription on its vertical face records that Glycon, son of Glycon (a wealthy but otherwise unknown citizen of Sardis), dedicated the statues of *Koros* and *Euposia* (Abundance and Fertility) to Caracalla and Geta (name erased), for the prosperity and flourishing of the city and territory of Sardis.[26] No trace of these statues was found.

Fragments of marble revetment and marble dado were found to have been preserved in uncommonly good condition on the walls of BE-C, including a section 8.50 m. in length in the center bay of the south wall, where the plaques of white marble were preserved *in situ* to a height of 0.90–1.20 m. over the floor level.

The corridor-like room, BE-E, providing the link between BE-C and BE-H was mainly excavated in 1964, except for a 2.0 m. wide strip of debris at its south end which was removed in 1972. The room is paved in fine *opus sectile* work,

but it appears that it fell into neglect and abuse sometime when the north one-third was closed off by a crude cross-wall. A remarkable array of vertical channels was provided in the masonry. A small staircase in the northeast corner appeared to have had some utilitarian purpose associated with the waterworks system (access to a roof reservoir?).[27]

A few test trenches laid in 1968 confirmed that the planning and the structural organization of BE-N are identical to its south counterpart. With the exception of BE-N, the area has been left unexcavated.[28]

Palaestra

The clearing of the vast Palaestra required several seasons of activity. The long hall on the north side of the Palaestra, LNH (Figs. 206, 220), was divided into three units. This was of considerable importance for the history of the Synagogue building because the division mirrored the arrangement of the pre-Synagogue hall on the south side of the Palaestra (see Fig. 271). The middle and east units, LNH 2 and LNH 3, were only partially excavated. It was obvious that there had been much late disturbance in this area, and neither one of these units had any paving, even rough subflooring preserved, although it was ascertained that the easternmost unit had been planned as a small peristyle courtyard much the same way as the forecourt of the Synagogue.[29] The full excavation of the west unit, LNH 1, in 1968 revealed a row of rectangular piers of ashlar; these piers had been originally projections of the two long walls, but were later cut back. The many large and small remodelings and rebuildings that this area must have gone through renders the original scheme quite incomprehensible. Of particular interest were three elaborate pottery kilns snugged between the north piers, indicating that at least at one stage (probably after the seventh century), LNH 1 and the north extension of the Palaestra, the "North Corridor," was the center of an industrial production of considerable magnitude.[30] The North Corridor, which originally provided the access into BE-N, specifically into BE-CC, was, perhaps, closed off during this period and made part of the industrial area. It would be logical to expect a timber truss system spanning between the piers in LNH 1, since no traces of a masonry roofing were found in any one of the three halls, and the walls are too thin to allow it. If LNH 2 once had an inner row of columnar supports, it has disappeared completely.

Palaestra South had already been excavated in 1966 and 1967 as a part of the overall Synagogue investigations (Fig. 206).[31] During the same season, work was expanded into Palestra East, concentrating around the central section which was expected to yield the main entrance of the complex. In 1968 the discovery of a triple-gate with heavy marble jambs at the exact center of the east boundary wall confirmed the hypothesis. Excavations were extended eastward and disclosed the existence of an outer colonnade along the east facade of the building which opened into the "East Road" (Figs. 206, 207, 210).

Both the outer colonnade and the inner ambulatories of the Palaestra are paved in mosaic, but the Palaestra East center area directly in front of the Main Gate and the Palaestra West area, in front of the Marble Court (Fig. 220), had been repaved by a layer of marble slabs over the mosaic. In fact, a raised "processional way" had been created connecting the east gate with the Marble Court straight across the Palaestra center. This appears to be a late feature added when the Marble Court was used as a ceremonial vestibule. The hard marble paving of the Palaestra center might belong to this phase also.

A number of deep trenches were laid across Palaestra South to study the stratigraphy.[32] Of these, the most important was the one between E52.0 and 62.0, which reached from the stylobate level of *97.70 down to *89.80. Between *95.0 and *91.0, Lydian wares made their appearance; at *90.80, some geometric Lydian sherds were found. The trench at E74.50–77.50 revealed a large vaulted drain running north-south under the Synagogue (Figs. 248:12; 271; top at *96.20, gravel bottom *92.70, diameter at extrados, 2.50 m.). One of the most significant results of the Palaestra South investigations was the discovery of a subterranean vault running east-west between N21.10 and 23.70 in the southwest corner (bottom at *92.0; height, 2.54 m.). The vault, constructed in rubble, is dated to early imperial times by pottery and partly by some badly eroded and sketchy fragments of painted fresco found on the end wall. It

is undoubtedly part of the artificial terracing and foundation system whose north extension had already been uncovered in 1965 under the Screen Colonnade of the Marble Court.

Reconstruction of the Marble Court

Apart from the excavations and routine small-scale repairs, a number of major restorations were undertaken in the complex. Undoubtedly, the single most important project was the reconstruction of the Marble Court between the years 1964 and 1973. Together with the Stoa of Attalos in the Athenian Agora and the facade of the Library of Celsus in Ephesus, this may be the most extensive reconstruction work undertaken in the Aegean in the last few decades (Figs. 211, 222–232, 235, 237).[33]

It was discovered that some 60–65% of the Court's columnar architecture in marble had been preserved, though the majority of the pieces had been damaged by the impact of the fall (Fig. 221), and many were in fragmentary form. Original elements, as much as was structurally possible, were joined by bronze dowels, lead, and epoxy glue; the missing parts were cast in concrete tinted to the proper color. Surface treatment and finish approximated the original materials and the ornamental design without attempting to hide the difference between the old and the new. The major problem of structural support was solved by building up the back walls of the Court and cantilevering the horizontal architectural members from a reinforced concrete frame embedded into the thickness of the massive rubble walls. In this system, the re-erected columns in two stories carry no overhead loads except their own (Figs. 226, 228, 229).

The reconstruction of the Marble Court was extended to its east colonnade ("Screen Colonnade"), as well as those of units of BE-S and BE-N. The architectural members of the east colonnade of BE-N, almost preserved intact, served as the model for determining the correct height and ornamental details of the first story of the Screen Colonnade, whose attractive "head-capitals" were replaced by plaster casts (Figs. 230–232).[34]

Continuation of the reconstruction work in the Palaestra during the seasons of 1972–1973 involved the *ananeosis* of the columns in the corners and the placing of the Ionic impost capitals, from a fifth century A.D. restoration, over some of them. In addition to this, the back walls of the Palaestra (the south wall of LNH and the east boundary wall of the complex) were rebuilt to a height of ca. 1.20–1.40 m. In BE-H, the ashlar piers and the double-ring brick arches of the west wall (Fig. 216) were fortified and repaired where needed.[35]

Structure

The structural system used throughout the complex can be described as one of load-bearing walls in mortared rubble and brick articulated by ashlar piers (Figs. 212, 214). The tall, massive piers in some of the major spaces—BWH and BE-C—project out of the wall and are organized in corresponding fashion to create a frame-like structure (Fig. 219). The piers, ordinarily, are connected in the lateral direction by double-ring brick arches (or vaults) which either carry the major vaulting of the roof directly (as in the aforementioned units) or support an upper zone of mortared rubble and brick wall section below the vaulting (as seen in BE-H; Figs. 216, 217). In the latter case, the load imposed by the main vault is not transferred to the piers directly, but to the wall section which acts as an intermediary structural element distributing the stresses uniformly into the system of arches and interconnected piers below (Fig. 233). Yet, despite the direct or indirect line of transfer of the roof loads to isolated points of support, the system cannot be said to represent a true "frame construction" because of the lack of structural ties and continuity between the piers in the transverse direction (no trace of ribs was encountered in the fallen remains of the brick vaulting; none were normally expected).

The piers are constructed of blocks of low-quality marble (Figs. 212, 219) from local quarries and consist of a rubble and mortar core, some of it material reused from structures destroyed in A.D. 17; the proportion of the core to the exterior ashlar work varies with the size and structural significance of the piers. Those of BE-H (Fig. 216) were found to be done in solid ashlar, and composed of much larger blocks (average 0.60–0.90 m. by 0.60 m.) than those from the piers of "B" or B-E (average 0.30–0.60 m.

by 0.40 m.). The piers of the west zone also display a more careful workmanship, with well-trimmed pieces fitted together by metal clamps, using no or minimal mortar whereas mortar has been used freely in B-E. All of the arches throughout the complex connecting the system of piers are in brick (full sizes, 0.39 × 0.39 × 0.05 m., or half-sizes, 0.39 × 0.19 × 0.05 m.) usually arranged in double rings (Fig. 214) with a 0.40 m. thick upper ring over a 0.60 m. lower one. In all instances, brickwork penetrates the full thickness of the wall. In some of the structural bays, the space under the brick arch is kept open to contain a door; in others, there is a solid, but essentially nonstructural, fill wall of rubble. The vaulting of the main barrel vaults or domical vaults (Figs. 233, 234, 236)—is also of brick, radially laid, with possibly a backing of rubble or mortar, especially at the haunches where compression devices are necessary.

The wall sections above the piers—or filling between the piers—are in rubble interlaced by bands of brick (Figs. 216, 233). The rubble presents an orderly facing of courses laid following regular, horizontal rows. The core of the wall (Figs. 214, 219), however, is a random and somewhat careless fill having large quantities of rubble, often with too little lime mortar. The brick bands occur at intervals of 0.60–1.20 m. in height and are ordinarily composed of four courses; like the arches, they invariably go through the entire wall in thickness (Fig. 233). It is significant that this type of construction, generally associated with the late Roman and early Byzantine work, was employed in large scale as early as the mid-second century A.D. in Sardis.

Of particular interest are the two partially preserved triangular brick sections in BCH, which were first noticed by A. Choisy in the nineteenth century and published as "pendentives" in his *L'Art de bâtir chez les Byzantins* (Paris 1883). It is impossible to prove that these corner constructions are indeed true pendentives since the maximum width preserved is not sufficient to show horizontal curvature; there is, however, a pronounced curvature in the vertical direction. If they actually were true pendentives, they could constitute one of the earliest known uses of this important structural element. In any case, the central unit BCH must have been roofed either by a domical vault (*volta a velo*) or a short barrel vault connected by semidomes (Figs. 234, 236).

Interior Decoration and Ornament

Apart from the ornament, which is part of the primary architecture of the building and exhibits a structural identity—columns, pediments, arches, niches, portals, and pools—the decorative program of the complex can be viewed under two major headings: (1) the decoration of surface elements, like floor pavings, wall and ceiling incrustation; (2) free standing monuments and sculpture.

The most lavish representation of architectural ornament from the complex undoubtedly comes from the Marble Court. The elaborately stacked and staggered columnar facades of the Court (Figs. 211, 222–224, 227) were designed to create the maximum visual impact by their astonishing variety of highly polished white and polychrome marble elements set against the marble-clad walls (Fig. 217) and the intricate pattern of the *opus sectile* floor (Fig. 235). The mixing of the Ionic, Corinthian, and Composite orders (Figs. 224–227) and the rich chiaroscuro of the deeply carved motifs are typical of the Marble Style of Asia Minor (Fig. 237) and provide a particularly good example of the full-blown baroque tendencies of Severan orament (Fig. 226). All of the white marble used for architectural ornament and most for the statuary comes from local quarries located some three miles south of Sardis, deep in the foothills of the Tmolus range (Magara Deresi Quarries).[36] The various breccias, cippolino, and onyxes belong to Phrygian sources.[37] A deep yellow-ochre marble identified as *giallo antico* and widely used for the first-story columns of the Marble Court—including the four gigantic spirally-fluted shafts (Fig. 225) of the central pedimented group—must have been imported from the Chemtou Quarries in Tunisia.[38]

The basic types of floor covering used in the complex are mosaic, slab paving in marble, and *opus sectile*. These different types are not necessarily contemporary and sometimes even overlay each other. It is difficult to determine what the original paving of the second century structure was like—possibly large rectangular slabs of white marble, as has been encountered in some of the less disturbed western units, BSH, BCH,

and in one instance, inside a pool in BE-H (Fig. 216). The most frequently encountered flooring, covering most of the entire east and southeast half of the complex as well as the exterior colonnades, is mosaic. Where preserved, it displays multicolored, geometric patterns divided into rectangular or square panels set off by runners and border; no figural or naturalistic representations have been found. Many of the designs are comparable to the Synagogue mosaics and probably date to the same era, ca. fourth to fifth century A.D. Perhaps the most handsome floors in the whole complex are the well-preserved marble *opus sectile* floors of the Marble Court, BE-N and BE-E (Fig. 235). Dated to the fourth and fifth century A.D. by coins trapped in the mortar bedding, these floors display rich and colorful variations of geometric patterns arranged in a checkerboard fashion of repeating square panels.[39]

Our knowledge of wall incrustation comes directly from scantily preserved portions of revetment *in situ,* especially the dado courses and the lower sections of walls, and indirectly from impressions left by marble plaques and from holes for revetment clamps on the wall surface where sufficient amounts of the backing mortar have remained (Figs. 212, 214; cf. 217). There was, of course, the actual evidence of the broken revetments themselves, found in copious quantities in the building debris. It seems that total revetment in marble was reserved for the more important spaces, such as the Marble Court, BE-H (the *frigidarium;* Fig. 217), and BWH (the *caldarium*). In other halls, like BE-S, BE-N, and BE-C, marble wall covering appears to have been restricted to the lower two-thirds of the wall, the upper reaches being finished in plaster and often painted with decorative-naturalistic designs or in geometric patterns and marble imitation. Some small fragments of painted stucco have been found in BE-A and BE-B.

The marble revetment scheme of the original phase seems to display a simple geometric and essentially rectilinear arrangement of rows of vertical plaques divided by flat horizontal bands and thinner molding, as quite clearly discernible on the north half of the west wall of BE-H through mortar impressions and clamp holes (Fig. 217). A number of ornate pilaster capitals and bases as well as other architectural respond elements found in BE-H, BE-S, BE-N, and BE-

C introduce the possibility of a more architectonic revetment scheme, although the small size of these elements suggests a second-story usage, perhaps in combination with stucco ornament. Only the walls of the Marble Court offer a fully worked out system of pilasters dividing up the wall behind the free-standing columns of the aediculae (Fig. 236). Of special interest is a small Corinthian pilaster capital with sculptural representation of a standing female figure ("Kore," "Anatolian Goddess"?) found in BSH (Fig. 148).[40] Dated in the second century A.D. on style and workmanship, this piece might be one of the rare elements preserved from the original decorative scheme of the building and might be taken as an illustration of the desire to incorporate sculptural motifs in the architectural ornamentation, as also represented by the head capitals of the Marble Court east colonnade. Large quantities of *skoutlosis* (small, thin pieces of marble, porphyry, and serpentine inlay of geometric shapes—squares, triangles, lozenges, circles, ovals, and "shields") found in the Marble Court must have belonged to the wall incrustation scheme of a later period (fourth to sixth century A.D.?) when the flat, abstract, and miniaturistic appeal of this kind of ornament was in vogue (see Figs. 264, 265).[41]

Based on the evidence of a considerable amount of stucco fragments with curved profiles, some still retaining clear impressions of mosaic cubes, and large quantities of loose *tesserae* found in the building debris, it is reasonable to propose that the curved interior surfaces of the major vaults (as well as the minor vaults and semidomes of niches) were finished either in plain or painted (or molded) stucco work, or multicolored mosaics, or both. Five gilded mosaic cubes found in one of the niches of BEH indicate a limited use of this Byzantine favorite.

Statuary

More than any other single building or area in Sardis, the bath-gymnasium complex has yielded free-standing statuary in marble, and bases for statues or statue groups now lost. (For statue bases with inscriptions see Figs. 213, 219.) Most of this material, unfortunately, is fragmentary and cannot be placed in its original and specific architectural context, though it is clear that the building was no exception in providing an ideal

setting for the exhibition of sculpture, as is generally true for most Roman baths. The wide variety of Classical types represented can be grouped as portrait heads, draped male and female figures, nude "athlete" (or Apollo/Dionysus types, a nude "Venus Pudica" type, and statues and statuette groups of satyrs and muses. Of the four or five portraits, some have been recognized as emperor or imperial types;[42] one is a bearded Zeus of Mylasa type[43] (from Palaestra West); and there is a late Roman bearded "philosopher" type of the late third century A.D. (Fig. 238, from the Main Avenue).[44] There were two or three nearly life-size draped female figures of the "Large Herculaneum Woman" type.[45] Of particular interest were the statuette groups, many representing Dionysiac themes: dancing satyrs, a group of Dionysus, Panther, and Satyr, and "Man and his dog" (from Palaestra South).[46]

Dionysus was closely associated with Sardis. According to the myth, he was born on Mt. Tmolus. His association with the city continued into the third century A.D., as is witnessed by his appearance on the city coins as late as A.D. 256. Hadrian was called Neos Dionysos—a reincarnation of Baki. The Marble Court was completed when Caracalla became sole emperor, and he may have been the first ruler to be worshiped there. We may assume a close connection between Dionysus and the Imperial Cult Hall at Sardis, which stressed Dionysiac subjects in its decorative program. In one particular capital from the Screen Colonnade, a merging of Caracalla with Dionysus may have been deliberately planned, as the god's features resemble those of the emperor.[47]

Planning

The plan of the bath-gymnasium complex of Sardis (Fig. 206) is recognizable as the Imperial type, composed of a series of rooms and halls arranged symmetrically around the main east-west axis and terminating in a single, large *caldarium*. Almost the entire east half of the complex is occupied by a square courtyard, the Palaestra, entered on the east through a gate with triple doors. The vaulted halls of the west half are intended for bathing. The three rooms on the north side, LNH 1, 2, and 3, appear to have served as rooms for exercise, undressing, or storage. Originally, the south wing of the Palaestra was occupied by simple rectangular halls similar to the north side in shape and function. Sometime in the third or early fourth century A.D., this wing was given over to the Jewish community of the city and rebuilt as a monumental Synagogue (Fig. 271).[48]

On the west side of the Palaestra, located directly on the central axis of the building, is the Marble Court, a rectangular space open to the sky (Fig. 236) displaying an impressive arrangement of columnar aediculae in two stories (Figs. 222–224, 237). This lavishly decorated hall, which appears to have been associated with the Imperial Cult, was reconstructed from the ground up between 1964 and 1973. According to the dedicatory inscription carved on the first-story architrave (Fig. 221), the Court assumed its present shape and rich columnar scheme under Septimus Severus and Caracalla. As recorded by the same inscription, this proud act of munificence was undertaken by the city of Sardis and two prominent Sardian women, C. Antonia Sabina and Flavia Politte.[49]

The Court opens into the Palaestra through a two-storied colonnade of double-engaged columns carrying Corinthian capitals with head motifs (Figs. 230–232). The aediculae of the south, north, and west walls are raised over a 2.20 m. tall continuous podium which displays a Byzantine inscription of the late fifth century A.D. recording a major renovation or redecoration, which may have been the occasion when passages were cut through the centrally located apses of the north and south walls into BE-S and BE-N (Fig. 237). The handsome marble *opus sectile* floor (Fig. 235) also seems to have been a part of this renovation activity. In the middle of the west side, between N51.60–70.40, the podium is interrupted for a monumental pedimented feature (Figs. 222–224); rising from the floor are two tiers of four gigantic spirally-fluted columns carrying a pediment broken by an arch. Originally, the columns and the arch of this ensemble framed an apse which may have contained an altar and a statue of the emperor—as they do in the apse of the *Kaisersaal* of the Vedius Gymnasium in Ephesus. Sometime in Late Antiquity (either in the fourth century A.D. or in the late fifth century, together with the north and south apses of the Court), the west apse, too, was cut through and made into a con-

venient passage leading into BE-H; this altered intentionally but effectively the function of the Court from an Imperial Cult Hall into a ceremonial vestibule.

The Marble Court probably never had a full roof except for a partial canopy of wood (coffered and gilded, even?) similar to those covering the stage building in Roman theaters and thus protecting the aedicular architecture below, displayed under the most effective light conditions.[50] The design has a fully "baroque" feeling which is created and enhanced by the variety of architectural types and the use of costly and multicolored marbles. There are plain, fluted, reverse-fluted, and spirally-fluted shafts of various colored marble, as well as some which are of square cross section. These shafts rise over simple Attic bases, tall square pedestal-bases, or in a few cases, over drums decorated by rich acanthus foliage resembling Corinthian capitals (Figs. 224, 237). There are Ionic, Corinthian, and palmette and lotus capitals, and some oval Corinthian ones displaying sculptured heads. All this seems to fit very well with the taste and tendency for exuberance that one encounters in the Roman architecture of the second and third century A.D., especially in Asia Minor, Syria, and North Africa, where the vogue towards eye-catching and decorative facade compositions applied on various public buildings such as stage fronts in theaters, nymphaea, city gates, and halls for ceremonial and Imperial purposes is unusually strong.[51]

The Marble Court is flanked by BE-S and BE-N (Figs. 206, 211), two square halls opening into the Palaestra through double columns *in antis*; these must have been vestibules leading into a symmetrically arranged group of halls to the north and south of the Court and the long hall behind it. This area is believed to have contained the changing rooms (*apodyteria*) for the use of the clients before they moved eastward into the Palaestra (Fig. 220) to engage in games and light exercise or continued westward, into the baths. The rectangular hall BE-H, west of the Marble Court, with the long pool with round ends (Figs. 216, 233, 234), must have been the *frigidarium* proper. It opens through triple arches into a squarish hall, BCH, on the west. This central hall (Figs. 234, 236) displays the same kind of pools and fountains inside the semicircular niches of its north and south walls

(Fig. 214) as the long walls of BE-H do, and can be considered as a spatial extension of the *frigidarium* (Fig 206). The units to the north and south of BCH are among the most monumental in the complex. They are a pair of identical oblong halls terminating in wide apsidal ends (Figs. 206, 212, 234). It is impossible to describe their function with any precision; they seem to have been intended largely for general use and social mixing—large, well-lighted spaces where the bathers could sit or stroll about in comfort and ease. Their marble-clad walls and floors and luxurious interior decoration also suggest a ceremonial and public character—one in keeping with and enhanced by the statue of Emperor Lucius Verus inside the south apse of BSH, elevated over the semicircular podium (Figs. 212, 213).

To the west of the BSH-BNH group lies the heated zone of the baths. A huge rectangular hall, BWH (Fig. 206), on the symmetry axis of the complex and divided into three bays by eight projecting piers has been securely identified as the *caldarium*. To the north and south of the *caldarium* there must have been a row of parallel and interconnected rectangular halls. Some of them, like BWH, must have contained heated pools between the piers. Undoubtedly they were well-lighted spaces, since large thermal windows could have been placed with ease under their east-west running barrel vaults. The unexcavated area between BWH and BCH appears to have contained a small chamber or passage acting as a "heat-lock" between the heated *caldarium* and the cold *frigidarium*. Normally, the bathing routine ended in a cold plunge in the *frigidarium* pool. Passages BE-E and BE-EE conveniently led the bather back into the *apodyteria*.

Usage

A visitor to the bath-gymnasium complex in the third century A.D. would enter the building by passing through the main gates on the east. Although there was no elaborate propylon, the axially situated entranceway could have been emphasized by a simple gable rising over the roof of the colonnade which lined the entire east face of the complex along the north-south street; this street joined the Marble Avenue in front of the Synagogue forecourt (Fig. 207).

Upon admittance, the visitor would step into an enormous courtyard of square proportions, the Palaestra, open to the sky in the middle but enclosed by tall Corinthian colonnades on all four sides. Since some kind of exercise or games usually preceded the hot baths, Sardians could be seen in the large central area wrestling, jumping, jogging, or engaged in various forms of ball games—the last preferred generally by the elderly as a less strenuous type of sport. Those who had already worked up a good sweat would be resting underneath the shaded colonnades, or discoursing with a friend while waiting for the hot baths to open. Before the newly-arrived visitor could join in these activities, he would have to undress and put on a short tunic. This required crossing the Palaestra to reach the changing rooms, the *apodyteria*, situated in the BE-S and BE-N area (Fig. 206). A secondary changing room located conveniently somewhere behind the colonnades would be a logical expectation, since the Palaestra served as an educational and athletic facility for the city and could be used independently of the baths. In fact, prior to the building of the Synagogue, both the south and the north sides of the Palaestra were occupied by a row of large rooms which must have served various sportive and communal functions. Just how long the building retained these functions is hard to determine. Although the gymnasium as an educational and athletic center had no place in the Christian world and faded fast during the fourth century A.D., this should not necessarily mean that they were all simply abandoned.[52] Already during the Roman Imperial era, the institution had been going through a slow and steady change from a physically oriented concern to an intellectually and socially oriented one.[53] Inscriptions of the fifth century A.D. carelessly scratched on the marble pavement of the Marble Court in Sardis mention the "place" for the city council and the *gerousia*.[54] Despite the ad hoc nature of these grafitti, they are important in illuminating the longevity and the later history of these administrative and cultural organizations in the city, and particularly in suggesting the continued use of the Palaestra for such civic functions long after its athletic meaning had come to an end.[55]

In the center of the west side of the Palaestra, facing the main entrance on the symmetry axis of the complex, could be seen behind a screen of double-engaged columns the sumptuously decorated Marble Court (Figs. 222, 224, 237). If the interpretation of the Marble Court as a space dedicated to the Imperial Cult is correct, it would be quite normal to expect its use during regular services and celebrations on the emperor's birthday and other important days of the cult calendar, as well as more informal but frequent use by bathers and athletes who would display their loyalty and respect for the emperor by simple offerings and homage at the altar, in front of his image. Exactly at which point this kind of observance took place during the course of the clients' stay at the establishment is impossible to know; probably there was no fixed time or order.

Eventually, the tintinnabulum announcing the opening of the hot baths would sound as a welcome invitation to the hot and dusty contestants. They would hasten along two identical paths into the building, north and south of the Marble Court, through BE-S and BE-N. These double vestibules led directly into BE-C and BE-CC, which appear to be major circulation centers connecting the Palaestra with the main bathing halls on the west. It was, perhaps, also here that the slaves and servants waited for their masters while keeping an eye on their clothing and belongings deposited in BE-A/BE-AA and BE-B/BE-BB, which are suggested as appropriate candidates for *apodyteria.*

The routine of bathing in Roman practice required a movement starting from the unheated areas through a series of warm rooms into the hot bathing hall, the *caldarium,* followed by a cold bath in the *frigidarium.* Along this typical circuit, the bather had the option of side-tracking, sometimes even backtracking, for a variety of activities: taking a sweat bath in the *laconicum,* getting a simple back-rub or a complete massage, or simply stopping to chat with friends. In Sardis the heated part of the baths was gained after going through the large apsidal halls BSH and BNH (Figs. 206, 236). Although the discovery of a statue base for Lucius Verus inside the south apse of BSH (Figs. 212, 213) gives a formal and ceremonial character to this space, it was perhaps a grand concourse and general gathering and mixing area within the sociable context of Roman baths. In his essay on "Baths of Hippias," Lucian describes a hall as being particularly suitable for "strolling about with profit." One can easily envisage a similar pattern in BSH and BNH, where the Sardians formed small groups, chatting and gossiping about politics and everyday events while a fair number gathered around the rich and the generous in the hopes of securing an invitation for dinner (Martial, *Epig.* I, 23; II, 14). The possibility of further use of these gigantic, vaulted halls of Sardis (Fig. 234) as indoor exercise areas during unfavorable weather should also not be disregarded.

The area west of the BSH-BNH alignment constitutes the heated zone of the baths (Fig. 206). Although the area is largely unexcavated, the results of a number of sondages indicate the presence of three large, rectangular halls parallel to each other. The visitor had to go through these intercommunicating halls before reaching the centrally located *caldarium,* BWH. All of these lofty halls must have received plenty of light through large windows on the west and contained basins and tubs of hot water; one of them, or a part of one, could have served as the *laconicum,* an overheated dry-steam room, but it was in the huge *caldarium* with its generous hot pools occupying the spaces between the massive piers where the ritual of bathing culminated. Judged by Seneca's famous fifty-sixth Letter about the nature of activities in the public baths, life in these lavishly decorated and brilliantly lit halls must have been noisy and somewhat hectic, but at the same time full of festive, community spirit. Apart from those who were busy washing themselves with the help of their servants or the bath attendants, or getting a professional massage, some were involved in forms of vigorous athletic exercise, while others splashed about noisily in the pools with great mirth. Vendors and hawkers were allowed in the baths, and they seem to have done a brisk business since eating and drinking were a popular part of the normal procedure of bathing. Ancient literature abounds in admonishing remarks and references about those who frequented the hot baths and exercised in the palaestra in order to indulge their gluttony better and to raise a thirst.[56]

After the *caldarium,* the visitor moved back eastward into the oblong hall BE-H (Fig. 206), identified as the *frigidarium;* the floor of this hall is almost entirely occupied by a swimming pool (Figs. 216, 233). This involved going first through a small space which acted as a kind of "heat-lock" between the heated and unheated areas (not delineated on the plan), then into BCH, the central hall (Figs. 234, 236), which is equipped with a number of small, circular pools (hip-baths) fitted neatly inside four semicircular niches (Fig. 214). BCH opens generously into the *frigidarium* proper through a wide archway. While in BCH, it was possible to omit cold bathing altogether and return to the changing rooms by going through the doors which connected this space with BNH and BSH; but most bathers probably enjoyed the swim in the large *frigidarium* pool and looked forward to it as a pleasurable and rejuvenating termination of the bathing procedure. Besides the public pool in the center, one could enjoy a private cold bath alone, or with a few friends inside the many small pools or basins which occupied the spacious niches of the two long walls. After the cold bath, a final massage complete with anointment and perfume was enjoyed by many, but it is hard to know where this activity took place in Sardis; perhaps there was no special room reserved exclusively for it.

The ancient sources also inform us that some of the clients, especially on hot summer days, preferred only a cold bath in the *frigidarium* following their exercises in the palaestra, without visiting the heated zone of the baths (*SHA, Alex. Sev.,* XXX). In Sardis, sometime in the fourth century A.D. (?), the swimming pool became directly and easily accessible from the Palaestra when the main west apse of the Marble Court was transformed into a gate (Figs. 223, 231). Normally, after having stayed in the baths two or three hours, the bathers would return to the changing rooms either by way of the corridor-like BE-E/BE-EE or by backtracking slightly into BSH and BNH.

Having dressed and anointed themselves, the Sardians were now ready to leave the baths and hurry to dinner. Some, probably, retired quietly through a minor door in BE-A which led directly into the Main Avenue. But the majority might have preferred a more ostentatious exit by way of the Palaestra and the East Gate. A few of the *nouveaux riches,* like Petronius' comical hero Trimalchio, might even have been bundled up in soft blankets and carried out on a litter accompanied by an army of servants, slaves, and well-wishers.

Analysis and Comparisons

The planning of the bath-gymnasium complex of Sardis represents a straightforward combination of a Roman bath with the palaestra of a Greek gymnasium. It is a type frequently and widely encountered in many of the Roman cities of Asia Minor. Major examples are to be found in Ephesus, Miletus, Aphrodisias, Hierapolis, Alexandria Troas, and even as far inland as Ancyra. The closest planning parallel to the Sardis complex is the Vedius Gymnasium (or Baths) in Ephesus. Both of those establishments display a scheme where the bathing and palaestral components have been pulled together and arranged symmetrically along a single, strong building axis.[57] The Ephesian building, much smaller in size, was dedicated to Artemis and Emperor Antoninus Pius by his wealthy friend, P. Vedius Antoninus.

The key position occupied by Asia Minor in the creation of a type so far freely referred to as the "bath-gymnasium" can be explained by a number of cultural and architectural traditions peculiar to the land.[58] Almost from its inception in the fifth and fourth centuries B.C., a certain kinship between the gymnasium and heated baths had always been a going concern. During the late Hellenistic period, simple washing and bathing facilities which were ordinarily included in the design of the Greek gymnasium were increased in size and elaborateness as the vogue for hot bathing for pleasure and recreation increased.[59] In the West, the development of the Roman baths was influenced only marginally by the palaestral component of the Hellenistic gymnasium. Because its real models, the gymnasium palaestrae, were lacking in the West, the interpretation was looser and freer. In Asia Minor and the East, where the influence of Greek culture and traditions had remained a vital factor, the two institutions, the Roman bath and the Greek gymnasium, merged into a new, composite architectural type: the bath-gymnasium.

Although the bath-gymnasia from Ephesus and the imperial complex of Sardis are representatives of the fully developed second century type, we are lucky to have a few examples that belong to an earlier stage in the development. The immediate architectural background for the type is best illustrated by the Capito Baths in Miletus—or similar projects since disappeared. Firmly dated by a building inscription in the reign of Claudius (A.D. 47–52), the Milesian building, with its strong emphasis on the east-west symmetry axis binding the bath and palaestra, can be claimed to have been the prototype for future planning of the bath-gymnasium type in Asia Minor earlier than any example from the

West.[60] Furthermore, the direct Hellenistic origins for the Capito Baths can be clearly traced to the second century B.C. Hellenistic Gymnasium, also in Miletus, adjoining the same baths on the south. Even a rudimentary comparison of the overall designs of this building with the Capito Baths of Miletus, and others of the imperial period from various sites, indicates that there is little reason to doubt the existence of a continuous thread of development for bath-gymnasium planning in Asia Minor based on the traditions of local, Hellenistic gymnasia.

Building History and Dating

The discovery of a statue base dedicated to Lucius Verus in BSH (Figs. 212, 213), one of the largest and better preserved vaulted halls, indicates that the overall construction of the bath block had been completed by the mid-second century A.D. at the latest. The work might have been started much earlier, since the imperial complex is only a part of a larger urban project that must have been prompted by the devastating earthquake of A.D. 17.

A circular base for a statue of Tiberius (IN 79.8) found at the east end of the excavations of the Main Avenue (S30–31/E135–137) may have stood between the columns or in front of the colonnade. The dedication is dated by L. Robert shortly after A.D. 41, in the reign of Claudius, and may indicate that the groundwork and terracing for the structure, as well as the basic street system and colonnades, were completed at that time.[61]

Judging by the difference in construction technique and materials, work on the gigantic building appears to have progressed from west to east, without any major breaks (Fig. 206). The marble decoration of the interiors may have taken quite some time; certainly, the Palaestra was not completed before the mid-third century A.D. The architectural ornament from the Marble Court, firmly dated to A.D. 211–212 by its dedicatory inscription (Figs. 226, 227), is quite typical of Severan ornament elsewhere in Asia Minor, and sets up a chronological standard against which others can be compared.[62] There is no reason to doubt, however, that the design of the entire complex was the product of a single, unified conception carried through a relatively long period of time.

During its long history, the complex must have gone through a number of major and minor renovations and adjustments. One of the most important of these was the rebuilding of the entire south wing of the Palaestra as an impressive Synagogue in the late third or early fourth century A.D. (Figs. 251–253). The present state of the Marble Court (as reconstructed) also represents the result of a number of earlier renovations. Originally, the Court was accessible only from the Palaestra, through the wide Screen Colonnade. The back walls carried centrally located apses which were partially blocked when the Severan aedicular scheme was applied; only the main, west apse could have been retained to house an altar or an imperial image. The other dedicatory inscriptions from the Marble Court record major renovation schemes involving the repairing of the floor and the redesign of the marble revetment of the walls. The earlier of these inscriptions, mentioning the name of one "Severus Simplicius" as the "Vicar of Asia," is tentatively dated to the late fourth century A.D.;[63] the date is supplied by coins of Constantine I and his sons found in the mortar bedding of the *opus sectile* floor.[64]

The second inscription comes from the top course of the podium (Figs. 221, 224) and records a major redecoration which might have involved areas other than the Court itself.[65] A mid- to late fifth century A.D. date has been assigned to the inscription on the basis of letter styles and literary form, which is composed partly in prose and partly in verse. A late coin of Zeno (A.D. 479–491) found between the lower mosaic floor and the upper marble slab paving of BE-S seems to support this date.[66] A number of Ionic-impost capitals from the Palaestra which replaced the original Corinthian ones have been dated in the same period on stylistic grounds.[67] It is, perhaps, during this late fifth century renovation that the north and south apses of the Marble Court were made into passages by cutting through the podium and the apse wall without altering the columnar architecture above (Fig. 237). The more momentous decision to convert the west apse and the pedimented group into a monumental gateway leading into BE-H (Figs. 206, 223, 236) might have belonged to the fourth century renovation if one could conceive of this architectural adjustment as a logical and effective response to the abolition of the Imperial Cult and its ritual under Christian rule.

The overall coin evidence from the excavated

areas, including drainage canals, indicates that the complex was in use throughout the fourth, fifth, and sixth centuries. It is likely that during periods of hardship certain sections of the gigantic complex were closed down to economize on expenses; this was technically possible. We know that during this period the much damaged row of shops was rebuilt and the earlier colonnade of the Main Avenue was replaced by a shorter one without much architectural pretense (Fig. 241). A tetrapylon terminating the new colonnade at the southeast corner of the complex might have been part of this scheme. At the southwest corner two public latrines (Fig. 215) were constructed adjacent to the building, one of them directly accessible from it by a door.

The last architectural reorganization of the building proper might have been the closing off of the east colonnades of the Marble Court, BE-S and BE-N (Figs. 206, 223), by a coarse rubble wall. This drastic alteration of the Court's original use and spatial integrity might have been necessitated by the various waves of approaching enemy threat during the third, but particularly in the late fourth century, when most of the city defenses were rebuilt and repaired. Sardis only narrowly escaped a plundering band of Goths in A.D. 399.[68] Destruction and abandonment finally came from the east by the Sassanian armies, which captured the city in A.D. 616. As suggested by numismatic evidence (especially from BE-B and BE-C), the south units appear to have temporarily sheltered the troops and contruction crews of Constans II, who were engaged about A.D. 660 in constructing a wide, cobbled road in front of the Byzantine Shops over the Roman Marble Avenue (Fig. 241). As the mighty structure was reduced to a state of ruin by the many earthquakes of subsequent centuries, the continuation of squatter settlements and lime-burning activity (Fig. 219) up until modern times is attested by the Middle Byzantine and Ottoman coins coming from upper levels.[69]

FKY

The Byzantine Shops

The importance of the Byzantine Shops can be summarized as completeness. No other shops from this period have been found with their contents, for all practical purposes, intact; no other shops from this period have provided such complete information about their occupants' trades, religions, and wealth. The economic historian can benefit from the information from the trades, coins, imported or local production of objects, and architectural form of the complex. The social historian or historian of religion can benefit from the evidence of Christians and Jews who shared a major urban complex, working in adjacent shops of modest scale. The art historian can benefit from the new iconographic evidence of sculpture, pilgrim flasks, and other objects. The political historian may benefit from increased data, as C. Foss's excellent book and articles already show.[1] Naturally, the greatest beneficiaries are archaeologists, who have in the Byzantine Shops an excellent sealed deposit of secure material to which they may compare over one hundred types of objects. We may be confident that as final publication continues, the Byzantine Shops will emerge as an even more important source of evidence in many disciplines and will create a broader and more detailed picture of ordinary human life in Early Byzantine times than has ever been possible before.

The Site

The center of Sardis in Roman and Byzantine times lay slightly north of the modern Izmir-Ankara highway and east of the modern village of Sart (Fig. 8). The modern highway (Fig. 5; Plan IV) is the successor to a number of other ancient roads, which have linked the west coast of Turkey with the interior. The Roman and Early Byzantine road was uncovered by the Harvard-Cornell Expedition in 1961, just north of the modern highway.[2] On either side of the ancient road, colonnades with mosaic floors provided shelter from sun and rain for pedestrians (Figs. 206, 207). Behind each of the two colonnades was a row of shops. One of these rows, the south, is still buried beneath the modern highway, but the north row, which extended the full length of the bath-gymnasium and Synagogue, has been almost completely excavated (Figs. 240, 241) except for two shops left unexcavated for control purposes. Should any future excavator wish to check the stratigraphy or apply presently unknown techniques, these last two shops will provide the necessary data.

The excavations which uncovered these shops

from 1958 to 1973 found them collapsed from their destruction in the Persian attack of A.D. 616.[3] Because of the suddenness of that attack, the inhabitants fled without removing their belongings. The contents of most of the shops were substantially intact.

The items from the Byzantine Shops at Sardis have provided valuable information about economic and religious life in a Late Roman/Early Byzantine city. While shops have been excavated at other cities in Asia Minor, no others have preserved such complete details about their inhabitants. Christians and Jews, merchants in glass, dye, paint, and hardware, and restaurateurs have left traces of their lives and livelihoods. These traces show us something of the lives of ordinary people, the submerged part of the historical iceberg, little mentioned by the historians of the day.

As one might expect, excavation of the Byzantine Shops produced large numbers of coins, in fact over 800. Most of them, except those found in later cleaning and in the 1972 and 1973 campaigns, were published by G. Bates and others were included by Buttrey.[4] The coins covered an enormous chronological span, indicating an unexpectedly long circulation. The earliest were Sardian local coins of the Hellenistic period issued after 133 B.C. The largest number of coins belonged to the fourth and fifth centuries A.D. The coins stop abruptly with a relatively small number of coins of Heraclius dated to A.D. 616. Because of the lack of later coins in the sealed deposit of the Byzantine Shops (later coins of Constans II were found at points where laborers were burning marble for road building in BE-C) and a similar pattern throughout the excavated areas of Sardis, G. E. Bates concluded that Sardis was destroyed in A.D. 616.[5]

The Excavations

The Byzantine Shops at Sardis were divided by the excavators into two groups: east and west. The dividing point was set by the "zero point" of the survey grid, which determined the recording for the entire complex (Figs. 8, 206, 239). The "zero point" corresponds exactly to the west wall of the main hall of the bath-gymnasium, which is called B. All shops west of this point were indicated by numbers preceded by W; all those east of it by numbers preceded by E. The

earliest excavations (1958) discovered parts of three of the west shops (W1–W3) and parts of the colonnade (W4–W6) which were not shops but were given designations as if they were.[6] In 1960 shops W7 and W8 were excavated.[7] Shops W9, 10, and 13 were excavated in 1972.[8] Excavation of the east shops began in 1962 with shops E13–E15.[9] Shops E13 and E15–E19 appeared in 1963 and 1964.[10] Shops E1–E11 were discovered in 1967 and 1968.[11] Recording for publication continued in 1969, and consolidation of the walls in 1972 and 1973.[12] Re-erection of five of the columns in front of the east shops (Figs. 240, 241) was also done in the 1973 season.[13] The excavation of the Late Roman/Early Byzantine road was done in 1961.[14]

There were three main levels of the road: Ottoman, Byzantine, and Roman.[15] The Ottoman level (*97.72) was of cobbled stones laid directly over the Byzantine Shops' colonnade and front wall and extending over the Byzantine and Late Roman/Early Byzantine roads. Its total width was over 12 m., and it remained in use until 1952, although when it was built is not certain.

The Ottoman road overlay the Byzantine road (*96.85). The Byzantine road, which had a cobbled surface above cemented rubble, was built in the reign of Constans II about A.D. 660.[16] At that time the Byzantine Shops and their contents were buried under the debris accumulated since their destruction in A.D. 616. No attempt was made to restore anything except the road, and the Byzantine Shops remained essentially a sealed deposit (cf. Fig. 210, taken in 1959, before most shops were excavated). The width of the Byzantine road was 15 m., slightly wider than the Ottoman road.

The Byzantine road overlay a Late Roman/Early Byzantine road (*96.21), which was the last phase of a Roman road laid out in the replanning of Sardis' urban center after the disastrous earthquake of A.D. 17. Like the Byzantine road, the Roman road was about 15 m. wide. Unlike the Byzantine road, however, it was paved with well-fitted marble slabs, some of them spoils from earlier monuments (Figs. 241, 243). This was the phase of the road associated with the Byzantine Shops. Epigraphic, typological, and other data from elsewhere at Sardis suggest a date around A.D. 400 for this restoration of the road, although we cannot say exactly when it was done.

The Byzantine Shops and their colonnade replaced another, more monumental building of early Roman phase, which was begun shortly after A.D. 17. Although little evidence of this phase remained, the large foundation walls below the stylobate and front wall of the shops (Fig. 187) and a fragment of a column larger than those used in the last phase suggested what the appearance of the earlier phase was like.[17]

The colonnade, shops, and road seem to have been designed with a 5-m. module (Figs. 206, 243). Most of the shops' partition walls were almost exactly 5 m. apart. The width of the colonnade mosaic was exactly 5 m. From front to back the shops were from 5 to 5.2 m. The width of the street was almost exactly 15 m., or three times the width of the colonnade. From the rough-finished areas on the stylobate, it was possible to tell that the columns of the colonnade were placed about 2 m. apart. It is possible that this is a reduction of 0.5 m. from a 2.5-m. interval in the early Roman phase. The column shafts of the Palaestra colonnade were 4.20 m. high, with pedestals 1.40 m. high. The original effect of columns 5.6 m. high can be judged from the re-erected columns and pedestals in the Palaestra (Figs. 220, 236; cf. 239).

In its final, Early Byzantine form the colonnade was rebuilt using disparate pieces gathered from many earlier buildings (Figs. 241, 243). Most of the capitals were Ionic, but Corinthian and Pergamene capitals were also found. Occasionally Attic bases for Ionic columns were reused as capitals by turning them upside down. Some short column shafts were raised to the correct height by placing them on pedestals rather than bases. Few, if any, new pieces were made for this phase, and parts which were too large or did not match were cut to fit. The last phase of the colonnade had a height of nearly 3 m., about half the size of the earlier phase.

The column shafts varied in diameter, but were usually about 0.35 m. Their smaller diameter and height were compensated by the use of a light, wooden entablature and beam structure, which supported a tile roof. This wood burned and collapsed in the Persian attack, forming a thick layer of ash, charcoal, and broken tiles on the colonnade floor. Most of the columns were found where they had fallen forward into the road. Two of the fallen column shafts had been incised with Latin crosses.

The flooring of the last phase of the colonnade was a mosaic of black and white tesserae (basalt and limestone) divided into square units of different patterns. Each square was separated from its neighbors by a frame with a guilloche pattern and conformed to a module of about 5 m. Patterns represented vine scrolls and leaves, circles, dots, and octagons containing squares. The entire mosaic is bordered by double guilloche and step forms.

Structure of the Shops

The structural system of the Byzantine Shops was a series of squared marble piers at their corners and door jambs (Figs. 239–243). The front wall was bonded to these piers, as were the partition walls. The partition walls abutted the south wall of the bath-gymnasium complex, but they did not bond with it. The piers were generally well cut, but were sometimes made of spoils from earlier buildings. The front and partition walls were made of mortared rubble, sometimes with brick leveling courses. Most of the stone used was fieldstone, but spoils often appeared. The mortar was friable and often little better than mud.

The Byzantine Shops were frequently altered by their owners, so it was common to find blocked-up doorways, niches roughly cut out of walls, enlarged doorways, and makeshift partition walls.

The Byzantine Shops were two-storied. Stairways existed in E4, E5, E7, and E12. Other shops probably had ladders to the second stories, as is frequent at Pompeii and Herculaneum.[18] The second stories had wooden floors which rested on rectangular or round wooden beams, which were let into holes cut out of the south wall of the bath-gymnasium complex and into put-log holes in the south wall of the shops. On top of the floorboards were placed bricks or square rooftiles; this is still a practice in modern Turkish village houses.

Above the second story were the slanted beams of the roof. Because of the collapse of the roof, it is uncertain whether these beams were continuous from the south wall of the bath-gymnasium complex (Fig. 207; reconstructed in Fig. 239) or if there were two rooflines, one for the second story, one for the colonnade. The latter solution seems more likely, because broken windowpanes were found with their leading. From their level, *96.60, they were in the upper story. If the colonnade had been continuous, the windows would have been right under the roof and almost useless. The roof was tiled, with the tiles resting on mud or plaster. During the day the open, bivalve doors of the lower stories allowed light and air to enter the shops from the colonnade. A few of the shops had first-story windows on the colonnade. E1 (Fig. 243), as a restaurant, served food through its window to customers in the colonnade. E8, whose first-story window was covered by an elaborate iron grille, presumably needed more light than the door afforded.

The floors of many of the shops were just packed earth, but shops whose floors had to be sturdier or impervious to liquids were made of bricks, rooftiles (Fig. 242), or even marble slabs (though this is unusual).

The inside walls of some of the shops still bore frescoes or fresco fragments. Frescoes can be inferred for some of the other shops from fragments found collapsed in the fill. Naturally, the collapse of the shops was most destructive to frescoes, so a dipinto found in E8 is a tantalizing but unreadable Greek inscription, smashed into hundreds of small fragments. On the back wall of E8, however, was a better preserved fresco showing a falling vase with red and black flowers and a black pannier of flowers flanking a square imitation of a fancy marble revetment. The shops varied so greatly that there were some with walls that were unplastered and unfrescoed as well.

The sanitary and waste disposal in the Byzantine Shops was achieved by vertical drains connected to a large drain running the full length of the complex along the back wall of the shops (Fig. 187). This drain connected with a large, barrel-vaulted drain which ran north-south under the Synagogue (Fig. 271; stage 1), Palaestra, and Long North Hall (Fig. 206), discharging downslope of the north side of the entire complex. The waste water from the bath-gymnasium was probably used to flush the whole system. Vertical drainpipes from the roof of bath-gymnasium complex buildings also entered the drain along the back of the shops at their corners.

Basins, vats, and large mortars which could also be used as vats in dyeing processes were found in several shops, most notably in E6 and W8–W9. These vats have drain holes in their lower sides, and the contents probably flowed into the main drain along the backs of the shops. This accounts for the placement of the vats in W8–W9 directly over the main drain.

The heating of the shops was done with braziers, as was the cooking in the restaurants. A well-preserved brazier was found in E4. Such braziers could have also been used to heat stones or bricks which may have been placed in vats to raise the bath temperature during dyeing.

Trades and Functions

In the Late Roman and Early Byzantine phase of occupation, the Byzantine Shops often served more than one function. It was common for the shopowner to live above the shop in which he worked, or in some cases, perhaps in the shop next door or nearby. Some of the shops were probably just storage areas. The people who lived and worked in the shops need not necessarily have been the owners, since wealthy owners might have lived elsewhere and hired workers to operate the shops for them.

On the whole the shops showed relatively little evidence of the production of goods, but much evidence of retail trade. Trades which involved production in the Byzantine Shops were paint and/or dyeshops (E6–E8, E13 and E14, W7 and W8). Restaurants cooked the food they sold, but did not produce it (E1–E2, W1–W3). Shops which sold hardware (E9–E11; Fig. 246) or glass vessels (Fig. 247) and windowpanes (E12) were strictly retail outlets. Practical reasons for this division between retail and production were lack of space and danger of fire. Smithies or glassworks would have endangered the entire central area of Sardis and required more room than a single or even multiple shop provided.

The presumed functions of the excavated Byzantine Shops (where known at all; Fig. 206, plan) are as follows: E1 and E2 (Fig. 243), restaurants; E2A, residence (converted from a dyeshop); E3, residence or restaurant; E4, residence or wineshop; E5, residence; E6–E8, paint and/or dye shop (E6, grinding room; E7, grinding and weighing room; E8, business office); E9–E11, retail hardware shop (Fig. 241); E12, retail glassware and windowpane shop; E13–E14 (Fig.

242), paint and/or dye shop; E15–E16, residences (?); E17, unknown; E18–E19, residences; W1–W3, restaurants; W4–W6, colonnade areas, not shops; W7, unknown; W8–W9, paint and/or dyeshop; W10–W11, unexcavated; W12, entrance to bath-gymnasium complex; W13, unknown.

The identifications of the functions just listed were made from the principal finds in each shop. The restaurants E1, E2, and W1–W3 contained many coarse black ware cooking pots. Occasionally, a fine red ware piece such as P 67.2:7284 (found in E1) occurred.[19] Especially important for the identification was the large number of food bones. Those identified from E1 included twenty sheep or goat bones, of which the highest percentage were mandibles and long bones (probably lamb chops and legs of lamb off which chunks could be cut for skewering); cow or horse (probably cow) bones numbered twenty-eight, over half of which were rib bones; three pig bones and mollusk shells occurred, suggesting that this restaurant would not have appealed to the Jews who lived and worked in the shops nearby. Knives and a small mortar were probably used in food preparation. E2 and W1–W3 had similar finds, so much so in W3 that it was nicknamed "the kitchen" during excavation. Benches inside and against the walls of E1 and E2 (Figs. 241, 243) were for patrons to sit on, while a column base was placed in front of the window of E1 for customers in the colonnade. A low brick bench was built into the colonnade in front of W1 for the same purpose.

Residence E2A (Fig. 243) contained household pottery and no large amounts of bones. That at one time it had been a dyeshop was inferred from the niche in the southwest corner with drain channels in the floor (filled with earth in the last phase) leading from it to the drain at the back of the shop.

Residence and/or restaurant E3 contained household pottery, but had benches similar to those in E1 and E2. Perhaps it had been a restaurant later converted into a residence.

Residence and/or wineshop E4 had the same household pottery along with two large bronze flasks with caps (M 67.29 and M 67.15). It also had a bronze brazier (M 67.5).[20] Residence E5 was the best furnished, containing a beautifully decorated ampulla with rabbits eating leaves with crosses on them on either side of a large Latin cross (Fig. 244); geese eating grapes were shown on the reverse (P 68.165). There was also a beautiful brass lamp in the shape of a lion with a cockle shell in its mouth (M 67.4; Fig. 245). An iron sword (M 68.23) and a dagger (uncatalogued) suggested the troubled state of the times.

The paint/dyeshops E6–E8 and E13 and E14 (which were probably all owned by a Jew, Jacob the Presbyter; Fig. 242) were identified from the quantities of red ochre, sulfur, a piece of Egyptian blue frit, and the numerous mortars and pestles used for grinding quantities of pigments. Steelyards and their weights were also found in E7 (M 67.31, one uncatalogued) and E13 (uncatalogued). Presumably different pigments were sold in different amounts and for different prices. Dyeshops W7 and W8 were identified by the large vat in the corner of W7.

The hardware store (E9–E11) had parts of 127 bronze and iron locks (Fig. 246), two sickles, two adze blades, some iron rings, a claw, a ladle, three chisels, one claw chisel, an iron sledgehammer head, two weights, and a bronze syrinx which had been bound with cloth. There was a large piece of iron, 0.195 × 0.14 × 0.1 m., which could have been used as a small anvil in lock assembly and repair.

The glass shop E12 contained 350 windowpanes, glass lamps, goblets (Fig. 247), concave vessel bases, and 7 or 8 globular vessels. From the number of windowpanes it seemed probable that the shop sold glass objects, not the contents of glass vessels. The frequent use of glazed windows in the shops themselves, modest as they were, suggested fairly general use of windowpanes.[21]

The preponderance of all the material found in the shops appeared to have been produced locally. All of the coarse red ware pottery had typically micaceous clay (the usual sign of Sardian clay),[22] and the coarse black ware was essentially the same but fired in a reducing atmosphere. The ochres in the paint and/or dye shops could have been made locally by burning ochre.[23] The "Egyptian blue" might have been imported, but the technique of its production was widely known.[24] The non-Sardian origin of some of the fine red ware objects seems likely, such as the plate with the cross (P 67.2; Fig. 282) and the ampulla (P 68.165; Fig. 244), but final word on many of the pieces must await further study.[25] A. von Saldern believed the glass at Sardis came predominantly from local works, and the metal objects were also presumably produced locally.[26]

Jews and Christians

Perhaps the most important discovery by the Harvard-Cornell Expedition for Late Antique studies was the Synagogue. The Byzantine Shops supplemented the evidence from the Synagogue with material of the following types: (1) epigraphic; (2) symbolic (religious symbols used as decoration on pottery and metal objects); and (3) legal (the presence of material such as pig bones, which would suggest a Christian owner by making a Jewish owner impossible).

The owners of restaurants E1, E2, and W1–W3 were Christians. The plate decorated with a Greek cross (P 67.2; Fig. 282) and the presence of pig bones and shellfish suggested this, as well as a graffito with a Latin cross and the name Kyriak . . . (Kyriakus) for E1 and E2. He may have been the owner of the restaurant. An ampulla (P 58.428) with a Latin cross embellished with circles was found in W1, which interconnected with W2. The residence/restaurant E3 had a Latin cross with a Rho top carved on the outside face of one of its west door jamb blocks. Residence/wineshop E4 had two mussel shells in it, implying a Christian owner. Residence E5 contained two ampullas with Christian symbols (P 68.165, Fig. 244; P 68.174). Paint/dye shops E6–E8 had a Jewish owner, probably the same Jacob who owned E14, since two graffiti mentioning him were found on pots in E7 (P 67.18; P 67.16). In E6 there was another graffito with the name Agumiou(?) with a branch-like design which might have been a lulav (P 67.17). On the inside face of a block of the west door jamb of E7, two menorahs were incised. The Jewish ownership of paint/dye shops E13–E14 (Fig. 242) was shown by three graffiti. Two of these found in E13 mentioned the names Theoktistos and Sabbatios; the last, found in E14, mentioned Jacob the Presbyter (of the Synagogue; P 62.371; P 62.394; P 62.23; IN 62.14). The presence of a small metal object with a cross on

it (M 62.90) may have been fortuitous, since a lamp with a Chi-Rho on its handle was found in a Jewish catacomb at Beth She'arim. The glass shop, E12, contained a graffito of the name John (P 67.147), a name that might be either Christian or Jewish. The discovery of a menorah incised on a marble slab (S 64.55) in the upper story fill of this shop made the Jewish denomination certain. The owners of the dye shops W7–W8 were certainly Christians because of Latin crosses on orbs decorating a vat in W8.

Comparisons

Similar buildings to the Byzantine Shops at Sardis have been excavated, were depicted in reliefs or mosaics, or also had evidence involving Jews, Christians, or trades attested at Sardis. Those most similar on architectural grounds have been found at Ephesus, Pergamon, Perge, and Side in Asia Minor. The closest of these to Sardis shops was the colonnaded street called the Arkadiane at Ephesus, which is similar in masonry style, shop width, colonnade width, street width, and probable date of construction (ca. 400 A.D.)[27] Only the diameter of the columns was substantially different; those at Ephesus were larger, more like the earlier phase of the Sardis colonnade. The colonnaded streets at Pergamon (Asklepieion),[28] Perge,[29] and Side[30] were similar in dimensions, except for larger column diameter, but different in masonry styles. These colonnades used rectangular, rather roughly dressed ashlar, as opposed to the Sardian and Ephesian mortared rubble and fieldstone with ashlar piers.

Dye shops have been found in the Ophel of Jerusalem which were destroyed in A.D. 612.[31] Another of Roman date was excavated at Athribis in Egypt.[32] A glass shop was found at Beth She'arim.[33] Restaurants were found at Pompeii and Ostia, although the former were built prior to A.D. 79.

Representations in mosaic or relief of trades found at Sardis were depicted at Antioch, where the border of the "Topographical Mosaic" shows wineshops and restaurants with patrons sitting on folding chairs similar to those found at Sardis.[34] Reliefs from Rome showed a hardware store,[35] while two others from Florence show cloth merchants before a colonnade.[36] Although these reliefs were made much earlier (first century A.D.) than the Byzantine Shops, the same sort of commercial life probably existed at both periods.

JSC

IX

The Synagogue and the Jewish Community

ANDREW R. SEAGER

A. THOMAS KRAABEL

The Building

Discovery and Excavation

The Synagogue enjoys one of the more prominent sites in the city, at what seems to have been the civic center of the Roman and Early Byzantine periods. It is not a freestanding building, but part of the monumental Roman bath and gymnasium complex described in the previous chapter (Fig. 206). It occupies the southeast part of the complex (0–N20/E34–E117), flanked by the palaestra of the gymnasium and a row of shops along the colonnaded Main Avenue, the principal thoroughfare of the city. Another colonnaded street runs along the front of the Synagogue, to the east, joining the Main Avenue at what seems to have been a public plaza or forum, at least from the late fifth century onward; a raised platform perhaps for speaking was built in the roadway just north of the intersection, and a rectangular monument was added over the pavement of the Main Avenue just around the corner. The upper walls and roof of the Synagogue would have been clearly visible rising above the shops and road colonnades (Fig. 207), and citizens walking past would have been able to look directly inside, when the doors were open, through the entire length of both rooms (Figs. 251, 253, 279).

There may have been a Jewish quarter nearby, in areas as yet unexcavated, but (at least in later years) the Synagogue was certainly not in the *midst* of a Jewish quarter. Jewish and Christian merchants were trading side by side in the shops outside the Synagogue at the time the area was abandoned, and the nearest contemporary dwelling house known, in the House of Bronzes (HoB) sector south of the Main Avenue, contained Christian objects and may have belonged to a high church official.[1]

In its final form, the Synagogue consists of two principal rooms: a colonnaded entrance court (Forecourt) and a long assembly hall (Main Hall). Both rooms are the same width, aligned on an axis which is emphasized by the symmetrical arrangement of furnishings. Together they occupy an area 20 m. wide and nearly 85 m. long. One door leads to the Forecourt from the east, on axis. Another door opens from the south, from the Main Avenue, through a short corridor between two of the shops (Figs. 206, 252:u, z).

Forecourt

The Forecourt had the form of a peristyle, roofed around the periphery but open to the sky in the middle (Figs. 206, 207, 253). Enough pieces were preserved to show that the colonnade originally extended around all four sides of the court, and also that there were originally fourteen columns in all: four at the corners plus three others along each of the north and south sides and two more at the east and west. The corner columns were heart-shaped in plan, and had Ionic capitals of an elegant and interesting design. Three of these capitals survived (Fig. 251). The colonnade may have been two stories high originally, though only one story has been restored; a two-story court would have been more in keeping with the scale of the Main Hall beyond (Fig. 207).

A fountain in the form of a large marble crater with volute handles stood in the center of the court (Fig. 251) and was served by an elaborate system of water pipes under the floor (there were two sets of pipes actually, one laid down when the fountain was first installed and the other put in later, in a renovation). A valve was fitted on the supply pipe to control the water flow.[2]

The walls of the court were initially covered with plaster, of which only traces remain. The floor was paved with stone mosaics around the outside of the colonnade laid out in carpet-like panels in complex and multicolored geometric patterns.[3] Four of the panels contain donor inscriptions in Greek. One reads: "Aurelios Polyippos, pious, having made a vow, I fulfilled it." The other three inscriptions are similar, but record the names of different benefactors (Fig. 254, Aurelios Eulogios).[4]

A balustrade of open-work screens ran from column to column around the court, separating the fountain area from the surrounding mosaic-paved sections. These may have been later additions, however. The balustrade top-rails are inscribed; one of them mentions a restoration or reconstruction, *ananeosis* in Greek.[5]

Perhaps as part of this same *ananeosis,* the plaster on the walls was removed and replaced by marble revetments. The marble pieces were installed a few centimeters from the wall, attached by metal hooks, and then secured by pouring mortar in the narrow space behind (Fig. 263). The decorative scheme included an arched frieze in shallow relief depicting urns and doves within bands of architectural ornament.[6] The recessed areas of the relief had been filled with red pigment, still faintly visible, to bring out the pattern.

The simply furnished Forecourt (Fig. 251) served as an anteroom or gathering place for entry into the Main Hall. It may also have housed certain community functions not directly connected with worship which did not require special facilities: public discussions and discourses, announcements, perhaps even study and instruction. There were no cooking facilities inside, however; a communal kitchen, if the Sardis Jews had one, must have been located elsewhere.[7] The fountain, the central feature of the court, probably served for the washing of hands before prayer. If this was the "Fountain of the Synagogue" (*krene tou synagogiou*) mentioned in an inscription listing public fountains at Sardis and their capacities,[8] then the Forecourt was a public space, accessible to anyone wishing to use it.

Thin partition walls forming a narthex cut off the west end of the court (Fig. 252, at mosaic panels N1 and S1) were late additions, prompted perhaps by a desire for greater differentiation of the space to accommodate varied activities or perhaps to gain more privacy for activities in the Main Hall. These partitions (which may not have risen all the way to the roof) were installed atop the mosaics, and after the revetments had been applied over the adjoining walls. A marble basin on a tall pedestal, not connected to water pipes, was found against the east side of the southern partition wall.[9]

Main Hall

Three doors (the northern one later blocked up) led from the Forecourt to the Main Hall, itself nearly 60 m. long (Figs. 252, 253, 258). It has been estimated that the Main Hall could hold nearly a thousand people[10] Two rows of massive piers, six on each side of the hall, rose to a height estimated to have been at least 9 m. above the floor.[11] There may have been a clerestory above the piers, adding an additional 5–6 m. in height. The roof itself probably was of timber trusses. Two pedimented shrines on masonry platforms stood against the entrance wall at the east, flanking the central door (Figs. 253, NS, SS, 266, 274). At the opposite, west end is a broad apse, occupying almost the entire width of the hall except for a narrow chamber on its south side. A three-tiered bank of semicircular benches at the base of the apse provided the only permanent seating (Figs. 253, 256, 257) separated from the rest of the hall by a railing.[12]

In front of the apse stood a huge marble table, unique in synagogues as far as we know, made up of stones from an earlier building or buildings. Its top was broken by the collapse of the roof and walls, but its supports—decorated with Roman eagles clutching thunderbolts—were still standing upright (Figs. 256, 257). The head of each eagle has been knocked off. The table was approached from the side of the apse and benches (west), where there is a pavement of polished marble slabs. Two pairs of marble lions (also in reuse here, perhaps associated with an image of Cybele originally!) flanked the table, standing guard (Figs. 256, 258). The heads of the lions have been battered but not entirely defaced.[13]

The floor of the Main hall was mosaic (Figs. 257–259, 267)—except for the area west of the table—in intricate geometric designs like those in the Forecourt for the most part. Again there are donor inscriptions (Figs. 260, 261). One panel, prominently placed in the semicircle of the apse, is a finely crafted figurative design showing twining vines growing from a golden, water-filled urn similar to the crater in the Forecourt. Here the inscription is in a brilliantly colored wreath. Two peacocks which flanked the urn were cut out in antiquity, but the tips of their crests and the outlines of their tails are still visible (Fig. 260).[14] The walls were covered with marble revetments, at least in their lower portions. Small pieces of carefully cut colored stones formed inlay panels of geometric, floral, and animal designs (including pomegranates, fish, and birds, but no human shapes) set within an architectonic frame (Figs. 262, 264, 265).[15] There was painted decoration too, according to an inscription, probably on the clerestory or the ceiling.[16] Bits of brightly colored glass mosaic from upper walls were found among the collapsed pier masonry.[17] Illuminated by daylight coming through windows high up in the walls or by many lamps at night, the colors and patterns covering so many surfaces must have been splendid, indeed.

One (or perhaps both) of the shrines on the entrance wall (Figs. 258, 266, 274) must have been a repository for the Torah, the scrolls of the Old Testament constituting the Jewish law; Torah shrines depicted in mosaics and on glass vessels are often just such pedimented structures.[18] The Torah would thus be housed at the end of the hall nearest Jerusalem. That there are two shrines at Sardis instead of one occurs in part at least because the building was not in-

tended originally as a synagogue but had to be adapted for that purpose. All of the fragments of Hebrew inscriptions (Fig. 269) found in the building lay at the foot of the southern shrine, and here too was a neatly incised marble plaque (Fig. 249) showing a seven-branched menorah, a *lulav* (palm branch), a *shofar* (ram's horn),[19] and two spirals which have been interpreted as Torah scrolls (Fig. 250).[20]

The table at the opposite end of the hall probably was used as a lectern for readings. Flanked by the guardian lions, the reader would have faced Jerusalem and the congregation simultaneously (Figs. 256, 257, 258). The table itself is an addition, its supports set into the floor in such a way that the mosaic pattern is interrupted. An earlier structure apparently stood on the same spot, however, and probably served the same purpose. The benches behind the table, on which seventy or more people could be seated (Figs. 256, 257), were most likely reserved for the community leaders, the "elders."

There was another furnishing in the hall, not yet mentioned, added some time after the mosaics were laid down. All that remains of it are four stone slabs set into the floor in the very center of the hall (Fig. 253) forming a square not quite 3 m. on each side. A dowel hole cut in the top of each stone once held a lightweight upright of some sort. A mosaic inscription in the midst of the four stones (Fig. 267, at top) is also secondary and may have been added at the same time. The inscription refers to a donation by a member of the community who was a "priest and *sophodidaskalos*" (wise teacher? teacher of wisdom? rabbi?). The association suggests that the four-pillared structure was the object which the *sophodidaskalos* gave, and further that it was the place from which he taught.[21] For a long time the structure was thought to have been a bima, or raised platform,[22] but a major difficulty with this interpretation has not been satisfactorily overcome: a platform at a plausible height would have obscured the inscription! The structure may instead have been a baldacchino or tabernacle, the four posts supporting a canopy overhead.

Two features long thought to be typical of assembly halls in ancient synagogues are absent at Sardis. There were no benches lining the side walls; worshipers must have stood or sat on the floor, perhaps on mats. There was neither evidence of a gallery or balcony to provide for women at worship separately from the men, nor a suitable staircase from which a balcony could be reached. Apparently women either prayed together with the men or were excluded from the assembly hall entirely.

Menorahs

More than a dozen representations of menorahs were found in and around the building in addition to the incised plaque already mentioned (Fig. 250)—carved in stone, scratched in pottery, cut from sheet bronze, and appliquéd on glass (Fig. 273). Such representations are reasonably common from Jewish settings. Much rarer is a real menorah from antiquity, with provision for attaching lamps. Part of one such menorah, originally with seven arms, was found in the Main Hall (Fig. 268). Carved from marble, it was about a meter wide when intact, but unfortunately it was burned in a fire and broken following the building's destruction. A bronze piece which may be from another, metal menorah was also found in the hall, and an inscription records the donation of a menorah by a man who may have been a goldsmith.[23]

Inscriptions

The great majority of inscriptions from the Synagogue are in Greek. There were over eighty Greek inscriptions all told, nearly all of them in mosaic on the floor or carved in marble plaques (Figs. 275, 277) which were mounted on the walls as part of the decorative scheme. These give information about members of the community and about some architectural features. Most of the inscriptions pertain to the gift of interior decorations (Fig. 270) and furnishings made in fulfillment of vows. One of them refers to the marble inlay decoration of the *nomophylakion* (Fig. 275), "the place that protects the Law," which must be the Torah shrine. The donors' names are often followed by the title "citizen of Sardis." Eight men are also identified as members of the city council (*bouleutes*), a hereditary position open only to the wealthier families in Greek cities under the Late Empire. One donor was a citizen and council member of the neighboring city of Hypaipa. Other office holders mentioned are an assistant in the state archives

(Fig. 272), a former procurator, and a count (Fig. 278). Three donors are identified as having been goldsmiths. Of the few inscriptions which do not pertain to donations, the most intriguing is a rectangular marble plaque (Fig. 276) found outside one of the doors to the Synagogue (where it may have been moved by plunderers after the building was abandoned). It enjoins, in Greek, "Having found and having broken open, read and observe."[24]

There are only a few fragments in Hebrew from the Synagogue, and only two are legible. One says *shalom* ("peace"; Fig. 269). The other, according to I. Rabinowitz, reads "Verus," perhaps honoring the co-Emperor Lucius Verus who ruled (with Marcus Aurelius) in A.D. 161–169. If so, the inscription must have been removed from its original position and reinstalled, for the wall from which the fragment apparently fell was built a century and a half after Verus' death.[25]

Earlier Building Stages

The land around the bath-gymnasium complex and Synagogue had been mostly abandoned during the late Hellenistic period, following the reorganization (*synoikismos*) of the city ordered by Antiochus III. A broad area of the lower city for several hundred meters on both sides of the Pactolus was then devoted to cemeteries and some small industrial operations (Plan III). Several late Hellenistic chamber tombs were excavated in the HoB sector south of the modern highway (Fig. 186). A Hellenistic mausoleum, never finished, lay beneath the south wall of the Synagogue (Fig. 187).[26]

Reurbanization of this district came about after the earthquake which rocked Sardis and several other cities of Asia Minor in A.D. 17. The bath-gymnasium and the surrounding streets were apparently laid out as part of this Roman "urban renewal" (Figs. 8, 206). Massive earth-moving operations were undertaken to form an artificial platform for the complex at a level well above the Hellenistic cemetery (Fig. 187, section 1). The complex remained under construction for a long time, perhaps two centuries, and underwent several alterations even after it was substantially completed.[27]

The area now occupied by the Synagogue was one of the more extensively and repeatedly remodeled parts of the complex. Numerous soundings were conducted below the mosaic floor in the Synagogue from 1964 to 1971 (Fig. 248), proceeding as mosaics were lifted for conservation. These soundings produced evidence of four distinct building stages, all within the same building boundaries and with floors at nearly the same level, but with substantially different plans (Fig. 271).[28] We are dealing, then, with a building that took shape over centuries, each stage influenced to some extent by its predecessors. Judging from the plans of the several stages, the site was turned over to the Jewish community for use as a synagogue only after having served other, secular functions for many years.

The original plan for the complex (stage 1) called for a suite of three rooms of roughly equal size along the south side of the Palaestra, with doors opening northward. The counterpart to the Synagogue on the north side of the Palaestra, Building LNH (Fig. 206), retains exactly this arrangement apart from a few Byzantine alterations; the Palaestra was to have been flanked by symmetrical buildings on the north and south. Both buildings seem to have been designed to serve the bathing and gymnastic activities in some capacity, perhaps as places for exercise, undressing, or storage.[29]

The southern building was never completed in its originally intended form. Some of the foundations begun according to that plan were abandoned, and those parts of the dividing walls which had risen above floor level were razed. The new plan (stage 2) was quite different. It consisted of a small vestibule at the east, open now to the streets bordering the complex rather than to the Palaestra, and a long basilican hall at the west. The hall was divided into a "nave" and "aisles" by two rows of columns, probably in two stories. The pavement was of polished marble slabs, in the "nave" at least; portions of this floor still survive. The apse appeared pretty much in its present form except that it was pierced by three niches and two diagonal passageways originally, all of which were later walled up. The passages probably emerged on a dais, ca. 1.5 m. above the floor, which was subsequently removed. No objects were found from which to judge the use of the building at this stage, but the plan itself leaves little doubt: stage 2 probably was a Roman civil basilica, with a *tribunal* in

the apse and the niches used for displaying statues of divinities or emperors.[30]

A third stage is attested by a small detail: the remains of marble revetments installed *after* the dividing wall between hall and vestibule of stage 2 was torn down but *before* the partition of the final plan was built. Little more is known with certainty. Stage 3 need not have been radically different from stage 2. The wall between hall and vestibule might have been opened up to merge the two rooms more fully while the rest of the structure was left pretty much intact. This is the minimal alteration which meets the evidence, though there may have been other adjustments as well. The uncertainty about the plan of the building in stage 3 extends also to its use. It may have continued as a civil basilica, or it may already have become a synagogue. This will be discussed further below.

Stage 4, then, is the Synagogue in substantially its final form. It came about after a thorough remodeling, involving not only renewal of the floor and wall surfaces but also some major structural alterations. The Forecourt was created, and in the new, shorter hall which resulted, the apse was converted to serve a new purpose. Also, a new focus was made at the opposite, east end of the hall by adding the shrines. The surviving donor inscriptions refer only to the interior decorations and furnishings, but the Jewish community must have been responsible for the structural changes as well.

Dating

Site work and the building of foundations for the bath-gymnasium complex were largely done during the first century A.D.; the earth fill for the artificial terrace on which the complex stands contains mostly Hellenistic and early Roman Imperial material. The upper parts were not finished until much later, however, with work progressing from west to east. The western block of rooms was complete in its main lines by the middle of the second century. Construction of the Palaestra, in the eastern half of the complex, continued into the century following (Fig. 207).[31]

The Synagogue could not have risen much faster than the Palaestra. Work was still proceeding according to the stage 1 plan well into the second century, judging from the masonry techniques used for the stage 1 walls. The revised plan—stage 2—was still under construction in the early part of the third century, if frieze blocks built into the apse foundation are correctly dated to the Severan period. Nothing was found in the bedding layers for the stage 2 floor or in the fill below which would provide a more precise date. The only coin from the bedding for the stage 2 floor is an issue of M. Aurelius Caesar (ruled A.D. 161–180) or Commodus (ruled A.D. 180–192).[32]

For dating stages 3 and 4 we have the far greater number of coins found in the thin (up to 0.30 m.) and disrupted layer above the stage 2 floor but below the final mosaics. This layer was rich in pottery, lamps, and other objects as well, but these could not be dated as closely as the coins. Nothing was noted among the other objects that contradicts the coin evidence.

There were about 400 coins from the layer just below the final floor all told, of which more than 300 were well enough preserved to be identified. Of these, 150 were recorded as lying beneath intact sections of the pavement (123 in the Forecourt, Fig. 254, and 27 in the Main Hall, Fig. 278); the remainder were from areas of mosaic loss. Because of the large number of sealed coins, the mosaics can be dated with some assurance to the middle decades of the fourth century A.D., with a few areas of later replacement and repair. Installation began in the Main Hall, where with one exception the latest of the sealed coins is dated A.D. 346–350 (Figs. 256–258).[33] In the Forecourt, most of the panels (Fig. 251) were installed in the period A.D. 360 to A.D. 370 or 380, according to the coin evidence. Two panels along the west side of the court (Fig. 254) are evidently somewhat later than the others; they may be replacements for sections damaged by a leak in the underlying water conduits.

The date for the floor is an upper limit for all major structural work in the building. The benches in the apse (Fig. 256), the piers in the Main Hall, the shrines and the wall which supports them, and the Forecourt peristyle (Figs. 251, 253) all must have been in place before the adjacent mosaics were laid down. A lower limit for much of the remodeling is provided, though not as firmly, by a coin of A.D. 321–324 found beneath some column fragments buried in the apse as supports for the benches and the apse mosaic (Fig. 260).[34] Assuming that the fragments

came from the colonnades which earlier held up the Main Hall roof, then the coin gives an approximate date for the destruction of those colonnades and for the erection of the massive piers which replaced them. The Synagogue in its final form thus seems to have taken shape beginning a decade or two before the middle of the fourth century, perhaps a bit earlier, (i.e., 320–340), with installation of the mosaics continuing a decade or more after mid-century.[35]

What, then, of stage 3? Indirect evidence comes from the fact that coins in the layer just below the mosaics in the Main Hall were stratified. Eight coins from the Main Hall were found at or near the bottom of this layer (below *96.15), and the latest of these are dated A.D. 270. All later coins were at higher levels. This stratification suggests a floor of the late third century (Fig. 259), torn up and replaced by the final mosaics about seventy or eighty years later. A date of ca. A.D. 270 for stage 3 cannot be far wrong; there is little leeway in light of evidence that stage 2 was finished not much more than half a century before that date, while the final floor followed by roughly the same interval.

On historical grounds, Kraabel believes that the most likely time for the building to have been given over to the Jews and made into a synagogue was before the reign of Constantine I, probably during the third century A.D.[36] If so, then stage 3 would be the Synagogue in its third century condition. Archaeologically there is not much evidence, except that some donor inscriptions from the Synagogue (Fig. 270) (and some of the pilaster capitals as well) were originally thought to date from the earlier period.[37] If some of the donor inscriptions somehow survived from stage 3, then stage 3 was certainly a synagogue. There is, however, a problem: throughout the building, wherever the meeting of mosaics and wall revetments could be observed, the revetments were found to have been applied *after* the mosaics were in place, and the mosaics in general are now firmly dated to the fourth century. The donor inscriptions on marble plaques can predate the mosaics only under one of two assumptions: (1) upper portions of the wall decoration were left intact while lower portions were replaced, or (2) donor plaques were carefully removed from the walls, saved, and reinstalled as part of the fourth century remodeling.

Later Alterations

Work continued on the building even after the fourth century A.D., though there were no further major structural alterations. The marble revetments on the walls of the Main Hall (Figs. 262–265) took two or three generations to complete, judging from the donor inscriptions, and there seems to have been a renewal or restoration of the Main Hall revetments still later, after the initial work was finished.[38] Other changes have already been noted. In the Forecourt, the wall revetments in their entirety were later additions, replacing the earlier wall covering of painted plaster (Fig. 254, upper left). Floor mosaics were repaired periodically, and some whole panels were replaced. Also, the pipe system serving the fountain was replaced by a second, parallel set of pipes. The four-pillared structure in the center of the hall (Figs. 252, 267) and the table in front of the apse were added (the table apparently replacing a similar structure which earlier stood on the same spot), and a narthex was created out of the west end of the Forecourt.

Several of these alterations may have been undertaken at the same time, as part of a general restoration in the bath-gymnasium and surrounding areas which seems to have occurred in the second half of the fifth century A.D., perhaps in response to an earthquake.[39] Other changes undoubtedly were made separately from the general *ananeosis* and for different reasons, continuing through at least the middle of the sixth century.

Craftsmanship declined in the later years, but no more rapidly in the Synagogue than in other parts of the complex and in other excavated buildings in the city too. The decline evidently represents deteriorating economic conditions not for the Jewish community alone but for Sardis at large,[40] and should not be taken as evidence of discriminatory measures against non-Christians. In any event, reasonably ambitious alterations indicating some degree of continuing prosperity were being made in the Synagogue long after Theodosius II banned the repair of synagogues except if they were in imminent danger of collapse. This law, promulgated in A.D. 438, apparently was not enforced at Sardis, and may not often have been enforced elsewhere.[41]

Coins found in the Synagogue continue through the early seventh century, and then cease abruptly; the Synagogue was abandoned along with the rest of the known city in A.D. 616, and partially destroyed. There is no evidence of activity anywhere in the area for several decades afterward, until ca. A.D. 660, when the Byzantine government under Constans II undertook a renewal of the main road and the Acropolis fortifications.[42] The troops or workers engaged in the road construction operated a limekiln in the suite of rooms immediately west of the Synagogue (Fig. 219), where they burned marble collected from the surrounding spaces.[43] A crude, tunnel-like passage cut through the wall between one of these rooms and the chamber south of the Synagogue apse probably was made by the road builders as a shortcut for carrying pieces to the kiln.[44] Two small rooms formed by partitioning off the eastern corners of the Forecourt may also have been the work of the road-building crews.[45]

The Jewish community was apparently dispersed after A.D. 616. No evidence is preserved in either the archaeological or the historical records of Judaism in Lydia from A.D. 616 until the fifteenth century.[46]

Restoration and Reconstruction

A partial reconstruction of the Synagogue was undertaken according to the terms of an agreement with the Turkish government in order to display the major discoveries in context and to preserve certain features which were already showing signs of deterioration from exposure.

In 1965, Alan M. Shapiro, then of the firm of Graves and Shapiro, began design and construction studies and proposals. Since 1967, all subsequent development in research, design and construction has been directed by A. R. Seager (Fig. 253).[47] The gigantic task of lifting, consolidating, and resetting ca. 12,915 sq. ft. (1,200 sq. m.) of mosaics was supervised by L. J. Majewski (Figs. 254, 259, 260, 267, 278, 279). It took from 1966 to 1973, with follow-up treatment lasting into 1975. The study and reconstruction of partial samples of marble revetments (Figs. 263–266) were undertaken by L. J. Majewski in collaboration with R. E. Stone, several Turkish architects and engineers, and epigraphist J. H. Kroll.[48] Seager also produced a catalogue of the decorative architectural parts of the building.[49]

The work began in earnest in 1967, starting with the two shrines. The masonry platforms for the shrines were raised to their full height and the wall behind built up to a level needed to support the entablatures. The "Tuscan" columns of the south shrine are the originals, repaired, with new capitals modeled after fragments found during excavation. The original north shrine columns, with spirally-fluted shafts, were badly fractured and were replaced by new marble columns turned on a lathe. The pediments of both shrines are the ancient stones, but the entablatures, which were missing, are entirely modern in the reconstruction (Figs. 266, 274).[50]

Other walls were raised to heights between ca. 1.0 m. and ca. 3.3 m., tallest where samples of the wall decoration were to be installed. The revetments as restored (Fig. 266, right) are conjectural in several details, but the overall outlines (and colors) of the decorative scheme are known from the combined evidence of the pieces found during excavations (pilaster shafts, bases, capitals, moldings, and friezes; Figs. 263, 264–265), the pattern of holes left by metal hooks which held the marble pieces in place (often the hooks were still *in situ*), and impressions which remained in the mortar backing (Fig. 263).[51] The lower course of the marble dado was pretty much intact all around and was preserved wherever possible. The inlay panels on the Main Hall walls were made from new stones shaped like the original *skoutlosis* pieces, many of which make up patterns found also in the mosaics. Red pigment was applied in the letters of the inscriptions and in the recessed areas of the arched frieze in the Forecourt, where traces of red remained from antiquity.[52]

In the Forecourt (Fig. 251) the preserved parts of the corner columns were reerected, and the remainder of the colonnade was cast in concrete.[53]

The floor mosaics were disintegrating rapidly, even when kept under an earth cover and even though edges of the loss areas had been cemented as a conservation measure. In consequence, the entire floor was lifted (in sections) and reset in modern mortar. The original apse mosaic (Fig. 260) and the inscription panels were replaced with hand-painted casts (Fig. 261).[54]

The supports for the table, the flanking lion statues (Figs. 256–258), and the crater which served as a fountain in the Forecourt (Fig. 251) are also casts of the originals.[55] The fountain was fitted with pipes so that it might be filled again some day, though there is no accessible water source at present.

Miscellaneous Furnishings and Finds

The major stationary furnishings have been described above, and Kraabel mentions yet another, a peculiar round Corinthian tempietto-shaped base (SYN 62.20; Fig. 256). Undoubtedly the Synagogue had plenty of textile adornments such as hangings and curtains, and vessels of precious metals and glass, but these were either plundered or saved by the congregation before the building was abandoned. Nowhere in the Synagogue was there a great accumulation of special vessels or lamps to indicate a particular function, but some objects were found which give hints of possible use. Among them are fragments of two miniature marble structures, one inscribed and the other part of a four-column building (tetrapylon).[56] Aurelius Basileides, former procurator,[57] gave something—another menorah?—on a small pedestal (Fig. 272). The heads of a sheep and a camel in marble-inlay (*skoutlosis*) technique (Fig. 262) may be parts of "marble-pictures" rather than the normal wall decoration.[58] Lions, birds (doves, peacocks), fish and dolphins were the animals seen in the Sardis Synagogue.[59] The Synagogue was undoubtedly lit by many lamps; the nobler kind, in bronze, is represented by chains and hooks. One chain was found near the south shrine.[60] Some clay lamps were also found.[61] Two fine bronze lion heads may come from a wooden chest, but since they were found outside the synagogue it is not quite certain where they belong.[62] A "grillos" gem[63] is probably not a sign of Gnostic leanings but, like the gem with a nude girl found in Jacob's shop,[64] a thoughtless use of gem devices current among their pagan fellow citizens.

The truly significant object was the menorah (Figs. 250, 268); a list of those known is given below. Some of them pose interesting questions—what, for instance, was weighted with the very small glass weights (Fig. 273)?[65] What was eaten from the bowls on which menorahs were incised?

Finally, there is a lamp which appears to have been found below the level of the synagogue

Menorah representations from the Synagogue
Main Hall:

T 63.41:5574	Brick with menorah. Photo 63.63:21
S 62.27a,b:4502	Incised menorah
Unnumbered	Stone fragment found under Eagle Table with incised menorah
S 62.26:4501	Menorah plaque by south shrine. Figs. 249, 250
M 63.55:5835	Sheet metal menorah
Kroll #76	Menorah incised on slab with inscription in round medallion. 73.91:36 (Seager, *Synagogue,* fig. 31). Fig. 277

Forecourt:

Kroll #72	Crowning member with menorah and accompanying objects, plus depiction of shrine?
Syn 68.14	Stylobate block with scribed menorah—see catalogue of architectural fragments

West Rooms:

P 66.173:7231	Sherd with menorah, and *lulav* on Roman white slip bowl. Photo 66.137:26,28
P 66.83:7112	Sherd with menorah on interior of plain red bowl.

Shops:

S 64.55:6587	Part of menorah? deeply and neatly grooved in marble slab. Photo 64.173:19 Were there others in the shop?
Unnumbered	Two menorahs incised on inside wall of shop E7; *BASOR* 215, 52

Main Road:

Unnumbered	Menorah incised on step of lion monument opposite shop E18, at E109/S11.70, *97.50, photo 73.8:7. *BASOR* 215, 52

Pa:

G 67.5	Menorah appliqué on glass. *Sardis* M6 (1980) *Glass* no. 674, pl. 16. Fig. 273.

NoEx:

S 66.8:7011	Incised menorah?

Summary: Sixteen representations listed here, plus two in the round (M 63.42 and Socrates menorah, Fig 268), also inscription #66 referring to the donation of a menorah, give a total of nineteen.

---

floor, and hence cannot belong to the latest synagogue. It is a lamp of late Hellenistic–early Roman type with premolded inscription: TO PHOS AGATHON—"The Good Light." This need mean no more than "this is a good lamp"; yet one wonders whether it was not intended to express some kind of *Lichtsymbolik*—if it belonged to an earlier synagogue.[66]

Mention has been made of the epichoric inscription in an unknown language built into a pier of the Synagogue (Fig. 157), of the Cybele shrine (Fig. 150),[67] and of other archaic sculptures. The inscribed stone may have been built into the walls before the building became a synagogue, but there can be no doubt that the relief of Artemis and Cybele (Fig. 93)[68] was put into the Forecourt face down by Jewish builders. They were obviously unafraid of these pagan demons, though few of them would know after a while that they were trampling on these abominations as the righteous man on the asp and the basilisk (Psalm 90:13). Given the high importance of these goddesses in pagan Sardis, the use of these stones in the Synagogue by permission of the city authorities who were closing the temples is another sign of the secure status of the Jewish community under Constantine and immediately thereafter.

An enigmatic find was made in 1970 in a small room at the east corner of the Synagogue, known as the "Packed Columns Area" (PCA; Fig. 252, south of "v") from the column shafts laid north-south over the floor in a very late phase of the Synagogue. Scattered between the columns and along a bench at the west wall were some 500 coins, mostly small cash, from the mid-fourth to the early seventh century A.D. Traces of a metal object led to a suggestion that this might have been the "poor box" of the Synagogue.[69]

Comparisons

What is perhaps most striking about the Sardis Synagogue from an architectural point of view is the extent to which it differs from other synagogues of the era. It has certain features in common with other synagogues, to be sure, notably the repository for the Torah on the wall of the assembly hall nearest Jerusalem. Taken as a whole, however, the building has no close parallels. It is far larger than any other extant ancient synagogue, first of all, and it occupies an unexpectedly prominent location. It lacks benches along the side walls of the assembly hall and apparently it had no women's gallery, yet these are features thought for a long time to have been standard. On the other hand, it has certain features which are unique among ancient synagogues, including the semicircular benches in the apse and the table in front of them, the twin shrines opposite, and the marble-inlay wall decoration.

Other synagogues have an overall plan organization very much like that at Sardis (Fig. 271:4): a colonnaded entry court followed by a basilical hall and an apse, all lined up on axis. Beth Alpha in present-day Israel is the best-known example.[70] The resemblance here is partly circumstantial, however. Among apsidal synagogues in general, the apse served as a repository for the Torah, typically occupying the Jerusalem-oriented wall. At Sardis the apse is a leftover from an earlier building stage, and it occupies the wall *away* from Jerusalem. It was reused, but not for the Torah. A place for the Torah was built at the *opposite* end of the hall.

The distinctiveness of the Sardis Synagogue should not be taken as proof that its builders departed from some canonical standard of design. It is, rather, part of the growing evidence that there was *no* clear-cut universal canon for synagogue architecture in the ancient world. The synagogue as a building type was a flexible conception, its form and materials determined to a

great extent by local circumstances and the locally prevailing architectural idiom. This has been demonstrated convincingly for the Diaspora, where circumstances of Jewish life and the relationship between Jews and the majority population could vary widely from city to city.[71] It seems to have been true in the Holy Land as well.

Two major synagogue types have long been recognized in the Holy Land. In the "early" or "Galilean" type, traditionally dated to the second and third centuries A.D., the facade typically faces Jerusalem. There is no permanent place in the assembly hall for the Torah, which is thought to have been carried in and out as needed. The "later" or "Byzantine" type, to which Beth Alpha belongs, has an apse for the Torah, typically on the Jerusalem-oriented wall.[72] Michael Avi-Yonah of the Hebrew University interposed a third, "transitional" type to account for synagogues which do not fit either of the original categories. These, he argued, resulted from "a period of experimentation with various architectural forms" such that "no two synagogues of that period are entirely similar."[73] Even so, he saw enough commonality among ancient synagogues of all types that he could conclude, in 1961, that "their homogeneity is assured owing to the uniform worship they served, and to a large extent also by their geographical proximity."[74] A decade later, however, Avi-Yonah altered his view. He perceived instead a "bewildering variety of plans" which "precludes any attempt to use them as a basis to determine chronology." Consequently, "the whole question of the development of synagogal plans from the third to the sixth century will have to be reconsidered, allowing more weight perhaps to local variants than to an overall style to be encountered throughout the country."[75]

The reconsideration which Avi-Yonah recommended is not complete, but this much is clear: ancient synagogues are not all basilicas with benches along the side walls; they are not all oriented to Jerusalem; evidence for women's galleries is scarce;[76] many examples do not fit neatly into well-defined categories; the established types may be local rather than universal forms. Ancient Judaism was far less monolithic than most scholars thought until recently, certainly as far as its architecture is concerned. The Diaspora will have to figure more prominently in the reevaluation than it did in the development of earlier theories, now that we have the evidence from Sardis to deal with.

ARS

Impact of the Discovery of the Sardis Synagogue

The Old Consensus and the Sardian Evidence

The importance of the discovery of the Sardis synagogue is simply that it reveals a Jewish community of far greater wealth, power, and self-confidence than the usual views of ancient Judaism would give us any right to expect. The older consensus is found in academic and (even more) in popular publications, by scholars, gentile or Jewish; if it is correct, then Sardis is a glaring exception—but we suspect that the consensus itself will soon undergo revision, with Sardis as catalyst.

This consensus, the usual view of the Jews under Rome, (1) tends to concentrate on ancient Palestine, (2) bases itself on the abundant *literary* evidence, and (3) often assumes that after Jesus, Judaism is compromised and drops into the background, unimportant, impotent—an ancient Christian bias still marvelously alive today.

If one assumes the first point of the consensus, then Jews outside ancient Palestine, that is, in the "Diaspora," are a ghetto people, without power, never "at home," outnumbered 10 or 20 to 1 by gentiles hostile to them. In this view, the only Jew at home in the Diaspora is the one who has compromised himself and assimilated to gentile society. But Jews were at home in Sardis; their ancestors had lived in the city for centuries *before* this synagogue was built. The first Jews to settle in the Sardis area probably did not come from Israel or Judah at all, but from exile communities in Mesopotamia and Babylonia; that is, they moved from one part of the Diaspora to another. The Sardis synagogue shows unmistakably that these Jews did not abandon their ancestral heritage, but affirmed it and gloried in it; at the same time they flourished among gentile neighbors who greatly outnumbered them.

The foundation of the old (consensus) view is the abundant literary evidence for the Jews of the Roman Empire, from the rabbinic literature to the writings of early Christianity to the brief and scattered references by pagan authors. This evidence is not so much incorrect as it is biased and incomplete—as might be expected in antiquity or in our own day when members of one racial or religious group write about another. And in the case of the rabbis, the evidence is for communities geographically distant and socially dissimilar, with few parallels to Sardis; yet most characterizations of the Jews who are contemporary with Roman Sardis turn out to be based on these nearly irrelevant data.

The third element of the consensus might be called a "Christian" bias, though for most students of this period it is a "given," an academic presupposition rather than a sectarian view. It occurs in the unexamined assumption that Judaism all but passed from the scene as Christianity moved out into the Roman Empire; or, alternatively, that the Jews of the late Roman Empire are not that much different from those in the New Testament, or even the Old Testament, so that what was true for an earlier era is valid too for this later one. A related assumption is that Jews from this period were preoccupied with their relation to non-Jews, to gentiles, and especially to Christians: trying to make converts, fearful of being converted themselves, cravenly adopting gentile practice and belief to a degree which amounts almost to apostasy.

The abundant Sardis evidence challenges this consensus at nearly every point, as will be made clear in the chapter which follows. Sardis may be only an exception to the norm; we predict, though, that it is more than that, and that this site will make a major contribution to establishing a new "norm," or rather, a new *group* of norms, a display of perhaps a dozen major forms which Judaism assumed under Roman rule in the first centuries of the common era. The result will be a more broadly documented, better understood image of Roman Judaism than students of the ancient world have ever seen before.[1]

History of the Jewish Community at Sardis

The first Jews known to have visited Sardis were refugees from the Babylonian destruction of Jerusalem in 587 B.C.; they are mentioned in passing in Obadiah 20, where Sardis is called by its Semitic name, Sepharad. It is possible, then, that the Sardis Jewish community began as early as the sixth century B.C.

A large group of Jews settled in the area in the late third century B.C. In an effort to pacify Lydia and Phrygia to the east, the Seleucid king Antiochus III brought in 2,000 loyal Jewish families from his holdings in Babylonia and Mesopotamia, provided them with houses, and gave them a decade's relief from taxation.[2] Since Sardis was the headquarters of the Seleucid governor responsible for the immigrants, it is likely that some of them came to settle in the city.[3]

By the first century B.C. Jews were well established in Sardis; the information provided by the Jewish historian Josephus makes the community come alive before our eyes. These Jews are an influential group: some of their rights are confirmed by an official of Rome itself, others by the city council of Sardis.[4] They also control their own meeting place, provided by the city; here religious ceremonies are carried out, and decisions are made on community matters, religious and nonreligious.[5] This meeting place could have been an entire building, an assembly hall, the forerunner of the mammoth synagogue described above; or it may have been nothing more than a designated space in some public building. In any case, these Jews enjoyed a considerable autonomy in the gentile city.

Finally, these Jews, so far from ancient Palestine in time as well as space, manifested some remarkably traditional religious practices; they faithfully transmitted the annual half-shekel tax for the support of the Temple in Jerusalem, a privilege guaranteed them by the Roman government.[6] They insisted on a supply of proper food for themselves; in all probability the food supply concerned them because they were observing the laws of *Kashrut*—the food was to be kosher.[7]

For the next century there is no direct information about the Sardis Jews; it may be assumed, however, that they lost their meeting place when the city "collapsed" (Tacitus) in the terrible earthquake of A.D. 17.[8] It is equally likely that some other place was assigned to them soon after for the same religious and communal purposes. Thus the present synagogue must have had at least two predecessors, one before the earthquake and one sometime thereafter.

In the late first century and into the second,

the life of Sardis Jews appears to have continued as before; at least their status in the city remains undiminished. If Rabinowitz correctly interprets one of the few Hebrew inscriptions, they formally honored the emperor Lucius Verus during his visit to the city in about A.D. 166; the city as a whole erected a statue of the young Verus in the gymnasium, and (Rabinowitz suggests) the Jews set up a commemorative inscription in Hebrew as well, probably in the community's meeting place or synagogue.[9]

At the same time the bishop of Sardis, Melito, is castigating "Israel" in his famous sermon *On Pascha;* the pointed and personal language of this bitter attack suggests that he has in mind Jews whom he knows personally, his neighbors at Sardis, as much as the Jews of the gospels. This does not mean a Jewish-Christian conflict in late second century Sardis; there is no evidence from the Jewish side for that, and in addition Jewish wealth and influence at Sardis in this period are such as to suggest Christian envy of the Jews from afar rather than an actual confrontation with them. The power of the Jewish community is perhaps even stronger than it had been earlier; before long they will control the largest synagogue ever found in the Roman world.

Not all Jews of this period are so fortunate: in ancient Palestine the century following the destruction of the temple (A.D. 70) is difficult indeed, and after the Bar Kochba revolt (132–135) Jews are forbidden even to live in Jerusalem; nationalistic political activism is discredited, and more and more the attention of Judaism here turns to its own inner development, under the leadership of some of its greatest rabbis. The "consensus" discussed at the beginning of this chapter would suggest that the Diaspora Jews too felt the pressure of Rome and lived a precarious existence as a result. Sardis is one exception to the consensus—and in the large Roman Diaspora there were probably others.

From this point on the history of the Sardis Jews is the history of their synagogue. This building, originally a public structure, came under their control and was turned into a synagogue in the third century, if not before. It was extensively remodeled late in the fourth century, and continued in use with minor repairs and alterations until the destruction of most of the city in 616.[10]

This period, "late antiquity," is of course

when Christianity moved into a position of great influence in the Roman world, putting many Jews very much on the defensive. At Sardis, however, the Jews' continuing prosperity suggests that they retained their old power despite Christian advances. The synagogue itself is our best evidence: it would have made a superb church, and synagogues and temples elsewhere were being taken over by Christians for that purpose; but not at Sardis! Until the city fell, the building remained a synagogue.

The relative prosperity of Sardis Jews in the late Roman Empire is probably the result of the interplay of power among Jews, Christians, and the remaining citizens of Sardis, here called "pagans" for lack of a better term. The strength of Sardis Jews and pagans together appears to have counterbalanced the Christians, resulting in a greater stability and security for the Jews here than was usually the case in this period.

The story comes to an end with the fall of Sardis in A.D. 616. The destruction by troops of Chosroes II was so severe that Sardis simply ceased to be a city for a considerable period. And after a life of perhaps a thousand years the Jewish community disappeared as well.

Sardis Jews and the Judaism of the Roman World

One of the best known incidents in the life of Anatolian Jews occurred in the first century B.C.: it is the attempt by the Roman governor Lucius Valerius Flaccus to divert to his own use the gold they were sending to Jerusalem to support the Temple. When prosecuted, Flaccus engaged Rome's most famous lawyer, Marcus Tullius Cicero, whose successful speech in Flaccus' defense, the *Pro Flacco,* may still be read.[11] Jewish funds deposited in four cities are mentioned, two in the interior, in Phrygia, and two in Mysia on the northwest coast. The speech reveals several things relevant to our story. These Jews took their traditional obligation seriously; far from ancient Palestine, they had not cut their ties to Jerusalem. Collectively they had substantial disposable income; over 200 pounds of gold were brought together. Inevitably their life in the Diaspora involved them with Roman authorities, officials who were in a kind of "diaspora" of their own; Flaccus held the office for the usual term of one year before returning home. (As it

happens he was replaced in Asia by Cicero's younger brother.) Thus even at this early date Jews were a part of the normal life of some, perhaps many, Anatolian cities. Roman provincial officials may have expected to have dealings with them, and venial ones may well have tried to exploit them; their vulnerability to Flaccus in this case, however, is not necessarily a sign of weakness, since he misappropriated funds from gentile communities as well, and even from Roman citizens.

Anatolian Synagogues

Several dozen Jewish communities have been identified in the Roman province of Asia; the important ones will be described briefly below, to fill in a picture of the Anatolian Judaism of which Sardis is a part.

Perhaps the most widely known synagogues from this area are the ones mentioned in the New Testament in Acts and Revelation. In several places in Acts (13:13; 14:1; 16:13; 18:19, 26; 19:8) Christian missionaries are described as beginning their work in Anatolian synagogues; this is due to the author's conviction that, in the very beginning of Christianity, missionary work in the Diaspora started with Jews for theological reasons. In Revelation 2:0 and 3:9 there are attacks on "synagogues of Satan" in Smyrna and Philadelphia, but these may be rival *Christian* groups. Thus the New Testament "evidence" must be used with great caution, perhaps with a substantial discounting of the Jewish-Christian hostility which they appear to reflect.

The following evidence is arranged roughly in chronological order, and may thus be put beside the account of the history of Sardis Judaism given in the previous section.

Miletus

By about the second century B.C. the coastal city of Miletus was so well known to Jews that a reference to it was inserted (at Ezekiel 27:18) into the Septuagint, the famous translation of the Hebrew Bible into Greek. The Miletus Jews of the Roman period were patrons of the magnificent theater there; an inscription reserves fine fifth-row seats for them.[12]

Acmonia

Of the dozen synagogues attested by inscriptions for this area, the earliest was at Acmonia in inland Phrygia; it is securely dated to the first century A.D. The Jewish community here must have been an attractive one, of social status equal perhaps to Sardis, since the Acmonia synagogue was a gift to the Jews from a gentile woman, Julia Severa, a magistrate of the city and at one time a priestess in one of the local pagan cults.[13] Beyond this we know very little about her, and nothing further about her philanthropic activities. Inscriptions indicate that the Jewish community was a large one, with a life extending over several centuries. Hebrew was known there; the only Hebrew inscription found in Asia Minor outside Sardis comes from here, perhaps from the synagogue given by Julia Severa. It is a "biblical" blessing: "(May there be peace upon) Israel, and upon Jerusalem and (upon this place to the time of) the end." It is also bilingual; the text is given in Greek as well.[14] Probably knowledge of Hebrew was limited to a few traditional blessings and other formulae; the Sardis fragments and the absence of Hebrew inscriptions elsewhere mean that in general the Jews of this area were at home only in Greek.

Aphrodisias

Aphrodisias in Caria is probably typical of more cities in this area than one would at first suspect: only a few years ago there was no indication at all of a Jewish presence there; now two lengthy inscriptions[15] of about the second century give names and occupations of a great many men of the Jewish community, and a graffito in the Odeum indicates the seats of certain Jews, as at Miletus.[16] These new data suggest that the Jews of this well-known Roman city may have been as influential as those of Sardis, and that other ancient cities in this area may also have had Jewish minorities, perhaps substantial ones, evidence for which has yet to be unearthed.

Hierapolis

For Hierapolis in Phrygia, just north and east of Aphrodisias, the evidence is more abundant—a good number of epitaphs from the second or third century. The Jewish community itself is designated a *Katoikia,* suggesting that it had a clear identity as a social unit within the city. Many citizens of Hierapolis were members of trade organizations, and the Jews were no exception; the city's Association of Purple-dyers and the council of the Association of Tapestry-makers were made responsible for memorial ceremonies for deceased Jewish members on Passover and Pentecost![17] These organizations contained gentiles as well as Jews; the conclusion must be that the Jews of this city maintained their Jewish identity and *at the same time* participated fully in the life of their city.

Apameia

Apameia, also in Phrygia, is east of Hierapolis; the two cities are connected by one of the main Roman roads. Apameia had a Jewish community of some size by the early first century B.C. It was one of the places where Flaccus confiscated funds intended for the Temple tax. The fascinating evidence here, though, is several centuries later—a series of coins minted in the first half of the third century, showing Noah and the Ark (*kibotos* in the Septuagint) from the biblical flood story. On each coin the scene is actually double: first Noah and his wife in the Ark (*kibotos*), which is shaped like a chest (also *kibotos*) with open lid; then Noah and wife standing outside the Ark with their right arms raised in thanksgiving. The name Noah appears on the Ark on the coins, making identification certain.[18] The background is fascinating and complex: there is literary evidence for the existence of pagan flood-legends in this area, and for their conflation with the biblical story. It is clear also that Apameia had a second name: it was sometimes called Apameia Kibotos, *kibotos* here meaning "chest," "container," "packing box," a reference to the city's importance as a commercial center. The various meanings of *kibotos* allow the link between the city's second name and Noah's Ark, and also led to the representation of the Ark as a *chest* on the coins. Some of the mint-masters who struck the coins may have been Jewish, although it is unlikely that all of them were who did so over a period of half a century. Because the imagery on the coins does not change over time, it has been suggested that there was a single pattern for them—a local painting, one on public view. Exactly contemporary with the Sardis synagogue, the coin is impressive evidence not just of close contacts between Jews and gentiles, but of something more: some sort of "official" acknowledgment of a traditional mythological bond of some antiquity between them.

Laodiceia

Nearby Laodiceia is also one of the cities where Jewish gold bound for Jerusalem was seized by

Flaccus. Much later, in the middle of the fourth century, it was the site of a council of Anatolian bishops; the council's formal decisions or "canons," still preserved, are among the most anti-Jewish known from the ancient Church. Canon 16, for example, stipulates that only New Testament texts are to be read on the sabbath (Saturday); possibly some Christians were following the synagogue practice and reading only the Old Testament at Saturday services, perhaps together with local Jews. Canon 29 orders Christians not to "Judaize" by resting on the sabbath; they are to rest instead on Sunday. Canon 36 forbids the making of Jewish ritual phylacteries. Canon 37 forbids keeping festivals with Jews or heretics, and receiving from them such gifts as are associated with these festivals. Canon 38 is more specific on the same point: Christians are not to receive unleavened bread from Jews. The conclusion of James Parkes regarding the canons seems plausible: "Taken together (they) certainly leave a strong impression that even in the fourth century there were not only Judaic practices in the Church in Asia, but that there was actual religious fellowship with the Jewish inhabitants," despite the opposition of church leaders.[19]

Priene

A dozen synagogues are known from the Jewish inscriptions of this area, but the only two buildings definitely identified are at Sardis and at the hillside, seacoast city of Priene, located between Ephesus and Miletus. Priene is a small place and its synagogue is small as well; it would fit easily into the *forecourt* of the Sardis synagogue. The Jews of Priene were less powerful, or perhaps less bold: their building was on a side street, not easily identified, surrounded by small rooms which may have also been under the control of the Jews. The synagogue itself was a plain room, 14 m. wide and 10 m. deep, with a niche in the east wall to contain the Torah-scrolls.[20]

Relations of Anatolian Communities with Palestine

There is some general evidence of communication among these Jewish communities (and others in the area omitted in this brief survey); since the cities were relatively close together and the road system was a good one, such contacts are to be expected.

Links with Jerusalem or (later) with the rabbinic authorities in ancient Palestine are more problematic. Before the destruction of the Jerusalem Temple in the first century, the two obvious connections between ancient Palestine and the Diaspora were the Temple tax and the pilgrimage to Jerusalem, the latter incumbent on Jewish men three times a year. We have already seen that the Jews of Asia Minor did contribute to the Temple by paying the tax. The obligation of pilgrimage three times a year could not be maintained in this period when the majority of Jews lived outside of ancient Palestine; pilgrims came as they were able, and as their piety demanded, and there is clear evidence that some who came were from Asia. Sardis was located on the main land route for pilgrims coming from the west,[21] and members of the Sardis Jewish community must have been among the pilgrims on occasion; the only Sardian who claims to have traveled to the Holy Land, however, is the second century bishop Melito.

The revolts in Palestine in the first and second centuries must have sent Jewish refugees and slaves into Asia Minor. There is no indication that Anatolian Jews took an anti-Roman position in these conflicts, or took part in the actual battles. Perhaps they viewed the revolt as nationalistic and political struggles which did not concern them; perhaps they did not want to endanger their own favorable position with the government. The Romans apparently made a distinction between the Jews in revolt and those Jews in other parts of the Empire who remained peaceful; at least, those in the latter group were not punished or restricted because they had a common religion and heritage with the former.[22]

After the Bar Kochba revolt the situation of the Palestinian Jews is greatly different from the way it had been a century earlier. The Temple with its cult no longer exists, and hope for its restoration is all but abandoned. There is no need for a priesthood, no goal for pilgrimage, no purpose for a Temple tax. The synagogue is now the central religious building, the rabbi is the community leader, and in Palestine the patriarch is recognized by Jews and Roman authorities as the head of the Jewish nation. The Temple tax from Diaspora Jews had been diverted to a special Roman treasury during the first revolt, but before long funds are coming in again from the Diaspora, this time in support of the patriarch;

these voluntary contributions are collected by the patriarch's emissaries, called *apostoloi*.

Could such *apostoloi* have come to western Asia Minor, or Sardis? This area was surely on the edge of the rabbinic world; little attention is paid to it in rabbinic literature. Even the meaning of the term "Asia" in the literary evidence is unclear; sometimes it designates what we have been calling Asia (Minor), sometimes a single city, sometimes a non-Anatolian location. For example, rabbinic texts tell of rabbis sent into the Diaspora as *apostoloi* of the patriarch, to collect funds and to keep the official ritual calendar synchronized with that of the partriarch. The famous second-century rabbi Meir once went to "Asia" for the second purpose, and when he found the community without a copy of the book of Esther (for the Purim festival) he wrote one out from memory. Meir is also reported to have died in "Asia." Did these two events take place in the same area of the same city? If an Anatolian community lacked Esther, was it because the community was so far out of touch with the majority of Jews as to even lack a complete text of the scriptures? Or was it because the people of "Asia" refused to accept the festival of Purim because of its political and anti-gentile emphases, that is, not because they were marginal Jews but because their kind of Judaism was self-consciously independent of the nationalism of the Palestinian homeland?[23]

In the last analysis, it is unlikely that the patriarch or the rabbis maintained any significant, systematic supervision over the Jews of Asia. The evidence available at present suggests that the *apostoloi,* the only body which might have carried out this function in the west, lacked the manpower and influence for so substantial a task.

The single piece of evidence on this issue from the Sardis excavations is the important mosaic inscription of Samoe, "priest and *sophodidaskalos*" (Fig. 267).[24] The second title means literally "teacher of wisdom" or "wise teacher," but in the Judaism of this period it is most likely the equivalent of "rabbi." The inscription is probably later than 429, by which date the patriarchy had been suppressed in Palestine. Thus the inscription may not be used as evidence for strong ties between Sardis Judaism and the patriarchate.

Two well-known features of Sardis Judaism

may provide the most helpful clue about the relations between this city and Palestine: the first is the use of Greek in the inscriptions, nearly to the exclusion of Hebrew; the second is the great age of the Jewish community here. These points, when taken with the other evidence reviewed in this chapter, lead almost inevitably to a picture of this community as strong and independent, with its own traditions, and "at home" in the Roman world; the Jews of Sardis had enduring respect for the homeland of their religion, but were not under its control. During centuries of life as a minority in the Diaspora, they must have worked out a form of Judaism more in keeping with that context than rabbinic Judaism could have been. If we knew more about Samoe, he likely would recall the earlier theologian and philosopher Philo of Alexandria, rather than any leader of the "rabbinic world" farther to the east.

The Jews in Gentile Sardis

Only three large cities of the Roman world contain Jewish minorities for which there is broad documentation. In the Empire's capital many Romans were put off by any foreigner: a Greek, a Briton, a Gaul, or a Jew. But in addition, Jews here were without political status and financial power; they lacked polish, often they were all but illiterate. Jews had lived in Alexandria in large numbers since its founding by Alexander the Great; the Septuagint and the writings of Philo are evidence for their intellectual activity in philosophy and theology. But the unstable Alexandrian citizenry was given to riot, and Jews frequently got caught up in clashes between local gentiles and the Roman authorities.

Before our excavations, the evidence for Sardis came chiefly from Josephus; the texts have been discussed above, and they could well give the impression that the Sardis Jews were a distinct group with strange practices and particular rights which must be protected by the authorities. One might assume that the status of the Jews in Sardis was not much different from the status of the Jews in Alexandria or Rome. But part of Josephus' purpose is to stress the long-held rights of Jewish communities, and the protection of those rights by the authorities. The result is to underemphasize the Jews as accepted members of a city's society. For Sardis at least, the picture changes considerably when archaeological evidence is added. Perhaps the situation of Sardis Jews improved after the period described by Josephus; all of the evidence to be discussed below comes from after the earthquake of A.D. 17.

Let us look again at Figs. 207, 240, 251–253; they show clearly the place of the Synagogue in Roman Sardis. As Seager notes, the upper walls and roof of the building must have been clearly visible above the shops and road colonnades (Fig. 239). The interior of the entire building could be seen by gentiles walking by when the doors were open. The Forecourt (Fig. 251) may have contained a municipally licensed fountain and may have been accessible to all.

The evidence from epigraphy buttresses the evidence from architecture. There are over eighty inscriptions from the Synagogue, and they differ strikingly at one point from the hundreds of other Jewish inscriptions known from the Roman world. Elsewhere, for example at Rome, the texts may emphasize one's status within the *Jewish* community; the Sardis inscriptions stress rather the status of Jews outside the Jewish community, in the city and its government, and even beyond. Many donors proudly identify themselves as *Sardianoi,* "citizens of Sardis," and no less than nine may use the privileged title *bouleutes,* "member of the city council"; perhaps because of their wealth, the latter must have possessed considerable social status. In addition, three donors held positions in the provincial administration: one was a *comes* ("Count"; Fig. 278), another a *procurator* (Fig. 272), another an assistant in the state archives.[25]

The inscriptions refer to more than thirty donors (Figs. 254, 268, 275, 278); only two names are Hebrew (Fig. 267), and one of these is followed by an additional name which is Hellenized Roman: "Samuel, known also as Julian"; this practice is found in other Jewish inscriptions and also in the New Testament, for example, "Saul . . . known also as Paul" (Acts 13:9). This preference for non-Jewish names is not surprising. Only 13% of the Jewish inscriptions of Rome display only Semitic names, while 46% have Greek names only, and 32% Latin names only; the rest have a mixture of Greek and either Latin or Semitic.

The few Semitic names from Sardis are fascinating in themselves: for example, the person of greatest religious importance in the synagogue bears a Semitic name, Samoe, the priest and *so-phodidaskalos* whose dedication was discovered squarely in the center of the Main Hall (Fig. 267). It is not surprising that a "rabbi" would manifest something traditional when other Jews were using names more common in the larger and largely gentile community. Four additional names are known from graffiti in the shops, three of Hebrew origin: Jacob, John, and Sabbatios. Perhaps the graffiti reflect more familiar names, the inscriptions more formal ones.

One synagogue inscription mentions "the tribe of the Leontioi." It is unclear whether this refers to a group within the synagogue community, or to the Jews as a whole within the larger Sardis community.[26] The choice of the term *Leontioi* was an inspired one, whatever the extent of the group to which it refers. *Leontes* is the Greek for "lions," a powerful symbol to those who speak Greek but think in biblical terms. In the Bible the tribe of Judah (Gen. 49:9), the tribe of Dan (Deut. 33:22), and finally all of Israel (Num. 23:24; 24:9) are all pictured as "lions." The great hero Judah the Maccabee could be described as a lion (1 Macc. 3:4–6), and in the Eagle Vision of fourth Ezra the lion is the Messiah himself (4 Ezra 12:31f.). The lion is a popular Jewish symbol in art as well as literature; the excavated synagogues of ancient Palestine have produced a score of examples. But in Greek literature the lion is associated with Sardis since the days of Herodotus. Lions are the subject of approximately one-third of all the sculpture published from Lydian and Persian Sardis, prompting Hanfmann to remark that "the Lydians suffered from a regular *leontomania.*"[27]

The recent excavations show very clearly what the Jews did with this powerful Sardis symbol. A massive Lydian lion (Fig. 240)—or possibly a pair of lions—was installed just outside the Synagogue Forecourt, and two pairs of lions from the Persian period (Fig. 256) bracket the great Eagle Table in the front of the Synagogue.[28] But the Jews were not simply "reusing" the lion statues; they were actually associating themselves in some way with this traditional Sardis image, combining it with the biblical one, using it as the story of Noah was used at Apameia in Phrygia. The culmination of this process appears in a Hebrew graffito to be published by Rabinowitz; the writer is a *ben Leho,* "son of Leo."[29] Apparently the lion became such a popular image among Sardis Jews that one of their number was given the name Leo, the *Latin* for "lion"; but in the graffito it is written in *Hebrew* characters!

The occupations of Jews in this part of the ancient world are not much different from those of gentiles; there is no clear indication that particular crafts were associated with Jews. Goldsmiths must have been in demand; three of the synagogue donors were Jews of that occupation. Others were merchants; some sold glass, some paints and dyes. One may have been a sculptor. As already mentioned, others held government positions.[30]

Since this is a sketch of the life of Jews in a gentile city, one final matter must be considered: what about anti-Semitism, gentile hatred of Jews? Our impression is that there was no anti-Semitism at Sardis while this synagogue was in use. (The special case of Melito, Christian bishop of Sardis, will be discussed below.) Modern descriptions of ancient anti-Semitism tend to generalize too quickly; on the basis of specific texts and incidents from particular locations, they extrapolate toward "*the* gentile attitude toward the Jews." But gentile attitudes toward Judaism were anything but monolithic! At about the time one gentile (a Roman general soon to be emperor) was destroying the Temple in Jerusalem, another gentile (an ex-magistrate named Julia Severa) was donating a synagogue to the Jews of Acmonia, in Phrygia not far from Sardis. In accounts of ancient anti-Semitism the Jew is a stranger and a threat; his religion forces him into an odd diet, peculiar work schedules, and strange cultic practices. He is forced to keep to himself, to live by himself, to avoid contact with gentiles. And yet he is eager to proselytize; it is an indication of his own insecurity that he must try to convert gentiles, or at least turn them into "sympathizers." His targets are the gullible of the gentile world: women, children, and the uneducated. Such a reconstruction of the past will not fit the Sardis presented in this volume; and because the Jewish community of Sardis is so well documented, the new evidence has the effect of calling into question long-held views of the relationships between Jews and gentiles in the entire ancient world.

Sardis Jews and Paganism

Until the discoveries at Sardis, the evidence for Judaism in western Asia Minor had been scattered and fragmentary. It was examined usually by those more interested in Christianity: Asia Minor is the first part of the Diaspora which Christianity penetrated, and it spread rapidly. In the Diaspora the Christian attitude toward Jews soon became generally negative. The idea grew up that Diaspora Jews had not remained true to biblical faith; particularly in Asia Minor, it was claimed, Jews adopted the vocabulary, the imagery, and even the theology of pagan piety. They came under the spell of the Anatolian god Sabazius; perhaps they thought that *Saba*zius was the *Sabb*ath. They sometimes used the eagle as a religious symbol; this too was seen as a descent into pagan ways, since the eagle was used as a religious and political emblem by Roman gentiles. Their cultic use of wine suggested that the Jews were secretly followers of Dionysus; according to Euripides, this god comes from Mt. Tmolus, immediately south of Sardis. In the Septuagint, God is frequently called "the highest one," *hypsistos;* in Anatolian inscriptions one deity or another may be called *hypsistos,* offering Jews here still another opportunity for syncretism, mixing their religion with pagan piety. Some Jews did these things because they were not very smart— they did not know any better; but most were deliberate, pathetically attempting to make themselves more "gentile." Thus the old view.

But if syncretism among Jews was as widespread as we have been told, there should be clear evidence for it in the Sardis data. From Lydia and from Sardis itself there is abundant evidence for Sabazius and Dionysus: was any of it found in the Synagogue? The Sardis Jewish community can now be extensively documented; is there any indication that mixtures of traditional Judaism and pagan piety were being concocted there? The answer to both questions is no.[31]

Frequent and generally friendly contact with gentiles must have been an accepted part of the daily life of Sardis Jews; clearly they worked, shopped, and lived side by side, and—like Philo—some Sardis Jews must have studied with gentiles. The Synagogue inscriptions provide strong evidence that they may have had a technical, philosophical vocabulary in common. Eleven inscriptions, dating from the third to the fifth centuries, use the term *pronoia,* "Providence"; the donors are stating that their gifts to the Synagogue are paid for out of resources bestowed by Providence. In an expression which seems strangely modern, the Sardis Jews used Providence to mean God. *Pronoia* is exceedingly rare in inscriptions for other synagogues, and never means "divine providence" (that is, God). Since the Sardis Jews use the term in a quasi-liturgical fashion in their inscriptions, it is probable that this use of *pronoia* became common in the synagogue community sometime before these inscriptions were composed. How did this idea reach Sardis, and why is it found only here, out of all the Jewish communities known in the Roman Diaspora?

The most likely possibility is gentile philosophy. In the thought of this period the concept of a systematic divine control over human events—a combination of plan and power building the cosmos—was an attractive alternative to the anthropomorphism of earlier Greek and Roman mythology. A number of treatises entitled *On Providence* were produced by pagan philosophers in this period, the most comprehensive by Plotinus in the third century.

If Jews and pagans studied together and lived side by side, it is possible that they joined forces against the Christians in Sardis' final religious conflict. Such a coalition would help to explain how the Synagogue building remained Jewish and was not expropriated, even during the reigns of such aggressively pro-Christian emperors as Constantius II (337–361), Theodosius I (378–395), Theodosius II (408–439), and Justinian (527–565).

The hypothesis which best explains the data is as follows: the religious situation of Sardis in the last two centuries of the city's existence was characterized by a coalition of Jews and pagans opposing a frequently divided Christian community that gradually grew to include a majority of the population. Because of this coalition the Synagogue did not pass into Christian hands. But this Jewish-pagan alliance did not lead to the "paganizing" of Sardis Judaism; the Synagogue itself remains our best evidence of that.

Sardis Jews and Christianity

Moving out from ancient Palestine, Christianity made a significant penetration into Asia Minor in the first century.[32] The New Testament contains letters written to Christian groups in Ephesus and Colossae, both on the Roman highway which runs south of Sardis, and the Christian missionary Paul directed one of his most im-

portant letters to Christians in Galatia, east of Sardis, in the interior. Revelation, written at the end of the first century, begins with brief letters to Christian communities at Sardis (Rev. 3:1–6) and six other nearby cities; people in Sardis had been Christian for some time by then, since the text pointedly contrasts their present low spiritual state with the good reputation which they had earned in the past. Other early Christian texts, still extant though not in the New Testament, come from authors personally familiar with Christianity in the Sardis area: the letters of Ignatius were written a decade or two after Revelation; the letter of Polycarp, Bishop of Smyrna, and the *Martyrdom of Polycarp* are from about the middle of the second century.[33] These texts and later evidence indicate that Christianity took several competing forms in Western Asia Minor; it was inchoate and still very young when it reached this area, and its often independent missionaries addressed different audiences in a variety of ways. There were conflicts not only with Jews, but also with "Judaizers," Christians who manifested more of Jewish belief and practice than Church authorities would prefer. Judaizers need not be converted Jews: apparently Jewish or Jewish-Christian practices were brought to the attention of some Anatolian gentiles when they became Christian, and they adopted them to the dismay of the Christian leadership. By the end of the first century there were many more Christians outside of ancient Palestine than within the Christian and Jewish homeland, and by the end of the second century the new religion was overwhelmingly gentile; "Judaizers" were increasingly unwelcome.

The best known Christian of ancient Sardis is the enigmatic Melito,[34] bishop there in the latter part of the second century; in Christian tradition he is one of the "great luminaries" of the early church in this area, along with the disciples Philip and John and the martyr Polycarp. The background of Melito's work has become much clearer thanks to the Sardis excavations, but the resulting picture is of a tangled set of relationships between him and second century Judaism, including the Sardis Jews in all probability. Consider the following: (1) the Old Testament was so important to Melito that he made a journey to the Holy Land to secure an accurate list of its precise contents; he is thus the first Christian pilgrim to Palestine of whom we are informed;

(2) he was a quartodeciman, like many other Anatolian Christians of his time: the Easter he celebrated was dated according to the Jewish Passover each year, and might thus fall on a day of the week other than Sunday. This practice has its roots in the Gospel of John but was repeatedly condemned as "Judaizing," particularly by western churches; (3) Melito's one extant sermon, the *On Pascha,* is an intricate, ornamented, often florid interpretation and application of the Passover story in Exodus 12, so central to Jewish piety.

None of this means that Melito was on good terms with Jews. Quite the reverse: in his *Apology* he calls them "barbarians," outside the boundaries of Greco-Roman culture. The *On Pascha* is a bitter attack on the Jews as responsible for the death of Christ; for this Melito has been called "the first poet of deicide" or "God-killing," the monstrous charge that all Jews and Jews alone are responsible for the death of Jesus. The attacks on the Jews in the *On Pascha* are bitter and prolonged; the section denouncing "Israel" occupies nearly a third of the whole text. There is nothing in quartodeciman Christianity which requires taking such a position; indeed, a quartodeciman sermon closely related to Melito in date and theology contains but a few references to Judaism—they are negative but quite brief. It is true that ancient Christianity produced substantial anti-Jewish literature, attacking Jews on theological grounds; but that tradition was just beginning at the time of Melito and he did not benefit from it.

The new Sardis evidence will permit Melito to be understood fully for the first time, by allowing us to see clearly the context out of which he wrote. Apparently he was battling on two fronts simultaneously. Among Christians he had to defend quartodeciman practice; what better way to meet the charge of "Judaizing" than by preaching sermons attacking "Israel"? But at Sardis the enemy must have been the Jews; the newly revealed Jewish community apparently had far more power locally than did Melito's Christians. There is no firm evidence that Sardis Jews were even aware of Melito, or that a direct hostility on their part provoked his attacks. But the present synagogue or its immediate predecessor, and the people who controlled it, made a profound and profoundly negative impression on him; of that there can be little doubt.

Two Christian martyrs are known from third century Sardis, but their conflict was apparently with the pagan state rather than with the Jews; there is no evidence whatever of Jewish contribution to Christian persecution at Sardis, although something of the kind had taken place in Smyrna, not far to the west.

With the reign of Constantine (306–337), relations among pagans, Jews, and Christians at Sardis become more complex. The substantial Church EA (Figs. 288–291) was built in a necropolis near the Pactolus River in about the middle of the fourth century; it is two-thirds the size of the Synagogue, an indication of Christian strength. But Christians were still divided into factions; there were reports of riots and violence among Sardis Christians into the fifth century. The laws of the now-Christian state bore down with increasing severity on pagans and Jews, but enforcement varied considerably from period to period and location to location. In Sardis, the combination of a still-living paganism and a divided Christianity may well have made it impolitic for local officials to apply sanctions on the Jews.

There are hints as well that relations between Sardis Jews and the Christian laity were not always hostile. The shops which were built against the outside of the Synagogue south wall are described in Chapter VIII; excavation has shown that shops owned by Christians existed side by side with shops owned by Jews (Figs. 239–243). The shops front on the main east-west street of the city, where Christian and Jewish shoppers and merchants encountered one another every day. There is no sign of a "Jewish quarter" or ghetto; from all indications Sardis Jews, Christians, and pagans lived side by side.

As a quartodeciman leader resident in Sardis, Melito the bishop was close to Jews in some points of theology and practice, and close to them also in his daily life; for his own reasons he attacked them strongly, making extreme statements which later become detached from their historical situation and made a substantial contribution to Christian anti-Jewish vocabulary. For Sardis Jews, he must have been an unpleasant person to have around. But the Jews also had Christians for neighbors, laity unlike Melito, and they may have had a more positive attitude toward them. We suspect that the larger history of Jewish-Christian relations at Sardis is something like this: something between antagonism and openness is to be assumed between the two groups. If the *On Pascha* is to be used as evidence, then the situation between Jews and Christians reflected in canons of the nearby council of Laodicea is also part of the picture—or so the new evidence would suggest.

Jewish Religious Life in Sardis

It is possible to enter the ancient Synagogue of Sardis; there has been extensive reconstruction (Figs. 251, 256–258, 280; cf. 253), so that visitors may examine the entire building, from front steps to apse. Anyone with more than a casual interest in this structure will surely want to know the answer to two central questions: How was this building used? And what does it tell us about Sardis Judaism? The simplest way to answer is to take an imaginary tour;[35] more questions will suggest themselves in the process.

Like the gymnasium itself, the Synagogue was designed to be entered at the east from the East Road colonnade (Figs. 239, 240, 243). What we see now is the fourth and last stage of the building (Fig. 271), from the fourth century; but in the latter part of stage three the building was already a synagogue, and even stage two could have been made to serve as such by blocking the northern passage in the apse, the only direct link in stage two between this building and the pagan gymnasium. In general, then, the building entered from the colonnade may be said to reflect the religious life of Sardis Jews from the third century until the destruction of the city in 616. But it did not serve the religious life alone. The ancient synagogue was a building of many uses. Particularly in the Diaspora, it may well have been the only large space in a gentile city where the Jewish community could assemble. In the first instance, it is the place where Jews gathered to pray and to hear the Scripture read; these tasks were the responsibility of the congregation and the community in general. The ancient synagogue had no professional priesthood, no formal liturgy of the kind associated with Christianity, no trace of any sacrificial rite as had been practiced in the Temple in Jerusalem. This synagogue was also a school, and it may have been used on occasion as a dining hall; since a main highway from the Aegean to the east was just outside, Jewish travelers must often have spent the night in the synagogue itself, or perhaps in a loft over one of the Jewish shops built against the outside of the south wall (Figs. 207, 239–242) next to the highway. It was pointed out above that one of the predecessors of this building was used by Sardis Jews for their own discussions and for the resolution of community differences, practices which must have continued in this building. Several features of the Sardis synagogue recall the famous Diplostoon, the "double-colonnaded" synagogue at Alexandria destroyed by Trajan.[36] The Talmud indicates that people were seated in the Diplostoon by trades—all the goldsmiths together, all the weavers together, all the carpetmakers together —so that a new person in the community thus associated himself with others in his profession in order to gain employment; the Sardis Synagogue too may have functioned as a kind of hiring-hall.

The first thing which strikes the visitor is the size and grandeur of the building, still inescapable today. The few other Diaspora synagogues which have been excavated are on the scale of a private dwelling;[37] the scale of this building is that of the great gymnasium and Marble Court of which it is a part (Fig. 207). In view of its central location, its size, and its embellishments, it is hard to avoid the conclusion that the building was intended to be a showplace of Judaism for Sardis gentiles. The richness of the Dura synagogue in Syria was hidden from strangers, walled off behind a complex of community meeting rooms; in contrast, this building appears to be "on display." The space which the Jews had received was substantial, and they could have used it more "efficiently," had they wished, or had they been following practices known from other Diaspora synagogues. The crosswall dividing the Forecourt from the Main Hall (Figs. 253, 266, 271) is a new feature in the fourth stage; it could have been erected much farther to the west, closer to the apse, and the space thus freed could have been devoted to a number of new, small rooms for various synagogue purposes. The present Forecourt too is more attractive than efficient: there were sunlight and shade, splashing water, brightly decorated floors and walls (Fig. 251), all in full view of anyone on his way from the Main Avenue to the gymnasium. To passersby, it all must have said quite good things about Sardis Judaism; we believe that was by design.

The Main Hall (Figs. 252, 253) is accessible only from the Forecourt, which may be entered through the main doors on the east or by a smaller passage from the south, convenient to the Jewish shops. It was customary to wash one's hands on entering the synagogue; a trough-like basin of marble for that purpose stood between the south entrance to the Forecourt and the south door leading from the Forecourt to the Main Hall. Water from the fountain might also have been used. Just before entering the Main Hall, the visitor would notice four comemorative inscriptions set into the mosaic floor on the west side of the Forecourt (Fig. 257), the first of many to be encountered in the building.

Just inside the Main Hall are the two marble shrines or aediculae, one on each side of the central entrance (Figs. 258, 266). The south shrine was evidently the more important (Fig. 274); the construction is of better quality, and the few fragments of Hebrew inscription (Fig. 269) from the building were found here. The shrines are in reuse; the capitals of each were notched so that a screen or curtain could be hung between them. In this way a wholly gentile architectural element became a synagogue furnishing, with all the essential features of the Torah Shrines known from other synagogues and from Jewish art.

When the Scripture was to be read aloud from the Eagle Table at the west end of the building (Fig. 256), the proper scroll must have been brought, perhaps in a formal procession, from the shrine over 40 meters away (Fig. 258); afterward it would be returned in the same fashion. This is perhaps as close to a formal liturgical activity as the Sardis community might come. The Sardis Jews erected two shrines for reasons of symmetry; there is no reason why both of them could not have been used as receptacles for scrolls. The crosswall and shrines are new to the fourth stage of the building; they indicate architecturally the increasing importance of the scripture in Diaspora Judaism, and permit the scrolls to be stored on the wall closest to Jerusalem, a feature seen also in Diaspora synagogues at Ostia outside Rome, and at Priene and Dura. The Sardis Jews had a significant name for such a structure; in one of the inscriptions it is called "that which protects the Law" (*nomophylakion*). The term is rare, and the choice of it revealing. The usual Hebrew, Aramaic, and Greek names

for the Torah Shrine reflect biblical imagery. This word does not; rather it underscores the purpose of such a structure at Sardis, and witnesses to the importance of the Law in this community.

Another inscription from the Synagogue makes the same point; it is not a dedication, but a kind of motto in formal, liturgical language: "Having found, having broken, read! observe!" The plaque bearing this inscription (Fig. 276) is designed to be free-standing, on a pedestal or perhaps on the Eagle Table itself (Fig. 257). "Breaking" may refer to "breaking open" a text, that is, discerning its meaning; or perhaps to breaking the seal of a scroll in order to open it. Both inscriptions are carefully done, intended to be impressive; each text is framed in a *tabula ansata*. The *nomophylakion* inscription was carved in raised relief; the depressed background was originally painted red (Fig. 275).

West of the aediculae in the center of the Main Hall is the Synagogue's most important inscription, the dedication by "Samoe, priest and *sophodidaskalos*"; the inscription is framed by four stone slabs set in a square, perhaps supports for a decorative baldacchino to mark the location (Fig. 267; cf. 252, Bay 4).

Samoe was a priest, although the Sardis Jews had no ritual of sacrifice; such things ended with the destruction of the Temple centuries before this inscription was created. A priest is not essential to the function of the synagogue, but Samoe was a descendant of the biblical high priest Aaron and bore the title proudly. *Sophodidaskalos* means "wise teacher" or "teacher of wisdom"; given the prominent location of the inscription, it is likely that he was the teacher for the synagogue, the closest thing that Sardis had to a rabbi. The inscription is in Greek, and Samoe must have taught in Greek, to judge from the overwhelming preference for Greek over Hebrew in the Jewish inscriptions of Sardis and of Asia Minor as a whole. (There is a higher percentage of Hebrew in the decorations of the typical American synagogue of today!) The precise center of the Main Hall is marked with this inscription and its baldacchino(?) (Fig. 252, Bima?) probably because this is just where Samoe taught, with his students around him, when the building was not given over to formal services. In synagogues in Asia Minor in this period, the Bible was read and then interpreted in

Greek; probably Samoe's teachings were homiletical and in some sense "haggadic," intended to instruct or to edify—but more than that we cannot say.

The west end of the Synagogue is the architectural focus of the building, and must be seen as a unit (Fig. 253); it is the culmination of this tour of the structure and this story of the Jews of Sardis. For the services, important members of the community and honored guests were seated on the benches of the apse; the wall behind them was decorated with colorful designs in cut marble and long commemorative inscriptions (Fig. 256). These personages looked out across a semicircular mosaic (Fig. 260), over the apse railing and the Eagle Table and out to the rest of the community. The table was flanked by pairs of marble lions (Fig. 256). The "Socrates" menorah (Fig. 268) may have stood on a small, carefully carved monument in the shape of a Corinthian round temple that was placed against one of the north piers (Fig. 256).[38] Eagles, lions, and menorah were all rich in symbolism for the assembled community. The scroll of the Scriptures was unrolled on the Eagle Table; a member of the community stood on a small pedestal at the table, his back to the apse, and read aloud the text designated for the day.

For centuries these are the things which characterized the ancient synagogue of Sardis and the community for which it was the center. In the Roman Empire there were many kinds of Jews, in different locations, on different social levels. About some of them we know a great deal: the rabbinic communities, Qumran, Palestine generally, Alexandria. Now with a directness which written evidence alone cannot convey, the Sardis building and its contents illuminate a Judaism almost unknown before. And because these Jews lived as they did in a city so important to the Greco-Roman world, they have a claim on our attention unmatched by remote Qumran with its Dead Sea Scrolls, or by the border village of Dura, despite its spectacular art. This must be the single most important building left to us by the Jews of the ancient world.

ATK

X

Christianity: Churches and Cemeteries

GEORGE M. A. HANFMANN

HANS BUCHWALD

Christianization of Sardis: Destruction and Construction

As the Hellenization of Sardis was the theme of our seventh chapter, so is the Christianization of the city the theme of this last chapter in our historical sequence. The history and character of Late Antique Sardis (A.D. 284–616) have been described in some detail by C. Foss.[1] We will summarize here only the most necessary information.

Under Diocletian's reform (ca. A.D. 300), Sardis, which was not a capital in the Roman province of Asia, became the capital of the new province of Lydia, which in turn was included in the diocese of Asiane.[2] That epochal change within the Roman Empire, the introduction of Christianity as the preferred religion under Constantine (A.D. 312?), has left no specific trace in the epigraphic or archaeological records of Sardis. The continuous series of bishops and metropolitans of Sardis, however, begins with the council of Nicaea (A.D. 325). Venerable as one of the Seven Churches of Asia, the metropolis of Sardis ranked high in Christian hierarchy —sixth after the Patriarchate of Constantinople.[3] Sardis remained an important military base with an Imperial arms factory. Among the military events, we have already mentioned the abortive attack which the Ostrogoths under Tribigild had planned against Sardis in A.D. 399.[4]

Between 284 and 616 Sardis seems to have suffered no damage from military attacks; there is, however, some probability that the widespread "renewal" (*ananeosis*) in the bath-gymnasium, and the Synagogue and the urban operations along the street to Hypaipa in the HoB area between A.D. 350 and 450, may have been necessitated by one or more earthquakes (and floods?) such as had hit Ephesus in A.D. 358 and 363. It was a flood that had isolated the city and prevented the Goths from attacking in 399. The great demand for construction workers reflected in the "Union" agreement in A.D. 459 also presupposes a more than normal activity.[5]

The signal political-military event in the history of Sardis is not mentioned by any historian. It is the destruction of Sardis by fire and sword which devastated the lower city in the spring of A.D. 616 and terminated its highly developed urban life.[6] Since this destruction—certainly not due to any natural causes—coincides precisely with the incursions of the Persian Sassanian King Chosroes II into Asia Minor, there can be no real doubt that it was the Sassanian Persians who largely demolished Late Antique Sardis.[7]

Classical Survivals

The important result of our excavations in combination with literary and epigraphic sources is the insight that in Late Antique Sardis continuity outweighed change. Despite the arrival of a religion as revolutionary as Christianity, the urban agglomerate remained largely the same, and may, indeed, have expanded (Plan IV).[8] The general style of life, the "Wohnkultur," too, does not seem to have much changed.

Paganism died hard at Sardis. Around A.D. 540 recalcitrant pagans were still being persecuted.[9] A statue of Dionysus, god of wine and protector of local vineyards, still stood in the basement of a wealthy Christian house.[10] Another group of Dionysus and Satyr was found in the latrine of the Byzantine Shops (Fig. 215).[11] Was it there to be mocked?

Not only pagan resistance but the survival of classical culture was closely linked with traditional education. Sardis was a branch of the characteristic pagan intellectual-theurgic school in the fourth century, which boasted such luminaries as the long-lived Chrysanthius (died ca. A.D. 390)[12] and Eunapius, who wrote on the lives of these late "sophists."[13] Yet we must see the gradations. Although its poems and epigrams use the customary bombastic Homeric tags and mythological allusions,[14] Sardis does not appear to have been a center of classical survival in the same sense as Antioch or Cyprus, where the educational-literary-intellectual paganism was massively represented in art by hundreds of mythological and literary mosaics.[15] So far, Sardis has yielded no mythological-literary figurative mosaics and only a few Late Antique sculptured pieces of this kind.[16]

Christianization of Daily Life

On the Christian side, too, no representations of the cross or other saintly signs have appeared in the Sardian mosaics. The attempts to recognize a possible symbol of St. John in the eagle of a mosaic from PN (Fig. 298) and the signs of Evangelists in certain incised reliefs have been rejected by experts.[17]

We have other signs for gradual Christianization of daily life. Crawford has enumerated the crosses engraved on the walls and incised on the plates (Fig. 282) in some of the Byzantine Shops. Even more spectacular are the two mighty crosses engraved on a cooling basin in Shop W8 (Fig. 281). Originally it was thought that the basin might have been transformed into a baptismal font, but informed opinion suggests that it was the water which was to be hallowed, as in a public fountain in Ephesus.[18]

In the gymnasium, in a unit which may have been on the way to the municipal gatherings, a late painted decoration bore the Aaronic blessing: "Blessed be the people."[19]

The most striking array of Christian and probably liturgical objects was the bronze incense shovel and censers found in the basement of the House of Bronzes (Fig. 283). Since they seemed to be objects for liturgical use, they led to the theory that the house may have belonged to a cleric.[20] A similar group with a lamp surmounted by a cross was found, however, in a shop.[21]

Besides the crosses, seals, rings (Fig. 299), and lamps from the graves, the most characteristic Christian objects were the so-called ampullae decorated with crosses and hares (Fig. 244), writing Evangelists, Virgin and Child, and, once, with a donkey. Some have been found in a guard room of the city wall, two in late Roman levels west of the House of Bronzes, two in the Byzantine Shops, and others among graves at Pactolus North.[22]

Yet it is not the finding of these and some other Christian objects which indicate the character of the daily life of Late Antique Sardis. It is rather that up to the destruction of 616, Jewish symbols appear in the Byzantine Shops alongside the Christian; and the same house found room for Christian liturgical objects and a Dionysus.[23] The process of Christianization was not quick, sudden, and all-embracing—and was not yet complete by A.D. 616.

Christianity and Urbanism

Christianity had come to Sardis early. "And unto the Angel of the Church in Sardis write; . . ." (Revelation 3:1). Whether the Angel was a spirit or a person,[24] he led an Early Christian community which was attuned to Jewish apocalyptic tradition and was presumably largely Jewish (ca. A.D. 90?). Some eighty years later the passionate Melito of Sardis attacked Israel for having killed Christ; but, as A. T. Kraabel justly notes,[25] Melito's position was far from simple. In a sense he, who tried to present an apology for Christianity to the Roman emperor, was competing for Imperial favor not only with the Jewish community —who at this very moment may have been asking for the concession of the synagogue building[26]—but also with the city of Sardis—who after invoking the THEOI PATRIOI, the gods of our fathers, proudly claimed the emperors as family members.[27] The Christian community Melito represented was no longer a small, esoteric "Jewish splinter group" but a powerful faith with ecumenical claims. Unfortunately, we have found nothing certain in the way of buildings or objects, and just possibly one grave to illustrate the life of one of the Seven Churches of Asia before the Peace of the Church.

With the sole accession of Constantine after the defeat of Licinius in A.D. 324, the challenge of Christianizing Sardis arose before the provincial and municipal authorities and the church. Constantine's own great building program at Constantinople, Rome, Antioch, Bethlehem, and Jerusalem aimed at giving architectural form to the most important places of worship and memorials of the new faith. The same task faced the governors and local authorities on a local level. How church and state began to cooperate in such Christian building programs we can see from literary sources in the example of Eusebius' basilica in Tyre: the bishop stimulates, the emperor commands, the governor carries out a Christian construction.[28] Now Sardis is beginning to provide us with a very interesting archaeological example of this process.

To look at the city as a whole (Plan IV), first, the civic-secular as well as domestic buildings normally remained untouched. Athletics, to be sure, disappeared from the gymnasium,[29] but the complex continued to function as a bath. Additional functions, such as serving for assemblies (and possibly dinners?) of the Council and the Senate replaced athletics, as we know from inscriptions in the Marble Court.[30] The bath CG, too, continued to function as a bath into the sixth century.[31] Commercial establishments continued operations, with Jews, pagans, and Christians trading side by side. When in the late fourth and fifth centuries a rather "makeshift" urban reconstruction of the city became necessary, it was apparently carried out with coordination of public and private resources. Thus the ananeosis[32] of the aleipterion of the gymnasium was carried out by Simplikios Severus, vicar of Asia, and that of the Marble Court apparently by an official called . . . onios; but something was "cleared out without public expense" in connection with the building of a stoa and a gate. The inscription and the gate advertised Christianity by conspicuous crosses.[33] Two other inscriptions may mention defensive constructions.[34] E. Kit-

zinger has suggested that "the ever-living ornament" kosmon aiezoonta with which "onios" adorned the Marble Court or the aleipterion may allude to Christian symbols in the redecoration; but none have been identified.

A second problem was that of "negative action," the need or desire to take over or destroy pagan temples and mysteria (houses of pagan cult associations). The fourth century was, of course, a period of transition. It was not until A.D. 435 that Theodosius II ordered the pagan temples closed and purified by the sign of the cross.[35] In Sardis, some destructive activity may be surmised to have taken place in connection with the removal by Constantine to Constantinople of diaphorai stelai,[36] various sculptural monuments, but this was not religiously motivated. The venerable temple of Artemis posed a problem in that it was also a temple of Imperial cult; it was, of course, precisely the refusal of the Christians to sacrifice to the genius of the emperor which had brought them into conflict with the Roman state. The temple was certainly not pulled down, as the eastern porch columns stand to this day. It seems that the colossal statues of Zeus (Fig. 176) and presumably of Artemis were pulled out, and a fragment of the head of Zeus was found built into the foundation of the small church M, which may have been built shortly thereafter.[37] The colossal statues of emperor Antonius Pius[38] and the empress Faustina, however, apparently remained seated until the acroliths collapsed from natural causes (decay of wooden cores?).[39] There is a curious parallel in this survival of neocorate statues to the fact that Sardis is still called "twice neokoros" that is, "twice warden of Imperial cult," in the "Union" agreement of A.D. 459, although the Holy Trinity is invoked in the oath in the middle of the document.[40]

As to the temple, some damaged parts may have been removed under Constantine.[41] The temple was liberally dedemonized with twenty-five incised crosses and a "Light-Life" inscription, possibly after the Theodosian decree.[42] The little chapel-church M was built against its east columns (Figs. 284–286) and the south colonnade utilized as a screened approach, perhaps even before A.D. 400. Then the Artemis Temple began to be dismounted and its parts burned for lime, beginning at the west entrance. The process was in full swing in A.D. 616.[43]

The temple of Hera and its image base (Fig.

177) must have been demolished by the time the east wall of the Main Hall in the Synagogue was built, that is, ca. A.D. 330–340;[44] for the image base was built into this wall. A slightly later date results for the destruction of the precinct of Cybele, since the Artemis-Cybele relief (Fig. 93) was built into the stylobate of the Forecourt of the Synagogue, perhaps around A.D. 360,[45]—assuming that like the lions of the Main Hall (Fig. 256) it came from the Cybele rather than the Artemis Precinct.[46]

Reuse of a monument to Mên Axioteinos as a table support in the House of Bronzes only shows that such stones were still available in the sixth century.[47]

In general, the archaeological data more or less agree with the statement of Eunapius that only "traces" remained of pagan temples by ca. A.D. 375,[48] when one Justus and the pagan governor of Lydia Hilarius tried to restore the pagan altars and temples.

As to takeovers, the Artemis Temple was not taken over *in toto* as a church, as was, for instance, the Parthenon in Athens. More remarkable is the fact that the Synagogue was not transformed into a Christian church.[49] Among the civic buildings, the Hall of Imperial Cult (Marble Court) became, ca. A.D. 400, a municipal meeting place. Here certainties cease. The preeminent position of the great church "D" (Fig. 287; Plan IV) and the great number of spoils from a large Roman building built into it suggest an earlier temple in this place. We do not know whose it was; a relief with a little frog seen by G. M. A. Hanfmann on a pier in 1957 (and since gone) is hardly sufficient to identify the owner as Apollo. Spoils built into the late Constantinian basilica EA probably come from several sources; those of the Lascarid Church E may come from one building, but there is no certainty that it was a temple.[50]

Constructive Christianization

The third aspect of Christian urbanism called for constructive action, for the creation of churches, baptistries, martyrions, and memorials. At Sardis we observe this action on a remarkable scale in a piece of urban planning rather than in individual construction. Sometime late in the reign of Constantine (324–337) or under his sons (337–361), the decision was made to build an entire "Christian quarter" just outside the city gate, *fuori le mura*—indeed, perhaps at the same time that the wall was being built (Fig. 208; cf. Plan IV).[51]

The new quarter was laid out along the ancient "Street of the Pipes" (Fig. 43), in an area where only a water tank and some cemetery plots had existed.[52] The choice may have been made because the land was available; but it remains an attractive though unproved conjecture that some important Christian martyr[53] was buried in this area. The work of rebuilding began with the laying of numerous pipes and drains under the Street of the Pipes; coins found in and around them provide the dating. The street itself was narrowed to provide a strip alongside the church complex, part of which eventually became the "North Chapel" and the rest a cemetery. A sizable basilica with various appendages (Fig. 289) was constructed on the south (southeast) side; a mosaic suite of three rooms was attached to the small bath on the north side, which may have been built somewhat earlier. It may have served some function in connection with the church complex. Its wonderful dolphin and animal hunt mosaics (Fig. 298) do not show anything Christian, but neither is the trident used as a symbol of the sea a confession of pagan worship to Poseidon. The "Eagle Mosaic" (5 m. by 4.5 m.; Fig. 298) hall makes the impression of having been intended for receptions. If not a bishop's residence, it might have been his reception hall.[54]

Excavations have not progressed very far into the ambient of the Early Christian basilica EA. It is clear that the basilica was part of a larger complex (Figs. 54, 288–290) which included more structures to the east and possibly to the south and west. What has been excavated is described by Buchwald (below); but it should be clearly understood that the south and west parts of the church are under the modern village roads, and much has been torn off by the Pactolus on the west. As our plans and drawings (Figs. 43, 289) clearly indicate, much remains to be done on the east. The "ancillary facilities" may have been far more extensive. The location, size, and type of the church (very appropriate to celebrate a martyr) make it very unlikely that this was the largest church or the cathedral of Sardis. Church "D" (Fig. 287) has a much better claim. It would therefore be incautious to suggest that the relative importance of the Christian and Jewish communities could be measured by comparing Church EA with the Synagogue, as is suggested by Kraabel and Buchwald.

The Complex of Church M

The region centering on the basilica EA was a creation *de novo*. The little chapel M (W83–100/S1242–1256) attached to the southeast corner of the Artemis Temple (Figs. 88–89, 284–286) was also a new building, but it was clearly intended to sanctify the Artemis Precinct and to provide a funerary chapel for a cemetery, which stretched along the south side of the Artemis Temple up to the front of Building L (Fig. 88).[55] When the church was built, the level of the temple colonnade had risen over a meter (from stylobate). Some 25 m. west of the church facade, two small columns standing on a threshold formed the entrance into a church precinct within the south colonnade. The church extends 17 m. east of the south edge of the temple stylobate. Its south wall continues the alignment of the south stylobate of the temple. Its north wall abuts one of the temple columns (Fig. 286). The original western chapel was a very simple apsidal hall with clerestory lighting (later blocked up) and a window in the apse. It measured 5.6 m. north-south and 7 m. east-west, plus an apse 3.15 in diameter. Built on shallow foundations of rubble alternating with brick courses and a marble floor of reused spoils, it had one door to north opening on a unit B, interpreted by Jacobs as a court. The west door was not on axis so as to avoid the temple column.[56] The interior of the church was originally stuccoed and frescoed. Purple bands on thin white plaster preserve a scheme of panels or simplified pilasters at the bottom of the apse. Yellow ochre and other pigments were used on other walls. The exterior, too, was originally stuccoed and painted in yellow, perhaps trimmed with green.[57] A block of sandstone laid on a marble support served as altar, one of the earliest known. Excavated originally by H. C. Butler in 1911–1914, the church was cleaned, restudied, and repaired by S. W. Jacobs in 1961, 1969, and 1973.

Just outside the north doorway, Butler found a hoard of coins which assured that the church was built before A.D. 400.[58] It is thus one of the earliest preserved churches in Western Asia Minor, "a social, historical, and architectural document of considerable value" (Jacobs).

In the sixth century a larger, outer apse, 5.04 m. in diameter, was added on the east, resulting in the peculiar arrangement known as *apse en échelon*.[59] The apse was covered by a half dome on inner shell only one brick thick, with two buttresses at the north and south; it had an attractive triforium which was reconstructed in 1973 after being lost with part of the wall (Fig. 285). The technique was a typically Justinianic mixture of stones and brick. The new eastern unit opened with one door into the "long, narrow service room A," and with another onto the cemetery area on the south.

Butler's plan showed a grave oriented north-south in the east apse; but he said nothing about finding one. Excavation of the east sanctuary in 1969 revealed two skeletons without grave-goods buried with their heads to the west. The freshness of the skeletons was such as to suggest that they must have been buried between 1914 and 1958, possibly during the hostilities in 1921–1922.[60] Although some Late Antique material was found in the fill, no evidence of an earlier grave was observed. It is likely enough that both sanctuaries were *martyria,* but the names of the martyrs remain unknown.

Both sanctuaries were buried by landslides and floods so that by the tenth century only the top of the church was exposed; by 1910 they had disappeared from sight.[61]

Other Christian Places of Worship

Among the houses of the Byzantine village that grew up on the north side of the Artemis Precinct (Fig. 88) was an ancient mausoleum of the fifth or sixth century(?) (Mausoleum U) built over a vaulted Roman tomb of ca. A.D. 100 (Fig. 188). There is, however, no proof that it had become a Christian chapel.[62]

A very different kind of funerary chapel with actual burials was found in the large cave hollowed out within what is at present the highest peak of the Acropolis. It has been conjectured that the cave had originated as a Lydian cistern, but the existence of Roman-Byzantine type of painted stucco observed by L. J. Majewski rules this out, at least for later times.[63] The date of the first use of the chapel is uncertain; it may well have come into existence during the Dark Ages

(A.D. 616 to ca. 800) or Middle Byzantine times to serve the much beleaguered citadel and its cemeteries.

Church D—The Cathedral of Sardis?

If any building holds the key to the greatness of Late Antique Christianity at Sardis, it is surely the mighty ruin at the east edge of the ancient city where the modern road dips down from the platform of the city site (Figs. 8:29; 287; Plan IV). The building stands north of the modern highway and commands a fine view of the Hermus plain. As R. L. Vann had pointed out,[64] the orientation of Church D follows the "bent axis" orientation of basilica "C," the Roman street at the mill, and so-called structure A, an orientation which must go back to the plan of A.D. 17, if not before. It is probable that the present building adopted this orientation from a temple. Although it was admired, discussed, and drawn by many travelers, among whom Choisy's drawing and comments deserve particular notice,[65] no inscription gives a clue to its identity. Butler dubbed it "D" and considered it a basilica; many archaeologists are inclined to see in it the major church, the cathedral of Sardis.[66]

Five rectangular piers with reentrant corners are preserved up to 10 m. in height above the surface of a vineyard. Their dimensions can be reconstructed to approximately 4.10 m. (east-west) by 5.35 m. (north-south). They are roughly and hastily constructed of spoils packed with small stones and laid by layers in poor mortar, and faced with irregular ashlar. Parts of pendentives and springing of sideways arches are preserved. A vault springing from one of the piers indicates that the building continued northward. Vann interprets the existing piers as forming two rectangular bays, ca. 14.30 m. (north-south) by 11.20 m. (east-west), originally covered by elliptical domes on pendentives. Choisy interpreted the remains as parts of a one-aisle basilica. Others see them as the central nave of a multi-aisled Justinianic church. Vann favors the one-directional arrangement of St. Mary ("Council Church") over the Latin cross plan of St. John in Ephesus.[67] The church is very deeply buried, and only an excavation can resolve the architectural problems and the equally vexing question—to whom was this major church of Sardis dedicated?

GMAH

Early Christian Basilica EA and Church E

Remains of several small domes visible west of the road leading to the Artemis Precinct were noted by H. C. Butler, who gave them the designation "Building E" and speculated with uncanny accuracy that they were fragments which had come from a Middle Byzantine inscribed cross church with five domes.[1] Church E was excavated in 1962 and 1963 by M. Del Chiaro and H. Detweiler.[2] At the same time portions of Church EA were also uncovered, but were not yet identified as the remains of an earlier church (Fig. 43).[3]

Excavations subsequently carried out in 1972 and 1974 by A. Ramage and G. M. A. Hanfmann, with the advice of H. Buchwald, uncovered large portions of the Early Christian basilica which had preceded the construction of Church E, and which was designated Church EA.[4] In the season of 1972 numerous fragments of masonry from Church E still embedded in the debris around the building were uncovered, cleaned, and accurately measured, making possible the reconstruction of the complex vaulting system and of the rich facade ornamentation used in the church, in spite of the almost total destruction of the building. A number of pits inside the church also permitted an accurate survey of the foundations to be made, which in turn led to valuable information concerning Byzantine structural practices. During the same season small portions of the apse of the earlier Church EA, including fragments of fresco and modeled plaster decoration, were uncovered by A. Ramage, although the full context of Church EA was not yet recognized. Subsequently G. M. A. Hanfmann developed the hypothesis that Church E might be located within an earlier and much larger church, as is the case at Side on the southern coast of Asia Minor. In the following season further excavation showed this hypothesis to be correct. The meticulous care used in the excavation of large parts of the apse, narthex, atrium, and other ancillary facilities, hampered by the existence of numerous medieval graves, provided the invaluable evidence which can be used to trace the gradual enlargement of, and the many changes to, the Church EA complex. In 1980, small but important excavations undertaken by B. McLaughlin and H. Buchwald clarified a number of details concerning the ancillary facilities to the east and west of the basilica and established the eastern and western limits of the building complex.

Church EA

The original construction of the church comprised a basilica with a nave flanked by two aisles and a narthex (Figs. 43, 288–290).[5] On the exterior a semicircular central portion of the apse was flanked on both sides by heavy buttresses. The extant walls of the church are straight on the interior and exterior, without visible articulation such as pilasters or other protrusions, giving the church a particularly simple, clear, geometrically pristine character. The overall dimensions of the church and its various features, which appear to be related according to a simple system of harmonic proportions (1:2, 1:3, 1:4—1:2:3:4), underscore the clear geometry which underlies the plan.[6]

The extant excavated walls of Church EA (Figs. 288, 290) include the entire north wall of the north aisle and the narthex, the eastern wall of the north aisle, the apse, and the northern portions of the western walls of the north aisle, the nave, and the narthex. Portions of the stylobates of both nave colonnades, but not the original column bases, were also found. The original intercolumniations could therefore not be determined. The other portions of the church, roughly comprising the south aisle and the southern half of the narthex, were not excavated.

The construction of all these walls is entirely consistent, with the exception that three brick courses were used in the apse (Fig. 288), a feature which does not occur elsewhere in walls preserved to the same height. Otherwise the masonry is mortared rubble faced with about 20 cm. of mostly untrimmed but very carefully ordered rounded fieldstones, most probably from the nearby river bed. While the sizes of the stones vary considerably, they are laid in horizontal courses, each of which is built of stones of roughly the same size. The colors of the stones also vary considerably, giving the masonry a particularly attractive polychrome appearance. The attractiveness of the masonry is, however, probably fortuitous, because on the interior, which has the same treatment as the exterior, the masonry was certainly covered by plaster and marble revetments, traces of which have survived (Fig. 290).[7]

The rubble core (Figs. 288, 290) is built of untrimmed, rounded fieldstones the same in character as those used in the facing; neither spoils, cut ashlar, nor brick were used. The mortar is fine-grained and hard, with little or no admixture of crushed brick except in the rubble core. Neither joints nor other fissures were found in the excavated walls except near the bottoms of the buttresses flanking the apse (Figs. 43, 288), indicating that the church was probably built in a single continuous construction effort.

The apse buttresses may not have been planned originally, but must have been added early during the construction of the building, for they are bonded with adjacent portions of the apse already at a level hardly higher than the original floor line. Doors which seem originally to have led directly from the church to the exterior were found in the west wall of the narthex and in the northern and eastern walls of the north aisle (Figs. 289, 290). The positions of the doors in the western narthex wall permit the reconstruction of three doors in the original western facade, one on the major axis and the others approximately on the axes of the side aisles. Fragments of original revetment door frames were found *in situ* on one of the doors in the north wall, and on the door in the eastern wall of the north aisle.

A door between the narthex and the north aisle, as well as the major entrance from the narthex into the nave, on the major axis of the church, was also excavated. A doorsill made of a reused Roman cornice fragment, with indentations in its upper surface for the door post and for a locking rod, was found *in situ* in the latter doorway, its surface incised by the repeated opening and closing of the door, perhaps on tiny wheels.

Numerous sections of the original mosaic floor of the church were preserved in the north aisle (Fig. 290), in the narthex, and near the southern colonnade in the nave. The extant portions of mosaic show only decorative patterns, but because the remaining mosaics belong to peripheral areas of the building, the existence of other, more elaborate, perhaps pictorial features in the central area of the church cannot be excluded.[8]

None of the numerous marble fragments of architectural members found in and near the excavations can be attributed to the original period of construction with certainty. While research has not been completed, a preliminary survey indicates that the column bases and fragments of column shafts came from numerous buildings of different periods. If they were originally used in Church EA, they could therefore have only been used there as reused spoils. On the other hand, these pieces could just as well have been brought to the site in the Middle Byzantine or Turkish periods. The same may be argued for the numerous fragments of door jambs found in the excavations. The nine recorded pieces belong to at least five individual doors, each with different profiles and presumably from various buildings and periods.

Only relatively minor marble fragments may cautiously be attributed to Church EA with the aid of circumstantial evidence. A number of fragments of double engaged columns were found, for instance, reused as spoils in two different repairs to Church EA and in several places within Church E, indicating that they were available on the site over a period probably spanning many centuries. The large number of fragments of this type, all quite similar in character, makes it unlikely that they were brought to the site at different times from elsewhere. The eight fragments belonged to at least six different double engaged colunmns. In spite of their rather small size, they could have served as the major supports of the nave colonnades.[9] It seems more likely, however, that they were used as supports of gallery colonnades or as intermediate supports in windows with two or more lights.[10] A number of fragments of marble string courses with similar profiles which were found in the debris or as reused spoils in various repairs could also have been used in the original construction of Church EA.

Aside from the mosaic floor, the fragmentary revetment door frames, and probably the double engaged columns and string courses, little is known concerning the interior decoration of the church. Near the northeastern corner of the north aisle, fragments of a simple, undecorated revetment composed of small, flat marble plaques were found in situ, and the cement bedding for this type of revetment was also found in other areas on the walls of the north aisle (Fig. 290). The only other feature of the decoration which was determined consists of a layer of fresco found for the most part clinging to small

pieces of plaster in the debris within the apse. Unfortunately, none of the fragments is large enough to permit anything more than recognizing the colors which were used.[11]

The period of construction of Church EA may at present best be determined with the aid of coins found in and near the excavated portions of the building. Two coins struck in the periods A.D. 341–346 and 346–350 were found in the bedding of the mosaic floor.[12] These coins provide a *terminus post quem* rather than a precise date for the construction, since it cannot be excluded that the coins continued to circulate for some time after they were struck. However, the fact that two coins were found dating from the decade between 340 and 350 makes it tempting to assume that the church was built at that time. The consistent character of the masonry and of other features attributable to the original construction and the relatively modest size of the building would argue for a short period of construction. Barring undue complications in the construction or the financing, for which there is at present no evidence, a period of one to two decades or even less would certainly have sufficed.

The evidence provided by other coins found in and near the church, while admittedly circumstantial, tends to support this interpretation. Two coins struck in the period 393–395 were found close to the exterior of the apse in earth 0.25 and 0.40 m. higher than the floor of Church EA, and a coin probably struck between 395 and 408 was found in the same general area about 0.60 m. above the floor line.[13] It is reasonable to assume that the ground outside the apse, which could easily be reached from the church by the door in the eastern wall of the north aisle, was at about the same level or even slightly lower than the church floor when the church was built. The slightly higher levels at which these coins were found, therefore, appear to represent accumulation of earth after the church first went into use. Moreover, coins struck in the periods 366–375, 395–408, and 400–408 were also found in various contexts in addition to the original church which will be described below, indicating that building activity had already shifted from the construction of Church EA to the expansion of ancillary facilities by the end of the century.

While taken individually none of the coin finds can be used to date the church or other features with precision, taken together the coin finds produce a convincingly logical sequence. The sequence of coins makes it difficult to avoid the conclusion that the church may have been built as early as the forties of the fourth century and was probably built before its last quarter.

The numismatic evidence is far more useful for establishing the construction date of Church EA than the scant stylistic evidence available at present. We know almost nothing of the superstructure of the building. Among the lacunae in our knowledge of the original appearance of the building are (1) the intercolumniation, the fenestration, and the forms of the column bases and capitals; (2) whether the capitals carried an arcade or a trabeated system; (3) whether the church was provided with galleries; and (4) the heights of the various features of the building. We know little more than the plan of Church EA near ground level (Figs. 43, 289), hardly enough to analyze a building in terms of architectural style. Just as detrimental for an effective stylistic analysis of Church EA is the lack of a sufficient number of dated comparable examples, particularly in Western Asia Minor. Over 300 Christian basilicas are known in Greece, an indication that those basilicas now known in Western Asia Minor probably represent a small portion of those which once existed. That relatively few basilican churches can be reasonably attributed to the fourth century outside Rome and the Holy Land limits still further the effectiveness of a stylistic analysis of Church EA.

A comparison of those forms of Church EA which have been firmly established in the excavations with similar forms in other buildings is therefore useful only in demonstrating that they do not require a later attribution of the church, and that there is no need, on the basis of the scant available stylistic evidence, to doubt the evidence of the coins. We do not suggest that the known features of Church EA can be used to attribute the church to the fourth century, but rather, that they permit the building to be attributed to the fourth century on the basis of numismatic evidence, without reservations concerning the stylistic criteria now available. Many if not all of these features seem to have been used, at least occasionally, also in the fifth and sixth centuries.

In the same context, it is relevant to note that not a single carved object with ornamentation typical of the fifth and sixth centuries was found in the excavations of Churches E and EA, even though numerous and well-preserved pieces carved in other styles were found. Moreover, excellent carving typical of the fifth to sixth century period was excavated in other Sardis buildings. The complete lack of even vaguely Theodosian details is particularly conspicuous, and the almost ascetic simplicity found in most features of the church would be surprising in many areas of the Byzantine sphere after the fourth century.

Later Additions to Church EA

Extensive remains of additions to Church EA, unfortunately in a very fragmentary state, were found to the west, north, and east of the original basilica. Probably the earliest is the atrium immediately to the west of the narthex (Figs. 289, 290). Its walls are not bonded with those of the narthex and are constructed of masonry somewhat different in character. The stones tend to be trimmed into squarish blocks, the courses are not as regular, and the polychrome effect achieved by the juxtaposition of stone, frequently marble, of different colors is reduced in favor of a more uniform use of a bluish-gray stone. Remains of the very poorly preserved mosaic floor of the atrium were found west of the northern portal, at a level about 0.10 m. higher than the narthex floor, probably a further indication that the atrium and the church are not contemporary.[14]

Similar masonry was used in the construction of three relatively small spaces north of the atrium. The east space is closed on the east by an exedral niche, leading to the suggestion that it was a chapel (North Chapel). The central space, which is the smallest, was probably originally a monumental vestibule leading from the street north of the EA complex into the atrium and has been designated Entrance Bay. The west space is in a particularly fragmentary state of preservation because its west end was washed away by the Pactolus River, making it impossible to determine its original extent or shape. Repeated repairs, changes, and additions are evident in all three spaces, but particularly in the Entrance Bay. The mosaic floor paving typical of the basilica, narthex, and atrium was found only in the Entrance Bay, while a relatively well preserved tile floor was found in the North Chapel.[15] A marble threshold between the Entrance Bay and the atrium was placed into its present position only after the completion of the mosaic, for the mosaic pattern in the atrium was interrupted by the threshold. The atrium and the Entrance Bay were probably constructed early in the fifth century. The date is suggested by a coin struck between A.D. 400 and 408 which was found in the north wall of the atrium,[16] and by the fact that the mosaic floor of the Entrance Bay had an exact equivalent in the floor of a house only a few meters north of the church, which can be dated to the same period on the basis of numismatic evidence.[17] The North Chapel had not yet been constructed during this period. After passing into the Entrance Bay from the street to the north, one continued either to the atrium on the south, or to a relatively narrow exterior courtyard on the east, which led to the north aisle of the church. The fact that the Entrance Bay, atrium, narthex, and church all had mosaic floors, while the courtyard leading to the north aisle was unpaved, suggests that those who used the courtyard were less privileged, perhaps the catechumens.[18]

The North Chapel was built somewhat later, utilizing the west end of the courtyard. With its construction the direct approach from the Entrance Bay through the courtyard to the north aisle was blocked, suggesting a change in the normal use of the church, perhaps caused by the declining number of catechumens.[19] At the same time the marble threshold seems to have been transferred from its original position, probably between the street and the Entrance Bay, to its present position between the Entrance Bay and the atrium. During this phase the Entrance Bay and North Chapel seem to have been open to the street, and the door closing the church complex was located between the Entrance Bay and the atrium. Somewhat later the open doorway between the street and the Entrance Bay was blocked by walls which created a large rectangular niche accessible only from the church complex. Another major entrance to the church complex must therefore either already have existed or have been created at the same time.

Most of these changes were probably carried out in the fifth century, not very long after the construction of the atrium and the Entrance Bay. For the most part, the character of the masonry used differs only slightly, and it is at times difficult to distinguish between the masonry of the various changes. Similar masonry was also used in the construction of two rooms which were partially excavated on the western side of the atrium. One had a mosaic pavement displaying an intricate pattern of crosses and interlocked circular elements formed of interwoven bands. The western walls of these rooms were constructed of particularly heavy masonry fortified by strong piers, indicating that the walls were expected to withstand the erosive action of the Pactolus, and perhaps also of other destructive forces. The western walls of these rooms, therefore, probably represent the western confines of the Church EA building complex. The existence of the rooms suggests that the atrium was flanked on the west, as on the north, and perhaps also on the south by a continuous series of spatial units. The form of the masonry and of the mosaic pavement indicates that the rooms west of the atrium were probably built in the fifth to sixth century period.

An apsidal unit which was also a small chapel, and of which only the eastern portions were excavated was located near the northwest corner of the atrium. It has been designated the West Chapel. Its masonry is poor in quality compared with that of other walls, and rests directly upon the mosaic floor of the atrium without a foundation. Its floor was paved with large, frequently carved, reused marble slabs, and a short column which supported an altar was located in the center of the apse. A considerable lapse of time between the construction of the atrium complex and this chapel must be postulated, and it seems reasonable to attribute the West Chapel to a construction phase after the Persian destruction of 616.

The character of the masonry in the walls of spaces added to the east of Church EA is also different from that of most walls in the atrium complex (Figs. 43, 289). Their location flanking the major apse of the basilica suggests that they may have been pastophories (rooms serving for storage of the Eucharist, also as vestries usually flanking the apse). The quality of the masonry and the character of fresco fragments found on one of the walls[20] suggests that these spaces were built before the Persian conquest of 616.[21]

Repairs and Restorations

Evidence of at least three distinct repairs or restorations to Church EA was found in the course of the excavations. Undoubtedly, the earliest is an *opus sectile* floor which was laid directly over the original mosaic floor. A similar floor which also replaced an original mosaic floor in the Sardis gymnasium dates from the late fifth or early sixth century, and the EA floor may well have been applied at roughly the same time.[22] Only small patches of the *opus sectile* floor were found, suggesting either that the other portions were destroyed in subsequent repairs or reconstructions, or that only small areas of the original floor were repaired with *opus sectile*. A fragment of a marble closure slab bearing an inscription (*tos archidiakon;* Fig. 293), as well as a short flight of steps leading from the north aisle to the north courtyard, may belong to the same renovation.[23]

A major restoration of Church EA was carried out in masonry reminiscent of that used in Constantinople, northern Greece, and Asia Minor in the late eighth, ninth, and early tenth centuries. When this type of masonry may have been used in Sardis has not been precisely determined, but it may well have been used here in the ninth century.[24] In this restoration, walls were constructed partly next to and partly over the stylobates of the nave colonnades, in places directly upon the *opus sectile* floor. The same type of masonry was also used to patch portions of the eastern and western walls of the basilica, suggesting that the church had suffered heavy damage. The nave walls may have served to support the roof of the basilica, replacing the original columns lost after the Persian destruction. It is also possible that they served to visually separate the nave from the side aisles, for comparable medieval walls are also found in other early basilicas in Asia Minor.[25]

A second layer of fresco over the original fresco of the apse may have been applied during this rather extensive reconstruction of Church EA, or earlier, perhaps in the restorations of the fifth to sixth century. The technique of the frescoes implies that the later date is more probable.[26] Even though the second layer of frescoes in the apse cannot be related to a specific reconstruction with certainty, this medieval reconstruction phase also seems to have included frescoes, because a section of masonry typical of this period was integrated into the walls of a pit of the late medieval Church E, and this masonry retains remnants of frescoes which must precede

the construction of Church E. A grave which was found underneath the floor of the pit in Church E contained ostensibly reburied bones and a glass bottle (G 72.1; Fig. 292), suggesting that they belonged to a particularly important person, perhaps a saint. Because the grave lies at a level below the floor of Church EA, and because a fourth century coin was found in the fill above the grave, the grave may already have existed in its present location when Church EA was built. However, neither the original mosaic floor nor the *opus sectile* floor of the first renovation were extant above the grave, and the grave bears a stronger relationship to the architectural features of the medieval restoration than to those of the original church, suggesting that the bones were transferred to their new location during that restoration. Underneath this burial was an earlier grave (G 73.19; Fig. 291) of the fourth century which had no gravegoods and was cut by the foundation wall of the late, medieval church.[27]

Evidence of at least one other, smaller restoration of Church EA was also uncovered, primarily in the form of patched walls and closed doorways. Probably at least some of these repairs were carried out after the building had been devastated and perhaps temporarily abandoned following the Seljuk invasion of Asia Minor in the late eleventh century.[28]

Church E

After the site of Church EA had been cleared and the remaining portions leveled, a much smaller but well-built vaulted church, Church E, was constructed within the eastern half of the nave of Church EA, in a final construction effort. Its foundations rest directly on the floor of EA (Figs. 43, 288). It is possible to reconstruct most features of the building in spite of its almost total destruction, undoubtedly due to an earthquake, with the aid of a careful analysis of numerous masonry fragments found in the rubble.[29]

The major features of the church were organized on the principle of the inscribed cross church type (Fig. 294), with the exception that the walls between the bema and the flanking chapels were replaced by columns, giving the nave an unusual basilican character. A narthex with doors on the north, south, and west preceded the nave. Small domes with cylindrical drums covered the corner bays of the nave immediately adjacent to the major dome, and pendentive domes covered the east bays of the side aisles. The exterior was richly articulated by blind arcades with stepped profiles, a reflection of the structural organization of the interior. Friezes of hollow quatrefoils (Fig. 295) formed of clay pipes inserted vertically into the wall surrounded the arches of the blind arcades, adding a strong chiaroscuro emphasis to the facade articulation. The four extant lunettes of the facade articulation were each decorated with a checkerboard pattern, while the lunettes of the arcades which decorated the major apse were filled with brick herringbone patterns. The drums of the minor domes were ornamented by simple brick meander bands, and the northern apse by a brick chevron frieze. The extant remains of the facade ornamentation permit the conclusion that the patterns used were unusually rich in number, that they were organized according to a carefully planned and ordered system, and that they were executed with meticulous care and precision.

The major features of Church E may be clearly distinguished from those of an early group of five domed inscribed cross churches which have been attributed to the period between the tenth and thirteenth centuries, and from those of a later, northern group which date from the late thirteenth to the fifteenth century. Church E has close parallels only in the five domed inscribed cross churches of Mistra and Nessebar, all datable to the period between the beginning of the fourteenth and the second quarter of the fifteenth century (Afentico, Metropolis, and Pantanassa in Mistra, Aleiturgitus in Nessebar). Most of the major features of the plans and of the vaulting systems of these churches are identical with those of Church E. The fact that only the churches of Mistra have galleries is undoubtedly to be explained by functional and iconographic considerations and therefore does not invalidate the comparison.[30]

A detailed examination of the brick ornamentation of Church E leads to a similar conclusion concerning the date of the building. The specific variations used here can, for the most part, be demonstrated only in the period between the late twelfth and the early fourteenth century.[31]

Historical and archaeological evidence permits the dating of Church E with greater precision. Activity at Sardis in the period immediately before the thirteenth century and after about 1260 appears to have been minimal. Turkish raids are reported in Lydia already during the reign of Michael Paleologus (1261–1282), and the hinterland of Sardis appears to have been under Turkish control towards the end of the thirteenth century. Sardis itself fell to the Turks at an unknown date not long after 1300. Only during the Lascarid rule from 1204 until 1261 does Sardis seem to have enjoyed the safety and prosperity during which the construction of a new church of the size and richness of Church E might be expected.[32]

A detailed comparison of numerous features of Church E, including the articulation of the apse and motifs used in the facade ornamentation, with those of a number of other buildings in Western Asia Minor which were probably built about the same time provides a stylistic framework which can be used to determine construction dates within somewhat narrower limits.[33] The interface between the proposed stylistic sequence and the thirteenth century history of Western Asia Minor permits an attribution of Church E to the period roughly between about 1230 and about 1245.[34] Indeed, it is possible that the church represents a style close to that of the imperial court of John Vatatzes (1222–1254), who took an active interest in the area. He spent much of his time in Nymphaeum and Magnesia on Sipylus, both not far from Sardis, and is known to have founded the monastery of Sosandria on Mount Sipylus, where he was buried.[35]

The Significance of Churches EA and E

The remains of Churches EA and E are extremely fragmentary, and numerous points in their reconstructions remain open. Large portions of the Church EA complex have not been excavated. Moreover, the comparable Byzantine architectural evidence is, for the most part, poorly dated, inadequately investigated and published, and spread over a vast area. The following observations concerning the significance of Churches EA and E are therefore certainly tentative. They seem, nevertheless, to be worth considering, if for no other reason than that they may stimulate further research concerning this valuable material.

1. Church EA (Figs. 43, 288–290) appears to be the earliest datable church now known in Western Asia Minor, and seems also to be one of the earliest extant churches now known outside Rome and the Holy Land. It was most probably built before any of the extant churches now known in Constantinople. As fragmentary as the remains of the church are, they therefore provide invaluable evidence concerning the early development of church architecture.

2. The proposed early date of Church EA is equally important as evidence of the Christian community in Sardis in the fourth century. A number of questions immediately arise in this context; the most important are the following: (1) Who built the church? (2) Why was it built at the edge of the city, outside the city walls? (3) Why would it have been built so much earlier than known churches in comparable cities? While definitive answers depend on further research and may never become available, the following observations should be considered: the modest size and peripheral location of the church seem to preclude an imperial donation, or a donation by a major public official; the dwellings north of the church were built at roughly the same time, in part by the same work crews, indicating that they may have been directly related to the church, and permitting the conjecture that they constituted a bishop's residence; the relatively small size and peripheral location of Church EA, as opposed to the central location of the roughly contemporary and very much larger Synagogue, probably indicate that the size and available means of the fourth century Sardis Christian community were limited compared with those of the Sardis Jewish community; the possibility that the location of Church EA was, at least in part, determined by the grave of a saint, perhaps martyred in the Diocletian persecutions, must be considered.[36] Although the lack of comparable and datable fourth century churches in other cities in the area may be due to accidents of preservation or of excavation, the fact that Sardis contained not only a very early church, but also a roughly contemporary and unusually large synagogue can hardly be ignored. The Sardis evidence permits the very tentative conjecture that the early date of Church EA can be explained by an unusually large Christian community in fourth century Sardis, and that this large Christian community

may, in turn, be explained by the existence of a sizable Jewish community there at the same time.[37]

3. The addition of ancillary facilities to the east, west, and northwest of the original basilica and the subsequent changes which were made in these areas may provide valuable information concerning how such spaces were used at different stages in the Early Byzantine period and when changes in usage may have taken place. For instance, there is clear evidence that the approach to the north aisle from the east, through the unpaved courtyard on its north side, had become superfluous in the course of the fifth century when it was blocked by the construction of the North Chapel, suggesting that that approach may originally have been used by the catechumens. There is also evidence which suggests that the unit north of the apse, perhaps a pastophory, was added no later than the sixth century, an observation which gains in importance when it is considered in the context of sixth century Constantinopolitan churches, which had no pastophories flanking the apse.

4. The pre-Lascarid medieval changes and repairs to Church EA are useful primarily for documenting the variations in the amount of medieval activity in Sardis. The architectural work is haphazardly constructed and inconsequential in design. Mostly it seems to have been limited to essential repairs, apparently made necessary by the Persian and Seljuk invasions of the early seventh and late eleventh centuries.

5. In contrast to the architectural remains, there is evidence that ornamental stone carving of high quality was created for Church EA in the pre-Lascarid medieval period. The carved epistyle of an altar screen and other fragments of architectural carving which can be attributed to these repairs are comparable in design and quality with pieces found in Aphrodisias, Ephesus, Heracleia on Latmos, Xanthos, and other sites in Asia Minor. Greek examples of roughly comparable material, mostly dated to the eleventh and twelfth centuries, are not as consistent in character and are usually inferior in quality. Moreover, similar carving does not seem to have existed in Constantinople. It therefore seems possible that the Sardis carving represents an independent style developed in Western Asia Minor, which has not until now been recognized.[38]

6. With the aid of evidence obtained in the ex-

cavation of Church E and numerous stylistic comparisons, a number of buildings in Western Asia Minor and on the Greek island of Chios can be attributed to the Lascarid period and to the years immediately following Lascarid rule.[39] Almost nothing was known of Lascarid architecture previously, a lacuna which was all the more frustrating because politically the Palaeologue dynasty, which initiated the final, extraordinarily rich period of Byzantine civilization, was the direct heir to the Lascarids in Asia Minor. Indeed, numerous features of Palaeologue architecture in Constantinople and other areas have strong similarities with features found earlier in Lascarid Asia Minor.

7. The major features of Church E seem to have been planned using the *quadratura,* a geometric system of proportions based on a series of diagonally inscribed squares. The *quadratura* was previously known in medieval architecture above all through its use in the sketchbook of Villard d'Honnecourt, roughly contemporary with Church E, and in the late fifteenth century treatise by Matthias Roriczer.[40] The importance of the use of the *quadratura* in Church E (Fig. 294) is emphasized by the further observation that the *quadratura* was also used in other Byzantine churches,[41] and that simple geometric constructions seem to have been used in the design of most Lascarid buildings.[42]

8. A number of Constantinopolitan features are found several decades earlier in Sardis Church E than in the comparable Palaeologue churches in Mistra and Nessebar. A transmission of at least some features from Constantinople to other provinces by way of Asia Minor may therefore be postulated. The forms may well have been transmitted by master builders or work crews escaping the Turkish onslaught in Asia Minor after the 1260s.[43]

9. Just as important as any of the points briefly outlined above seems to be the observation that Churches EA and E represent over a thousand years in the history of a single building complex in Western Asia Minor. The excavation serves as a yardstick which can be used to measure the impact of history on Sardis from the late Constantinian period through the Ottoman occupation, until the building's final destruction by an earthquake, probably in 1595.[44]

HB

The Cemeteries

It was a widespread belief in Classical antiquity that death means pollution and that ordinary mortals should not be buried within a sanctuary. This was certainly true of Artemis and Apollo,[1] and the placing of a Roman chamber tomb within the limits of the Artemis sanctuary at Sardis (Fig. 188) must have had special reasons.[2] The Christian attitude was very nearly the opposite. Precisely because the graves were the places where the dead entered life eternal, they were venerable—doubly so, if their owners had attained the crown of life through martyrdom. Although the exact way of the resurrection of the body was from the beginning a controversial subject,[3] there was a considerable body of opinion which held that resurrection would be of bodies as they were in life.[4] This could lead to the feeling that the tombs should be protected. We mentioned above the law of A.D. 386 calling for construction of churches for veneration of the saints, presumably often over the tombs or relics of martyrs. Both the basilica EA and the chapel M may well belong to this category. Two martyrs associated with Sardis are known by name—Therapon and Apollonius[5]—but so far nothing has emerged to link them either to churches or to graves. In fact, no pre-Constantinian Christian graves have been safely identified.

The principal interest of the Christian cemeteries at Sardis lies in the continuity of communal life and worship to which they attest across the great divide of the destruction of A.D. 616. Just as the Churches EA and E constitute a thousand years of continuous Christian worship, so too does the cemetery at these two churches attest Christian burials over a thousand-year period (ca. 350–1350). Part of the same span is seen in the cemeteries on the Acropolis (Fig. 74; ca. 500–1100?).

These burials illustrate the thin line of survival in the life of the Christian community. They also illustrate in a specific way what kind of population had survived; for much the largest number of better preserved skeletal remains has come from people buried in these Christian cemeteries. Some general results of anthropological researches have been published, but eventually something more detailed may be learned about the makeup of age, sex, health, illness—provided the material now in Ankara is preserved and available.[6]

On the other hand, in Late Antique times and during the "Dark Ages," the notion of grave-goods seems to have been felt to be pagan. Except for the lamps of the mass burial at Bin Tepe,[7] only small personal possessions such as seals, finger rings (Fig. 299), and simple jewelry (usually of bronze) were buried with the dead and even those only in a few cases. It is striking that even tombstones and inscriptions are very rare, perhaps because of the belief that "their names are known to God."[8]

The crude and austere PN burials are perhaps to be considered as expressing the new attitude toward the dead. The painted chamber tomb, on the other hand, was most definitely a continuing form of Roman burial architecture. Recent discoveries (since 1976) have established beyond a doubt that a local school of tomb painters flourished at Sardis from the mid-fourth into the early fifth century. We have even learned the name of one of the painters, Flavius Chrysanthios, a Christian, who, surprisingly, was an official of the Imperial arms factory. He calls his vaulted chamber tomb (Fig. 297) a *heroon,* as did his pagan(?) contemporary Aurelius Zotikos.[9] The group of chamber tombs discussed below reveals a very interesting example of Christianization of a traditional burial type.

A unique case of the reuse of a Lydian chamber tomb for a Christian mass burial in the late sixth or early seventh century presents a mystery which is as yet unsolved. It pertains, in any case, to the region of Bin Tepe rather than the city of Sardis. Common burials for association (guild) members continued the tradition of Roman times. This is attested by an inscription with two crosses which speaks of a *kamara* (camera) of the Clothes-Dealers' Assistants; the stone closed the entrance to a late Roman tomb on the south side of Seytan Dere.[10]

Location of Cemeteries

HoB/Highway Area
In the HoB area, the small painted chamber tomb of the fourth century A.D. piously preserved under Unit 16 of the House of Bronzes

(Fig. 186)[11] may perhaps be considered as part of the Hellenistic-Roman cemetery along the highway. Within the House of Bronzes, the vaulted subterranean Unit 2, served as a depository for bones; but the bones might belong to a quick burial made after the disaster of A.D. 616. That the Christians used the Roman cemetery, which stretched along the highway west beyond the bridge and included the mausoleum of the *femina consularis,* Claudia Antonia Sabina (died ca. A.D. 215),[12] is proved by the painted tomb with a chrestogram (no. 3, below) found in 1913 across from Claudia's sepulcher.

Sector PN, Churches EA and E, Pactolus Bank
As we noted in Chapter VII, a late Hellenistic mausoleum (Fig. 129, M) became after the A.D. 17 earthquake part of a small Roman burial precinct. A Roman chamber tomb with a bed ("Ch") was built askew onto the ruined Hellenistic monument. Two Roman brick sarcophagi of the late second and early third centuries A.D., and two tile graves, one possibly Julio-Claudian, the other perhaps late Roman,[13] were placed in the area around the chamber tomb. When the precinct was built over with the "Mosaic Suite" (Late Antique Villa),[14] a window was put in the basement so that the north side of the mausoleum was visible (and accessible for offerings?). This window was walled up in A.D. 518. It seems that until that time, the owner of the Hellenistic mausoleum and his successor(s) in the chamber tomb "Ch" had enjoyed special respect.

The reason for describing this precinct is that it provides the best proof that a Roman cemetery preexisted in the area of the basilica EA. In fact, the precinct is only a little over 10 m. distant from the north wall of EA (Fig. 43). It is not clear whether another supposed Roman funerary precinct further to the northwest was already Christian.[15] The Roman cemetery probably extended at least 50 m. south (from the church area). There the painted "Peacock Tomb" (Figs. 8:12; 296) cut through two Roman tile graves (G 61.24 and G 61.25) of the first or second century A.D.[16]

The Christian Cemetery at the Churches EA and E
Of the 112 graves excavated in 1961–1962 and 1972–1973, only one was of the Roman brick-tile type and possibly pre-Constantinian. It lies within the strip of ground alongside and north of

the church, which was separated by a low wall from the street (Fig. 43; cf. 289) and which M. Del Chiaro named the "Roman Garden."[17] This strip was probably from the beginning intended for a small cemetery.

The Two Graves under Church E

Was the presence of tombs of martyrs or saints the reason which led to the construction of the basilica EA? H. Buchwald suggests with regard to Grave 72.2, found under a peculiar stepped area of the Lascarid Church E (Fig. 291), that the bones of a saint along with a late Roman glass bottle (Fig. 292, G 72.1) were transferred to the then new thirteenth century Lascarid church from an earlier place of burial. He does not discuss an earlier burial which lay underneath Grave 72.2 and is numbered Grave 73.19 (Fig. 291).[18] Carefully built of large stone slabs, this grave was cut into by a foundation wall of the Lascarid church. The bones were not discarded but deposited in the east part of the grave. There were no gravegoods. The grave lay under the tiled subflooring of the Early Christian basilica EA. Below the subfloor but above the grave was a coin of Valentinian (A.D. 382–392). The grave must be earlier, but we cannot tell by how much. It may well belong to one of the Christian saints for whom the basilica was built.

Types of Graves and Gravegoods

In addition to the two graves described above, two wooden caskets were inferred with certainty from the position of iron nails, one of them from the burial of a wealthy child after the mid-thirteenth century.[19] Two Lydian bathtub-like sarcophagi were reused.[20] These were the exceptions. Otherwise, the more than a hundred graves containing over 150 individuals were oblong or boat-shaped, constructed of reasonably carefully joined reused bricks, tiles, and stones. The covers, too, were made of reused schist or marble pieces. Only four graves had crosses on the marble covers—on the underside, turned inward toward the dead.[21] Not one grave had the name of the dead inscribed. All buried people had their heads to the west. Among the small personal belongings were one bronze cross, three pairs of bronze earrings, and two bronze necklaces.[22] The very exceptional burial of a small girl, mentioned above, which lay along the south side of the Lascarid Church E, yielded a gold earring and a fine, faceted rock-crystal bead.[23]

Development of the Cemetery at PN

The series of burials stretches from ca. A.D. 350, when the first burials were made against the apse of the basilica EA, to ca. A.D. 1360–1390, the dates of the Islamic coins found in the reused Lydian sarcophagus placed against the north side of the Lascarid Church E.[24]

As noted above, the first step in the formation of a Christian cemetery was taken during the reconstruction of the Roman "Street of the Pipes" and simultaneously with the construction of the basilica EA between A.D. 340 and 400 (Figs. 43, 289). A strip 4 m. wide was reserved along the north side of the church. A coin of Valentinian I (366–375) on the "walking floor" dated the early phase of the use of this part.[25]

By virtue of location and by coin finds we can distinguish the following sequence.

1. Graves built against early parts of the basilica EA; apse, Grave 73.6 (infant burial); 62.20.
2. Graves built against the pastophory and south aisle of EA: 62.19; 62.20; 73.13; 73.1?
3. Graves made within the basilica, under its floor, while the church was functioning: 62.47; 62.38; 62.49; 62W. Parallels for such "chaotic" burials found within a church in Apamea are dated by J. Balty to the eighth and ninth centuries.[26]
4. Graves made after the mosaic and sectile floors of the basilica were destroyed: 62.32; 62.33; 62.36; 62.39. These graves should certainly date after A.D. 616. Stages three and four may correlate with the restoration work dated to the eighth to tenth centuries, as observed by Buchwald (above).
5. Graves made after the narthex and atrium of the basilica EA had been abandoned (W239–246/S386.5–392): 73.23; 73.24; 73.29; 73.37; 73.28; 73.30; 73.32; 73.33; 73.267. Three coins of Constantine X and Romanus IV, 1059–1067; 1067–1071 were found. Stage five may be related to the very late repairs made after temporary abandonment due to Seljuk raids in the eleventh century.
6. Graves cut into the area of basilica EA after its abandonment: 73.2; 73.11 (apse); 73.7

(pastophory); 73.4; 73.5; 73.9; 73.10; 73.12; 73.15; and on top of north aisle: 62.40.

7. Graves associated with Lascarid Church E (1220–1250). North side: 62.1; 62.2; 62.18; 62.27; 73.12; south side: 73.21; 73.22; 73.25; west side: 62.38; 62.45; 62.46; 62.47. In narthex of church: 4 graves (not numbered).

At a time not yet closely determined but certainly not later than the construction of Lascarid Church E, the "Street of the Pipes" was abandoned and the cemetery spread across the 6 m. wide road up to the walls of the "Mosaic Unit" ("Roman Villa," Fig. 43), which may have served as a residential adjunct to the basilica ("bishop's residence").[27] The latter may have been restored (if indeed, it had been abandoned) and briefly reused during the thirteenth century. Church and cemetery probably ceased to function about the same time, possibly around 1400 or sometime in the fifteenth century; the exact dating hinges on the dating of the Islamic village which was built over the cemetery.[28]

Some 30 m. west (W265–275) and 15 m. north (S320–350) of the Christian cemetery was a Roman barrel-vaulted tomb revetted with marble slabs and four other graves with burials of at least nine individuals. The chamber tomb was tentatively dated to the fourth or fifth century A.D. There was, however, no definite indication that this assemblage, interpreted as a funerary precinct, was Christian.[29]

Southward the same uncertainty prevails with regard to the "Peacock Tomb," ca. 50 m. south of Church EA (no. 7, below; Fig. 296).

The Barrel-Vaulted Chamber Tombs

The painted and/or marble-revetted chamber tomb was clearly an upper-class type of sepulcher. We have noted earlier the development of the rubble and brick walled, brick and tile vaulted Roman chamber tomb from its Hellenistic forerunners with flat ceilings. The very interesting wall decorations range from the "First Pompeian" tectonic panel style executed in stucco to the late Roman and Late Antique freefield compositions.[30]

Structurally, two types were current in the late Roman period: the small vaulted chamber tomb with access from one of the ends,[31] and the large barrel-vaulted tomb. The form and general size of the latter were highly standardized. Usually, a trap door covered with a lid of schist or reused marble opened at one end to corbel steps set into the end wall (Fig. 188). The walls were plastered, stuccoed, and painted.[32]

Such chamber tombs have been found along the Main Highway (Fig. 129, plan of tombs and cemeteries), west of the Pactolus bridge; under the House of Bronzes (no. 5 of the list below); outside the Roman city wall opposite (north of) the mausoleum of Claudia Antonia Sabina (no. 3); along the east bank of the Pactolus with the "Peacock Tomb" (no. 6); and in and above the Artemis Precinct three other unopened tombs[33] (nos. 1–2). Since 1976, a group of chamber tombs has been reported in a valley 200 m. north of the Pyramid Tomb (E30/S620; Fig. 8:14). Three of them had been opened by 1979.[34]

These chamber tombs present a classic example of Christianization of a preexisting Roman sepulchral architectural type and decoration. Christianization was achieved by the simple device of introducing a chrestogram ("Morey's Tomb," no. 3) in the painted lunette or by a Christian formula in the inscription (Flavius Chrysanthios, no. 4). One tomb is definitely earlier and Roman (Artemis Precinct, Tomb 2, no. 1, below); another is also probably Roman ("Shear's Tomb," no. 2). The others remain indeterminate as to religion of the owners. The sequence adopted in the following list reflects this uncertainty.

List of (Painted) Chamber Tombs

Roman:
1. Artemis Precinct, Tomb 2 (Fig. 188). Painting: bird and branch. *Sardis* 1 (1975) 59, figs. 68, 72, 74. *Sardis* (R9) *Wall Painting* (forthcoming): WP 69.1. Finds under tomb: lamp; Hellenistic Apollo-club coin. Probably first century A.D. Strocka, *Ephesos,* 8:1, 60 n. 167.
2. Kagirlik Tepe. Location: *Sardis* 1 (1975) fig. 1, no. 34, "Roman Chamber Tomb." Shear, "Chamber Tomb," 19–25, figs. 1–3, pls. 1–6. Painting: "freefield" design: stocking-garlands, flowers, birds; flower baskets; peacocks; grapes; *Sardis* (R9) *Wall Painting:* WP 69.2. Shear (ibid., fig. 3) dated lamps found in the tomb to the first or second century A.D. He also dated the wall paintings to this period, but they seem close in style to the following:

Christian:

3. Location: west of Pactolus Bridge, opposite (north of) the mausoleum of Claudia Antonia Sabina; see *Sardis* R2 (1978) fig. 1, no. 32.2, "Painted Tomb," ca. W550/N50, pls. 4–5. Painting: "freefield" design, "scattered" flowers, bird, one stocking-garland, one basket, two peacocks, Constantinian chrestogram. *Sardis* I (1922) 174, 181–183, ill. 18, color pls. 4–5. Strocka, *Ephesos* 8:1, 60. A.D. 330–350.

4. Tomb of Flavius Chrysanthios and his family (Fig. 297). Location: "ca. 200 m. east of sector PC, ca. 200 m. north of Pyramid Tomb" (E30/S620). *BASOR* 229, 61–64, figs. 4–7. *BASOR* 233, 4–6, figs. 3–9. Mellink (1977) 308–310, fig. 19. Greenewalt, "Twentieth Campaign," 105. Painting: "freefield" "dense" flowers, birds, cornucopia, wreath, rectangular panels with inscriptions. The inscriptions state that Chrysanthios was *dukenarios, zographos, fabrikesios,* a high official of the Imperial arms factory and also a painter. The inscription in the lunette wreath uses the Christian formula "God Help," *Kyrie boethei.* Chrysanthios took the family name of the House of Constantine; hence probably A.D. 340?–400?

Uncertain:

5. Tomb under House of Bronzes, Unit 16. Location (Fig. 186): *Sardis* R2 (1978) fig. 1, no. 4 and *BASOR* 157, 26, figs. 9, 13. Painting: flowers, fillets. Probably fourth century A.D., possibly Christian, as it was carefully preserved under a Christian residence of the sixth century.

6. Pactolus North, Grave 67.3. Location: W265–275/S320–335. Barrel-vaulted mausoleum with reused large white marble revetments. *BASOR* 191, 10–11. Fourth to fifth century A.D.?

7. The "Peacock Tomb." Location: ca. 50 m. north of PN. *Sardis* R2 (1975) fig. 1, no. 12. *BASOR* 166, 30–33, fig. 26; 199, 56–58, figs. 44–45, removal of paintings to Manisa Museum. Painting: "dense" flowers, birds, garlands, peacocks, flower baskets (Fig. 296). *Sardis* (R9) *Wall Painting:* WP 61.1. Strocka, *Ephesos* 8:1, 41–42.

The chamber tomb was built over Roman tile graves of the first or second century A.D. (Graves 61.24; 61.25). In the floor was the burial of an adult aged 60 (Grave 61.14). There were dispersed bones from other burials. Coins in earth: Honorius (393–423) to Phocas (602–610). It seems that the tomb, which closely resembles no. 3, was built and painted in the later part of the fourth century and was subsequently used for secondary burials. There are no definite indications that it was Christian. Hansen and Strocka date it to the fifth century.

8–10. These chamber tombs from the vicinity of the tomb of Chrysanthios, no. 4, were excavated in 1979.

8. Excavated by Manisa museum. Absence of birds. Use of compass in outlining swags, baskets of fruit, medallions. "Overall tone of artistic sobriety" (C. H. Greenewalt, preliminary manuscript report). Skeletal remains of two individuals; two gold diadems; pair of gold earrings; coin of Valentinian II (375–392).

9. Excavated by K. P. Erhart in 1979. Painting: "freefield" style, pheasant-like birds and partridges.

10. Unpainted tomb. Excavated by K. P. Erhart in 1979. Coin of the fifth century A.D.

Excepting the Tomb no. 2 (list no. 1) in the Artemis Precinct, all Sardian painted chamber tombs, including the two definitely Christian mausolea (nos. 3–4), seem to be the work of one workshop active in late Constantinian times (A.D. 324–361) and perhaps before and after. In design, there may be a workshop connection between the peacock mosaic in the apse of the Synagogue (Figs. 260, 261) dated after A.D. 324 and the paintings of the tomb of Chrysanthios and the "Peacock Tomb" (nos. 4, 7). The dating of this group to the mid- and late fourth century is confirmed by the coin of Valentinian II (375–392) found in tomb no. 8. If the coin of Honorius belongs to the earliest burial in the Peacock Tomb (no. 7), then the paintings might be as late as ca. 400. The new evidence also confirms C. R. Morey's dating of no. 3 based on the Constantinian monograms of A.D. 355 and 360.[35]

The beautiful painted tomb found in 1967 at Nicaea (Iznik) has the same general motifs, including a "Constantinian monogram" and peacocks. On the basis of architectural framework parallels with more ambitious figured paintings in the tomb at Silistra (Bulgaria, pre–A.D. 376–378), Firatli dated the Nicaea paintings to the mid-fourth century.[36]

In the emerging panorama of late Roman and Late Antique painting, the Sardis ("Chrysanthios") group of painted tombs is of considerable importance as a safely localized and fairly well dated school. Stylistically it represents a mixture of the architectural framework style of panels imitating marble revetments ("incrustation," *skoutlosis*) with the "floral," "freefield" or scatter style analyzed long ago by Rostovtzeff from examples of the second and third centuries A.D. in the Roman tombs of South Russia.[37] In the hypogaeum at Nicaea, *skoutlosis* panels, quite similar to those reconstructed for the Sardis Synagogue (Fig. 266), are used in the main zone of the wall.[38] In Sardian paintings the architectural element is reduced to the rendering of polychrome marble panels on the lower wall (nos. 3, 4, 7). With the newly discovered examples in Anatolia, which include houses in Ephesus,[39] it is probable that this "style" or manner of decoration developed in Asia Minor and Syria.

Ideologically, the Sardis sequence illustrates very clearly the Christianization of generalized symbols of immortality. Idyllic motifs such as flowers, garlands, fruit baskets, peacocks, doves, and pheasants probably symbolized Paradise for the Christians; for the pagans they could allude to the Elysian fields[40] or to the offerings of flowers and fruit brought to the grave.[41]

The ambivalence and ambiguity of this visual vocabulary are characteristic of Late Antiquity. If we are tempted to assume because of two Christian sepulchers that all the uncertain examples are Christian, we should remember that the Christian arms maker and painter Flavius Chrysanthios (died 350–375?) had a famous pagan namesake and contemporary, Chrysanthius, leader of "sophists" and theurgist (A.D. 310 to ca. 390), who promised the initiates immortality in a celestial paradise;[42] and that as late as ca. A.D. 450 the leading light of Neoplatonism, Proclus, could count on finding friends at Sardis.[43] Such upper-class believers in a pagan paradise could well be buried in a tomb like the Peacock Tomb (no. 7; Fig. 296).

Cemetery at Church M on the South Side of the Artemis Precinct

We have already described the location of this cemetery in relation to Church M and the Artemis Temple (Figs. 88, 89).[44] It stretched from at least W80 to W200 to the end of Building L and from the south side of the temple (S1260) to ca. 1300,[45] and sloped rather steeply east to west (from ca. *103 to *99). In addition to many simple burials, it is known to have included at least four chamber tombs. The lower walls of two survive. They were originally barrel-vaulted, with traces of ivory and yellow stucco on the interior. A Lydian sarcophagus was probably also reused. Neither the chamber tombs nor a number of poor stone and tile graves, some covered with

reused inscriptions, yielded finds which permit a date for the duration of the cemetery.[46] It seems logical to assume that it coincided with the estimated lifetime of chapel M (Fig. 284; ca. A.D. 400–800?) and like the chapel, was buried by landslides and flooding.

The Mass Burial at Duman Tepe (Bin Tepe)

A most remarkable Christian burial was discovered by the Harvard-Cornell Expedition in a standard Lydian chamber tomb (BT 66.1)[47] in 1966. According to J. Savishinsky's estimate, some 150 individuals were buried in the dromos and Chamber I and to the south in Chamber II in as many as three layers, with their heads to the east.[48] Some 50 lamps were found, most of them used only once. According to local sources, some 300 lamps were illicitly removed before our excavation. Thus one or more lamps accompanied each individual. This suggests a ritual comparable to that of the Eastern church, when during the funerary mass candles are lit and then, at a certain point in the service, extinguished. The lamps are said to include types that range from the fourth to the seventh century.[49] Bits of textiles, fragments of wooden combs, portions of bronze mirrors, bracelets, and earrings, and remains of shoe nails are analogous to the finds in the cemetery at PN. The dead were buried wearing clothes or shrouds, some personal ornaments, and shoes, but there were no other gravegoods except lamps. A very fine bronze ring with an archangel carrying a cross (Fig. 299) proves that this mass burial is Christian. Iconographic parallels are dated to the sixth century.[50]

The skeletal material was very carefully excavated by the physical anthropologist J. Savishinsky, but unfortunately, illicit diggers had disturbed the positions and partly destroyed the skeletons. According to the findings of Savishinsky and the follow-up study by D. H. Finkel, no clear traces of violent deaths were observed. Finkel thought that he could discern some possible family relationships.[51]

The preliminary anthropological study has failed to provide support for the obvious theory that the mass burial may be connected with the capture of Sardis by the Sassanian Persians in A.D. 616. The alternative is to assume that we have found a cumulative depository of the dead resembling a "bone house" or "charnel house" of medieval and later times. In this case, it would represent several generations of inhabitants of one or more estates and villages at the southeast end of the Gygean Lake. The reason for selecting this particular Lydian chamber tomb escapes us.

The Cemeteries on the Acropolis

A cemetery on the southward slope in the central part of the Acropolis (AcT) consisted of typical oblong or boat-shaped graves of Byzantine type built of tiles, bricks, stones, and reused blocks, and oriented east-west.[52] The cemetery may have been started in Early Byzantine times, perhaps in the seventh century under Constans II, ca. A.D. 660, when the Acropolis fortress wall was probably built.[53] A bronze reliquary in the shape of an even-armed cross was probably Early Byzantine.[54] Yet another grave was clearly dated to the tenth or eleventh century by a fine medallion with an Anastasis on one side and a cross on a stepped base on the other.[55]

We may distinguish two Byzantine building phases in the occupation of the Acropolis, one extending from the sixth to the tenth century and the other from the eleventh or twelfth to the fourteenth century. The cemetery may belong to the first phase; the structures of the second phase were built over it.[56] In his reconstruction of the history of Byzantine Sardis, C. Foss postulates that the Acropolis was abandoned between the time of the Arab attacks (ca. A.D. 718) and the tenth century.[57] The cemetery, however, seems (to G. M. A. Hanfmann) to continue across this gap. It would prove that the fortress continued to be occupied or at least to be utilized as a burial ground.

There were other graves in the "Cave Chapel" in the north peak of the Acropolis, but they cannot be closely dated.[58] It is not likely that any Christian graves postdate the occupation of the citadel by the Turks early in the fourteenth century.

Our Christian finds have not brought forth any direct clues for the Angel of the Church at Sardis and the life of the Early Christian community prior to the Peace of the Church. What we have been given are enlightening and tantalizing glimpses of a city in transition in the time from Constantine to Heraclius: a Christian quarter with a very early basilica being built on the Pactolus; the temple of Artemis taken over and replaced by a small chapel; Jews and Christians trading side by side in the most central commercial area along the Main Avenue; the Synagogue left unmolested all through Late Antiquity; Christians and pagans going to their last rest in mausolea painted with the same paradisiac themes—and the old Sardian god of wine, Bacchus, adorning one room of the same house that yielded Christian liturgical implements (Figs. 210, 283). Thus the curtain is being lifted in spots. The entire stage will not be revealed until further excavations uncover the major cathedral (Church D) of Christian Sardis.

GMAH

XI

Conclusion

GEORGE M. A. HANFMANN

The image of Lydian culture and history in the literary sources is dominated by two ancient historians—the Lydian Xanthus, who wrote in Greek, and the Greek Herodotus, born in Asia Minor, who knew Lydia at first hand. Mythical and miraculous matters were to the fore in Xanthus—such as the glutton King Cambles, who ate his wife—but Xanthus had also preserved some genuine Lydian-Anatolian traditions of history and legend—for instance, episodes from the struggle for power between the two dynasties of the Dascylids and Tylonids before the accession of Gyges. The "Father of History," Herodotus, on the other hand, viewed the history of Lydia as a prelude to the struggle of Greece and Persia. In addition, the rise and fall of the Mermnad dynasty in general, and of Croesus in particular, were to Herodotus a "model" of human fallibility and of the unpredictability of human fate.

Herodotus and the scanty fragments of earlier archaic Greek poets agree that Lydian kings were powerful and immensely rich in gold; that the Lydians were superlative horsemen (Mimnermus); that Sardis was the center of fashions (Sappho) and sophistication (Alcman); that Ionian Greeks had learned "useless softnesses" (or "luxuries") so that they appeared "clad in purple cloaks . . . drenched in scented unguents" (Xenophanes), so that "Lydian living" became synonymous with "soft living" (Anacreon).

Hellenistic poets had enlarged this vision to include the mythical past with Midas, Marsyas, and Arachne. This mythical and paradigmatic Sardis of Croesus and his forebears was seen by later ages in a golden haze of timeless unreality. The darkness of the actual later history of the city was pierced only by the drama of Achaeus as related in Polybius and by the fiery admonition of the Revelation to the Angel of the Church at Sardis.

As a result of the Harvard-Cornell researches, the concrete, "archaeological" city of Sardis is beginning to emerge as a complex, millennial phenomenon, a cumulation of superposed cultures from the Late Stone Age to modern times. Although twenty years of excavations and soundings covered but a small percentage of the total area of the ancient city, it is no longer a matter of conjecture where the Lydian city of Croesus lay; and the general lineaments of the development of human communities at Sardis are emerging.

The story of Sardis begins with scattered signs of human presence in the Late Stone Age, in the fifth and fourth millennium, perhaps already in contact with the amazing pioneering communities of Southwest Anatolia, such as Hacilar with their astounding sculptural creations (Fig. 21). Then, in the Early Bronze Age of the third millennium B.C., around the Gygean Lake in the Sardis region we encounter manifestations of the metal-using farming communities of the West Anatolian Bronze Age, a culture first defined at the classical sites of Troy and Yortan but becoming better known from new sites every year. Even the two small cemeteries excavated (Figs. 11–13) reflect the pattern of small villages and hamlets quite densely arrayed on the fertile slopes around the lake. Already the region is a meeting place of east and west: the large jar burials (Fig. 14) point inland toward Central Anatolia; the chest-like cist graves (Fig. 15) from the same cemeteries come from the Mediterranean coast and the Aegean island cultures.

We do not as yet know when the city site of Sardis was first settled. At present a gap of several hundred years intervenes between the Early Bronze Age cemeteries on the Gygean Lake and the first signs of settled life at the ford across the Pactolus several miles to the south, the place where the east–west road into the interior was joined by a road coming down from the Troad (Figs. 2, 5, 31).

It is in the Late Bronze Age, in the fourteenth or thirteenth century B.C., that a hut and a cremation burial (Figs. 23–25) offer the first firm evidence for settled life at the site of the city. They are quite Anatolian; and Anatolian pottery traditions dominate the traces of denser habitation which succeeded the hut at the Pactolus ford (HoB area). Sudden, perhaps violent contact with the Aegean world is suggested by a burned level associated with a small quantity of Aegean-type painted pottery of Submycenaean and Protogeometric affinities (Figs. 26, 28). Novel too is the appearance of iron, including some of the earliest iron tools known from the Eastern Mediterranean. This situation could be plausibly explained as caused by the arrival of Greek warriors roaming the coast of Asia Minor after the Trojan War. According to Herodotus, "sons of Herakles" took over the rule in Lydia sometime in the twelfth century B.C.

The limited data gained from three deep soundings prove that at least a village existed at Sardis in the Late Bronze Age; but nothing has been found to prove that Bronze Age Sardis had a fortified citadel and palace in the manner of Hittite cities of Central Anatolia, or that it can be identified with one of the kingdoms with whom the Hittites were embroiled in the West.

The foundations for Lydia's greatness must have been laid in the three centuries between 1000 and 700 B.C. Again, it is only the area at the ford (HoB), now more legitimately described as Lydian Trench or Lydian Market, that attests continuity. More walls and storage pits begin to suggest a possibly urban conglomeration. Slowly and steadily a Lydian Geometric style of painted vase decoration (Figs. 36, 37, 65) begins to emerge, with obvious links to Eastern Greek and Cypriote–South Anatolian ceramic traditions. Imported Greek pottery confirms contacts with Ionian and Aeolic cities on the coast of Asia Minor; and around the mid-eighth century B.C., the Greek mainland center of Corinth sends vases (Fig. 38) from the first distant overseas source.

A sudden expansion of the city area and a dynamic upsurge of activities occur in the next phase (Plan I), the phase of the Lydian Kingdom (680–547 B.C.), as A. Ramage rightly saw. The settlement on the Pactolus becomes a recognizable market and residential area ("Lydian Market"). Traces of Lydian structures are found a half-mile north of the modern highway, and Lydian houses go up the Pactolus Valley, appearing on the east banks at Pactolus North (PN) and Pactolus Cliff (PC); further up toward the Acropolis at Keklik Suyu and Şeytan Dere; and above the Artemis Precinct (NEW). For the first time the Acropolis weighs in with datable finds. The town stretches in archaic congestion and irregular plan for nearly two miles north–south along the Pactolus. The general urban type is clearly that of an "Acropolis" or "arx" city, with a citadel dominating a lower town (Plan I). We have traces of the palace terraces (Fig. 79) and of the triple fortifications of the citadel (Fig. 73, AcS). We have the mighty walls of the lower city (MMS; Fig. 133). Two religious areas are marked by altars, one in the precinct of Artemis (Fig. 95), the other, sacred to Cybele, in the Gold Refinery (Fig. 49). If our finds give only hints of the life of the king and the aristocracy and have not produced any temple, they reveal the dwellings and shops of craftsmen and tradesmen, the market, and the factory. Indeed, the new type of organization of skilled labor and the new technology required to bring about the Lydian economic revolution toward monetocracy could not be more cogently presented than in the Gold Refinery precinct found on the Pactolus (Figs. 42–58, 139). On the other hand, the concentration of power in the hands of kings such as Gyges, Alyattes, and Croesus, and their massive ambitions to rival the great royal cities of Mesopotamia, are clearly manifested in the colossal mudbrick fortifications of the lower city (MMS) and in the three huge royal mounds of the cemetery of Bin Tepe (Figs. 97, 105), which Herodotus compared to the pyramids.

As western capital of the Achaemenid empire (547–334 B.C.) Sardis looms large in literature and written history, but archaeology seems to indicate a period of détente. The city remained basically Lydian in its material culture. This is all the more surprising since the fire of 499 B.C., when the Greeks attacked Sardis, should have presented an opportunity for rebuilding the archaic city of reed huts described by Herodotus. Yet the riverstone and mudbrick houses excavated on PC and PN speak more of gradual Hellenization of households than any sudden change of life-style. The picture may be incomplete. The new monumental wall (MMS) was apparently rebuilt by the Persians (after 547? or 499?), and they may have moved the city limits eastward (Plan I).

Were it not for the chance survival of some marble blocks reused in the Synagogue, we should never suspect that the Metroon of Cybele was rebuilt in marble, probably in the Persian period (Fig. 169). As it is, a pediment illustrates satrapal life (Fig. 138), and Lydian inscriptions with Persian regnal years indicate that the Persian bureaucracy was recruiting Lydians. A hitherto quite unsuspected confrontation between the native Anatolian and official Iranian cults is revealed in the inscription of the satrap or high official Droaphernes (Fig. 166).

Hellenistic Sardis can be much better understood now that new epigraphic evidence, old historical sources, and archaeological results combine to show that the destruction by Antiochus III in 213 B.C. and the destruction by earthquake in A.D. 17 sharply separate the earlier, Seleucid city (Plan II) from the Pergamene-Roman Sardis (Plan III), and the latter, in turn, from the city as renewed under the Roman Empire.

In general, Sardis fits into the overall pattern of Hellenization of Anatolian cities. No longer a unique capital of the Lydian kingdom or the western capital of the Persian empire, it becomes a typical Hellenistic *polis* with theater, gymnasium, stadium, and temples. The progress of Hellenization is attested by the disappearance of Lydian (last inscription on stone ca. 280 B.C.) and the complete dominance of Greek in inscriptions.

In the Seleucid phase (280–190 B.C.) the great royal fortress is in theory distinct from the city. Only some traces from the siege of 215–213 B.C. remain on the citadel; but it is probable that the great building program that included the colossal temple of Artemis and the marble theater, both attached to the periphery of the city area, was, in fact, inspired by the royal presence. New evidence (1981) indicates that the eastern quarter between the Lydian wall MMS and the theater was being built up in a terraced composition prior to 213 B.C. (Plan II). The western part of the city, however, remained in the archaic Lydo-Persian agglomerative state, as shown by houses on the Pactolus that survived until 213 B.C.

That Antiochus III had fiercely punished Sardis and destroyed its western quarter is attested by "destruction fills" (Plan III, DF). Clearly he did not have time between 213 B.C. and the battle of Magnesia in 190 B.C. to carry out his plans for a new *synoikismos* of Sardis as revealed in his inscriptions (Fig. 169).

Under the rule of the Pergamenes and the Roman Republic, Sardis declined (190 B.C. to A.D. 17; Plan III). The city withdrew from the Pactolus eastward; Hellenistic mausolea and cemeteries replaced Lydian residential structures in the Lydian Market and Pactolus North areas. There was local industrial activity in pottery, mostly dependent on Pergamene models (Figs. 185, 192–193); but very little survives of the Hellenistic city, at least in the western areas excavated. The reason for the near-total disappearance is the earthquake of A.D. 17 and the subsequent gigantic urban renewal by the Romans. Damaged Hellenistic structures, especially houses, were used in massive fills for terraces and platforms, while masonry from major buildings was stockpiled and reused in such public structures as the gymnasium complex (Figs. 5, 212, 216, 217). That the Hellenistic period, which was culturally the most critical in the life of Sardis and which produced the grandest building in Sardis history in the temple of Artemis (Figs. 88–90, 285), should leave so little trace is dismaying but not unique—neither

Ephesus nor Miletus had many Hellenistic structures left. Survey work done between 1976 and 1981 holds out promise that significant alignments and even structures of the Hellenistic city may be discernible in the area between the Lydian wall MMS and the theater. Eventually, we may learn when the bent-axis plan and the terraced composition of the eastern part of the city were planned and realized (Plans II–III).

The Roman renewal of Sardis was planned between A.D. 20 and 30. The Main Avenue was complete by ca. A.D. 40, the water supply by 54; yet the actual construction for the ambitious plan was slow going and continued for two centuries into the Severan period. It made Sardis a typical creation of the Asiatic variant of Roman architecture, much like Ephesus, Pergamon, Aphrodisias, Smyrna, and Miletus, all opulent, flourishing cities of Rome's richest province. According to our results Sardis may claim one of the earliest colonnaded avenue (ca. A.D. 20–40) and perhaps the finest of the characteristic civic centers, the so-called bath-gymnasium, a skillful synthesis of Greek and Roman components. As described in Chapter VIII (Figs. 206–240), it was built in stages, probably from ca. A.D. 100 through 166 to the dedication of the Marble Court in A.D. 211. The discovery that is unique to Sardis is the Jewish Synagogue, not an original architectural creation but a structure adapted (ca. A.D. 270?) from a Roman basilica which was previously a part of the gymnasium. With its decorations and inscriptions, the Synagogue of Sardis has opened entirely new vistas upon the Jewish communities of the Diaspora and, indirectly, has led to reassessment of the role of the Christian community at Sardis as well.

Another lesson has been taught by Roman–Early Byzantine Sardis with a clarity not quite matched in other Asiatic cities. This is the strong continuity of Graeco-Roman *polis* life and culture, a continuity lasting almost exactly six centuries, from the earthquake of A.D. 17 to the destruction of A.D. 616. Despite the important spiritual changes brought about by the interplay of religions and the ultimate Christianization of the city (Plan IV), it is the continuity and the recurrent civic activity, with vigorous rebuilding and renovation, that impresses the historian. In the most basic sense Sardis remained a "classical *polis*" city until its end.

Finally, if we glance over the entire span of the life of Sardis as a human community, we perceive that in the early phase, from the Late Stone Age through the Early Iron Age, Sardis seems to grow and develop in step with most other major communities of Western Anatolia, such as Troy, Smyrna, or Ephesus, from a Prehistoric village to a fortified town, showing no particular preeminence nor great backwardness. Then an extraordinary outburst of creativity, which lasted somewhat over a century (680–547 B.C.), lifts the capital of Lydia to world leadership, reflected in the large expansion of area and the rise of monumental regal and military architecture. This brilliant peak of achievement is followed by a gradual descent lasting some three centuries (547–213 B.C.) when the city was the center of the important satrapy of Sparda and a major stronghold of the Seleucid kingdom. Rising from a low point in late Hellenistic times, Sardis in its last major phase emerges as a prosperous Graeco-Roman and Late Antique city, one of many equals, overshadowed by Ephesus but in step with such congeners as Smyrna and Pergamon. The final individual distinction of Sardis was its sudden death as a city. This violent doom has preserved for posterity a treasure of knowledge which our generation of archaeologists has just begun to explore.

Notes

I. The City and Its Environment

General Topography and Ecology

1. This discussion is based on the more extensive treatment of ecology in *Sardis* R1 (1975) Chapter II, 17–34, "Regional Setting and Urban Development" by C. Foss and G. M. A. Hanfmann, supplemented by data reported by several geologists in Campbell; Olson, "Landslides"; and other recent research. Earlier valuable descriptions of Sardis are in *Sardis* I (1922): H. C. Butler, Chapter II, 15–36, "The Site"; W. Warfield, Appendix I, "Report on the Geology of Sardis," 175–180, with L. T. Emory's topographic map, pl. 1. A brief, well-phrased description is found in Pedley, 21–24. Ecological aspects are considered throughout in *Sardis* M4 (1976) 1, 35–52, 98–100. A new geological study was launched and a detailed geological map prepared in 1978 by D. F. Belknap, University of Delaware. Canet-Jaoul, *Geologie de la region de Manisa-Gördes,* and other systemic reports on the region filed with the Maden Tetkik ve Arama Enstitüsü, Ankara, were not available for detailed use. An invaluable source of information is Köy Işleri Bakanligi report made available through G. W. Olson.

2. Dewdney, 100, fig. 8, shows the general location of Demirköprü. See also *Sardis* R1 (1975), fig. 2.

3. Brinkmann, 171. For a more detailed account of the Bozdag see Izdar, in Campbell, 495–500, figs. 1, 2 (with Sardis region) after which Fig. 3 in this volume. Description of the mountain world and the settlements and roads of the Tmolus is given by Foss, "Explorations," 22–61.

4. For the geological aspects, see Harta Genel

Müdürlügü Basimevi 1946, Manisa 87:2, Philippson, *Topographische Karte* (1910); *Deutsche Heereskarte* Türkei, Blatt-Nr. GIII (1941); and the forthcoming study and map by D. F. Belknap made for "Stage II" of the Sardis fieldwork. For limits of Sardis region, see *Sardis* R1 (1975) 19, 20, fig. 2, "Regional Map of Sardis."

5. Sart Mahmur population in 1978 was 2,300; Sart Mustafa, 1,700.

6. The new road has cut out the traditional passage along the southern foothills between Turgutlu (Kassaba) and Kemal Pasa Pass. It was completed in 1968 (Hanfmann, *Letters 226*). The course is shown on automobile maps, Highway Dept. 1: 850,000.

7. Built as unsurfaced vehicle road in the late 1960s. For its course across the Tmolus see Foss, "Explorations," 33, 34.

8. February and March 1966: *BASOR* 186, 38.

9. In 1963–1964, cotton and tobacco constituted 31% of crops cultivated in the Vilayet Manisa, which to some extent corresponds to ancient Lydia; wheat was 31%, barley was 22%, grapes were 14%. See *Sardis* R1 (1975) 20.

10. *Sardis* R1 (1975) 7 (S. L. Carter); for maps, see n. 4 *supra*.

11. Izdar, *Petrographisch-geologische Untersuchungen* (unpublished, in Turkish, 1969). A number of articles in Campbell are of interest for this region of western Turkey and have large-scale maps: J. C. Dewdney, "Physical, Human, and Economic Geography," 83–108, fig. 11; M. Kamen-Kaye, "A Review of Depositional History and Geological Structure," 111–138; R. Brinkmann, "The Geology of Western Anatolia," 171–190, with discussion of Bozdag-Tmolus, 171, figs. 6, 13; F. van der Kaaden, "Base-

ment Rocks," 201, on Menderes massif; G. Evans, "The Recent Sedimentation of Turkey," 385–406, fig. 1, geological map with Gediz region; E. Ilhan, "Earthquakes in Turkey," 431–442, fig. 1, seismic zones and fault patterns; Izdar, "Introduction to Geology and Metamorphism of the Menderes Massif of Western Turkey," 495–500. In 1978, D. Belknap (University of Delaware) initiated work on a new geological map of the Sardis area.

12. *Sardis* R1 (1975) 7, 8 (S. L. Carter). The grids used and their variations from the SAS map are discussed by Carter, *supra*. The Harvard-Cornell Expedition was able to make occasional use of aerial surveys not made specifically for the site; and for the area of Bin Tepe, it was able to consult copies of the new photogrammetric survey on 1:5,000 scale being prepared for this region of Turkey. Photogrammetric experiments with balloon photography were made in individual sectors by J. and E. Whittlesey, but no systematic coverage of the entire site could be arranged. (See Whittlesey, "Tethered Balloon," 181.)

For the region, a number of maps are listed by R. S. Thomas in *Sardis* (M11) *Bibliography* (forthcoming), category 2, Maps and Plans, including those by Kiepert and Philippson, as well as the theoretically unpublished British and German military maps. The German map has superior indication of vegetation and hydrography. *Harta Genel Müdürlügü* (1946) is the basis for many other published maps. Philippson, *Topographische Karte* (1910) Blätter 3, 4. General Staff, *Asia Minor, Alshehr* (pre-1914). War Office (1961) Izmir, 1:500,000. OKH Gen. St.d.H. (German) (1941) (Manisa). With classical names: Kiepert, *Karte von Kleinasien. National Geographic Society,* "Classical Lands," (1949). Calder-Bean, "A Classical Map of Asia Minor." A roughly colored map of the Vilayet Manisa, locally printed, provides a general idea of relief and vegetation.

13. Herodotus 5.54 = *Sardis* M2 (1972) no. 191; Xenophon, *Hellenica* 3.2.11; Pedley, 21.

14. *BASOR* 166, 40–45, figs. 32–34; a test pit in 1961 failed to reveal definite traces of a Persian or Lydian road under the Roman Main Avenue. For the discovery in 1976 of a Lydian structure which may be a road gate, see *BASOR* 229, 64, 65. For the literary tradition on the Royal Road: Herodotus 5.52 = *Sardis* M2 (1972) no. 191. For its significance for Sardis: *Sardis* R1 (1975) 19, fig. 8, map of Anatolia and Aegean. A Lydian road was found in 1980.

15. See *Sardis* R1 (1975) 18, 19, fig. 8 and the discussion by Foss, "Explorations," 27–37.

16. See Brinkmann, 171, figs. 6, 13; and G. van der Kaaden, 201.

17. The location of the marble enclave and the Magara Deresi torrent is shown on E. Izdar's sketch

map in Campbell, 499, fig. 2 (Fig. 3 in this volume) and is labeled "quarry" on the map in *Sardis* R1 (1975), fig. 3 (*Sardis* I [1922] pl. I). For the description of the quarry, see the work by D. Monna and F. H. Whitmore, *Sardis* R2 (1978) 17 and 4–7, with Table 1 for semiquantitative spectrographic analyses.

18. *Sardis* R1 (1975) 78.

19. *Sardis* R1 (1975) 151, nos. 3–5, lithocalcarenite.

20. *BASOR* 166, 54–56; 170, 59–60; 174, 56–68.

21. Olson, "Landslides," with Table 1, description of collection soil samples and study sites; Table 2, physical analyses of soil samples; Table 3, chemical analyses of soil samples. For additional data of interest for archaeological research, see his earlier paper (1970), "Field Report." More general points of view are in "Ancient Cities of the Dead," 39–44 (Tikal and Sardis); and with G. M. A. Hanfmann, "Some Implications of Soils for Civilizations," 11–14.

22. Kamilli, "Mineral Analysis of the Clay Bodies," in *Sardis* M5 (1978) 12–15, with table 2 in which sherd mineralogy of Lydian mold-made architectural terracottas and contemporary Lydian wheel-made lamps is compared to ceramic assemblage of 100 pot sherds; table 3, elemental composition of white slips on architectural terracottas.

23. Olson, "Landslides"; *Sardis* R1 (1975) 25 (alluvial fans).

24. Cf. *Sardis* R1 (1975) 17; and for the exact title in Turkish, 192. It means translated: "Report on Gold Prospecting of the Alluvium between Turgutlu and Salihli with a Detailed Study of Gold in the Area around Sart Çay," Maden Tetkik ve Arama Enstitüsü (Ankara 1963). For his conclusions see Hanfmann, *Letters,* 141, 142. For a possible mine south of Sardis, see Foss, "Explorations," 38, 39.

25. On the occasion of the prospecting for well-water by the expedition in 1963, see Hanfmann, *Letters,* 144. Since 1976 new studies of geology and hydrology have been initiated by D. F. Belknap and D. G. Sullivan.

26. Olson, "Landslides," 270.

27. E. Ilhan, in Campbell, 431, 433–437, fig. 1; see Olson, "Landslides," 261; Robert, "Séismes," 405, with a survey of earthquakes in Asia Minor.

28. Ambraseys, 376, 378, fig. 2, with detailed analysis of ancient sources and their references. *Sardis* M2 (1972) nos. 219, 220.

29. *Sardis* I (1922) 20, 21; *Sardis* R1 (1975) 21 n. 20; *Sardis* M4 (1976) no. 39 (Katip Çelebi, ca. 1650).

30. Erinç, "The Gediz Earthquake of 1970," in Campbell, 443–454.

31. Theater area: Vann, "Theater and Stadium Complex," in *Sardis* (M14) *Early Travelers and Unex-*

cavated Buildings (forthcoming); gymnasium and House of Bronzes: *BASOR* 162, 43, fig. 26; 166, 49; 187, 53, 54, 58; 203, 11, fig. 7; inscription on reconstruction of a shrine of Hera "after the earthquake": *Sardis* R2 (1978) no. 275, figs. 467, 468; see ibid., Appendix I, on the inscription of Puteoli, for measures after the earthquake; L. Robert, "Séismes," 405.

32. *Sardis* M4 (1976) 59 would date the earthquake before or in the reign of Constans II (641–668); see Olson, "Landslides," 264. Particularly suggestive is the condition of the toppled north wall of the Synagogue: *BASOR* 182, 53, fig. 42; 191, 28.

33. H. Warfield, Appendix I in *Sardis* I (1922) 178–180, made an attempt for the Artemis Precinct which, however, needs correction; see *Sardis* R1 (1975) 54–56, chronological summary. For the deposition rate in a wadi, the sector NEW provides very characteristic data. See *Sardis* R1 (1975) 118, 119; *Sardis* I (1922) 149, 154.

34. The quick formation of such a wadi from an excavation dump on the Acropolis led M. J. Mellink to suggest that perhaps one could retrieve the stratigraphy of the Acropolis in reverse by making a stratification probe through the material fallen from the south side. See Olson, "Landslides," 270, fig. 20; see also figs. 5, 8, 12–14.

35. J. Dewdney, in Campbell, 88, 89, figs. 3, 4, temperatures and precipitation from 600 to 1000 mm. A table of temperature data for Vilayet Manisa and of average monthly rainfall for Salihli, 9 km. east of Sardis, is given in *Sardis* R1 (1975) 25, after information of Village Works Ministry. Note the contrast between 258.3 mm. for Dec.–Feb. and 29.7 mm. for June–August.

36. *Köy Işleri Bakanligi*, 11–12. The authors note that the erosion of the upper Gediz (Hermus) Valley through floods threatens the fertility of the lower valley.

37. Strabo 13.4.7 = *Sardis* M2 (1972) no. 279: "Some state that Lake Coloe [alternate ancient name for Gygean Lake] is man-made to contain the floods which occur when the rivers overflow."

38. Garbrecht, "Fragen der Wasserwirtschaft Pergamons," 43–48, a valuable outline of proposed systematic research and a note on work in 1967. Preliminary reports have appeared in *Mitteilungshefte der Technischen Universität Braunschweig, Leichtweiss-Institut für Wasserbau*: G. Garbrecht and G. Holtorff, "Die Madradag-Leitung," 37 (1973); G. Garbrecht and H. Fahl, "Die Kaikos-Leitung"; K. Hecht, "Zwei Aquedukte der Ketios-Leitung"; K. Hecht, "Zwei weitere Aquädukte der Kaikos-Leitung." In 1967 a plan for a similar detailed study of the water supply of Sardis was discussed with Professor Garbrecht but

was not carried out because of difficulties of scheduling and financing.

39. List of public fountains: *Sardis* R1 (1975) 27 n. 73; *Sardis* VII.1 (1932) no. 17.

40. *BASOR* 162, 23; *Sardis* R1 (1975) 26–28. While the water level in the plain (CG) has risen 2 to 3 m. since ancient times, it seems to have stayed the same in the Pactolus Valley.

41. *Sardis* R1 (1975) 129, 130, 135, 140, 165, figs. 333, 335. For the general effects of the disruption of the water supply system, see *Sardis* M4 (1976) 72–76.

Agriculture, Pastoralism, Hunting, Forestry

1. G. W. Olson, letter of August 1, 1978.

2. *Köy Işleri Bakanligi*.

3. See Olson, "Landslides," 262–263, who states that "overgrazing and overcutting continues at Sardis to the present day." On desolation of cultivated land and increase of pastoralism in the seventeenth and eighteenth centuries, see *Sardis* M4 (1976) 98–103.

4. See McDonald-Rapp, 247, where McDonald and Hope Simpson apply a formula of 112 people per hectare.

5. *Köy Işleri Bakanligi*.

6. *Sardis* R1 (1975) 20, table 2.

7. For vegetation of the Tmolus and special plants noted by ancient authors (hazel and chestnut, saffron), see Foss, "Explorations," 22; *Sardis* M2 (1972) no. 26, with reference to "aspects of the Sardian dinner table"; Greenewalt, *Dinners*, 34, 38–39, 52–54, with detailed discussions of such famous dishes as *kandaulion* and *karyke*.

8. Herodotus 1:94 = *Sardis* M2 (1972) nos. 23, 24. G. A. Wainwright, "Meneptah's Aid to the Hittites," 24–28, and "The Teresh, the Etruscans and Asia Minor," 197–213; Hanfmann, *Sardis und Lydien*, 14, 15.

9. Roebuck, 60, says there was no import of grain from Lydia.

10. See Greenewalt, *Dinners*, 13–15, on Lydian wine cups and jugs, and 36 n. 10, on the reputation of Lydian wines with ancient references. See also *Sardis* R1 (1975) 22, for mention of wine vessels from an estate in the Sardian Plain.

11. "Bread trays," *Sardis* M5 (1978) 8, fig. 18; also excavation numbers T 61.80:3781, T 61.84:3822, T 65.15:6842, all from "Lydian Trench" (HoB), possibly from one building (E5-8/S90–93, *98.60–70), the model house "H," *Sardis* M5 (1978) 7, 8, fig. 15.

12. Plutarch, *Moralia, De Pythiae oraculis* 16 = *Sardis* M2 (1972) no. 68.

13. *Sardis* R1 (1975) 6, 22–23.

14. McDonald-Rapp, 128, 254–256.

15. Galen, *De cognoscendis curandisque animi morbis,* chap. 5; Hanfmann, *Croesus,* 49 n. 33.

16. *Sardis* R1 (1975) 21.

17. Doguer et al., 56, Table 1. The present statistics are based on the report of a team of veterinarians from the University of Ankara. See also *Sardis* R1 (1975) 171 n. 18; *BASOR* 229, 66 (S. Payne).

18. Greenewalt, *Dinners,* 18–26, 31–39. He believes that the puppies found in special vessels along with iron knives were prepared for the divinity but not eaten by the worshipers.

19. Polyaenus, *Strategemata* 7.2.1. "The war dogs of Alyattes would perhaps have been big, like the fighting dogs on the Pergamon frieze," according to Greenewalt, *Dinners,* 24 n. 29. Basing his argument partly on the analysis of puppy bones by Sebastian Payne, Greenewalt, *Dinners,* 19–26, Greenewalt suggests that the breed represented by the puppy bones may have been similar to the so-called "Lakonian" hounds of medium size. Representations: terracotta friezes, *Sardis* X (1926) 27–30; *Sardis* M5 (1978) 17, 19, nos. 7, 14, figs. 37, 46, frontispiece (color). For an earlier geometric representation of a hunter, mid-seventh century B.C., see *BASOR* 162, 34, fig. 17.

20. Mimnermus 13 = *Sardis* M2 (1972) no. 44.

21. Hanfmann, "Horsemen," 570–581. *Sardis* M5 (1978) 20–21, nos. 18–22, figs. 49–53, horses in terracotta friezes. Cf. horseman as feudal knight, Roebuck, 32–34.

22. M. Littauer states by letter that no definite identification of the Lydian breed of horses is known to her.

23. *Sardis* R1 (1975) 21. Doguer et al., 56, Table 1. Savishinsky, FR 1966: *Human and Non-Human Bones* (unpublished), unhesitatingly described the skeleton from the Submycenaean level as donkey.

24. Doguer et al., 56, table 1. The terracotta legs of a large statuette found in mid-sixth century B.C. context were identified by T. Çalişlar, Veterinarian Faculty, University of Ankara, as the legs of a camel, *BASOR* 174, 11–12, fig. 5; Greenewalt, "Exhibitionist," 45 n. 49, with references to Herodotus, Xenophon, and modern literature; K. Schauenburg, "Die Cameliden im Altertum," 64–65; Cook, "Old Smyrna-Ionic Black Figure," 123, 124, pl. 30. See also Vereshchagin, 154, 156, 219–221, 785.

25. Late Roman representation of a camel rider: *BASOR* 174, 22, fig. 13.

26. Bones: Doguer et al., 56, Table 1. Herodotus 1.80 = *Sardis* M2 (1972) no. 115. A seventh century representation of hunt: *BASOR* 162, 34, fig. 17.

27. Greenewalt, "Lydian Graves," 118–120, 129, pls. 4, 5; for shells, see ibid., 124, 125, nos. 17, 18; *BASOR* 229, 65 (oyster shell).

28. *Sardis* R2 (1978) 20–22, "On Lions," with references, especially n. 67, for lions seen in Asia Minor as late as 1873.

29. Boar killed Croesus' son: Herodotus 1.34 = *Sardis* M2 (1972) no. 89. Terracotta friezes: *Sardis* M5 (1978) 18, 19, figs. 43, 44. Pottery: Greenewalt, "Elements," 40, 41, pls. 16, 18; *BASOR* 203, 9, fig. 4. Ring: *Sardis* XIII (1925) no. 98, pls. 9:11, 11:4; Boardman, *Gems,* pl. 292; idem, "Pyramidal Seals," pl. 8:95. Bronze: *BASOR* 162, 39, fig. 24. Cybele monument: *Sardis* R2 (1978) 48, fig. 46.

30. Tmolus: Foss, "Explorations," 21–23; *Sardis* R1 (1975) 20, 171 n. 14.

31. Diodorus Siculus 2.25.1-2 = *Sardis* M2 (1972) no. 70. The terracotta model of a Lydian boat found in a chamber tomb looks like a lake or river canoe; see n. 34, *infra.*

32. Wooden couch in BT 63.2: *BASOR* 174, 55. Greenewalt-Majewski, "Lydian Textiles," 138 n. 39. The C-14 date for the couch is 1100 B.C. ± 250 years. Wooden stretchers: *Sardis* I (1922) 159.

33. Timbers in monumental mudbrick structure (MMS): Greenewalt, "Twentieth Campaign," 106.

34. Wooden and terracotta boats: *Sardis* VI:1 (1916) 56, 57, detail with inscription, ill.; *Sardis* VI:2 (1924) no. 30; Gusmani, *LW,* 262 no. 30, from a square chamber tomb "on the eastern slope of Acropolis Hill."

35. Wooden knife handles and sheath: Greenewalt, *Dinners,* 18.

36. *Sardis* I (1922) 159.

37. Wooden (oak) ashes above Alyattes tomb: *BASOR* 170, 55, fig. 40; above Keskinler Tomb: *BASOR* 206, 14.

38. Timber in buildings: *Sardis* M5 (1978) 4. A. Ramage comments on the striking lack of traces of the use of timber in domestic construction. On the other hand, detailed representations of wooden roof and wall construction are seen in the Lydian-Mysian chamber tombs: Kasper, "Nekropole," 72–77, figs. 2, 3, 6–8.

39. Gordion wooden chamber and furniture: R. S. Young, "Gordion 1956," Tumulus P, 325–331; 326, wood identified (black pine, boxwood, yew, pear, poplar), pls. 91, 95, 96. R. S. Young, "Gordion 1957," 148–154, pls. 23–25, 27; "Phrygian Contribution," 12–15, 19–20.

Mineral Resources

1. A list with ancient references and modern geological findings is cited in *Sardis* R1 (1975) 21 nn. 19, 20. It has been updated by J. C. Waldbaum in the section on "Mineral Resources and Mining" of her volume *Sardis* (M8) *Metalwork* (forthcoming).

2. *Sardis* R1 (1975) 171 n. 19; Waldbaum, *Sardis* (M8) *Metalwork.* For ancient sources see Magie, 1:45.

3. Collignon, "Bijoux," 188–191; Dominian, 581–584; *Sardis* I (1922) 16 n. 1.

4. Philippson, *Reisen,* 172.

5. Ravndal, 140–141; Ryan, 6, 7; Pamir and Erentöz, Geological Map of Turkey, Explanatory Text, 98, 99.

6. Consulted only in manuscript (unpublished), Birgi; Saydamer. For the collaboration on analyses with MTAE and Çekmece Nuclear Research Center, see *BASOR* 199, 11; and Hanfmann-Waldbaum, "New Excavations," 313–315.

7. Foss, "Explorations," 37–39, identifies the place as the ancient settlement at Metallon.

8. Archilochus fragment 22, Diehl 3, 1:3–49. Huxley, *Ionians,* 59.

9. Dominians, 581–584; de Jesus, 83–85; Diod. Sic. 3.12–14.

10. Herodotus 6.47 (Thasos). Cf. Roebuck, 91 nn. 23, 24, with literature.

11. Pedley, 73, 74; Dominian, 581–584.

12. Plutarch, *Moralia, De mulierum virtutibus* 27 (262E–263).

13. *Sardis* (M8) *Metalwork,* "Introduction" (forthcoming). Citing Darius' Persian inscription from Susa: *Sardis* M2 (1972) no. 303.

14. *Sardis* XIII (1925) 11–13, nos. 1, 2, 8, pl. 1.

15. Ryan, 7, 66; Pliny, *HN* 5:30, 22; *Sardis* (M8) *Metalwork,* "Introduction" (forthcoming).

16. Worked gold: MTAE (1968), N. Bayçin, A. Uluocak, reported in Hanfmann-Waldbaum, "New Excavations," 314. Native gold: chemical analysis cited by Birgi—14.5%. Neutron activation analysis 24.9% ± 1.5%. Okar, Aydin (1969) 6, 8, 9.

17. Gentner, 273–284, esp. 283.

18. Siglos: *BASOR* 170, 11, Inv. C 62.25. Although issued by the Persian kings, these Persian silver coins seem to have been struck by the mint at Sardis as successors of Croesus' silver coins, with which they were found in Asia Minor boards. See *Sardis* XI (1916) 44, nos. 416, 417, two sigloi.

19. *Sardis* (M8) *Metalwork* (forthcoming).

20. *Sardis* (M8) *Metalwork* (forthcoming): near Aydin, Söke, Izmir, Ayvalik, following Ravndal, 141. This refutes Roebuck's skepticism, 90 n. 87.

21. Waldbaum, *Bronzes* 35, 69 (metallographic analysis).

22. *Sardis* (M8) Metalwork, "Introduction" (forthcoming); Ryan, 30; Ravndal, 140, 141.

23. *Sardis* (M8) *Metalwork,* "Introduction" (forthcoming). Ryan, 6, 7 mentions a lead, silver, and gold deposit near Alaşehir. R. H. Brill has done work on isotopes of lead on some samples from Sardis.

24. *Sardis* (M8) *Metalwork* (forthcoming); Strabo 13.1.56; Ryan, 7, lists deposits in Manisa region.

25. *Sardis* R1 (1975) 21 n. 20, with references to ancient authors, where C. Foss cites the locations of

ancient and modern cinnabar workings. For the sulphur springs near Sardis, see Philippson, *Reisen,* 71, 72; *Sardis* 1 (1922) 20; *BASOR* 154, 27 n. 50. Yellow ochre was found in the Hellenistic Haci Oglan sarcophagus 61.3. W. and E. Kohler, FR 1961: *Haci Oglan Sarcophagi* (unpublished).

26. *Sardis* R1 (1975) 21 n. 21; *Sardis* R2 (1978) 4–7, with analysis of F. E. Whitmore.

27. *Sardis* R1 (1975) 21 n. 21; Pliny *HN* 33.126; Theophrastus, *De lapidibus,* 45–47; Caley-Richards, 156–158. Sard: Pliny *HN* 37.105 = *Sardis* M2 (1972) no. 137.

28. *Sardis* (M10) *Small Finds* discusses the occurrence of rock crystal; see Greenewalt, "Elements," 42.

29. Claybeds: Olson, "Landslides," 255. A mineral analysis of the clay bodies of terracottas, lamps, and pottery is given by D. Kamilli in *Sardis* M5 (1978) 12–14. For the restoration project see *BASOR* 229, 67–70. Hostetter, 56–59.

30. In her section of the volume on *Sardis* (R5) *Pottery,* I. Hanfmann has collected pieces of thirty-six molds for the making of Hellenistic relief ware.

31. Lydian kiln, HoB, 1958: *BASOR* 154, 28. Byzantine kilns built in LNH part of the gymnasium: *BASOR* 154, 28.

Industry

1. Roebuck, 50–60. Greenewalt, "Elements," 37–45, pls. 13–20. *Sardis* M4 (1976), 74–76, 84, 110–115.

2. Mitten-Yügrüm, "Ahlatli," 25 and ills. Hanfmann, "Prehistoric Sardis," Neolithic type celts: 163–166, fig. 1. Stone head: *Sardis* R2 (1978) 155; no. 299, figs. 396–399.

3. Protogeometric: *Sardis* (M10) *Small Finds* (forthcoming), Seal 66.1:7109, green schist, *BASOR* 186, 36, fig. 15.

4. Boardman, "Pyramidal Seals," 20, 21; for Lydian inscription, see Hanfmann, *Croesus,* 19, figs. 43, 44.

5. Greenewalt, "Lydian Graves," 125, 126, pl. 10, onyx on goldwire.

6. *Sardis* (M10) *Small Finds* (forthcoming) and section "Rock Crystal," with eight objects including the sixth century lion; *BASOR* 177, 7, fig. 7. Also cited are rock crystal objects found by the first Sardis expedition, *Sardis* XIII (1925) nos. 49, 50, 114 and Boardman, "Pyramidal Seals." Greenewalt, "Elements," 42.

7. *Sardis* (M10) *Small Finds* (forthcoming), Boardman, *Gems* 380–382, fig. 316. *LSJ* (1968), *s.v.,* gives the reading as *daktylokoiloglyphos* and takes it as a misreading of *daktylioglyphos:* the publication cited is *IGRR* 4, no. 1648 (Philadelphia).

8. *Sardis* (M10) *Small Finds* (forthcoming), no. 17 = Seal 59.1:2151. Also cited is a rock crystal bead from a thirteenth century Byzantine grave, *BASOR* 215, 14, fig. 10.

9. *Sardis* (M8) *Metalwork* (forthcoming).

10. *BASOR* 199, 15, 16, figs. 4, 5.

11. Waldbaum, *Bronze*, 69.

12. *Sardis* M2 (1972) no. 292. Roebuck, 101 n. 87. Herodotus 1.34–36 = *Sardis* M2 (1972) no. 89.

13. *Sardis* M4 (1976) 36, fig. 8; on its administration, see 14, 15.

14. See the sections "Pactolus North" and "Goldworking Installations and Techniques" in Chapter III, *infra*.

15. *Sardis* M2 (1972) nos. 73–83. Roebuck, 90, 92. Testimonia will also be included in *Sardis* (M8) *Metalwork* (forthcoming). See also Greenewalt, "Elements," 42, 43.

16. Bull: Amandry, *BCH* Supp. 4 (1977) 273–293. Chryselephantine heads: K. Koubetsos, *Tachydromos* 26 (29 June 1978), 36–41, eight color reproductions. *Archaeological Calendar 1980*, pl. Nov. 24–Dec. 7.

17. *Sardis* XIII (1925). Gold plaques: see Oppenheim, 172.

18. A goldsmith was among the people sentenced to death for assault on the sacred Embassy of Artemis, ca. 330 B.C.(?): D. Knibbe in Bammer-Fleischer-Knibbe, 95–97; no. 1631.

19. J. H. Kroll, "Greek Inscriptions," in *Sardis* (R4) *Synagogue* (forthcoming) and *BASOR* 187, 32.

20. Indere: Greenewalt, "Lydian Graves," 125, 135, pl. 10:1; idem, "Elements," 42, 43.

21. Hawk: Greenewalt, "Lydian Graves," 126, 135, 136, pl. 10:3. Silver phiale mesomphalos: *Sardis* I (1922) 82, 83. This tomb, Butler's no. 213, contained also a silver bowl. Oliver, in Hanfmann, *Studies*, 115, 116 has reconstructed its contents. For other silver objects: *Sardis* (M8) *Metalwork* (forthcoming). *Sardis* I (1922) 83, bowl, ladle, little dishes, ointment stirrers, rings. *Sardis* XIII (1925) nos. 83, 84.

22. Greenewalt, "Elements," 41. Mirrors and bronzes of animals with folded legs: Oliver, 113–120, pls. 29–31, ca. 500–400 B.C. For bronzes found by the first Sardis expedition see *Sardis* I (1922) 84, ills. 77 (Hellenistic), 82 (Persian).

23. *Sardis* (M8) *Metalwork* (forthcoming); *Sardis* (M19) *Byzantine Shops* (forthcoming): E10, E11.

24. Greenewalt-Majewski, "Lydian Textiles"; Greenewalt, "Elements," 43, 44, pl. 19. See *Sardis* R1 (1975) 21 n. 23, for literary sources. According to a communication from C. H. Greenewalt, textile material was found in a tumulus-chamber tomb at Allahi near Ahmetli by K. Nayir of the Manisa museum (1979). Nayir, 124, fig. 29.

25. Gold-woven chitons: Lydus, *De magistratibus*

3.64. Heracleides Cumanus in Athenaeus 12.514, ca. 350? B.C. Greenewalt, "Elements," 43 n. 15.

26. Greenewalt-Majewski, "Lydian Textiles."

27. BT 63.2; Greenewalt, "Elements," 43, pl. 19:15,16.

28. Greenewalt-Majewski, "Lydian Textiles."

29. Ibid. For Phrygian mosaics as a possible reflection of rugs, see R. S. Young, "Early Mosaics," 13.

30. *Sardis* M5 (1978) 15, 16, no. 2, fig. 33 and the frontispiece (in color); Hanfmann-Detweiler, "Heights," 3–12 and cover; Hanfmann, *Letters*, pl. II.

31. Greenewalt, "Exhibitionist," 42–48, pl. 14.

32. For the leather industry and mentions of leather workers at Sardis in Homer, see *Sardis* R1 (1975) 21. Other references: Roebuck, 56 (sandal thongs, bells, shoes).

33. Homer, *Iliad* 4:131–137. Cheek pieces of this kind have been found in Gordion but they are imported (Syrian?), not Phrygian: R. J. Young, "Gordion 1961," 167, pl. 47. Barnett, "Ivories," 18. Pedley, 108, 109, argued in favor of a Sardian ivory carving school.

34. Bone disks of animal style: *Sardis* (M10) *Small Finds* (forthcoming) nos. 54, 55 (BI 65.2:6636), (BI 61.27:3934) with literature, including *BASOR* 211, 33, 34, fig. 11. P. Gaber, "A Chape in the Boston Museum and the Problem of Scythian Scabbards" (Qualifying Paper, Harvard University, 1976, unpublished) denies, however, that these are chapes. *Sardis* (M10) *Small Finds*, preface, and Chapter II, "Bone-Ivory," discusses all of this material. The Lydian ivory pieces came from "Lydian Trench" (HoB) and PN; *Sardis* (M10) *Small Finds*, nos. 60, 65–67.

35. Ephesus ivories: Cecil Smith, "The Ivory Statuettes" and "Other Ivory and Bone Objects" in Hogarth, *Ephesus* (1908), 155–198. Akurgal, *Kunst Anat.*, 195–204, figs. 150–161, 165–173. Jacobsthal, 85–95. B. Freyer-Schauenburg, *Elfenbeine*.

36. Ivory head, Archaeological Museum, Istanbul 4657. "Found in a plundered tomb of early type," *Sardis* I (1922) 140, 162–164, ills. 156, 182, plan; *Sardis* XIII (1925) no. 87, pl. 8:8–10. D. Curtis assumed that like the heads in Delphi, it had a gold portion with hair on back of head. Barnett, *Nimrud Ivories*, no. 2, fig. 20, pl. 11:c. ? Smithsonian Institution, *Art Treasures of Turkey*, fig. 115. Akurgal, *Kunst Anat.*, pl. 7:6. *Sardis* R2 (1978) 14 n. 6. *Sardis* (M10) *Small Finds*, Introduction, "Carved Figures" (forthcoming).

37. See Amandry, *BCH* Supp. 4 (1977) 273–293, on the finds at Delphi. K. Koubetsos, *Tachydromos* 26 (June 29, 1978) 36–41, eight color plates —Apollo or Croesus? Artemis or Croesus' wife?

38. The references on *baccaris* from Croesus through the fifth century B.C. are collected in *Sardis* M2 (1972) no. 131 and in C. H. Greenewalt's Ph.D.

dissertation (University of Pennsylvania) on the Lydians. Cf. Greenewalt, "Elements," 38, pl. 13.

39. The Lydian building techniques are discussed in detail by A. Ramage, *Sardis* M5 (1978) 3–10.

40. *BASOR* 174, 34; the text is still unpublished (IN 63.118). See, however, the translation by L. Robert, Chapter VII, Appendix.

41. *Sardis* M4 (1976) 16, 19, 110–112, no. 14; see also "Building Inscriptions," 113–115.

42. *Sardis* M4 (1976) "Industry and Commerce," 14–19: "with the exception of gold, all resources which made Sardis a major center of industry in earlier times were available in late antiquity."

43. *Sardis* M6 (1980) 1–2. See R. H. Brill, "Glass Finds," *BASOR* 170, 62–65.

44. For the technique of "dichroic" vases, which according to tests at Wembley (General Electric Research Laboratory) entailed purposeful addition of gold, see Harden, "The Rothschild Lycurgus Cup," 10. For the dating by decomposition layers, see R. H. Brill and H. P. Hood, "A New Method for Dating Ancient Glass," 18–21. R. H. Brill, "Weathered Glass," 21–23.

45. *Sardis* M4 (1976) 75, 76. *Sardis* M6 (1980) 1–4.

46. *Sardis* M4 (1976) 92, 97. H. Crane, *BASOR* 228, 51–53.

47. *Sardis* M4 (1976), index *s.v.* "Limekilns," 50, 73–74, 83, 92. N. H. Ramage, in *Sardis* R2 (1978) 81 n. 5, lists the evidence for limekilns and pits. Gymnasium: J. Schmidt, "Aus Constantinopel und Kleinasien," 151.

Regional Settlement Pattern: Prehistoric to Twentieth Century

1. D. G. Mitten, *BASOR* 191, 7–10; 199, 12–15; Mitten-Yügrüm, "Eski Balikhane"; Mitten-Yügrüm, "Ahlatli."

2. See the survey by D. H. French, "Prehistoric Sites," 41–98. Numerous Yortan cemeteries, e.g. at Gölde, were illicitly excavated in the Lydia-Kekaumene region in recent years. For the Yortan-type tripod vase at Ahlatli Tepecik see Mitten-Yügrüm, "Eski Balikhane," 195, fig. 9.

3. Boysal, "Excavations in Caria," 46. Cf. Mee, 128.

4. A. Ramage–N. Ramage, 141–160, fig. 1.

5. *BASOR* 206, 11–15.

6. Plutarch, *Moralia, Mulierum virtutes* 262 D, E.

7. Ramage, "Architecture," 73, 74.

8. *Sardis* VII.1 (1932) 3, no. 1; see Buckler-Robinson, 41–51 for a discussion of these villages and towns. Atkinson, 48, 49, 69–75. For translation and discussion of economic points, see Cavaignac, *Population* (1932) 122–128.

9. Actually, these "village" units often include several hamlets.

10. Official statistics after *Manisa* 1967, 107. The district of Salihli (map, ibid., 77) probably corresponds pretty closely to the immediate ecological area of Sardis, except that the ancient land may have extended somewhat farther westward into the present district of Turgutlu, at least along the Hermus and the southern shore of the Gygean Lake (Marmara Gölü).

11. *Sardis* R1 (1975) 19, 20, "Territory of Sardis." Roebuck's notion that "Lydia should be envisaged as a land of peasant and herder villages with one great center, Sardis," is surely inaccurate. In addition to known towns mentioned in the text, Hypaipa, Tyre, and probably Kula were cities in Lydian times.

12. Mersindere: *Sardis* VII.1 (1932) no. 144. Metallon and Üç Tepeler: Foss, "Explorations," 30, 31, 33, 34, 37–39, 52–54. Çaltili: *Sardis* VII.1 (1932) no. 146 and unpublished Sardis inscriptions IN 58.9, IN 68.11. Sart Çamur Hamamlari: *Sardis* VII.1 (1932) 97; no. 209, also IN 60.40.

13. Allahdiyen: Foss, "Explorations," 40, 43–45. Tatar Islamköy: Sardis inscriptions IN 59.64, IN 64.57; this site was apparently adjacent to the village of Tatar Dere (which has now disappeared or merged with its neighbor) where Keil and Premerstein saw numerous ancient and Byzantine remains; Keil-Premerstein, II: 8. The two villages are mentioned as separate but adjacent by Arundell in *Seven Churches,* 176. Yeşilkavak (formerly called Monavak): Buresch, 186; Keil-Premerstein, II: 9–10. There are no remains now visible, but a tumulus stands above the village.

14. Sites at and around Durasalli: Buresch, 194; Keil-Premerstein, II: 9; III: 10–14; there are no remains now to be found at Durasalli. Mounds: A. Ramage–N. Ramage, 149. Lydian inscription: Keil-Premerstein, III: no. 16. Thymbrara: Xenophon, *Cyr.* 6.2.111; 7.1.45; Diodorus 14.80.2 (there called Thybarna); Buresch, 194.

15. Çapakli: Buresch, 133; Keil-Premerstein, I: 67, 68; an occasional fragment is still to be found in the village; mounds stand nearby at Gebeç and Tepecik Çiftligi. North side of plain: Sardis inscription IN 68.1 (Yagbasan Köy): *BASOR* 177, 35–36. South side of lake: unspecified findspot: *Sardis* VII.1 (1932) nos. 5, 153, 160; Ahlatli Tepecik: *BASOR* 191, 12–15; Eski Balikhane: *Sardis* VII.1 (1932) no. 139; Mitten-Yügrüm, "Eski Balikhane," 191. West side of lake: Keil-Premerstein, I: 64, unpublished milestones from Kanbogaz; the remains of a large stone building stand beside the modern road, and a fragmentary inscription mentioning an aqueduct is built into a local fountain.

16. Gürice: Buresch, 184; Keil-Premerstein, II:

4–8; Buckler notes that tombs and fragmentary inscriptions are visible at the site, which seems to have been fairly considerable. On Lübbey Yaylasi and Bozdag, see C. Foss, "Explorations," 31, 39–43, 34–36. Antiquities found at Bozdag were made available for inspection through the courtesy of Bay Mütahhar Başoglu of Ödemiş and Bozdag, who is well versed in the history and archaeology of this relatively unexplored region.

17. A new inscription from Ephesus, dating between Flavian and pre-Hadrianic periods, has added ten unknown units to the *conventus iuridicus* (*dioikesis*, "diocese") of Sardis, among them at least one going back to the Persian era. Others sound as if their names go back to Lydian times. Habicht, "Asia," 67, 68, 71–77. L. Robert, *Bull.* 89 (1976) 533, 534; no. 595. C. Foss, "Explorations."

18. For the route of the Third Crusade see the narratives of Ansbert and the *Historia Peregrinorum*, 75, 153, 154. The other routes were followed by Turkish attacks in 1110: Anna Comnena 14.1.6.

19. Late antique and Byzantine remains have been found at Gürice, Kilcanlar, Kemerdamlari (unpublished), Eski Balikhane, Bin Tepe, Tatar Dere, Durasalli, and Lübbey Yaylasi; on these sites see the references *Historia Peregrinorum*, nos. 35–40, and *BASOR* 186, 47–52. Unpublished inscriptions show that the sites at Çaltili and Sart Çamur Hamamlari were inhabited in late antiquity (IN 68.11, IN 60.40). Villages in the neighborhood of Sardis are mentioned in the narratives of the Third Crusade; see *Historia Peregrinorum* no. 41. To judge by its name, the village of Candaules, mentioned only in the life of some obscure martyrs of the Great Persecution, was probably in the vicinity: Delehaye, *Synaxarium*, 16.

20. For the administrative centers of Saruhan, see the extremely useful work of M. Çagatay Uluçay, 2:10, ii and 37–117. The latter section is a publication of archival documents of the province classified according to regional centers; the documents include the names of many villages.

21. For the towns and villages of the vilayet of Manisa in the seventeenth century see Uluçay, ibid., 1:16, 17, n. 43.

22. For the Ottoman highway system see the map at the end of vol. II of Fr. Täschner, *Wegenetz*. Relevant texts of the travelers will be published by J. A. Scott in *Sardis* (M14) *Early Travelers and Unexcavated Buildings* (forthcoming).

23. For the caravan trade of Izmir, see in addition to the travelers, Täschner, *Wegenetz*.

24. Salihli is mentioned as a large and inhabited village by Sieur Paul Lucas, 305, who passed through ca. 1705. By the time of Arundell, who visited Salihli in 1826 and 1832 (*Seven Churches,* 176; *Discoveries* I: 30, 31), it was an important market town. Thus the local story that the town was first settled around 1790 by a camel driver named Sadik Dede may be dismissed; for that see *Manisa* 302. This story is related in Türkdogan, 11, where a brief sketch of the history and geography of the town is given. According to Türkdogan, Salihli became the administrative center of the region in 1875.

II. Prehistoric and Protohistoric Periods

Early Bronze Age Sites on the Gygean Lake

1. *BASOR* 186, 40–43, fig. 18; 191, 7–10, figs. 1–6; 199, 12–16, figs. 1, 2; *TürkArkDerg* 16:2 (1967) 77, 78; 17 (1968) 125–127. Mitten-Yügrüm, "Ahlatli," 22–29; G. M. A. Hanfmann, "Ahlatli Tepecik," in Mellink (1969) 209; and Sardis Field Reports.

2. *BASOR* 199, 15, 16, figs. 1, 4–5, *TürkArkDerg* 18:1 (1969) 61, fig. 1. Mitten-Yügrüm, "Eski Balikhane," 191–195; G. M. A. Hanfmann and D. G. Mitten, "Sardis—Eski Balikhane" in Mellink (1970) 163; and Sardis Field Reports.

3. *BASOR* 191, 10.

4. For more detailed information about metal objects see *Sardis* (M8) *Metalwork* (forthcoming). Cf. Hanfmann-Waldbaum, "New Excavations," 311–315.

5. Arik, *Alaca Höyük 1935,* CCLIV-CCLV, A1. 1731–1737.

6. *Sardis* R2 (1978) no. 229.

7. Ibid., no. 1.

8. Mitten-Yügrüm, "Ahlatli."

9. Wheeler, "Bronze Age Burial," 415–425.

10. Mellink, "Karataş-Semayük and Elmali, Lycia," 293–307; Mellink (1969); and Angel, "Karataş People," 385–391.

11. Kadish, "Prehistoric Remains at Aphrodisias, 1967," 49–65; idem, "Prehistoric Remains at Aphrodisias, 1968–1969," 121–140.

12. Collignon, "Yortan," 810–813.

13. Bittel, "Yortankultur," 1–28.

14. Levi, "Campagne 1961–1962," 555–571; idem, "Le campagne 1962–1964," 505–546.

15. Wheeler, "Bronze Age Burial," 418–420.

16. Mitten-Yügrüm, "Ahlatli," 27. Blegen, *Troy,* 52, fig. 11 (Troy I pottery) and 80, fig. 19 (Troy II pottery). Podzuweit, 165–173, 240–242, pls. 7–8, 11, 16.

17. Mellaart, *Early Bronze Ages,* 128–132, fig. 39; French, "Prehistoric Sites," 64, 65; for comparison of

pottery: Orthmann, "Keramik der Yortankultur," 13–16, fig. 6.

18. Mellaart, *Early Bronze Ages,* 140.

19. *Sardis* (M8) *Metalwork* (forthcoming).

20. Mitten-Yügrüm, "Ahlatli," 27.

21. Karataş-Semayük: Mellink, "Karataş-Semayük and Elmali, Lycia, 1968," 323, pl. 74:16 (also reference to Yortan example); Yortan: R. Duru, "Jewelry," 123–135, and Mellink (1973) 175. Kocumbeli and Karayavşan: Mellink (1968) 148. Alaca Höyük: Mellink, "Karataş-Semayük and Elmali, Lycia, 1968," 323 n. 10. Arik, *Alaca Höyük 1935,* pl. 179, A1 317–348, Tomb B.

22. *BASOR* 199, 16.

23. Mitten-Yügrüm, "Eski Balikhane," 194.

24. D. Stronach, "Diffusion on Metal Types," 96.

25. The absolute dating of Bronze Age sites is controversial. The Early Bronze Age was long thought to have begun not before 3000 B.C., with EB II arriving ca. 2750 B.C.: Mellink, "Anatolian Chronology," 101–131; Mellaart, *Early Bronze Ages.* But recently, D. F. Easton, "Chronology," 145–173, has proposed much earlier dates, using C-14 figure and comparisons of Balkan, Helladic, and Anatolian sites, and wishes to push back the beginning of Troy II to ca. 3000 B.C. and the beginning of the Bronze Age much earlier.

26. *BASOR* 191, 10.

27. Ibid., 7.

Late Bronze and Early Iron Age in the City Area

1. *BASOR* 162, 9–16.

2. *BASOR* 170, 4–9.

3. *BASOR* 186, 31–37.

4. For similar impressions in Neolithic Greece, see S. Weinberg, "Elateia, 1959."

5. T. Özgüç, *Bestattungsbräuche: Ausgrabungen in Kultepe,* and *Ausgrabungen in Kultepe-1949.*

6. Blegen, *Troy III,* 377–379.

7. Blegen, *Troy III,* 6–7, 18, 370–379.

8. Blegen, *Troy III,* 18.

9. Güterbock, "Boghazköy," 211–216. Bittel, "Osman-Kayasi," 37–47; idem, *Bogazköy 1906–1912* 4–6, pls. 21, 22; idem, *Die hethitischen Grabfunde von Osmankayasi.*

10. Akurgal, *Hittites,* 103. Mellink, *Cemetery.*

11. On Troy: Blegen, *Troy III,* 370–379 n. 6. Bogazköy: Bittel, *Bogazköy III,* pl. 22. Beycesultan: Lloyd-Mellaart, "Beycesultan Excavations: First Preliminary Report," 75–78: figs. 16, 17 (Level II pithoi) and 84–87; fig. 20 (Level I pithoi). Gordion: Mellink, *Cemetery,* 15 n. 10; pl. 25.

12. M 62.64:4557: *Sardis* (M8) *Metalwork* (forthcoming).

13. *Sardis* R2 (1978) no. 2.

14. Kenna, *Cretan Seals,* 30 n. 3, 31, 85, 107; no. 134 (1933.415); pl. 6. Also in Boardman, *Gems,* 34, 91; color pl. 39:4.

15. Kenna, *Cretan Seals,* 66, 143; no. 396 (1889.279); pl. 15.

16. See note 14, *supra.*

17. Hanfmann-Waldbaum, "New Excavations," 309. C. Özgunel termed *BASOR* 186, fig. 9, Submycenaean. See Fig. 26.

18. G. F. Swift, *BASOR* 186, 37. Cf. Mee, 144, 148 and Desborough, *Dark Ages,* 184.

19. *Sardis* (M8) *Metalwork* (forthcoming).

20. *BASOR* 186, 36 n. 7. Hanfmann-Waldbaum, "New Excavations," 308 n. 13. O. W. Muscarella has dated the piece Geometric (by letter to J. C. Waldbaum). The fibula is said to fit Blinkenberg's Type IV:C. Blinkenberg, 87–106. *Sardis* (M8) *Metalwork* (forthcoming).

21. *Sardis* M6 (1980) nos. 821, 828–830, 846.

22. *Sardis* (M10) *Small Finds* (forthcoming); *BASOR* 186, 36, fig. 15.

23. *BASOR* 186, 36.

24. *BASOR* 162, 16 n. 14; Pedley, 25–29; Hanfmann-Waldbaum, "New Excavations," 308, 309.

25. Huxley, *Achaeans and Hittites,* 33. For the controversy on Tudhaliyas, see n. 28, *infra.*

26. Herodotus 4.45; Pedley, 26.

27. Pedley, 26.

28. Mellaart, "Anatolian Trade," 189–193, 196, argues that the Kingdom existed in the Balkans and dealt in tin, and he denies that Greeks settled in Western Anatolia in numbers sufficient to have a kingdom. For controversial dating of Ahhiyawa documents, which also involves Tudhaliyas, see Otten; Houwink ten Cate, 63–65, 76.

29. Weickert (1956); (1959–1960); Kleiner, *Alt-Milet;* Desborough, *The Last Mycenaeans,* 16, 219.

30. Gultekin-Baran, "Mycenaean Grave," 125–133.

31. Hanfmann, "A Hittite Priest," 1.

32. Hanfmann-Waldbaum, "New Excavations," 309. *Sardis* R1 (1975) 173 n. 85; *Sardis* M2 (1972) no. 26.

33. Barnett, "Mopsos," 140; idem, "Phrygia and the Peoples of Anatolia in the Iron Age," 27.

34. Boysal, "Excavations in Caria," 46–47, pl. 31–32. Mee, 121–156.

35. Mee, 128, no. 35, 144. Hanfmann-Waldbaum, "New Excavations," 309 n. 15. C. Özgünel, Ankara, has kindly advised on some of the Sardis sherds (1980).

36. Blegen, *Troy IV,* 53, 156.

37. Goldman, *Tarsus II,* 206.

38. Hanfmann-Waldbaum, "Two Submycenaean Vases," 52, 53.

39. Hanfmann-Waldbaum, "Two Submycenaean Vases," 53; Hanfmann proposes Submycenaean links between Carian and Greek legends.

40. Swift, *BASOR* 186, 37.

III. Lydian Excavation Sectors

House of Bronzes/Lydian Market: Stratification Sequence and the Lydian Levels

1. For G. F. Swift's observations, see *BASOR* 182, 8-18; 186, 31-37; 199, 28-29; 203, 8-10. It may be preferable, ultimately, to turn this scheme around so that Lydian I is at the beginning of the sequence rather than the end. Lydian I would be used as the first Iron Age level, and additional numbers could be added for the most recent levels.

2. *BASOR* 186, 22, fig. 5.

3. Ibid., 33.

4. See Schmidt, *Alishar Hüyük,* 115, for remarks on modern, medieval, and ancient grain storage pits.

5. *Sardis* M2 (1972) nos. 49-51.

6. J. Schaeffer's work on Corinthian pottery is due to appear in *Sardis* (R5) *Pottery:* "Corinthian" (forthcoming).

7. FR 1975: *Corinthian Pottery,* 3 (unpublished).

8. *BASOR* 154, 28.

9. *BASOR* 157, 30.

10. See *BASOR* 154, 28 for extensive description.

11. *BASOR* 157, 30-32, fig. 9, Unit 24.

12. Herodotus 1.94 = *Sardis* M2 (1972) no. 23. *BASOR* 170, 11-13 ("H").

13. *BASOR* 182, 12, general fittings; 13, figs. 1-2, pots and loom weights.

14. *BASOR* 174, 8.

15. *BASOR* 174, 8.

16. *BASOR* 157, 28.

17. *Sardis* R2 (1978) 14.

18. *BASOR* 191, 7-10; Mitten-Yügrüm, "Eski Balikhane."

19. Herodotus 1.70 = *Sardis* M2 (1972) no. 104; Strabo 13.4.5.

20. Nicolas of Damascus, *FGrHist* 90 F. 47 = *Sardis* M2 (1972) nos. 10, 29, 30, 32, 35, 45, 53, 64, 126.

Pactolus North

1. *BASOR* 162, 25; *Sardis* R2 (1978) no. 8, figs. 51-54.

2. *Sardis* 1 (1922) 33 E; Buchwald, "Church E."

3. Herodotus 5.101 = *Sardis* M2 (1972) no. 282.

4. *BASOR* 162, 26.

5. *BASOR* 166, 22.

6. *BASOR* 199, 16; Hanfmann-Waldbaum, "New Excavations," 310; *Sardis* M5 (1978) 2, 9. For new developments in studies of ancient silver sources, see Gentner, 273-284.

7. See V. Biringuccio, *Pirotechnia* IV, Chapter 7 and other contemporary writings; Ramage, "Gold Refining," 729-735.

8. Tylecote, 80, fig. 15, with notes and references.

9. Herodotus 1.94 = *Sardis* M2 (1972) no. 132. Balmuth, "Earliest Coin," 3-7.

10. Herodotus 1.50-52 = *Sardis* M2 (1972) no. 99.

11. *BASOR* 191, 13.

12. *Sardis* M5 (1978) no. 42.

13. *BASOR* 199, 18.

14. Barnett, "Ivories," 22, cites Aelianus, *NA* 12:4: mermnos (a hawk) was sacred to the mother of Gods (Cybele).

15. Gusmani, "Name," 158-161; *Sardis* M3 (1975) 28.

16. *BASOR* 166, fig. 14 (partial).

Goldworking Installations and Techniques

1. Special thanks are due to Turkish colleagues at Çekmece Nuclear Research Center, Istanbul. Director General Sait Akpinar, Professor Talat Erben, and Dr. Sevim Okar provided data from neutron activation of the gold samples. Director General Sadrettin Alpan of the Maden Tetkikve Arama Enstitüsü in Ankara and Dr. Nilüfer Bayçin, Director of the Technical Laboratory, provided spectrographic analysis. The Faculty of the Institutes of Geology and Zoology at Ege University in Izmir made microscopes and macrophotography equipment available to us. We thank Ozcan Dora, Erol Izdar, Dr. Mehmet Arod, Dr. Heinrich Bremer, Dr. Orhan Kaya, and Dr. Inan Ullah Tareem. Andrew Ramage, the primary archaeologist in PN, was most helpful. Professor Lawrence J. Majewski and R. E. Stone, Sardis conservators, assisted us in the early phases of the discovery of the industrial area. It was Stone who confirmed Ramage's suggestion that the site was a metalworking area, in fact, a cupellation floor. Professor C. S. Smith, Dr. A. Gordus, Professor H. Lechtmann, and A. Beale have provided invaluable suggestions.

2. Herodotus 5.49.5; Aristogoras of Miletus is explaining a map of Anatolia to Cleomenes of Sparta.

3. Herodotus 1.94 = *Sardis* M2 (1972) no. 132.

4. Roebuck, 58; J. G. Milne, 85-87, champions the innovation of a bimetallic coinage by Croesus. W.

L. Brown, "Pheidon's Coinage," 179, considers it the invention of coinage.

5. Perrot-Chipiez, *History of Art*, 248.

6. Bean, 261: "The gold for these Lydian coins was obtained, in part at least, from the river Pactolus, a small stream which flows down from the Tmolus through Sardis to join the Hermus . . . The Pactolus itself was quickly exhausted . . . It had, however, sufficed to make the names of Gyges and Croesus proverbial for wealth."

7. The most complete recent compendium of literary references is Pedley, *Sardis* M2 (1972), esp. nos. 66–84, 93, 97, 98, 100, 103, 124, 130–132, 140, 144.

8. For the chronological sequence of the goldworking industry and the altar of Cybele (Figs. 42, 45); see Hanfmann, *Croesus*, 6.

9. The area is near the village, and many children play in the excavations despite attempts to control this activity. Visitors to the site unwittingly break up floor areas and crumble walls which are not reinforced with a concrete topping.

10. Ramage, *BASOR* 199, 23–25; a detailed report on the use of these furnaces will be presented, including E. Wahle's important cementation complex reconstruction drawings (Figs. 55, 139), in *Sardis* (R7) *Pactolus* (forthcoming).

11. Goldstein, *BASOR* 228, 57, fig. 11.

12. Goldstein, *BASOR* 199, 26, 27.

13. These analyses were carried out only on samples of furnace refractory material and glassy slags.

14. Hanfmann-Waldbaum, "New Excavations," 313.

15. J. H. Kroll, University of Texas, Austin, first referred us to S. Bolin, 23, Table 1, showing known weights of the so-called "Lion-Head" series (half-stater weights vary from 4.38 to 4.76 grams), to which now a considerable hoard from Gordion must be added. See A. R. Bellinger, 10–15. Bolin's Table 2, showing the variations in fineness of the "Lion's-Head" series, is based primarily on the specific gravity analyses of J. Hammer, "Der Feingehalt," and B. V. Head, *BMC, Lydia*, 1. See Pászthory, 152–156, analyses of three "Lion's-Head" coins: one was electrum-plated silver.

16. Goldstein, *BASOR* 228, 54–57, fig. 8.

17. W. J. Young, "Fabulous Gold"; Whitmore-Young, 88–95; R. E. Ogilvie, "X-ray Detector." Pászthory, 155–156, found no platiniridium in three analyzed coins.

18. A. Ramage, "City Area: Pactolus North," *BASOR* 191, 13, fig. 13.

19. For recent research on the matter of lead studies, see Brill-Shields, "Ancient Coins," 282–284, no. 617.

20. *BASOR* 199, 16–26; 215, 43, 44; 228, 53–57. *TürkArkDerg* 18:1 (1969) 61, 62; 24:1 (1977) 116, 117. Hanfmann, *Letters*, 230–234, 248, 249, 253; idem, *Croesus*, 5, 6; Hanfmann-Waldbaum, "New Excavations," 310–315.

21. *Sardis* (R7) *Pactolus* (forthcoming).

Pactolus Cliff

1. *BASOR* 157, 12; 162, 17; 166, 33; Hanfmann-Detweiler, "Heights," 7–8, figs. 8–10.

2. A sherd of monochrome ware: P 60.398:2853, *87.40; *BASOR* 162, 20 was tentatively described as Bronze Age, but this was before the Early Iron Age wares from HoB and PN became known.

3. *BASOR* 162, 19–24, figs. 7–11.

4. *BASOR* 162, 24, fig. 10.

5. Strabo 13.4.8; *Sardis* M2 (1972) 50. The pottery found under Level II, above Level III, included a Protocorinthian jug (P 60.80); a Protocorinthian kotyle (P 60.107), late eighth century B.C., according to J. S. Schaeffer, *Report on the Corinthian Pottery at Sardis* (1977–1978) 3 (unpublished) and a letter of March 11, 1980; a Rhodian jug, ca. 650 or 660 B.C. (P 60.149); and an Eastern Greek plate, Hanfmann-Detweiler, "Heights," 8, fig. 8, which is not Ephesian, according to C. H. Greenewalt, Jr., "Ephesian Ware," 92 n. 3. Nothing demands a date earlier than 650 B.C.

6. *Sardis* M5 (1978) no. 43, fig. 86; no. 79, fig. 107; *BASOR* 162, fig. 8. Ramage now dates this type before 500 B.C.

Pyramid Tomb

1. *Sardis* I (1922) 155, 167–170.

2. Ibid., 170, ill. 185.

3. *Sardis* (R6) *Acropolis* (forthcoming); Hanfmann, *Letters*, figs. 192–193.

4. *BASOR* 199, 38.

5. *BASOR* 166, 28.

6. Stronach, *Pasargadae*, 41.

7. Ibid., 17, 41. Hanfmann-Waldbaum, n. 10, *infra*.

8. Nylander, *Ionians*, 97.

9. Xenophon, *Cyropedia* 7.3.4–5, 7.3.15 = *Sardis* M2 (1972) nos. 276, 277; Hanfmann, *Letters*, 92.

10. Hanfmann-Waldbaum, "New Excavations," 316; *BASOR* 162, 31 n. 45.

11. Hanfmann-Waldbaum, "New Excavations," 317, pl. 38. Stronach, *Pasargadae*, 23; Susa Building Tablets DSF (Darius, Susa F) 35–55 = *Sardis* M2 (1972) no. 303.

The Acropolis

1. *Sardis* R1 (1975) 9–12. The coordinates given in this discussion of the Acropolis have been converted to the B grid from the original Acropolis grid records.

2. *BASOR* 170, 37.

3. Hanfmann, *Croesus,* 6.

4. Shear, "Sixth Report," 401.

5. W. Warfield, Appendix I in *Sardis* I (1922).

6. For instability of soil, see Olson, "Landslides," 261–262; for grabens and faults, see Ilhan, 433. A new geomorphological study was begun by D. F. Belknap and D. G. Sullivan in 1978.

7. Herodotus 1.84 = *Sardis* M2 (1972) no. 116.

8. *Sardis* M2 (1972) nos. 49–51.

9. *BASOR* 182, 10.

10. Lydian pottery found on the Acropolis (Figs. 71, 76): Greenewalt, "Wild Goat," 57–59, 65, 79–80, no. 8, pl. 6: 3–4 "rectangular box lid" attributes Fig. 71 to a "Sardis Style" group around 600 B.C. *BASOR* 162, 34; for Phrygian sherds: *BASOR* 166, 35–36; for plaque: *BASOR* 162, 34, fig. 18.

11. Herodotus 1.84 = *Sardis* M2 (1972) no. 116.

12. Ibid.

13. Arrowheads: *Sardis* (M8) *Metalwork* (forthcoming); *BASOR* 162, 36.

14. Herodotus 5.99–102 = *Sardis* M2 (1972) nos. 150, 272, 382.

15. Plutarch, *De Herodoti malignitate* 24 (861 B.C.) = *Sardis* M2 (1972) no. 154.

16. Arrian, *Anabasis* 1.17.3–6. = *Sardis* M2 (1972) no. 235.

17. *BASOR* 215, 31–33, fig. 1.

18. Hanfmann, "On Lydian Sardis," 100–104, figs. 15–19.

19. Greenewalt, "Twentieth Campaign," 106–107.

20. Polybius 7.15.6 = *Sardis* M2 (1972) no. 283.

21. For the walls, see *BASOR* 166, 37, fig. 28; for the method of construction, see *Sardis* M5 (1978) 5.

22. *Sardis* M5 (1978) no. 19, fig. 50; *BASOR* 170, 33, fig. 22.

23. *BASOR* 162, 34.

24. See the section "Acropolis Tunnels" later in this chapter.

25. *BASOR* 162, 36, fig. 19; Hanfmann, *Letters,* 77, figs. 48–49.

26. *Sardis* R2 (1978) no. 23, figs. 87–89; *BASOR* 162, 36, fig. 20.

27. Herodotus 1.84 = *Sardis* M2 (1972) no. 116.

28. *Sardis* R2 (1978) 20–21; *BASOR* 162, 36–37, fig. 20.

29. Jenkins, no. 20 (BM1928); Balmuth, 3–7, pl. 1a; Weidauer, 59–62, 94–106.

30. Arrian, *Anabasis* 1.17.6 = *Sardis* M2 (1972) no. 235. Hanfmann, "Palace," is a comprehensive discussion.

31. *BASOR* 162, 37–39, figs. 21–22; 206, 15–20, fig. 5–7. Hanfmann, *Croesus,* 8–9, fig. 17.

32. *BASOR* 162, 37.

33. For stylistic comparisons, see *BASOR* 177, 31–33; Hanfmann, "Palace," 151; for limestone chips and pottery, see *BASOR* 206, 19. *Sardis* M3 (1975) no. BI6, figs. 43–44.

34. D. P. Hansen, "Bronze Boar," 27–36. *BASOR* 162, 39, fig. 24. For Ephesus, see Hogarth, *Ephesus,* 176, fig. 33.

35. Stronach, *Pasargadae,* 20.

36. Ibid., 12, 20.

37. Nylander, *Ionians,* 89–91. Nylander also supports the idea of a strong Lydian element in the formation of the technical, stylistic, and structural features of the Tall-i Takht.

38. *AASOR* 43, 67–69; *BASOR* 228, 48–50, fig. 2.

39. From just above the top of the conglomerate, that which would be the bottom of the shelf, came a piece of a gray ware fish plate rim, indicating that the fill above was not earlier than the Hellenistic period.

40. Vitruvius 2.8.9–10 = *Sardis* M2 (1972) no. 291.

41. Hanfmann, "Palace," 152–153.

42. *Sardis* M5 (1978) no. 17, fig. 38.

43. The wording is preserved by Aristotle, *Analytica posteriora* 94 a–b = *Sardis* M2 (1972) no. 148.

44. Hanfmann, "Palace," 147.

45. Vitruvius 2.8.9–10 = *Sardis* M2 (1972) no. 291.

46. *Sardis* M2 (1972) no. 149; Byzantine Fortress, Building C (Fig. 8:23).

47. Hanfmann, "Palace," 154.

48. For Philadelphia: Y. Boysal, "Caria," 46; for Aphrodisias: Akurgal, *Civilizations,* 174, and K. Erim in M. J. Mellink (1977), 297; for Pergamon: W. Radt, *Pergamon;* Akurgal, *Civilizations,* 69; Ziegenhaus-De Luca, *Pergamon* XI.2, 99–102.

49. Thus the sketchy investigation of the large hollow space within the top hillock of the Acropolis turned up only traces of painting and Christian graves, disproving its use as a cistern in late times: L. J. Majewski, *BASOR* 206, 15–16 n. 3. Another underground space is now inaccessible except by rope. In addition to the extant Roman and Byzantine cisterns (*Sardis* M4 [1976] 70), circular rock cuttings on AcT and AcS platforms seem to be bottoms of cisterns (*BASOR* 162, 34).

50. *Sardis* X (1926) 1–2; on "lower slope at northwest end," presumably our AcN, see Shear, "Sixth Report," 401; for the Harvard-Cornell discoveries see *Sardis* M5 (1978) nos. 7, 19, 38, 47, 104.

51. Hanfmann, "On Lydian Sardis," 103–104, figs. 15–19.

52. For views of the Athenian Acropolis during

the Turkish Age see Travlos, *Dictionary,* fig. 65; idem, *Poleodomike Exelixis,* 200–207, figs. 134–135.

53. Although the walls proved to be Lydian, the coins of Antiochus III, the Hellenistic fill, and the marble chips may still relate to the reconstruction of the defenses under Antiochus III after the siege of 213 B.C.: *BASOR* 162, 38–39 nn. 62–63; for Hellenistic fill on AcN, see *BASOR* 228, 50.

Acropolis Tunnels

1. *BASOR* 166, 5; 170, 35–37, fig. 24; 177, 8–10; Hanfmann, *Letters,* 105–106, figs. 69–70.
2. *Sardis* R1 (1975) 27. A Lydian sherd came from the deepest level of earth in the top chamber. *BASOR* 177, 8.
3. H. J. Kienast, "Der Tunnel," 97.
4. Wace, 98–99; Verdelis, 129–130; E. T. Vermeule, 161. For the Mycenaean Spring House on the Acropolis at Athens, see Travlos, *Dictionary,* 72–75, ills. 92–96.
5. Gall (1967) 585–587.

The Northeast Wadi

1. *Sardis* R1 (1975) 118; *BASOR* 199, 35.
2. *Sardis* 1 (1922) 151–152.
3. Shear, "Sixth Report," 400–410.
4. *BASOR* 199, 35; Hanfmann, "Prehistoric Sardis," 174.
5. *Sardis* R1 (1975) 119.
6. Ibid., 118, 120.
7. V. J. Harward, FR 1977: "Northeast Wadi Field Report for 1977," 10 (unpublished).
8. Mudbrick remains resting on stone socles have been recovered *in situ* at HoB and PN. *Sardis* R1 (1975) 124: HoB: Buildings H and K (Figs. 35, 39); PN: Unit XXVII (Fig. 44). For mudbrick architecture in pre-Hellenistic Sardis, see *Sardis* M5 (1978) 4–10.
9. *Sardis* R1 (1975) 122, fig. 307.
10. *Sardis* 1 (1922) 151; Hanfmann, "Horsemen," 570–579.
11. For illustrations of the finds in 1969, see *Sardis* R1 (1975), figs. 299, 301–313.
12. V. J. Harward, FR 1979: "Northeast Wadi Field Report for 1977," 11 (unpublished).
13. Ramage, "Architecture," 8.

The Artemis Precinct and Altar in Lydian and Persian Times

1. The area is ca. 210 m. north-south by ca. 200 m. east-west. *Sardis* I (1922) 25–26. The number of standing columns has changed over the years.

Edmund Cheshull noted six in 1690; Richard Chandler saw five in 1764; C. R. Cockerell counted three in 1812; and H. C. Butler found only two in 1910.

2. *Sardis* I (1922), plans II and III; *Sardis* R1 (1975) 74.
3. 1958: *BASOR* 154, 8–12; *TürkArkDerg* 9:1 (1959) 15–16; 1960: *BASOR* 162, 29–31; 1961: *BASOR* 166, 34; *TürkArkDerg* 11:12 (1961) 44; 1968: *BASOR* 199, 29–35; *TürkArkDerg* 17:11 (1968) 114; 1969: *BASOR* 199, 29–35; *TürkArkDerg* 18:11 (1969) 62–63; 1970: *BASOR* 203, 7; *TürkArkDerg* 19:1 (1970) 99; 1972: *BASOR* 211, 17; 1973: *BASOR* 215, 41.
4. *Sardis* R1 (1975) 53.
5. *BASOR* 199, 32–33.
6. *Sardis* R1 (1975) 107–115.
7. *Sardis* R1 (1975) 107. Antefix: ibid., 85, fig. 176, *Sardis* M5 (1978) 32, no. 80.
8. *Sardis* R1 (1975): Northwest Quarter: 57, North Terrace: 62–64, Northeastern Sector: 65. See also *Sardis* 1 (1922) 125–127 for North Terrace.
9. *Sardis* VI.1 (1916) 38–39; *Sardis* I (1922) ills: 136, 137, 138; *Sardis* R2 (1978) no. 274, figs. 465–466. For Baki, see Gusmani, *LW,* 74.
10. *Sardis* R1 (1975) 66; *Sardis* I (1922) 132, ill. 146.
11. *Sardis* R1 (1975) 73.
12. Ibid., 74–87.
13. Butler believed that the purplish sandstone (calcareous tufa) had been the characteristic building material used by the pre-Persian era Lydians: *Sardis* R1 (1975) 88; for Butler's interpretation see *Sardis* I (1922) 81, 103; for the column bases see *Sardis* R1 (1975) fig. 120, nos. 11, 12, figs. 121, 122; see also H. C. Butler, "Columns," 51–57.
14. *Sardis* XI (1916) v–vi; *Sardis* I (1922) 74–76.
15. Butler, "Columns," 51–57; Gusmani, *LW,* no. 21.
16. See Chapter VII, the section on "The Artemis Sanctuary."
17. *Sardis* R1 (1975) 85.
18. The fragment of marble astragal molding (NoEx 78.15/IN 78.4) probably is from one of the Artemis Temple columns which had stood in the east pronaos, although it was found reused in a rubble wall. Gusmani by letter (Sept. 1978) has dated the inscription (*Srkastulis SV*) to late fourth or early third century B.C. *Srkastulis* is probably the patronymic, "Son of Srkastus." For another appearance of the name *Srkastus,* see Gusmani, *LW,* no. 21. Gusmani intends to publish the new inscriptions in "Incontri Linguistici" (forthcoming).
19. *Sardis* R1 (1975) 76–80. K. J. Frazer, ibid., 75–76, has proposed that the first sanctuary had an image base with a small shrine or the earliest altar; during the reign of Croesus (ca. 550 B.C.) an archaic

temple modeled on the Artemision at Ephesus was erected. Frazer suggests that the altar (Figs. 94, 95) dates from the same building effort.

20. K. Knibbe, "Inschriftstele Inv. 1631," in Bammer-Bleischer-Knibbe, 95–97.

21. F. Eichler (1962) 50–51. First publication with transcription, Knibbe, "Religiöser Frevel," 175–182. F. Sokolowski, "Testimony," 427–431. L. Robert-J. Robert, *Bull.* 76 (1963) 163–164, no. 211 (after Eichler): 78 (1965) 155, no. 342 (after Knibbe); 79 (1966) 422, no. 369; *Sardis* R1 (1975) 6. R. Fleischer, 200–201, thinks as Sokolowski, that the sanctuary of Artemis of Ephesos was a different, smaller shrine. Robert dates 340–320 B.C., Knibbe in Bammer, 325–300 B.C., Hanfmann in *Sardis* R1 (1975) 6, ca. 300 B.C. Because Sardis is not treated as a Greek polis in this inscription, the attack probably occurred before the beginning of the Seleucid rule in 280 B.C.

22. *Sardis* R2 (1978) 17, figs. 70–71.

23. *Sardis* VI.1 (1916) no. L17, 23–28; VI.2 (1924) 1–4; VI.1, no. L11, 48–51; VI.2, 4–7; VI.1, no. L., 41–44; VI.2, 8–11; VI.1, no. L25, 38–39; VI.2, 38; Gusmani, *LW,* no. 1, 258.

24. Tacitus, *Ann.* 4.55.

25. *Sardis* R2 (1978) no. 3, figs. 9–10.

26. Ibid., no. 12, figs. 63–64. Dated ca. 500 B.C. by Hanfmann, fourth century B.C. by E. B. Harrison.

27. See Chapter V, the section on "Religious Life," under *Artemis.*

28. *Sardis* R2 (1978) 32, no. 19.

29. Ibid., no. 246, figs. 426–427.

30. Ibid., 62, fig. 176.

31. *Sardis* R1 (1975) 88–103.

32. *Sardis* II (1925) pl. A.

33. Ibid., ill. 97.

34. Nylander, "Clamps," 136, 144; *Ionians,* 42–45, figs. 10–11, 65–67, 19–20; Martin, *Manuel,* 273.

35. *Sardis* R1 (1975) 94, fig. 208.

36. *Sardis* R2 (1978) no. 51, fig. 161. Limestone crown: *Sardis* R1 (1975) 94095, fig. 210.

37. *Sardis* R1 (1975) 94 n. 17.

38. Ibid., 79.

39. Ibid., 103.

Peripheral Sectors

1. *BASOR* 162, 49, fig. 31; Hanfmann, *Letters,* 84.

2. *BASOR* 162, fig. 32.

3. *Sardis* R2 (1978) 9, figs. 58–60.

4. Richter, *Korai,* nos. 119, 120, figs. 377–384. (Acropolis 670–683); Harrison, *Agora XI,* 21, no. 75, fig. 228.

5. Akurgal, *Kunst Anat.,* 54–60, 86; Hanfmann-Waldbaum, "Kybele," 267.

6. *BASOR* 229, 66–67.

7. *Sardis* R1 (1975) 12, 27.

8. A. Ramage, "Architecture," 73.

9. C. H. Greenewalt, Jr., E. L. Sterud, D. F. Belknap, E. E. Freedman, *BASOR* 229, 58–61; 233, 1–4.

IV. Lydian Graves and Cemeteries

The Burial Mounds

1. Herodotus 1.93; Xenophon, *Cyropaedia* 7.3.15 = *Sardis* M2 (1972) no. 278; Strabo 13.4.7 = *Sardis* M2 (1972) no. 279; Hipponax F 42 = *Sardis* M2 (1972) no. 280; Nicander, *Theriaca* 630–635 = *Sardis* M2 (1972) no. 281; Chandler (1775); Texier (1862); Sayce.

2. Von Olfers, 539–556.

3. Choisy, "Tombeaux," a basic study for Bin Tepe.

4. *Sardis* I (1922) 9–10.

5. Ibid., 10; this has been the experience of the Harvard-Cornell Expedition as well.

6. Ibid., 156.

7. *BASOR*: 170, 51–60; 174, 52–58; 177, 27–35; 182, 27–30; 186, 38–52; 206, 11–15; 229, 70–71; 233, 9–19 (this tomb is not at Bin Tepe but is located much nearer the city). *TürkArkDerg* 12:1 (1962) 26, 32, 33; 12:2 (1963) 14; 13:2 (1964) 61–62; 14:1–2 (1965) 152–153; 15:1 (1966) 71–6. *Sardis* R1 (1975) 1, 5, 11–12, 22, 28, 95; *Sardis* R2 (1978) 3, 36, nos. 230–231; *Sardis* M2 (1972) 76–78, nos. 276–281; *Sardis* M3 (1975) 67–71, no. B15; *Sardis* M5 (1978) 6; Hanfmann, *Letters,* 108–109, 118–120, 131–132, 146–147, 152–159, 164–165, 183–186, 193–194, 300, 319, 320, 322.

8. Duman Tepe: *BASOR* 186, 47–52 (Duman Tepe), 47 (Cambaz Tepe, Kuş Tepe), 42–43, fig. 23, Grave BT 63.3; *BASOR* 229, 70 (two tumuli at Kestelli).

9. See *Sardis* R1 (1975) 22. For location of major Lydian tumulus sites, see A. Ramage–N. Ramage, 143–160; Kasper, "Nekropole," 71–81. Nayir (1979) 115–120, pls. 1–9.

10. Spiegelthal's map shows a road, of which no trace remains, leading straight toward the Alyattes mound; the location of the ford over the Hermus north of Sart-Mahmut supports him. According to Hipponax (F 42), there was a major east-west road to the coast leading past the three "Royal Mounds"; this may have passed by the lake and the freshwater spring of Süyütlü Çeşme shown on Spiegelthal's map.

11. Since no Lydian mound has been completely excavated, little is known about the number of graves

and burials any one mound might contain. Certainly, a number have only one chamber, but there are several which contain or probably contain two or more. So far, BT has yielded only two (Lydian-Persian) cist graves, but exploration is far from complete.

12. See Hanfmann, "Markers" (unpublished ms.).

13. "Alyattes Mound," "Karniyarik Tepe." 62.4, 63.2, 63.5, *infra*.

14. His information was used by Perrot-Chipiez. The only other firsthand accounts were by Butler and Shear, *Sardis* I (1922). There are important comparisons in Kasper, "Nekropole," 72–85.

15. Choisy, "Tombeaux," 76. Bin Tepe: 8–11, 154–155; City: 164–165.

16. Muscarella, "Phrygian or Lydian?" (1971) 63, and "Tumuli at Şe Girdan," 23 n. 1, also claims that the chambers are off-center and that "it seems almost certain that the idea was borrowed from the Phrygians." For Phrygian tumuli see R. S. Young: "Gordion 1953," 1–18; "Gordion 1957," 147–154; "Gordion 1959," 227–233; "Gordion 1965," 267–269; *From the City of Midas* (1958–1959), esp. "Site Map"; "History," (1953) 159–166; Hanfmann, "Lydian," 101; Mellink, "The City of Midas," 100–109. Cypriote parallels, Karageorghis, "Tomb Architecture," 364.

17. Choisy, "Tombeaux," 174.

18. Ibid. Ramage, however, has noticed a high incidence of ca. 2.0 m. measurements, and speculates that it may represent a measure of 7 Lydian feet, as indicated by other structures and sources: *Sardis* M5(1978) 6. Length varies from 1.86 to 4.35 m. (BT 66.5; BT 66.1), width from 1.35 to 2.37 m. (BT 63.2; Alyattes), and height from 1.19 to 2.25 m. (Choisy, "Tombeaux," 4; Alyattes); inner volume ranges from 5.23 to 17.37 cu. m. (BT 63.2; Alyattes). *BASOR* 206, 11–15, figs. 1–3, (BK 71.1); 233, 9–19, figs. 7–23 (T 77.1).

19. Kasper, "Nekropole," 77, figs. 6–8.

20. Nylander, *Ionians,* 42–45, figs. 10a, 11: 1a, 5a; 64–67, 79–81; cf. Nylander, "Clamps"; *Sardis* R1 (1975) 93–94, figs. 204–207; *BASOR* 170, 58, fig. 42.

21. Similar doors are shown by Choisy, "Tombeaux," figs. 1–4; and Butler, *Sardis* I (1922) 11, fig. 3 = Bossert, *Altanatolien,* 26, fig. 151.

22. *BASOR* 229, 70, built of marble. A similar tomb is mentioned by Butler in *Sardis* I (1922) 155.

23. In his 1980 report, Greenewalt speaks of an "unroofed forecourt," *TürkArkDerg* (forthcoming).

24. BT 63.2: *BASOR* 174, 55; BT 66.5–6: *BASOR* 186, 52; Choisy, "Tombeaux," 74.

25. Examples: *BASOR* 170, 58, figs. 42–43; 186, figs. 28–29 (roofed).

26. See material on the Alyattes mound below.

27. Nylander, *Ionians,* 66–67.

28. A. Ramage–N. Ramage, 143–160.

29. Kasper, "Belevi[1]," 12; and idem, "Belevi[2]," 129–167.

30. See Muscarella, n. 16, *supra*.

31. Kurtz-Boardman, 38, 56, 75, 79–81, 176–177; "Ionia and Aeolis," 185–186; H. von Gall, *"Paphlagonische Felsgräber."* Idem, "Felsgräber der Perserzeit," 585–595. For Urartian chamber tombs, see B. Ögün, 639–678. For Lycian tumuli, see Zahle, 77–94. For Mysia, Caria, Paphlagonia, Urartu, see Kasper, "Nekropole," 81–82. Karageorghis, "Tomb Architecture," 363–368: Anatolian influences in Cypriote tombs.

32. *Sardis* M2 (1972) no. 23.

33. Though published originally in 1848 and revised in 1878, the Etruscan travels of G. Dennis took place between 1842 and 1847, *The Cities and Cemeteries of Etruria,* 1: Introduction, 381, 434–437.

34. *Sardis* I (1922) 9, "during the seventies and early eighties"; cf. 7, his dig in Artemis temple in 1882.

35. The Cucumella, "hillock, barrow," ca. 200 feet in diameter, had supposedly two towers, as Dennis conjectured, two of the original five. The Cucumella was excavated by Prince of Canino in 1829. It had at the time a crepis of masonry and sundry small sepulchral chambers: *BdI* (1829) 50. Description by Dennis, 1: "Vulci," "La Cucumella." The ruin is virtually unreadable and overgrown now (1972). In his excellent short article on "Vulci" M. Torelli remarks about Cucumella: "Still not well known": *PECS* (1976) 991. He seems to date Cucumella ca. 600 B.C.

36. Porsenna: Varro in Pliny, *HN* 36:13.91. Dennis, 437. Correctly in K. O. Müller, *Die Etrusker,* 2: 226–227. Brendel, *Etruscan Art,* 459–460 n. 17.

37. Monterozzi: Dennis 1: 381 and n. 1, "These tumuli are among the most ancient description of tomb in Etruria." In n. 1 he says on the authority of a much-traveled friend that no masonry is visible around the Alyattes base and mentions numerous mounds, none of them having basements of masonry: "The Turks call them the Thousand One Hills."

38. Pallottino, *Necropoli Cervetri,* 7.

39. Ibid., 11, fig. 26 and esp. 30. Giglioli, *L'arte etrusca,* pl. 93. More detailed publication: R. Mengarelli (1927) 145; idem (1937) 77. Final publication Pace-Ricci, 346, fig. 73.

40. A brief survey accepting an eastern origin of tumuli is Boethius, *Etruscan Culture,* 40–42, 65–75, with fine pictures of rock-cut tombs and tumuli of Cervetri, figs. 74–80. Cf. Demus-Quatember, 61–62, 75–76. See Kasper, "Nekropole," 82, with special reference to newly opened Lydian-Mysian chamber tombs near Soma.

41. An imitation of a hut with a thatched roof,

Pace-Ricci, 346, fig. 73; Boethius, *Etruscan Culture,* fig. 74, the tumulus may well be around 700 B.C. For a chamber tomb dated to the eighth century see F. Prayon, 165–179, pls. 41–50.

The Royal Mounds

1. Herodotus 1:93 = *Sardis* M2 (1972) no. 278; for date see *BASOR* 170, 55; Hanfmann, "Central Marker" (Alyattes Mound) (unpublished ms., 1975).

2. Maps: *BASOR* 170, 59, fig. 38 (BT-2); *Sardis* R1 (1975) fig. 2; Hanfmann, *Letters,* Map 2; von Olfers, fig. 1; Bossert, *Altanatolien,* fig. 153.

3. Published in von Olfers, 539–556, pls. 1–5; repeated in Perrot-Chipiez 5, 265–285; see also Sayce, 169–170. The mound's crepis was the basis of measurements by Herodotus and by Spiegelthal (Herodotus 1:93; von Olfers, 545), who recorded the following dimensions: diameter 355.2 m., circumference 1115.32 m., height 61.46 m. It has a photogrammetric survey marker of 183.93 m. a.s.l.

4. *Sardis* I (1922) 8–11.

5. *BASOR* 170 (1963) 52–57, figs. 38–41; *TürkArkDerg* 12:1 (1962) 26, 32, fig. 25; and (1980, forthcoming); Hanfmann, *Letters,* 118–120, fig. 88.

6. Herodotus 1:93. It is unclear as to whether or not these markers were intended as phalli; the term *ouros* ("marker," "guardian") is neutral. See Perrot-Chipiez 5 (1890), 239; *Sardis* R2 (1978) 6, 23; Paton, 67–69, fig. 7; travelers earlier than Spiegelthal in Olfers, 540; Hanfmann, "Central Marker" (Alyattes Mound) (unpublished ms., 1975), for complete history and bibliography.

7. Von Olfers, 546, pl. 3:2; *Sardis* I (1922) 9.

8. For exact measurements, location, and orientation of all fragments see Hanfmann, "Central Marker"; found in the overturned earth was a handle from a Byzantine or Roman cup.

9. Von Olfers, 546, pl. 3:1–2.

10. Hamilton, 1, 145.

11. Spiegelthal made a careful drawing of the door construction (now lost) showing the use of drafted edges. *BASOR* 170, 52–57, figs. 39–41. Antechamber: von Olfers, pl. 4:4. Cf. *TürkArkDerg* (1980, forthcoming).

12. Von Olfers, 549, 550, pl. 5 (5:10 for alabastron). The dating was kindly provided by R. W. Hamilton of the Ashmolean Museum.

13. *BASOR* 170, 56–57; unpublished: P 62.250:4539; P 62.379:4719.

14. *BASOR* 229, 71, fig. 19.

15. *BASOR* 170, 55, fig. 10. Hittite kings are known to have been cremated in a ceremony involving a "stone house"; see *BASOR* 170, 55, n. 55; Otten, "Totenritual," 3; S. Kasper, "Nekropole," reports that a layer of charcoal lay above the ceiling of the so-called "Sphinx Tomb" in a Lydian cemetery northwest of Soma.

16. Kleeman, *Sarkophag,* 54, pl. 15:2 dates to 570–560 B.C.; Alyattes died in 561–560 B.C.

17. Nylander, *Ionians,* 66; Stronach, *Pasargadae,* 20.

18. Hanfmann, "Forerunners" (unpublished; Congress of Iranian Art and Archaeology, Oxford 1972); Stronach, *Pasargadae,* 40–42.

19. Hipponax F 42 = *Sardis* M2 (1975) no. 280.

20. *Sardis* I (1922) 9; for up-to-date discussion, see Kaletsch, 1–47.

21. Karniyarik Tepe is the highest mound of Bin Tepe, with a photogrammetric survey marker (A) of 227.72 m. a.s.l. It lies 38 m. above the quarried limestone edge of the mound. This edge is ca. 105 m. from the center of an approximate diameter of 210–220 m.

22. *BASOR* 174, 53–58, fig. 34; 177, 27–35, fig. 27–33; 182, 27–30, fig. 21–25; 186, 43–47, fig. 25–26; *TürkArkDerg* 12:2 (1963) 14; 13:2 (1964) 61–62, figs. 22–29; 14:1–2 (1965) 152–153, fig. 12; 15 (1966) 75, fig. 8; *Sardis* R1 (1975) 1, 5, 95, fig. 5; Hanfmann, *Letters,* 146–147, 152–159, 164–165, 193–194, 319, 320, 322, figs. 106–112; Pedley, 62–70, fig. 3.

23. *BASOR* 174, 56.

24. *BASOR* 174, 55; *TürkArkDerg* 12:2 (1963) 14; Hanfmann, *Letters,* 131–132.

25. *BASOR* 177, 28; Hanfmann, *Letters,* 154.

26. Hanfmann, *Letters,* 157; *BASOR* 177, 30, figs. 27–29; *TürkArkDerg* 13:2 (1964) 62, figs. 23–24.

27. *BASOR* 177, 30, fig. 28; oral communication, November 1964.

28. *BASOR* 177, 28–33, figs. 27, 30–32; 182, 27, figs. 22–24; 186, 45–46, figs. 25–26; *TürkArkDerg* 13:2 (1964) 62, figs. 26–27; 14:1 (1965) 152–153, fig. 12; 15 (1966) 75, fig. 8; *Sardis* R1 (1975) 5, 95, fig. 5; Hanfmann, *Letters,* 153–159, figs. 109, 111–112; Pedley, 66–68, fig. 3.

29. This theory was first suggested by Mrs. Jacquetta Hawkes Priestley, then visiting the excavation; *BASOR* 177, 31.

30. *BASOR* 182, 27–29, fig. 22; cf. *BASOR* 177, 31–33, *TürkArkDerg* 13:2 (1964) 62; 14:1–2 (1965) 153.

31. *BASOR* 177, 34, fig. 33; 182, 27, fig. 22; *TürkArkDerg* 13:2 (1964) 62, figs. 28, 29; 14:1–2 (1965) fig. 12; *Sardis* M3 (1975) 57–61, no. B15, figs. 38–42; Hanfmann, *Letters,* 154–156, fig. 107; Pedley, 67–68.

32. *BASOR* 177, 34.

33. *Sardis* M3 (1975) 67–68.

34. *BASOR* 177, 34; 182, 27; *TürkArkDerg* 13:2

(1964) 62, fig. 29; Hanfmann, *Letters,* 156; the affiliations of these signs are discussed by Gusmani in *Sardis* M3 (1975) 68, figs. 40–42; the red paint was perhaps used in planing the surface of the blocks, as suggested by C. Nylander; C. H. Greenewalt, FR 1966: "Karniyarik Tepe and Promenades," 7 (unpublished).

35. *BASOR* 174, 55; 186, 46.

36. *BASOR* 177, 30.

37. *BASOR* 182, 27.

38. *BASOR* 182, 27, fig. 23; *TürkArkDerg* 14:1–2 (1965) 153.

39. *BASOR* 182, 7. This was C. H. Greenewalt's opinion.

40. Nylander, *Ionians,* 84; Stronach, *Pasargadae,* 20. Karageorghis, "Tomb Architecture," 365, calls attention to resemblances with Mound Tomb 3, Salamis, dated ca. 600 B.C.

41. Hanfmann, "Forerunners" (unpublished ms. 1972); idem, "Lydian Relations," 26, 27.

42. Hipponax F 42 = *Sardis* M2 (1972) no. 280; Pedley, 63.

43. *BASOR* 174, 55, 56, fig. 34; 186, 57, fig. 23; 191, fig. 1.

Rock-Cut Chamber Tombs

1. *Sardis* I (1922) 157; Greenewalt, "Lydian Graves," 115 n. 5 calculates that Butler's (1910–1914) and Shear's (1922) records total 1,154 graves.

2. *Sardis* I (1922) 56, 158.

3. *Sardis* I (1922) 158.

4. *Sardis* I (1922) 159.

5. *Sardis* I (1922) 116, 118, 159–160, ills. 122, 124, 177–179.

6. *Sardis* XIII (1925) pls. 2:3, 10:1, 11:20.

7. *Sardis* I (1922) 116.

8. *Sardis* R2 (1978) 25 n. 109, with bibliography for contents of Tomb 813.

9. *Sardis* I (1922) 79, ills. 75a and b, 159; Price, "Naucratis," 207, fig. 36.

10. *BASOR* 157, 10–12.

11. See plan, Fig. 129.

12. Neg. 59.35:25–27, Sardis Expedition.

13. Cf. lekythos from Butler Tomb 43 in *Sardis* I (1922) ill. 75B, top.

14. P 59.238:1606.

15. Drawing 59.12; 59.1, Neg. 59.24:21–23. P. 59.188:1540; P 59.189:1541; P 59.239:1607.

16. *BASOR* 157, 11.

17. *Sardis* R2 (1978) 23 n. 84. Some fragments, now in the Metropolitan Museum, which came from graves opened by Butler, resemble Greek "Protogeometric" wares of the ninth to seventh centuries B.C.

18. T. Özgüç, *Bestattungsbräuche,* 116, thought that no cave burials or chamber tombs earlier than the eighth century B.C. were known in Anatolia. This is not to be taken literally; there are Mycenaean chamber tombs at Miletus: Kleiner, *Ruinen,* 24, 125. Lydia/Mysia: Kasper, "Nekropole," 71–85, with references to other Lydian and Mysian examples and literature for Caria, Phrygia, Paphlagonia, and Urartu. Lydia/Phrygia: Akurgal, *Kunst Anat.* 106–110, 127–130, 162, Phrygia, Lycia, Caria, figs. 67, 75, 81–84, 110–111, pl. 4 a–b. For the various regions cf. von Gall, *Paplagonische-Felsgräber,* 120; Ögün, 638–678 (Urartu); von Gall, "Felsgräber der Perserzeit," 585–595. Continuity from Mycenaean to historic times is possible for some regions of Greece (Crete, Rhodes): Kurtz-Boardman, 171, 175. Cyprus: Karageorghis, "Tomb Architecture," 363–368.

19. Kasper, "Nekropole," 71–85; Hanfmann-Waldbaum, "New Excavations," 316.

20. One of the two mounds inspected in 1976 was Hellenistic: *BASOR* 229, 70. Butler mentions reuse of Lydian chamber tombs in Hellenistic times. Some of the burial material he published is unquestionably Hellenistic: *Sardis* I (1922) 74, 81, ills. 76–77.

Furnishings

1. BT 63.2 and Cambaz Tepe: *BASOR* 186, 47. Other possible instances of wooden couches or biers placed on couches are mentioned in *Sardis* I (1922) 159. Use of wooden grave furniture is well attested by the finds from the Phrygian tumuli; see "The Burial Mounds," *supra,* and De Vries, 34, figs. 8–10.

2. Pre-Hellenistic Lydian textiles: Greenewalt-Majewski, "Lydian Textiles," 133–140; Nayir, 124, fig. 29, from Alahidir.

3. Dimensions vary: length of bed averages ca. 2.15 m.; width ranges from 0.58 to 1.12 m.; thickness of slab varies from 0.10 to 0.32 m.; legs are around 0.2 m. thick and are flush with the edges of the sides. Overall height is 0.50–0.70 m. A couch leg decorated with egg (leaf) and cannelures was found at Şeytan Dere in 1967 (unpublished).

4. *BASOR* 206, 11–15, figs. 1–3. Choisy, "Tombeaux," 78–81.

5. *Sardis* R2 (1978) 156, nos. 230–231, fig. 400–401.

6. Choisy does note finding "splinters of resinous wood" which he assumed to be from a coffin; *Sardis* R2 (1978) 78.

7. Hanfmann, *Croesus,* 14, fig. 35; Pryce, 99, n. 5, *supra.*

8. *Sardis* R2 (1978) nos. 18, 234, figs. 72, 404; Ramage, "Banquet"; Hanfmann-Erhart, "Mausoleum," 87–89, figs. 4–7. Stool and table: *Sardis* R2 (1978) no. 71, figs. 70–72.

Cist Graves

1. *BASOR* 166, 24–27; 174, 54, 58; 186, 42–44, 47, 52. *TürkArkDerg* 11:2 (1961) 45; 15:1 (1966) 75; *Sardis* R1 (1975) 12; Hanfmann, *Letters,* 85–86, figs. 56–58; Greenewalt, "Lydian Graves," 113–145; Hanfmann-Detweiler, *ILN* (7 April 1962) 542–544.

2. *BASOR* 166, 24–27, figs. 19–23; *TürkArkDerg* 11:2 (1961) 45; Hanfmann, *Letters,* (1972) 85–86, figs. 57–58; Greenewalt, "Lydian Graves," 113–145, pls. 1–10.

3. Greenewalt, "Lydian Graves," describes and illustrates these and several of the uncatalogued finds: from G 61.1, the lekythos-jug, 117, no. 3, pl. 3:2; from G 61.2, the lydion, 123, no. 13, pl. 9:1; the streaked skyphos, 121, no. 8, pl. 6:1; the lekythos-jug, 123, no. 12, pl. 3:2; the two closed vessels, 124, nos. 14, 15, pl. 9:2; shells, 124–125, nos 17, 18; sheep knucklebones, 125, no. 19; bits of carbonized wood, 125, no. 20.

4. For a discussion of the possible Phrygian derivation of this bowl, see Knudsen, "Lydian Imitation," 59–69.

5. *BASOR* 174, 54, fig. 1; 186, 42–44, fig. 23; *TürkArkDerg* 15:1 (1966) 75.

6. *BASOR* 186, 43, fig. 24. This protome, or bust-vase, is of excellent Samian workmanship. It has a white chiton and red cloak over the right shoulder, with the wavy hair cut short above the shoulders as in Clazomenian vases.

7. *BASOR* 186, 52, fig. 35; M. Kunt, FR 1966: "BT/DU Final Report," 14 (unpublished). Kasper, "Nekropole," 76, nos. A1–3, fig. 10, with lid.

8. *BASOR* 186, 47.

9. Shear, "Sixth Report," 395, figs. 2 (tile), 4 (pottery). For terracottas: *Sardis* M5 (1978) 26, 38, no. 42, fig. 51. For NEW pottery: *Sardis* R1 (1975) 122–125, figs. 307, 310, 314, 318.

Sarcophagi

1. *Sardis* I (1922) 81.

2. *BASOR* 186, 31–32, fig. 17 (view of grave), object list at end of section.

3. Recep Meriç, FR 1966: "Şeytan Dere Report" (unpublished).

4. Published upside down in *BASOR* 186, 38, fig. 16. Correctly, *Sardis* R2 (1978), 74–75, no. 46, figs. 150–151; Hanfmann, "Stelai," 37, fig. 2.

5. *BASOR* 166, 30, fig. 25, plan; Hanfmann, *Letters,* 86, fig. 60 (during opening).

6. *Sardis* R1 (1975) 67.

7. *BASOR* 170, 17, fig. 13. *Sardis* M7 (1981).

8. *BASOR* 170, 17, fig. 13; Buchwald, "Church E," 296–297.

9. *BASOR* 170, 15.

10. *BASOR* 157, 10–12 and "Rock-Cut Chamber Tombs," *supra.*

11. *BASOR* 162, 31; 166, fig. 24, plan.

12. *BASOR* 166, 28–29, fig. 24.

13. *BASOR* 166, 30.

14. *Sardis* I (1922) 81, ill. 80; cf. 143–144, two intact terracotta sarcophagi.

15. Kurtz-Boardman, 269, pl. 70, date the Clazomenian series 530–460 B.C. They name for other examples Erythrae, Ephesus, Lesbos, Pitane, and for other decorated sarcophagi, Samos, Chios, Kameiros. Plain clay sarcophagi were used in Samos, Chios, Rhodes, Abdera, Kavalla, and Sicily. See R. M. Cook, *Clazomenian Sarcophagi,* 146–147.

16. An example of this kind is in the Museum at Tire in the Cayster valley.

Lydian Burial Rites and Beliefs

1. Herodotus 1.93 says the mound of Alyattes, which it must have taken years to pour with ox-drawn carts and donkeys, was built by traders, craftsmen, and girls who work for money (prostitutes), whose share of work was the greatest. That was clearly a levy on the lower classes, but it still seems probable that money rather than muscle alone was contributed.

2. Kurtz-Boardman 21, 25–26, 73–74 (Attica, Crete), 174 (Rhodes), 177 (Pitane), 182 (Boeotia), and particularly Homer, 180; Lorimer, *Homer,* 103–121; Hanfmann, *JNES* 12 (1953) 230–233; Snodgrass, *Dark Ages,* 35, 147–176, 187–190, 326–327, 375, 391.

3. *BASOR* 170, 55. Otten, "Totenritual," 3; Naumann, *Architektur,* 2d ed., 407–409.

4. *Sardis* I (1922) 81–87; Butler rightly saw that marble chest-like urns and painted pottery urns are characteristic of Hellenistic and Roman cremation burials, and noted that they invaded Lydian chamber tombs as secondary burials.

5. J. Savishinsky, FR 1966: "Bones," Report (unpublished); E. H. Kohler, FR 1961: "Bones in Tombs 61.3 and 61.4 (Haci Oglan)" (unpublished).

6. *Sardis* I (1922) 141, untouched sarcophagus with gold and jewelry, 143–144.

7. Shear, "Sixth Report," 395.

8. *Sardis* I (1922) 10, citing Bacon's description of Dennis's excavations.

9. The wetness and other factors imperil the survival of skeletal material at Sardis. Butler repeatedly comments on the way in which skulls collapsed in opened burials, *Sardis* I (1922), 144. Lydian skeletal material found in the city was at times better preserved. The articles by our collaborator Enver Bostanci do not include any material from the Lydian

graves: Bostanci, "Skeletal Remains"; "Skulls" 1967; "Skulls" 1969.

10. *BASOR* 186, 33 n. 5. The data on five individuals and their relationship can be found in D. J. Finkel, "Bones," Report (1967; unpublished). Other skeletal remains such as that of a girl, 8–9 years old, whose skull was crushed by the burning house, and other scattered remains found in the burned level caused by Kimmerian destruction, do not qualify as burials.

11. For couches, see Choisy, "Tombeaux"; Dennis, *Sardis* I (1922) 10. The idea of outlining the body came from Egypt to Eastern Greece (Samos), where it is used in sarcophagi: Kurtz-Boardman, 288, fig. 58.

12. Ahura Mazda: *Sardis* XIII (1925) 13, no. 8, Tomb 27A, pl. 1:8. Achaemenid sphinxes and rosettes: *Sardis* I (1922) 143, ill. 158; *Sardis* XIII (1925) 12, nos. 1–4, 6, pl. 1, Tomb no. 836, First Nekropolis, "Tomb near the top of ridge extending westward from the first tomb hill and on its north face." This tomb is dated by two silver sigloi of Artaxerxes I (465–404 B.C.) or II (404–349 B.C.). See *Sardis* XI (1916) 44, nos. 416, 417. For golden plaques on garments, see Oppenheim, 172; Hanfmann, *Sardis und Lydien,* 16, 17 n. 3. Cf. *Sardis* I (1922) 144, "ornaments sewn onto dress."

13. *Sardis* I (1922) 144. See *Sardis* XIII (1925) 1–35, for some fifty pieces of Lydian jewelry from the graves.

14. *Sardis* I (1922) 83–86, ills. 82–86.

15. Shear, "Sixth Report," 396–400, figs. 7, 8; idem, "Hoard," 349–352; Oliver, "Lydia," 197, ills. 26.59.6 (the jar), 25.59.2–5 (coins). BT 62:4: *BASOR* 170, 57. Tomb 836: *Sardis* XI (1916) nos. 416, 417, not illustrated; see n. 12, *supra.*

16. *BASOR* 170, 58.

17. *BASOR* 174, 55.

18. *BASOR* 157, 10–12; 170, 58, 59; 186, 47–53, and the sections on graves, *supra.*

19. *Sardis* I (1922) 141, "untouched sarcophagus containing bronze pitcher, two seal rings, and other jewelry"; 144, "two terracotta sarcophagi absolutely intact." Greenewalt, "Lydian Graves," 115, has calculated that 160 of 1,154 graves opened by Butler and Shear had yielded objects.

20. Kurtz-Boardman, 204, 205.

21. *BASOR* 166, 30.

22. Kurtz-Boardman, 75, 76, 205: "offerings often disposed of by burning on the ground or in pits."

23. We count lydion, aryballos, lekythos, and alabastron as vases for oil, ointment, or perfume; skyphus and so-called wine bowl, as drinking vessels. The statistics given are based on elucidation of the use of these types and other pouring vessels and large containers. Complete data are given in field reports and fieldbooks. See Kurtz-Boardman, 209, "offering of oil seems to have become a regular practice" (aryballoi, lekythoi). For alabastra see *BASOR* 157, 12; 166, 30; 186, 43, 51, 52, fig. 33; Von Olfers, 549, 550. Greenewalt, "Lydian Graves," 137, pl. 9:3 (Indere) notes that twenty-two alabastra of alabastron and thirty-eight of clay were found by Butler. For a probable food plate, see Knudsen, "Lydian Imitation," 62, 69, pls. 8, 9.

24. Tomb no. 23a: *Sardis* I (1922) 119-121, ills. 125, 126, with datable Attic olpe. Butler speaks of "more than fifty vases"; Greenewalt, "Lydian Graves," 127 n. 9, counts thirty-six complete items. The side-spouted pitcher was to strain barley beer, according to Chase, "Two Vases," 114–117, fig. 2; Oliver, "Lydia," 199. The boat-shaped vase is inscribed: *Sardis* VI:2 (1924) 52–54, no. 30; Gusmani *LW,* 105, 213, no. 30. It may carry a dedication of the type: "Titi gives my contents to Atvas Kitvas." For water jars (hydriae) and wine vessels (oinochoai, craters), in Greek burials, see Kurtz-Boardman, 204–210.

25. *Sardis* I (1922) 10, 158, ill. 175.

26. None of the vases we found had any trace of their original contents. For the term *lydion,* attested by Greek graffiti, and its use as ointment container, see the detailed discussion by Greenewalt, "Lydian Graves," 132–135 n. 27; Rumpf (1920) 165; and Roebuck, 56. Concerning contents, W. C. Kohler mentioned some "ungerminated seeds" in his report on sarcophagus Haci Oglan 61.3, but in view of the presence of mice, the age of the seeds is uncertain. For water and wine vessels, and "the dead, who are always thirsty," see Kurtz-Boardman, 204, 209–211.

27. Greenewalt, "Lydian Graves," 118, 137, 138, nos. 17, 18, records shells of salt-water (*Macta corallina*) and fresh-water variety clams, and suggests that the pierced salt-water specimen was an ornament, and the other shells were "containers." See *BASOR* 229, 65, for an oyster shell from domestic context. Greenewalt cites Myrrhina, Samos, and Rhodes for Greek parallels. See Kurtz-Boardman, 215, for Greek seashells offered as foodstuffs.

28. Knucklebones: Greenewalt, "Lydian Graves," no. 19, 138, 139, reports 156 game pieces from Grave Indere 61.20. He links this find with the Lydian invention of games (Herodotus 1.94) but also cites Greek parallels and the Greek epigram *Anth.Pal.* 6.308, which records the award of eighty astragals as a prize in a writing contest.

29. Plutarch, *Moralia, Mulierum virtutes* 27 (262E–263C).

30. Hanfmann, *Croesus,* 14, fig. 35. Arias-Hirmer, 322, pl. 131.

31. Semicircular hole: *BASOR* 186, 48, fig. 28.

See Kasper, "Belevi²," 148–150, pl. 2, libation pipes. Kurtz-Boardman, 205, 206, mention pipes for libation in a South Russian mound burial.

32. Traces of charcoal in Indere 61.2 and the burned layer on top of Alyattes chamber might be considered in this connection, but no traces of burned objects or animal bones were found. For the burning of objects on pyres, see Kurtz-Boardman, 65, 75, 205.

33. *BASOR* 170, 58; 174, 55; BT 66.31: J. Savishinsky, FR 1966: "Bones" (unpublished); Greenewalt, *Dinners,* 47, with detailed discussion and literature. For pet dogs buried in Greek graves, see Kurtz-Boardman, 66, 215. Cf. the man and dog stele, *Sardis* R2 (1978) no. 17, fig. 70.

34. For the Greek practices of animal sacrifices, see Kurtz-Boardman, 64–67, 215.

35. Herodotus 1.93 says that "writing was cut into the five markers on top of the mound." The tomb of Abradatas (Pyramid Tomb? see Chapter VI, under "The Satrapal Court," *infra*) also had "Assyrian writing"; cf. Xenophon, *Cyropaedia* 7.3.2 = *Sardis* M2 (1972) nos. 276, 277, and *BASOR* 162, 31.

36. For markers from Şeytan Dere Cemetery, see *BASOR* 186, 37–38, NoEx 66.1, 66.2; for Pactolus-Necropolis West, NoEx 73.1. These are discussed by Hanfmann, "Sepulchral Markers" (unpublished ms.). For other regions of Asia Minor see Kurtz-Boardman, 242.

37. Surviving stelai, inscribed and uninscribed, are discussed in *Sardis* R2 (1978) 23–29; their texts are published in *Sardis* VI:2 (1924) 1–3, 5–12, 15–18, 22, 24, 26; Gusmani, *LW,* nos. 1–3, 5–6, 8–18, 22, 24, 26, 29, 41, 46; *Sardis* M3 (1975) AI 2, 3, 4.

38. *Sardis* I (1922) 160–162.

39. *Sardis* M3 (1975) nos. AI 1, 2, 3. None were found *in situ.* See *Sardis* I (1922) 160, and Gusmani *LW,* nos. 1–2, 41, for other stelae dated by Persian regnal years; idem, "Lydiaka," 272, for dates. The use of Persian regnal formula may indicate that the dead wanted to underline their loyalty; they probably served the Persian administration.

40. *Sardis* R2 (1978) 23–26, 182, nos. 234, 241, figs. 404 (330–329 B.C.), 420. Cf. Gusmani, *LW,* 250, no. 1.

41. *Sardis* R2 (1978) 56–57, no. 17, figs. 70–71; no. 18, fig. 72; no. 234, fig. 404; N. Ramage, "Banquet." Hanfmann-Erhart, "Mausoleum," 82–90, figs. 4–7.

42. *Sardis* R2 (1978) 24–26, nos. 45–49, 240–242, figs. 148–157, 419–421. As in Greek stelai, the basic symbolism of the *anthemion* ("flower") stele is that of the new life of plants growing over the grave.

43. Gusmani, *LW,* 63, 64, 156, 163, 188, no. 1. For Kufavk, see idem, "Lydiaka," 266.

44. *Levs:* Gusmani, *LW,* 160; *Sardis* M3 (1975) no.

A III 2, fig. 32. *Baki-illi, Baki-valis:* Gusmani, *LW,* 74–75; idem, "Lydiaka," 268.

45. Gusmani, *LW,* 59, 189, 190, 222; a sample of such information is the Lydian-Aramaic bilingual stele of 394 B.C. which speaks of stele, vault, wall, land, and antechamber; ibid., no. 1.

46. For the Lydian curses, see Gusmani, *LW,* 21 and the examples in n. 37, *supra.* For the Daskylion stelai, see Hanfmann, *Croesus,* 18, 19, figs. 40, 41; Cross, "Daskylion," 7–13. The Semitic influence on the curse formulae in Sardis, Maeonia, and Phrygia in later times is discussed by Robert, "Maledictions," 241–289, especially 249, Sardis-Maeonia.

47. "Seven Brothers," partly visible in Hanfmann, *Sardis und Lydia,* 5, fig. 20.

48. *Sardis* I (1922) 34, 35, 78–86, and especially 158–167; South cemetery, 162, well to the south of the city, where Butler cites tombs from west bank, ill. 155 and east bank, ills. 182, 183; "Southwest Cemetery," 164, ill. 183, may be the western part of the South cemetery. Unfortunately, Butler left no map of these cemeteries. For a concise survey of Sardis cemeteries see also Greenewalt, "Lydian Graves," 112–116, especially nn. 4–6.

49. Shear's cemetery, "Sixth Report," 396–400, fig. 6, may be the northern continuation of Şeytan Dere ("Devil's Gorge") cemetery: *BASOR* 186, 37, 38, fig. 17. It seems to have gone up both sides of the gorge to the Pyramid Tomb on the south bank; an opening high in the north bank leads into a chamber tomb. See Fig. 8:14, 54. The location was checked in 1979 by Greenewalt.

50. Tumulus chamber tomb above Lydian houses: Greenewalt, "Twentieth Campaign," 105.

51. See Chapters VII and VIII, *infra.*

52. A. Ramage, in Chapter III, *supra,* speaks of the culmination of the Lydians' first move toward prosperity.

53. This is clear in Homer's *Iliad* 16.456, 457, where the Lycians will give due burial with mound and stele to Sarpedon: "Such is the honor of the dead," cf. 11.371, mound and stele of Ilos. The mound itself, too, is a *sema,* a "sign," *LSJ, s.v.*

54. *Sardis* R2 (1978) no. 18, fig. 72; no. 234, fig. 404. N. Ramage, "Banquet"; Hanfmann-Erhart, "Mausoleum," 82–90.

55. For the Greek wine-vat, *lenos,* cf. F. Matz, *Dionysische Sarkophage,* 126–174. Bakivalis: Gusmani, *LW,* 74, 75; *Sardis* R2 (1978) no. 274, fig. 465. Dionysus born on the Tmolus: Euripides, *Bacchae* 461–464 = Sardis M2 (1972) no. 257.

56. *Sardis* VI:2 (1924) 52–54, no. 30. Gusmani, *LW,* no. 30; cf. n. 22, *supra.* A wooden boat was reportedly found in a mound at Bin Tepe. On Pythes/Pythios' boat, see Plutarch, *Moralia, Mulierum virtutes* 27 (263).

57. Bacchylides, *Epinicia* 3:23–62 = *Sardis* M2 (1972) no. 124.

58. See Herter's "Lydische Adelskämpfe," 31–60; Pedley's overview (Pedley, 30–48); and Balcer's "By the Bitter Sea: The Landed Gentry in Western Anatolia, c. 700–411 B.C." (forthcoming).

59. For the dating by regnal years, see n. 39, *supra;* for Achaemenid jewelry, see n. 12, *supra,* and Hanfmann, *Sardis and Lydien,* 16, 17 n. 3.

60. Naumann, *Architektur,* 407–409. Phrygian burials: see R. S. Young, *Gordion Guide,* 44–53. There were Mycenaean rock-cut chamber tombs at Miletus, and a link is not impossible. It is noteworthy that in Homer, Trojans and Lycians, as well as Achaeans, use mound burials; the mounds of the Trojans Ilos and Myrrhina date from "olden days."

61. *Sardis* I (1922) 81, 82. For the origin and development of sarcophagi, see the sarcophagus of Ahiram, Jidejian, *Byblos,* 29–33, figs. 92–96, and for archaic (seventh century and later) Greek sarcophagi from East Greece (Chios, Samos, Kyme, Rhodes) see Kurtz-Boardman, 266–270.

62. Indere 61.1–3: Greenewalt, "Lydian Graves," 116, pl. 2; BT 63.3; *BASOR* 186, 42, 43, fig. 24; terracotta slabs (reused) in a cist tomb of ca. 550 B.C.: Shear, "Sixth Report," 395, figs. 2, 4. For the date see *Sardis* M5 (1978) 28, 39, no. 34.

V. Lydian Society and Culture

The Progress of Research

1. Radet, *Lydie,* 302–304. To the Assyrian annals, there were added the references to Lud in the Bible, and eventually the appearance of Lydians at the court of Babylon; see n. 4, *infra.*

2. Buerchner-Deeters-Keil, 2161–2202.

3. The Indo-European character of the Lydian language was determined in F. Sommer's and P. Kahle's basic treatment of the Lydian-Aramaic bilingual (Sommer-Kahle, 18–86) in 1927. Meriggi, "Der indogermanische Charakter," 283–290. See O. Carruba, "Lydisch," 383–385, for a survey of previous research. For the unitarian concept of Anatolia, see Bossert, *Altanatolien,* 22–27, figs. 141–198, "Lydien." Bossert was prepared to see Lydian relations with Hittites in the time of the mythical Atyad dynasty and "the Hittite Empire (1475–1192 B.C.)." See also Götze, 206–209.

4. Meantime, more Near Eastern references had been found: *Sardis* I (1922) 1–3. For the Assyrian texts, see Radet, *Lydie,* 177, citing Menant's publication of 1874. For up-to-date editions, see *Sardis* M2 (1972) nos. 292–296, which include the Babylonian "Nabonidus Chronicle" dealing with deeds of Cyrus. Bible: Ezek. 30:5 (dated 592 B.C.); Jer. 46:9 (Lud archers in Egyptian army of Necho, 608–605 B.C.); Gen. 10:22, 1 Chron. 1:17, Lud among children of Shem; Isa. 66:19, named with Tarshish, Pul, Tubal, Yavan. Lydians (hostages?) receive rations at the court of Babylon under Nebuchadnezzar II, see Weidner, "Jojachin," 923–924, 934; *Sardis* R2 (1978) 14 n. 5.

5. Bittel, *Grundzüge* (1950) 97. Akurgal's account of Lydian art, *Kunst Anat.,* 150–159, was still based only on Butler's results.

Stratigraphy and History

1. A. Ramage, Chapter III, *supra,* under "House of Bronzes/Lydian Market," mentions fragments of Hittite-like red pottery from his Level (I) at HoB/Lydian Market, presumably pre-1400 B.C. (Chart A, Chapter III, *supra*). See *BASOR* 162, 5 n. 12, fig. 3 (P 61.563:4055), "extrusive from 1960 deep pit." For PN, see *BASOR* 166, 24 (P 61.550), a hint that the Bronze Age was represented along the Pactolus. For the arrowhead found in mixed fill of "Road Trench," i.e., in the general vicinity of HoB/Lydian Market, see *Sardis* (M8) *Metalwork* (forthcoming), "Introduction," 1400–1200 B.C. Hittite seals: Dussaud had tried to claim as Lydian the famous "Tyskiewicz seal" in the Boston Museum of ca. 1500 B.C., but E. Porada terms it Syrian-Cypriote (by letter); Dussaud, 43–53.

2. Strabo 13.4.5, "less old than Troy." That Sardis previously bore the Homeric name of Hyde (Homer, *Iliad* 5.43, 44) may be learned Hellenistic speculation. Xanthus in Lydus, *De mensibus* 3.20, allegedly called Sardis "Xuaris." This comes close to the known Lydian name of *Sfar, Svar, Suar.* Cf. *Sardis* M2 (1972) nos. 15, 16, 234; Gusmani, *LW,* 201, 202.

3. If the beginning of the rule of Gyges is placed at 680 B.C., the date is 1185 B.C.; if at 687 then it is 1192 B.C., almost exactly the date also for the fall of the Hittite empire.

4. Herodotus 1.7 and 1.86 = *Sardis* M2 (1972) no. 26. Since Herodotus says the descendants of Herakles ruled 22 generations or 505 years, he must include the rule of the last Heraklid, Kandaules, in the 505 years, and calculate to the accession of Gyges. For Tylon, Tylonids, and Mopsos/Moksos, see Hanfmann, "Lydiaka," 68–76, with ancient sources.

A. Ramage, Chapter III, *supra,* under "House of Bronzes/Lydian Market," does not comment on the burned level which separates his Level (III) (Chart A, Chapter III, *supra*) from the Submycenaean-Protogeometric Level. If this burning signifies the attack on Sardis by "the sons of Herakles," then the date of the beginning of Level (IV) is ca. 1200 B.C. Waldbaum, *Bronze,* 35, tries to lower the date for this level without giving the reason. For the spread of Mycenaean-type pottery in Western Anatolia, see Mee (1978) 144 (Sardis).

Huxley, *Ionians,* 202 n. 81, notes that "Tylonians" occur among the Milesian phratries and the Lydian "Herakleidai" in the inscriptions of Colophon and Klaros.

5. Records of the physical anthropologists establish the presence of at least fifteen individuals in the relatively small area of the burned "Kimmerian" level in HoB. Most seem to have perished from fire. This overwhelming evidence rules out any attempt to dissociate the destruction from the Kimmerian attack, such as is hinted at by A. Ramage, Chapter III, *supra,* under "House of Bronzes/Lydian Market." The "absolute" historical date of the attack may waver by seven, ten, or even twenty years; the correlation is far more secure than the correlations underlying the allegedly certain ceramic Greek chronology.

6. Thirty small pits were dug in 1973. They reached Lydian houses under the "Gold Refinery" and yielded one Protocorinthian Linear fragment (P 73.6:8237). Cf. *BASOR* 215, 33, and for the chronology of Protocorinthian and Corinthian imports at PN see J. S. Schaeffer, "Note on Chronology of PN," unpublished.

7. G. M. A. Hanfmann is now inclined to date the vases under the floor of Level II somewhat later than he did in *BASOR* 162, 21–22. This would allow a span of ca. 650?–638 B.C. for the duration of the level, which was terminated by Kimmerian attack under Ardys.

8. Kaletsch, 25, 46–47. See *BASOR* 162, 12 n. 8; Pedley, 44–45; *Sardis* M2 (1972) nos. 292–295. Ardys: Herodotus 1.15 = *Sardis* M2 (1972) no. 52.

9. For the Kimmerian question, see Gimbutas, 90–92, for origins; H. Kothe (1963) 1–37; and especially the symposium on "Dark Ages and Nomads ca. 1000 B.C.," with papers by R. Ghirshman, R. S. Young, M. J. Mellink, et al. (1964).

10. Schefold, *Die Griechen,* 284–288, including the Sardis piece, pl. 342a. For Sardian metal finds associated with Scythians, including the Sardis references, see Waldbaum, *Sardis* (M8) *Metalwork* (forthcoming).

11. Herodotus 1.88–89. Nabonidus chronicle: *Sardis* M2 (1972) no. 296. Kaletsch opts for 547, Mallowan, "Cyrus," 7, 12, for 545 B.C.

12. Previous interpretation in *BASOR* 162, 12; 166, 8–10, had placed the abandonment in 499 B.C., except for "Unit 24"; *BASOR* 157, 30, fig. 15, with a Laconian (not "Eastern Greek") vase; *BASOR* 162, 12

n. 7. Black- and red-figure sherds and a Persian siglos show that the area was used during the Persian period; see *BASOR* 157, 30 n. 26; 166, 9, 10; *ILN* (1 April 1961) 537, fig. 7; also *BASOR* 170, 11, siglos, fig. 10 (Attic red-figure).

13. See Chapter III, *supra,* under "Pactolus North." This is the case of Lydian structures under and in the apsidal buildings in PN; see *BASOR* 166, 23, 24, fig. 14 (plan), figs. 16, 17 for pre-547 objects probably including a Croeseid silver obel. Hanfmann now agrees with A. Ramage that the apsidal buildings may have been built before 547 B.C. A heavy layer of burned matter at ca. *87.7, which contained fragments of a fine Attic black-figure vase of ca. 540 B.C., *BASOR* 170, 24, fig. 19, may be the destruction level of 499 B.C.

14. *BASOR* 157, 18, Lydian walls are sealed at *89.8 level by a strong deposit of carbonized matter, 0.10 m. thick, is retracted, *BASOR* 162, 18 n. 21, where the burning signifies the end of Level II, and perhaps the last Kimmerian assault; see n. 6, *supra.*

15. Herodotus 5.101 = *Sardis* M2 (1972) no. 282; and the independent tradition of Charon of Lampsacus, ibid., nos. 148–149, 155.

16. *BASOR* 162, 19, "a continuous deposit with carbonized matter at ca. *91.1 may possibly be linked with the destruction of 499 B.C." Note that the star and scroll terracotta found in this level (Fig. 66), *BASOR* 162, fig. 8, is now dated to ca. 540 B.C. by A. Ramage, *Sardis* M5 (1978) no. 43, fig. 86 and frontispiece.

17. See n. 13, *supra. Sardis* M5 (1978) 5, suggests the apsidal buildings were built by Lydians before 547 B.C.

Urbanism and Architecture

1. Hanfmann, *Croesus,* 4–10, a study in which Sardis is integrated into the development of urbanism in Western Anatolia. Hanfmann, "On Lydian Sardis," 99–131, a study of the major aspects of Sardian urbanism compared with Gordion. For the position of Sardis in the political-constitutional development toward the Greek city state, see Hammond-Barton, *City,* 144–147, 466–468, "Phrygian Gordion and Lydian Sardis."

2. Hanfmann, *Croesus,* 5, 9, 25; R. Martin, *Agora,* 150–274, 283–287.

3. Herodotus 5.101 = *Sardis* M2 (1972) no. 282.

4. Polanyi, 67; idem, "Comparative," 333–334.

5. *Sardis* I (1922) 76–78, 149, 154, pl. I; Shear, "Sixth Report," 400, 401; *Sardis* X (1926) 1; *Sardis* M5 (1978) 40. NEW: see *Sardis* R1 (1975) 118; marked "Terrace" and "NE Wadi" in fig. 7.

6. Discussions of the urbanistic aspect of Sardis:

Sardis R1 (1975) 28–34. Hanfmann, *Croesus,* 4–10; Hanfmann, "On Lydian Sardis," 99–107. Architecture: *Sardis* M5 (1978) 4–10, based on A. Ramage, *Architecture;* Hanfmann, "Palace," 147–154.

7. Greenewalt, "Lydian Graves," 113–115.

8. Artesian well: *BASOR* 229, 60, 65–66; Greenewalt, "Twentieth Campaign," 106–107. Estimate of north-south extension in grid terms: Well, N650; "750 m. south of Artemis Temple," ca. S2000; total, 2,650 m. East-west extension: MMS, E140; 0–Pactolus, ca. W300; subtotal, MMS–Pactolus, 440 m.; estimated extension west of the Pactolus, ca. 600 m.; total, ca. 1,040 m. This estimate and Plan I alter the tentative proposals by A. Ramage and G. M. A. Hanfmann, *Sardis* R1 (1975) fig. 7; but the new plan is closer to Ramage's.

9. Herodotus 1.78, 80–81, speaks of *proasteion* and *teichos.*

10. So-called "Road Trench," *BASOR* 166, 45, figs. 33, 34 (Section). E18–20/S15–18, to *94, *93.2, dug in 1961, yielded no clear evidence. The new excavations at MMS (1980) revealed four levels of a graveled roadbed: *TürkArkDerg* (forthcoming).

11. *Sardis* R1 (1975) 47 n. 52; *Sardis* R2 (1978) 69, 70, no. 34, figs. 125–129 (550–530 B.C.).

12. *Sardis* I (1922) 30, pl. 18, H. *Sardis* M5 (1978) 40. The branch road shown in *Sardis* R1 (1975) fig. 7, follows an old village road.

13. PN, at W244–247/S378–381: *BASOR* 170, 25, fig. 20.

14. Part of the Lydian east-west road has begun to appear in Section MMS (1980). It was graveled.

15. The possibly paved street may have issued into the main north-south road; *BASOR* 162, 20, fig. 7. See Chapter III, *supra,* and Fig. 64.

16. HoB, "Refinery," PN: see Chapter III, *supra,* under "House of Bronzes/Lydian Market" and "Pactolus North."

17. *Sardis* M5 (1978) 3, figs. 5, 6, 12, 16, 27. For a typical village plan and houses (Fig. 130) see Hanfmann, *Croesus,* 3, fig. 5 (Çeltikci).

18. See Figs. 22 (HoB), 44 (PN overall); *Sardis* M5 (1978) fig. 3: Fig. 64 (PC), and the new sector MMS: *BASOR* 233, 21–26, figs. 26–30. For Ephesus, Miletus, and Old Smyrna, see Hanfmann, *Croesus,* 9, 10, figs. 8 (Ephesus), 18 (Old Smyrna), 50, 51 (Miletus): J. M. Cook, *Greeks,* 74.

19. For use of animal spaces, see F. K. Yegul in Hanfmann, *Croesus,* 3 n. 6 (Çeltikci), up to 30% animal space; and *Yassihüyük.* Almost every house in Sart Mustafa village has animal spaces, either in the lower story of the dwelling or in separate barns and stables around the yards; see *Sardis* M5 (1978) fig. 27.

20. R. Martin, *Urbanisme,* 222, with an admirable

chapter on "Éléments de la structure génerale" and "L'habitat," figs. 40, 43, 44; see especially the plans of Athens and Colophon.

21. These wells were previously thought by G. M. A. Hanfmann to be typical of the Persian period, but A. Ramage argues for Lydian origin. Five early wells were excavated. They are carefully built of stone, narrowing at the well-head. Diameters vary from 0.70 to 0.90 m., just enough for one person to descend, and depths to 8–9 m. in PN, up to 20 m. in HoB. The site of a well at PN (1): W286/S332, top ca. *87, bottom *79.7, opening in side of wall just above present level of water, is the best example for a possible public area (Fig. 44); *BASOR* 182, 21–23, fig. 15. Others in PN (2): W238/S352, destroyed curbing *87.3, *BASOR* 177, 6; (3) W255/S381, *88.30, *79.6, *BASOR* 166, 20; figs. 14, 15. "W1," diameter 0.70 m. At HoB the well near structure F, W3/S113, top pr. *99.66, had not reached bottom at *80.80, diameter 0.90 m., filled in probably 213 B.C.: *BASOR* 174, 12, fig. 2, had 1 m. water when digging stopped. (4) W254/S378, *BASOR* 166, 23, fig. 14, "W2," partially destroyed, excavated only 2 m. (Lydian low level).

22. Chapter III, under "Pactolus North"; *BASOR* 166, 20; 182, 21–23.

23. A covered channel led spilled water from the well into Unit (3) at PN. See *BASOR* 182, 22, and *Sardis* M5 (1978) fig. 3.

24. It is located at the east end of the gorge of the north branch of Şeytan Dere (Fig. 8 E200/S720 and Plan I).

25. Strabo 13.4.7 = *Sardis* M2 (1972) no. 279.

26. *Sardis* R1 (1975) 35–37. The literary source overlooked there is Herodotus 1.89. Even if Herodotus wrote a "Croesus Romance," he would not run the danger of being disproved about a place as well known to Greeks of his time as Sardis. MMS: *BASOR* 229, 64, 65; Greenewalt, "Twentieth Campaign," 106, 107.

27. *BASOR* 215, 31–33, figs. 1, 2. For a detailed comparison with the city wall of Gordion, see Hanfmann, "On Lydian Sardis," 103–104, figs. 15–19.

28. MMS, n. 26, *supra.* An expert in military architecture, F. E. Winter, surmised that the Lydian defensive and siege techniques were indebted to Near Eastern military engineers, of whom the Assyrians were the most prominent; see Winter, 129 n. 17, on Phrygian kings and their Lydian successors. Hanfmann, *Croesus,* 7 n. 21, with references to "Lydian Fort" at Gordion; Mellink, Review in *AJA* 61 (1957) 324, pl. 89. Alliance of Gyges and Ardys with Assyria: *Sardis* M2 (1972) nos. 292–295. Greenewalt, *BASOR* 223, 25–26, notes Late Hittite and Syrian parallels to MMS.

29. *Sardis* M5 (1978) 9, 10.

30. There is an excellent discussion of mudbrick-pisé structures in *Sardis* M5 (1978) 4–8, figs. 6, 11–27. For masonry construction, clamps, drafted edges, see *Sardis* R1 (1975) 92–94 (K. J. Frazer).

31. *Sardis* M5 (1978) 5, 6; he also discussed "the brick which is called Lydian in Greek," according to Vitruvius 2.3.3, proportioned 3:2 (1½ by 1 foot). It may be represented in MMS; other Lydian bricks run to 4:3:1. See *Sardis* M2 (1972) no. 134. *BASOR* 182, 12 n. 6.

32. *Sardis* M5 (1978) 39.

33. See Chapter IV, *supra.*

34. See Chapter III, *supra.*

35. If the superstructure had been built of masonry, one would expect to find some trace of it. For the combined technique in Mesopotamia see Lloyd-Mellaart, *Beycesultan* I, 58–68; for Achaemenid Iran: Schmidt, *Persepolis III,* 55, 56; Krefter, *Persepolis,* 24–25, 85–86; for late Hittite: R. Naumann, *Architektur,* 86–104. The combination was known in Greece, e.g., in the Heraeum of Olympia, but the ambitious Lydian kings who knew about Assur, Babylon, and late Hittite castles are not likely to have imitated the small Greek kinglets. Cf. Dinsmoor (Sr.) (1975) 53 and index, *s.v.* brick.

36. A marble head of a goddess may go back to 600 B.C. or earlier. If the marble quarry at Magara Deresi is ever excavated, it may be possible to determine if it was in use before the Hellenistic Age. *Sardis* R2 (1978) 4–8, 40, 41, no. 3, figs. 9, 10.

37. Theodorus did a silver bowl for Croesus, but he was an inventor and "technical consultant" at the Croesus-endowed Artemisium of Ephesus. Herodotus 1.51 = *Sardis* M2 (1972) no. 99; Pollitt, 19, 22–23, 37 (Diog. Laert 2.103). At Ephesus, Croesus must have worked with the Greek architects Chersiphron and Metagenes. Holloway, "Architect and Engineer," 280–290. See Hanfmann, *Croesus,* 7–8.

38. See Chapter III, *supra,* under "The Acropolis."

39. *Sardis* M5 (1978) 7–9, figs. 3, 4, 15, 21–23; *BASOR* 182, 12–14, figs. 1, 4.

40. *Sardis* M5 (1978) 6–8, figs. 7–15; *BASOR* 157, 19, 30–32, fig. 17; 162, 12, 20, 28–30, figs. 3, 7, 13, 14. Apsidal structures: *BASOR* 166, 5–14, 19–24, 37, figs. 2, 14, 28; 170, 10–13, 24, 25, figs. 7, 14. They had more ambitious plans for interiors and better furnishings than the really rustic hut described by Ovid for Philemon and Baucis, *Metamorphoses* 8, 618–723; cf. Hanfmann, *Croesus,* 3.

41. *BASOR* 191, 13, with cobbled courtyard. It is, however, possible that other houses in PN and NEW had courtyards: *BASOR* 177, 4, fig. 1; *Sardis* M5 (1978) figs. 21–23. (The Hellenistic? courtyard; Fig. 181; W294–300/S325–331; Units XIX, XX); NEW: Fig. 84; "trapezoidal room or courtyard," *Sardis* R1 (1972) 124, fig. 283, c, d, e, f; internal dimensions 4.5 by 3 m. Priene: Dinsmoor, 322, fig. 117.

42. Examples from Sardis: *Sardis* M5 (1978) figs. 5–13; Celtikci: Hanfmann, *Croesus,* fig. 6; and Fig. 130.

43. Pithoi: *BASOR* 182, 10. Pits: Small, stone-lined, *BASOR* 182, 18 (PN, Unit XV A). Circular bins carefully built of stones: NEW: *Sardis* R1 (1975) 120, 124, figs. 283 (a), 293 "circular wall 'a,'" diam. 1.33, P.H. 0.82 m.; PN: *BASOR* 182, 24; 199, 9, figs. 7, 8, plan, probably HoB (plan HoB 83) circular Unit E, W393, S333; W282, S328; W275, S239; W282, S348. Rectangular, "basement storage spaces": NEW, *Sardis* R1 (1975) 124, fig. 283, f, i, j, k; also Greenewalt, "Twentieth Campaign," 106; PN: *BASOR* 166, 23, fig. 14; 170, 25, fig. 20.

44. Representative examples: NEW d–e (courtyard), *Sardis* R1 (1975) 122, bones of young cattle, sheep, goats with butchering marks. PN: unit XVB, *BASOR* 182, 18–20, fig. 15, plan XVII R. "Cattle, sheep/goat, pig, bird, dog," *BASOR* 229, 66, many sheep and goat, fair amount of cattle, small number of pig and horse. Overall statistics of animal bones found 1958–1963: sheep and goat 50%, cattle 25%, horse 16%, pig 8%.

45. *Sardis* M5 (1978) 8–9, fig. 3, unit XXVIII; *BASOR* 199, 17–18, fig. 8 (detailed plan) 28; PC: Figs. 63, 64.

46. See Chapter IV, *supra,* under "Lydian Burial Rites and Beliefs."

47. Hanfmann-Erhart, "Mausoleum," 81–85, figs. 1, 6, 7. Writing desk, chair (Fig. 159): *Sardis* R2 (1978) no. 17, figs. 70–71. For literature see *Sardis* M2 (1972) nos. 128, 133.

48. Comparison with Gordion: Hanfmann, "On Lydian Sardis," 102, fig. 13; idem, *Croesus,* 4, 9, fig. 7, Smyrna: fig. 18; J. M. Cook, *Greeks,* 74; idem, "Old Smyrna," fig. 3 (plan). Akurgal, *Bayrakli,* 75–79, pls. 4–5, fig. 1; house plan somewhat similar to "House of Priest," Fig. 45.

49. Evidence for precinct(s) to the north is a dump, *BASOR* 199, 25, fig. 9, at W304/S324, which "extends into undug area to north." The very tentative reconstruction by S. M. Goldstein and E. Wahle has nineteen workmen in the precinct (Fig. 139), but this does not include people who brought ore, coal, galena, and other supplies; nor any guards or superintendents.

50. The refinery continued operation in a more restricted area after 570–560 B.C. *Sardis* M5 (1978) nos. 28, 30, fig. 3.

51. Rock crystal: see Chapter I, *supra,* under "In-

dustry"; jewelry: *BASOR* 191, 13, fig. 13, gold disk pendant; 25, fig. 15, jewelry mold.

52. See Chapter III, *supra,* under "House of Bronzes/Lydian Market."

53. *BASOR* 157, 34, pit in W13 to *92, Protocorinthian sherd; griffin terracotta: *Sardis* M5 (1978) no. 17 (from BS W13); *BASOR* 166, 45, figs. 33, 34, two test pits, E15–20/S15–25 area to *92.3. See *TürkArkDerg* (forthcoming).

54. See Chapter III, *supra,* under "House of Bronzes/Lydian Market."

55. Lamps: *BASOR* 162, 12, fig. 3 (plan: Text—E14/S97, Plan—E16/S98.5; Hanfmann, *Letters,* 80, fig. 51. The location is slightly misplaced on the plan (E16/S98.5 instead of E14/S97.)

56. *Sardis* (M8) *Metalwork* (forthcoming) nos. 950–953.

57. Mold: *BASOR* 166, 11, fig. 8; unfinished ibex: *BASOR* 170, 10, fig. 11, within a meter of the mold.

58. *BASOR* 154, 28, figs. 8 (plan), 9 (view), 10 (section), 14 (repaired hydria), 15 (bichrome amphora); 157, 30, fig. 9, at "96.8".

59. Siglos: *BASOR* 170, 16. Pseudo-coin with rosette: *ILN* (1 April 1961) fig. 9.

60. *BASOR* 174, 9–11, fig. 3, before restoration. Greenewalt, "Exhibitionist," 29–46, pls. 8–15; G. M. A. Hanfmann does not agree with the restoration of the figure as phallic. Demon: *BASOR* 166, 10, fig. 5.

61. *BASOR* 177, 13, fig. 13; Gusmani, *Sardis* M3 (1975) 38–39, no. AIII 2, figs. 32–33. The piece (P 64.43; IN 64.15) was in the west part of HoB/Lydian Market trench between Buildings "G" and "H" (W31–34, 155–120 *100.70–100) but at a higher level, in association with sherds of ca. 550–500 B.C. It appears to belong to Swift's Lydian Level I, ca. *99.0 of which a floor and a wall of small stones is mentioned at W34. The dative *labλ* speaks for a dedication.

62. *Sardis* M3 (1975) 79–111, and dating, 107. Two of the Carian inscriptions (IN 66.1, 66.2) were found in the same place, just outside an archaic Lydian structure in HoB, north of Building D in Fig. 39 (W13–4/S89–91). The levels were *98.8, *98.4, if correctly given.

63. See Greenewalt, *Dinners,* 4–9, 27–30, for the chronology, 42–47, rejecting Carian war god as recipient; *thyma Karikon:* see Pedley, "Carians," 99.

64. Even if cautiously worded, Gusmani's remark, *Sardis* M3 (1975) 106, that the presence of Carians as mercenaries or prisoners of war is "thinkable" and that the finds indicate a separate Carian city quarter should not become a dogma yet.

65. Chapter III, *supra,* cites all important sources.

66. A separate unit for gold storage is implied in the account of Alcmaeon's visit to Croesus. Herodotus 6.125 = *Sardis* M2 (1972) no. 77, cf. also 75. There is no specific mention of the mint building in ancient sources.

67. For the palatial economies of the second millennium B.C. in the Near East and Aegean, see Polanyi, 67; Hammond-Bartson, *City,* 40, 43, 89; Hanfmann, "On Lydian Sardis," 106 n. 56; for the semirural "Homeric" economy of the Gordian palace(s), see DeVries, 33–42.

68. Hanfmann, *Croesus,* 8–9, 17–18, fig. 39 (Larisa); idem, "Palace"; Lycia: Eichler, *Gjolbaschi-Trysa,* 7, 8, 23–26, 61–62, pl. 18 A 7–8, B10, fig. 8; Nylander, *Ionians,* 117.

69. Xenophon, *Cyropaedia* 7.2.1 = *Sardis* M2 (1972) nos. 113–122; most plausible account of Persian success: a slave of one of the Lydian guards knew the secret way. Incidentally, the story implies a secret way to the water, in this case the Pactolus.

70. *BASOR* 162, 32–37; 166, 35, 36, fig. 28, "hollows in the conglomerate which may be bottoms of storage bins or cisterns."

71. Arrian, *Anabasis* 1.17.3 = *Sardis* M2 (1972) no. 235. From the fact that the "Council of the Elders" (*gerousia*) moved into the royal palace, one might deduce that this city-representation, common in the Near East, predated the Hellenistic constitution of Sardis. For the traditions on *gerousia* see Hanfmann, "Palace," 145–147.

72. PC: See Chapter III, *supra. BASOR* 162, 19, figs. 7, 10–11; Hanfmann-Detweiler, "Heights," 8, figs. 8, 9.

73. Hanfmann, "On Lydian Sardis," 105–106, figs. 20–26.

74. Price-Trell, fig. 244. For the possible cult of Zeus Lydios in the vicinity of HoB/Lydian Market, see n. 61, *supra.* A Roman glass stamp with Zeus Lydios does not have a known findspot: *Sardis* M6 (1980) 32, no. 216, pl. 10. Representations in Greek and Roman sculpture and coins: *Sardis* R2 (1978) 84, no. 107.

75. *Sardis* M5 (1978) 9; see Hanfmann, *Croesus,* 6, 14, figs. 10, 33, 34, for Delphi altar and Etruscan parallel for placing of lions.

76. See Chapter III, *supra,* under "The Artemis Precinct."

77. Lydian names, *infra.* Greek gods: Keil, "Kulte," 250–266. Anatolian: L. Robert, *Noms indigènes.* Cf. *Sardis* R2 (1978) 16, 17 (iconography), nos. 6, 7.

78. Dede Mezari, *BASOR* 162, 48, 49; 229, 66, figs. 10–12 (Ionic capital, ca. 500 B.C.); *Sardis* R2 (1978) 52, 53, no. 9, figs. 58–60, relief of Aphrodite or votary.

79. Hanfmann, *Croesus,* 10–12, figs. 23–26;

Sardis R2 (1978) 37, 38, 42–50, nos. 6, 7, figs. 16–50.

80. *BASOR* 174, 38, figs. 21, 22; see also the Ionic capital of ca. 500 B.C. (also post-499 B.C.) from Dede Mezari, *BASOR* 229, 26, figs. 10–12.

81. *BASOR* 174, 34, *parastades tou Metroou.*

82. *Sardis* M5(1978) 40, nos. 4, 17, 23–30, 68, figs. 34, 48, 54–63, 103; *Sardis* X (1926) pls. 3, 5.

83. *Sardis* R2 (1978) 71, no. 39, figs. 137, 138 (ca. 400 B.C.).

84. Gusmani, *LW,* 150, 151; *Kaves, Kaoueis* was still used for priestess of Artemis in Roman times. *Sardis* VII.1 (1932) nos. 90–93 and *s.v. iereus;* in Lydian, male priests are attested for Artemis, Baki, Armas (no. 22:9, 10), and Demeter (no. 26:2).

85. Chapter III, *supra,* under "Pactolus North," Fig. 44, units XXVIII–XXX; *Sardis* M5 (1978) 9, fig. 3.

86. For a discussion of the altar, see Chapter III, *supra; Sardis* R1 (1975) 94, 95, figs. 124, 125. For Lydian and Persian finds at the Roman Building L, see ibid., 107, 110, 116; but no architectural traces were found.

87. Possibly predecessor of Building "D" and structure north of it (Fig. 39, and n. 62, *supra*). Building "D" had two floors at *99.3, *99.1, and yet a lower floor? It had a hearth and a circular bin. The spectacular terracotta "Exhibitionist" (Figs. 142, 143) and some of the finest wine drinking Lydian vessels were discarded into a refuse heap next to the building. These are dated between 600 and 550 B.C. *BASOR* 174, 8, figs. 2–4, 6, 7.

88. Hanfmann, "On Lydian Sardis," 101, figs. 11, 12, 14; both Sardis and Gordion are cities at east-west crossings of river fords on the Royal Road.

89. Hanfmann considers as erroneous the attribution to Proto-Fikelura and the dating (600–570) of the terracotta lid with primitive animals found on the Acropolis (Fig. 71); Greenewalt, "Wild Goat," 59, 65–67 n. 27, no. 8, pl. 6.3–4. For Phrygian pottery on the Acropolis see *BASOR* 166, 35–36.

90. Hanfmann, "On Lydian Sardis," 99–101, figs. 1–6.

91. *Sardis* M2 (1972) nos. 292–295; Weidner, "Jojachin."

92. Greenewalt, "Twentieth Campaign," 105, "Tumulus of the Lydian Period." *BASOR* 233, 19, fig. 24, Tomb 77.1. Hanfmann-Erhart, "Mausoleum," 82, figs. 1, 7.

93. Polybius 7.15–17 = *Sardis* M2 (1972) nos. 283–285; *Sardis* I (1922) 17 n. 1. Polybius' account suggests that "the so-called Persian Gates" were located in the continuation of a city wall which apparently made use of or passed close by the Theater (Fig. 8:26); scarp at ca. E900–1000/S300–N100; *Sardis* R1 (1975) fig. 1, no. 26.

94. Radet, *Lydia,* 284–287; Gerôme's painting of Rhodope and Candaules in the Museo de Arte de Ponce, Puerto Rico, was noticed by A. H. Detweiler: J. S. Held, ed. Museo de Arte de Ponce, *Catalogue* 1, *Paintings of the European and American Schools* (Ponce, P. R. 1962) 72, fig. 112, no. 63.0353.

95. Hippodamos and Piraeus: J. R. McCredie, 95–100.

96. Thucydides 1.10: "If the city of the Lacedaemonians should be deserted and nothing left . . . but its temples and foundations of other buildings . . . after a long lapse of time (one) would find their renown incredible . . . and yet, they occupy two fifths of the Peloponnese . . . Sparta is not built in urban fashion . . . has no temples and costly buildings . . . they live in villages."

97. *Sardis* M5 (1978) 10.

Production and Trade

1. See Chapter I, *supra,* under "Mineral Resources."

2. See Chapter III, *supra.*

3. Roebuck, 86, 87; Waldbaum, *Bronze,* 38–58 with statistical tables; 67, she notes "the dearth of objects in precious metals."

4. Phoenicians: Herodotus 6.47 = *Sardis* M2 (1972) no. 31; Roebuck, 91, no. 23. Meles: Balmuth, 3–7, cites "half shekels" cast by Sennacherib (705–681 B.C.) and silver ingots inscribed by King Barrekub in 730 B.C.

5. Roebuck, 89, 90, with references.

6. See Chapter III, *supra,* under "Goldworking," with references. Pászthory, 151–156, Table 2.

7. Bolin, 23–27; credibility: Frankel, 15–17; L. H. Clark, *Wall Street Journal,* January 20, 1981.

8. This preposterous argument was actually used by Bolin. For the analyses of Pactolus gold see Chapter III, *supra,* under "Goldworking." Hanfmann-Waldbaum, "New Excavations," 310–315.

9. The restoration by Goldstein and Wahle shows sixteen people without the supporting crews and guards. For evidence of a workshop north of the present refinery, see *BASOR* 199, 25, plan fig. 9, W303/S324 (marked "dump").

10. Tribute: Burn, *Persia,* chart opposite 122 (Herodotus); Thasos: Herodotus 6.46; Roebuck, 91–92. Siphnos: Herodotus 3.57–58; Roebuck, 90–91.

11. Thirty staters in "Pot of gold," Shear, "Sixth Report," 396–400, figs. 7, 8. Smyrna and Gordion yielded comparable small hoards. Smyrna: Akurgal, *Kunst Anat.,* 151, 155, fig. 106, where the coins are not Lydian; but Lydian connection is suggested by the lydion used as a piggy-bank; and Gordion: Bellinger, 10–15. Weidauer, 23, no. 71–75, lionhead

with "rayed wart," pl. 9. Mercenaries: R. M. Cook, "Speculations," 257; Alcaeus fragment 42, Diehl; Roebuck, 54 n. 62.

12. Pászthory, 155–158.

13. Head, *BMC, Lydia,* xviii–xx, 5 (Croesus, "Babylonic" standard). Idem, *HN,* 643.

14. E. G. S. Robinson, "Coins Reconsidered," 156–160; Jacobsthal, 85–95. Robinson placed the beginning of the imageless coins at 630 B.C.

15. Weidauer, 54 type XV, XVI, 108–109, pl. 107; she dates the Lydian lionhead series XV–XVIII to 650–625 B.C.

16. Weidauer, Catalogue 22–28, 54, type XVIII, nos 59–115, pls. 8–12; 59–66, esp. 63, 71, types XV, XVI (lions), XVII (*Valvel*), XVIII (*Kalil*) attributed to Sardis; 99–107.

17. The arguments entail a consideration of the chronology of the foundation deposit in Ephesus. Since we do not believe that the equation *valvel* = "Alyattes" has been eliminated, the entire argument leading to a date of pre-626 B.C. for the deposit is not necessarily valid. Even if we accept the redating of the destruction by three decades, Weidauer's attempt to refute Jacobsthal's archaeological dates does not carry conviction. All comparisons are of the kind that permits the coins compared to be dated between 640 and 620 B.C.

18. Cahn, *Knidos,* 185, and Weidauer, 13, admit "Oriental origins." For the terms "stater" = *Ishtar;* "shekel" = *siglos;* "mina" = *mna,* see Olmstead, *Persian Empire,* 188; Balmuth, 3–7.

19. E. G. S. Robinson, "Coins Reconsidered," 159–160, linked the "wart" to Assyrian prototypes. Weidauer, 22–25, 99–10, pls. 8–10, distinguishes two lion types on early electrum coins, one with four-rayed wart (XV), no. 59–85, the other with "many-rayed wart" (XVI), no. 86–90. She arrives at a date "in the decades of the third quarter of the seventh century," i.e., 650–630 B.C.; a non-Lydian lion is dated even earlier, 660 B.C., idem, 94–97 (XLIII), no. 180–184, pl. 20, 29:1.

20. *Pace,* Weidauer, 62–63. Hanfmann suggests that Phanes, too, is the name of a king or prince or tyrant of some Greek city in Asia Minor. We know very little even about the history of archaic Miletus to which the coin is very tentatively attributed, let alone about smaller Eastern Greek places.

21. As witness the controversies about the real names of Meles, Candaules, and the so-called Sadyattes. *Sardis* M2 (1972) nos. 30–37. Gusmani, *LW,* 220–221, seems to exceed the evidence when he says the legend "has certainly nothing to do with the name Alyattes."

22. Balmuth, 7, nos. 29, 32, rightly points to widespread use on Aramaic and Hebrew weights. The Lydian formula used by Croesus on the Ephesus

column ended in *-lis,* "belonging to" but was translated into Greek: *Kroisou Basileos.* Hanfmann, *Croesus,* 11, fig. 22. The Hesychios' gloss—*koalddein,* "king" in Lydian, *Kualdn? Qldan*—might be rendered with a *Kal?* See Gusmani, *LW,* 188, 274. Or is this the same name as that of King Kadys mixed up with Ardys, in Nicolas of Damascus: *Sardis* M2 (1972) no. 30?

23. *Sardis* (M8) *Metalwork* (forthcoming) nos. 949–953.

24. See the reference in n. 56, *infra.*

25. Waldbaum, *Bronze,* 55, 69.

26. *Sardis* M2 (1972) no. 297.

27. See Chapter I, *supra.*

28. *BASOR* 170, 11–13; Greenewalt-Majewski, 133–140, also for literary sources. R. S. Thomas, *Sardis* (M10) *Small Finds* (forthcoming).

29. Figs. 108–110. See Chapter IV, *supra,* under "The Royal Mounds."

30. According to observations made in 1980 (J. A. Scott), the Alyattes marble may have come from quarries at Mermere, ca. 20 km. away by road. See *Sardis* R2 (1978) 4–6; *Sardis* R1 (1975) 21, fig. 2.

31. In the Gyges mound crepis wall: *BASOR* 117, 33.

32. Cook, "Old Smyrna" (1959) 24, 25.

33. *BASOR* 233, 23–26, figs. 28–29; *TürkArkDerg* (forthcoming).

34. *Sardis* M5 (1978) 12–14. Table 2: "Quartz; untarnished feldspar; biotite; muscovite; lomatite stain and grains" as basic ingredients. See the analysis of a Sardis sherd in Goldman, *Tarsus III,* 403, fig. 112.

35. H. G. Crane, "Traditional Pottery Making in the Sardis Region" (unpublished, originally prepared for the present study).

36. *BASOR* 154, 27, 28, figs. 8 (plan), 9; 157, 30, fig. 9 (plan): Hanfmann, *Letters,* 46–48, figs. 24–27. A lower "firebox" and part of a curving upper chamber had survived, but everything else had been cut by later (Roman) buildings. Excavation to the north, south, and west did not reveal other kilns or the usual piles of rejects. G. M. A. Hanfmann, who had previously studied Iron Age kilns found at Tarsus, thought the identification plausible, but the loss of immediate surroundings where rejects, coal, and refuse of firing might be expected makes certainty impossible. Similar doubts prevail with regard to structure "E" (Fig. 39) in HoB. *BASOR* 174, 8.

37. Crane, "Traditional Pottery Making in the Sardis Region" (unpublished).

38. Coarse wares: *BASOR* 162, 23, figs. 10, 11 (pithoi, PC). See *BASOR* 154, 29 (90% brown, gray, black below "Potter's Workshop"); 157, 30, fig. 17 (Unit XXIII); 166, 15 (HoB).

39. *BASOR* 154, 30. See J. Mellaart, "Southern Anatolian," 115–136; Hanfmann in Goldman, *Tarsus* III, 50, on Cilician; Brein, 726–728, pls. 224–226, on Ephesian Black-on-Red.

40. C. H. Greenewalt, "Wild Goat," 57–89, pls. 1–18, nos. 1–18; *Sardis* R1 (1975) 121–124, figs. 302, 307, 313–316, 318. They feature not only wild goats, dogs, and lions but also bizarre griffins and sphinxes and even a *Potnios* or *Potnia Theron*. Greenewalt dates the Sardis group ca. 600–575 B.C. For common shapes of wine jugs, bowls, fruit stands, see the basic discussion in Greenewalt, *Dinners,* 13–17.

41. Greenewalt, "Lydian Graves," 129–134, pls. 3–9; "Ephesian Ware," 91–122, pls. 1–13; *Dinners,* 114, 120–122, imitations. For Corinthian craters, see *Sardis* M5 (1978) 39, fig. 132; for the popular Lydian skyphos imitated from the Corinthian kotyles, see Greenewalt, *Dinners,* 15–16, pls. 17–28, 31.

42. Knudsen, "Lydian Imitation," 59–69, pl. 8; Chase, "Two Vases," 114–117, fig. 2; Greenewalt, "Elements," 38, pl. 13:2; Greenewalt, "Lydian Graves," 132 n. 25 lists other Phrygian reflections and imports; *BASOR* 166, 35–36.

43. Thought by Knudsen to imitate Phrygian metal bowls, "Lydian Imitation," 59–69, pls. 8, 9; see also Greenewalt, "Lydian Graves," pl. 8. Omphalos bowl (phiale): Greenewalt, *Elements,* 38, 39, pls. 14:3, 4. In household discards: *Sardis* R1 (1975) 122–123, fig. 317. See Luschey, *Phiale,* for origins and development of the shape; Oliver, 116.

44. Marbling, "streaking": Greenewalt, "Elements," 38–46, pls. 13–15; *BASOR* 166, 37, fig. 29. Lydion: Greenewalt, "Elements," 36, pl. 13, white stripes and dots; Akurgal, *Kunst Anat.,* 151; *Sardis* M5 (1978) fig. 32; *Sardis* R1 (1975) figs. 229, 308, 310. Cf. *Sardis* I (1922) 79, ill. 75A, Tomb 43.

45. NEW: *Sardis* R1 (1978) 122–123, lists thirteen different shapes from 38 vessels. PN: *BASOR* 182, 18–20, 14 skyphoi, 5 plates, 8 jars, 2 cooking pots. HoB near "D," *BASOR* 174, 8–13, figs. 6–7. Graves: Greenewalt, "Lydian Graves," 127–128, gives statistics and references including the tumulus at Gordion.

46. Greenewalt, *Dinners,* 11–17, pls. 17–32, a thorough discussion of jugs, oinochoai, skyphoi, dishes, with capacities.

47. See Greenewalt, *Dinners,* pls. 17–28, esp. 23 profiles, pl. 42, "coarse gritty fabric of cooking ware," example recovered from a hearth of Building "D" in HoB, and many parallels from other Anatolian sites, nn. 5–6. He also notes the connection with the technique of modern potters at Gökeyüp observed by H. G. Crane, "Traditional Pottery Making in the Sardis Region" (unpublished).

48. *BASOR* 154, 27, 28, fig. 14; Hanfmann, *Letters,* 46, fig. 27 (two views). This ware was made in many Eastern Greek workshops and was also imitated locally; Goldman, *Tarsus* III, 324.

49. See Chapter VI, *infra.*

50. *BASOR* 162, 12; Hanfmann, *Letters,* 80, fig. 31.

51. *Sardis* M5 (1978) 12–14.

52. *Sardis* M5 (1978) 11, 12; *BASOR* 229, 69, 70, figs. 15–17.

53. *Sardis* M5 (1978) 11.

54. R. S. Thomas, *Sardis* (M10) *Small Finds* (forthcoming). Bearded heads: *BASOR* 166, 10, fig. 6 (P 61.289). Protomai and dove: *Sardis* I (1922) 118, fig. 124 (Tomb 813, dated ca. 500–480 B.C. by the black figure oinochoe, Beazley, *ABV,* 533, no. 10. Cf. *Sardis* R2 (1978) 75.

55. *BASOR* 170, 11–13, fig. 7 (plan) "H," *98.8.

56. DeVries, 40–42. For the palace-oriented economies of the Near East and the Aegean in the second millennium, see Hammond-Bartson, *City,* Chapters II-XIII with bibliography. Hanfmann, "On Lydian Sardis," 107 n. 56.

57. Roebuck, 52, really applies to pre-Mermnad Lydia; Hanfmann, "Homeric Asia," 135–155. Balcer, "By the Bitter Sea" (forthcoming).

58. Pottery: Lydian Protogeometric and Geometric is as yet to be analyzed. Ramage, Chapter III, *supra* remarks on two traditions—that of circles and semi-circles and that of rectangular patterns. For Greek Protogeometric imports, see *BASOR* 154, 9, 29, 30, fig. 13, Artemis Precinct; 162, 14, 15, fig. 3; 177, 14, (*96.4, P 64.351, 364); 186, 34–36, figs. 11–13; *Sardis* R1 (1975) 107, fig. 238; Hanfmann, "Lydian Relations," 28, fig. 2 (HoB). For the ceramics of Eastern Greek cities see Coldstream, Chapter 12, "East Greek Geometric," 262–302, pls. 50–64. Desborough, *Last Mycenaeans,* 160 (Sardis sherd), 169 (Miletus, Smyrna). Cf. Mee, 144. Phrygian fibulae, copper, tin; *Sardis* (M8) *Metalwork* (forthcoming). Muscarella, *Fibulae,* 44.

59. Herodotus 1.93–94. He names the *agoraioi,* the craftsmen, and "the girls who work" as the three classes who worked on the mound of Alyattes.

60. Xenophon, *Anabasis* 1.5.6., 401–400 B.C. In Mesopotamia, the "Lydian Market" raised prices to four sigloi for a *pithe,* supposedly fifty times the going price in Athens.

61. Mesopotamia: e.g., the famous banking house of Murasu, even though it was active in the Persian period, G. Cardascia (1951). The Greek examples: Kolaios of Samos, Herodotus 4.152, who traveled to Spain; Pamphaes of Priene, who lent money to Croesus, *Sardis* M2 (1972) nos. 64–66; and Sostratos of Aegina, possibly commemorated by a marble an-

chor dedicated at Gravisca in Etruria, Harvey, "Sostratos," 206-214. For the theory that bankers struck their own money, see Weidauer on Phanes, 64-65; she thinks him a moneyer who signed his coins. For Lydia: Pythes/Pythios, "The richest man of whom we have knowledge," Herodotus 7.27, must have traded in gold.

62. Mnesimachus: *Sardis* VII.1 (1932) 3, no. 1; *Sardis* R1 (1975) 22, 180 n. 44, with literature. Lydian property texts: Gusmani in *Sardis* M3 (1975) 23-24 (IN 71.1), no. AI4; *LW*, 21, nos. 13, 22-24, all from the Artemis Precinct. Gusmani considers nos. 23-24 as transactions involving the temple; the new inscription (Fig. 154) as possibly a financial agreement among members of a family.

63. Hanfmann, *Croesus*, 4-5, with literature on temple economics, especially D. van Berchem, "Ephèse," 24-26; Xenophon, *Anabasis*, 5.3.4-8. It is not said whether the Megabyzos could use the money in Xenophon's absence. The money was supposedly a tithe for Artemis, but nonetheless Xenophon got it back.

64. Herodotus, 1.69 = *Sardis* M2 (1972) no. 103. On the position of the king in the "exchange" and redistributive proceedings, see H. Frankfort, "Kingship"; Polanyi; and M. I. Finley, *Odysseus*, 110-113, 140-141. Darius was reproached with being a *kapelos* (huckster); Roebuck, 59 n. 83, a careful discussion of the term in Herodotus.

65. The Lydians controlled Adramyttion (Troad) on the gulf of the same name but left Cyzicus to the Greeks. They must have had Lydian merchants negotiating shipments and travel by sea with the Greeks at such ports as Smyrna and Ephesus. Hanfmann, *Croesus*, 9-10.

66. Herodotus 3.48 = *Sardis* M2 (1972) nos. 57-58.

67. Herodotus 1.70 = *Sardis* M2 (1972) no. 104. *Sardis* R2 (1978) 30. The Spartans were making a "counter-present" (*antidounai*), perhaps for Croesus' gift of gold for the statue of Apollo at Thornax, Herodotus 1.69.

68. Plutarch, *Moralia, Mulierum virtutes* 27 (263), and Pythes/Pythios' boast to Xerxes in Herodotus 7.28: He had counted his property and was worth "two thousand talents of silver, and of gold four million Daric staters lacking seven thousand."

69. See Chapter III, *supra,* under "The Acropolis."

70. L. Robert, *Bull.* 78 (1965) 155, no. 342.

71. Presents: *Sardis* M2 (1972) nos. 97-103.

72. Scaraboid seal from Naucratis: *BASOR* 170, 25, fig. 21. E. Porada referred to *Naukratis* 1: 36, pl. 37: 28; *Naukratis* 2: pls. 18, 62. R. S. Thomas, *Sardis* (M10) *Small Finds* (forthcoming). For grain trade of

Naucratis see Roebuck, "Naukratis," 212-220. It should be noted that one Lydian graffito was found in Upper Egypt in the sandstone quarry at Silsilis, Gusmani, *LW,* no. 49.

73. Babylonian seal: *Sardis* XIII (1925) 45, pl. 11, no. 120, identified by E. Porada (by letter). Ivory: Chapter I, *supra.* Both Egypt and Mesopotamia had supplies of ivory; Barnett, *Nimrud Ivories,* 163-166.

74. Roebuck, 50, rightly notes that the authority for Phrygian overlordship in ancient sources is weak, but the overall picture lends credibility to the idea of some sort of Phrygian suzerainty in the eighth century; see Hanfmann, "On Lydian Sardis," 99-102, 106-107. Roebuck's useful survey of Phrygian products, ibid., 33-50, should be supplemented for Lydia by Greenewalt, "Lydian Graves," 131-132; for fibulae and copper: Muscarella, "Phrygian or Lydian?" 57; and *Fibulae,* 44.

75. Hanfmann, "Lydian Relations," 26-27, citing Schol. Plato *Republic,* 566 = *Sardis* M2 (1972) no. 102, on marriage of daughter of Alyattes with Astyages (after 585 B.C.).

76. Lydians were part of the population of Ephesus from pre-Greek times: Pausanias 7.2.8. Neither at Ephesus nor at Smyrna has the Lydian material been systematically collected. Ephesus: "Base hoard," Robinson, "Coins Reconsidered," 163-166; literary references, see "Religion," *infra;* Roebuck 56-57; pottery, Brein, 727-728, fig. 17, might be Lydian. He notes that Ephesian and Sardian Black-on-Red "look practically alike." Smyrna: "lydion" as saving box, Akurgal, *Kunst Anat.,* 151, 155, fig. 106; other evidence, Cook, "Old Smyrna," 17 (Lydian writing), 29-31 n. 82, 87, pl. 42. 31; "There appears to have been a considerable Lydian element present," citing presence of Lydian wares, one or two Lydian graffiti, a tumulus burial with offerings of a Lydian, and Lydian coins in a hoard with darics. See Thompson-Mørkholm-Kraay, no. 1789, for hoards allegedly from this region.

77. Dunbabin, *Greeks.*

78. Coldstream, 262-302, pls. 50-64. Brein, 721-728, pls. 220-226.

79. Rhodes, Aeolis: *BASOR* 157, 13, 28, fig. 16; 162, 34 n. 55, fig. 17; 166, 23, fig. 16 (Aeolic); 177, 6, fig. 5 (Aeolic); 182, 13, 14, fig. 6 (Rhodian bird cup). Greenewalt, "Exhibitionist," 42, 43 n. 40; idem, "Lydian Graves," 128-130; idem, "Fikellura," 163-164.

80. *BASOR* 199, 14, fig. 3.

81. *BASOR* 157, 30, fig. 15, misidentified as "Eastern Greek," 560 B.C.; 182, 21, fig. 17, Laconian II, ca. 600 B.C. A complete "lakaina" on tall foot from Butler's Tomb 720: Chase, "Two Vases," 111-114,

pl. 4; A. Lane, "Lakonian," 151; Oliver, "Lydia," 199, was found with an Attic olpe (not Corinthian), ca. 560?–550? B.C. Laconian cups: see Beazley-Ashmole, 23. Historical background: Roebuck, 58.

82. N. H. Ramage, "Attic Pottery" (unpublished, originally written for this study) considers a deinos fragment close to the Gorgon Painter as the earliest of 200 Attic fragments found by the Harvard-Cornell Expedition. She does not include the pieces found by Butler, of which the olpe, n. 81, *supra,* is early. See *Sardis* I (1922) 118, ill. 124, oinochoe T813, 500–480 B.C.; *Sardis* R2 (1978) 75; *Sardis* I (1922) 119, ill. 125, olpe, T720? (or 43?); cf. lekythos with Herakles (T348, MET no. MMA 14.30.23); Alcmaeon, Solon: Herodotus 6.125; 1.28–32 = *Sardis* M2 (1972) nos. 77, 84.

83. Roebuck's account is excellent, 54–58.

84. The largest amounts were in bullion or art works, as in the presents to the Greek sanctuaries and later tribute to Persia, or the wagon load of silver sent by Croesus to Pamphaes, *Sardis* M2 (1972) no. 66. Payment in coin: 2,000 gold staters to Lesbos (n. 9, *supra*); 30 silver *minas* from Pamphaes of Priene to Croesus, ibid., may be supplemented by finds made outside Lydia: Gordion, Bellinger (1968) 10; Weidauer, 23, nos. 71–72, 74–75. Ephesus: E. G. S. Robinson, "Coins Reconsidered." Smyrna: Cook, "Old Smyrna," 30 n. 82. Persepolis: Schmidt, *Persepolis* II = OIP 69, 111; Thompson-Mørkholm-Kraay, index 402, *s.v.* Lydia, esp. no. 1789; Nippur, in Oriental Institute Excavations, according to M. Gibson (oral communication).

85. *Lydion-Bakkaris* (unguent): Rumpf, "Salbegefaesse," 163–170; Roebuck, 56 n. 70, a thorough summary with references to exported Lydian lydions in Athens and Corinth, imitations in Aegina and Italy. He thinks Lydians handled exports inland (to Gordion), Ionians, the overseas shipments. Greenewalt, "Lydian Graves," 132–134; idem, "Elements," 38, pl. 13:1. On the unguent *bakkaris,* see *Sardis* M2 (1972) no. 131. Already the ancients were not sure whether it was (also?) a perfume.

86. R. M. Cook, "Speculations," 257. While still a prince, before 560 B.C., Croesus hired mercenaries with money lent by Pamphaes; Nicolas of Damascus, *Sardis* M2 (1972) nos. 64, 66. For fifth century ratio of gold and silver, see Eddy, 101–112.

87. The only definitely excavated Lydian coin is a silver obel from the apsidal building (fountain house?) at PN. A. E. M. Johnston, *Sardis* M7 (1981) Greek no. 133. *BASOR* 166, 22.

88. *Sardis* M2 (1972) nos. 297–300, with references.

89. "Pot of Gold," n. 11, *supra.* It is remarkable that in the story of Pamphaes, n. 86, *supra,* as well as in a fragment of Hipponax, thirty silver *minas* are

used in the sense of "much money" ("a million dollars"). There were thirty staters in the "Pot of Gold."

90. As some numismatists argue from the existence of tiny fractions of electrum and silver. E. G. S. Robinson, "Coins Reconsidered," 163; Roebuck, 55: "Apparently the money was used in ordinary small scale transactions." Polanyi, "Comparative," 333–334.

The Lydian Society

1. Bostanci, "Skeletal Remains," 121–123, 126; Bostanci, "Skulls" 1967, 2, 14; Bostanci, "Skulls" 1969, 109–114; also E. Bostanci, FR 1966: "Progress Report, July 16, 1966" (unpublished). See also E. H. Koehler, *BASOR* 170, 60–62. This section draws on Field Reports by J. Savishinsky (1966), J. S. Henderson (1967), and D. J. Finkel (1968). It concerns only skeletal remains of the Lydian period.

2. E. Bostanci, "Skulls" 1969, 109–114. For possible linguistic relations, see sections on progress of research, *supra,* and languages, *infra* (in this chapter).

3. J. Savishinsky, FR 1966: "Human and Non-Human Bones, July 21, 1966" (unpublished); D. J. Finkel, FR 1968: "Final Report" (unpublished).

4. R. and M. Ascher, *BASOR* 182, 18.

5. The description is from J. Savishinsky, FR 1966: "Human and Non-Human Bones, July 21, 1966" (unpublished). The "pit" is mentioned in *BASOR* 186, 33 n. 5. It is referred to, not quite aptly, as a "charnel house" by A. Ramage in Chapter III, *supra,* under "House of Bronzes/Lydian Market."

6. A "family group" of two men, two women, and one child.

7. *BASOR* 186, 33, 34, fig. 5; Hanfmann, *Letters,* 185, fig. 139. Savishinsky assumed that death was caused by asphyxiation; the damage to skull was done afterwards.

8. From data of the graves one may deduce a fairly short life span. The data from the city are distorted by representation of a special disaster.

9. Herodotus 1.7 = *Sardis* M2 (1972) no. 26; Hanfmann, "Lydiaka," 71, 72 nn. 41–43, 45, for the possible equation of Herakles with a native hero Tylos.

10. Homer, *Iliad* 3.401; 10.431; 18.291; 20.302. Cf. Buerchner-Deeters-Keil, 2167: "Iphition, a local prince from the central plain of Sardis." The names of these Homeric Maeonians are Greek, not Lydian.

11. See Chapter III, *supra,* under "House of Bronzes/Lydian Market."

12. Herodotus 1.69, Mimnermus F 13 = *Sardis* M2 (1972) nos. 44, 103; and Cook, "Old Smyrna" (1959) 27–28, "Mimnermus." See Hanfmann, "Horsemen."

13. Buerchner-Deeters-Keil, 2124, cite Aristotle,

Fr. no. 506 (Rose) = Stephanus Byzantius, *s.v. Adramytteion.*

14. Rendered *lud* in Assyrian; Slavic: *liud, liudva.*

15. The key passage for Lydian social classes is Herodotus 1.93–94. Cf. Roebuck, 59. Lydian terms are certain only for *kaveś*—priest or priestess, Gusmani, *LW,* 278. *LW,* 275; Jongkees (1938) 147. King *qldans:* Gusmani, *LW,* 274. *Briga,* "freeman" (Hesychius) from *Phrygos.* Gusmani, *LW,* 273 compares "frank" from the ethnic "Frank." *Nekyrtas,* O. Masson, ed. Hipponax F 28, 32, n. 3, 121, denies that the word is Lydian. Gusmani did not include it in *LW.*

16. Xenophon, *Cyropaedia* 7.2.3–4 = *Sardis* M2 (1972) no. 122, "A Persian who had been a slave of one of the guards" (on the Acropolis).

17. Plutarch, *Quaestiones Graecae* 45 (302A) = *Sardis* M2 (1972) no. 4. The double axe is a frequent symbol of Hittite gods.

18. Plutarch, ibid., Herodotus 1.8 = *Sardis* M2 (1972) nos. 4, 33–41.

19. Hanfmann, "Lydiaka," 66–68.

20. *Sardis* R2 (1978) 20–23, no. 23, figs. 87–89. Strocka, "Löwen," 512.

21. Plutarch, *Quaestiones Graecae* 45 = *Sardis* M2 (1972) no. 4. Hanfmann, "Lydiaka," 76.

22. See Chapter III, *supra,* under "The Acropolis."

23. Baking women: Herodotus 1.50. Heralds, messengers: *Sardis* M2 (1972) nos. 99, 292–295. Moneyers: Weidauer, 62.

24. Our figure is after the famous vase in the Louvre: Arias-Hirmer pl. 131. Hanfmann, *Croesus,* 14, fig. 35. For another Attic representation see J. D. Beazley, "Fragments," 319, pl. 85; Beazley *ARV²* 1, 571, no. 79. For possible royal monogram of Gyges, see Fig. 110.

25. See Figs. 45–48, 139.

26. Smyrna mound: see under "Architecture," *supra;* the Ephesus tower later called "The Traitor" was "upturned," *anetrape,* Aelian, *VH* 3.26 = *Sardis* M2 (1972) no. 69. This could be done by undermining the tower so that it would tip out of the wall line. The event was regarded as a near miraculous *tour de force.* For an actual attack of this kind in A.D. 256, see Hopkins, 242–249.

27. A. Ramage–N. Ramage, 143–160. Note that Pythes/Pythios came to Kelainai rather than Sardis, hence his properties were probably in that region. Herodotus 7.26–27. Unquestionably there were other "leading families" in places like Hypaepa, Tyre, near Kula, and around Thyateira (settlement near Harmandali).

28. *BASOR* 162, fig. 17, still geometric in style, ca. 650 B.C. at latest.

29. See Hanfmann, "Horsemen," 570–581, with discussion of social status of equestrians. Battle, char-iots, horsemen: *Sardis* M5 (1978) nos. 12, 14, 18, 20–21, figs. 44, 46, 49, 53.

30. *Sardis* M5 (1978) 15–16, no. 4, frontispiece and fig. 33, ca. 560 B.C., interpreted as horsemen by A. Ramage. Greenewalt, "Exhibitionist," 29–46, describes the details of dress and armor. Hanfmann feels sure the "Exhibitionist" wears a cuirass of red leather. Greenewalt interprets his attire as Persianizing.

31. Aeschylus, *Persae* 44–47 = *Sardis* M2 (1972) no. 186, where Pedley wavers between four- and six-horse chariots. Aeschylus speaks of two- and three-pole teams, probably three- and four-horse chariots.

32. Either we accept the two statuettes (Horseman P 63.607:8; Camel T 63.48) as being post-547 B.C., after the defeat of the Lydians, as suggested by Greenewalt, "Exhibitionist," 29–46; or the Lydians were aware of camels before. Greenewalt, "Exhibitionist," 37–46, has argued that the horseman is dressed like an Iranian and must date after the defeat of Croesus in 547 B.C. The camel's leg is clearly of the same make as the horseman. One might, indeed, ask whether it was a camel rider—not a horseman—but the camel leg base seems too small: *BASOR* 174, 11–12, fig. 4 (T 63.48). "There is no way of proving that this is the beast on which the horseman sat" (Hanfmann).

33. Ezek. 30:5; Jer. 46:9; cf. Gen. 10:22; 1 Chron. 1:17; Isa. 66:19. Archers are represented on one of the Sardis terracotta friezes, *Sardis* M5 (1978) no. 5, figs. 35–36.

34. Lydian inscriptions: n. 15, *supra,* "Religion," *infra;* "Sacrilege" inscription: Knibbe, "Religiöser Frevel" (1961–1963) 175–182; Robert, *Bull.* 78 (1965) 155; Gusmani, *LW,* 278; *Sardis* VII.1 (1932) nos. 51–55, 90–93.

35. Aristophanes, *Nubes* 598–600 = *Sardis* M2 (1972) no. 186. Aelian, *NA* 12.9 cites Autocrates in *Tympaniastae,* a play of the fourth century B.C., delightfully describing their dance = *Sardis* M2 (1972) no. 184. Autocrates calls them "virgins."

36. Robert, "Règlement perse" 319.

37. *Sardis* R2 (1978) nos. 4–5, figs. 11–15. It is not known whether they were priestesses of Cybele, from whose sanctuary much of the Lydian material reused in the synagogue appears to derive.

38. *Sardis* R2 (1978) 56, no. 17, figs. 70–71. Hanfmann then thought the man might be a priest, but now prefers the interpretation as the "new ideal" of account-keeping *kapelos*—merchant.

39. *Sardis* M5 (1978) 4–10, especially Building "H" (HoB) and PN units 1, 2, 3.

40. See Chapter III, *supra,* under "Pactolus North" and "Goldworking."

41. *BASOR* 199, 14 (600–580 B.C.).

42. Phyle Asias, after Asies, Herodotus

4.45 = *Sardis* M2 (1972) no. 11, with literature, including H. Th. Bossert, *Asia; Sardis* VII.1 (1932) 179; Robert, "Tribu," 155–158; *Sardis* R2 (1978) no. 211. Pelopis, IN 62.41, here Fig. 170.

43. Apollonios of Tyana in Philostratos, *Epistolae* 39; Penella, 308, "Shameful are the names of your tagmata *Koddaroi* and *Xyrisi-tauroi* (one who shaves the sexual parts). Your wives and daughters are like your tribal (tagmata) names and even more brash." *LSJ* suppl. (1938) 106, translates tagmata as "clubs."

44. Angdistis in 367 B.C.: Robert, "Règlement perse"; "Religion," *infra*. Pessinus legend: Pausanias 7.17.9; Roscher, *Lex* 1, 100–101. Omphale: *Sardis* M2 (1972) nos. 1–6. Vermaseren, *Attis,* 31–38.

45. Euripides, *Bacchae,* ed. E. R. Dodds. For possible connection with service to Cybele, see *Sardis* R2 (1978) 47, 51. Cf. "Religion," *infra*.

46. Omphale, n. 44, *supra*. *Sardis* M2 (1972) no. 30 (Nicolas of Damascus): The king's wife "Damonno . . . took a handsome cousin of her husband . . . as a lover . . . and with him plotted the death of her husband." Wife of Candaules, Herodotus 1.8 = *Sardis* M2 (1972) 34; in Nicolas of Damascus' divergent story, she is chaste and her name is Toudo; ibid., no. 35.

47. Priestesses: even in Roman times the most honored position was that of priestess of Artemis with the old title *kaoueis:* Buckler-Robinson, "Inscriptions III," 353–370; Gusmani, *LW,* 278, patronymic, ibid. nos. 1–10. This designation also in the "Sacrilege" inscription in describing Sardians. On the question of matriarchy, see Pembroke, 4.

48. Bacchylides, *Epinicia* 3.33–35 = *Sardis* M2 (1972) no. 124, poetic and not necessarily reliable.

49. Arachne, *Sardis* M2 (1972) no. 133, with references. G. D. and S. S. Weinberg, "Arachne," 262–267, fig. 1, pl. 33.

50. "Traditional Pottery Making in the Sardis Region" (unpublished) reports that women only are engaged in making special cooking pots at that village.

51. Herodotus 1.8 = *Sardis* M2 (1972) no. 34. Among the representations of men, the komasts on the Cybele monument (Fig. 152) are not quite nude, and are in any case presumably mythical. Cf. *Sardis* R2 (1978) 46, figs. 35–36.

52. No. 67: Robert, "Règlement perse," 322. Bath of blood: Stephanus Byzantius *s.v.* Mastaura: Hanfmann, "Lydiaka," 66, 82 n. 11.

53. *BASOR* 166, 11, fig. 7, at W10/S100, *99.2, "together with a pothoard." Greenewalt, "Exhibitionist," 35–36, pl. 12.

54. The join is not really perfect and the emerging composition most peculiar. Hanfmann cannot believe that such a phallic vase could be intended as a portrait. Greek phallic vases depict general apotropaic types.

55. Roman *genius,* "the begetter," H. J. Rose, *s.v. genius* in *OCD,* 461, with references.

56. If one does not include such matters as representations of pomegranates, doves, and other objects of possible fertility symbolism. Some of these were found by the first Sardis expedition among the grave-goods. For representations of Artemis, Cybele, and possibly Aphrodite, see "Religious Life," *infra*.

57. Boys sent to Croesus by Periander, "Trade," *supra*. Women: "In the second book of Lydiaka, Xanthus says that Adramytes, king of Lydia, was the first to sterilize women and use them instead of male eunuchs." Athenaeus had some doubt about the authenticity of the passage, since some ancient critics attributed this version of Xanthus to Dionysius Scytobrachion, a notoriously unreliable writer. Athenaeus 12.515 = *Sardis* M2 (1972) no. 130. As attributed to Xanthus, the passage might be construed to imply prevention of Lesbian relations—or just elimination of men from the harem.

58. Sappho F 218 (96) 1–9 = *Sardis* M2 (1972) no. 138; "in Sardis . . . now she is preeminent among the ladies of Lydia."

59. Herodotus 1.94, strictly speaking says only: "The Lydians use customs rather close to those of the Greeks except that they make whores out of the female children . . ." or "make the female children go as whores." The remark leaves much unexplained—generally? sometimes? where? to what purpose? The assumption about the dowry is based on the Babylonian parallel, Herodotus 1.196. *Sardis* M2 (1972) no. 132.

60. The story must be seen against the practice in ancient warfare of castrating the boys, as the Persian generals threaten to do to the Milesians, Herodotus 6.10. This kept men alive as slaves, but effectively ensured the death of enemy population within a generation. In the case of the youths from Corcyra, however, the fact that they came from the highest families may point to uses more special than just slaves.

61. Herodotus 1.84 = *Sardis* M2 (1972) no. 116, speaks of a *palake,* a mistress of Meles. Alyattes had a Carian and an Ionian wife: Plutarch, *Moralia, De Herodoti malignitate* 18 (858 E) = *Sardis* M2 (1972) no. 67; Herodotus 1.92 = *Sardis* M2 (1972) no. 100.

62. There was apparently no primogeniture, though a special position is claimed for the eldest son by Pythes/Pythios in the Xerxes story.

63. "Shameful are the names of your *tagmata—Koddaroi* and *Xyrisitauroi* ("one who shaves sexual parts"). Your wives and daughters are like your *tagmata* names and even more brash." Philostratus, Apollonius of Tyana, *Letters* 39. Cf. n. 43, *supra*.

64. The story of Lydians abroad, which begins with the appearance of *ho Lydos,* "The Lydian," and "Croesus" as proper names (Beazley, *ABV,* 106;

Richter, *Kouroi*, 115) in Athens of the mid-sixth century B.C. continues with the appearance of Lydian slaves in the comedy and girls named Lyde and Lydia in Greek and Roman poetry.

65. Herodotus 7.38.

66. See Chapter IV, *supra,* under "Lydian Burial Rites."

Languages and Writing, Intellectual and Musical Life

1. The most recent treatments and bibliographies: Gusmani, "Lydische Sprache," 134–142, with bibliography after *LW;* idem, *LW,* 9–14, bibliography, 16–18, state of research; idem, *LW,* 1, 10–13, bibliography; idem, *Sardis* M3 (1975) xi–xii; V. V. Sevoroskin, *Lidiyskiy Yazik;* A. Heubeck, "Lydisch," 397–427. The basic collection of the first Sardis expedition is *Sardis* VI.2 (1924) by W. H. Buckler. Important comments and criticism by O. Carruba, "Grammatik," 39–83; and articles by R. D. Barnett, "Lydian Seal," 21–24; O. Masson, "Beletras," 193–196, and G. Neumann, "Verknüpfungen," 217–225.

2. W. H. Buckler, *Sardis* VI.2 (1924) published fifty-one items; Gusmani, *LW,* 269, sixty-one; Gusmani, "Lydische Sprache," ninety-five. More have been found so that the known texts number ca. one hundred. See Gusmani, *LW* 1.

3. *Sardis* M3 (1975) 11–24, no. A I 4, figs. 6–7, incomplete. Gusmani recognizes *taada*—father, *kana*—wife, *ena*—mother, and possibly *det*—money(?), possession.

4. *Sardis* M3 (1975) no. A II 5, figs. 12–13; and A III 2, figs. 32–33. *labλ*—from *Levs,* ca. 540 B.C.

5. *Sardis* M3 (1975) 52–53, chronological table of Lydian inscriptions. The earliest is the monogram on the Gyges wall (Chapter IV, *supra,* under "Royal Mounds"), followed by the *Kuvava* inscription which is no later than 550 B.C. and may be as early as 600 B.C. (Fig. 50). *Sardis* M3 (1975) 28–30; Gusmani, "Name der Kybele," 158–161. The earliest datable Phrygian inscriptions date from the late eighth century B.C., R. S. Young, "Phrygian Alphabet," 270–275.

6. *Sardis* M3 (1975) 59–61.

7. Carruba, "Grammatik," 39–40, with select bibliography.

8. *Sardis* M3 (1975) 81–111, figs. 56–66, nos. C I 1–6, C II 1–3, "Karische Sprachdenkmäler."

9. Herodotus; Plutarch, *Moralia, Quaestiones Graecae* 45 (302A) = *Sardis* M2 (1972) no. 4.

10. Carruba, "Lydian Inscription," 195, 196, pl. 3:2.

11. Roebuck, 54 n. 63.

12. Herodotus 1.92 = *Sardis* M2 (1972) no. 100.

13. IN 66.1, 66.2 were found just outside the archaic Lydian structure north of Building D. *BASOR* 186, 33–34, figs. 6–7, levels *98.8, *98.4.

14. Hanfmann-Masson, 123–134; *Sardis* M3 (1975) 89, with concordances and commentaries on texts, 106–111. While Gusmani is right in saying that the earlier graffiti might coincide with Ardys' attacks through Caria (Herodotus 2.15), G. M. A. Hanfmann does not believe that the graffiti were left by mercenaries. The HoB/Lydian Market seems to be a purely commercial area.

15. *Sardis* M3 (1975) 115–132, figs. 67–76, esp. 118 ill.—"Teil D. Die Inschrift der Synagoge."

16. *Sardis* M3 (1975) 131, possibly Maeonian; G. Neumann, "Synagogen-Inschrift," 95. Torrhebian language "differs only a little" from Lydian, according to Xanthus. Dionysius of Halicarnassus, 1.28.2.

17. Donner-Röllig, 305–309, no. 260, with bibliography; *Sardis* R2 (1978) 162, no. 241, fig. 420, with bibliography; *Sardis* VI.2 (1924) no. 1. This famous text must definitely be dated to 394 B.C.

18. Chapter II, *supra.*

19. IN 63.31, P 63.113: *BASOR* 174, 52, fig. 33.

20. *Sardis* VII.1 (1932) no. 102, a funerary stele.

21. *BASOR* 162, 34–36, fig. 19; Hanfmann, *Letters,* 77, figs. 48, 49. N. H. Ramage, in her unpublished "The Attic Pottery," seems to date it as early as 570–560 B.C.

22. Xanthus: *OCD,* 1140 with reference to *FHG,* Pearson, *Historians,* Chapter 3. H. Diller, 66–78.

23. Robert, "Règlement perse," 310. *Sardis* R2 (1978) 176, 177, no. 273, figs. 463, 464 (text).

24. Nannas: *Sardis* R2 (1978) 177, 178, figs. 465, 466, no. 274.

25. Matis: *Sardis* R2 (1978) no. 134, figs. 267, 268; Hanfmann-Polatkan-Robert, 45–56.

26. L. Robert and J. Robert, *Bull.* 78 (1965) 155, no. 342; Knibbe, "Religiöser Frevel," 175–182; Bammer-Fleischer-Knibbe, 95–97, no. 1631; Kawerau-Rehm, *Milet* I:3, no. 135.

27. These are the two dedications on the reused smaller columns in the pronaos of the Artemis Temple: *Sardis* VI.2 (1924) 21; Gusmani, *LW,* no. 21; newly found fragment, Greenewalt, "The Sardis Campaign of 1978" (forthcoming). The dating of these columns is still controversial, but if they do not come from an earlier building (fourth century), then they and the inscriptions must date after 280 B.C.

28. Radet, *Lydie,* 284–287; *Sardis* M2 (1972) Part II, "From Accession of Gyges to the Fall of Sardis," nos. 39–139; Buerchner-Deeters-Keil, 2161–2202.

29. Hanfmann, *Croesus,* 11, figs. 21–22; Pryce, *BMC* L:L, figs. 31–69.

30. Hanfmann, "Lydiaka," 68–72; *Sardis* M2 (1972) nos. 16–34, especially no. 31; Gusmani, *LW,* no. 21, on the contents of inscriptions.

31. Gusmani, *LW,* no. 22; Meriggi, "Der Charakter," 283–290.

32. Lydian mode: Wegner, *Musikleben,* 48, 141, 227.

33. Terpander: Athenaeus 635 D. *OCD* (1970) 1045. A seven-stringed kithara is shown on a sherd found at Smyrna, Hanfmann, "Ionia," 16, fig. 5. Terpander was supposedly inspired by Lydian musical instruments. Wegner, *Musikleben,* 48, 141, 227.

34. Schefold, *Die Griechen,* 167–168, pl. 32 a–c, fig. 7, reconstruction.

35. Autocrates: *Sardis* M2 (1972) no. 184.

36. *Sardis* R2 (1978) 47, fig. 32, no. 7.

37. Dice: *BASOR* 154, 9; Hanfmann, *Letters,* fig. 12; *Sardis* R1 (1975) 107, fig. 245, T58.5; knucklebones: Greenewalt, "Lydian Graves," 36; Lydian bricks: *Sardis* M2 (1972) no. 134.

38. *Sardis* M5 (1978) 6.

Religious Life

1. Keil, "Kulte," 239–266. For an attempt to reconstruct some Lydian divinities and myths, see Hanfmann, "Lydiaka." Other studies up to 1973 are listed by R. S. Thomas, *Sardis* (M11) *Bibliography* (forthcoming), Category 21, "Religion and Mythology."

2. For the Artemis Precinct see *Sardis* I (1922) 38–55, 61–76, 89–115, 123, 135, 145–154; *Sardis* II (1925); and *Sardis* R1 (1975) 53–73. Sculpture: *Sardis* R2 (1978) 21, 32, 82, 84, nos. 62, 72, 79, 102, 137, 237, 251, 252. Coins: *Sardis* M7 (1981), especially in the "Introduction" by A. E. M. Johnston. Gems: *Sardis* (M10) *Small Finds* (forthcoming).

3. For names of gods in Lydian see Gusmani, *LW,* 63–65 (*Artimu*); 74–75 (*Baki*); 156 (*KuFa[d]*); 160 (*Lev*—Lydian Zeus); 188–189 (*Qldan*). According to Heubeck, *Qldan* is equivalent of Mên, who is *not* an early Anatolian god. Carruba, "Lydisch" (1963) 404; Jongkees, "Gottesnamen," 355–367. Kore: see Hanfmann-Balmuth, 261, pls. 34–35; *Sardis* R2 (1978) 84, fig. 344, no. 194. *Qldans:* Gusmani, "Neue Inschriften," 131–133; festival Chrysanthina: Robert, "Fête," 51–52.

4. Essentially, the theory is in Radet's *Cybébé.* The chance survival of the Artemis Temple led early explorers to see in it the temple of Cybele mentioned by Herodotus. Butler considered the "syncretism" solution. In the pre-excavation article "Lydiaka," G. M. A. Hanfmann mistakenly defended the Artemis-Cybele theory. It still haunts the numismatists, who also are worried because not Artemis, but the Kore of Sardis appears on Roman coins as the major divinity of the city. See Fleischer, 196–199; "Supplement" 343. Price-Trell, 137, 141, figs. 240–243, and A. E. M. Johnston in *Sardis* M7 (1981). For correct

statement on relation of Artemis and Cybele, see Hanfmann-Waldbaum, "Kybele," 264–269.

5. Bammer-Fleischer-Knibbe, 95–97, no. 1631.

6. Artemis *sfardak, ibimśiś, kulumśiś:* Gusmani, *LW,* 63, no. 1.2. Koloene: Strabo 13.4.5 (626). Keil, "Kulte," 252, 262 n. 1. Hanfmann, "Lydiaka," 73–74, 85 n. 50. "To the Chitons," as a locality, L. Robert and J. Robert, *Bull.* 78 (1965) 155, no. 342. Fleischer, 200–201, interprets *theoron apostalenton hypo tes poleos epi chitonas tei Artemidi* as "after the city sent out sacred messengers (to invite people) to the feast of The Chitons for Artemis." Bammer-Fleischer-Knibbe, 95–97, no. 1631.

7. Hanfmann-Waldbaum, "Kybele," 265–266, ill.; *Sardis* R2 (1978) 58–60, figs. 78–83, no. 20.

8. *Sardis* R2 (1978) 55–56, figs. 70–71, no. 17: *Sakardas artimuλ ibśimlλ fēnčan.*

9. Hanfmann, *Croesus,* 11. Lydian girls: Aristophanes, *Nubes* 598–600; Autocrates, *Tympanistae* cited by Aelian, NA 12.9 = *Sardis* M2 (1972) nos. 184, 186. We should remember, however, that Lydians may have taken part in the Artemis cult at Ephesus long before Croesus, if they were the "aboriginal" settlers; cf. Pausanias 7.2.8; "The greater number of the inhabitants (before the Greeks came) were Lydians." In his fundamental study, Fleischer, 116–137, especially 131–132, agrees that the cult is pre-Greek and that the goddess was called "Our Lady of Ephesus," *Despoine Ephesia,* "before Artemis was ever heard of."

10. Gusmani, *LW,* 188, no. 23, limestone block found in the Artemis Precinct. On *Qldans,* see n. 50, *infra.*

11. Terracotta frieze in the Louvre: Radet, *Cybébé,* pl. 1; *Sardis* X (1926) 13–15, pl. 3, ca. 600 B.C. A figure with winged creatures (Fig. 153) may be a god or a goddess: *Sardis* M5 (1978) fig. 34, no. 4. Reconstructed plate: Greenewalt, "Wild Goat," 68–70, 84–85, pls. 10–13, seems to prefer snakes to lions, in which case the parallel would be with the snakes of the Cybele shrine. Figs. 149, 150; *Sardis* R2 (1978) 42–43, no. 6; 43–45, no. 7, figs. 16, 17, 20–28. Greenewalt dates the plate to 620–590 B.C.

12. Radet, *Cybébé.*

13. Strabo 13.4.5 (626); Keil, "Kulte," 252; Gusmani, *LW,* nos. 1–2: bilingual of 394 B.C. Hanfmann, "Lydiaka," 73–76, presented a theory that the original "Artemis" was a goddess connected with a fish-cult, a very natural connection in a sanctuary on a lake teeming with fish. Strabo mentions a *kalathoi* ("baskets") dance in her honor; but the reading and the meaning are not quite sure. In two Lydian texts, the Lydian Aramaic bilingual of 394 B.C.: Gusmani *LW,* no. 1, and the similar sepulchral inscription: ibid., no. 2, *artims ibimśiś asti muh kulumśiś* is rendered in Aramaic as "Artemis of Ephesos and

Koloe"; but *artimun ibśimnar kulumnak* in no. 2, "Artemis of Ephesos and Koloe" remains the same goddess, once in Aramaic and once in Lydian. The imprecation of *LW*, no. 1, says: "Now whoever something damages, Artemis of Ephesus and Artemis of Koloe to his court and house . . . shall bring destruction"; see *Sardis* R2 (1978) 162, no. 241, for Gusmani's translation.

14. Reported by von Olfers, 542, pl. 1: "Der Koloenische See, an dessen Ufer die Trümmer des Tempels der Artemis Koloene oder Gygaie gefunden wurden . . . gleich von Tempelruinen S. P. begegnet man den ersten kleinen Grabhügeln." His map pl. I shows the temple clearly as a rectangular structure with projection at the southeast corner of the lake. It should be due north and slightly west from the mound of Alyattes. Nothing indicating a temple has been observed by the Harvard-Cornell Expedition members.

15. *BASOR* 177, 35-36, fig. 34. For the location of Saz Köy see *Sardis* R1 (1975) fig. 2 (map). The monument is of the second century A.D. It is therefore impossible to determine how far back the cult may go. In general, "Mother of Gods" was taken to be Cybele, not Artemis. The sanctuary claimed more than local significance.

16. The later fortunes of the Artemis of Sardis and her relation with the Persian goddess Anahita are discussed in the section on religious life in Chapter VII.

17. *Sardis* M3 (1975) 28-30, A II 5, figs. 12-13 (IN 68.18; P 68.140): *kuvav* with detailed commentary; also Gusmani, "Name der Kybele," 158-161. *BASOR* 199, 22; under cupellation floor A, 600-570 B.C. *Kuvava* was named with the gods *Santaś* and *Marivda(s)* as protectress of the grave on a stele carved in imitation of a wooden door, Gusmani, *LW*, no. 4, *Sardis* I (1922) 56, ill. 49.

18. *Sardis* R2 (1978) 21, 66, figs. 105-117, nos. 27-29. Jongkees, "Gottesnamen," 355-367.

19. *Sardis* R2 (1978) 40, 41, no. 3, figs. 9, 10. Much of the vast literature on Cybele is listed in Vermaseren, *CCCA*, 3 (1977) xi-xxviii; 7 (1977) ix-xv.

20. *Sardis* R2 (1978) 45, no. 77 (530 B.C.), figs. 20, 27, 28; cf. 42, no. 6, figs. 16-19 (560 B.C.); 139, no. 193, fig. 343 (Roman); C. H. Greenewalt, "Wild Goat," 69 n. 41, collects representations of snakes associated with potnia figures. The snake appears as a symbol of immortality with Lydian Tylos-Masnes myth: Hanfmann, "Lydiaka," 69, 70. B. Trell, "Prehellenic Sanctuaries," notes that two snakes appear next to the altar of Zeus Lydios on Roman coins and compares the Sardis Cybele, Figs. 147, 149, 150. Tylos, like the Greek agricultural hero Triptolemos, rides a snake chariot on Roman coins, Hanfmann, "Lydiaka," 84 n. 42.

21. Herodotus 1.78.

22. *Sardis* R2 (1978) 45-50.

23. E.R. Dodd in his edition of Euripides, *Bacchae*, 76, thinks of a Divine Mother Cybele and a Divine Son Bakkos worshiped with dances and mountain roamings (*oreibasia*); cf. *Sardis* R2 (1978) 50, figs. 32, 35-37.

24. *Sardis* R2 (1978) 48, no. 7, figs. 44, 45, Panel M. Possibly a pine tree, symbol of Attis?

25. Herodotus 5.102 = *Sardis* M2 (1972) no. 272.

26. The fundamental study is by Laroche, 113-118; supplemented by Hanfmann-Waldbaum, "Kybele," 265, 266; also *Sardis* R2 (1978) nos. 6, 7, 19, 20, 21; literary sources: 31, nos. 12-13; images: nos. 6, 7, 9, 20, 21; and for some aspects: Henrichs, "Despoina Kybele," 435-503.

27. *Sardis* R2 (1978) 139, 140, no. 194, fig. 344; Hanfmann-Balmuth, 261-269, pls. 34, 35; Fleischer, 187, 193-201, pls. 78-83, with good illustrations of gems and coins; he believes the moon sickle to be a Roman addition.

28. On *Chrysanthina* and the Kore coins, see Robert, "Fête," 49-56 esp. 51, 52 n. 17; idem, *Rev. phil.* (1958) 29; *Sardis* M7 (1981) "Introduction." Robert says "the golden flowers" commemorated the flowers which Kore was picking when she was carried off and those given to the victors in the games. The earliest mention of *Chrysanthina* or *Koraia* is ca. A.D. 150-175. Cf. Moretti, *Inscr. Agonistiche,* 154, no. 75; *Sardis* VII.1 (1932) no. 77.

29. Coins: Hanfmann-Balmuth, 263-268, pl. 35:3-5; Fleischer, *Artemis,* 188-191, pls. 79-80; *SNG, Aulock* 8: pl. 100:3141. Cf. Robert, "Fête," 54 n. 34; A. E. M. Johnston, *Sardis* M7 (1981) "Introduction"; Price-Trell, 137-138, 141, figs. 240-243. Fleischer, 187-201, reidentifies the Kore as Artemis, arguing that she appears on coins of other cities where Artemis was worshiped.

30. *BASOR* 211, 27; *Sardis* R2 (1978) 178-179, no. 277, fig. 470 (text); and 180-181, on the base of Puteoli and Euthenia.

31. Strabo 14.1.44, cited by B. V. Head, *BMC, Lydia,* CX.

32. *Kait* in Hattic is *Halki* ("grain") in Hittite. H. G. Güterbock cites the description of a statuette of wood "of a woman seated, veiled, the grain goddess *Halki*" in the Bogazköy table to (BO 2318 plus 30 8042) and in his article on "Kumarbi," *Reallexikon des Assyriologie* (forthcoming). Hanfmann is indebted to Güterbock for his authoritative elucidation.

33. Hanfmann has considered Kore among the possible interpretations for the goddess of prosperity and the young boy who represent Sardis on the base of A.D. 30, found at Puteoli, *Sardis* R2 (1978) 181, fig. 472.

34. As proposed by Fleischer, 198–199. A Sardian coin (A.D. 218–222) shows the temple with the "Kore" image and the three temples of the Imperial cult, one of which was the Artemis temple, where the colossal statues of Antonius Pius and Faustina were found (*Sardis* R2 [1978] nos. 79, 251). B. Burrell, *Neokoroi* (unpublished), first saw that the coin rules out the equation of Artemis and Kore. Illustrated in Price-Trell, 136, fig. 242.

35. Apollonius of Tyana, in Philostratus, "City of Demeter," *VA*, 75. *Sardis* M2 (1972) no. 217: "One would think your city belonged to the Furies and not to Demeter." Cf. Penella, 308.

36. *BASOR* 177, 13, fig. 13; *Sardis* M3 (1975) 38–39, A III 2, figs. 32–33; *kâλ:labλ: vr it[takm.* Cf. Gusmani, *LW*, 160, nos. 3, 50. *Levs* will punish the violator in the relief of the funerary stele dated 329 B.C. *Sardis* R2 (1978) 157–158, no. 234, fig. 404, from vicinity of Tire of the Alexander era.

37. *Sardis* M7 (1981) no. 216, pl. 10. Trell, "Prehellenic Sanctuaries," 119, pl. 37:40; 38:41. Cf. Kraft, pl. 37:59b; 51:5. A. E. M. Johnston, *Sardis* M7 (1981) Greek, nos. 231–234. For the Hellenistic coins, see Metraux, 158–159, pl. 36:8, who conjectures that a Hellenistic statue of Zeus Lydios was made before 225 B.C.

38. Eumelus fragment 18, *EGF* (Kimbel), Joannes Laurentius Lydus, *De mensibus* 4.71 = *Sardis* M2 (1972) no. 14; A. B. Cook, *Zeus*, 2:2, 957.

39. *Sardis* R2 (1978) 147, figs. 373–375, no. 213; Hanfmann, *Croesus*, 57–58, fig. 120.

40. Hittite and Semitic storm gods: Gusmani, *LW*, nos. 3, 4–5, 5–6; *Sardis* R2 (1978) 157–158, fig. 404, no. 234.

41. Fig. 166. See Chapter VI, *infra*.

42. See Chapter VII, *infra*. Arrian, *Anab.* 1.17, 3.

43. Robert, "Règlement perse," 314–321; *Sardis* R2 (1978) 128, 129, no. 161, figs. 308, 309, mentioning the *therapeutai* of Zeus.

44. He first appears on coins of ca. 226–223 B.C.; Metraux, 158, 159. Two Antonine marble heads may be from statues of Zeus Lydios. See *Sardis* R2 (1978) 106, nos. 107, 108, figs. 231–233. Zeus Lydios on coins: Seyrig, "Monnaies Hellenistiques" (1963) 35.

45. Gusmani, *LW*, no. 29; *Sardis* R2 (1978) 177, 178. no. 274, figs. 465, 466.

46. Two graffiti starting *BA* might have belonged to names like *Bakivas, Bakivalis. Sardis* M3 (1975) 20, 36, no. A II 17, figs. 26, 29.

47. Gusmani, *LW*, 190 (*santo*), 201 (*santa*), no. 4 a 3. *Santaś* was named as protecting avenging god with *Kuvava* and *Marivda*. For equation with Santas see H. Bossert, *Santaś und Kupapa*. For Sandon see H. Goldman, "Sandon," 164–174. Note also the name of the wise Lydian Sandanis: Herodotus 1.71 = *Sardis* M2 (1972) no. 110. The passage in Joannes Lydus, *De magistratibus* 3.64, deals with *Sandyx*—a flesh-colored garment, and reports a tradition from Varro that Sandon-Herakles was a son of Omphale. For the confused Greek and Roman tradition, cf. *MythLex* 4 (1915) 318–333, *s.v. Sandaś*. On Herakles and Omphale on Roman coins, see Trell, "Prehellenic Sanctuaries," 119–120, pl. 38:42–46. For cremation as royal ritual, see n. 59, *infra*.

48. Heubeck, *Lydiaka*, 16. Mên is known at Sardis from Roman inscriptions and late Hellenistic reliefs. Robert, *NIS*, 31–33, pl. 3, gives a survey of material from Sardis starting from the reused inscription to Mên Axiottenos. He appears on coins of Sardis from Nero on. The late Hellenistic relief of Mên as horseman in Oxford is perhaps the earliest evidence, *Sardis* VII.1 (1932) no. 17, line 17; *Sardis* R2 (1978) 166, fig. 436, no. 253; E. Lane, *CMRDM* 1 (1971) no. 78 (horseman), no. 79 (Menogeion), no. 80; 2 (1975) 41–46, pls. 17–18, coins with Mên Askaenos; 3 (1976) 17, 43, 113: "There is no real evidence for seeing Mên as an indigenous Anatolian divinity. The principal element seems to be Persian." For Mên, Lord of Axiotta, see P. Herrmann, "Mên, Herr von Axiotta," 415–423.

49. For the moon attributes of Kore, cf. n. 27, *supra*. The moon sickle on an archaic ivory head is not clearly local Lydian. Cf. Akurgal, *Kunst Anat.*, 159, pl. 72. Wilamowitz-Mollendorff, "Apollon," 575. H. Cahn, "Löwen," 29 n. 58, with literature.

50. *Pldans, Qldans* with *Artimuλ* Gusmani, *LW*, 188, no. 23, line 1. The Mitratastas inscription comes from the Artemis sanctuary of the Persian era. For Apollo Pleurenos and his mystai, see *BASOR* 177, 36, from Kemerdamlar, IN 64.4.

51. H. Cahn, "Löwen," 28–31. Cf. the story of the lion which a mistress bore to King Meles and which he carried around the Acropolis wall: Herodotus 1.84 = *Sardis* M2 (1972) no. 116.

52. *Sardis* M5 (1978) 16–17, fig. 34, no. 4; see n. 11, *supra*.

53. Greenewalt, "Wild goat," 68–69, 84–85, pls. 10–13, no. 16.

54. Greenewalt, *Dinners*, 45–52; O. Masson, *Hipponax*, 106, a "dieu-loup."

55. *Sardis* R2 (1978) 52–53, figs. 58–60, no. 9.

56. Charon of Lampsacus in Photios, *Biblioteca, s.v. Kybelos*. Cf. Hanfmann, "Lydiaka," 81 n. 4.

57. Dioscurides, in *Sardis* M2 (1972) no. 13. Gusmani, *LW*, 69, nos. 9:1, *atelis* ("son of Ates") and 30.2, *atal* on the archaic terracotta boat in Princeton are personal names, but the name *Atys* is undoubtedly very old in Lydia. The legend of Zeus and the boar: Pausanias 7.17.9. For recent excavations at Pessinus by P. Lambrechts, see Akurgal, *Civilizations*, 277–278, 388.

58. *Sardis* VII.1 (1932) no. 17.6 (Fountain In-

scription, ca A.D. 200). *Sardis* R2 (1978) nos. 159 (as tree?), 164, 224. M. J. Vermaseren's vast, illustrated corpus of monuments of Cybele and Attis: *CCCA* vols. 3 (1977); 7 (1977) promises a very full coverage.

59. Cremation of kings may be evidenced for Alyattes and Croesus; see Figs. 101, 126.

60. Hanfmann, "Lydiaka," 68–72; L. Robert, "Tribu," 155–158. For possible appearance of Tylos in Puteoli base of A.D. 30, see *Sardis* R2 (1978) 180, 181, fig. 472.

61. Wilamowitz-Mollendorff, *Herakles,* 318, thought of Creophylus of Samos, an early epic Greek poet, as inventor of the story; but Omphale is clearly a mixture of a native (early) goddess and a possibly historical queen. Hanfmann, "Lydiaka," 72, 84 n. 44. For an interesting study of the iconographic reading given the figures of Herakles and Omphale in a painting by Rubens, see Huemer, 562–574.

62. Tantalus: the sources are collected in (Scheuer) *MythLex* 5 (1924) 75–85. It is noteworthy that a Lydian tradition of Xanthus, Nicolas of Damascus, makes Tmolus the father and Daskylos one of the sons of Tantalus. Pelops: (Bloch) *MythLex* 3:2 (1909) 1866–1875; Pindar, *Olympia* 1; Apollodorus, *Bibliotheca* 3.2. For Pelops and his (Late Bronze Age) grave at Olympia see Drees, *Olympia,* 17, 18, 27–31, 77, 78. Already H. R. Hall, "Mursil and Myrtilos," 19–22, called attention to the resemblance of Myrsilos with the Hittite name Mursilis (II, 1334–1306); Barnett, "Oriental," 215, 216.

63. The Hittites not only had horses but also had treatises on horsemanship. A "horse-master" (charioteer) of the Hittite kings, "a man of some importance," had ridden with both the Hittite king and a prince of the Achaeans. He served as messenger to the king of Ahhiyawa. Cf. O. Gurney, *The Hittites,* 105; Barnett, "Oriental," 215, 216.

64. Tacitus, *Ann.* 4.5 = *Sardis* M2 (1972) no. 221. Coins: Head, *BMC, Lydia,* nos. 132, 133. Tribe Pelopis: IN 62.41, a Hellenistic urn, before 100 B.C. (Fig. 170) (to be published by L. Robert).

65. *Sardis* R2 (1978) 49, fig. 48, panel P.

66. As pointed out in *Sardis* R2 (1978) 14, a very few art objects may derive from "Late Hittite" and Phoenician types. Bases: Greenewalt, "Wild Goat," 55–69, esp. 61–65, pls. 1–18; Greenewalt, "Lydian Graves," 119, 120, 126, 129, 135, 136, pls. 4, 5, 10:3 (fishes, birds, hawk); Greenewalt, "Elements," 39–41, figs. 7, 8 (wild goats, boar). Sculpture: *Sardis* R2 (1978) 17, 18, 20–23 (lions); nos. 22–44, figs. 86–147 (animals and monsters). Terracotta: *Sardis* M5 (1978) nos. 9-30. Metal: *Sardis* (M8) *Metalwork* (forthcoming). See also R. S. Thomas, *Sardis* (M10) *Small Finds* (forthcoming). It is instructive to compare the iconography of the Persian period in the

Achaemenid style seals: see Boardman, "Pyramidal Seals," 26–37, figs. 6–10, pls. 1–2. His orientalizing *potniai,* sirens, lions, birds of prey, griffins, and winged horses may be relevant to the Lydian period.

67. Kleiner, *Ruinen,* 127, figs. 92–93: Gabelmann, 119, no. 114; cf. also the Lion Tomb, Xanthos: Pryce 1, 118–122, figs. 176–177, pl. 18; Strocka, "Löwen," 511–512.

68. The boar is a damager of fields and the most dangerous attacker in hunting. Real life experience (cf. Croesus' son named Atys and his boar hunt, Herodotus 1.34–44) is mythologized in the legends of Attis (*supra*) and Adonis. Barnett, "Oriental," 221–222, pl. 19:1, suggests that the Attis boar hunt may be represented in the Hittite sculptures of Alaca Hüyük (early fourteenth century B.C.). Lydian boars: Greenewalt, "Elements," 40–41, pls. 16:7–8, 18:14; *Sardis* M5 (1978) 18–19, figs. 43–44, no. 12, terracotta. A. Ramage cites the seal ring, *Sardis* XIII (1925) no. 98; Boardman, "Pyramidal Seals," pl. 8.195.

69. Hawks, eagles: *Sardis* R2 (1978) 14, 16–17, and the discussions, nos. 160–177, 238, figs. 413–415. Greenewalt, "Lydian Graves," 135–136, no. 23, pl. 10:3. For the links with Cybele and Artemis see Barnett, "Ivories," 1–25, pls. 1–13; von Gall, 588.

70. *Sardis* R2 (1978) 160, figs. 413–415, no. 238; *Sardis* (M8) *Metalwork* (forthcoming).

71. Gyges: G. Neumann, *Untersuchungen,* 69–71. Dionysius of Halicarnassus, *Antiquitates Romanae* 2.16. Mermnos: Aelian, *NA* 12.4.

72. Sphinxes: *Sardis* R1 (1975) fig. 307; *Sardis* R2 (1978) nos. 41, 42, 239, figs. 142–145, 415–418. Cf. *Sardis* M5 (1978) no. 27, figs. 60–61; Kyrieleis, 138. Dessenne, 13–23, 124–127.

73. *Sardis* R2 (1978) 71–72, figs. 139–141, no. 40, ca. 530–500 B.C.

74. The following items are treated by R. S. Thomas in *Sardis* (M10) *Small Finds* (forthcoming): Protogeometric seal, scarabs; *BASOR* 186, 36, fig. 15; 182, 14; *TürkArkDerg* 14:1–2 (1965) 152, fig. 5 and seal 63.1, *BASOR* 182, 13, fig. 7; 170, 25, fig. 21. Possible amulets are also a rock crystal lion: *BASOR* 177, 7, fig. 7; ivory foot: *BASOR* 166, 8. For finger rings, seals, and a rattle, see *Sardis* XIII (1925) pls. 7–11 and Boardman, "Pyramidal Seals," 19–45, a group, 38, "from early years of Persian administration to late fifth century."

75. Processions and dances on the Cybele monument, Figs. 150–152. Cf. the processions on the Croesus columns in Ephesus, Hanfmann, *Croesus,* 12–13. Dances at Ephesus: *Sardis* M2 (1972) no. 184. Anatolian rituals may be hidden in the perambulation of a fortress wall with a divine lion image by King Meles, *Sardis* M2 (1972) no. 116, and in

Croesus' strange boiling together of a ram and a tortoise, Herodotus 1.47–48. The account of Croesus by Herodotus is full of omens, sacrifices and purifications, but they would require a special study.

76. Bammer, *Artemision,* 3 n. 11, with references; Akurgal, *Civilizations,* 178, 179, fig. 61.

77. Figs. 42, 49, 94, 95, "alternating layers of ash and earth, charred bone and horn(?) at bottom." We may recall that the Persians seem to have objected to burnt offerings for Sabazius in the regulation of 367 B.C. L. Robert, "Règlement perse," 324–325. For the animal offerings at the late Classical Artemis Altar at Ephesus, see Bammer-Brein-Wolff, "Tieropfer," 107–115, with goats-sheep (62.5%) and oxen (29%) accounting for virtually all animal sacrifices.

78. "Rhea (Cybele) was also called Ma and a bull was sacrificed to her among the Lydians," Stephanus Byz. *s.v. Mastaura;* Hanfmann, "Lydiaka," 82 n. 11; however, the inscription of 367 B.C. seems to treat the mysteries of Ma as a divinity different from Cybele; Robert, "Règlement perse," 322–323, emphasizes that her presence may be due to Persian "converts." Bull representations: *Sardis* X (1926) 9, 16, 17, 21, pl. II, IV; *Sardis* M5 (1978) no. 13; cf. Hanfmann, "Lydiaka."

79. Greenewalt, *Dinners,* 30.

80. The itinerant priests of Magna Mater must have become a familiar sight by the early Hellenistic period. Alexander of Aetolia (third century B.C.) says that had Alcman been raised in seventh century Sardis he would have become a kernos-bearing priest, or a eunuch clad in gold beating the chattering kettledrums (of Cybele) = *Sardis* M2 (1972) no. 39.

81. Robert, "Règlement perse," 322–325; *Sardis* R2 (1978) 177, no. 273; Apollo Pleurenos, *BASOR* 177, 36.

Cultural Perspectives

1. For some of the views on Lydian culture, see the discussion of the progress of research at the beginning of this chapter. Recent assessment within the framework of the developments of Asia Minor: Hanfmann, *Croesus,* 1–14, 96; Hanfmann, "Lydian Relations," 31; Greenewalt, "Elements," 37–45; and for the political-constitutional aspect: Hammond-Bartson, 144–147.

2. For the methodical problem see C. B. Moore, ed., *Complex Societies.* For a comprehensive discussion of the concept of culture see Kroeber's classic survey, Kroeber-Kluckhohn, *Culture.*

3. Xenophanes, F 13 in Diehl 1³; cf. *Sardis* M2 (1972) nos. 127, 130.

4. Finkel, *Dynamics,* 36, 39, 40, 48, 50, 69, 86,

and especially 123–216. The study encompasses 33 sites and 49 populations. For Sardis, he used principally the published Roman and Byzantine material. He noted a slight heterogeneity in Sardian statistics but dismissed it as insignificant. In his "superpopulation" Group 1, he includes Troy, Sardis, Ephesus, Bodrum (Halicarnassus), Karataş, (Lycian), and Lapethos (Cyprus). The case against the Eurasian steppes origin is not very strongly supported as it rests on only one South Russian site of ca. 1200 B.C.

5. By "direct archaeological evidence" we mean that no written documents of the second millennium B.C. in Lydian or a kindred earlier language have been found in the Sardis area. The much discussed inscriptions of Kara Bel warrior reliefs appear to be Hittite rather than Luvian. Cf. Akurgal, *Kunst der Hethiter,* 46–47, 83, versus Huxley, *Achaeans and Hittites,* 40–42. See also Bittel, "Karabel," 188. Mellaart, "Western Anatolia," I, 493–526.

6. Barnett, "Oriental," 217; Akurgal, *Civilizations,* 7.

7. Troy: Naumann, 341–345; Blegen, *Troy.* Beycesultan: S. Lloyd and J. Mellaart, *Beycesultan* I; S. Lloyd, *Beycesultan* II; Hanfmann, *Croesus,* 4, with literature, n. 8, "Hittite archives imply royal palaces at Ephesus and Miletus. Eighth century Gordion seems to continue the pattern." The only imposing defensive installations of the Late Bronze Age in Western Anatolia have been found at coastal sites where actual Mycenaean-Aegean presence is likely: Miletus, Teos, and Troy. It is only in the case of Gordion that "Late" Hittite influence is probable.

8. This triple division underlies the discussion of Western Asia Minor in Hanfmann, *Croesus,* 1, 96; for Lydian culture, see ibid., 2–14.

9. Pre-Indo-European cultures: Hanfmann, *Croesus,* 3; A. Ramage, *Sardis* M5 (1978) 1–10. The localism of the Anatolian religion has been well noted by L. Robert, *NIS,* 35, 36, pl. 3:1; see also Hanfmann, *Croesus,* 57, 58.

10. Seal: *Sardis* XIII (1925) 45, no. 120, pl. 11. The identification as Neo-Babylonian was made by E. Porada (by letter).

11. See Hanfmann, "Lydian Relations," 31, for the methodical distinction between "extensive, popular," and "high level sporadic" cultural contact.

12. Meles, Assurbanipal: *Sardis* M2 (1972) nos. 31, 292, 294. For the gold riches of Iran in the tenth to eighth century see Porada, *Iran,* 90–103.

13. L. Oppenheim, 172–193.

14. On the relations to Phrygia, see Muscarella, "Phrygian or Lydian?" 49–63; Greenewalt, "Lydian Graves," 130–132; Hanfmann, "On Lydian Sardis," 101–107; Heubeck, "Lydische Schrift," 55–66.

15. Hanfmann, "Lydian Relations," 26, 28.

16. J. S. Schaeffer, *Sardis* (R5) *Pottery* (forthcoming).

17. See the discussion of "Production and Trade" in this chapter, *supra.*

18. Coulton, *Architects,* 16, 45–46, 141–144; for a good technical explanation, see Holloway, "Architect and Engineer," 281–290. Hanfmann, *Croesus,* 11, 12. Both the problems and preliminary solutions of quarrying, transporting, and lifting heavy loads (Egyptian colossi; Assyrian lamassu) had been developed in the Near East and Egypt; we have indications that Theodorus and Rhoecus got their knowledge directly from Egypt.

19. Preliminary assessment: Hanfmann, "Lydian Relations," 25–31, and *Sardis* R2 (1978) 14–18; Greenewalt, "Elements," 37–45.

20. Pindar, *Pythian Odes* 1.93 = *Sardis* M2 (1972) no. 101.

VI. The Persian Period

The City Under the Persians

1. A. T. Olmstead, *Persian Empire,* 41, 59, 110, and "Map of Satrapies." Buerchner-Deeters-Keil, 2171–2179. For the relations of Sardis to Persia, see also Hanfmann, "Lydian Relations," 25–35, pls. 7, 10. J. M. Balcer and M. Weiskopf kindly responded to requests for information on satraps of Sardis. Balcer's "By The Bitter Sea: The Landed Gentry of Western Anatolia, c. 700–411," in preparation, and Weiskopf's forthcoming thesis will greatly contribute to the neglected subject of the satrapies of Asia Minor under the Achaemenids.

2. Herodotus 1.80 = *Sardis* M2 (1972) no. 115.

3. Xenophon, *Cyropaedia* 7.4.12 = *Sardis* M2 (1972) no. 144.

4. Herodotus 1.154–157.

5. Herodotus 5.99–102 = *Sardis* M2 (1972) nos. 150, 272, 282.

6. Herodotus 7.32 = *Sardis* M2 (1972) no. 157.

7. Herodotus 8.117 = *Sardis* M2 (1972) no. 158.

8. Xenophon, *Hellenica* 3.4.21 = *Sardis* M2 (1972) no. 178. J. K. Anderson, "The Battle of Sardis in 395 B.C.," *CSCA* 7 (1975) 27–53.

9. Arrian, *Anabasis* 1.17.3–6 = *Sardis* M2 (1972) no. 235.

10. Herodotus 5.101 = *Sardis* M2 (1972) no. 282; M5 (1978) 9–10.

11. Herodotus 5.101.

12. Herodotus 5.102 = *Sardis* M2 (1972) no. 272.

13. Stronach, *Pasargadae,* 110.

14. De Francovich, "Problems," 207–208.

15. Xenophon, *Oeconomicus* 4.20ff = *Sardis* M2 (1972) no. 289.

16. Xenophon, *Agesilaus,* 30. Sardis M2 (1972) nos. 171–178.

17. Arrian, *Anabasis* 1.17.3–6 = *Sardis* M2 (1972) no. 235.

18. For PN, see *BASOR* 162, 26.

19. *Sardis* (M8) *Metalwork* (forthcoming).

20. For PN, see *BASOR* 162, 26; for HoB: 162, 9; 174, 5; and for PC: 162, 9.

21. *BASOR* 162, 12; 166, 22, fig. 21. A. Ramage, Chapter III, *supra,* under "Pactolus North," suggests that the apsidal buildings were built before 547 B.C.

22. *BASOR* 177, 4.

23. *Sardis* (R5) *Pottery* (forthcoming): "Lydian," "Attic." See also *BASOR* 166, 8 (P 61.263:3624); 170, 11, fig. 10; 174, 12.

24. *BASOR* 174, 12.

25. *BASOR* 170, 11, fig. 9. *Sardis* (M8) *Metalwork* (forthcoming) no. 87.

26. Chapter III, *supra,* under "House of Bronzes/Lydian Market." *BASOR* 166, 8.

27. *Sardis* M7 (1981) no. 382; *BASOR* 170, 11.

28. Chapter III, *supra,* under "House of Bronzes/Lydian Market."

29. *Sardis* M5 (1928) 5.

30. Ibid., 30–31, 35, 39. A star and scroll sima; no. 43, fig. 86; *BASOR* 162, 21, fig. 8, is dated early in the Persian period (540 B.C.) by A. Ramage, after 499 B.C. by G. M. A. Hanfmann in the first (1960) report.

31. A. Ramage, FR 1970; Pactolus North, *Sardis* (R9) *Mosaics and Wall Painting* (forthcoming).

32. Hanfmann, *Croesus,* 16.

33. Herodotus 6.42; Welles, *Royal Correspondence,* 91, no. 18, ll. 27–28.

34. Kraay, *Archaic Greek Coins,* 32. Price-Waggoner, 97.

35. Kraay, *Archaic Greek Coins,* 32.

36. Ibid.

37. Ibid., 31.

38. Ibid.

39. Olmstead, *Persian Empire,* 189, 191; for lack of coinage in empire and attendant problems, 298.

40. Kraay, *Archaic Greek Coins,* 32.

41. Ibid., 271.

42. Ibid., 278.

43. See Chapter III, *supra,* under "Peripheral Sectors."

44. Nylander, *Ionians,* 93, 97; Hanfmann, *Croesus,* 14–15, figs. 37–38; Stronach, *Pasargadae,* 20.

45. Hanfmann, "Pediment," 295–296.

46. Coupel-Demargme, *Xanthos III,* 157, "autour de 400."

47. Borchhardt, *Limyra,* 22.

48. *Sardis* R2 (1978) no. 18, figs. 72–74.

49. For the "Nereid Monument" at Xanthos, see n. 46, *supra.* For the Heroon at Limyra, see Borchhardt, *Limyra,* 22.

50. Stronach, *Pasargadae,* 20; Nylander, *Ionians,* 84–85.

51. Darius, Susa fragment: *Sardis* M2 (1972) 303.

52. Olmstead, *Persian Empire,* 115.

53. Arrian, *Anabasis* 1.17.3ff. = *Sardis* M2 (1972) 235.

54. Strabo 13.4, 5.625.

55. Foss, "Explorations," 47.

The Satrapal Court

1. Athenaeus 15.690b–d = *Sardis* M2 (1972) no. 131.

2. Athenaeus 12.515d–f = *Sardis* M2 (1972) no. 130.

3. Ibid.

4. Keil identified eleven satraps who had ruled Lydia in his 1927 list, Buerchner-Deeters-Keil, 2175–2178: Oroites 547–?, Artaphernes 511–492, Mardonios 494–491, Artaphernes 491, Pissuthnes 450–415, Tissaphernes 415–407, Kyros 407, Tithraustes 395–394, Tiribazos 394–392, Autophradates 392–388, Tiribazos 388–380, Autophradates 380–350, Rhosakes 350–?, and Spithridates 334. For the addition of Droaphernes to the list see n. 10, *infra.*

5. Olmstead, *Persian Empire,* 152, 156.

6. Ibid., 358–363.

7. Ibid., 110.

8. *Sardis* M2 (1972) no. 289.

9. *AASOR* 43, 61.

10. Robert, "Règlement perse," 312. M. Weiskopf (by letters of May 11 and June 11, 1981) points out that *hyparchos* may designate an official lower than a satrap; and that Artaxerxes I (ruled 464–426/5 B.C.) also had a thirty-ninth regnal year. Because Autophradates is conjectured to have been satrap of Sparda in 367 B.C., Weiskopf proposes 427–426 B.C. as the date of the Droaphernes document, if Droaphernes was a satrap.

11. *AASOR* 43, 63.

12. Ibid., 61. M. Weiskopf by letter (n. 3, *supra*) suggests that Artaxerxes I and 427–426 B.C. are a possible alternative.

13. Boyce, 456.

14. Ibid.

15. *BASOR* 191, 11–12. For fire altars, see Boyce, 456.

16. For a representation of a fire altar, see Akurgal, *Kunst Anat.,* 173, pl. 120.

17. Pausanias 5.27.5 = *Sardis* M2 (1972) no. 273. He mentions Hypaipa, neighbor of Sardis and Hierokaisareia, in this context.

18. IN 73.5 = NoEx 73.25, *BASOR* 215, 52; for IN 64.58, see *BASOR* 177, 19.

19. Inscriptions: *Sardis* VII.1 (1932) nos. 47, 48; temple of Zeus Polieus: *Sardis* I (1922) 114, 115, 124.

20. Robert, "Règlement perse," 321. *Sardis* R2 (1978) 84, 104 and no. 273.

21. Seyrig, 36–38, pl. 3:6. Kleiner-Noë, 83–85, pl. 31:19b. Price-Trell, 139, figs. 244, 245.

22. *Sardis* XIII (1925) 13, pl. 1, no. 8.

23. Robert, "Règlement perse," 322. Sokolowski, "Enpyra," 65–69.

24. *AASOR* 43, 61.

25. Ibid.

26. Gusmani, "Iranica," 3, 7–8; *LW,* 23–24.

27. Boardman, "Pyramidal Seals," 20–21, 28, 37–39.

28. Ibid., 39, no. 1, 38; Gusmani, "Iranica," 1–8.

29. Gusmani, *LW,* 18, 250–251, 264, nos. 1, 2, 41; *Sardis* M3 (1975) 7, cf. 49, 240, 242 (figs. 157, 419, 421).

30. Hanfmann, *Croesus,* 19.

31. *Sardis* VI.1 (1916) 21–38; Gusmani, *LW,* 1.

32. Hanfmann, *Croesus,* 15.

33. *Sardis* XIII (1925) pl. I, 1–11.

34. Ibid., pl. II, 1–13; pl. III, 1–14; pl. IX, 1–8; pl. V, 1–7.

35. Oliver, 118–120.

36. Mellink, "Archaeology 1967," 172, pl. 59.

37. Hanfmann-Waldbaum, "New Excavations," 316.

38. *Sardis* (M8) *Metalwork* (forthcoming), "Introduction." For the ibex as a Persian motif, see Amandry, "Un motif Scythe en Iran et en Grece," 149–160.

39. For red-figure ware, see *Sardis* (R5) *Pottery* (forthcoming): *Attic; BASOR* 170, 11, fig. 10 (crater).

40. Olmstead, *Persian Empire,* 70.

41. Heracleides Cumanus, *Persica* 1 fr. 1.

42. Lydus, *De magistratibus* 3.64, from an earlier source, Leisander, poet of Laranda in Lycaonia, *RE* 19.1 (1937) 144–146.

43. Greenewalt-Majewski, "Lydian Textiles," 136.

44. Aristophanes, *Acharnenses* 122; *Pax.* 1174 and scholion.

45. Plato Comicus, frag. 208 (ed. Kock) apud Athenaeus 2.48A–B.

46. Greenewalt-Majewski, "Lydian Textiles," 138–140, figs. 7–10. Cf. Nayir, 124, fig. 29.

47. Greenewalt, "Exhibitionist," 38–40. See the descriptions of Persian garments in Olmstead, *Persian Empire,* 238–239.

48. *Sardis* R2 (1978) no. 46, figs. 150–151.

49. Ibid., 25; *Sardis* XIII (1925) 12, 14, nos. 3, 12. Hanfmann, "Pediment," 300–301.

50. *Sardis* R2 (1978) 27, no. 233, fig. 403.

51. Hanfmann, "Stelai," 18–20, no. 71, figs. 40–41.

52. S 69.14:8047; Istanbul, Archaeological Museum 4030 (*Sardis* VI.2 [1924] no. 7); Stockholm, Nationalmuseum SK936 (*Sardis* R2 [1978] no. 234; not illustrated).

53. Dentzer, "Banquet," 215–231.

54. Hanfmann-Erhart, "Mausoleum," 82–90.

55. Dentzer, "Reliefs en Banquet," 221; Borchardt, "Epichorische gräko-persische Reliefs"; Hanfmann-Erhart, "Mausoleum," 82–90; Hanfmann, "Pediment," 295–296.

56. Hanfmann, "Pediment," 299.

57. *Sardis* R2 (1978) no. 234, fig. 404.

58. Ibid., no. 18, figs. 72–74. Hanfmann-Erhart, "Mausoleum," 82–90, figs. 1, 4–8.

The Lydian Survivals and the Greek Impact

1. *Sardis* VI.1 (1925) 23–28; Gusmani, *LW,* 18–19; *Sardis* M3 (1975) 1, 3, 24, 26, 30–33, 36, 39, 75.

2. *Sardis* VI.1 (1925) 23–28; Gusmani, *LW,* no. 1.

3. The typical amphora in the "Tomb of the Lintel" is as late as 175 B.C. and is still visibly derived from Lydian antecedents, *BASOR* 157, 18; to be published by A. Oliver, *Sardis* (R5) *Pottery* (forthcoming): "Hellenistic."

4. *BASOR* 154, 30. Cf. Figs. 194, 195.

5. *BASOR* 166, 8–9; 170, 10–11; 174, 8; 177, 4, 6; 186, 33; 203, 8.

6. Greenewalt, "Dinners," 11–19.

7. *BASOR* 170, 11; observation of J. E. Bickermann.

8. Ibid., 52–55.

9. Ibid., 28.

10. Ibid., 29–30.

11. *Sardis* M5 (1978) 5.

12. *Sardis* M2 (1972) nos. 43–48, 62–63, 69–72; Pedley, 47–48, 51–52, 80.

13. *Sardis* M2 (1972) nos. 41, 103; Pedley, 46, 87–88, 130.

14. *Sardis* R2 (1978) 29, no. 3; see Hanfmann, "Lydian Relations," for Persian and Greek elements in the Lydian culture.

15. Greenewalt, "Wild Goat Style," 55–89, and "Ephesian Ware," 91–122.

16. Greenewalt, "Fikellura," 153–180.

17. See Chapter III, *supra,* under "The Acropolis."

18. *Sardis* (R5) *Pottery* (forthcoming): "Attic."

19. The "poor glaze" begins not later than 458–400 B.C., but continues through the Hellenistic Age; *Sardis* R1 (1975) 100; *BASOR* 154, 30.

20. Many more models come from the Aeolic and Ionian cities.

21. PN: *BASOR* 182, 22–25.

22. LA: *Sardis* R1 (1975) 100.

23. *Sardis* R2 (1978) 21–22.

24. Hanfmann, "Pediment," 293; *Sardis* R2 (1978) no. 18, figs. 72–74.

25. *Sardis* R2 (1978) 30, no. 11.

26. Ibid., no. 8, figs. 51–54.

27. Ibid., no. 40, figs. 139–141; no. 41, figs. 142, 143.

28. Ibid., no. 9, figs. 58–60; no. 19, figs. 75–77; no. 20, figs. 78–83.

29. Ibid., 25; Hanfmann, "Stelai," 38–39, 43.

30. *Sardis* R2 (1978) 24.

31. Ibid.

32. Ibid., no. 45, figs. 148, 149.

33. Ibid., no. 19, figs. 75–77.

34. Ibid., no. 233, fig. 403.

35. Ibid., 27, no. 20, figs. 78–83.

36. Ibid., 22, no. 38–39, figs. 135–138.

Conclusion

1. Aeschylus, *Persae* 41–47 = *Sardis* M2 (1972) no. 185.

2. Hanfmann, "Lydian Relations," 25–35.

3. Olmstead, *Persian Empire,* 227–228, 234–236, 303–304, 373–374, 402–404, 437–441.

4. Olmstead, *Persian Empire,* 110–113.

VII. The Hellenistic Period

Previous Research and the Harvard-Cornell Excavations

1. *Sardis* I (1922); II:1 (1925). Cf. *Sardis* R1 (1975) 53–55.

2. *Sardis* VII:1 (1932) and Robert's important review *RA* 6 (1936) 233–246.

3. *Sardis* XI:1 (1916) iv–vi, the so-called Basis Hoard and Pot Hoard. The latter should not be confused with the Lydian "Pot of Gold Hoard" found in 1922 (see Chapter V, *supra,* under "Production and Trade." For the exact date of the Basis Hoard (220–215 or 190–188 B.C.), see Newell-Mørkholm, *WSM* (1977: after original edition of 1938) 187, no. 154. Noe, *Hoards* (1937) no. 925. Franke, "Chronologie,"

197-208, especially 205. Seyrig, "Monnaies Hellénistiques" (1963) 23-24. *Sardis* R1 (1975) 179-180 n. 22. Few would agree with Bell, *Sardis* XI (1916) v, that the Pot Hoard "found in connection with a graveyard of the Byzantine period" though "not in a grave" (see *Sardis* M4 (1976) 48 n. 124 for the graveyard) was a medieval collection. For the discussion of the mint of Sardis see Newell-Mørkholm, *WSM* (1977) 242-271; Thompson, "Lysimachus," 165-173; Mørkholm, "Mint of Sardes," 6-20; all kindly pointed out by A. Houghton III.

4. Sculptures still extant are included in *Sardis* R2 (1978); see 2-4, for summary of present state. See Figs. 174-176, 183.

5. See *Sardis* I (1922) viii-x: "the later pottery has perished"; "lamps . . . completely destroyed"; "bronze mirrors, stone, ivory, and all the glass apparently perished." For final state see *Sardis* R1 (1975) 2-3. Some material from the tombs was illustrated: see *Sardis* I (1922) 79, Tomb 43, ills. 75 B (secondary burial), 76 (Anadyomene terracotta); 121, ills. 127 (relief bowls and jar), 128.

6. For an earlier summary see *Sardis* R1 (1975) 29-30.

7. Ephesus: relocation of city by Lysimachus, "Die Lysimachische Stadt" in Keil, 20-22; Akurgal, *Civilizations,* 143. Recent plans, views, commentaries: Oberleitner, *Funde aus Ephesos* (1978) 11; plans 14, 15.

8. Cf. the location of MMS, the Lydian city wall (?), discovered in 1976-1979, at E116.8-E138.5 (Fig. 132), Greenewalt, "Twentieth Campaign," 106. *BASOR* 233, 21-26.

9. *BASOR* 166, 7-9; 170, 10-11, fig. 7; 174, 16, fig. 2 ("fallen debris marked the destruction of Building C in Hellenistic times").

10. A coin of Antiochus I (293-261 B.C.) and a stamp handle of Hellanicus (ca. 250 B.C.) make any date in the second half of the third century possible for Building "C" and "Industrial Circle." Rubble from 213 B.C.: *BASOR* 182, 15. A floor above the Lydian Building F (Fig. 39; *Sardis* M5 (1978) fig. 4), at ca. *100, W5-10/S109-115, excavated by Hanfmann in 1963, yielded the spectacular Hellenistic relief sherd with helmet and dolphins, P 63.223 (IH 138), and other relief ware sherds of the second century B.C.

11. Cemetery: *BASOR* 157, 28, fig. 9; chamber tombs *j, k, n;* similar tombs found in 1953 reached as far as ca. W230. "Hellenistic Steps": *BASOR* 174, 47-50, fig. 30, and 182, 40-42. Similar in construction to Hellenistic Steps, CP in Sector WWB, "not enough was freed in deeper levels to determine whether it antedated the structures aligned on the Roman gymnasium grid": *BASOR* 191, 38-40.

12. These Units XIX, XX, XXI are described by A. Ramage, Chapter III, *supra,* under "Pactolus North." For the destruction fills at W273-278/S348-350; W256-246/S331-333; W275-295/S320-335, ca. *87 (87.5-86.4), see *BASOR* 177, 4; and especially 182, 24-25. A coin of Antiochus II (261-246 B.C.; C 64.56) was found below and a coin of Antiochus III (223-187 B.C.; C 64.97) above the destruction fill.

13. *BASOR* 174, 22, fig. 11: "built just before or just after the earthquake of A.D. 17."

14. Hellenistic kiln: *BASOR* 177, 4; 182, 25. Lamps: in so-called Pactolus Industrial Area (PIA), *BASOR* 191, 38.

15. *BASOR* 182, 25.

16. PC: *BASOR* 157, 16-18, figs. 2, 5, 6; 162, 18-19. Oliver, *Sardis* (R5) *Pottery* (forthcoming): *Hellenistic,* "Introduction."

17. *Sardis* R1 (1975) 109-110, "earlier floors."

18. *BASOR* 162, 38; a coin of Achaeus was not well stratified, ibid. 39, no. 63 (C 60.56).

19. *AASOR* 43 (1974) 69.

20. *BASOR* 162, 23 (on Byzantine destruction); 166, 37: "a coin of Philetairos (C 61.216) found on a Lydian floor may be at most taken as indication that the floor continued to be used in the Early Hellenistic period"; 170, 32, no. 26, "scattering of Hellenistic pottery," at northeast edge of AcT. Six Hellenistic relief ware fragments were found on AcT (communication of I. Hanfmann).

21. As described in *BASOR* 162, 33, thousands of stones from earlier structures were built into the Early Byzantine Acropolis wall. They have not been systematically scrutinized for possible reused Hellenistic masonry.

22. *BASOR* 166, 30, fig. 25; see the discussion of graves and cemeteries, *infra.*

23. *Sardis* R2 (1978) 114, figs. 267-268, no. 134.

24. UT: *BASOR* 157, 19-22; for the situation under the gymnasium and the Synagogue, see *BASOR* 157, 36-38, late Hellenistic or early Roman floor with late Hellenistic mold of lovers and sphinx (Fig. 193), 4 m. below surface; 174, 47-50, fig. 30, "Hellenistic Steps," 3 m. below floor of Byzantine Shops and Synagogue, with many Hellenistic finds; 182, 40-42, the other part of the mausoleum; 191, 45 (twenty-two tests made); 338 pieces of Hellenistic relief ware came from this fill under the Synagogue (communication of I. Hanfmann).

25. *BASOR* 174, 34; IN 63.118-121. Robert is at work on the *editio princeps* of these texts. He has kindly sent a translation, printed as Appendix to this section.

26. The date of the city decree is later because it incorporates Laodice's reply.

27. For the career of Zeuxis, prior to discovery of the new texts, see Robert, *NIS,* 11-15.

28. IN 60.1: Robert, *NIS,* "Decret Hellénistique de Sardes," 9–21, pls. 1–2.

29. Johnson, "Sabazios," 542–550. Kraabel, "Paganism" (1978) 30–31. Cf. *BASOR* 154, 34.

30. *Sardis* R2 (1978) no. 211, fig. 371, *Phyles Tmolidos.* Phyle Pelopis: IN 62.41; urn of Menodorus, *phyles Pelopidos,* is dated by the Stephanephoros Charmos. See Robert, *NIS,* 7, on the proposed study of "Tribus et monnaies de Sardes."

31. *Sardis* R2 (1978) no. 275, figs. 467–468. Robert, "Séismes," 405.

32. Robert, *NIS,* L. and J. Robert's preliminary comments appear in *BASOR* reports.

33. Newell-Mørkholm, *WSM,* 242, 271. Seyrig, "Monnaies Hellénistiques" (1963) 35–38. Thompson, "Lysimachus," 165–173; Mørkholm, "Mint of Sardis," 5–19.

34. Noe, "Cistophoric Coinage," 29–41. Hansen, *Attalids,* 221–223, 483–484. Johnston (n. 35, *infra*) holds that the coins were struck by Pergamon for the various cities. Kleiner-Noe, 83–85.

35. See *Sardis* M7 (1981), "Pattern of Finds"; "Notes on Major Finds," and the history of the Sardian mints and coinages in "Notes to Greek Catalogue."

36. *Sardis* M6 (1980) 6–8, "Hellenistic Bowls."

37. These contexts are discussed in the sections on industrial architecture and cemeteries, *infra,* and also in A. Oliver, G. M. A. and I. Hanfmann, *Sardis* (R5) *Pottery* (forthcoming): *Hellenistic.*

Historical Background

1. Buerchner-Deeters-Keil, "Lydia," 2179–2190, "Historischer Teil," pt. 4; Magie 1: 6, 11, 225, 246, and especially 121–122, 974–976, a valuable survey with documentation. Rostovtzeff, *Hellenistic World,* 81, 426, 465, 477, 495–496 (Mnesimachus). Bengtson, *Strategie* 2: 90–119 (1944). Jones, *Greek City,* 43–44. Will, *Histoire* 1: 123, 131, 265–266, 268–269; 2: 39–41, 181–185, 354, 356. *Sardis* M2 (1972) 57–63, nos. 192–216, 235, 283–286, 290–291.

2. See Chapter V, under "Religious Life," "Cultural Perspective"; and VI, under "The Lydian Survivals," *supra.*

3. Gusmani, *LW,* 251, no. 3. *Sardis* R2 (1978) 27, fig. 404, no. 234.

4. Hanfmann-Polatkan-Robert, 45–56, pls. 9–10. *Sardis* R2 (1978) 114, figs. 267–268, no. 134.

5. See Gusmani, *LW,* no. 21; a second inscription of this kind was found in 1978: Greenewalt, "Campaign of 1978" (forthcoming). For the Hellenistic date of these smaller Ionic columns, see *Sardis* R1 (1975) 179, no. 10; compare the characteristically bilingual (Lydian-Greek) dedication on a column base

from Athena Temple, Pergamon: Gusmani, *LW,* no. 40.

6. *Sardis* M3 (1975) 53–54, also A II 7, "destruction fill of 213 B.C."; A II 15, Hellenistic relief ware, second or possibly early first century B.C.; figs. 15, 24. The tile stamp monogram for Artemis, A III 1, fig. 31, may be a conscious archaism, like the use of *kaoueis-kaveś,* "priestess," in Roman Imperial inscriptions. Hanfmann does not believe with Gusmani that the graffiti are chance uses of Lydian letters.

7. For the history of the Sardis mint, see Thompson, "Lysimachus," 165, 172–173. In her "Notes" on coins of Alexander III, Philip III, and Antigonus found in the Harvard-Cornell excavations, Johnston, *Sardis* M7 (1981) says: "It is not certain that there was a mint in Sardis" prior to Lysimachus. Cf. Newell-Mørkholm, *WSM,* 187, 242–271.

8. Arrian, *Anabasis* 1.17.3–6 = *Sardis* M2 (1972) no. 235.

9. Sacrilege inscription: Knibbe, "Religiöser Frevel," 175–182. Robert, *Bull.* 78 (1965) 155; 79 (1966) 422, dating 340–320 B.C. Bammer-Fleischer-Knibbe, 95–97, no. 1631; cf. *Sardis* R1 (1975) 178 n. 52.

10. Rehm, *Milet,* 1:3, 286, no. 135. *Syll.,* no. 273. Magie 2: (vol. 2) 975, no. 5. The treaty is often dated before Alexander's death in 323 B.C., but Magie points out that the situation could "apply equally well to the time immediately after Alexander's grant, before any public officials could be created."

11. See the Appendix to the preceding section: IN 63.118–121. *BASOR* 174, 34.

12. Robert, *NIS,* 9, IN 60.1, line 4.

13. *Sardis* VII.1 (1932) 53, no. 30: for the relation of the meeting place of the *gerousia* to the palace and seat of governor.

14. According to Buckler, the earliest *stephanophoros* is Chondros; *Sardis* VII.1 (1932) 46–47, no. 21, which mentions the cult of Athena Nicephorus, is presumably of the Pergamene period (ca. 150 B.C.?); Menophila, a young girl, was *stephanophoros,* apparently also before 133 B.C. *Sardis* VII.1 (1932) 108–109, no. 111, figs. 100–121; *Sardis* R2 (1978) 164, fig. 425, no. 245 (Istanbul 4033).

15. Robert, *NIS,* 9: IN 60.1, line 4.

16. Rostovtzeff, *Hellenistic World,* 526–530, discusses the problem of "freedom" and the royal authority.

17. Thompson, "Lysimachus," 65, 72–73.

18. *Sardis* M2 (1972) no. 306.

19. Mørkholm, "Mint of Sardis," 5–20, has worked out the following (still hypothetical) chronology on the basis of coins attributed to the Sardis mint: 229–228 B.C., Hierax leaves Sardis; 228–226 B.C., Seleucus II holds the city; 222–220 B.C., coins for Antiochus III are struck by Achaeus; 220 B.C.,

Achaeus coins on his own, n. 20, *infra*. We owe the knowledge of this article to A. Houghton, III.

20. Loyalty to Antiochus: Polybius 4:48.8–10. Siege and execution: Polybius 7:15–17; 8:15–21. Hanfmann, "Donkey Man," 233–235, pl. 51, reviews the evidence and literature on the execution of Achaeus, including Fleischer's interesting theory that the famous Hellenistic group of hanging Marsyas was intended to mythologize the punishment of Achaeus; cf. Fleischer, "Marsyas und Achaios," 105–122. Coins of Achaeus: Hanfmann, *Letters*, 125, fig. 92; *Sardis* M7 (1981) no. 379; Bank Leu, *Auktion 20, Antike Münzen* (Zurich, 25 April 1978) no. 160.

21. See the Appendix to the preceding section. *BASOR* 174, 34, IN 63.121. On Laodice, see L. Robert, *Annuaire* (1971–72) 516.

22. Josephus, *AJ*, 12.147–153, reports a letter from Antiochus III to Zeuxis ordering the transfer of 2,000 Jewish families from Mesopotamia to "the fortresses and most necessary places"; cf. Robert, *NIS*, 12. Hanfmann-Waldbaum, "New Excavations," 318–319, present arguments for assuming that Sardis was one of "the most necessary places."

23. Zeuxis' career is sketched in Robert, *NIS*, 11–15, prior to discovery of new inscriptions. He was *ho epi ton pragmaton*, "Charged with the Affairs" (of the King), really a prime minister, and in effect, Viceroy of Asia Minor. Other cities in the vicinity had suffered: see *Sardis* VII.1 (1932) 8–9, no. 2, where a town appeals to Antiochus III and his son, hence 209–193 B.C. The town had been burned; most of the citizens had lost their property and had perished. Robert, *NIS*, 20, no. 1, eliminating the false reading of T(molus), considered hesitantly that Sardis might be intended, but, in addition to Buckler's reasons, the payment of 20 minae annual tax does not seem sufficient for Sardis.

24. Robert, *Hellenica* 6 (1948) 16–26. Habicht, "Asia," 71–72, fig. 2, and 65, 78, on a settlement called Makedones in the *conventus* of Sardis.

25. On Mnesimachus, who had received his grant from Antigonus, see Rostovtzeff, *Hellenistic World*, 495–496. Cf. Atkinson, 45–74, with wrong date and a complete confusion with regard to the Cybele and Artemis temple. Cf. *Sardis* R1 (1975) 180–181 n. 44. For Andromenes, see Hanfmann-Polatkan-Robert, 55–56.

26. For these "Lydians who call themselves Persians," see Pausanias 5.27.5 = *Sardis* M2 (1972) no. 273. Robert, *Hellenica* 6 (1948) 19–20; idem, in Hanfmann-Polatkan-Robert, 56; idem, "Règlement perse," 326–328. See Habicht, "Asia," 74, a propos of Mabazani in the *conventus* of Sardis. We must assume that the sanctuaries of Anaitis in Hypaipa, Hierocaesareia, and Hieracoma continued to be important centers of Persian religion. The last mention of Persian Artemis in Sardis before Roman times refers to 322 B.C.: Pausanias 7.6.6. Was her name suppressed by Macedonian rulers? Cf. Hansen, for Pergamene kings concerning themselves with the privileges of the temple: *Attalids*, 143, 179–180.

27. Rostovtzeff, *Hellenistic World*, 492–511. Bickerman, *Institutions*, 176–185.

28. Appian, *Syriaka*, 36. Polybius 21.16.1–2; Livy 37.44–45 = *Sardis* M2 (1972) nos. 206, 207, 209. Will, *Histoire* 2:181–185.

29. *Sardis* VII.1 (1932) 10–12, no. 4. For the later fate of the stele, see *Sardis* R1 (1975) 58, 60, 68, fig. 75.

30. A royal dedication (of trophies) on a marble "label" found near the north side of the temple was, according to Buckler and Robinson, "attached to the wall of the temple near the offerings to which it was related"; they conjecture that Eumenes II dedicated enemy armor after the battle of Magnesia (190–189 B.C.), but the crucial name of the king is missing. *Sardis* VII.1 (1932) 93, fig. 75: the priestess of Artemis, Moschion, daughter of Diophantos, gave marble blocks for the temple after 133 B.C., presumably because construction was unfinished: *Sardis* VII.1 (1932) 95, no. 93.

31. Sculpture: perhaps the Herakles herm (Fig. 205), *Sardis* R2 (1978) 93, no. 71, figs. 186–187, is a mythological portrait of an Attalid king; they traced their descent from Herakles. Cf. Sardian gymnasium with "mysteries for Hermes and Herakles," *Sardis* VII.1 (1932) 46, no. 21. On the relief vase from the Tomb of the Lintel (Fig. 185), see *BASOR* 157, 16–18, fig. 6, and G. M. A. and I. Hanfmann on Pergamene import of appliqué ware and influence on Sardian relief ware, *Sardis* (R5) *Pottery* (forthcoming).

32. See *Sardis* VII.1 (1932) 46–47, no. 21, where Dionysius (pre-133 B.C.) contributed something to the festival of Athena Nicephorus as well as golden images; no. 27, Iollas (between 100 and 50 B.C.) conducted at his own cost Panathenaic and Eumenian games, a clear sign that both were in Sardis. The Sardians sent sacred ambassadors to Delphi (167, 162 B.C.) to request acceptance, which was granted, of the Panathenaic and Eumenian games established by the People (*Demos*) of Sardis which included musical, athletic, and horseracing contests. Hansen, *Attalids*, 458. Pouilloux, 159–169. Magie 2: 975, no. 7. An Athena possibly of the Nicephorus type: *Sardis* R2 (1978) 108, no. 113 (Berlin), fig. 239. For evidence on Athena Nicephorus on coins and the festival of which he dates the beginning to 166 B.C., see Robert, "Alcée," 345, no. 1, with references to his earlier discussions.

33. IN 58.11: Johnson, "Sabazios," 542–544, pl. 1. Stratonice, wife of Eumenes, brought the cult to Pergamon: Fränkel, *Inschriften*, no. 248. Welles,

Royal Correspondence, 267–270, no. 67. As pointed out in Chapter VI, *supra,* Sabazius was known in Sardis before 367 B.C.; see L. Robert, "Règlement perse," 307–310, 324–325. A later Sardian devotee of Sabazius in Maeonia: J. and L. Robert, *Bull.* 75 (1962) 202, no. 293.

34. Johnston, *Sardis* M7 (1981) "Notes."

35. *Sardis* VII.1 (1932) 13–15, no. 6. See Robert, "Alcée," 343, for the date 98–94 B.C. and the proconsul Q. Mucius Scaevola.

36. L. and J. Robert, *Bull.* 76 (1963) 165, no. 220; Hephaistion, son of Alcaeus, Sardian.

37. L. Robert, "Alcée," 344–346 has pointed out that the person known from Plutarch, *Pompey* 37.2, as the victim of Mithradates between 88 and 85 B.C. was eponymous priest of Zeus Polieus for Sardis at the time of the treaty with Ephesus, *supra,* n. 35 (ca. 98–94 B.C.), and an exact contemporary of Socrates, son of Polemaios, Pardalas. He identifies Alcaeus with the magistrate (moneyer) of the autonomous issues: Head, *BMC, Lydia,* 243, nos. 57–58, with bust of Artemis and standing Athena Nicephorus.

38. Organization of province of Asia: Magie 1: 154–176. Hansen, *Attalids,* 159–163. The *conventus iuridicus* or judicial district was an arrangement for the Roman governor to appear and hold court in central places, theoretically for provincials other than inhabitants of "free and autonomous" cities. Magie 1: 171–172. The organization has been brilliantly discussed by Habicht in his commentary on a new inscription from Ephesus, which shows the *conventus* of Sardis with 28 or 29 members extending from Daldis (near Nardi) in the west to Cabala (south of Usak) in the east: Habicht, "Asia," 67–77, sketch map, fig. 2.

39. *Sardis* VII.1 (1932) 94–95, no. 91; and nos. 22, 122. He is named as priest of Roma in the Pergamene version of the treaty with Ephesus (98–94 B.C.); see Robert, "Alcée," 344, no. 5. Since the inscription of his grandchild Ioulia Lydia dates after A.D. 17, *Sardis* R2 (1978) 178, figs. 467–469, nos. 275, 276, and since he was already priest of Roma between 98 and 94 B.C., he cannot have been born later than ca. 115 B.C. and must have had a long life. Alexarchus: *Sardis* VII.1 (1932) 95–96, no. 93.

40. Iollas: *Sardis* VII.1 (1932) 50–51, no. 27.

41. Plutarch, *Vit. Brut.* 34.1 = *Sardis* M2 (1972) no. 214.

42. "When Marcus Antonius *Autokrator* was eponymous official" is the dating formula on two Sardian marble urns, one new, IN 69.10, the other previously known, *Sardis* VII.1 (1932) 117, no. 129.

43. See Magie 1: 447, 470, on Augustan reorganization, on the temple erected to "Roma and Augustus" by the Koinon (Commonalty) of the province of Asia, and on local cults, with Appendix on cults of Roma and Augustus; 2: 1613–1614, where he lists

Sardis as having a cult of Augustus alone. The temple is mentioned in 5 B.C., *Sardis* VII.1 (1932) 17, 20, no. 8, I, ll. 13–14, "to consecrate an image of him [Gaius Caesar] which they shall install in his father's [Augustus'] temple."

44. *Sardis* VII.1 (1932) 16–21, no. 8.

45. Ambraseys, 375–379. Robert, "Séismes," 405.

Urban and Architectural Development

1. Owing in part to post-1975 excavations, the present, still tentative interpretation differs in some essentials from the sketch presented in *Sardis* R1 (1972) 29–30, nn. 91–113.

2. The detailed architectural study and plotting of unexcavated ruins were carried out from 1970 to 1972 by R. L. Vann. See Vann, "Unexcavated Buildings," in *Sardis* (M14) *Early Travelers and Unexcavated Buildings* (forthcoming). The account was to appear in *Sardis* R1 but had to be omitted for financial reasons. The results are treated in a larger setting in Vann, *Construction.* Important work has been done by the survey carried on since 1976 in this region; some of the results through the summer of 1981 are taken into account in this chapter.

3. See Bikerman, *Institutions,* 53–55, on major Seleucid strategic fortresses including Sardis. For the fortress-minded Hellenistic mentality with reference to Sardis, see Winter, *Fortifications,* 324–325, citing Polybius 7.15 = *Sardis* M2 (1972) no. 203: "Trusting in the natural or artificial strength of their defenses, they neglect to keep proper guard."

4. Hansen, *Attalids,* 166–298; Martin, *Urbanisme,* 127–151, figs. 16, 17, 19, pls. 8–9, and 57–63 on *astynomoi.* Ward-Perkins, *Planning,* 18, 117, figs. 14–15 (reconstruction).

5. See *BASOR* 162, 33; 166, 3–40; 170, 31–33; and Chapter III, *supra,* under "The Acropolis," for a detailed description of the Acropolis. During the 1960–1962 seasons three competent archaeologists tried their best on the central and southern peaks, and each reported as his conclusion that the situation was hopeless.

6. Arrian, *Anabasis* 1.17.3–6 = *Sardis* M2 (1972) no. 235. Hanfmann, "Palace," 147; "Lydian Sardis," 103–104, figs. 15, 17.

7. Winter, *Fortifications,* 318–324.

8. Hanfmann, "Palace," 151–153, figs. 2–4. See Chapter III, *supra,* under "The Acropolis."

9. Newell-Mørkholm, *WSM,* 242. Bengston, *Strategie,* 90–119. Seleucus I, Antiochus II, Achaeus, and Antiochus III stayed in Sardis. From 276 to 274 B.C. Antiochus I "left his court, his wife, and the crown prince to keep a strong guard": *Sardis* M2 (1972) no. 306. Throughout the Persian era, the sa-

traps withdraw to the citadel, and *ta basileia* and *ta akra* are interchangeable.

10. Vitruvius 2.8.9–10 = *Sardis* M2 (1972) no. 291. Hanfmann, "Palace," 145–147, 154. Polyaenus 4.94 = *Sardis* M2 (1972) no. 237, specifically says that the treasures of Lysimachus were with the commander of the citadel, Theodotus. Mithrines, too, surrenders the treasures and Acropolis, *akran kai ta chremata,* to Alexander. Arrian, *Anabasis* 1.17.3–6 = *Sardis* M2 (1972) no. 235.

11. Welles, *Royal Correspondence,* 90–100, nos. 18–19.

12. For the king's court, see Bikerman, *Institutions,* 31–50; for permanent garrisons, see ibid., 51–53. Hanfmann, "Palace," 149–151, 154, figs. 1–2.

13. *Sardis* R2 (1978) 4–7; the Hellenistic relief in the quarries, ibid., 126, figs. 301–303, no. 156, as well as Hellenistic parts of the temple prove the date.

14. See "Historical Background," *supra.*

15. It may have existed in the Lydian city plan; see Chapter V, *supra,* under "Urbanism and Architecture," and Plans I, II.

16. See Chapter III, *supra,* under "Pactolus North."

17. Polybius, 1.17.6; 18.5–7 = *Sardis* M2 (1972) no. 285, with Pedley's interpretative notes. Hanfmann does not believe, however, that the "Persian Gates" lie to the west.

18. Vann, *Sardis* (M14) *Early Travelers and Unexcavated Buildings* (forthcoming), places the theater within the walls. Given Polybius' account and the character of the site, it is quite possible that the east side of the theater was serving as part of the wall or was overtopped by it.

19. See Chapter III, *supra,* under "The Acropolis."

20. Vitruvius 2.8.9. Hanfmann, "Palace," 145. Blake, *Construction* 1, Chapter VII, "Sun-dried and Semi-baked Bricks," 278–280, shows that in Arezzo (pre-87 B.C.) these were semi-baked bricks.

21. *Sardis* R1 (1975) 36, 38, figs. 1, 10, 11, nos. 31–34.

22. Vann, *Sardis* (M14) *Early Travelers and Unexcavated Buildings* (forthcoming), and *Construction,* 99–103. Vann's treatment also features a full bibliography of early travelers and modern investigators.

23. Mentioned in *BASOR* 157, 14, as "profiled marble blocks." Their true purpose was explained by L. Robert, who thought the letters probably late Hellenistic. Others have been found as far afield as the Acropolis; they are theater seats decorated with lion's legs, all of the same type, and are kept presently at Sardis camp. For the statue, Fig. 174; *Sardis* R2 (1978) 88, figs. 166–168, no. 55; G. M. A. Hanfmann now agrees with N. Ramage that a pre-A.D. 17 date and reuse are likely, especially as the head was

made separately and could have been replaced. Cf. Linfert, *Kunstzentren,* 144 n. 571.

24. Discussed by Vann, *Sardis* (M14) *Early Travelers and Unexcavated Buildings* (forthcoming), here Figs. 169–170, with previous literature. The north side is a single barrel vault 194 m. long (east-west). The stadium is 35–40 m. wide (north-south). There are six vaulted chambers preserved at the eastern end. The present construction certainly dates from the first century A.D. Vann does not speculate about the Hellenistic forerunner. He compares for the relation to the theater, Aizanoi and Pessinus, both unexcavated.

25. *Sardis* R1 (1975) 119, figs. 59, 282.

26. There are marble blocks in the bottom of the torrent and ashlar masonry east and west of the torrent, just east of the "Byzantine Fortress," Fig. 8:41. Vann describes it as "a massive stone foundation (E750/S340, *182), that must have supported a building of substantial size, judging from the numerous large blocks . . . in the bed of the wadi." The column base was kindly shown to G. M. A. Hanfmann by W. E. Mierse, C. Ratte, and T. N. Howe.

27. See the Appendix to "Previous Research," *supra*: IN 63.118; cf. *BASOR* 174, 34.

28. *Sardis* VII.1 (1932) 8–9, no. 2.

29. Martin, *Urbanisme,* 57–63.

30. See Chapter V, *supra,* under "The Progress of Research."

31. For the Lydian location, see Herodotus 5.101 = *Sardis* M2 (1972) no. 282; the Hellenistic Agora is mentioned in 5 B.C. (*infra*). Some scholars have proposed as Roman Agora the vast platform of so-called complex A, and other areas adjacent to the west, Fig. 8:24, 37, 38, a suggestion Hanfmann finds appealing. Butler, however, thought of a gymnasium, *Sardis* I (1922) 31; and Foss sought to locate the late Roman Imperial arms factory in "A": see *Sardis* M4 (1976) 36–37, fig. 8.

32. See the discussion and plan in *Sardis* R1 (1975) 19, 29–30, figs. 10 (alignments) and 11 (present roads).

33. See the dedication by Eumenes(?) and the gift of marble blocks by Moschion, *infra;* "Historical Background," n. 30, *supra.*

34. See Fig. 8:57, "Street of the Pipes." This is deduced from the location of Mausoleum "M," *BASOR* 174, 22–24, where, however, the "grand alignment" is termed post-A.D. 17. Since the monument antedates the earthquake of A.D. 17 and is late Hellenistic, the street is likely to have existed in some form.

35. This is deduced from deviations of 9° and 22° north, seen in the facades of mausolea "CP" and "Hellenistic Steps" north of the Roman road. See Figs. 8, 167; Plans II, III. It is certain that the Helle-

nistic road, too, passed between the "Hellenistic Steps" (E85–90/S3–5; Fig. 187) on the north and the row of late Hellenistic chamber tombs (Fig. 186; E0–10/S50–60?) to the south of the Roman Main Avenue. Current (1979) excavations promise to clarify some phases in the history of the east-west road.

36. See *Sardis* R1 (1975) 38, figs. 1, 10, 11, 21, 22; sections 31–34.

37. Structure MMS, a Lydian fortification wall, has been traced northward from S51–58 to S10 uphill. Ramage thinks it was abandoned by the Persians, but with the heights to which it is preserved (to 6 m. plus), it may have continued to stand and could have been rehabilitated by Hellenistic builders.

38. Martin, *Urbanisme,* 161, 180, figs. 24, 32; see also 110, fig. 9 (Olynthus). Cf. Ward-Perkins, *Planning,* figs. 31 (Selinus), 37 (Chersonesos), 49 (Ostia). At Sardis the axis bends at ca. E130–150; see *Sardis* R1 (1972) figs. 1, 9, 10. In many instances (Selinus, Ostia) the bending is a result of an old city quarter being expanded; this could also have happened in Sardis already in Lydian or Persian times.

39. *Sardis* R1 (1975) 30, fig. 10. Erroneously, in n. 106 the bend is said to be at E1000!

40. Priene: Martin, *Urbanisme,* 113–114, fig. 11, pl. 9; Wiegand-Schrader, *Priene,* 49–50, fig. 28.

41. See n. 31, *supra,* for some of the suggestions.

42. *Supra,* and Chapter V, *supra,* under "Urbanism and Architecture."

43. Fig. 8:62; Street of the Pipes, 8:57; *Sardis* R1 (1975) fig. 9, view; fig. 11 is clearest in showing the present course.

44. Polybius, 1.17.6; 18.5–7 = *Sardis* M2 (1972) no. 285. For a larger map of the area, where the road dips, from the city hillock at Church D, see *Sardis* R1 (1975) fig. 335. For the Persian Gates, see n. 17, *supra.*

45. *BASOR* 229, 61, fig. 4.

46. Seager, *Synagogue* (1974) figs. 27–28. *Sardis* R1 (1975) 46, fig. 49.

47. See *Sardis* R2 (1978) no. 20, fig. 79; and especially 118, fig. 277, no. 141. Cf. *Sardis* VII.1 (1932) no. 28, fig. 20, second to first century B.C. A late Hellenistic example in real architecture is the shrine of Mithradates VI in Delos: Lawrence, *Architecture,* 219, fig. 122.

48. *Sardis* R2 (1978) 118, no. 277, figs. 278–279.

49. *Sardis* R1 (1975) 63, 65, figs. 81–82, 88, 94–95.

50. This development has been studied by Vann, *Construction,* who also cites the so-called Odeion, now known as "Hillside Chambers," *Sardis* (M14) *Early Travelers and Unexcavated Buildings* (forthcoming) and *Sardis* R1 (1975) 109 (on mortared rubble construction in Sardis), figs. 1, 11:27. For the vaulted tombs, see *Sardis* R1 (1975) figs. 72–74.

51. As pointed out by Vann, *Construction,* 99–103 n. 30, the builders tried to devise a flexible wall system to counteract earthquake shocks.

52. *Sardis* VII.1 (1932) 10–12, no. 4. With Baki being equated with Greek Dionysus in the *Nannas Bakivalis* inscription of ca. 350 B.C., *Sardis* R2 (1978) no. 274, it is possible that the Lydian sanctuary of Baki (location unknown) was hellenized even before the Hellenistic period. The tribe Dionysias, too, is undoubtedly a translation of "Baki-tribe." Dionysius: *Sardis* VII.1 (1932) 46–47, no. 21. For a possibly Hellenistic herm of Herakles (Fig. 205), see *Sardis* R2 (1978) 93, figs. 186–187, no. 71.

53. *Sardis* VII.1 (1932) no. 21, Dionysius may have given an image; ibid. 69–70, no. 55, a priestess of the Sardian Artemis is also a priestess of Athena Nicephorus, but if the inscription is a decree of Pergamon (second century A.D.), it proves nothing for survival or non-survival. Buckler and Robinson assume that there was no cult in Sardis in Imperial times.

54. This is virtually certain from the correct translation of IN 58.11, kindly supplied by L. Robert (May 1981). See Johnson, "Sabazios," 542–544, 549–550, for Sardis IN 58.11. See Welles, *Royal Correspondence,* 266–273, nos. 66–67, for Stratonice introducing cult of Zeus Sabazius in Pergamon. Cf. Kraabel, "Paganism," 30–31, on the role of Sabazius at Sardis.

55. A striking number of Cybele monuments and the inscribed blocks from the *parastades* of the Metroon (Fig. 169, correspondence and decrees relating to 213 B.C.) were built into the Synagogue. This suggests that the sanctuary of Cybele was not far away. See *Sardis* R2 (1978) 33, where the evidence is given in detail, and L. Robert's translation in the Appendix to "Previous Research," *supra.*

56. The evidence is in the Menogenes decrees, dated 5–1 B.C. *Sardis* VII.1 (1932) no. 8; text IV, line 49; VI, line 72: dedication of *gerousia* in *presbeutikon;* XI, line 128: statues of Menogenes in the agora; XI, line 130: painted image of Menogenes' son in the *paidikon.* Dionysius: *Sardis* VII.1 (1932) no. 21, he was a gymnasiarch for boys. Hanfmann, "Palace," 145–147, presents a detailed discussion of the possible relation of the *presbeutikon* to a Gymnasium of Seniors, mentioned only in the Roman (ca. A.D. 200) List of Fountains, *Sardis* VII.1 (1932) no. 17. See also 52–53, no. 30, for the earliest mention of *gerousia.*

57. Seyrig, *Monnaies Hellénistiques* (1963) 35–36, no. 1, pl. 3:5. Price-Trell, 139, figs. 244–245. Johnston, *Sardis* M7 (1981) 10–11.

58. See *Sardis* R2 (1978) 178, no. 275. Robert, "Séismes," 405; and on Socrates Polemaiou Pardalas, "Historical Background," n. 39, *supra.*

59. Apollo figures importantly on autonomous coins after 133 B.C., see Johnston, *Sardis* M7 (1981); Mên is represented by a late Hellenistic relief, *Sardis* R2 (1978) no. 253; possibly also no. 163; and his strong popularity from the early Imperial age on argues an earlier cult. He appears on autonomous coins from Nero on. Cf. Robert, *NIS,* 32–34; Lane, 43.

60. *Sardis* VII.1 (1932) no. 8, text XII, ll. 131–132; for a possibly Hellenistic inscription, see *Sardis* R2 (1978) 128, figs. 308–309, no. 161, with references to Robert's theory that the "servants of Zeus" in this inscription descend from the cult personnel of Zeus Baradates. A treaty with Ephesus, too, was set up in the sanctuary of Zeus, ca. 98–94 B.C.; see *Sardis* VII.1 (1932) no. 6.

61. Roma is attested first around 100 B.C. See the treaty with Ephesus (Socrates Polemaiou Pardalas as priest of Roma) and the Alexarchos and Moschion inscription, *Sardis* VII.1 (1932) 95–96, no. 93; *OGIS,* no. 437.

62. Robert, *NIS,* 38. *Sardis* M2 (1972) no. 212. Josephus, *AJ* 14.235. On the background, and possible connection with Jewish veterans brought by Zeuxis, see Hanfmann-Waldbaum, "New Excavations," 318–319. Cf. Chapter IX, *infra.*

63. Martin, *Urbanisme,* 144–151.

Artemis Sanctuary

1. The beautiful Hellenistic bases are enlivened by little creatures: lizards, scorpions, snails, and slugs. Some of them and some of the Hellenistic capitals survived the earthquake and were used in the Roman reconstruction, *Sardis* II (1925) 61, 135–139, ill. 66.

2. Berve-Gruben, 470–473. Dinsmoor, 226–229; Müller-Wiener, 239–240.

3. Though not reported by Butler, the north stylobate profile rises by 0.045 m. A detailed discussion of the work at the Artemis Temple and precinct and its results appears in *Sardis* R1 (1975), chapters 4–7.

4. *Sardis* I (1922) plan III, pl. II, 110. *Sardis* II (1925) pl. A and Atlas, pl. I, 140–143. Prior to the publication of *Sardis* R1 in 1975, two other building chronologies were published for the Artemis Temple. In 1961, G. Gruben, 155–196, after making his own study of the temple remains at Sardis, determined that there had been an early Hellenistic phase (270–200 B.C.) when the cella with a deep pronaos and a short opisthodomos was built; a Pergamene phase (post-188 B.C.) during which time the pseudo-dipteral plan was adopted; and a Roman phase (A.D. 140–160) when the two-cella arrangement was made to accommodate the cult figures of Antonius Pius and Faustina. Martin in Charbonneaux-Martin-Villard,

Hellenistic Art, 5–7, 351, figs. 388–390, published in 1973, suggested that there had originally been an esplanade and altar. In the early third century B.C. the naos was built as a "compromise between the traditional Ionian and more classical rules of Pitheus (Pytheos) at Athens and Priene." The temple was then left until the Antonine Age, at which time Artemis was installed in the east cella and Faustina in the west cella.

5. *Sardis* R1 (1975) 86–87.

6. Ibid., 56.

7. *Sardis* VII.1 (1932) no. 85.

8. A beginning between 334 and 281 B.C. cannot be entirely ruled out. In A.D. 22–23, Sardians pleaded for renewal of the right of asylum before the Roman senate: "They cited a gift of Alexander the Great," *Alexandri Victoris id donum.* Tacitus, *Ann.* 3.36. The temple is not named; but the other cities were pleading for their largest and most famous ancient sanctuaries: Artemis of Ephesus, Artemis Leukophryene of Magnesia, Aphrodite of Aphrodisias, Apollo of Didyma; hence Artemis is probable, even though the temple was in ruins after the earthquake. For the Alexander era the passage proves the existence of the sanctuary probably with customary right of asylum, possibly within the confirmation of Lydian customary laws (Arrian), in 334 B.C. It does not prove that Alexander started building a temple.

9. *Sardis* VII.1 (1932) no. 86; this attribution to Stratonice, Seleucus I's queen, is contested by Franke who thinks the dedicant was a private person; Franke, 206–208.

10. For relations between the Seleucid kings and the great temples of Asia Minor, see Rostovtzeff, *Hellenistic World,* 502–507.

11. Bammer, "Amazonen und das Artemision," 93–94.

12. Welles, *Royal Correspondence,* 89–104, nos. 18–19; *Sardis* II (1925) 104.

13. *Sardis* VII.1 (1932) no. 1; the amount of the loan was substantial, 2,650 gold staters. Atkinson believes the inscription dates rather to about 200 and refers to events which took place after 213; Atkinson, 62–68. A further indication of the early use of the Artemis sanctuary is the Euthymos dedication which Buckler and Robinson date to the mid-third century B.C.; *Sardis* VII.1 (1932) no. 87.

14. *Sardis* R1 (1975) 84, 87.

15. Ibid., 87.

16. See *Sardis* R1 (1975) 179–181 n. 22, for complete literature. A detailed discussion of the image base investigation is reported, ibid., 76–80.

17. Ibid., figs. 140–142.

18. *Sardis* I (1922) 66, fig. 61. The cult image was probably an acrolith.

19. Newell-Mørkholm, *WSM,* 265, pl. 60:1–2.

Sardis R1 (1975) 75; *Sardis* R2 (1978) no. 102, figs. 223–225. Bank Leu, *Auktion 20, Antike Münzen* (Zürich, 25 April 1978) no. 160.

20. For Artemis facing west, see *Sardis* R1 (1975) 75. It is Hanfmann's theory that the Lydian and Greek inscriptions attest to three distinct cult aspects to Artemis: Artemis of Sardis, Artemis of Ephesus, and Artemis of Koloe; but no image of the archaic Artemis of Sardis is known. A relief of ca. 400 B.C. (Fig. 93) represents Artemis holding a stag in the crook of her arm; to her right is the figure of Cybele holding a lion, *Sardis* R2 (1978) no. 20. It represents an image of ca. 450 B.C. of the Artemis of Sardis, not Ephesus, where the type is virtually unknown. A colossal image of Artemis was set up in the Seleucid temple to balance with the colossal Zeus (220–200 B.C.). After the collapse of the temple in A.D. 17, a second Artemis colossus was put up. Originally alone, she later shared her base with the colossal statue of Faustina (after A.D. 148). Possible fragments of the Antonine Artemis have been identified, *Sardis* R2 (1978) no. 252.

Fleischer presents an opposing theory (Fleischer, 193–201). A wooden *xoanon* known from a representation on a second century A.D. capital (Fig. 148) and usually identified as Kore (*Sardis* R2 [1978] no. 194) was established as the image in ca. 600 B.C. It was regularly presented with a new dress and continued to be worshiped in Hellenistic times. It was to the ceremony of "Chitons for Artemis" that the sacred embassy from Ephesus was headed when it was attacked (see Knibbe, "Ein religiöser Frevel," 175–182.) According to Fleischer, the Sardian coins with the Kore *xoanon* (third century A.D.) refer to this version of Artemis.

It is Hanfmann's view that Fleischer's theory is ruled out by the following: the appearance of Artemis in non-*xoanon* form (*Sardis* R2 [1978] no. 20); the improbability of a colossal temple housing a *xoanon;* and a Sardian coin which shows three Imperial temples, one of which we know was that of Artemis, as well as a separate temple with an image of Kore.

21. Vitruvius 3.3; 4.3; 7 *Praef.* Herrmann, "Antiochos," 43–44. Hanfmann, *Croesus,* 30 n. 54. Linfert, *Kunstzentren,* 164 n. 652.

22. For Eumenes' dedication, see *Sardis* VII.1 (1932) no. 88; for the marble blocks given by Moschion, see ibid., no. 93.

23. Ibid., no. 8.

24. *Sardis* R1 (1975) 26, 75. A cylindrical statue base with a dedication to Tiberius was discovered in 1979.

25. Ibid., 80.

26. *Sardis* II (1925) 141. A short, incomplete text in Lydian, inscribed on a fragmentary apophyge of a column shaft of the Temple of Artemis (NoEx 78.15/IN 78.4), was found ca. 60 m. north of the Artemis Temple and just outside the Expedition compound ca. W213/S1167.5. The fragment's height and estimated diameter associate it with the smaller columns inside the temple peristyle. The parallel instance of a Lydian inscription on one of the two elevated columns in the east porch (Gusmani, *LW,* no. 21) suggests that the fragment belongs to one of the elevated columns in the west porch. The letters have the breadth, symmetry, and small serifs of late-Classical Hellenistic Greek inscriptions and not the cursive, narrow, closely spaced style of Lydian. Text *srkastulis sv* is part of a personal name (son of *Srkastus,* resident of Sardis? *sv/sfard*), to be published by Gusmani; cf. *LW,* no. 40, Athena.

27. *Sardis* II (1925) 82–83.

28. See Chapter III, *supra,* under "The Artemis Precinct."

29. *Sardis* R1 (1975) 99.

30. A detailed discussion of the investigations of LA 1 and LA 2 can be found in *Sardis* R1 (1975), chapter VI.

31. *Sardis* R1 (1975) 95–96, 101.

32. Ibid., 96.

33. For list of finds from LA 2, see ibid., 100.

34. Bammer, 7–12, 41–42, figs. 5, 7b, 37, 42, 43.

35. Berve-Gruben, 480, fig. 140.

36. Akurgal, *Civilizations,* 183.

37. Bammer, *Artemision,* 7 n. 36.

38. *Sardis* II (1925) pl. A, ill. 97; *Sardis* R1 (1975) 88–89, figs. 179, 180.

39. *Sardis* R1 (1975) 103.

40. Lloyd-Müller-Martin, 350, 360–362, pls. 484–487. Martin wrote the essay in the volume on Greek architecture.

41. Xenophon, *Anabasis* 1.6.7 = *Sardis* M2 (1972) no. 271.

42. *Sardis* M2 (1972) no. 270 + Pausanias 7.6.6; *Sardis* R2 (1978) 31–32, no. 18.

43. Pausanias 5.27.5 records the worship of the Persian Artemis in Hypaipa.

44. *Sardis* R1 (1975) 110, 112.

45. Ibid., 65–66.

46. Ibid., 65, a suggestion made by H. A. Thompson. Cf. Thompson-Wycherley, 65, 202, fig. 21, pl. 41b, basin-like water clock in Athens Agora, with reference to other Greek water clock constructions.

47. *Sardis* (R5) *Pottery: Hellenistic Relief Ware* (forthcoming); *Sardis* M7 (1981), xxi.

48. *Sardis* R1 (1975) 64.

Private Buildings

1. *BASOR* 166, 7–8, fig. 2; *BASOR* 170, 10–13, fig. 7.

2. Swift, FR 1965: "The House of Bronzes Area at Midseason," 2 (unpublished).

3. *BASOR* 166, 7; *Sardis* (M8) *Metalwork* (forthcoming): "Introduction."

4. *BASOR* 174, 8, 13–14.

5. *Sardis* (R5) *Pottery* (forthcoming): *Hellenistic,* "Black Glaze."

6. *BASOR* 170, 10. *Sardis* M7 (1981), A. Johnston has identified C 62.178 as a coin of Alexander III or Successors, mint Lampsacus (no. 7); C 62.345 she lists as a coin of Alexander III or Successors, mint uncertain (no. 10); C 61.217 is a coin of Antiochus III, Sardis mint (no. 365).

7. *BASOR* 199, 28.

8. *BASOR* 157, 26, 28.

9. *BASOR* 170, 13, figs. 11–12. The columns were taken to have been burnt at a later date for lime (post-A.D. 17).

10. Complex: *BASOR* 182, 24. Coin finds: *BASOR* 182, 23. A. Johnston recognizes coins C 65.86, C 65.143, C 65.147 as being from the mint at Ephesus, date 305–288 B.C., *Sardis* M7 (1981) no. 81; C 65.110 as an Alexander III or Successors, mint unknown, ibid., no. 17; and C 65.130 as an early third century B.C. issue, ibid., no. 24.

11. Oliver accepts the pre-213 B.C. date for the pottery found in the complex, *Sardis* (R5) *Pottery* (forthcoming): *Hellenistic,* "Coarse Ware" and "Black Glaze." Attic black glazed ware P 65.252.

12. *BASOR* 177, 4; 182, 24–25.

13. *BASOR* 177, 6; 182, 22–23, 25, fig. 19.

14. *BASOR* 182, 25.

15. The fragment of a tile was found near the kiln (uncatalogued).

16. C 64.97 (W272/S341, *87.75) = *Sardis* M7 (1981) no. 381.

17. *BASOR* 174, 22.

Graves and Cemeteries

1. *BASOR* 166, 30, fig. 25; Hanfmann, *Letters,* 86, fig. 60.

2. C 61.23. *Sardis* M7 (1981) Greek no. 10.

3. There were four white-painted alabastra, a lekythos, and plates with concentric circles. See Oliver, *Sardis* (R5) *Pottery:* "Hellenistic" (forthcoming).

4. *Sardis* M6 (1980) no. 858.

5. See Oliver, n. 3, *supra,* who compares Goldman, *Tarsus* 1, 230, nos. 234, 238, figs. 135, 187, for the unguentarium.

6. Keil, *ÖJh Beibl* (1935) 135–318, figs. 52–53. Hanfmann, *Croesus,* 37–38, fig. 80, with literature on the dating controversy.

7. *BASOR* 186, 52, fig. 35. Similar tombs have been found near Soma: Kasper, "Nekropole," 76, fig. 10.

8. It was found by farmers. No clear traces of the tomb could be discerned in the vineyard. Hanfmann-Polatkan-Robert, 45–56; *Sardis* R2 (1978) 114, figs. 267–268, no. 134.

9. *Sardis* R2 (1978) 115–118, figs. 269–279; 164, fig. 425, no. 245. This does not include stelae without figures. Comparisons: Pfuhl-Möbius 1:79–110, 128–186, especially nos. 228, 503, 633, 666; 2:332–335, nos. 1393–1418, with illustrations.

10. *BASOR* 229, 70.

11. "Hellenistic Pottery" (Introduction), *Sardis* (R5) *Pottery* (forthcoming). Cf. *BASOR* 186, 52. Among the finds were a wavy-line amphora, the foot of a late Lydian scyphus, an unguentarium, a fragment of a black-glazed closed vessel, blue glass from a cored vessel, G 66.9:7140, *Sardis* M6 (1980) no. 5; and a lamp (L 66.49:7196 rim), similar to Broneer type VII, Broneer, *Corinth* 4:2, 45. BT 66.3 had bottoms of Hellenistic unguentaria (P 66.75:7102).

12. Kurtz-Boardman, 272–283, figs. 60–64, with literature. Makaronas-Miller, 248–259. Miller, *Hellenistic Macedonian Architecture: Its Style and Painted Ornamentation* (Ph.D. dissertation, University of California at Berkeley, 1974, unpublished): cited by Lehmann, "Lefkadia," 226–229, pl. 57.

13. *BASOR* 157, 16–17, figs. 3, 5, 6; 162, 18.

14. *BASOR* 157, 28, figs. 8–9.

15. *BASOR* 174, 20, fig. 11, tomb "Ch." It was built against the Hellenistic monument "M" (*infra*) after A.D. 17.

16. *BASOR* 157, 28. For the imitation of masonry in the "First Pompeian Style," see Bruno, "Antecedents," 305–317. Lehmann, "Lefkadia," 228; and P. W. Lehmann, *Samothrace* 3, 138, 206.

17. *Sardis* R1 (1975) 59–60, figs. 59, 69, 72–73.

18. Skeletal remains were found on the benches and the floor and in a large amphora in the Tomb of the Lintel.

19. *BASOR* 157, 18, fig. 6. Hanfmann, *Letters,* 64, fig. 41. Hellenistic "Lagynos" ware: Oliver, *Sardis* (R5) *Pottery:* "Hellenistic" (forthcoming). Cf. *Sardis* I (1922) 120, ill. 128.

20. *BASOR* 170, 51, fig. 37; 174, 47–49, figs. 29–30. In general see *Sardis* M4 (1976) 42–43, fig. 19; M6 (1980) Plan IV.

21. *BASOR* 182, 40–41. "Three walls forming an enclosure 3.84 m. wide . . . these walls correspond in orientation to the Hellenistic Steps." The south wall diverges in orientation from the south wall of the Synagogue. The top of the "Hellenistic Steps" is at *93.85; that of the new walls, *93.80. The width of HS at the top is 6.27 m., 3.40 m. more than the width of HS; hence the 1965 walls are foundation

walls for the inner (shrine-like?) structure. The (bottom?) brick grave is at *91.42, 2.38 m. under the floor level of the mausoleum.

22. Its position is shown in *BASOR* 174, 49, fig. 30, next to the legend "Roman Pipes."

23. *BASOR* 174, 48. "Head of Apollo; club, oak wreath" (Gr 178) C 63.232. E8.5/S2.7, *92.7. There were five autonomous Sardis coins and one coin of Pergamon found close to the structure. See *Sardis* M7 (1981) no. 198 and "Notes on Some Archaeological Contexts."

24. *BASOR* 191, 39, and fig. 1 (location at Sector West).

25. *BASOR* 174, 22, fig. 11 (plan). For the possible monument see Kurtz-Boardman, 301–302, fig. 74, Alyzia, "stepped altar . . . contained an early Hellenistic sarcophagus."

26. *Sardis* I (1922) 78, 79, 85, 157.

27. *BASOR* 228, 50–51.

28. NoEx 75.6, 75.7, 75.8, 75.9.

29. *Sardis* R2 (1978) no. 227, fig. 394; for the tomb, see *BASOR* 157, 28.

30. *Sardis* VII.1 (1932) 105–107, nos. 105–109. The *stephanophoros* and the Priest of Roma eponymy were both used by Alexarchos, ibid., 95–96, no. 93.

31. Ibid., 109–113, nos. 112–115 are "Priest of Roma"; nos. 116–117, "Priest." The Priesthood of Roma was certainly used by 98–94 B.C.

32. Ibid., 112–115, nos. 118–124; 117–119, nos. 129–132.

33. The urn IN 69.10, *Epi Markou Antoniou Autokratoros,* confirms the validity of another urn with similar dating, *Sardis* VII.1 (1932) 117, no. 129. Buckler-Robinson suggest either 41 B.C. when Antony was acclaimed as Dionysos, or more probably 33–32 B.C. when he and Cleopatra were wintering in Ephesus, Magie, 428, 439.

34. IN 68.6 has *epi Polemaiou* on one side and *Pardala* on the other. This may be the father of the distinguished Socrates Polemaiou Pardalas, Priest of Roma between 98 and 94 B.C.

35. IN 75.1: the suggestion was made by C. Foss. The Corpus of these marble urns is being readied by Nuşin Asgari. Two other inscribed urns are in Leyden and Rome, the former probably dating to the late first century B.C. or the first century A.D., and the latter to ca. 100 B.C.: L. Robert, *RA* (1936) 238–239.

Economy and Industry

1. Magie, 45.
2. See Chapter I, *supra,* under "Agriculture, Pastoralism."
3. Magie, 45; E. V. Hansen, *Attalids,* 207–209.

4. Magie, 46.
5. Theophrastus, *Hist. Pl.* 5:5, 4.
6. For animal breeding during the centuries of Lydian rule, see Chapter I, *supra,* under "Agriculture, Pastoralism."
7. Rostovtzeff, *Hellenistic World,* 307–308, 357–358.
8. Strabo 13.4.5 = *Sardis* M2 (1972) no. 234. Robert, *NIS,* 10, 15–16 remarks that ten staters or 200 drachms is not a great amount.
9. *Sardis* VII.1 (1932) no. 8.
10. *Sardis* VII.1 (1932) no. 1.
11. Rostovtzeff, *Hellenistic World,* 495. Balcer, "By The Bitter Sea" (forthcoming).
12. Xenophon, *Anabasis* 7:8, 7; E. V. Hansen, *Attalids,* 9–10.
13. Rostovtzeff, "Economic Policy," 372–375.
14. For the policies of the Seleucid monarchs regarding Greek and Macedonian colonization, see Rostovtzeff, *Hellenistic World,* 472–502.
15. *Sardis* M6 (1980) 6–8, "Hellenistic Bowls," nos. 6–14.
16. *Sardis* (R5) *Pottery:* "Hellenistic" (forthcoming).
17. Schäfer, 25, lists twenty molds, pls. 27–30: erotic; 34: plants.
18. *Sardis* (R5) *Pottery:* "Hellenistic Relief Ware" (forthcoming).
19. *Sardis* (R5) *Pottery:* "Hellenistic" (forthcoming).
20. *BASOR* 157, 16–18, fig. 6.
21. *Sardis* (R5) *Pottery:* "Hellenistic" (forthcoming).
22. Magie has suggested that much of Lydia's wealth was derived from a combination of trade and home industry, 46. Jones, *Greek City,* 259–260.
23. Pausanias 7.6.6 = *Sardis* M2 (1972) no. 270. The Lamian War (322 B.C.) in which Adrastos fought and for which he was being honored with the statue was against the Macedonians; therefore, the statue must date from a time when the Macedonian control of Sardis had come to an end, *Sardis* R2 (1978) 31–32, no. 18.
24. In addition to the three statues of Iollas to be gilded, there were four other bronze statues. Both Pausanias and Pliny refer to a bronzecaster, Theomnestos of Sardis. Pausanias credits him with creating a statue of Ageles, the victor of the boy's boxing at Olympia (Pausanias 6.15.2); Overbeck, *Schriftquellen,* no. 2046. According to Pliny (*HN* 34.91) he did bronze sculptures of "athletes, armed men, hunters, and sacrificers." Overbeck, *Schriftquellen,* no. 2047. There is also an inscription from Chios but known only through Muratori's copy—*Theomnestos Theotimou kai Dionysios Astioulepoiesan;* Muratori II, 1014,

11; Overbeck, *Schriftquellen,* no. 2048; E. Lowy, *Inschriften Griech. Bildhauer,* no. 286. Picard believes Theomnestos was active during the fourth century B.C., Picard, *Manuel,* 194.

25. *BASOR* 199, 51, fig. 42. *Sardis* (M8) *Metalwork* (forthcoming) no. 731.

26. *Sardis* (R5) *Pottery:* "Hellenistic Relief Ware" (forthcoming).

27. Ibid.

28. Wrabetz, "Serenus Stamping," 195–198. R. Zahn, "Thongeschirr," 437.

29. *Sardis* (R5) *Pottery:* "Roman" (forthcoming).

30. See Chapter VI, *supra,* under "The Lydian Survivals."

31. Rostovtzeff, "Economic Policy," 380–382; Rostovtzeff, *Hellenistic World,* 564; Magie, 47–48; Hansen, *Attalids,* 214. For preserved gold thread from a Roman burial, see Greenewalt-Majewski, 135–137, fig. 4. For weaving workshops in the later Roman era, but perhaps reflecting the Hellenistic setup, see A. H. M. Jones, "Cloth Industry," 183–192.

32. The 1979 discovery and 1980 follow-up are to appear in C. H. Greenewalt's report to the *TürkArkDerg* (forthcoming). For the first Sardis expedition's jewelry finds, see *Sardis* XIII (1925) no. 101, pl. 9: 14, 15. For the earring, see *BASOR* 199, 51, fig. 42; for the seal, see *Sardis* (M10) *Small Finds* (forthcoming).

33. *Sardis* R2 (1978) 85, no. 106, figs. 229–230.

34. Ibid., 4–6.

35. Ibid.

36. M. Thompson, "The Mints of Lysimachus," 163–182. A. Houghton, III (by letter of October 24, 1979), kindly summarized the arguments in favor of Newell's contention that Alexander, Philip III, and Antigonus operated a mint at Sardis.

37. *Sardis* M7 (1981) 3, 79.

38. Kleiner-Noe, 78–85, pls. 29:1–g, 30:1, 31:1–5, 7, 9, 10. Seyrig, "Monnaies Hellénistiques," 35–38. Cf., however, Mørkholm, "Reflections," 50–51, 53.

39. *Sardis* XI (1916) nos. 139–145. *Kistophoroi* are mentioned in the inscription *Sardis* VII.1 (1932) no. 195, according to L. Robert, "Inscriptions de Sardes," 240.

40. *Sardis* M7 (1981), catalogue, nos. 381–384.

41. For the banking function of the great temples of Asia Minor, see Rostovtzeff, *Hellenistic World,* 231, 495.

42. *Sardis* VII.1 (1932) no. 1.

43. Ibid., no. 4.

44. Ibid., no. 3.

45. Rostovtzeff, *Hellenistic World,* 493; Atkinson, 65.

46. Magie, 225.

47. *Sardis* VII.1 (1932) no. 27.

48. Ibid., no. 8.

Religious Life

1. Keil, "Kulte," 255–266, especially 262–263. Cf. Hanfmann, "Gods" (forthcoming).

2. A. E. M. Johnston, "Greek Coins," in *Sardis* M7 (1981). Apart from L. Robert's *NIS* and inscriptions mentioned in preliminary *BASOR* reports, the new epigraphic finds are largely unpublished. The exemplary treatment and commentary of *all* Sardis inscriptions known to the authors (W. H. Buckler and D. M. Robinson) in *Sardis* VII.1 (1932) will continue to be the indispensable foundation of Sardian studies until a comparable treatment of the recent material is published. For sculpture, see *Sardis* R2 (1978).

3. Apart from the large block of Synagogue inscriptions (Chapter IX, *infra*) to be published in *Sardis* (R4) *Synagogue* (forthcoming), the new finds encompass many fragments and few long texts. Even *Sardis* VII.1 (1932) contains few Hellenistic inscriptions, by far not enough to reconstruct a history of the city. Considerable guesswork is involved in attribution and dating of coins of Sardis. The pioneering B. V. Head thought a number of autonomous coins were issued between 189 and 133 B.C.; Head, *BMC, Lydia,* xcviii-c. A. E. M. Johnston probably rightly assumes that none (except the "Seyrig" series) were struck at Sardis before the end of the Pergamene rule in 133 B.C. This kind of fundamental decision is still a matter of argument, and will remain so until a careful historical coordination of the moneyers' names and epigraphic material is achieved.

4. *Sardis* VII.1 (1932) 65–66, no. 50; R2 (1978) 164–165, figs. 426–427, no. 246. Moschine is not specifically designated as priestess of Artemis, and the dating of her statue is stylistic. For women named after Artemis, see a new inscription IN 61.49, probably first century B.C., and *Sardis* VII.1 (1932) no. 3.

5. *Sardis* VII.1 (1932) no. 8, line 139: Isidorus, son of Menogenes.

6. Priest: Gusmani, *LW,* 188, and no. 23. Priestesses: *Sardis* VII.1 (1932) nos. 50–55, 90–93. The earliest, no. 90, may date ca. 175–150 B.C., according to Buckler; three date between 133 and 50 B.C.; the others date from the second century A.D.

7. Neokoros Timarchus: *Sardis* VII.1 (1932) no. 4, and "Previous Research," *supra;* cook, lyre player, ibid., no. 3. The name of the lyre player, Seddis, seems Lydian.

8. *Sardis* R2 (1978) 20, 58–60, figs. 79–81, no. 20. A. E. M. Johnston, "Introduction," *Sardis* M7 (1981) and Catalogue. Head, *BMC, Lydia,* nos. 53–

59, pl. 24:16. The long neck and hairdo may reflect the style of the die-cutter rather than that of a third century B.C. (?) original. Approximate dating of the coins is provided by the moneyer Polemaios, possibly father of Socrates Pardalas, priest of Roma in 98 B.C., and Alcaeus, who died in 86 B.C. See L. Robert, "Alcée," 344–346. For "Hellenistic Rococo," see Bieber, 136–156.

9. *Sardis* R2 (1978) 166–167, fig. 435, no. 252; 98, fig. 201, no. 88.

10. The crucial text is *Sardis* VII.1 (1932) no. 8, ll. 132–139, of 2 B.C.: "those dwelling in the sanctuary of Zeus Polieus and Artemis." Cf. L. Robert, "Règlement perse," 320–321 n. 52; with other texts on Zeus Polieus. See "Zeus," "Artemis," *infra.*

11. Archaeological-linguistic: Chapter III, *supra;* also Hanfmann, "Gods" (forthcoming); *Sardis* R2 (1978) 58–60, no. 20.

12. See the discussions in Chapter V, *supra,* under "Languages" (*Kuvava*) and "Religious Life"; and Cybele, Meter, *infra.* Price-Trell, 137, figs. 240–243: "The temple of *Artemis-Kore* was erected in the Hellenistic period." Trell's account of Sardian coinage and architecture is utterly confused and confusing. Artemis idol: Fleischer, 181–201, pls. 77–83, thinks that "man die lydische Kore in hellenistischer und römischer Zeit mit Artemis gleichsetzte," a view rejected by L. Robert, "Hypaipa," 47 n. 103.

13. L. Robert, "Hypaipa," 32–36.

14. The first Chrysanthia and Artemis Chrysanthe: *Sardis* VII.1 (1932) 82–83, no. 77. The date has been corrected by Moretti, *Iscr. Agonistiche,* 154, no. 75. Cf. A. E. M. Johnston in *Sardis* M7 (1981).

15. *Sardis* R1 (1975) 57, 73–76, 100–103; R2 (1978) 82, 166, nos. 79, 251. *Sardis* M4 (1976) 48–49.

16. Strabo, 13.4.5 = *Sardis* M2 (1972) no. 234.

17. Knibbe, "Religiöser Frevel," 175. Fleisher, 200–201; for other bibliography and discussion, see Chapter V, *supra,* under "Religious Life," with n. 6.

18. Callimachus, *Hymns* 3.242–247 = *Sardis* M2 (1972) no. 188. Written after 270 B.C.?

19. Xenophon, *Anabasis* 1.6.6–7 = *Sardis* M2 (1972) nos. 270–271; Pausanias 7.6.6. *Sardis* R2 (1978) 31–32, no. 18.

20. The commander of the garrison of Sardis in 215–213, Aribazus had a Persian name. See Polybius, 7.7.10, 18.4.7. For late Hellenistic examples, see Metrodorus Mithreous and Mithres Metrodorou, among the *mystai* of Apollo Pleurenos, IN 64.4; and the potter Mithres of late Hellenistic pottery.

21. L. Robert, *NIS,* 23–33, in discussing a new inscription and one previously known, 32 n. 1, notes the "faible importance" of the cult of Anaitis at Sardis in Roman times. Cf. *Sardis* VII.1 (1932) no. 95, probably first or second century A.D.

22. L. Robert, "Hypaipa," citing Pausanias 3.16.8; Diogenes Tragicus in Athenaeus 14.38 (636 a–b). Welles, *Royal Correspondence,* no. 68.

23. Coins: *Sardis* M7 (1981) Catalogue. Head, *BMC, Lydia,* nos. 53–59, pl. 24:16. *Sardis* VII.1 (1932) no. 55, ca. A.D. 124–150. Buckler thought this a decree of Pergamon and referred the priesthood to the Athena cult in Pergamon. Dionysius contributed a statue for Athena, ibid., no. 21:10–11, ca. 150 B.C. Panathenaia and Eumenia, ibid., no. 27:13 (Iollas, before 50 B.C.). Embassy of 166 B.C.: n. 58, *infra.*

24. See n. 23, *supra.* The late Hellenistic copy of an Athena Nicephorus also speaks in favor of a local cult: *Sardis* R2 (1978) no. 113. She is represented on autonomous coins of Sardis with Artemis: *Sardis* M7 (1981) Catalogue. Head, *BMC, Lydia* nos. 53–59.

25. *Meter theon: Sardis* R2 (1978), priest of, no. 160, second century A.D. or earlier; dedication, no. 256, third century A.D. *Meter oreia: Sardis* VII.1 (1932), no. 101 b, date uncertain. *Meter Lydias,* from Lake Koloe: *BASOR* 177, 35–36, fig. 34; see n. 16, *supra.*

26. Sophocles, *Philoctetes* 391–401. Timotheos, *Persians,* 116–117; *Sardis* R2 (1978) 30–31, commentary. Henrichs, "Kybele," 267–276. For Hellenistic Metroon, see under "Urban and Architectural Development," *supra.*

27. *Sardis* R2 (1978) 126, figs. 301–302, no. 156.

28. *Sardis* R2 (1978) 60–61, 168–170, nos. 259 (Hellenistic), fig. 447; no. 256, fig. 442 (Roman). Coin: *Sardis* M7 (1981) Catalogue. Head, *BMC, Lydia,* no. 210.

29. *Sardis* R2 (1978) no. 256.

30. 226–223 B.C., Seyrig, "Monnaies Hellénistiques" (1963) 36–38, pl. 3.6: "Pseudo-Alexander"; reverse, head of city goddess in front of seated Zeus Olympius; *Sardis* M7 (1981) Catalogue, ill. (5 pieces found); "Oriental": Head, *BMC, Lydia,* nos. 49–52, pl. 25:15, after 133 B.C., on obverse; Zeus Lydios on reverse. The same Tyche type reappears on coins from A.D. 200–253. Head, *BMC, Lydia,* nos. 90–91, pl. 26:2.

31. *Sardis* R2 (1978) 88, 134–135, figs. 259–260, no. 128.

32. *Sardis* R2 (1978) 127–128, fig. 306, no. 159. The piece was found near the village of Matdere, not at Sardis, and may come from a countryside sanctuary.

33. IN 65.15, in a wreath on a large architectural pier. *BASOR* 203, 14. See L. Robert, *Hellenica* 11–12 (Paris 1960) 23–25.

34. *Sardis* R2 (1978), 180-181, fig. 472, "The City Goddess of Sardis on the Base from Puteoli."

35. Head, *BMC, Lydia,* nos. 60-61, pl. 24:17. Peplos, wheat stalks in r., long torch in l. Moneyer Asclepiades. Normal Hellenistic Dionysus on obverse. Sophocles, *Philoctetes* 391-401. See n. 26, *supra.* Coins: *Sardis* M7 (1981). Head, *BMC, Lydia,* no. 72, pl. 25:7. "City of Demeter," Apollonius of Tyana in Philostratus, *Letters* 75; *Sardis* M2 (1972) no. 217. Penella, 308-311.

36. Head, *BMC, Lydia,* nos. 98-101, pl. 26:4. *Sardis* R2 (1978) 181.

37. By Charon of Lampsacus in Photius, *s.v.* Kybelos.

38. *Sardis* (M10) *Small Finds* (forthcoming). *Sardis* I (1922) 81, ill. 76, thought by Butler an import from Myrina. *Sardis* R2 (1978) 83, 107, fig. 237, no. 111.

39. A. E. M. Johnston in *Sardis* M7 (1981) 85, no. 285. Head, *BMC, Lydia,* no. 135. Price-Trell, 137-139, figs. 31, 266 (color, Paphos). It is interesting that at Tamassos on Cyprus next to the sanctuary of a very Ishtar-like Aphrodite there has come to light a sanctuary of Cybele, pointing to possible early relations.

40. Koraia/Aktia: *Sardis* VII.1 (1932) no. 77; the basic discussion of coins is now A. E. M. Johnston, *Sardis* M7 (1981) Catalogue and Commentary. Fleischer, 187-191, has good coin illustrations and valuable material on the occurrence of the same statuary type in other Lydian cities (Tmolus, Daldis, Gordus Iulia, Maeonia, Silandus), pls. 77-83. See also Price-Trell, 136, figs. 240-243. Dedication in Rome: *IGRR* 1 (1911) nos. 88-89. Chrysanthina: L. Robert, *Bull.* 76 (1963) 169 n. 34: "A notre avis, la fête de Sardis était célébré en l'honneur de Kore," with references; see n. 13, *supra.* Children of Kore, *BASOR* 211, 27, fig. 8. *Sardis* R2 (1978) 178-179, fig. 470, no. 277.

41. Von Aulock, *SNG* 8, pl. 100, no. 3141. Fleischer, *Artemis,* 189.

42. Hanfmann-Balmuth, 261-269, pls. 34-35, with earlier coin literature (here Fig. 148). *Sardis* R2 (1978) 139, fig. 344, no. 194.

43. *Sardis* R2 (1978) no. 102. See under "Urban and Architectural Development," *supra.*

44. Treaty with Ephesus, 98 B.C.: *Sardis* VII.1 (1932) no. 6; cf. the copy found in Pergamon, *OGIS,* no. 437.

45. See Robert, "Règlement perse," 320-321, on *therapeutai*; ca. 100-50 B.C. (honors for Pardalas); also *Sardis* VII.1 (1932) no. 22; late Hellenistic(?) altar of Demetrios, *Sardis* R2 (1978) no. 161; *Megistos: Sardis* VII.1 (1932) nos. 47-48 (under Trajan).

46. Robert, ibid.

47. Arrian, *Anabasis* 1.17.3 = *Sardis* M2 (1972) no. 235.

48. Seyrig, "Monnaies Hellénistiques" (1963) 36-38, no. 2, pl. 3:6. There is no cogent evidence for the posture of the colossal Zeus-Achaeus in the Artemis temple, though a seated "Olympian Zeus" image is possible (see Fig. 201:2). His later *synnaos,* Antoninus Pius, was seated. *Sardis* R2 (1978) nos. 102 (Zeus); 79-87 (Antoninus).

49. 329 B.C.: *Sardis* R2 (1978) 31, nos. 17 and 234. Gusmani, *LW,* no. 3. Artemis-Qldans temple: Gusmani, *LW,* 188, and no. 23, line 1. "King" is Gusmani's preference.

50. Seyrig, "Monnaies Hellénistiques" (1963) 35-36, pl. 3:1; *Sardis* M7 (1981) Catalogue, ill. (5 pieces), with discussion of type; Head, *BMC, Lydia,* no. 7, pl. 42:10, inscribed "Sardis year 6," calculated as 133 B.C. minus 6 equals 127 B.C.; ibid., no. 96, Augustus. See Kleiner-Noe, 78-85, pls. XXIX-XXXI.

51. Price-Trell, 138-140, figs. 244-245.

52. *BMC, Lydia,* no. 76, pl. 25:9, with Thea Roma seated on the other side.

53. Metraux, 158-159, pls. 35-36, with comparisons of coins. *Sardis* R2 (1978) no. 107. The style is definitely Hellenistic, different from what the severe, full-figure Lydian Zeus leads us to expect.

54. *Eis to Dios: Sardis* VII.1 (1932) no. 17. This sanctuary was near the sanctuary of Mên, hence presumably in town. For Zeus Lydios on the Tmolus, see Chapter V, *supra,* under "Religious Life." The Phrygian Zeus Petarenos, *Sardis* VII.1 (1932) no. 100, has nothing to do with Sardis.

55. L. Robert, "Règlement perse," 308, 324-325. Welles, *Royal Correspondence,* 266-273. S. E. Johnson, "Sabazios," 542-550. Kraabel, "Paganism," 30-31.

56. A. E. M. Johnston in *Sardis* M7 (1981) Catalogue, Commentary. "Apollo-club," 42 new pieces. See Head, *BMC, Lydia,* nos. 10-21, pl. 24:7. "Herakles-Apollo," 77(?) new pieces, and Head, *BMC, Lydia,* nos. 22-31, pl. 24:8-9. Johnston discusses the relation of the two series and sees them as largely parallel. Pre-133 B.C. cistophori with club: Head, *BMC, Lydia,* nos. 2-3.

57. G. Daux, "La Liste Delphique," 658-661. L. Robert, *Bull.* 91 (1978) 461-462, no. 403.

58. Comparisons of Apollo figure with Head, *BMC, Lydia,* pl. 24:8-9.

59. IN 64.4 (unpublished). See *BASOR* 177, 36.

60. See Hanfmann, "Lydiaka," 68-72, 84 n. 44, on Tylon, Herakles, and Omphale. *Sardis* R2 (1978) 48-49, fig. 47, no. 7-O (Nemean Lion). For sources on Omphale, see Rose, *OCD,* 753-754, including

Apollodorus, *Bibl.* 2.131 and Ovid, *Heroides* 9.53–118. *Sardis* M2 (1972) nos. 1–4, 130 (Dionysius Scytobrachion) and Ion (tragedy Omphale).

61. *Sardis* VII.1 (1932) no. 21, inscription in honor of Dionysius. The name of Herakles is plausibly restored after an analogous phrase in a Pergamene inscription. Fig. 205; *Sardis* R2 (1978) 93, figs. 186–187, no. 71. N. H. Ramage compares Ptolemy IV, but historical reasons speak for an Attalid. One would expect Eumenes II or Attalus II or III, but the profile really resembles most the gem with the founder Philetairos: Richter, *Portraits* 3, 273, fig. 1916.

62. Herakles-Omphale: *BASOR* 157, 18. Hanfmann, *Letters,* 65, fig. 42. See A. Oliver in *Sardis* (R5) *Pottery:* "Hellenistic" (forthcoming), for the date of Tomb of the Lintel and description. The famous Pompeian painting of Herakles and triumphant Omphale is generally regarded as following a Pergamene original: Pfuhl, *MuZ* 3, 826–828, fig. 664 (color).

63. Head, *BMC, Lydia,* nos. 22–31, 39, pl. 24:9, 11.

64. Head, *BMC, Lydia,* no. 37, pl. 24:10. Cf. Richter, *Portraits* 3, 275, fig. 1930 (Louvre). Bieber, 121, figs. 482–487. E. Thomas, following H. Kähler, identifies the Herakles of the Pergamon relief with Eumenes II (Thomas, *Mythos,* 17).

65. Head, *BMC, Lydia,* nos. 79–80, pl. 25:11. *Sardis* M7 (1981) Catalogue, four coins, dated A.D. 90–100, perhaps Nerva. Price-Trell, 140, fig. 248, dated A.D. 175. The walking type does not correspond to the Pergamene painting, n. 62, *supra.*

66. *Sardis* R2 (1978) no. 156; see the "folk" graffito, no. 166.

67. Head, *BMC, Lydia,* nos. 81–82, pl. 25:12. Price-Trell, 139–141, fig. 247, with head of Zeus Lydios (inscribed) on obverse.

68. Price-Trell, 138–141, figs. 245–246; for altar of Zeus Lydios see n. 51, *supra.* Torso: *Sardis* R2 (1978) 108, fig. 240, no. 114.

69. See Chapter V, *supra,* under "Religious Life."

70. *Sardis* VII.1 (1932) no. 21. Coins: Head, *BMC, Lydia,* nos. 8–9, pl. 42:12. *Sardis* R2 (1978) 126, no. 156, fig. 303.

71. Head, *BMC, Lydia,* nos. 8–9, pl. 42:12. *Sardis* R2 (1978) 126, fig. 303, no. 156.

72. *Sardis* R2 (1978), 15, 86, figs. 431–432, no. 249.

73. Nannas: Gusmani, *LW,* no. 29. *Sardis* R2 (1978) no. 279, with literature. Head, *BMC, Lydia,* nos. 47–48, pl. 24:14. *Sardis* M7 (1981) Catalogue, four coins. *Sardis* VII.1 (1932) nos. 4, 123; R1 (1975) 31, 175 n. 123. Three large acroteria with emphatic grapes (Manisa Museum) may have belonged to a late Hellenistic temple of Dionysus. *BASOR* 215,

44, fig. 12. One was found in Church "EA," the others in the Synagogue.

74. *Sardis* VII.1 (1932) no. 4, Timarchus is to be crowned at the annual Dionysia in the god's own place, the theater. *Phyle:* ibid., nos. 12, 126.

75. Head, *BMC, Lydia,* nos. 40–44, pl. 24:12, 14. Cf. *Sardis* M7 (1981) Catalogue, with other references.

76. *Sardis* R2 (1978) 107, fig. 236, no. 110. N. H. Ramage, "Herm," 253–256. Coin of the Ionic League by M. Cl. Fronto: Englemann, 190–191.

77. Sculpture: *Sardis* R2 (1978) nos. 117–119, 162 (goat sacrifice), *Sardis* (M10) *Small Finds* (forthcoming): terracottas including Hellenistic actors' masks. Pottery: Papposilenus, maenads, on Hellenistic local ware (IH 303), P 67.9; 63.571, and many vines. See G. M. A. Hanfmann and I. Hanfmann, *Sardis* (R5) *Pottery,* "Hellenistic Relief Ware" (forthcoming).

78. *Sardis* VII.1 nos. 13, 14. Inscriptions of *Dionysoutechnitai:* both inscriptions celebrate Hadrian as *Neos Dionysos,* but this actors' association was already quite active in Hellenistic times, with its early center located in Teos: Magie, 80–81; 2, 899–901.

79. Of the three best preserved Roman sculptures, works of the second or third century A.D. copying earlier originals, one shows Dionysus supported by a satyr and the others were table legs. The first was found in the latrine of the "Byzantine Shops"; one of the table legs was found in the "Byzantine Shop" of the fifth to sixth century, BS E 19, another standing on the floor of the basement of "House of Bronzes," which dates probably after A.D. 540. See *Sardis* R2 (1978) nos. 122, 223, 225. C. Foss, *Sardis* M4 (1976) 155: "Himerius mentions the worship of Dionysus as if it was current . . . in the late fourth century."

80. Hera: *Sardis* R2 (1978) no. 275. Hecate: ibid., no. 246.

81. A nice relief group of Asclepius and Hygieia from a jug neck of Greek mainland(?) black-glazed ware is imported: *Sardis* (R5) *Pottery,* "Hellenistic Relief Ware" (forthcoming). Statuette and fragments: *Sardis* R2 (1978) no. 125. NoEx 59.2; 69.25, unpublished. Dedication of an "Asclepius" to the Nymphs, *Sardis* VII.1 (1932) no. 94.

82. See Chapter V, under "Religious Life," *supra,* on "Qldans," and n. 50, *supra,* with complete references to the material collected by Lane, *CMRDM* 1: nos. 78, 79, 80; 2: 41–46, pls. 17–18 (coins with Mên *Askaenos*); 3: 17, 43, 113. Robert, *NIS,* 31–33, new inscriptions up to 1964. Others yet unpublished, all Roman. Cf. *BASOR,* 157, 24; Hanfmann, *Letters,* 58, fig. 35. In 67.2, *Meni Ourani(o),* second century A.D.; 67.4, *Meni Axiotteno,* A.D. 235; IN 67.8,

Meni . . . otto; 67.10, *Axiotteno.* All four inscriptions found in 1967 came from the Synagogue or the Byzantine Shops; and Robert's inscription, IN 58.8, from the House of Bronzes, thus from a limited area along the Main Avenue. This is a possible indication that the sanctuary of Mên was nearby. Cf. *Sardis* VII.1 (1932) no. 17, line 16: *peri to Menos.* Possibly, it belonged to "Mên, Lord of Axiotta," whose original location P. Hermann, "Mên," 415–423, situates in the region of Saitta and Silandus. On the other hand, it is Mên *Askaenos* who officially appears on coins of Sardis. Cf. Lane, *supra;* an up-to-date discussion, *Sardis* M7 (1981) Catalogue, (Vespasian); see Von Aulock, *SNG* 8 no. 3147. Inscribed: *Askenos,* Head, *BMC, Lydia,* nos. 95–96, third century A.D. He is shown standing, with Phrygian cap, holding scepter and pine cone.

83. *Sardis* VII.1 (1932), no. 96 a; R2 (1978) no. 253.

84. A study of the Sardian theophoric names is yet to be made. Menophila is still of the second century B.C. See *Sardis* R2 (1978) no. 245.

85. Dioscorides, *Anth. Pal.* 6.220, third century B.C. *Sardis* M2 (1972) no. 13: "From Pessinus he intended to journey to Sardis . . . in frenzied state." Catullus, *Poem* 63. Ovid, *Fasti* 4.221–244. Walton, *OCD,* 146–147 gives the basic sources for the legend. See also Vermaseren, *Attis,* esp. 3, 31, and *CCCA,* vols. 3, 7.

86. *Sardis* VII.1 (1932) no. 17, ll. 6–7: *krene mysterioi Attei entantia, aporrhytos eis to Dios.* Zeus-Angdistis: Pausanias 7.17.9.

87. A table leg, ca. second century A.D., may represent Attis but is not in his usual type. *Sardis* R2 (1978) no. 224.

88. *Sardis* VII.1 (1932) 13–15, nos. 6, 93: *OGIS,* no. 437, line 92. Alexarchos, priest of Roma, late second century B.C.? and 98 B.C. *Sardis* VII.1 (1932) nos. 112–114, funerary chests dated by priests of Roma.

89. Head, *BMC, Lydia,* no. 76, pl. 25:9, with inscribed head of Zeus Lydios on obverse. She is shown in the standard seated type of the Ara Pacis with Victory in hand.

90. IN 63.121. Flight: Livy 37.33; *Sardis* M2 (1972) nos. 206–207.

91. *Sardis* R2 (1978) no. 102. P. Herrmann, "Teos," 43–44. Hanfmann, *Croesus,* 23 (Achaeus), 72, no. 54.

92. See under Athena, *supra.* An embassy went to Delphi in 166 B.C. to obtain recognition of the Eumenia. They are mentioned in the Iollas inscription, ca. 50 B.C. Timarchus: *Sardis* VII.1 (1932) no. 4. Curtius, *Wandmalerei,* 336–339, color pl. 9. *Sardis* M2 (1972) no. 39, Alexander of Aetolia.

93. *Sardis* R2 (1978) no. 72. C. Vermeule,
"Cuirass," 97. Dedication: *Sardis* VII.1 (1932) no. 88.

94. *Sardis* VII.1 (1932) no. 8, Part I, lines 13–14. Cf. Magie, 1614. Augustus on autonomous Sardian coins: Head, *BMC, Lydia,* no. 96, with Zeus Lydios, standing.

95. *Sardis* VII.1 (1932) no. 89.

96. Altar: *Sardis* R2 (1978) no. 158; on the "diluted" use of *heros,* see L. Robert, ibid., 175, no. 270 (not from Sardis), where a baby or child is called *heros.*

97. *Sardis* R2 (1978) no. 141 (horseman); no. 135, "Zeus-like" dead between two small servants.

98. *Sardis* R2 (1978) no. 134, with reference to L. Robert's commentary, Hanfmann-Polatkan-Robert, 45–56. *Sardis* R2 (1978) no. 245. *Sardis* VII.1 (1932) no. 104.

99. *Sardis* VII.1 (1932) no. 27.

100. *Metragyrtai:* known already in the fourth century to Aristotle, as nickname of Callias, *Rhet.* 1405 a 20. On *metragyrtai* see Nilsson, *GGR,* 616–630; *RE* 30, 1471–1472. The wonderful mosaic of *metragyrtai* by Dioscurides of Samos is likely to reflect a Pergamene painting, then used as illustration of New Comedy, as was its counterpart, Menander's "Women at Breakfast." Curtius, 337–340, color pl. 9. Alexander of Aetolia probably projects contemporary Hellenistic experience when he speaks of a "*bakelas* clad in gold . . . beating chattering kettledrums (tympana)." *Sardis* M2 (1972) no. 39. *Anth. Pal.* 7.709.

101. L. Robert, "Hypaipa," 28–40, especially 30–31, inscription of Theophron.

102. For the Persian names, and especially Mithres, see, most recently, L. Robert, "Hypaipa," 31, 35, new Sardian inscription n. 51. Secure late Hellenistic examples of Mithres are graffiti on a Hellenistic Relief molded bowl and on a piece of Eastern Sigillata B (ca. 30 B.C.–A.D. 40): *Sardis* (R5) *Pottery* (forthcoming): J. F. Wrabetz, "Hellenistic and Roman Sigillata Wares," Introduction. Cf. *Sardis* VII.1 (1932) no. 224. IN 64.4; *Metrodoros Mithreou* and *Mithres Metrodorou* (late Hellenistic stele). For the origin and spread of the Mithras cult in Asia Minor, see Saxl, *Mithras,* who thought that the canonic bull-slaying type in art was created in Pergamon in the second century B.C.

103. On the general phenomenon see Hanfmann, *Croesus,* 45, 56, 66–68, 74, with references to the work of C. P. Jones and G. W. Bowersock. For intentionally emphasized Lydianism, see L. Robert, "Hypaipa," 30 n. 24: Sardis is capital "of all Lydia"; Mother of Gods is "of Lydia."

104. See the discussions of the evidence under Artemis, Kore, Demeter, Zeus Polieus, and Zeus Lydios, *supra.* It is clear that the reconstruction of the

Artemis–Zeus Polieus temple and precinct went on into the second century. Inscriptions to Artemis reappear around the time of Trajan.

105. Basic surveys: Robert, *NIS,* 37–38. Hanfmann-Waldbaum, "New Excavations," 318–319. *Sardis* R1 (1975) 29–30 n. 101. Josephus, *AJ* 12.147–153, cites Antiochus III's letter to Zeuxis as speaking of "rebelling," *neoterizontes* Phrygians and Lydians, thus avoiding the mention of Achaeus.

106. Josephus, *AJ* 14.135 (L. Antonius); 16.172 (C. Norbanus Flaccus), 14.259–261 (City of Sardis). *Sardis* M2 (1972) nos. 212, 275, with references. Kraabel, "Paganism," "The Evidence from Josephus," 14–18, is a recent commentary (1978). See also the discussion in Chapter IX, *infra,* under "The Building" and "Impact of Discovery."

107. Kraabel, "Paganism," 16.

Conclusions and Cultural Perspective

1. Some results of Sardis work are integrated in the overview of Anatolia in "Hellenization Takes Command," Hanfmann, *Croesus,* Chapter II.

2. *PECS,* 360–361 (R. S. Young).

3. See the Appendix to "Previous Research," *supra.*

4. Hanfmann, *Croesus,* 4. *Acts of the Apostles* 14.11–12 (Lycaonian).

5. See *Sardis* VII.1 (1932) no. 27 (Iollas); and J. C. Waldbaum in *Sardis* (M8) *Metalwork,* "Sources."

6. Pausanias 6.15.2. Picard, *Manuel* 3:1, 194.

7. Bieber, 194. Cedrenus, *Hist.,* 306 B. Metraux, 156. *Sardis* R2 (1978) no. 107. The attribution of the Mylasa-Boston head to Bryaxis was proposed by G. Lippold, and approved by A. Adriani and Ch. Picard. The Mylasa head has indisputable similarities to the Zeus head found in Sardis and considered by Metraux as possibly Zeus Lydios. Zeus from Artemis Temple, *Sardis* R2 (1978) no. 102.

8. That Hermogenes must have influenced the design of the "pseudodipteral" porch of the temple has been argued by G. Gruben (1961) 155–196, and R. Martin, in Lloyd-Müller-Martin, 350, 360–362. Cf. *Sardis* R1 (1975) 75. Date of Hermogenes: Linfert, *Kunstzentren,* 164–165.

9. *Sardis* VII.1 (1932) no. 21 (Dionysius).

10. Nilsson, *Die Hellenistische Schule,* 30–82. F. A. G. Beck, "Hellenistic Education," in *OCD,* 371.

11. Strabo, 13.4.9. *Sardis* M2 (1972) no. 216.

12. Menophila: *Sardis* VII.1 (1932) 108–109, figs. 100–101; R2 (1978) no. 245. Cumont, *Recherches,* 26–27, 306–307. "Philaenis," *RE* 19:2 (1938) 2122. Elephantis: Weitzmann, *Roll²,* 67–68, with references. Reflected in Pergamene appliqué ware: Schäfer, 79, no. 94, literature. Similar scenes on appliqué ware found at Sardis: *Sardis* (R5) *Pottery:*

"Hellenistic Pottery" (forthcoming). It is not yet clear whether all are imported from Pergamon.

13. The mold, P 59.475, is certainly local; *BASOR* 157,36; probably first century B.C.; to be published in *Sardis* (R5) *Pottery:* "Hellenistic Pottery" (forthcoming). Illustrated love and adventure romances: Weitzmann, *Ancient Illumination,* 99–110, on "love, adventure, bucolic, allegorical romances."

14. See *Sardis* M2 (1972) 3–4, for a listing of relevant fragments.

15. Callimachus, *Hymns* 3.242–247; *Iambus* 4 = *Sardis* M2 (1972) no. 188. Henrichs, "Despoina Kybele," 271–273.

16. Ovid, *Met.* 11.85–193.

17. Ovid, *Met.* 6.9–16.

18. Ovid, *Heroides* 9.53–118.

19. Dioscorides, *Anth. Pal.* 6.220 = *Sardis* M2 (1972) no. 13.

20. Alexander of Aetolia, *Anth. Pal.* 7.709 = *Sardis* M2 (1972) no. 39.

21. For a sample of Graeco-Roman *topoi,* see the sections "Pactolus" and "Tmolus" in *Sardis* M2 (1972) nos. 242–267 (Dio Chrysostomus, Horace, Juvenal, Lucan, Ovid, Philostratus, Propertius, Seneca, Varro, Virgil, Lycophron, Silius Italicus, Statius). The imagery in later European arts of Sardis and Lydia is being collected. For a nice late medieval example of Arachne, see S. and G. Weinberg, "Arachne," 267, pl. 35, an Ovid illustration.

VIII. The Roman and Late Antique Period

Introduction

1. The periodization followed here is that proposed in *Sardis* R1 (1975) 30–31; it differs from the scheme outlined in the "Chronological Terminology," ibid., 6, where the period is presented in a tripartite division: Early Imperial, A.D. 17–284; Late Roman, 284 (280)–395; Early Byzantine, 395–616. In C. Foss's chronology, *Sardis* M4 (1976), 1–52, this is followed by "Dark Ages," 617 to ca. 800. The tripartite scheme has the advantage that it correctly designates as transitional the time from Diocletian through Theodosius I (A.D. 284–395). However, since the publications of Sardis sources (M2, 1972; M4, 1976) have adopted the twofold division A.D. 17–284; 284–616, we are following this division. By "Late Antique" we understand approximately the period 284–616, as suggested in a bracketed alternative of "Chronological Terminology," *supra.* For numismatic periodization, see *Sardis* M1 (1972) 1.

2. See *Sardis* R1 (1975) 2–3, for the situation prior to the Harvard-Cornell excavations. The decisions to excavate the huge, clearly Roman building "B" (gymnasium), which stood high above ground, the large bath CG, the Artemis Precinct, and eventually the Acropolis were taken jointly by G. M. A. Hanfmann and A. H. Detweiler, who as President of the American Schools of Oriental Research had been asked by the Bollingen Foundation to certify that the site was "diggable." Other excavations of Roman and Late Antique material developed out of attempts to reach Lydian levels (HoB, PN, PC). The development of digging and the early uncertainties (CG was to be a city gate) are described in Hanfmann, *Letters*, 32–34, 36–37, 40, and passim.

3. Serious consideration was given from 1958 to 1962 to the possibility of excavating a major Roman complex, either in the center (Fig. 167:37, 23, 41) or in the east part of the site (Church D, theater; Fig. 167:25, 29). Exorbitant land expenses and commitment of available staff and labor to ongoing projects (especially the Synagogue and Bin Tepe cemetery) thwarted these plans.

4. F. K. Yegul's account of *Early Travelers and Modern Excavations*, under "The Bath-Gymnasium Complex," *infra*, with reference to the incompletely excavated gymnasium (1958–1974), well illustrates the difficulties of coping with an overburden of 6–9 m. above floor levels. The same situation, with overburden up to 10 m., prevented complete excavation of the bath CG, where in fact the lower floors were not reached; see *Sardis* R1 (1975) 134, 144. The huge church "D" is buried as deeply or more deeply than the gymnasium. Only a mechanized assault with front loaders, conveyor belts, cranes, and a fleet of trucks could produce results in the large buried Roman buildings.

5. *BASOR* 154, 22–27; 157, 22–28; *Sardis* M4 (1976) 43–44 n. 113, literature.

6. This project was led by R. L. Vann. See *Sardis* (M14) *Early Travelers and Unexcavated Buildings* (forthcoming).

7. See Yegul, "Marble Court," 169–194.

8. For illustrations see Seager, *Synagogue*, figs. 3–35; Hanfmann, *Letters*, figs. 126–130, 144–147, 167–168, 182–184, 189–201, 212–217, 222–226, color pl. V for a pictorial account; and Majewski, *BASOR* 187, 29–50, figs. 46–52 (mosaics, revetments, pilasters), and "Conservation," Kansas City, 99–104, fig. 5, for methods used.

9. See nn. 6, 7, *supra*. Figurative (but not floral decorative) sculpture including architectural pieces is published in *Sardis* R2 (1978) Parts V–VI. A full account of mosaic and wall painting is to appear in *Sardis* (R9) *Mosaics and Wall Painting* (forthcoming).

10. Dedicatory inscriptions of 211–212 (Fig.

227); of Severus Simplikios, ca. A.D. 400; and of the fifth century A.D.: see "Bath-Gymnasium Complex," *infra*, nn. 14–16, 47, 55, 58, with references. *Sardis* M4 (1976) 40, "Sources," nos. 15, 16 (Greek texts), with correction on the position of Severus Simplikios as Vicar of Asia by C. Foss, "Atticus Philippus," 175–177.

11. See in general the synopses in Chapter I of *Sardis* M7 (1981) (Greek Imperial by A. E. M. Johnston; Roman by T. V. Buttrey); also *BASOR* 211, 34–36, for a preview; *Sardis* M6 (1980); and (all forthcoming): *Sardis* (M8) *Metalwork*; (R5) *Pottery*, especially "Sigillate" by J. F. Wrabetz; (M12) *Lamps*; (M10) *Small Finds and Terracottas*. At the time of writing, no work was being done on plain Roman and Byzantine pottery.

12. It should perhaps be put on record that the identification of the destruction of Sardis with the Sassanian invasion in A.D. 616 was first proposed by G. M. A. Hanfmann, *BASOR* 154, 17 n. 32, suggesting A.D. 615. The argument was bolstered and the time of destruction defined as the spring or summer of A.D. 616 by G. E. Bates, *Sardis* M1 (1971) 1–2, by close analysis of coins found in the Byzantine Shops. An attempt by Charanis, "A Note," 175–180, to undermine the synchronism was convincingly refuted by C. Foss; see Foss, "Fall of Sardis"; see also *Sardis* M4 (1976) 53–55.

13. *Revelation* of St. John the Divine 3.1–6: "And write to the angel of the Church in Sardis." *Sardis* M2 (1972) no. 224. On letters to the Seven Churches, most recently, see Lähnemann, 517–539; on that to Sardis, ibid., 532–533. For the interplay of forces see the appreciation by Kraabel, "Paganism," 13–33. For Late Antique–Early Byzantine Christianity in Sardis, see *Sardis* M4 (1976) 27–34, "Pagans, Jews, and Christians."

14. Seager, *Synagogue*.

15. See *BASOR* 215, 33–41, figs. 3–10, the most extensive report. *Sardis* M4 (1976) 45–47, figs. 24, 27.

16. *Sardis* M4 (1976) 38–52.

17. See *Sardis* M4 (1976) 40 f., 44, 50–52; and R2 (1978), 49, 85–86, for reuse of sculpture.

18. The dating of the Roman city walls based on coins is A.D. 350–400, favored by Hanfmann in *Sardis* R1 (1975) 45, and Müller-Wiener (1979) 237; in *Sardis* M4 (1976) 3, fig. 1, Foss argued for the late third century. He plausibly dates the Acropolis wall to the period of Constans II (641–668), successor of Heraklios, under whom the Main Road was repaired in the lower city.

19. It is arguable that the great Christian construction program as well as the major part of the Synagogue decoration was begun under Constantine and his sons.

20. *Sardis* M4 (1976).

21. *Sardis* R1 (1975) 31–32. For the integration of Sardis results into the broader picture of Roman and Late Antique Asia Minor, see Hanfmann, *Croesus,* 42–44, 52–55, 87–90, figs. 87, 102, 106, 157, 158, 183, 184, with special reference to renovation of the city, bath-gymnasium, and Synagogue.

22. Tacitus, *Ann.* 2.47. C. H. Moore translated "administer relief" for *refoveret. Sardis* M2 (1979) no. 220, omits appointment of Ateius, for which see Dio Cassius 1.7.17.

23. For instability and seismicity, see Chapters I and II, *supra.* Most recently, see Ambraseys, 376–377, a seismologist who seeks to establish cycles of seismicity; L. Robert, "Séismes," 405, within a survey of inscriptions of Asia Minor which mention earthquakes.

24. *BASOR* 157, 20, figs. 1, 8.

25. *BASOR* 177, 14–15: according to G. F. Swift, the dump was built up between the "late Hellenistic" and "late Roman" periods, i.e., ca. A.D. 17–400.

26. *BASOR* 170, 50–51, fig. 37; 174, 47–50, figs. 29–30 (section).

27. *BASOR* 177, 27, fig. 25 (section), vaulted passages under east screen colonnade of the Marble Court.

28. Aqueduct: *Sardis* VII.1 (1932) no. 10. Latin and Greek, northeast bastion of the Acropolis, A.D. 53–54. A statue base from the south colonnade of the Main Avenue found during the summer of 1979 (E135–137/S30–31 near MMS, *99.7, H. 1.61 m., diam. 0.61 m.) carries an inscription (IN 79.8) dedicated to Tiberius, "founder of the city" and uncle of emperor Claudius; hence the Main Avenue was begun under Tiberius and finished under Claudius. L. Robert (by letter, October 1979) conjectures that this statue was a counterpart to a statue of Claudius erected shortly after Claudius' accession, in A.D. 41.

29. Although briefly mentioned by Butler and recorded in the survey, *Sardis* I (1922) pl. I, the aqueduct traces have not been properly recorded; the aid of a hydrologist would be required. It may have been a pressure aqueduct. It is not included in R. L. Vann's *Sardis* (M14) *Early Travelers and Unexcavated Buildings* (forthcoming). See also *Sardis* R1 (1975) 6–7, 27–28, 31, 33, 83.

30. *BASOR* 170, 21–22, fig. 13. *Sardis* R1 (1975) 27.

31. R. L. Vann, *Sardis* (M14) *Early Travelers and Unexcavated Buildings* (forthcoming); and *Construction* (unpublished). An average example, Building D: *Sardis* R1 (1975) 108–116, figs. 257, 273, 274.

32. A similar situation with reuse of large ashlar masonry seems to have occurred in the Roman Northeast Stoa, late first or second century A.D., *Sardis* R1 (1975) 119, fig. 282.

33. *Sardis* R1 (1975) 132, 143, 146, fig. 424.

34. Visible in *BASOR* 157, 34–35, fig. 19. See n. 47, *infra.*

35. A penetrating analysis of this system is given by Yegül, "Bath-Gymnasium," under *Structure;* cf. Fasolo, "L'Architectura Romana di Efeso," 1–92.

36. *Sardis* VII.1 (1932) no. 10.

37. He had a distinguished counterpart or forerunner in Cossutius, a Roman citizen, but perhaps a Greek, who built for the Seleucids (175–163 B.C.) the aqueduct at Antioch. The Sardis aqueduct is quite Roman in type, and with a project sponsored by the emperor, the experts were likely to come from Rome. For an example of a Roman army surveyor so employed, see R. MacMullen, "Imperial Building," 200–210; and for the tug-of-war for such experts, see Hanfmann, *Croesus,* 46. For Cossutius' aqueduct, see Downey, *Antioch,* 102–103.

38. We speak in terms of design, not execution. The actual colonnades at Antioch, erected under Tiberius, were also built later than the street. Those of Olba and Pompeiopolis may be contemporary with Sardis. See Hanfmann, *Croesus,* 49; and n. 39, *infra.*

39. Downey, *Antioch,* 173; cf. Ward-Perkins, *Planning,* 32.

40. One may surmise inspiration from the baths of Agrippa, built in 25 B.C. *ERA,* 186, fig. 87. Nash, 2:429. For the Augustan colonies, see Ward-Perkins, *Planning,* 29–32, figs. 52, 63; for arrangement of public buildings, figs. 65–67; and for the Imperial Works Office: Hanfmann, *Croesus,* 42 n. 8, with references.

41. *Sardis* R1 (1975) 30, figs. 1, 10, grid squares E100–900.

42. Vann, *Sardis* (M14) *Early Travelers and Unexcavated Buildings* (forthcoming), with description of stadium.

43. *Sardis* VII.1 (1932) no. 17, line 11.

44. Hanfmann, *Croesus,* 44–45, with examples from Prusa and Nicaea.

45. By Julia Lydia, granddaughter of the famous Socrates Polemaiou Pardalas, on whom see Chapter VII, *supra,* under "History," n. 39. *Sardis* R2 (1978) no. 275; L. Robert, "Séismes," 405.

46. *Sardis* VII.1 (1932) no. 181, with figs. 168–182, pl. 12: "My torus and my foundation-block are each a single stone, and of all (the columns) *I am the first to rise again* built of complete (*holon*) stones not furnished by the people (not from city funds) but from stones given by friends." Buckler on general epigraphic grounds favored the earlier part of the first century A.D., but others (L. Robert, orally) prefer the second century.

47. Yegül, "Bath-Gymnasium Complex," under *Building History and Dating, infra,* cautiously leaves the date of the beginning open. The *petit appareil*

technique used in the west wall has parallels from the late first and early second century in Pergamon and Ephesus: see *BASOR* 211, 29, and *ERA,* 346, 584.

48. Head, *BMC, Lydia,* 171; Price-Trell, 137, fig. 242; Burrell, *Neokoroi,* no. 65–66.

49. *Sardis* R1 (1975) 37–39, 42–43, fig. 11.

50. *BASOR* 215, 33–41, figs. 3–9.

51. *Sardis* M4 (1976) 3, and 149 n. 3; for Pactolus North villa and church, see ibid., 46–47, figs. 24–27.

52. *Sardis* R1 (1975) 44, 48–49. Zosimus 5.18; *Sardis* M4 (1976) 108, no. 7, A.D. 399.

53. Müller-Wiener (1979) 237.

54. *Sardis* VII.1 (1932) no. 8.

55. *Sardis* R2 (1978) no. 250, dated by V. H. Poulsen after A.D. 14.

56. IN 65.14: *Germanikon Theon,* posthumous, *BASOR* 203, 14. For the visit and coin, see Magie, 497–498, n. 1357. *Sardis* M7 (1981) *Catalogue.* Cf. C. Vermeule, *Imperial Art,* 187–190, 461.

57. Rome: *Sardis* R2 (1978) 181; *Sardis* VII.1 (1932) nos. 9, 34 (Phyle *Tymolis*). For the new statue base IN 79.8, see n. 28, *supra.*

58. Temple: Tacitus, *Ann.* 4.55–56. It is on this famous occasion that the Sardians claimed kinship with the Etruscans. Caesareia: *Sardis* VII.1 (1932) no. 38; family group with Claudius: nos. 37, Antonia; 35, Drusus, son of Germanicus.

59. *Sardis* M7 (1981). For devices see *BASOR* 211, 35: "Zeus Lydios, Demeter/Kore, Dionysos predominating." Roman tile grave 61.21: *BASOR* 166, 32 n. 54.

60. HoB: *BASOR* 157, 28, fig. 9. A coin of Domitian showed that the cemetery lasted into the late first century A.D. or longer. Finds: terracotta charioteer, *ILN* (9 July 1960) 61, fig. 1; marble urn, *Sardis* R2 (1978) no. 227, here Fig. 189. Kagirlik Tepe: *Sardis* R1 (1975) 125–128, figs. 320–330. Bin Tepe–Ahlatli Tepecik: *BASOR* 191, 9–10, thirty-one Roman graves with coins from A.D. 50–117. Finds: terracotta "Aphrodite with Flavian hairdo" (T 67.14:7495). Glass: *Sardis* M6 (1980). Pottery: Wrabetz in *Sardis* (R5) *Pottery,* "Sigillate" (forthcoming).

61. Chamber tombs: it is not clear whether the chambertomb south of the railway, *BASOR* 228, 47–48, 50–51, with cinerary chests is pre- or post-earthquake of A.D. 17. Artemis Precinct, Tomb 2, *Sardis* R1 (1975) 59–60, figs. 72–74. Apollo/club coin and Eastern sigillata B permit a date before A.D. 17; certainly not much after.

62. Plutarch, *Praecepta* 813F, 825D. W. H. Buckler, *Sardis* VII.1 (1932) 116 n. 1, considered the father of G. Iulius Pardalas, high priest of Asia, ca. A.D. 4–12, as a possible adversary of Mark Antony 41–31 B.C. but rightly said: "Possibly Plutarch refers to some Sardian, whom Menemachus had personally known." See *Sardis* M2 (1972) nos. 227–228. L. Robert, *Bull.* (1974) Sardis: nos. 30, 528; cf. L. Robert, *Annuaire* (1973) 485–486.

63. Plutarch, *De exilio,* "On Exile" from *Plutarch's Moralia* 7, 513–571, trans P. H. Lacy and B. Einarson. The *Praecepta* dates after Domitian, A.D. 96; *De exilio* after *Praecepta,* and before A.D. 117. C. P. Jones, *Plutarch,* and "Chronology," 72. *Sardis* M2 (1972) no. 218.

64. Apollonius, *Letters* in Philostratus, *The Life of Apollonius of Tyana* 2, trans. F. C. Conybeare, nos. 38–41, 85–86. He says that children, young people, men, old men, girls, and women were all involved in "truceless war," in the city of "Furies rather than Demeter." In the earlier letters he taxes the Sardians with indecency and with winning the first prize for "vice" (*kakia,* badness).

65. Magie, 581, 600, with other instances of class struggle. R. McMullen, *Enemies,* 180–183.

66. *Sardis* VII.1 (1932) no. 47. The name is a conjecture by Head after a coin in the British Museum. The person was also "Priest of Tiberius Caesar," showing that Tiberius had a cult and a temple(?) as late as A.D. 100.

67. Magie, 581 n. 39, after Robinson and Rostovtzeff.

68. This rests on the acceptance of the Beast of the Revelation as Domitian, not Nero.

69. Trajan: *Sardis* XI (1916) nos. 282–284. A. E. M. Johnston, *Sardis* M7 (1981), the inscription is *Dakikos:* proconsul Lucius Balbius Tullus, A.D. 108–109; Magie, 1583. Cf. C. Vermeule, *Imperial Art,* 252. In contrast, N. H. Ramage, U. Hiesinger, and Hanfmann consider *Sardis* R2 (1978) no. 76 as a poorly preserved head of Trajan; the relief, no. 191, might be Trajanic. For Tiberius Iulius Celsus Polemaeanus, see *Sardis* VII.1 (1932) no. 45; Bowersock, *Augustus,* 120, 142; *PIR*² 4:3 (1966) no. 260. Hanfmann, *Croesus,* 43 n. 12, literature.

70. Cl. Ant. Lepidus gave statue of Lucius Verus (A.D. 166?) and was the first to administer the newly built gymnasium: *Sardis* R2 (1978) no. 276. L. Robert, *Bull.* 200, no. 290. He also gave a statue of Faustina Minor, wife of Marcus, after her death in A.D. 176: *Sardis* VII.1 (1932) no. 59. For this and the following, see the list of statues and inscriptions and the comments of C. Vermeule, *Imperial Art,* 461; 270, 276, 293, 318. There is no entry for Lepidus in *PIR.*

71. Strictly speaking, they and the city "gilded the work," which might have been known as "The Golden Court" had the gilding survived. For Claudia Antonia Sabina and her mausoleum and sarcophagus at Sardis, see Hanfmann, *Croesus,* 43–44, 52, 68, fig.

143. Flavia Politte was named first among ladies sacrificing to Juno at the *ludi saeculares* in Rome in A.D. 204. *PIR²* 2 (1936) no. 1070; Sabina: 3 (1943) no. 434 (Politte).

72. *Sardis* VII.1 (1932) nos. 13–14, concerned with a privately endowed penteteric festival. See Magie, 617–618. For the visits of Hadrian to Sardis, see *Sardis* M2 (1972) no. 307, from Polemon's *Physiognomica*. Bowersock, *Sophists*, 120–123. On coins: *Sardis* M7 (1981) Catalogue, with comments by A. E. M. Johnston, who cites Kienast, "Hadrian-Augustus," 11, 61–69 (1960). N. H. Ramage identifies a head from Sardis in Manisa as a portrait of Hadrian's wife Sabina, who may have accompanied Hadrian, *Sardis* R2 (1978) no. 78.

73. The first neocorate of Sardis is not safely identified: Burrell, *Neokoroi*, Section "Sardis." It is not clear what happened to the temple of Augustus mentioned in 5–1 B.C., before the earthquake: *Sardis* VII.1 (1932) no. 8, I, line 13.

74. Burrell, *Neokoroi; Sardis* VII.1 (1932) Index, *s.v. neokoros*.

75. *Sardis* R2 (1978) nos. 79, 251. Inscription IN 70.4: *BASOR* 203, 14. Altar: *Sardis* R2 (1978) no. 161.

76. *BASOR* 158, 10, no. 4. *Sardis* R2 (1978) no. 276, fig. 469. Burrell, *Neokoroi*, "Sardis," Inscriptions no. 1. Hanfmann has suggested that Lucius Verus may have come to Sardis when he traveled to Ephesus returning from the Eastern campaign in A.D. 166. Faustina Minor, wife of the emperor Marcus, who had a statue, *Sardis* VII.1 (1932) no. 59, may be represented in a terracotta bust found near the Roman Northeast Stoa: *Sardis* R1 (1975) 119–120, figs. 289–290, T 69.3.

77. Coins with the head of Albinus were struck in A.D. 196. Magie, 673 n. 24; Head, *BMC, Lydia,* no. 146. Burrell, *Neokoroi*, Coins, no. 1.

78. The dedicatory inscription on the entablature of the first-story pavilions of the Marble Court (Fig. 227) is still unpublished *in toto*. It was composed after the death of Septimius Severus in February 211 and before the death of Geta in February 212. Geta's name is erased.

79. Burrell, *Neokoroi*, Coins, no. 32, British Museum. Statue base: *BASOR* 177, 23, fig. 23. L. Robert, "Inscriptions grecques," 41, 48 n. 6. Dating from Caracalla's sole rule, A.D. 212–217, the inscription of Demostratos Damas names his son Aurelius Damas, one of the dedicants, as *xystarchos* and (*ho*) *epi balaneion tou Sebastou*, "President of the Athletes and Overseer of the Emperor's Baths." (Only *bal* is preserved.) *Sardis* VII.1 (1932) no. 79, ll. 24–26.

80. Magie, 684–685; 1551–1553. Reusch, 39.

81. L. Robert, "Fête," 52–53. He discusses the coins with Elagabalia. The third neocorate was apparently bestowed upon Sardis by Elagabalus. Temples: Head, *BMC, Lydia,* no. 171. Price-Trell, 137, fig. 242. Burrell, *Neokoroi*, "Sardis," Coins no. 65.

82. Septimius; *Sardis* VII.1 (1932) no. 71 (Latin); a huge (over 2 m. high) pedestal (or architectural pier?) later engraved with the "Union of Builders Inscription" of A.D. 459, ibid. no. 18. *Sardis* VII.1 (1932) no. 73 (Greek); Alexander, ibid. no. 72.

83. See *Sardis* R2 (1978) no. 254, considered by N. H. Ramage a private portrait rather than Julia Mamaea.

84. That the *xystos* (in the sense of athletic race rather than athletic association) and palaestra were probably ready at the same time or shortly after the Marble Court, perhaps for Caracalla's possible visit in A.D. 214–215, appears from the Aurelius Damas inscription, n. 79, *supra*. For the unidentified basilica, again of Caracalla's time, see *Sardis* VII.1 (1932) no. 63.

85. For the festivals—Koraia/Aktia, Chrysanthina, Elagabalia—see *Sardis* VII.1 (1932) 82–83, nos. 77–79. L. Robert, "Fête," 51, 54; A. E. M. Johnston, *Sardis* M7 (1981). It is generally said that inflation and the decline of farming began under Septimius Severus, but in contrast to the complaints of Lydian farmers, the picture of urban Sardis shows only prosperity. See Magie, 678–682. The greater importance assigned to large autonomous bronzes versus silver, ibid., 682, may, however, have helped the spirit of self-assertion on these local coins.

86. See the very useful list of *neokoroi* coins in Burrell, *Neokoroi*, where references to modern publications are given; also *Sardis* M7 (1981) Catalogue. The "educational" use of inscriptions recalls the great expansion of labels on late Roman, especially on Eastern Greek, mosaics (Antioch, Cyprus, Cilicia). Nonnus' *Dionysiaca* (fifth century A.D.), the literary equivalent of this late antique, encyclopaedic learning, has several passages of interest for Sardis. See Foss, "Explorations," 38, and *Sardis* M4 (1976) 10, Sources no. 8 = Nonnus 13.464, 41.354.

87. *Sardis* VII.1 (1932) no. 79. *Sardis* R2 (1978) nos. 153–155, with references to other reliefs in L. Robert, *Les gladiateurs;* two animal hunts, *Sardis* R2 (1978) nos. 146–149.

88. Magie, 703–707.

89. A. R. Seager, Chapter IX, *infra,* under "The Building," seems to assign all known decoration to the fourth century but leaves open the possibility that donors' inscriptions and marble decoration of a third-century phase were reused.

90. *Sardis* M4 (1976) 3, 31–32, Foss suggests that the bishop of Sardis became a metropolitan, at the same time or shortly after Diocletian made Sardis the

capital of Lydia. In later Byzantine times, the metropolitan of Sardis ranked sixth after the patriarch of Constantinople.

91. Extension: *Sardis* R1 (1975) 32, 600 acres. A.D. 395–616 greatest expansion; C. Foss, *Sardis* M4 (1976) "The Expansion of the City in Late Antiquity," 39–52, Plans II and III, graphic presentation; but excavations and survey since 1975 have increased the area north and south; see *BASOR* 229, 57–61, fig. 1.

92. Population: Magie, 585. Galen, *De cognoscendis curandisque animi morbis,* Ch. 9: translated in Hanfmann, *Croesus,* 49 n. 33. The present estimate for Sardis is somewhat more flexible than that in *Croesus;* see *Sardis* R1 (1975) 32–33, for estimate of population in Lydian times, and Foss, *Sardis* M4 (1976) 2, "perhaps 100,000" in the second century A.D.

93. Location of modern watermill, *Sardis* I (1922) 116; evidence for ancient watermill, *Sardis* VII.1 (1932) no. 169; *Sardis* M4 (1976) 16–18.

94. Information given by Orhan Araz, August 1971.

95. *Sardis* VII.1 (1932) no. 17. *BASOR* 191, 29–30.

96. Vitruvius 2.8.9–10, *gerousia;* see Hanfmann, "Palace," 146–147, 154. Fountain inscription, *Sardis* VII.1 (1932) no. 17; Menogenes documents, ibid., no. 8, mention temple of Augustus and Gaius, Agora, *Presbeutikon* (Hall of Elders), *Paideutikon* (Hall of the Boys), Precinct of Zeus Polieus and Artemis; no. 63, basilica; no. 79, Baths of the Emperor; no. 145, archives. See the list of buildings built after the earthquake, this section, *supra.*

97. IN 63.A 1. *BASOR* 174, 46; on a Roman column base, reused.

98. IN 68.19–20. *BASOR* 199, 29, fig. 16. Foss in *Sardis* M4 (1976) 44–45, interprets the inscription in relation to the "HoB Colonnaded Street" (Fig. 8:58), possibly laid down anew and a gate "cut" for the road to Hypaepa.

99. Houses above HoB (Middle Terrace): *BASOR* 162, 17; 170, 13; 174, 6–8; *Sardis* M4 (1976) 44. Ephesus: Vetters, "Stockwerkbau," 69–92. Strocka, *Ephesos* 8:1 (1977) 8–28.

100. *Sardis* VII.1 (1932) no. 12.

101. Area south of Main Avenue in HoB: see Chapter VII, and this section, *supra.* C. Foss, *Sardis* M4 (1976) 43, assumes an initial date in the fourth century for the House of Bronzes, which is not, so far, supported by definite evidence. The only definite indication is a coin of Justin II, A.D. 565–578, found sealed in the floor of "Unit 16": *BASOR* 157, 26. There were some large, earlier walls in the area, either third or fourth century A.D. For the various buildings of clubhouses or "confraternities" (*mysteria*), see *Sardis* VII.1 (1932) no. 17.

102. *Sardis* M4 (1976) 7–8, 14–15, 106, Sources nos. 1–2. A new inscription of a *doukenarios fabrikesios: BASOR* 229, 61, fig. 7; Greenewalt, "Twentieth Campaign," 105. Mellink (1977) 308–310, fig. 19, "high salaried official and director of factory." Hanfmann, "Painter," 87–88.

103. See Chapter IX, *infra.*

104. For the Severan dedication inscription with the city, Antonia Sabeina, and Flavia Politte contributing the gilding, see this section, *supra,* and n. 71; fifth century: *Sardis* M4 (1976) 114, Sources no. 16: "golden-roofed . . ."

105. *Sardis* VII.1 (1932) no. 18; M4 (1976) 19–20, with literature n. 51, text, translation, 110–113, Sources no. 14.

106. For Demeter see *BASOR* 211, 35; Head, *BMC, Lydia,* nos. 98–100; and *Sardis* M7 (1981) Catalogue, nos. 250–251. It is noteworthy that immediately after the earthquake, Livia is shown as Demeter. Demeter as well as Demeter with Kore—and the "Lydian Kore"—are frequent in the Sardian coinage from A.D. 197 to 256. Burrell, *Neokoroi,* "Sardis," Coins. For Sardis as city of Demeter, see n. 4, *supra.* Kore's children: *Sardis* R2 (1978) no. 277. Watermills: M4 (1976) 16–17, and 111, Sources no. 10.

107. *BASOR* 154, n. 50 (sulphur in pithos, used for bleaching?), tank: 157, 24. The stone basins possibly used in olive oil production are as yet unpublished.

108. For the material from Byzantine Shops, see "Byzantine Shops," *infra,* and the detailed final publication, forthcoming in *Sardis* (M9) *Byzantine Shops;* the discussion by J. C. Waldbaum in *Sardis* (M8) *Metalwork* (forthcoming); also Crawford, "Lamp," 291–294; *BASOR* 154, 22–23, figs. 11–12; D. Hansen, "Sardi cristiana," 169–174. *Sardis* M4 (1976) 43–44, fig. 21.

109. See this section, *supra,* nn. 28–29. *Sardis* R1 (1975) 27–28, lists most of the material for water supply; see M4 (1976) 72–73, on the disruption of the system in A.D. 616. The drainage system, very elaborate in the bath-gymnasium, next section, n. 21, *infra,* has not been systematically investigated in other sectors.

110. *BASOR* 157, 35, fig. 19. Hospital: *Sardis* VII.1 (1932) no. 19.

The Bath-Gymnasium Complex

1. Its exact position on the Sardis "B-Grid" is NS0-N122.60/W52.10-E117.20; the floor is roughly *96.0–*96.6. On Sardis topography and B-Grid, see *Sardis* R1 (1975) 7–11.

2. De Peyssonnel, 343–344.

3. Texier, 254.

4. *Sardis* I (1922) 31–33, ill. 18.

5. *BASOR* 166, 40–46, figs. 32, 33, 34, 35.

6. *BASOR* 154, 13–16, fig. 4; Johnson, *BASOR* 158, 7–10, figs. 2, 3. *Sardis* R2 (1978) 178, no. 276, fig. 469; Hanfmann, *Letters,* 33, figs. 17–18. For Claudius Antonius Lepidus, see *Sardis* VII.1 (1932) no. 59.

7. *BASOR* 157, 35–38.

8. *BASOR* 211, 23–24, figs. 5, 6.

9. *BASOR* 157, 34, fig. 19.

10. *BASOR* 166, 48–49.

11. *BASOR* 211, 29.

12. *BASOR* 157, 38.

13. *BASOR* 162, 40–43; 166, 46–48; 170, 37–38; 174, 25–26. Burrell, *Neokoroi* (unpublished); *Sardis* (M15) *Inscriptions* (forthcoming).

14. Hanfmann, *Croesus,* 51–52.

15. *BASOR* 162, 42. Hanfmann, *Croesus,* 51–52.

16. *BASOR* 177, 21–23; 182, 31–32; 187, 53.

17. *BASOR* 199, 42.

18. *BASOR* 177, 23, fig. 23, and previous section, nn. 79, 80, *supra.*

19. *BASOR* 211, 21–22, fig. 4; *Sardis* M4 (1976) 21, 40–41, 114–115, no. 17; *Sardis* R1 (1975) 173, no. 75; *Sardis* R2 (1978) 179, no. 278, fig. 471.

20. *BASOR* 211, 23.

21. *BASOR* 177, 25; 182, 30–31; 187, 54–58, fig. 64.

22. *BASOR* 191, 33.

23. *BASOR* 187, 10–21.

24. *BASOR* 211, 26.

25. *BASOR* 177, 25–26; 187, 10. See also J. H. Kroll in *Sardis* (R4) *Synagogue* (forthcoming): "Greek Inscriptions." L. Robert, "Rhéteur," 249 n. 47.

26. *BASOR* 211, 27–28, fig. 9; *Sardis* R1 (1975) 32; *Sardis* R2 (1978) 178–179, no. 277, fig. 470.

27. *BASOR* 177, 25.

28. *BASOR* 199, 42.

29. *BASOR* 191, 33.

30. *Sardis* M4 (1976) 74–75, fig. 36: Foss dates the kilns to the tenth century and considers them suitable for the making of glazed pottery.

31. *BASOR* 187, 50–52.

32. *BASOR* 191, 29.

33. *BASOR* 177, 26–27; 182, 32–34; 187, 58–60; 191, 34–35; 199, 43–44; 203, 18–20; 206, 24–25. See also Yegul, "Marble Court," 169–194. A detailed account of the reconstruction by M. C. Bolgil will appear in *Sardis* (R3) *Gymnasium* (forthcoming).

34. Hirschland (Ramage), 12–22; *Sardis* R2 (1978) 82, nos. 198–206, figs. 351–363.

35. *BASOR* 206, 29–31; 211, 19–21; 215, 46.

36. *Sardis* R1 (1975) 17, 21.

37. On Phrygian marble types and sources, see Alpan, *Türkiye Mermer Envanteri;* Röder, "Marmor Phrygium," 253–312. Ballence-Brogan, "Roman Marble," 35, in Campbell.

38. An inscription kindly brought to our attention by J. B. Ward-Perkins mentions columns of the same marble imported from the Numidian Chemtou quarries to be used in the Agora and the Basilica of Smyrna. Spirally-fluted shafts of comparable size and type to the Sardis examples are still visible among the architectural fragments on site in Izmir Agora. For the inscription, see *IGRP* IV no. 1431 = *CIG* 3148.

39. *BASOR* 182, 31; 177, 25; 187, 52.

40. *BASOR* 154, 33; *Sardis* R2 (1978) 139, no. 194, fig. 344 (see also no. 193, fig. 343 for a comparable figure capital from Sardis); Hanfmann-Balmuth, "Anatolian Goddess," 261–269, pls. 34–35, figs. 1–5.

41. *BASOR* 187, 46–47. For stylistic tendencies in Late Antique wall decoration, see Deubner, 14–41; Krautheimer, "Constantinian Basilica," 127; and Asemakopoulou-Atzaka, 8–9, 30, 56 n. 7, 62–63, 71–72, 108, pls. 10, a (apse), b (sheep), c (dove-crater).

42. *Sardis* R2 (1978) 101–102, nos. 94, 95, figs. 212–214; *BASOR* 177, 25, fig. 24; 187, 27, fig. 44; Hanfmann, "Late Portraits," 290–295; *Sardis* M4 (1976) fig. 3.

43. *Sardis* R2 (1978) 106–107; no. 107, figs. 231–232; *BASOR* 191, 33, fig. 30; Metraux, 156–159, pls. 35–36.

44. *Sardis* R2 (1978) 100, no. 92, figs. 206–207; *BASOR* 166, 45, fig. 37; Hanfmann, *Roman Art,* 100, no. 90, 183, fig. 90; Hanfmann, *Croesus,* 71, fig. 151.

45. *Sardis* R2 (1978) 89, 91, nos. 60, 64, figs. 174, 178.

46. *Sardis* R2 (1978) nos. 114, 117–120, 122, 129, figs. 240, 243–248, 250–251, 261. See above entries for full bibliography. See also *BASOR* 211, 27; 157, 35.

47. *Sardis* M7 (1981); *Sardis* VII.1 (1932) nos. 13, 14. The concept of Dionysus' connection with the emperor appears to enter the decorative program of the Vedius bath-gymnasium in Ephesus, where panels representing the god visiting the poet Menander have been found inside the hall: Miltner, Ephesos, 58–68, 75–78. *Sardis* R2 (1978) no. 198, figs. 351–352.

48. See Chapter IX, *infra,* under "The Building." Seager dates the third phase to the later third century and the fourth phase (the Synagogue) to the early fourth century, under *Earlier Building Stages* and *Dating.*

49. *BASOR* 162, 42; Hanfmann, *Croesus,* 52; *Sardis* R2 (1978) 163, no. 243, fig. 422.

50. For roofing, see Theater of Aspendos, reconstruction drawing; Lanckoronski-Niemann, pl. 27; Robertson, *Architecture,* fig. 117.

51. Hanfmann, *Croesus,* 52–53; *ERA,* 405–406

52. The last reference to ephebic training and contests is in A.D. 323, *P. Oxy,* 42; to gymnasia, A.D. 370, *P. Oxy,* 2110. On the disappearance of the Greek gymnasium, see D. Claude, *Byzantinische Stadt,* 76; Jones, *Greek City,* 253.

53. G. M. A. Hanfmann points out that the location of Justin the Martyr's philosophical dispute with the Jew Tryphon in Ephesus is a gymnasium. Hanfmann, *Croesus,* 55; Justin, *Dialogue with Trypho.* See Eusebius, *Hist. Eccl.* 4:18.

54. *BASOR* 206, 25, fig. 27; C. Foss, *Sardis* M4 (1976) 41, fig. 2.

55. Although the civic and administrative institutions of the classical city, like the *boule* and the *gerousia,* increasingly lost their meaning and importance after the fourth century A.D., many cities did retain some semblance of a council and a fairly wealthy curial class into the sixth century. The administrative authority was definitely and irrevocably transferred to the bishops and the agents of the imperial government by the reforms of Anastasius. Jones, *Greek City,* 200–210; Claude, *Byzantinische Stadt,* 102; Jones, *Roman Empire,* 763.

56. Martial, *Epig.* XII, 70; Columella, I, 16; Seneca, *Ep.* 15, 3.

57. For Ephesian bath planning, see Keil, *Führer durch Ephesus,* 53–55, 69–75, 123–124; Miltner, *Ephesos,* 43–48, 58–68, 75–78; Fasolo, "L'Architettura Romana di Efeso," 1–92; Maccanico, "Ginnasi romani ad Efeso," 32–60.

58. F. K. Yegul, "The Bath-Gymnasium Complex in Asia Minor During the Imperial Roman Age," 77–202 (unpublished).

59. Delorme, 243–250.

60. See Gerkan-Krischen; Kleiner, *Ruinen,* 93–97, fig. 63; but especially Tuchelt, "Bemerkungen," 147–164.

61. To be published in the forthcoming field report for the 1979 season.

62. *BASOR* 162, 42; 174, 26–30; 177, 25.

63. *BASOR* 187, 54, fig. 63; *Sardis* M4 (1976) 40, 113–114, no. 15. The rank and titulature of Simplikios as *comes primi ordinis* identifying him as a vicar of Asia (rather than a governor) is discussed by C. Foss in "Atticus Philippus," 175–177. Foss's placement of the inscription in the late fifth century based on "archaeological evidence" is, however, erroneous. Whatever archaeological evidence there is that can be associated with the inscription actually belongs to the late fourth century A.D. But this does not invalidate Foss's argument on titulature, as he points out that a vicar with the rank of the first order of *comes* could belong to the fourth as well as the fifth century.

64. *BASOR* 177, 25; 187, 52.

65. *BASOR* 162, 42–43; *Sardis* M4 (1976) 40, 114, no. 16. This inscription will be published by L. Robert.

66. *BASOR* 182, 31.

67. Yegul, "Capitals," 265–274.

68. *Sardis* R1 (1975) 36; *Sardis* M4 (1976) 3, 4, 9, 10, 108, Source, no. 7.

69. *Sardis* M1 (1971) 149; *Sardis* M4 (1976) 53–54.

The Byzantine Shops

1. *Sardis* M4 (1976); Foss, "Fall of Sardis"; "Byzantine Cities."

2. *BASOR* 166, 40–46, figs. 32–37. For excavations of the area after 1975, see *BASOR* 228, 50.

3. *BASOR* 154, 16–18; 157, 32–35; 162, 40; 166, 40–46; 170, 49–51; 174, 45–47; 177, 19–20; 191, 16–22; 199, 44; 211, 29–30; 215, 51–52.

4. *Sardis* M7 (1981), "Roman Coins"; "Byzantine Coins."

5. *Sardis* M1 (1971) 2.

6. *BASOR* 166, 40–46.

7. *BASOR* 162, 40.

8. *BASOR* 215, 52.

9. *BASOR* 170, 49–51.

10. *BASOR* 174, 45–57; 177, 19–20.

11. *BASOR* 191, 16–22; 199, 44.

12. *BASOR* 211, 29–30; 215, 51–52.

13. *BASOR* 215, 46.

14. *BASOR* 166, 40–46.

15. *BASOR* 166, 40–46.

16. *Sardis* M4 (1976) 57.

17. F. K. Yegul, "The Earlier Phase of the Byzantine Shops Colonnade," in *Sardis* (M9) *Byzantine Shops* (forthcoming). In 1979 part of a statue base, IN 79.8, inscribed in honor of Tiberius, uncle of Claudius, was found on the south side of the Main Avenue. If it comes from the original south colonnade, then it indicates that the colonnades were begun under Tiberius and finished under Claudius.

18. Deiss, 95–96. Ladders: Spinazzola, *Pompei,* 114, fig. 138; stairs: ibid., 116, fig. 141.

19. Three pieces of Eastern sigillata B will be discussed by J. Wrabetz in *Sardis* (R5) *Pottery,* "Sigillate" (forthcoming): P 59.461; 63.563; 63.650.

20. See *Sardis* (M8) *Metalwork* (forthcoming) "Introduction."

21. For detailed study of the major individual objects of glass from the shops see *Sardis* M6 (1980) nos. 277, 279–281, 287, 291, 292, 295, 297, 300, 302–303, 311, 312, 316, 318, 340, 342, 345, 346–

348, 369, 371, 375, 377–379, 395, 444, 445, 454–456, 458, 466, 484–486, 488, 499, 502, 503, 516, 519, 520, 522, 523, 549, 557, 558, 560, 561, 577, 594–597, 602, 603, 628, 629, 632, 633, 654, 668–670, 676, 677, 679–681, 683–688, 711, 717, 721, 726.

22. For a description of the clays of Sardis used in pottery, see *Sardis* (R5) *Pottery* (forthcoming) "Sigillate," and D. Kamilli in *Sardis* M5 (1978) 12–14.

23. Pliny, *HN* 25.16.38: "It (red ochre) is also manufactured by burning ochre in new earthen pots with lids stopped with clay." Vitruvius, 7.7.2: "Abundant red ochre, also, is extracted in many places."

24. Noble, "Faience," 435.

25. Hayes, 409, pl. XXIIIa (P 67.2).

26. *Sardis* M6 (1980) 1–2.

27. Miltner, *Ephesos,* 17; Wilberg, *Ephesos,* I, 132.

28. Ziegenaus, "Hallenstrasse," 448–449.

29. Lanckoronski-Niemann, 41–44.

30. Mansel, *Ruinen von Side,* 17–18.

31. Mazar, "Excavations," 25–40; idem, *Mountain,* 248–254; idem, *Jerusalem;* idem, *Temple Mount.*

32. Leix, 423; S. Robinson, *Dyed Textiles,* 15.

33. Mazar, *Beth Sh'arim* 1, 211, 218–220; Brill, 261.

34. Levi, *Pavements,* 330; Downey, *Antioch,* ills. 56, 60.

35. Meiggs, *Ostia,* pl. 36; 428, pl. 29.

36. Rostovtzeff, pl. 30:2, and E. Simon in Helbig-Speier, 305–306, no. 400.

IX. The Synagogue and the Jewish Community

The Building

1. *Sardis* M4 (1976) 43–44.

2. On the pipe system, see *BASOR* 191, 29–31, fig. 23. On restoration of the crater, see *BASOR* 199, 48, 51–53, figs. 38, 43.

3. A plan of the Forecourt showing the mosaic panels and patterns is given in *BASOR* 191, fig. 23.

4. Inscriptions (IN 62.297–300): *BASOR* 170, 47; L. Robert, *NIS,* 38–47, pls. 4, 5. For Greek inscriptions from the synagogue in general, see L. Robert, *NIS,* 37–58, pls. 4–11; *BASOR* 170, 47; 187, 27–32 n. 26; 206, 20, fig. 10; J. Kroll, "Greek Inscriptions," forthcoming in *Sardis* (R4) *Synagogue.*

5. Inscribed balustrade (IN 62.111): *BASOR* 187, 27; L. Robert, *NIS,* 53 n. 2.

6. *BASOR* 187, fig. 60, shows some of the arched frieze fragments prior to reconstruction.

7. The road colonnade east of the Forecourt was partitioned off in a late remodeling (sixth century A.D.?) to create what seems to have been a restaurant: *BASOR* 174, 47. Whether it was a public facility or associated with the Synagogue remains uncertain. Occasional travelers might have been housed in the two interconnecting shops (E17, E18) which opened from the corridor leading into the Forecourt from the south, or in lofts above other shops, or perhaps even in the Forecourt. No real hostelry has been discovered, however. Nor was there a *mikveh,* as required for ritual bathing, either in the Synagogue or in surrounding rooms. If there was a *mikveh* and/or hostelry, they must have been some distance away, in places not yet excavated.

8. *Sardis* VII.1 (1932) no. 17, line 7.

9. *BASOR* 170, 46–47, figs. 26, 32.

10. A room the size of the Main Hall would hold nearly 1,000 people using the standards for *modern* churches and synagogues (assuming pews or benches): Kraabel, "Diaspora Synagogue," n. 29 (forthcoming).

11. The piers were built of reused stones for the most part, taken from a variety of buildings and monuments dating from archaic to Roman times. Several of the pier stones (and other pieces reused elsewhere in the Synagogue) may have belonged to a sanctuary of Cybele originally: *Sardis* R2 (1978) 33, 38, nos. 4, 6, 7, 19, 20, 25, 26, 39. Also *BASOR* 174, 34, 38–43, figs. 18, 21, 22–27, 31; 182, 41–42, fig. 33.

12. For the apse and benches, see *BASOR* 174, 30–33.

13. Table: *Sardis* R2 (1978) no. 217, figs. 379–382; Goodenough, 12:195, fig. 4; *BASOR* 174, 34–36, fig. 19. Lions: *Sardis* R2 (1978) no. 25, figs. 92–101; *BASOR* 174, 38, fig. 23.

14. For the Main Hall mosaics in general, see *BASOR* 187, 32–46, figs. 46–56. For the apse mosaic, see *BASOR* 174, 30–33, fig. 17; Mitten, *Synagogue,* fig. 4; Seager, *Synagogue,* 7, fig. 21. Inscriptions: *BASOR* 187, 27–32; L. Robert, *NIS,* 38. On the revetments, see *BASOR* 187, 46–50, figs. 57–59, 71; 191, 32, fig. 26.

15. See n. 59, *infra.*

16. Inscription (IN 62.182–185): L. Robert, *NIS,* 48–53, pl. 6 top, no. 7; *BASOR* 187, 27.

17. Glass mosaic: *BASOR* 206, 20, 37. For the interior decoration in general, see Majewski, "Interior Decoration of the Synagogue," in *Sardis* (R4) *Synagogue;* see also *Sardis* (R9) *Mosaics and Wall Painting* (both forthcoming).

18. Pedimented shrines occur in synagogue mosaics at Khirbet Sussiya, Beth Alpha, Hammath-Tiberias, and Beth Shean, photographs conveniently collected in Shanks, 98, 113, 114, 129. For examples

of shrines on glass vessels, see Goodenough, 3: figs. 967, 973, 974. Other depictions have round-headed shrines.

19. Menorah plaque (S 62.26:4501): *BASOR* 170, 43, fig. 33; Hanfmann, *Letters,* fig. 85.

20. Shiloh, "Torah Scrolls," 54–57.

21. For the four bases, see *BASOR* 182, 44–45, fig. 35. For the inscription (IN 66.3), see *BASOR* 187, 29, fig. 48; also Seager, *Synagogue,* fig. 30.

22. On analogy with the wooden *bema* at the *diplostoon* of the Jews at Alexandria (destroyed A.D. 116), according to the rabbinic description. On the *diplostoon,* see Goodenough, 2:85.

23. Marble menorah, bearing the name "Sokrates" on the crossbar (S 63.50:5645 and S 63.63:5826; IN 63.130): *Sardis* R2 (1978) no. 226, figs. 391–393. Bronze menorah? (M 63.42: 5629) and inscription (IN 63.49): *BASOR* 174, 36–38, fig. 20. Talmudic injunctions prohibit the making of a seven-branched menorah similar to the one in the Jerusalem Temple, but the interpretation of these is debated. The arguments are reviewed by Yarden, 21 and Shanks, 108–115. Gutmann, "Temple Menorah," 290, notes that the prohibition appears only in the Babylonian Talmud, not in the Palestinian Talmud.

24. See the preliminary report on the Greek inscriptions by J. Kroll, *BASOR* 187, 27–32, and final report forthcoming in *Sardis* (R4) *Synagogue. Nomophylakion* plaque (IN 63.124, 125) and the injunction to "read and observe" (IN 63.77): Seager, *Synagogue,* figs. 33–34. On the injunction to "read and observe," see also "Impact of Discovery," *infra.*

25. Hebrew inscriptions, *shalom* (IN 62.66a, b) and "Verus" (IN 62.79): *BASOR* 170, 43; 187, 25. Rabinowitz notes physical evidence that the "Verus" plaque was indeed cut away from a larger stone for the use in a second locus: "The Sardis Hebrew Inscriptions," forthcoming in *Sardis* (R4) *Synagogue.*

26. On the *synoikismos,* see *Sardis* R1 (1975) 29–30 and literature, nn. 91, 95, 101–113. The evidence consists in part of Hellenistic inscriptions found in the Synagogue, reused as pier masonry: *BASOR* 174, 34. On the mausoleum beneath the Synagogue (the "Hellenistic Steps") see *BASOR* 170, 51; 174, 47–50, figs. 29–30; 182, 40–41.

27. For the earthquake and subsequent reconstruction, see *Sardis* R1 (1975) 31.

28. Evidence detailed in Seager, "History," 425–435, figs. 1–11.

29. On LNH, see Chapter VIII, *supra,* under "Bath-Gymnasium Complex."

30. On the building as a civil basilica, see *BASOR* 187, 21–25. For Roman civil basilicas see Crema, 167–170, 370–375, 515–521 (esp. 515–517, figs. 672–674, the Severan basilica at Leptis Magna).

Stage 2 is not suitable for a synagogue because of the connection, via the northern passage in the apse, to the palaestra of the pagan gymnasium.

31. See Chapter VIII, *supra,* under "Bath-Gymnasium Complex."

32. Coin (C 71.268).

33. Coin (C 71.229): *Sardis* M7 (1981) no. 374. None of the coins below floor level in the Main Hall, including those from areas of mosaic loss, were minted A.D. 350 to 383; yet coins of that period are commonplace in other contexts.

34. Column fragments: *BASOR* 182, 43–44, fig. 34. Coin (C 67.754): *BASOR* 191, 26 (where it is misidentified as an issue of Maximian, A.D. 284–308); *Sardis* M7 (1981) no. 147.

35. The many pagan monuments reused in the Synagogue in the fourth-century phase may have come from sanctuaries destroyed under Constantine: *Sardis* R2 (1978) 38.

36. See "Impact of Discovery," *infra,* this chapter.

37. The interpretation of stage 3 in Seager, "History," is according to the older dating. The third century dating for many donors' inscriptions was originally proposed by L. Robert on the strength of the frequent occurrence of the Aurelii, who had taken Caracalla's family name after receiving Roman citizenship with the *constitutio Antoniniana* of A.D. 212; the controversy is discussed by J. H. Kroll, *Sardis* (R4) *Synagogue* (forthcoming).

38. *BASOR* 187, 27; Kroll, "Greek Inscriptions," *Sardis* (R4) *Synagogue* (forthcoming).

39. The *ananeosis,* the late fifth-century remodeling in the gymnasium area, included reconstruction of the palaestra and Main Avenue colonnades: *Sardis* M4 (1976) 40; F. K. Yegul, "The Building History and Dating of the Bath-Gymnasium Complex" (unpublished); F. K. Yegul, "Reconstruction Study of the Marble Avenue Colonnade," 2 (unpublished). A new colonnaded street was built through sector HoB "after the gate had been cut out and the whole area cleared": *Sardis* M4 (1976) 44–45, sources 18, 19.

40. *Sardis* M4 (1976) 10–13, 34, 42 documents the deteriorated conditions in Asia Minor during the sixth century despite the magnificence of Justinian in the capital. *Sardis* R1 (1975) 32 notes signs of decline already in the fourth and fifth centuries.

41. *Novellae Theod.* 3:3 = *Codex Justinianus* 1.9.18; for translation and comments: Pharr, 489 n. 3.

42. *Sardis* R1 (1975) 32–33; *Sardis* M4 (1976) 53–60.

43. *Sardis* M1 (1971) 2; *Sardis* M4 (1976) 57. On the road rebuilding, see *BASOR* 166, 45; 186, 28–29. On the late occupation in rooms west of the Synagogue, see *BASOR* 187, 14, 16, 20; 211, 26–28, fig. 9.

44. The suite of rooms west of the Synagogue was once thought to have been a synagogue annex: *BASOR* 187, 10–21.

45. Alternatively, occupation of the partitioned-off corners may have been associated with the disruption of life caused by the Persian incursion of A.D. 616. A much earlier date is impossible; one of the partitions contained a coin of A.D. 614/615: *Sardis* M1 (1971) 101, no. 905.

46. *Sardis* M4 (1976) 156 n. 80, 172 n. 42.

47. *BASOR* 182, 34; 186, 22, 25; 187, 60–62, fig. 63 (proposed conservation reports); Seager, *BASOR* 191, 31–32, figs. 24, 26 (start of restoration of South Shrine); 199, 47. Hanfmann, *Letters,* 217, fig. 168, shows drawings by A. R. Seager and A. M. Shapiro working out the design and conservation problems. See also *The Ancient Synagogue of Sardis: A Progress Report* (Sardis Office, Fogg Museum, Cambridge, Mass., 1969).

48. See n. 47, *supra,* and *BASOR* 187, 27–32 (J. H. Kroll, Inscriptions); L. J. Majewski's comprehensive survey "Evidence for the Interior Decoration of the Synagogue," *BASOR* 187, 32–50, figs. 49–60; 191, 29–32, figs. 23–26, including proposals for wall decoration system; 199, 47–55; 203, 17–18, figs. 11–12; 206, 20–23, figs. 8–10 (setting of mosaics); 211, 30–31, setting completed; 215, 52, copies of mosaics, casts of lions installed (1973).

49. This catalogue comprises pieces arranged according to typology. The actual pieces are kept in a special storage at the site. They are numbered SYN.

50. *BASOR* 191, 31–32, fig. 25. Seager, *Synagogue,* 9, figs. 27–28.

51. See Majewski in *BASOR* 187, 46–50; also *Sardis* (R4) *Synagogue* (forthcoming) "Interior Decoration of the Synagogue"; Hanfmann, *Letters,* 196, 257, figs. 146–147, 182.

52. *BASOR* 187, 49–50, fig. 60. Seager, *Synagogue,* 6, fig. 10. Visible in the background in Hanfmann, *Letters,* color pl. 5, and fig. 212. Cf. Shanks, 173, ill.; Hanfmann, *Letters,* fig. 215.

53. *BASOR* 199, 47–48, fig. 38. Hanfmann, *Letters,* 264, color pl. 5.

54. Mosaics: *BASOR* 187, 27–46, figs. 46–56; 191, 29–32; 199, 45–47, 53–54; 203, 17–18, figs. 11–12; 206, 20–23, fig. 8–10. Hanfmann, *Letters,* 246, 277–278, 305, figs. 183, 199, 200, 212–213, 217, various stages of setting and lifting. Seager, *Synagogue,* 5, 13, figs. 13–14, 19–21. The originals are in the Manisa Museum.

55. See n. 13, *supra;* and Hanfmann, *Letters,* 264, fig. 197. Other references, *Sardis* R2 (1978) 148–149, no. 217, figs. 379–382, including state as found. Cf. Seager, *Synagogue,* 5, fig. 11 (photo). Lions: *Sardis* R2 (1978) 63–65, figs. 92–101, 382; for discussion of findspot on fourth century A.D. mosaic floor, and

for the actual date of the lions as 450–430 B.C., see *Sardis* R2 (1978) no. 25. Crater: *BASOR* 199, 51–52, fig. 43; Hanfmann, *Letters,* 247, fig. 184; 264, color pl. 5 (cast in place).

56. The first consists of two segments of a plain crowning(?) plinth; for inscription, see Kroll in *Sardis* (R4) *Synagogue* (forthcoming), "Greek Inscriptions," no. 73. Tetrapylon: *Sardis* (R4) *Synagogue,* "Furnishings," no. 36.

57. For Aurelius Basileides, see Kroll, in *Sardis* (R4) *Synagogue,* "Greek Inscriptions," no. 70. *BASOR* 187, 32, *apo epitropon* (IN 63.92).

58. Hanfmann, *Letters,* 174–175, fig. 130; Seager, *Synagogue,* 7, fig. 22.

59. Peacocks: apse mosaic, cut out: *BASOR* 174, 30–33, fig. 17; Hanfmann, *Letters,* 137–138, fig. 95. Fish, birds, doves, lions: *BASOR* 170, 45–46; Seager, *Synagogue,* 7, figs. 22, 23; Hanfmann, *Letters,* 286, fig. 214.

60. Bronze lamps: at least five bronze chains for lamps were found, one near the South Shrine (E89/N6, *96.9–*96.5). They are discussed by J. C. Waldbaum, *Sardis* (M8) *Metalwork* (forthcoming) nos. 597–600.

61. Clay lamps: *BASOR* 170, 46. A report is in preparation by J. A. Scott, *Sardis* (M12) *Lamps* (forthcoming). More than seventy-five lamps of fourth to fifth century, Ephesos Type III–IX, were found under Forecourt mosaic panels S1 and S2, according to J. A. Scott and E. Kessin.

62. *BASOR* 177, 20, fig. 21. Hanfmann, *Letters,* 141, fig. 103.

63. *BASOR* 170, 46, fig. 35 (Seal 62.3) Grillos. See R. S. Thomas, *Sardis* (M10) *Small Finds* (forthcoming) no. 12.

64. Nude girl: *BASOR* 170, 50, fig. 30 (Seal 62.1).

65. Glass weights: *BASOR* 191, 28, fig. 20 (G 67.5:7401); *Sardis* M6 (1980) no. 674, pl. 16.

66. Lamp (L 65.9:6765). Hanfmann, *Letters,* 178, fig. 133: "Roman gray-ware lamp . . . probably used in a building destroyed by earthquake in A.D. 17." Yet as was shown in the discussion in this chapter, there is no other architectural or other remnant indicating an earlier synagogue in this location. This does not rule out a Jewish grave.

67. Inscription: "There is no evidence for any covering of the inscription . . . it was visible when reused": *Sardis* R2 (1978) 176, no. 272, fig. 462, M3 (1975), "Die Inschrift der Synagogue," 115, 122, figs. 67–76. Gusmani notes that the rough trimming precludes any idea of intentional display, figs. 67–76. The situation of the piece as found is shown in *BASOR* 174, 34, fig. 18.

68. *Sardis* R2 (1978) 58–60, no. 20, figs. 79–83. For the piece as found, see Hanfmann, *Letters,* 243, fig. 180.

69. *BASOR* 177, 17–18, fig. 18 (plan); 203, 14–15; Hanfmann, *Letters,* 275–276, fig. 96 (420 coins, imprint of box of bronze and a lead container). The Byzantine but not the Roman coins from an earlier lot from the same room found in 1963 were catalogued by G. E. Bates, *Sardis* M1 (1971) 152–153: "Description and Index of Hoards," N, O, T, list 89 coins. The bulk seems to be very small change from ca. 330 to 420, but the latest coins are of the seventh century. For a discussion with parallels, see *Sardis* M7 (1981) "Archaeological Contexts," xxiii–xxiv.

70. Beth Alpha synagogue: Sukenik, *Beth Alpha:* Sukenik, *Synagogues,* 31; Goodenough, 1: 241; 3: figs. 631, 641. On courtyards in synagogues, see Seager, "Dura and Sardis," 92–98.

71. Kraabel, "Diaspora Synagogue"; Kraabel, "Synagogues, Ancient," 436–439. See also Seager, "Dura and Sardis."

72. This typology, with only slight variations, is followed by Sukenik, *Synagogues,* 31; Goodenough, 1: 181–225, 238–264; Avi-Yonah, "Synagogues, Classical," cols. 158–173, 179–187; Meyers, "Synagogues, Architecture," 843; and others, most recently Shanks, 48–53. For the synagogues individually, see Saller; Hüttenmeister.

73. Avi-Yonah, "Synagogues, Classical," col. 173. Cf. the "Broadhouse" type of others, e.g., Goodenough, 1: 225–237; Meyers, "Synagogue, Architecture," 843; Shanks, 50.

74. Avi-Yonah, "Synagogues, Classical," col. 188.

75. Avi-Yonah, "Ancient Synagogues," 41–42.

76. Safrai, "Women's Gallery," 329–338.

Impact of the Discovery of the Sardis Synagogue

1. Other parts of the old consensus are being dismantled from the side of Jewish studies, chiefly by Jacob Neusner of Brown University and his students. Neusner's work begins with the history of the large Jewish community in Babylonia, beyond Roman control; see his *History.* Increasingly and inevitably, however, it has a direct impact on our understanding the Judaism of the Roman Diaspora; see for example the articles on Jewish symbolism and the Dura synagogue collected in Part 3 of his *Early Rabbinic Judaism.* In what follows, general statements are not usually footnoted; rather reference is made here to the following studies: Avi-Yonah, *Jews;* P. R. L. Brown, *World; Compendia;* Leon; Smallwood, *Jews.* Also A. T. Kraabel, *The Jews of Western Asia Minor under the Roman Empire* (forthcoming).

2. Josephus, *AJ* 12.147–153.

3. L. Robert, *NIS,* 9–21.

4. Kraabel, "Paganism," 14–18.

5. Josephus, *AJ* 16.235 = *Sardis* M2 (1972) no. 275; *AJ* 14.259–261.

6. Josephus, *AJ* 16.171 = *Sardis* M2 (1972) no. 212.

7. Josephus, *AJ* 14.261.

8. Tacitus, *Ann.* 2.47 = *Sardis* M2 (1972) no. 220.

9. Rabinowitz in *Sardis* (R4) *Synagogue* (forthcoming), no. 1 (IN 62.79); *BASOR* 187, 25.

10. *Sardis* M4 (1976), "Late Antique Sardis."

11. Cicero, *Flac.* 66–68.

12. *CII,* 748.

13. *MAMA* VI, no. 264 = *CII,* 766.

14. *MAMA* VI, no. 334.

15. Mellink, "Archaeology" (1977) 306.

16. Cameron, *Circus Factions,* 315.

17. *CII,* 775, 777.

18. Kindler, 24–32; Kraabel, "Paganism," 23; Goodenough, 2:119, 3:700.

19. Parkes, 175.

20. Kraabel, "Diaspora Synagogue," 489–491.

21. See Map V in *Compendia,* 196.

22. Smallwood, *Jews,* 356–357.

23. Babylonian Talmud, *Megillah* 18b; Cohen, "Rabbi Meir," 51–59. Generally on the *apostoloi,* see *Compendia,* 205–210; Smallwood, 475.

24. *BASOR* 187, 38, fig. 48. On Samoe, see *infra,* in the section on "Jewish Religious Life in Sardis."

25. On the inscriptions, see "The Building," this chapter, *supra,* nn. 24–25.

26. L. Robert, *NIS,* 45–46, pl. 5, considers it "certain" that the Leontioi were not a municipal tribe.

27. *Sardis* R2 (1978) 15, 20–23.

28. *Sardis* R2 (1978) nos. 31, 25.

29. Rabinowitz in *Sardis* (R4) *Synagogue* (forthcoming), "Hebrew Inscriptions."

30. *BASOR* 187, 32.

31. Generally, see Kraabel, "Hypsistos"; "Paganism"; *Sardis* M4 (1976) "Late Antique Sardis."

32. Generally, see Johnson, "Asia Minor."

33. Ignatius, etc., in *Apostolic Fathers.*

34. Kraabel, "Melito," 77–85; *Melito of Sardis.*

35. A review of the plates and plans in Seager's description of the building, *supra,* will serve to stimulate the imagination.

36. Goodenough, 2:85.

37. Kraabel, "Diaspora Synagogue," 489–491.

38. *Sardis* R2 (1978) nos. 25, lions: 217, Eagle Table (supports); 226, Socrates menorah. "Corinthian" monument base (SYN 62.20), restored 1970–1971, is described by A. Seager, *Sardis* (R4) *Synagogue* (forthcoming), "Main Hall," pier N1. It consists of a hexagonal structure with attached Corinthian half-columns capped by an architrave with Ionic dentils, height 1.30 m., diameter 0.70 m. According to

G. M. A. Hanfmann, it dates ca. A.D. 200. A cast is on display in the Sardis Synagogue. Original parts are at Sardis camp and in the Manisa Museum.

X. Christianity: Churches and Cemeteries

Christianization of Sardis: Destruction and Construction

1. *Sardis* M4 (1976) Chapter I.
2. *Sardis* M4 (1976) 4–5.
3. Ibid., 135.
4. For the factory: Foss, ibid., 7, notes that Constantine rather than Diocletian may have created the great arms factory. Goths: see ibid., 9 and 108, Source 7 = Zosimus 5.18.
5. Foss, *Ephesus*, 188–191. Hanfmann, *Croesus*, 87. *Sardis* M4 (1976) 21–22, 113–114, Sources 14 ("Union" agreement), 15–16. Some of the damage to the Synagogue could be best explained by a flood, since the bottoms rather than the tops of the walls were damaged.
6. Skeletons, sword in HoB: *BASOR* 154, 24; 157, 24.
7. See *Sardis* M4 (1976) 53–55, for the background.
8. C. Foss in *Sardis* M4 (1976) 39–52, "The Expansion of the City in Late Antiquity."
9. *Sardis* VII.1 (1932) no. 19; M4 (1976) 28, 29, 116, Source 21.
10. House of Bronzes. Described as a table leg in *Sardis* R2 (1978) no. 225, the statue was made ca. A.D. 200–250. It was, therefore, an heirloom. Find circumstances: *BASOR* 154, 27. In his poem written about the time when the House of Bronzes was flourishing (ca. A.D. 550), Macedonius Consul has the city of Sardis speak enthusiastically of Dionysus (Bromios), whose nurturer Sardis was, and claim that wine was first squeezed out of grape "in our meadows." *Anthologia Graeca* 9.645 = *Sardis* M4 (1976) 109–110, Source 9. But if the statue with a damaged face was meant to serve such "learned-decorative" use of ancient myths (as Nonnus, presumably a Christian, did in his *Dionysiaca*), why was it in the "servants' basement"?
11. Dionysus group in the latrine: *BASOR* 157, 34–35. *Sardis* R2 (1978) no. 122.
12. *Sardis* M4 (1976) 23–27.
13. *Sardis* M4 (1976) 26–27. Eunapius, *Vitae Sophistarum*, ed. I. Giangrande (Rome 1956).
14. *Sardis* M4 (1976) Sources 4, 9, 16, 20 (Ajax, Achilles, Patroclus; Hermes, Zeus, Bacchus).

15. Levi, *Pavements*, passim. For Cyprus see the newly discovered "House of Dionysus" at Paphos.
16. Helios, *Sardis* R2 (1978) no. 167; one could imagine the strange relief no. 214 as late antique.
17. Crosses do appear in the frame of the apse mosaic in the Synagogue, Seager, *Synagogue*, fig. 21, a classic example of a non-Christian cross. See Kitzinger, 645 n. 36. The most ambitious figurative mosaics of Sardis are the dolphin and the eagle-animal mosaics of the Christian "bishop's residence"(?) mosaic suite at PN (see Buchwald, next section, *infra*). They are described by W. C. Kohler in *BASOR* 170, 22–24, 26–31, figs. 14–18. Hanfmann, *Letters*, 106, figs. 73–75 (plan). Some had thought to recognize a bearded head in the medallion on the eagle's chest (Fig. 297), but this turned out to be an optical illusion.

Reliefs with roughened background (*epipedogly-pha*): *BASOR* 162, 43 n. 77. Found near south door of Marble Court. S 60.10; two leaves, lion, bull. E. Kitzinger stated that numerous examples are known from Greece, Italy, and Crimea, with an earlier group of the fifth to sixth centuries A.D. and a later group of the Middle Byzantine period.
18. *BASOR* 157, 32–33, fig. 18. Hanfmann, *Letters*, 55–56, fig. 33. Ephesus: Akurgal, *Civilizations*, 161, fig. 58:6.
19. *Eulogeit(os ho laos)*: IN 64.1, *BASOR* 177, 26; correct reading in *BASOR* 187, 10. This inscription was thought to be Jewish and was one of the reasons why Unit BE-A was thought to belong to the Synagogue. Since then, A. R. Seager has determined that there was no connection between BE-A and the Synagogue before the destruction of A.D. 616; the crude opening was due to workmen doing later repair operations on the Byzantine version of the Main Avenue (see Chapter IX, under "The Building," n. 44, *supra*). Consequently, the inscription is now assumed to be Christian, although L. Robert has reservations.
20. *BASOR* 154, figs. 11, 22, 23. *Sardis* M4 (1976) 43–44, fig. 21. D. Hansen, "Sardi cristiana," 172–173, pls. 10B–11.
21. *BASOR* 174, 45, fig. 28. Shop E18 ("Pithos" Shop), E106/S2.5: M 63.5, lamp stand; M 63.60, incense burner; M 63.61, lamp with cross. This shop was next to the south entrance into the Synagogue.
22. The official definition of ampulla is "a vase of baked clay often bearing the image or symbol of the saint, which was used to preserve oil from light burned in the martyria," *ODCC*, 45 *s.v.* ampulla; E. Iosi, *EC* 1 (1949) *s.v.* "Ampolla," 1113–1115. *BASOR* 182, 15–18, figs. 12–13, with a list of Sardian examples. *Sardis* R1 (1975) 47, figs. 52–53 (guardroom). D. Hansen, "Sardi cristiana," 179, pl. 11B. Hanfmann, *Letters*, 166, 250, figs. 122, 123,

185. *BASOR* 199, 70, fig. 37. Donkey: Byzantine intrusion in PN Christian graves: P 67.90, *BASOR* 191, 11. Interpreted by Hanfmann as Entry into Jerusalem, John 12:12-16.

23. See n. 10, *supra,* for Dionysus in the House of Bronzes. In an important note on survival of pagan rites, C. Foss recalls the visit of the Neoplatonist Proclus, who studied ancient rites that were still preserved in Lydia around A.D. 450. *Sardis* M4 (1976) 155 n. 73.

24. Foss takes "the Angel" to be the leader of the Sardis church, *Sardis* M4 (1976) 135, List of Bishops of Sardis. Foss's careful review of Christianity at Sardis and S. E. Johnson's "Christianity in Sardis" are recent surveys. According to one Menologion, a Clement, the first gentile to believe in Christ, was the first bishop of Sardis; he has sometimes been identified with Clement, the fellow laborer of St. Paul (*Philippians* 4:3, A.D. 59-61?); but the traditions are contradictory. *Sardis* M4 (1976) 30.

25. See Chapter IX, *supra,* under "Impact of Discovery."

26. See also Kraabel, "Melito," 79 n. 13; idem, "Paganism," 29, with ref. Melito was trying to present his *Apology* to Marcus, co-ruler of Lucius Verus, to whom the Jewish community, according to I. Rabinowitz, may have set up an inscription in Hebrew, *BASOR* 187, 25. Previously, Hanfmann had speculated that Lucius Verus might have been asked by municipal authorities and the Jewish community for approval of the transfer of the gymnasium basilica to the Jews.

27. The great dedicatory inscription of the gymnasium, dated to A.D. 211, starts: *THEOIS PATRIOIS,* followed by the Emperors; and the city calls herself *oikeia ton kyrion hemon,* "Member of the House of Our Lords," *familiaris.*

28. For the Constantinian program, see Krautheimer, 17-14, "Constantinian Church Building"; for Tyre (A.D. 318), see ibid., 24-25. Eusebius, *HE* 10.4.44.

29. *Sardis* M4 (1976) 24. A. H. M. Jones, *Greek City,* 253.

30. *Sardis* 4 (1976) 5-6, IN 71.6, fig. 2.

31. *Sardis* R1 (1975) 139, 164-165.

32. *Sardis* M4 (1976) 113-114, the Union of Builders inscription envisages both public and private construction. Fines from defaulting workmen are to be used for public works.

33. On the term *aleipterion,* which is of wider application than "oiling room," see Foss, "Aleipterion." Simplikios and . . . *onios: Sardis* M4 (1976) 113-114, Sources 15, 16.

34. Acholios: *Sardis* M4 (1976) 115, Sources 20. *Sardis* VII.1 (1932) no. 83. A new inscription in

verse speaks of someone who had created *krepeida krateren,* "a strong foundation," *BASOR* 203, 14; IN 70.7.

35. *Codex Theod.* 16.10.25. *Sardis* M4 (1976) 49, 159, n. 128, citing A. Frantz, "From Paganism to Christianity in the Temples of Athens," 187-188; and F. W. Deichmann, "Fruhchristliche Kirchen," 107.

36. Pseudo Codinus in *Script. Orig. Const.,* ed. A. Preger, 189. *Sardis* M4 (1976) 107, Source 6.

37. See "Complex of Church M," *infra.* The fragment is shown *in situ* in the foundation, *Sardis* R2 (1978) 104-105, fig. 226, no. 103.

38. Antoninus: *Sardis* R2 (1978) no. 79. His head fragment was found in the Byzantine cistern within the temple.

39. *Sardis* R2 (1978) no. 251. Found in the center (apparently within the former western cella) of the temple.

40. *Sardis* M4 (1979) 110, 112; *en tei lam(protatei) kai dis neokoron Sardianon metropolei,* "in the most distinguished metropolis of the Sardians twice honored with an emperor's temple," occurs in the preamble. Burrell, *Neokoroi* (unpublished), notes that this is the latest known occurrence of the title and speculates that it might have been copied from an inscription. Later, the artisans swear "by the Holy and Life-Giving Trinity and the Safe Preservation and Victory of the Lord of the Inhabited World, Flavius Leo, everlasting Augustus and Emperor."

41. A coin of Constantine (A.D. 324-330) was found with marble fragments of a temple column in Trench 2 of the peristyle in 1972. H. C. Butler also noted that coins of Constantine were the earliest in the "late antique level"! *Sardis* R1 (1975) 82, 102. Possibly some columns were removed because they were damaged or were reused in Constantinople?

42. *Sardis* M4 (1976) 49.

43. *Sardis* I (1922) 49, 67-68. *Sardis* M4 (1976) 50.

44. *Sardis* R2 (1978) no. 275. The crosswall between the Main Hall and the Forecourt, into which the base was built, must date from the beginning of the last phase of the Synagogue, not later than 330-340.

45. *Sardis* R2 (1978) 58-60, figs. 78-82, no. 20. For the circumstances of the find, see *BASOR* 199, 48-50. Hanfmann, *Letters,* 243, figs. 180, as found, 181. According to Seager's current chronology, the reuse of the piece occurred around A.D. 360.

46. Lions: *Sardis* R2 (1976) no. 29, esp. fig. 92; other pieces possibly from the Cybele precinct, 38. The point is that by the architectural chronology the Artemis-Cybele relief and the lions must have been used after the accession of Constantine and the de-

struction of sanctuaries; there is some doubt in cases regarding pieces built into the long walls of the Synagogue.

47. L. Robert, *NIS,* 33–34, pl. 3:2. For the position of the piece as part of a makeshift support of a marble table, see *BASOR* 157, 24.

48. *Sardis* M4 (1976) 116–117, Sources 22. Eunapius, *Vitae Sophistarum* 503.

49. John of Ephesus, *Sardis* M4 (1976) 34.

50. *BASOR* 170, 15; 20, fig. 13; 174, 19, fig. 10. Buchwald, "Church E," 270, 272, states that each of the five reused preserved column bases of the interior was somewhat different, probably indicating that material in good condition from the classical buildings was no longer available in large quantities.

51. For the best and most up-to-date overall plans and axonometric reconstruction, see *BASOR* 215, 33–42, figs. 3, 4, 5. See also *Sardis* M4 (1976) 45–47, figs. 24, 27. For the general location see *Sardis* R1 (1975) figs. 1, 10.

52. *BASOR* 174, 20–24, fig. 11, plan; 170, 13–23, fig. 13 (plan); though superseded by the 1973 excavations for the interpretation of church units, these plans are important for the relation of buildings to the graves.

53. See *BASOR* 215, 33–37, fig. 6 for the description of the two graves within the church, G 72.2 and 73.19. G 72.2 is the grave considered by Buchwald as a possible reburial. Grave 73.19 (Fig. 291), however, belongs with the church. For the law of Theodosius I (A.D. 386) encouraging the building of churches over the saints' graves, see *Sardis* M4 (1976) 46, cited by Foss in connection with the basilica EA. *Codex Theod.* 9.17.7; for translation Pharr, 240.

54. Mosaics: *BASOR* 170, 22–30, figs. 14–18. The suggestion of a bishop's residence is Buchwald's: see "Early Christian Bascilica EA," *infra.* To understand the plan of the mosaic unit, it should be remembered that the suite continued northward beyond the Eagle Mosaic room, as is best shown in *BASOR* 215, 34, fig. 3. The reconstruction of this building and the adjoining bath has not been worked out yet.

55. *Sardis* I (1922) 145–146. *BASOR* 154, 11. Except for the chamber tombs and a sarcophagus, the tombs are not shown on our plan, *Sardis* R1 (1975) 66–67, n. 42, fig. 59; Foss, *Sardis* M4 (1976) 48–49, n. 124, appropriately recalls the tomb stones found by the first Sardis expedition: *Sardis* VII.1 (1932) nos. 165–167, 169, 170, 173.

56. In August 1973, the late S. W. Jacobs took out to Sardis (in typescript form) a careful descriptive analysis and account of restorations in which he entered a number of corrections. The manuscript was being readied for inclusion in *Sardis* R1; but Jacobs was not satisfied with the available reconstruction drawings and withdrew the manuscript, to which he also wanted to add a conclusion. It is hoped to make his account the basis of a publication in the forthcoming volume on *Churches of Sardis* (*Sardis* [M13]). The description in this section draws on Jacobs's observations. The following accounts are of value: H. C. Butler, *Sardis* I (1922) 112–115, ills. 118–119, good though incomplete plan and section. S. W. Jacobs, *BASOR* 166, 49–54, figs. 39–40, up-to-date plan, account of 1961 restorations. *BASOR* 199, 34–35, excavation in east apse; 215, 43, reconstruction of triforium. *Sardis* R1 (1975) 26, 54, burial of church and flood deposits; M4 (1976) 48, figs. 30–31, general account. Two unusual views in Hanfmann, *Letters,* 266–267, figs. 197–198; for S. W. Jacobs at Sardis, see ibid. 303.

57. S. W. Jacobs, Manuscript (unpublished); L. J. Majewski, "Wall Paintings," *BASOR* 199, 54, WP 69.3.

58. *Sardis* I (1922) 113; XI (1916) viii.

59. S. W. Jacobs cites K. J. Conant, 26–27, for this arrangement in ninth century churches in the early medieval west.

60. *BASOR* 199, 34–35; Hanfmann, *Letters,* 266.

61. *Sardis* R1 (1975) 26, 54; I (1922) 90–91.

62. *Sardis* R1 (1975) 58–60, figs. 57, 67–75; M4 (1976) 49 n. 127. *BASOR* 199, 29–35. The painted tomb underneath dates to the first century A.D. The stele of Timomachus, ca. 150 B.C., was placed in front of the structure—because the family claimed him as ancestor?

63. *BASOR* 206, 15–16 n. 3.

64. This account is based on R. L. Vann, "Unexcavated Buildings," to appear in *Sardis* (M14) *Early Travelers and Unexcavated Buildings* (forthcoming). For an orientation and alignment map, see *Sardis* R1 (1975) fig. 10.

65. A. Choisy, *L'art de bâtir chez les Byzantins* (Paris, 1883), 73.

66. *Sardis* (M14): Vann gives a full listing of previous discussions. Butler, in *Sardis* I (1922) 33, ill. 18, "Basilica D." See also *Sardis* M4 (1976) 39, fig. 11, described straightforwardly as "Justinianic basilica." As Foss, *Sardis* M4, 158 n. 104, notes, A. H. S. Megaw first suggested the time of Justinian. A detailed description with drawings of what was visible in 1970 will be published in R. L. Vann's "Unexcavated Buildings," *Sardis* (M14).

67. Keil (1964), figs. 33, 13. Krautheimer, 80–81, figs. 26–27, 175–176, figs. 67–68, pl. 84. Vann notes that elliptical domes on pendentives occur in the Justinianic churches of St. John in Ephesus, Basilica B, Philippi, and St. Titus, Gortyn.

Early Christian Basilica EA and Church E

1. *Sardis* 1 (1922) 33.

2. *BASOR* 170, 15–16; 174, 14–20. The plans and reconstruction published at the time were based on incomplete evidence and are incorrect in numerous details.

3. *BASOR* 170, 18–22. Those portions of Church EA and its ancillary units which were excavated were designated "Southwest Building," "Roman Garden," "Long South Wall," and "Long Mosaic Unit" by the excavators.

4. *BASOR* 211, 17–19; 215, 33–40; *TürkArkDerg* 21 (1975) 60; 24 (1977) 117; Hanfmann, FR 1973: "Report on Excavations within and around Church E" (unpublished); L. J. Majewski, FR 1973; "Report on the Study of Wall Paintings and Mosaics at Sardis" (unpublished); H. Buchwald, FR 1972: "Work on Church E" (unpublished); idem, FR 1973: "Work on Church E and Church EA" (unpublished); idem, FR 1975: "Report on Churches E and EA" (unpublished).

5. A detailed account of the excavation and an evaluation of the findings will appear in *Sardis* (M13) *Churches* (forthcoming).

6. Hanfmann, FR 1973, 10.

7. The exterior was probably also plastered, but no direct evidence concerning its treatment has survived.

8. See particularly *BASOR* 215, fig. 8, Majewski, FR 1973, 4; also R. Koehler, *BASOR* 170, 26–31.

9. Double engaged columns were used to support the nave colonnades of other Early Byzantine basilicas in Asia Minor, for instance at Bin Bir Kilise. This reconstruction would assume that none of the columns or column bases found in the excavation, including the bases reused in Church E and the base found on the stylobate of Church EA, belonged to the original construction.

10. Double engaged columns were used in Early Byzantine churches as window mullions, but none of the extant Church EA fragments shows signs of attachments which must have been used to fix the window frames, making this reconstruction seem less tenable. Therefore, they were most likely gallery supports. While there is no other evidence of galleries in Church EA, numerous basilicas with galleries are known in Greece, Constantinople, and Asia Minor, and double engaged columns have been suggested as gallery supports for a basilica in Miletus.

11. *BASOR* 211, 18 (fig. 2); Majewski, FR 1973, points out that two layers of fresco can be traced on some of the fragments, and most of the distinctive features belong to the second layer. The fragments of plaster ornamentation, which included a cross, and which were also found inside the apse, cannot be attributed to the first construction with any degree of certainty.

12. Hanfmann, FR 1973, 11. C. Foss rechecked the numismatic evidence with H. Buchwald at Sardis in 1980.

13. Ibid.

14. Majewski, FR 1973, 5.

15. *BASOR* 170, 18–22.

16. Hanfmann, FR 1973, 12.

17. *BASOR* 170, 18, 30.

18. The other alternative is that this approach to the church was used by the women, but this interpretation seems less likely, particularly because of the changes mentioned below. While a stairway leading to a gallery could also theoretically have been located in this area, no trace of a stairway has been found and there is no reason to believe that one existed here.

19. This interpretation seems convincing because of its obvious logic and simplicity, although other interpretations, such as changes in usage or liturgy, are also possible. These alterations in the ancillary spaces west of Church EA may prove to be useful in clarifying the still open questions concerning the purpose of side aisles in Early Byzantine basilicas.

20. Majewski, FR 1973, 2 suggests that the fresco was stylistically similar to the so-called Peacock Tomb (Fig. 296), tentatively dated fourth to sixth century, and notes that pigments were used which do not seem to have been employed after the sixth century.

21. A well-built tile drain underneath the floor of the space north of the major apse could lead to the interpretation that the space was used as a baptistery (Fig. 291); however, no font was found in the floor, and the drain seems to have continued at least as far as the south wall of the room. The drain may, therefore, have served another function.

22. Hanfmann, FR 1973, 13.

23. Hanfmann, *BASOR* 215, 40 and fig. 9. The fragment cannot be related to Church EA with certainty, for it may have been brought to the site at a later period. No comparable pieces have been found in the excavation. If the closure slab (Fig. 293) was indeed made for Church EA, it must have been created for a fifth to sixth century renovation rather than for the original construction of the basilica because of the paleography of the inscription.

24. Buchwald, *Sige,* 57, for the masonry. Foss, *Sardis* M4 (1976) 73f., points out that activity in this part of Sardis resumed in the ninth century.

25. In the basilica located above the theater at Hieropolis (Pamukkale), for instance, the side aisles seem to have been completely sealed off from the nave in a medieval reconstruction.

26. Majewski, FR 1973, 1.

27. Grave 72.2: *BASOR* 215, 37, fig. 6; *TürkArk-*

Derg 21, 60, and particularly fig. 5. The glass bottle found in the grave is dated to the fifth century (around A.D. 400) by A. von Saldern, *Sardis* M6 (1980), Bottle Type 7, no. 509. See Buchwald, "Church E," 275, for a more detailed description and arguments concerning the date of the grave and frescoes. Grave 73.19: *BASOR* 215, 37, fig. 6. See "The Cemeteries," this chapter, *infra.*

28. *BASOR* 215, 40; Hanfmann, FR 1973, 12; three coins all dating to the period between 1059 and 1071 were found in debris and in graves located in the northeast corner of the atrium and in the north part of the narthex. The *terminus post quem* provided by the coins coincides exactly with the date of the battle at Manzikert, in which the Byzantine forces were crushed by the Seljuk Turks. The fact that the main door to the narthex was made smaller at this time probably means that either the lintel over the door or the wooden door leaves had been destroyed and could not be replaced in their original dimensions.

29. See n. 2, *supra,* for the excavation, and *BASOR* 215, 33–40, and 228, 37, for further work carried out after 1972. See Buchwald, "Church E," for a summary of the findings and reconstruction.

30. See Buchwald, "Church E," 277, for details and references.

31. See ibid., 283–295, for a detailed analysis of the ornamentation, comparable examples, and references.

32. See ibid., 295–299, for a summary of the evidence with further references.

33. Buchwald, "Lascarid Architecture," *JÖB,* 259.

34. Ibid., 288.

35. Ibid., 260, with further references, and 288.

36. This possibility was first proposed by Buchwald after the reburial was found underneath the "pseudo-crypt" of Church E in 1972. See also n. 27, *supra,* for further references. Because of considerations which will be published in detail in *Sardis* (M13) *Churches* (forthcoming), Buchwald no longer finds this hypothesis as convincing.

37. For a somewhat different view, cf. Kraabel, Chapter IX, *supra,* under "Impact of Discovery."

38. This material will be published in detail in *Sardis* (M13) *Churches* (forthcoming).

39. Buchwald, "Lascarid Architecture."

40. Buchwald, "Church E," 271, with references.

41. Ibid., 281; Buchwald, "Lascarid Architecture," 292.

42. Buchwald, "Lascarid Architecture," figs. 4–9.

43. Ibid., 289; Buchwald, "Church E," 281. See also "Lascarid Architecture," 294 on, for other important considerations concerning the possible influence of Church E on Palaeologue imperial church types.

44. See Buchwald, "Church E," 268 n. 10, for the destruction of the church. The building seems to have served domestic and industrial functions for almost 300 years before its destruction, but there is no evidence that it was ever used as a mosque.

The Cemeteries

1. The classic case is the purification of Apollo's entire island of Delos by the Athenians in 543 and 425 B.C. See Kurtz-Boardman, 189, 198: "in sanctuary area birth, death, and burial were normally forbidden." Thucydides 3.94.2.

2. *Sardis* R1 (1975) 59–60, figs. 59, 60, 72–73, Tomb 2.

3. *ODCC* 1158, *s.v.* "Resurrection of the Dead," describes as the prevailing view that "the resurrection will be a restoration of the whole psychic-physical organism," but already St. Paul, 1 Cor. 15:35–54, spoke of a new spiritual body at resurrection.

4. Tertullian, *De resurrectione carnis,* 63.

5. *Sardis* M4 (1976) 117–118, Sources: 23 (May 26, A.D. 257), Therapon; 24 (July 10, third century A.D.), Apollonius.

6. See Bostanci, "Skeletal Remains," "Skulls" 1967 and 1969; *BASOR* 170, 60 (PN cemetery). See also Field Reports, especially 1962–1963, 1966–1967.

7. *BASOR* 186, 49. See "The Mass Burial at Duman Tepe," *infra.*

8. *Sardis* M4 (1976) 110 lists *Sardis* VII.1 (1932) nos. 166–169. A tombstone found in 1961 (IN 67.30) and interpreted by L. Robert invokes the curses of 318 Fathers (of the Council of Nicaea). It probably belongs to the eighth or ninth century.

9. *Sardis* VII.1 (1932) no. 166. A member of the *gerousia* and municipal bread-seller, Zotikos and his wife Aurelia Hesychion belonged to the moneyed classes.

10. Ibid., no. 168.

11. General location: *Sardis* R1 (1975), fig. 1, no. 4. *BASOR* 157, 26, fig. 9, 13 (section). This is no. 5 of the tomb list, *infra.* A small brick tomb, L. 2.5 m., W. 0.60 m., H. 1.0 m., was stuccoed and painted with flowers and fillets. It contained "but a few bones." A large chamber tomb with burials of the fourth century was excavated just west of HoB in 1980.

12. *Sardis* V (1925) 3–5. For the destruction of Claudia Antonia Sabina's mausoleum by its landowner, see *BASOR* 211, 31–32. The *venatio* reliefs, *BASOR* 215, 47, fig. 1; *Sardis* R2 (1978) nos. 147–149, probably also belonged to a mausoleum in this area.

13. *BASOR* 174, 22–24, fig. 11.

14. *BASOR* 170, 22–26, figs. 13–18; 174, 20–22, 24, fig. 11 (plan), *Sardis* M4 (1976) fig. 26 (axonometric view).

15. *BASOR* 191, 10–11.

16. *BASOR* 166, 32. Location: *Sardis* R1 (1975), fig. 1, no. 12.

17. *BASOR* 215, 41, Grave 73.37 (plan fig. 4). The numbers of excavated graves are as follows: 1962: 49; 1972: 5; 1973: 47; plus two unnumbered graves, 1961, *BASOR* 162, 25. For the "Roman Garden" see *BASOR* 170, 20, fig. 13, plan of 1962; corrected in *BASOR* 215, 33–41, fig. 4, which includes graves found through 1973.

18. *BASOR* 215, 37, fig. 6, Grave 73.19. For the glass bottle see Bottle Type 7, *Sardis* M6 (1980) no. 509. The lower Grave 73.19 was made before the Lascarid Church E was built; the church foundation wall cut through the western end of the lower Grave 73.19: see "Early Christian Basilica EA," *supra*.

19. One of the wooden caskets was traced in 1962; the other, Grave 73.22, was within a tile box: *BASOR* 215, 41, fig. 10, rock crystal, J 73.5; gold earring, J 73.3.

20. One sarcophagus, Grave 62.1, was along the north side of Lascarid Church E: *BASOR* 170, 17, fig. 13; 215, fig. 4, G 62. It contained Islamic coins, C 62.186–188. The other sarcophagus was being used as a water tank in the Turkish workshops which occupied the church. It was not assigned a burial number: *BASOR* 170, 15. It seems very likely that it, too, was reused as a Christian burial before being reused by Turkish craftsmen.

21. Graves 73.23; 62.45 (on column); 62.42; 62.50. See *BASOR* 170, 17; 215, 41. A bronze cross in the grave: Grave 61.33.

22. Bronze rings: Graves 62.47; 73.24. Necklaces: Grave 73.6; for other examples see *BASOR* 170, 17.

23. *BASOR* 215, 41, fig. 10. See n. 19, *supra*.

24. *BASOR* 170, 17 n. 7a. Grave 62.1 (n. 17, *supra*). Preliminary identifications by G. C. Miles: C 62.186–187: Sarukhanid, 1374–1388; C 62.188: Ottoman, Murad I, 1360–1389. Final publication: *Sardis* M7 (1981) nos. 2, 3, 204. It does not seem that this burial could be Turkish; more probably the coins were dropped in by chance shortly after the Turkish craftsmen took over the church.

25. *BASOR* 170, 18–23, fig. 13 (plan); 215, 40–41, figs. 3–4.

26. Balty, *Colloque* (1972) 197, pl. 80:2–3.

27. See the plans showing the graves, *BASOR* 170, 18–23, fig. 13; 215, fig. 4. For steps leading to Mosaic Unit Room D, when the street was already occupied by the cemetery, see *BASOR* 170, 22; 162, 25–

26, Middle Byzantine glazed wares found within "Mosaic Suite."

28. *BASOR* 174, 14; 215, 41; and 228, 51–53, figs. 3–7. A general account: *Sardis* M4 (1976) 91–92.

29. *BASOR* 191, 10–11. Grave 67.3. List of tombs, *infra*, no. 6.

30. For incised "First Style" decoration see *BASOR* 157, 28. A very fine, well-preserved "First Pompeian" stucco masonry was discovered at HoB in 1980.

31. As probably the tomb under Unit 16, HoB and PN 67.3. See list of tombs, nos. 1, 5, *infra;* and nn. 11 and 29, *supra*.

32. Known dimensions: Artemis Precinct Tomb 2 (list, no. 1): Int. L. 2.92, W. 2.12, H. 1.85; Shear's tomb at Kagirlik Tepe (list, no. 2): L. 2.82, W. 2.43, H. 2.11; Tomb of Chrysanthios (list, no. 4): L. 3.50, W. 2.80, H. 1.70; Peacock Tomb (list, no. 7); L. 3.06, W. 2.33, H. 1.91.

33. Their positions are shown in *Sardis* R1 (1975), fig. 1, nos. 33, 47.

34. *BASOR* 229, 61, 64: "Ca. 220 m. north of Pyramid Tomb," at ca. E30/S620, "the tops of three or four other hypogaea were recognized immediately northwest of the tomb of Flavius Chrysanthius . . . another with painted decoration was exposed in north." Reports as yet unpublished tell of the opening in 1979 of the sepulchers listed below as nos. 8–10.

35. *Sardis* I (1922) 183 n. 2.

36. Firatli, "Hypogaeum," 919–932, pls. 330–340a (Nicaea), pl. 340b (Silistra).

37. Rostovtzeff, "Wall Painting," 144. Morey in *Sardis* I (1922) 181–183. Minns, 314, figs. 225–231.

38. Firatli, "Hypogaeum," 924–929, figs. 130–131. Very close in style to the Synagogue panels are the wall paintings in Ephesus, H 1/b, Strocka, *Ephesos* 8:1, 31–38, figs. 39–41.

39. Strocka, *Ephesos* 8:1, 57–64, 69–70, 110, H 2 A; H 2 /SR 1; H 2/14 d, for three examples of *Streumuster,* figs. 79–82, 117–118, 236–243 (color plates).

40. They derive from flowered meadows such as are seen in the Tomb of the Octavii, Rome, ca. A.D. 220, where little souls inhabit the meadows and the symbolic Rape of the Soul to Immortality is depicted in the Rape of a Psyche-Prosperina by Pluto. Swindler, 404, fig. 623. For simplified examples of such Roman pagan "paradisiac" decoration, see the Roman casket graves near Amasya, dated by coins to the second or third century A.D.: Tokaz, 109–111, ills. A thoroughly documented, comprehensive survey of the rose-garden, Elysian fields, scattered flow-

ers theme in Roman and Early Christian painting is given by Strocka, *Ephesos* 8:1, 58–63. He tends, however, to date all Ephesian examples somewhat schematically to ca. A.D. 400. See Strocka, *Ephesos* 8:1, 63, a recent survey, on meaning of "eternal spring" and on peacock as a symbol of paradise.

41. In a Christian peacock mosaic from near Hama, the Greek inscription speaks of the donors as *karphoresantes,* literally "bringing fruit," the usual term for "offering" in which yet the "first-fruit" theme was still felt. S. Adbul Hak, *Musee Damas,* 69, pl. 33.2. That the Christian significance was established by the end of the fourth century A.D. is proved by the use of these "paradisiac" motifs in the famous Catacomb and Church complex of the Seven Sleepers in Ephesus, now correctly redated by M. Restle, 77, 187, and Strocka, *Ephesos* 8:1, 59, figs. 93–94, to the last quarter of the fourth century. A coin of Valentinian I (364–375) was found in 1973 under the mosaic floor of the church. This provides another secure date for the "scatter pattern" or "freefield" flower designs.

42. *Sardis* M4 (1976) 23–24. Based on Eunapius, 500–505 and passim.

43. Marinus, *Vita Procli,* 15. *Sardis* M4 (1976) 155 n. 73.

44. See "Christianization of Sardis," this chapter, *supra,* n. 54.

45. *Sardis* R1 (1975) 66–68; see figs. 59 and 96.

46. *Sardis* I (1922) 134, 145–146, fig. 101: "a poor medieval Byzantine cemetery" along the south side of the temple. The upper levels with these

graves yield "a few late coins, some bronze utensils, plates and bowls . . . Fragmentary Greek inscriptions served to line or cover the graves."

47. BT 66.1; see Chapter III, *supra,* under "Pactolus North."

48. *BASOR* 186, 47. Hanfmann, *Letters,* 185–186, figs. 135–137.

49. *BASOR* 186, 50. Some of the lamps are seen in Hanfmann, *Letters,* fig. 137.

50. *BASOR* 186, 50, fig. 31. Hanfmann, *Letters,* fig. 138. A similar archangel appears on coins of Justin I (518–527).

51. D. H. Finkel, FR 1967: "Bones" (unpublished). Cf. Bostanci, "Skeletal Remains" (1963); "Skulls" 1967 and 1969.

52. *BASOR* 162, 33; 166, 37–40, with plan, fig. 30.

53. *Sardis* M4 (1976) 57–60.

54. *BASOR* 166, 39, Grave 61.12; M 61.83.

55. *BASOR* 166, 39 n. 66, fig. 13; Grave 61.40; M 61.93.

56. *BASOR* 170, 31–33; 166, 39. The tomb with the Anastasis medallion, n. 48, *supra,* was built over by structures of this phase.

57. *Sardis* M4 (1976) 70.

58. See "Christianization of Sardis," this chapter, *supra,* on "Acropolis Cave Chapel"; especially n. 63; *BASOR* 206, 15–16, "closely grouped graves of indeterminate date." See *Sardis* M4 (1976) 70 for a general description of the Acropolis settlement, where Foss also takes the chapel "excavated into the rock and covered with frescoes" to be Middle Byzantine.

Illustrations

Plan I   Lydian city: hypothetical sketch plan.

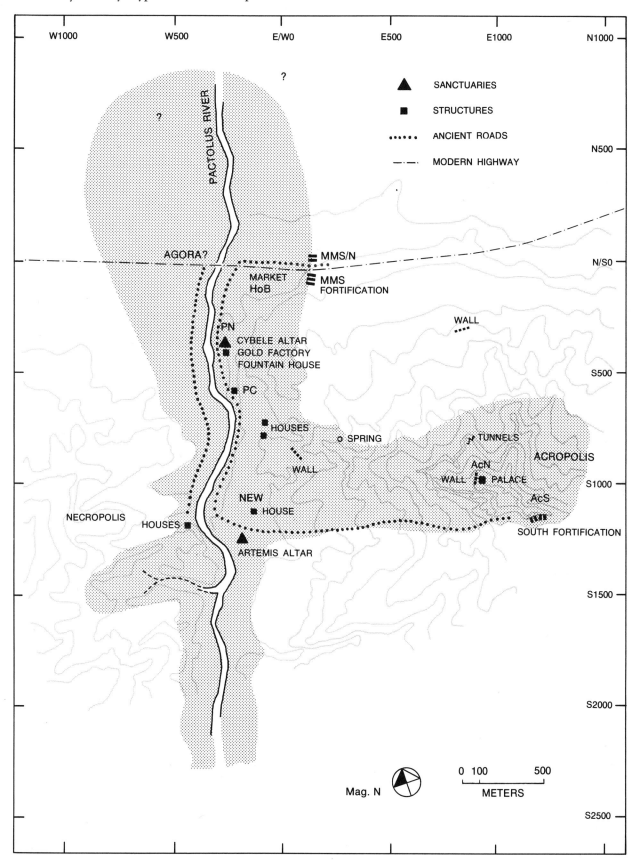

Plan II Seleucid city before 213 B.C.: hypothetical
sketch plan.

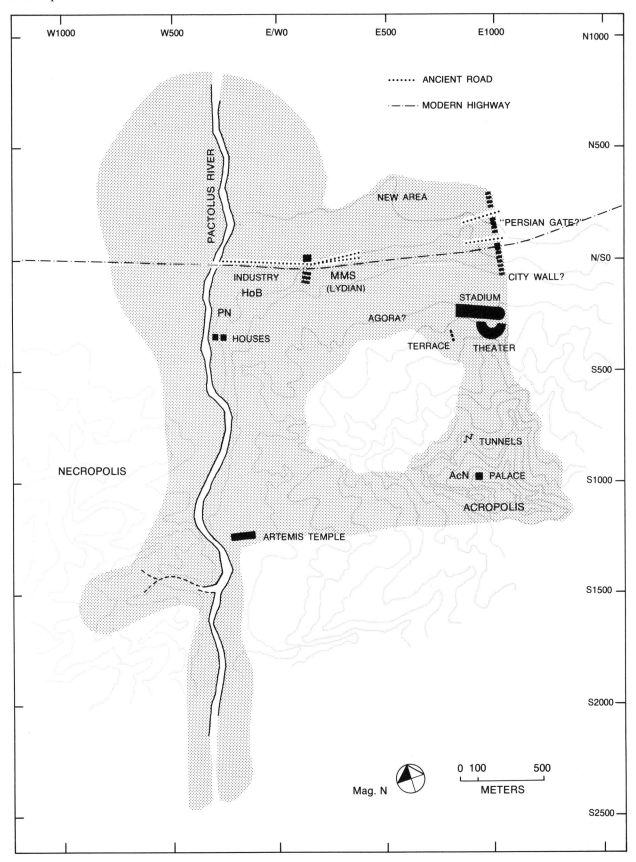

Plan III Pergamene and Roman city, 213 B.C. to
A.D. 17: hypothetical sketch plan.

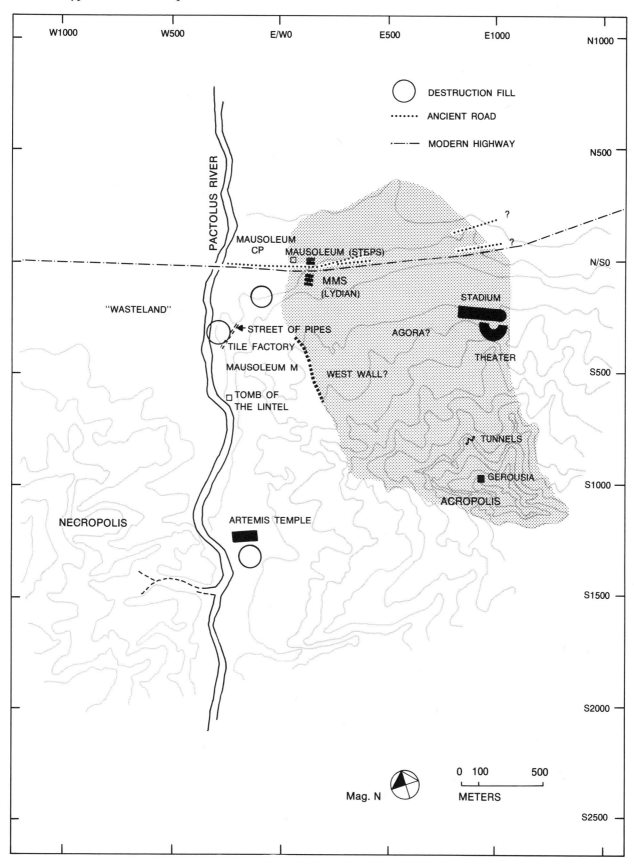

W1000 W500 E/W0 E500 E1000 N1000

○ DESTRUCTION FILL

···· ANCIENT ROAD

–·–·– MODERN HIGHWAY

N500

PACTOLUS RIVER

N/S0

MAUSOLEUM CP

MAUSOLEUM (STEPS)

MMS (LYDIAN)

STADIUM

"WASTELAND"

STREET OF PIPES

TILE FACTORY

MAUSOLEUM M

AGORA?

THEATER

S500

WEST WALL?

TOMB OF THE LINTEL

TUNNELS

GEROUSIA

S1000

NECROPOLIS

ACROPOLIS

ARTEMIS TEMPLE

S1500

S2000

Mag. N

0 100 500
METERS

S2500

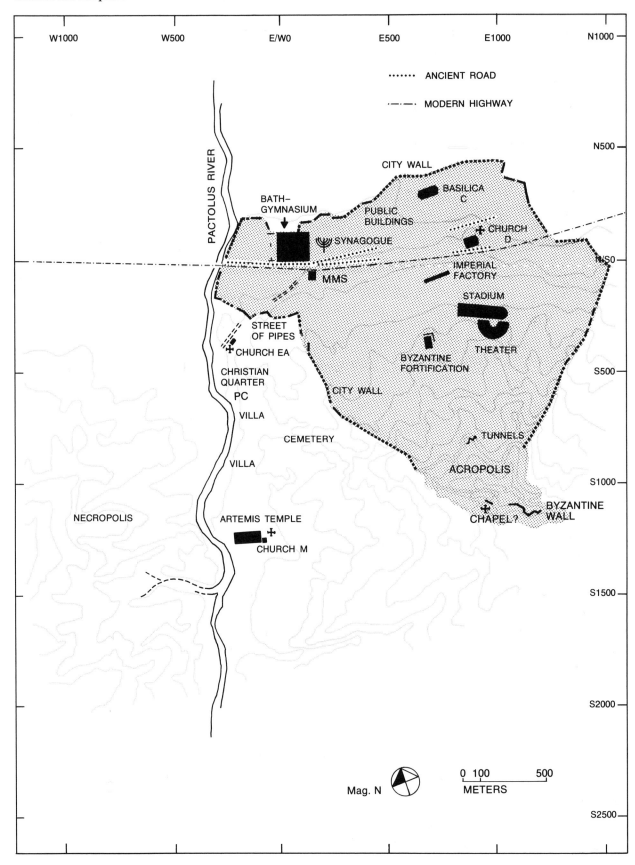

Plan IV Late Roman city, A.D. 400–616: hypothetical sketch plan.

········ ANCIENT ROAD

—·—·— MODERN HIGHWAY

PACTOLUS RIVER

CITY WALL

BATH–
GYMNASIUM

PUBLIC
BUILDINGS

BASILICA
C

SYNAGOGUE

✝ CHURCH
D

MMS

IMPERIAL
FACTORY

STADIUM

STREET
OF PIPES

✝ CHURCH EA

BYZANTINE
FORTIFICATION

THEATER

CHRISTIAN
QUARTER

PC

VILLA

CITY WALL

CEMETERY

VILLA

TUNNELS

ACROPOLIS

NECROPOLIS

ARTEMIS TEMPLE

✝
CHURCH M

✝
CHAPEL?

BYZANTINE
WALL

Mag. N

0 100   500
METERS

W1000   W500   E/W0   E500   E1000   N1000

N500

N/S0

S500

S1000

S1500

S2000

S2500

Fig. 1 Location of Sardis and the Royal Road.

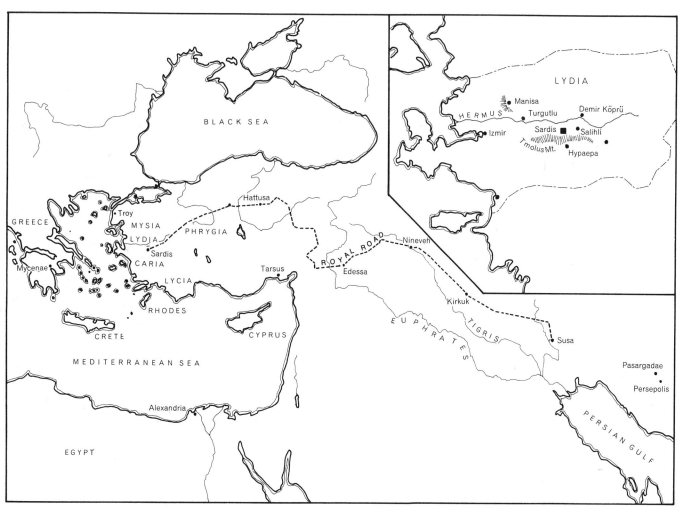

Fig. 2 Sardis and vicinity.

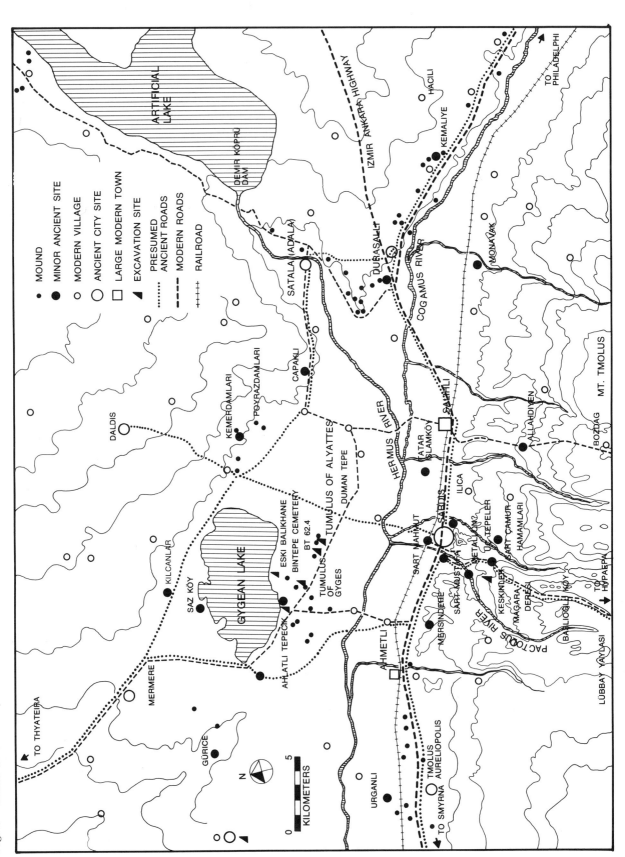

MOUND
MINOR ANCIENT SITE
MODERN VILLAGE
ANCIENT CITY SITE
LARGE MODERN TOWN
EXCAVATION SITE
PRESUMED ANCIENT ROADS
MODERN ROADS
RAILROAD

ARTIFICIAL LAKE

DEVIR KÖPRÜ DAM

IZMIR ANKARA HIGHWAY

HACILI

TO PHILADELPHI

KEMALIYE

SATALA (ADALA)

DURASALLI

ÇOG AMUS RIVER

MONAVAK

ÇAPAKLI

KEMERDAMLARI

POYRAZDAMLARI

DALDIS

TATAR ISLAMKÖY

SALIHLI

ALLAHDIYEN

HERMUS RIVER

TUMULUS OF ALYATTES

DUMAN TEPE

MT. TMOLUS

BOZDAG

ILICA

KILCANLAR

SAZ KÖY

GYGEAN LAKE

ESKI BALIKHANE
BINTEPE CEMETERY
BT 62.4

TUMULUS OF GYGES

SART MAHMUT

SARDIS

SART MUSTAFA

METALON?

SART ÇAMUR HAMAMLARI

TEPELER

KESKINLER

DEREKÖY

MERMERE

MERSINDERE

MAGARA

PACTOLUS RIVER

BAĞLIOĞLU KÖY

AHMETLI

LÜBBAY YAYLASI

TO HYPAEPA

TO THYATEIRA

GÜRICE

N

KILOMETERS
0   5

URGANLI

TMOLUS
AURELIOPOLIS

TO SMYRNA

AHLATLI TEPECIK

Fig. 3 Geological map of Tmolus region: plan and
profile (E. Izdar).

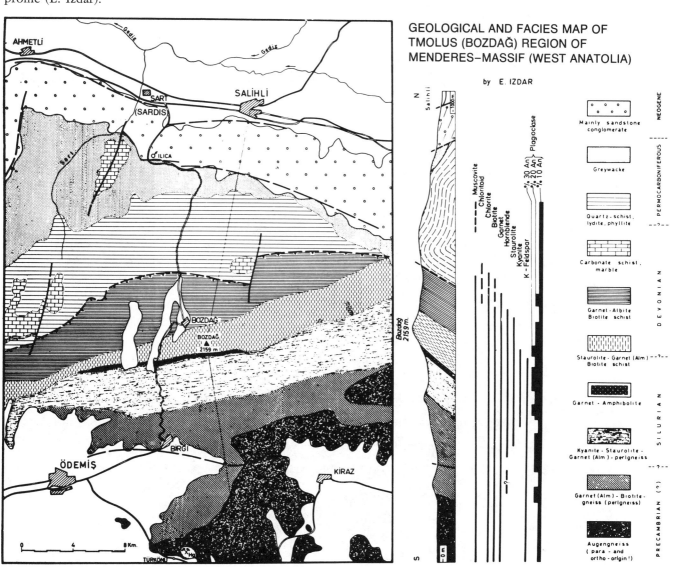

GEOLOGICAL AND FACIES MAP OF
TMOLUS (BOZDAĞ) REGION OF
MENDERES–MASSIF (WEST ANATOLIA)

by E. IZDAR

Fig. 4 View of Sardis from west.

Fig. 5 View of Sardian plain from the Acropolis
after gymnasium area restoration (1973).

Fig. 6 View of the Acropolis of Sardis from the
north showing vegetation of various types and
Roman-Byzantine ruins of Hall C and Complex A.

Fig. 7 Pactolus Valley with Expedition camp,
Artemis Temple, and west flank of the Acropolis.

Fig. 8 Site plan with excavations and ruins of Sardis.

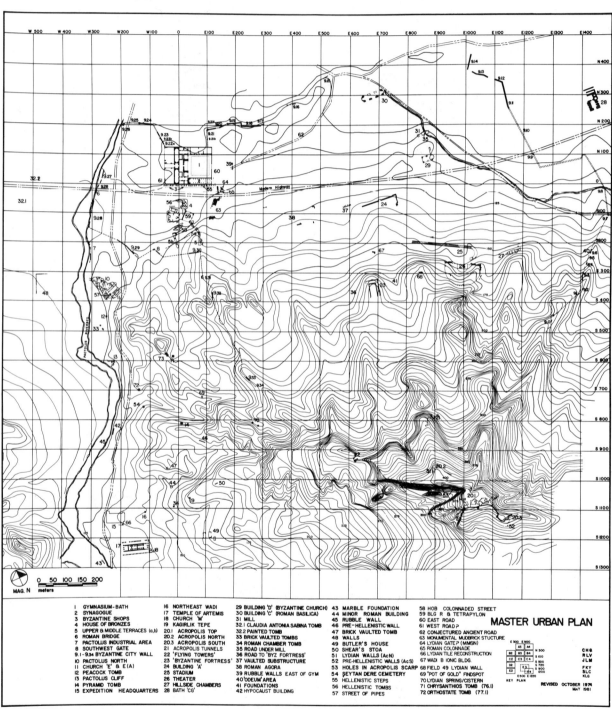

MAG. N

0 50 100 150 200
meters

1 GYMNASIUM-BATH
2 SYNAGOGUE
3 BYZANTINE SHOPS
4 HOUSE OF BRONZES
5 UPPER & MIDDLE TERRACES (a,b)
6 ROMAN BRIDGE
7 PACTOLUS INDUSTRIAL AREA
8 SOUTHWEST GATE
9.1-9.34 BYZANTINE CITY WALL
10 PACTOLUS NORTH
11 CHURCH 'E' & E(A)
12 PEACOCK TOMB
13 PACTOLUS CLIFF
14 PYRAMID TOMB
15 EXPEDITION HEADQUARTERS

16 NORTHEAST WADI
17 TEMPLE OF ARTEMIS
18 CHURCH 'M'
19 KAGIRLIK TEPE
20.1 ACROPOLIS TOP
20.2 ACROPOLIS NORTH
20.3 ACROPOLIS SOUTH
21 ACROPOLIS TUNNELS
22 'FLYING TOWERS'
23 'BYZANTINE FORTRESS'
24 BUILDING 'A'
25 STADIUM
26 THEATER
27 HILLSIDE CHAMBERS
28 BATH 'CG'

29 BUILDING 'D' (BYZANTINE CHURCH)
30 BUILDING 'C' (ROMAN BASILICA)
31 MILL
32.1 CLAUDIA ANTONIA SABINA TOMB
32.2 PAINTED TOMB
33 BRICK VAULTED TOMBS
34 ROMAN CHAMBER TOMB
35 ROAD UNDER MILL
36 ROAD TO 'BYZ FORTRESS'
37 VAULTED SUBSTRUCTURE
38 ROMAN AGORA
39 RUBBLE WALLS EAST OF GYM
40 'ODEUM' AREA
41 FOUNDATIONS
42 HYPOCAUST BUILDING

43 MARBLE FOUNDATION
44 MINOR ROMAN BUILDING
45 RUBBLE WALL
46 PRE-HELLENISTIC WALL
47 BRICK VAULTED TOMB
48 WALLS
49 BUTLER'S HOUSE
50 SHEAR'S STOA
51 LYDIAN WALLS (AcN)
52 PRE-HELLENISTIC WALLS (AcS)
53 HOLES IN ACROPOLIS SCARP
54 ŞEYTAN DERE CEMETERY
55 HELLENISTIC STEPS
56 HELLENISTIC TOMBS
57 STREET OF PIPES

58 HOB COLONNADED STREET
59 BLG R & TETRAPYLON
60 EAST ROAD
61 WEST ROAD?
62 CONJECTURED ANCIENT ROAD
63 MONUMENTAL MUDBRICK STUCTURE
64 LYDIAN GATE? (MMS/N)
65 ROMAN COLONNADE
66 LYDIAN TILE RECONSTRUCTION
67 WADI B IONIC BLDG.
68 FIELD 49 LYDIAN WALL
69 "POT OF GOLD" FINDSPOT
70 LYDIAN SPRING/CISTERN
71 CHRYSANTHIOS TOMB (76.1)
72 ORTHOSTATE TOMB (77.1)

MASTER URBAN PLAN

KEY PLAN

CHG
RLV
JLM
FKY
SLC
KLG

REVISED OCTOBER 1974
MAY 1981

1·2000

M26 U 101

Fig. 9 Artemis sanctuary and west bank of the
Pactolus with Necropolis Hill and Lydian tombs.

Fig. 10 Map of Asia Minor with Lydia and other
Iron Age countries. Courtesy of Archaeological Institute of America.

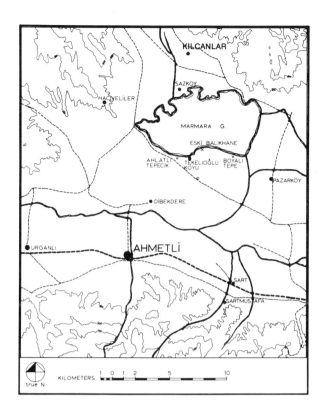

Fig. 11 Sardis region map with locations of Prehistoric sites on Gygean Lake.

Fig. 12 View of Ahlatli Tepecik, looking west.

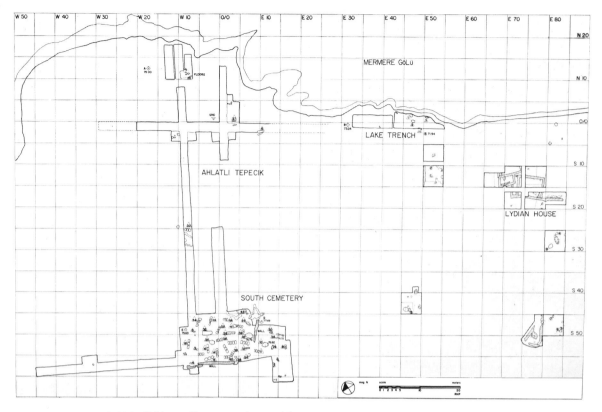

Fig. 13 Plan of Ahlatli Tepecik excavations with South Cemetery and Lydian house.

Fig. 14 Early Bronze Age pithos burial (AT 68.8) at Ahlatli Tepecik.

Fig. 15 Early Bronze Age cist burial at Ahlatli Tepecik (AT 67.29).

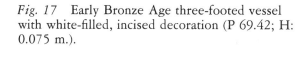

Fig. 16 Gravegoods from pithos burial at Eski Balikhane (EB 69.3): pottery, gold "earplugs," copper dagger, silver ram pendant (M 69.5–8).

Fig. 17 Early Bronze Age three-footed vessel with white-filled, incised decoration (P 69.42; H: 0.075 m.).

Fig. 18   Silver ram (M 69.6; L: 0.027 m.) from pithos burial (EB 69.3) at Eski Balikhane.

Fig. 19   Early Bronze Age red ware jug (P 67.60; H: 0.095 m.). Ahlatli Tepecik.

Fig. 20   Mesolithic lunate microlithic tool (S 68.17; L: 0.015 m.). Chance find, Sardis.

Fig. 21   Neolithic stone head (R2, no. 229; H: 0.04 m.). Chance find, Sardis.

Fig. 22 HoB, overall plan showing location of
deep soundings of 1962 and 1966.

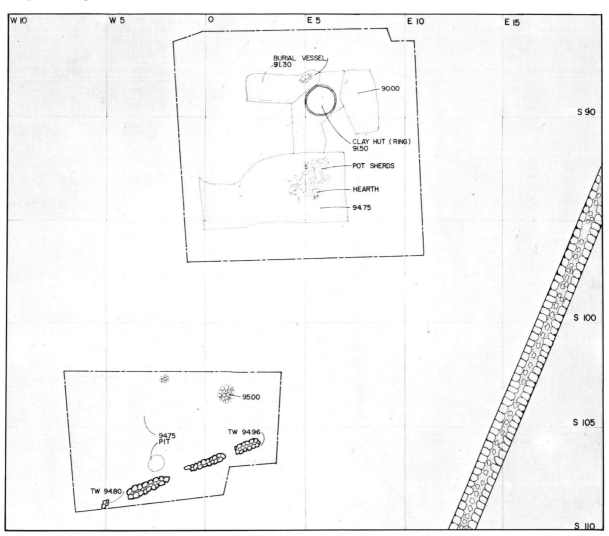

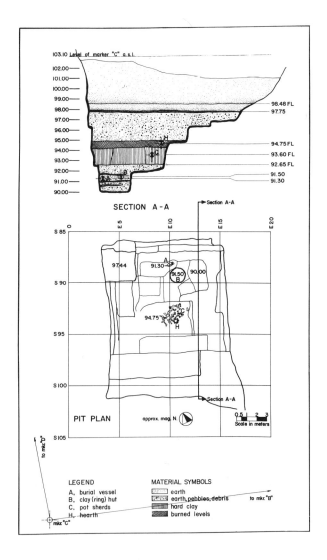

Fig. 23 HoB, plan and section of 1962 deep sounding.

Fig. 24 HoB, view of hut floor and burial in 1962 deep sounding during excavation.

Fig. 25 Bronze Age pithos (P 62.463; H: 0.52 m.) from HoB 1962 deep sounding.

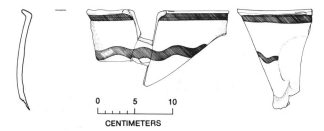

Fig. 26 Sherds of a Mycenaean crater from 1966 deep sounding (P 69.119).

Fig. 28 Lydian Protogeometric cup (P 66.107; H. with handle: 0.135 m.) from 1966 deep sounding.

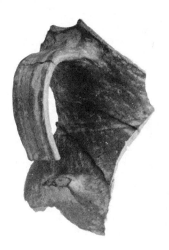

Fig. 27 Gray ware: jug neck and band handle (P 60.552; 0.05 × 0.05 m.).

Fig. 29 Bronze arc fibula (M 66.13; H: 0.035 m; W: 0.046 m.) from 1966 deep sounding.

Fig. 30 Iron sickle blade from 1966 deep sounding.

Fig. 31   HoB general view (1964) with Lydian
houses of Levels I–II and deep sounding of 1962
(on the right, beyond Roman wall).

Fig. 32   HoB, Lydian Level III with stone wall and
bothroi.

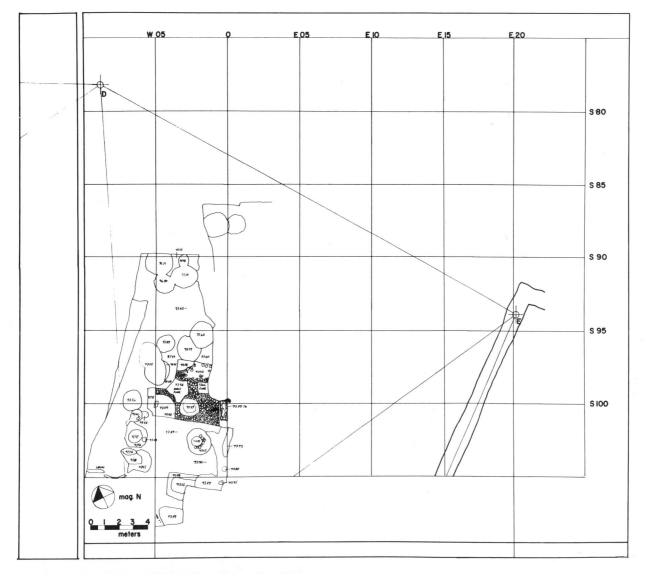

Fig. 33   HoB, plan of Lydian Level III.

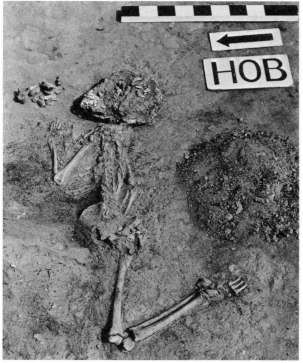

Fig. 34   HoB, skeleton of a small girl in conflagration level.

Fig. 35 Southwest part of HoB with market(?)
wall and units H and G. Balloon photograph (J.
Whittlesey).

Fig. 36 Lydian vase fragment of close style (P 66.66; P.H.: 0.20 m.). HoB, Lydian Level III.

Fig. 37 Lydian high-footed bowl of loose style (P 66.55; complete H: 0.08 m.). HoB, Lydian Level III.

Fig. 38 Corinthian trefoil oinochoe, HoB, ca. 750 B.C. (P 65.224; H: ~0.20 m.).

Fig. 39 HoB, plan of Lydian Levels II and I and
Hellenistic Building C.

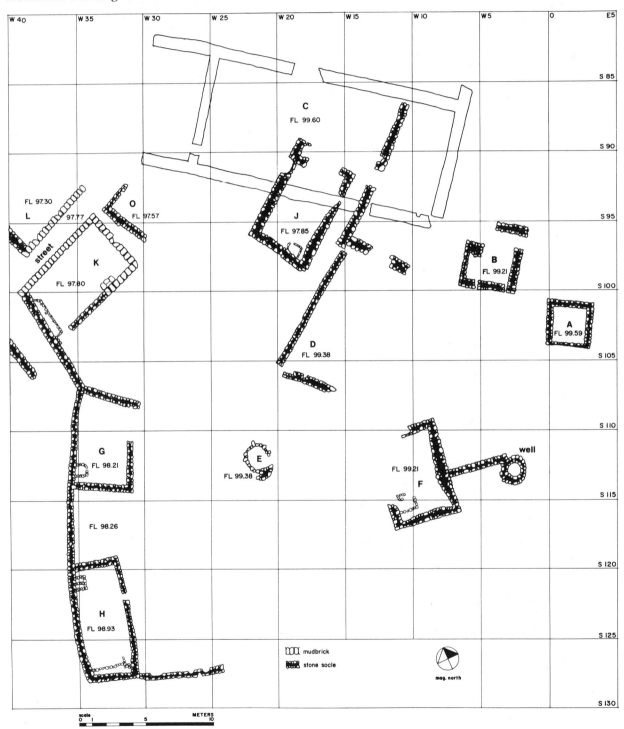

Fig. 40   HoB, Lydian Building H, interior from above.

Fig. 41   HoB, plan of Persian and Hellenistic
levels.

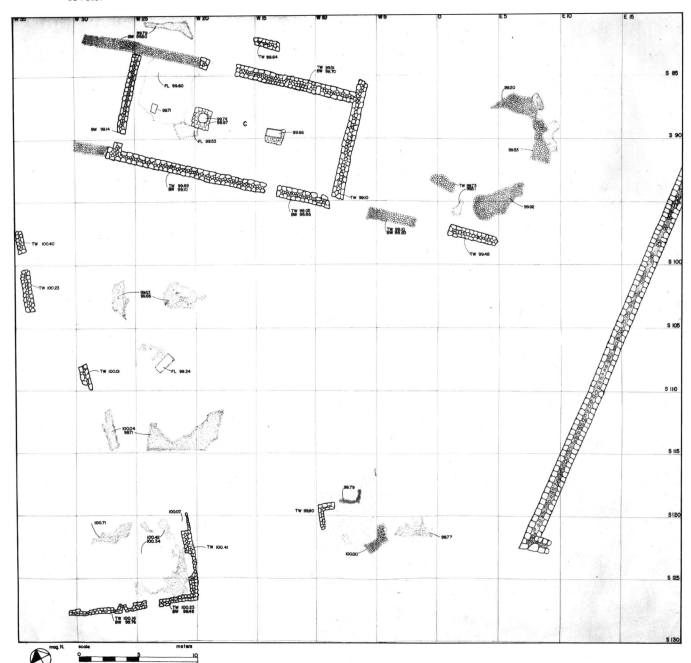

Fig. 42 PN, Lydian goldworking installation and
altar of Cybele looking west, 1968.

Fig. 43   PN, axonometric drawing of all periods (1973).

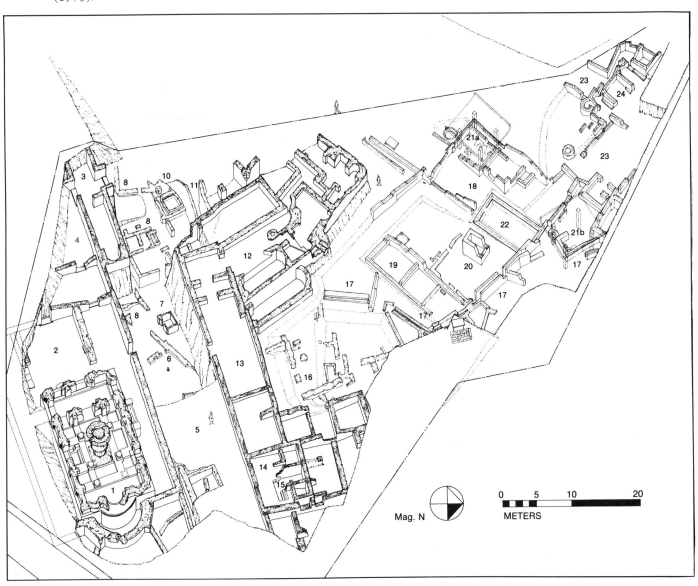

Mag. N

0   5   10   20
METERS

1 CHURCH 'E' (13TH CENTURY)
2 CHURCH 'EA' (4TH CENTURY)
3 NORTH CHAPEL (6TH CENTURY)
4 ISLAMIC VILLAGE HOUSE (17TH CENTURY)
5 ROMAN STREET (4TH CENTURY)
6 PERSIAN WALLS (5TH–4TH CENTURY B.C.)
7 LYDIAN BASEMENT (7TH–6TH CENTURY B.C.)
8 LYDIAN HOUSES (7TH–6TH CENTURY B.C.)
9 PERSIAN WELL (5TH–4TH CENTURY B.C.)

10 PERSIAN FOUNTAIN HOUSES (5TH–4TH CENTURY B.C.)
11 LANE
12 LATE ROMAN BATH (4TH–5TH CENTURY)
13 MOSAIC SUITE
14 ROMAN FUNERARY PRECINCT (1ST–3RD CENTURY)
15 HELLENISTIC MONUMENT (BEFORE 17 A.D.)
16 LYDIAN AND PERSIAN HOUSES (6TH–5TH CENTURY B.C.)

17 LYDIAN–HELLENISTIC WATER SYSTEM
18 LYDIAN GOLD-PROCESSING WORKSHOPS
19 HOUSE OF THE PRIEST
20 ALTAR OF CYBELE ca. 570 B.C.
21a,b LYDIAN FURNACE AND CUPELS
22 RECTANGULAR LYDIAN ROOM
23 LYDIAN AND PERSIAN HOUSES (6TH–5TH CENTURY B.C.)
24 HELLENISTIC ROOMS DESTROYED IN 213 B.C.

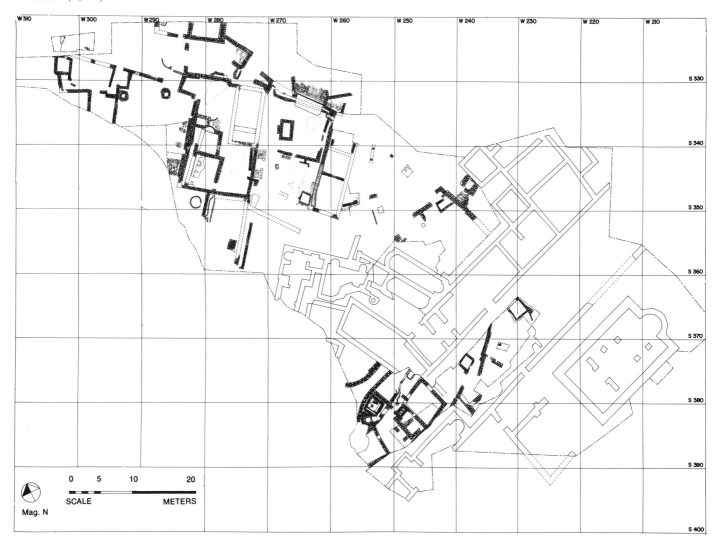

Fig. 44 PN, plan of main Lydian and Persian
levels (1970).

W 310   W 300   W 290   W 280   W 270   W 260   W 250   W 240   W 230   W 220   W 210

S 330

S 340

S 350

S 360

S 370

S 380

S 390

S 400

0   5   10   20

SCALE   METERS

Mag. N

Fig. 45 PN, plan of goldworking area with "cupels" and furnaces.

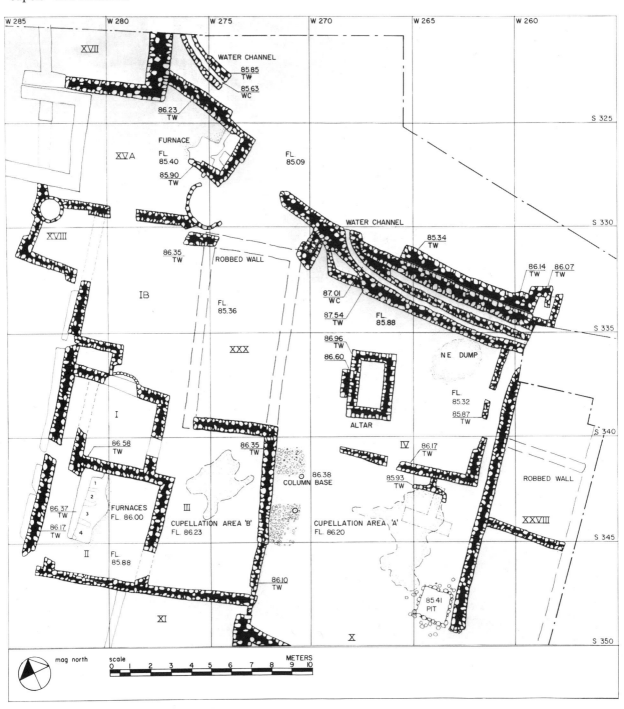

Fig. 46 PN, Cupellation Area A, two strata of
cupels.

Fig. 47 PN, furnaces in Furnace Area A.

Fig. 48 Schematic drawing of "cementation" process (after A. Ramage, "Gold Refining"): (A) gold; (B) cementation mixture.

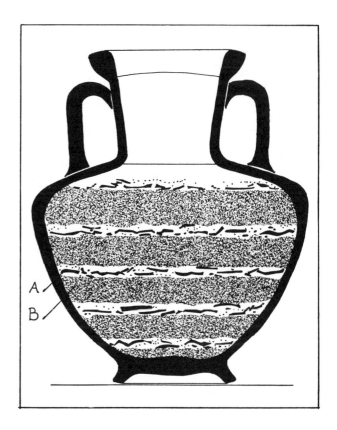

Fig. 49 Altar of Cybele after restoration (1973). Lions not in exact findspots.

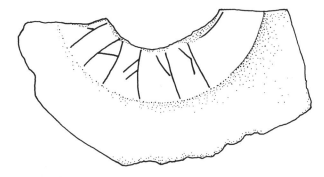

Fig. 50 Lydian graffito naming *Kuvava* (Cybele) (IN 68.18–P 68.140; H: 0.045 m.).

Fig. 51 Bronze hawk's head filled with lead (M 68.1; H: 0.025 m.).

Fig. 52 Lion immured in southeast corner of Cybele altar (S 67.32).

Fig. 53 PN, apsidal structures and Hellenistic
wall, looking east.

Fig. 54 General view of PN during excavation
(1968).

Fig. 55 PN, detail of work in the "Cementation"
Complex. Reconstruction by S. M. Goldstein and
E. Wahle (1975).

Fig. 56 PN, Cupels 5–7.

Fig. 57 PN, fragments of a tuyere and iron blow-
pipe (Samples 39–41).

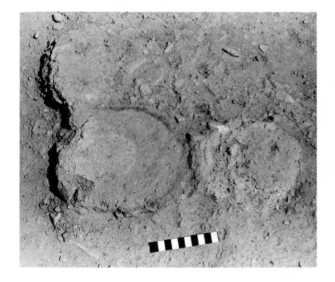

Fig. 58 PN, plan showing concentrations of gold
finds.

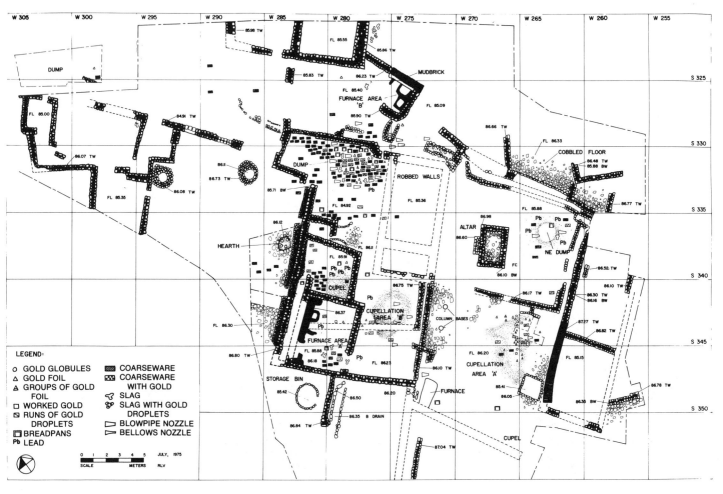

Fig. 59 PN, cut lump of gold (Sample 15). Weight 180 mg.

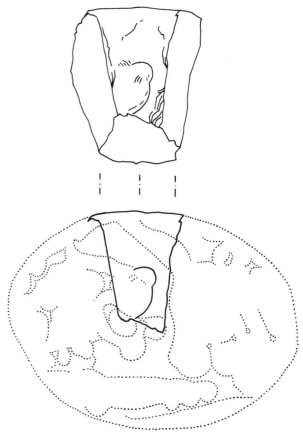

Fig. 61 Gold hecte of Croesus (C 63.1).

Fig. 60 PN, reconstruction of gold lump (Sample 15) with part of Lydian lionhead coin device (S. M. Goldstein and E. Wahle).

Fig. 62 Golden earring with ram (J 67.3; H: 0.01 m.).

Fig. 63   PC (Pactolus Cliff) Lydian structures,
looking north across Wall 3 to corner of Walls A
and B (1960).

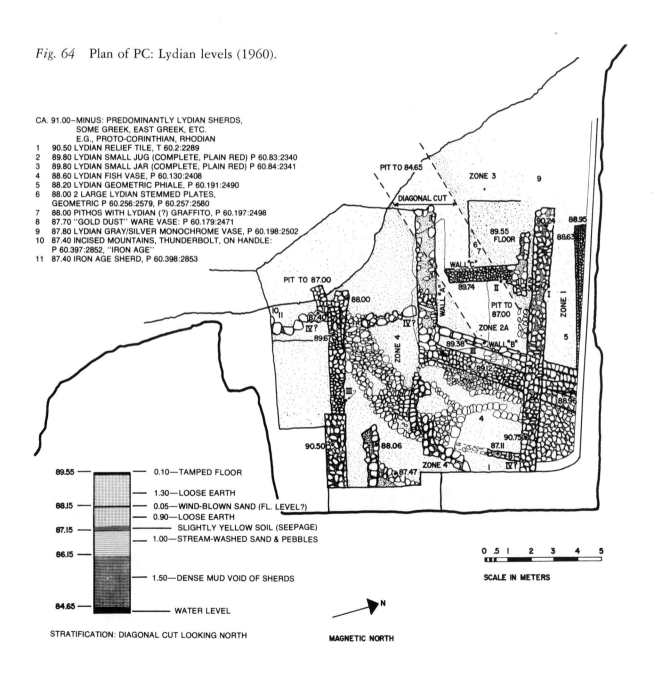

Fig. 64 Plan of PC: Lydian levels (1960).

CA. 91.00–MINUS: PREDOMINANTLY LYDIAN SHERDS,
          SOME GREEK, EAST GREEK, ETC.
          E.G., PROTO-CORINTHIAN, RHODIAN
1   90.50 LYDIAN RELIEF TILE, T 60.2:2289
2   89.80 LYDIAN SMALL JUG (COMPLETE, PLAIN RED) P 60.83:2340
3   89.80 LYDIAN SMALL JAR (COMPLETE, PLAIN RED) P 60.84:2341
4   88.60 LYDIAN FISH VASE, P 60.130:2408
5   88.20 LYDIAN GEOMETRIC PHIALE, P 60.191:2490
6   88.00 2 LARGE LYDIAN STEMMED PLATES,
          GEOMETRIC P 60.256:2579, P 60.257:2580
7   88.00 PITHOS WITH LYDIAN (?) GRAFFITO, P 60.197:2498
8   87.70 "GOLD DUST" WARE VASE: P 60.179:2471
9   87.80 LYDIAN GRAY/SILVER MONOCHROME VASE, P 60.198:2502
10 87.40 INCISED MOUNTAINS, THUNDERBOLT, ON HANDLE:
          P 60.397:2852, "IRON AGE"
11 87.40 IRON AGE SHERD, P 60.398:2853

89.55	0.10—TAMPED FLOOR
	1.30—LOOSE EARTH
88.15	0.05—WIND-BLOWN SAND (FL. LEVEL?)
	0.90—LOOSE EARTH
87.15	SLIGHTLY YELLOW SOIL (SEEPAGE)
	1.00—STREAM-WASHED SAND & PEBBLES
86.15	
	1.50—DENSE MUD VOID OF SHERDS
84.65	WATER LEVEL

STRATIFICATION: DIAGONAL CUT LOOKING NORTH

N

MAGNETIC NORTH

0 .5 1   2   3   4   5

SCALE IN METERS

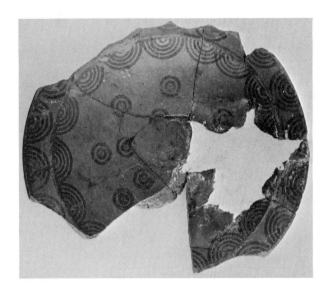

Fig. 65   Lydian black and red plate (P 60.191; diam.: 0.36 m.) from PC Level 3.

Fig. 66   Lydian terracotta sima (T 60.2; H: 0.18 m.) from PC Level 1.

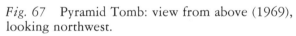

Fig. 67   Pyramid Tomb: view from above (1969), looking northwest.

Fig. 68 Pyramid Tomb (reconstruction by S. Kasper).

A. NORTHWEST AXONOMETRY
B. VIEW FROM THE NORTH
C. VIEW FROM THE WEST
D. LONGITUDINAL SECTION
E. GROUND PLAN

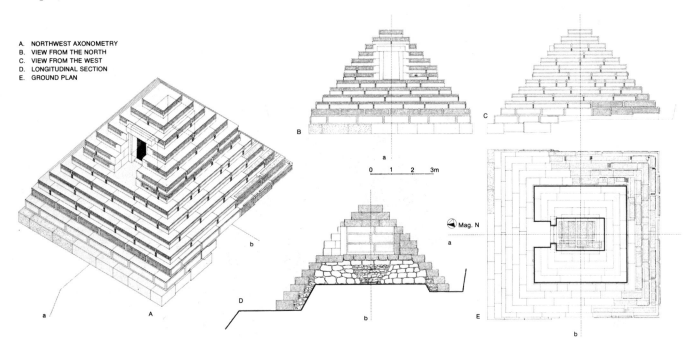

Fig. 69   Pyramid Tomb: detail of east side (1961).

Fig. 70 Acropolis area plan (1974) including "Flying Towers" ("fortification").

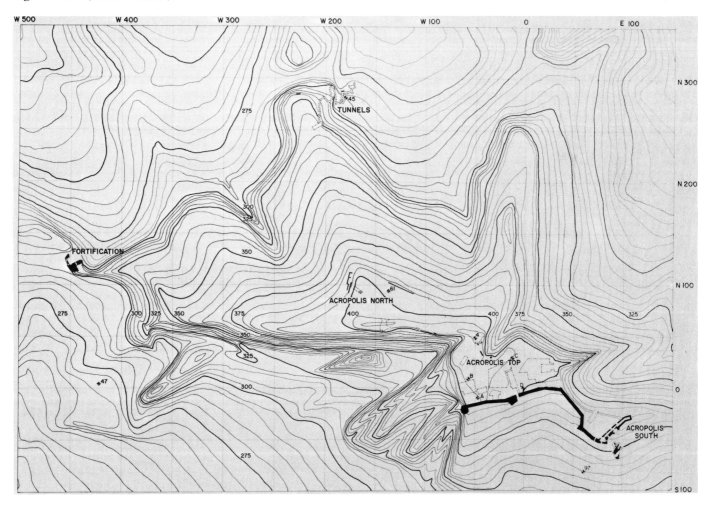

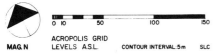

MAG. N

ACROPOLIS GRID
LEVELS A.S.L.   CONTOUR INTERVAL: 5m   SLC

Fig. 71 Polychrome Lydian terracotta lid or plaque from the Acropolis (P 60.496; 0.045 × 0.056 m.).

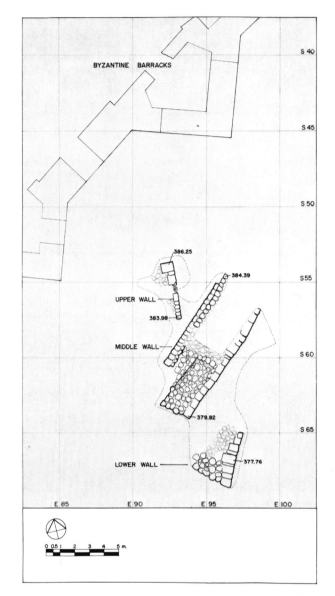

Fig. 72 Acropolis South (AcS): plan of pre-Hellenistic fortification walls.

Fig. 73   AcS, middle and lower pre-Hellenistic
wall, looking west.

Fig. 74   Acropolis Top (AcT): corner and floor of
Lydian structure, with Byzantine houses and storage jar in background.

Fig. 75 Archaic terracotta relief (T 62.5; tile H: 0.16 m.) from a Lydian building. Winged horse (AcT).

Fig. 76 Rim of "marbled" Lydian crater with geometric birds (P 61.380; H: 0.057 m.) found under Lydian floor on AcT.

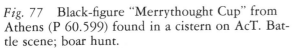

Fig. 77 Black-figure "Merrythought Cup" from Athens (P 60.599) found in a cistern on AcT. Battle scene; boar hunt.

Fig. 78 Double-sided marble relief of a lion from the Acropolis (S 60.31; H: 0.42 m.).

Fig. 79 Acropolis North (AcN), monumental limestone and sandstone masonry Walls 1–3, possibly the supporting terraces of Lydian royal palace. Looking northeast.

Fig. 80 AcN, elevations of Walls 1, 2, 3.

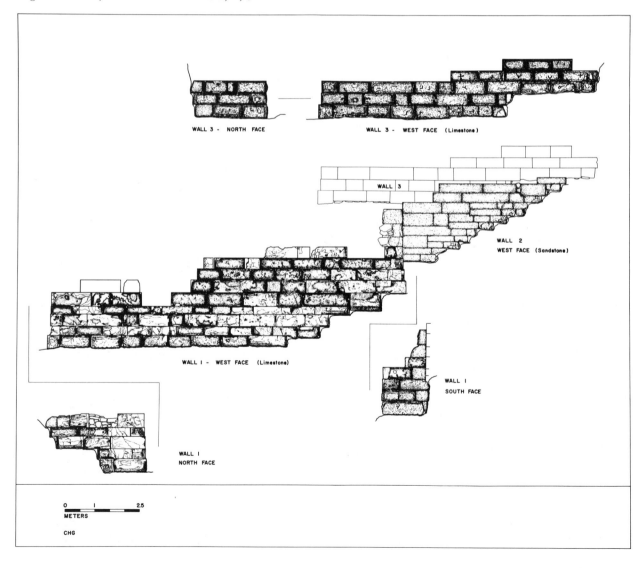

Fig. 81 Archaic Lydian bronze boar (M 60.24; L: 0.095 m.) found below AcN Wall 1.

Fig. 82 Acropolis tunnels (1962): elevation, plan, and section.

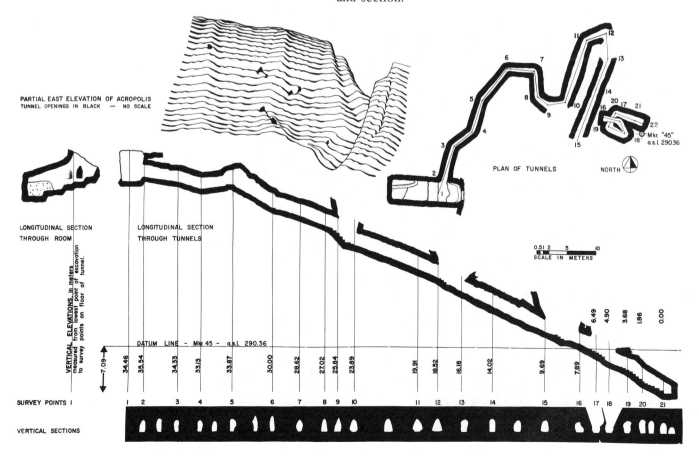

PARTIAL EAST ELEVATION OF ACROPOLIS
TUNNEL OPENINGS IN BLACK — NO SCALE

PLAN OF TUNNELS

NORTH

⊕ Mkr. "45"
a.s.l. 290.36

LONGITUDINAL SECTION
THROUGH ROOM

LONGITUDINAL SECTION
THROUGH TUNNELS

0.5 1 2   5   10
SCALE IN METERS

VERTICAL ELEVATIONS, in meters
measured from lowest point of excavation
to survey points on floor of tunnel.

DATUM LINE - Mkr. 45 - a.s.l. 290.36

6.49 4.90 3.68 1.86 0.00

7.09

34.46 35.54 34.33 33.13 33.87 30.00 28.62 27.02 25.84 23.89   19.91 18.52 16.18 14.02   9.69   7.89

SURVEY POINTS   1   2   3   4   5   6   7   8 9 10   11   12   13   14   15   16 17 18 19 20 21

VERTICAL SECTIONS

Fig. 83 Acropolis tunnels, view looking north.

Fig. 84　Sector NEW and Acropolis (1969).

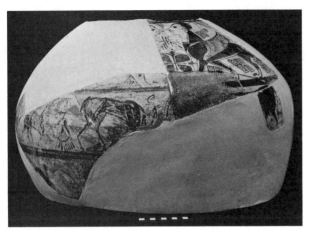

Fig. 85 NEW, sherds from Lydian sphinx amphora with orientalizing decoration (P 69.71; max.
P.H.: 0.36 m.).

Fig. 86 NEW, Lydian imitation of Corinthian crater (P 69.56).

Fig. 87 NEW, Lydian pottery *in situ* between
Walls b, c.

Fig. 88 Plan of Artemis Temple and Precinct.

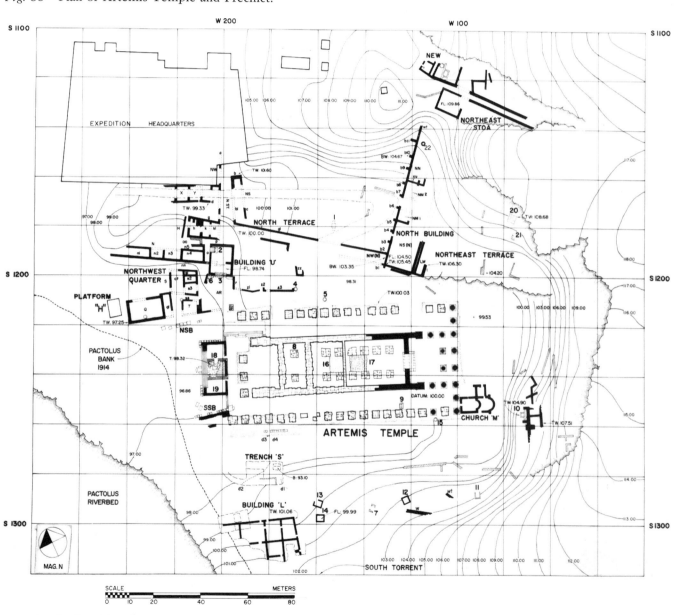

1. Lydian Lion-Eagle monument
2. Vaulted tomb
3. Marble steps, Building U
4, 5. Terracotta wells
6. Stelai
7. Sarcophagus
8. Mortgage inscription on wall
9. Two small columns
10. Exedra monument
11-14. Vaulted tombs
15. Terracotta well
16. Concrete base
17. Sandstone base
18. Building LA, Lydian Altar
19. Perimeter structure
20, 21. Bases
22. Well

Fig. 89 Plan of Artemis Temple with exploratory
trenches (1972).

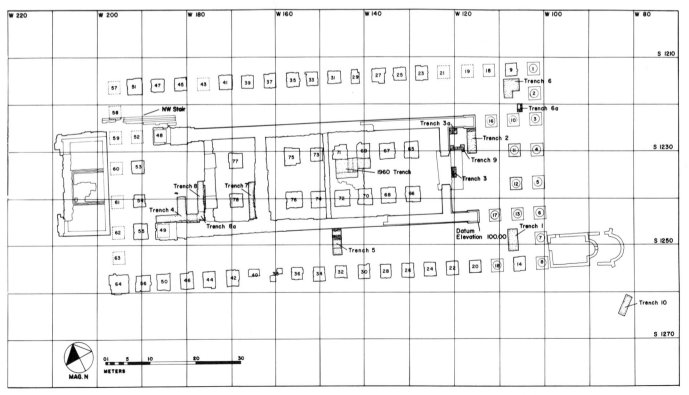

Fig. 90 Stratification in 1960 pit next to east image base with west cella behind it and Necropolis (West Cemetery) Hill in background.

Fig. 91 Silver tetradrachm of Achaeus found at Sardis. Obverse: Achaeus (C 63.21).

Fig. 92 Silver tetradrachm of Achaeus. Reverse: fighting Athena. Inscribed: *Basileos Achaio(u)* (C 63.21).

Fig. 93 Stele with Artemis and Cybele, fourth century B.C. (S 68.6).

Fig. 94 Plan of Artemis Altars LA 1 and LA 2.

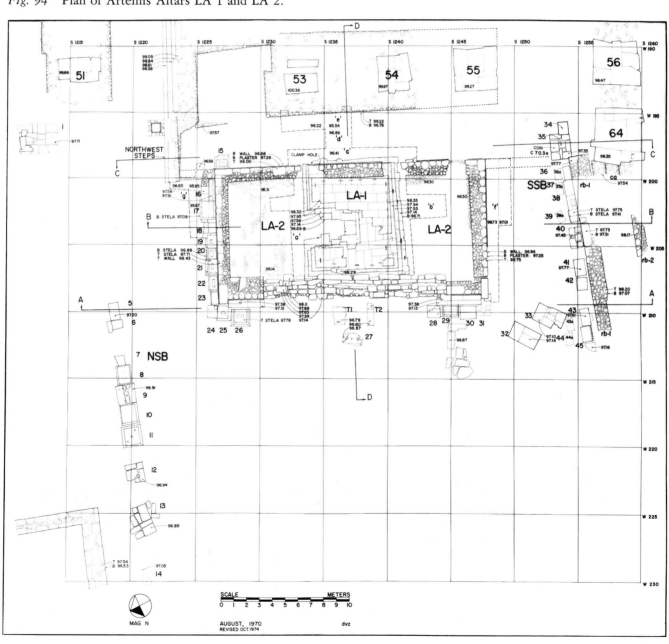

Fig. 95 View of Artemis Altars LA 1 and LA 2, looking south.

Fig. 96 Sketch plan of Bin Tepe, central and eastern part.

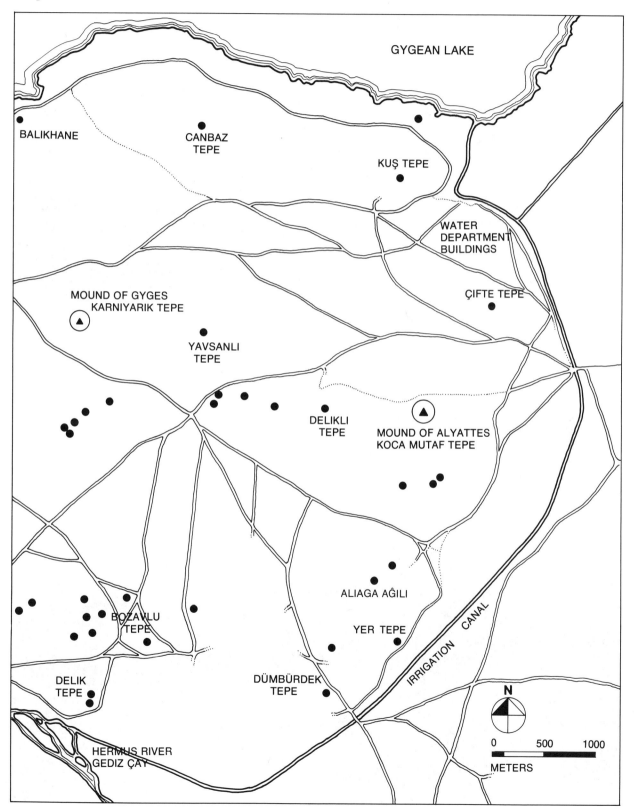

GYGEAN LAKE

BALIKHANE

CANBAZ
TEPE

KUŞ TEPE

WATER
DEPARTMENT
BUILDINGS

ÇIFTE TEPE

MOUND OF GYGES
KARNIYARIK TEPE

YAVSANLI
TEPE

DELIKLI
TEPE

MOUND OF ALYATTES
KOCA MUTAF TEPE

ALIAGA AĞILI

BOZAYLU
TEPE

YER TEPE

DELIK
TEPE

DÜMBÜRDEK
TEPE

IRRIGATION CANAL

N

0   500   1000

METERS

HERMUS RIVER
GEDIZ ÇAY

Fig. 97   Bin Tepe: view of Alyattes Mound from
southeast.

Fig. 98   East central and eastern part of Bin Tepe
from Kir Mutaf Tepe (Western Royal Mound) with
Gyges Mound (Karniyarik Tepe) on upper left.

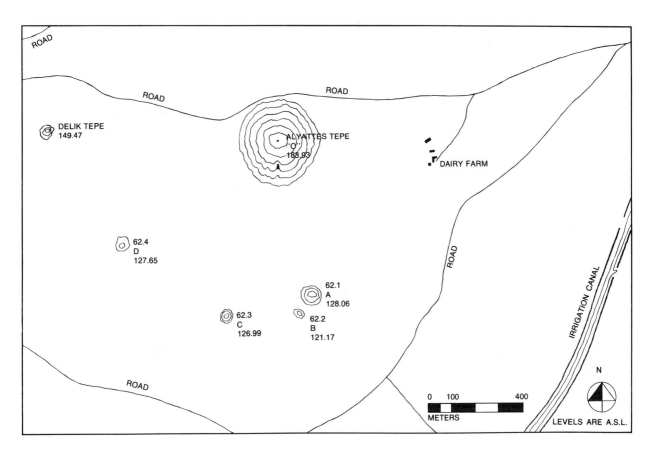

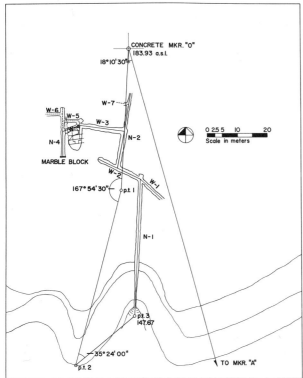

Fig. 99   Plan of region around Alyattes Mound.

Fig. 100   Alyattes Mound: plan of tunnels (1962).

Fig. 101   Alyattes Mound: plan and sections of
grave chamber (1962).

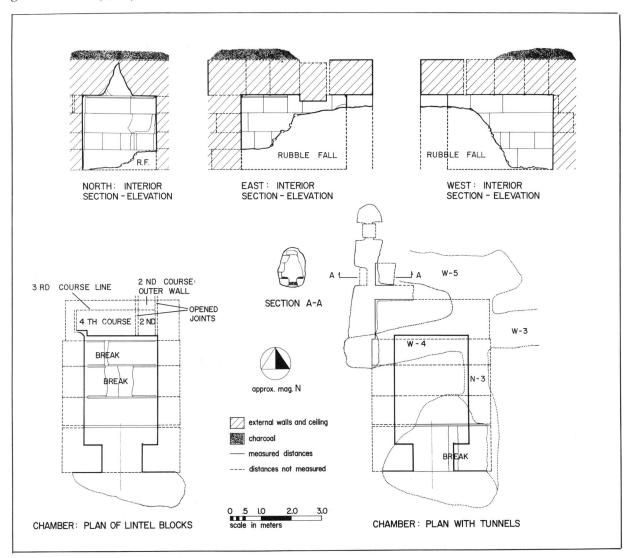

NORTH: INTERIOR
SECTION – ELEVATION

EAST: INTERIOR
SECTION – ELEVATION

WEST: INTERIOR
SECTION – ELEVATION

R.F.

RUBBLE FALL

RUBBLE FALL

SECTION A-A

A ⌐─────┐ A

W-5

W-3

W-4

N-3

BREAK

approx. mag. N

3 RD COURSE LINE
2 ND COURSE
OUTER WALL
OPENED
JOINTS
4 TH COURSE 2 ND

BREAK

BREAK

external walls and ceiling
charcoal
measured distances
distances not measured

CHAMBER: PLAN OF LINTEL BLOCKS

0 5 1.0   2.0   3.0
scale in meters

CHAMBER: PLAN WITH TUNNELS

Fig. 102 Corner of grave chamber in Alyattes Mound (1962).

Fig. 103 Alyattes Mound: left jamb of door into chamber seen from antechamber (1980).

Fig. 104 Drilling with oil rig on Gyges Mound
(Karniyarik Tepe, 1963).

Fig. 105 View of Karniyarik Tepe, looking north
(1963).

Fig. 106 Plan of tunnels at Karniyarik Tepe (1966).

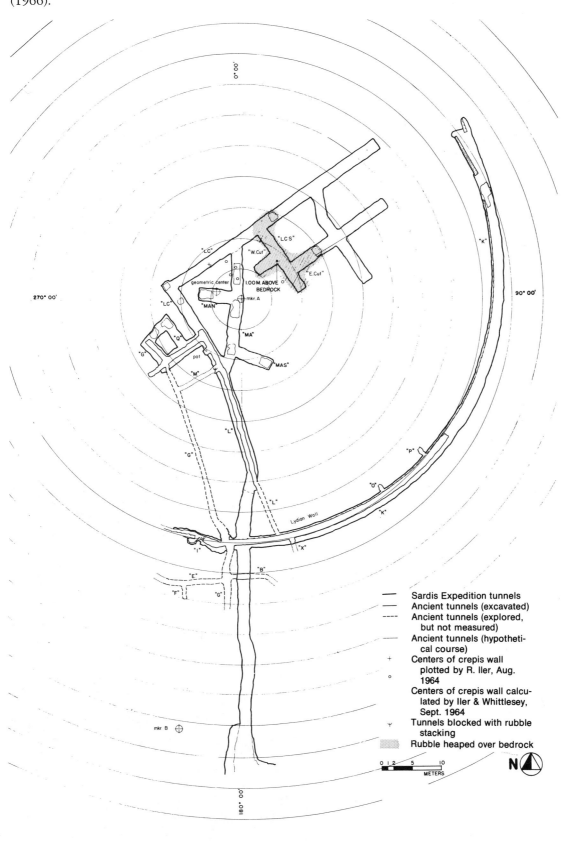

0° 00'

270° 00'

90° 00'

"LCS"
"W.Cut"
"LC"
"E.Cut"
geometric center
1.00 M. ABOVE BEDROCK
"LC"
mkr. A
"MAN"
"MA"
"Q"
"MAS"
"G"
pot
"M"
"K"
"L"
"G"
"P"
"L"
"O"
"I"
"K"
Lydian Wall
"X"
"E"
"B"
"F"
"G"

180° 00'

mkr B

mkr G

───── Sardis Expedition tunnels
─────── Ancient tunnels (excavated)
‑ ‑ ‑ ‑ Ancient tunnels (explored, but not measured)
········· Ancient tunnels (hypothetical course)
  +   Centers of crepis wall plotted by R. Iler, Aug. 1964
  o   Centers of crepis wall calculated by Iler & Whittlesey, Sept. 1964
  Ψ   Tunnels blocked with rubble stacking
  ▓   Rubble heaped over bedrock

0 1 2   5   10
METERS

N

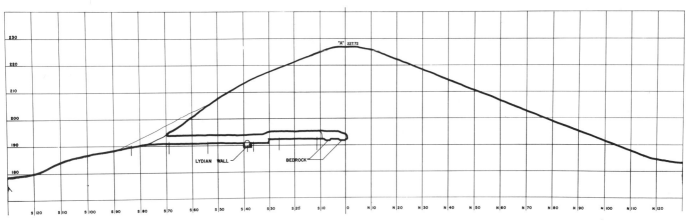

Fig. 107 North-south section through Karniyarik Tepe (1964).

Fig. 108 Karniyarik Tepe: Lydian crepis wall, looking east.

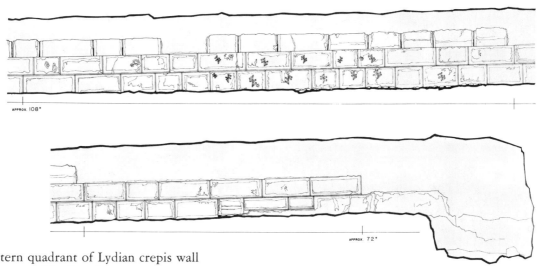

Fig. 109 Eastern quadrant of Lydian crepis wall showing placement of Lydian signs.

Fig. 110 Lydian "GuGu" sign (H: ~0.27 m.).

Fig. 111 Roman jug found in grave robbers' tunnel (P 64.365; H: 0.165 m.).

Fig. 112 Karniyarik Tepe: stratification in Tunnel L, with pit to solid rock.

Fig. 113 Tomb 813 excavated by first Sardis expedition (*Sardis* I [1912] ill. 178): plans and restored facade. Courtesy of Princeton University, Research Photograph Collection.

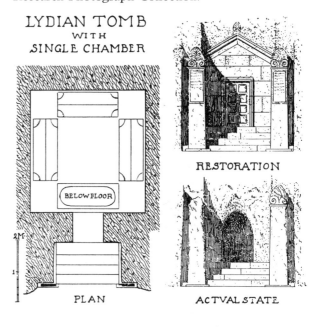

LYDIAN TOMB
WITH
SINGLE CHAMBER

BELOW FLOOR

PLAN

RESTORATION

ACTVAL STATE

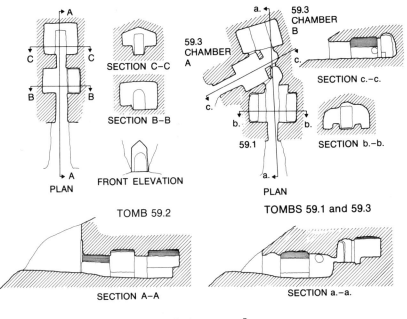

SECTION C-C

SECTION B-B

FRONT ELEVATION

PLAN

TOMB 59.2

59.3 CHAMBER B

59.3 CHAMBER A

SECTION c.-c.

59.1

SECTION b.-b.

PLAN

TOMBS 59.1 and 59.3

SECTION A-A

SECTION a.-a.

0 1   5

SCALE IN METERS

Fig. 114 Plans and sections of Tombs 59.1–3.

Fig. 115 Example of built chamber tomb (BK 71.1).

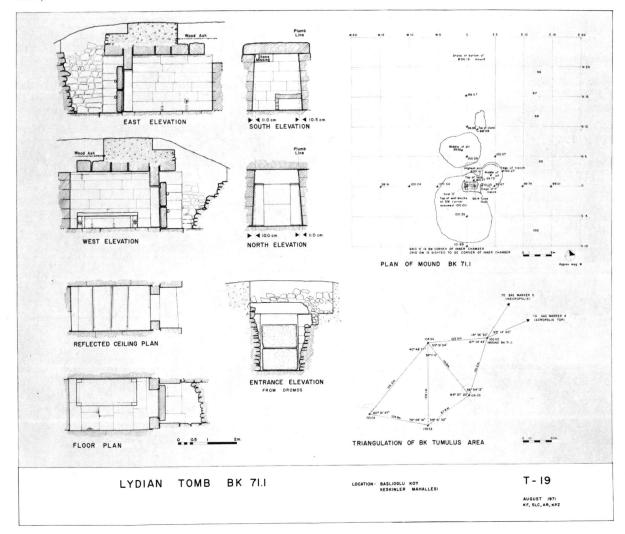

Fig. 116 View of chamber with couch, chamber tomb BK 71.1 (Başlioglu Köy).

Fig. 117 Detail of couch in chamber tomb BK 71.1.

Fig. 118 Cist graves Indere 61.1 and 61.2.

Fig. 119 Pottery group from Indere grave T 61.2: imitation of metal bowl, fish and bird cups, Lydian skyphoi, rosette cup (bowl).

Fig. 120 Jewelry: silver pendant in shape of hawk (J 61.3; H: 1.75 cm.).

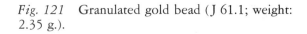

Fig. 121 Granulated gold bead (J 61.1; weight: 2.35 g.).

Fig. 122 Pendant of onyx bead on gold wire (J 61.2; L: 2.4 cm.).

Fig. 123 Hellenistic rock-cut cist grave, BT 66.5.

Fig. 124　Sarcophagi (61.3–4) found at Haci
Oglan.

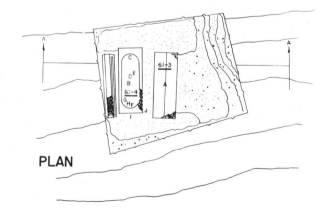

PLAN

SCALE IN METERS

APPROX. MAGNETIC NORTH

A.　RIB FRAGMENT, CHARCOAL & SKULL
B.　BRONZE HELLENISTIC COIN
C.　2 SKULLS
D.　HELLENISTIC UNGUENTARIA
E.　LOWER FRAGMENT - ALABASTRON
F.　BRONZE HELLENISTIC COIN
G.　SAME AS D, BUT LARGER
H.　UPPER FRAGMENT- ALABASTRA
I.　4 CLAY ALABASTRA
J.　SAME AS D

Fig. 125　Sarcophagi (61.3–4): plan, section, location of gravegoods.

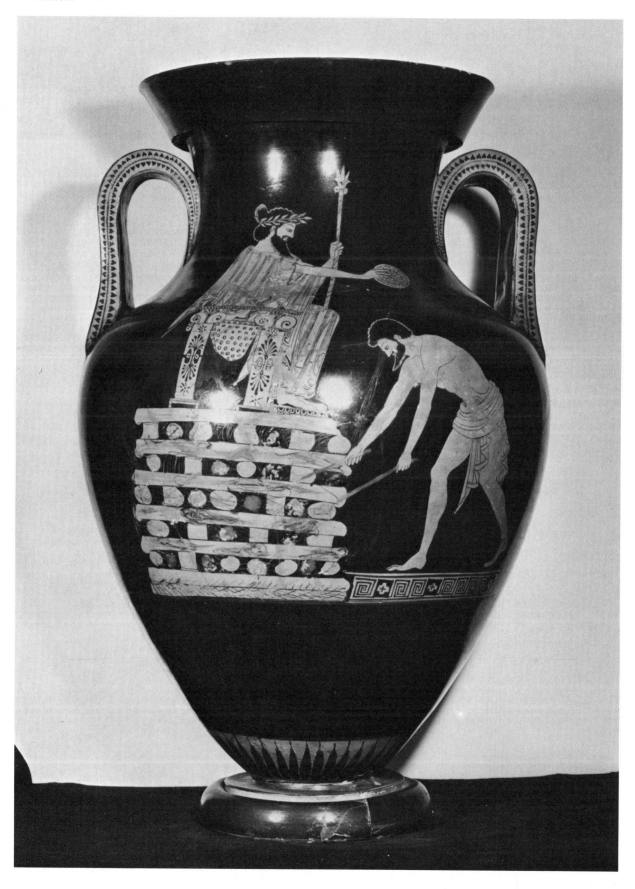

Fig. 127 Lydian pottery from Tomb 43 excavated by the first Sardis expedition. Courtesy of Princeton University, Research Photograph Collection.

Fig. 128 Anthemion of a Lydian grave stele (NoEx 73.1; P.H.: 0.69 m.).

Fig. 129 Plan of Sardis showing location of Lydian, Persian, and Hellenistic graves and cemeteries.

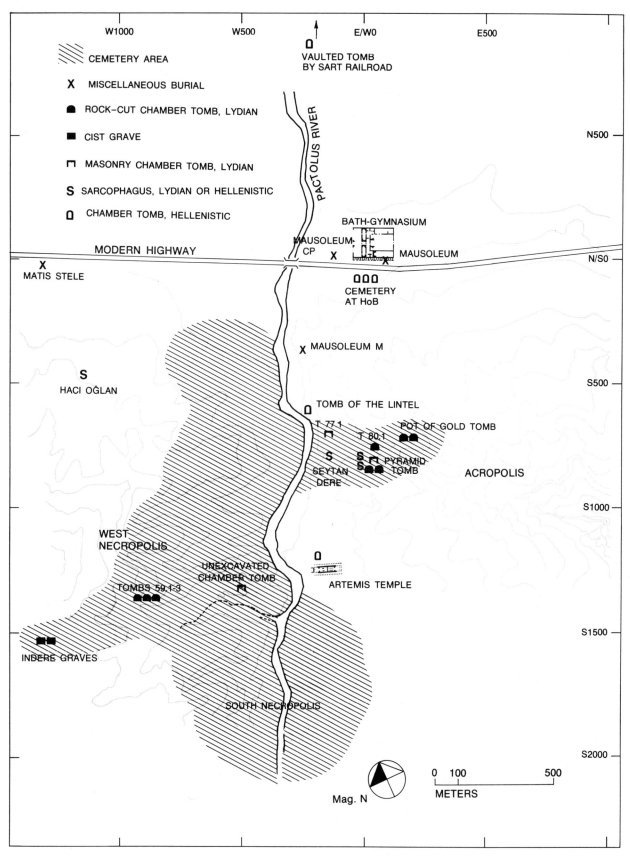

CEMETERY AREA

X   MISCELLANEOUS BURIAL

◓   ROCK-CUT CHAMBER TOMB, LYDIAN

■   CIST GRAVE

⊓   MASONRY CHAMBER TOMB, LYDIAN

S   SARCOPHAGUS, LYDIAN OR HELLENISTIC

◻   CHAMBER TOMB, HELLENISTIC

W1000   W500   E/W0   E500

VAULTED TOMB
BY SART RAILROAD

PACTOLUS RIVER

N500

BATH-GYMNASIUM

MODERN HIGHWAY

MAUSOLEUM-
CP   X   MAUSOLEUM

N/S0

X
MATIS STELE

CEMETERY
AT HoB

X   MAUSOLEUM M

S
HACI OĞLAN

S500

◻   TOMB OF THE LINTEL

T 77.1

⊓   T 80.1   POT OF GOLD TOMB

S   S ⊓   PYRAMID
SEYTAN   S ◓◓   TOMB
DERE

ACROPOLIS

S1000

WEST
NECROPOLIS

◻

UNEXCAVATED
CHAMBER TOMB   ⊓
TOMBS 59.1-3   ◓◓◓

ARTEMIS TEMPLE

INDERE GRAVES   ◓◓

S1500

SOUTH NECROPOLIS

S2000

Mag. N

0   100   500
METERS

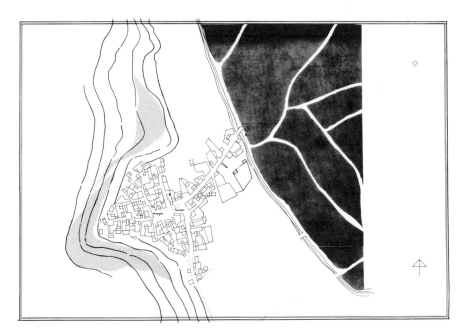

Fig. 130 Plan of a Turkish village in Western Anatolia.

Fig. 131 View of Sardis village from PC: looking south to camp, new road to Ödemiş, and the Tmolus range.

Fig. 132　MMN/MMS location plan.

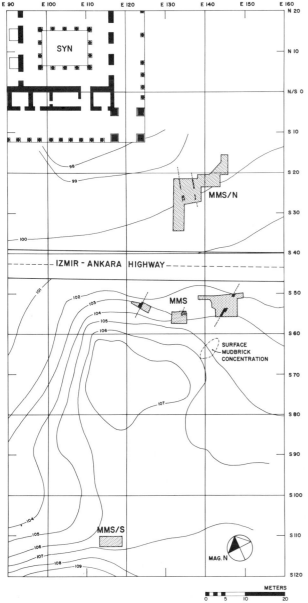

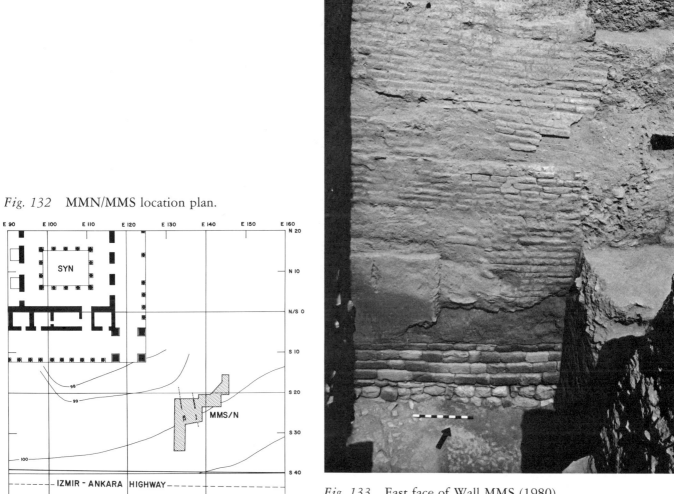

Fig. 133　East face of Wall MMS (1980).

Fig. 134   Modern pisé wall in Sart-Mustafa village.

Fig. 135   Isometric reconstruction of Unit "H" in HoB.

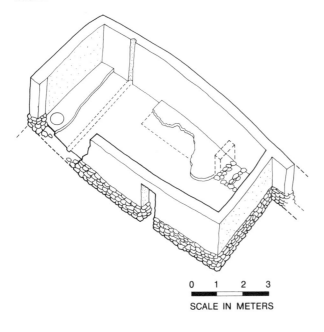

Fig. 136   Isometric sketch of Units I, Ia, II in PN.

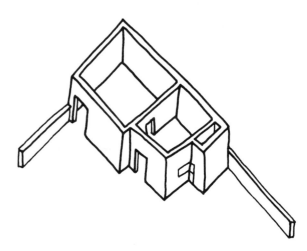

0   1   2   3
SCALE IN METERS

Fig. 137   Units I, Ia, II in PN, looking northeast.

Fig. 138   Satrap(?) and family dining: pediment
from a Lydian mausoleum (S 69.14, H: 0.58 m.,
max. L: 1.30 m.; NoEx 78.1, max. H: 0.595 m.).

Fig. 139   Goldworking installation in operation.
Reconstruction by S. M. Goldstein and E. Wahle
(1975).

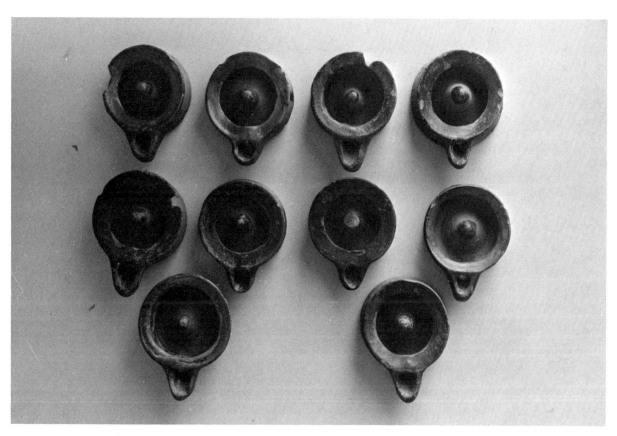

Fig. 140 Unused lamps from Lydian Market/HoB
(L 60.37).

Fig. 141 Repaired Lydian wavy-line hydria from
potter's shop, Lydian Market/HoB (P 58.587; H:
0.325 m.).

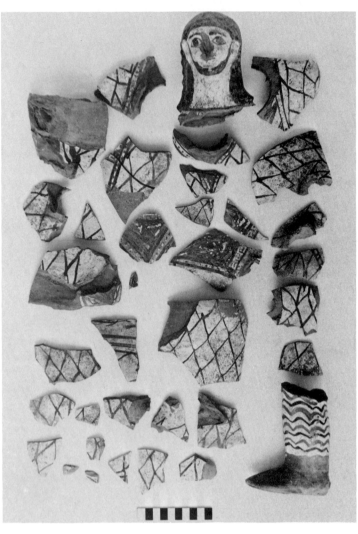

Fig. 142 Fragments of Lydian horseman vase before restoration (P 63.307).

Fig. 143 Lydian horseman vase partly restored (P 63.307; P.H.: 0.35 m.).

Fig. 144 Lydian inscription painted on archaic vase dedicated to Lydian Zeus (*lab*λ; P 64.43; H: 0.05 m.).

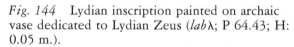

Fig. 145 HoB, "Ritual Dinner" sets cd 13 and cd
14 *in situ*.

Fig. 146 HoB, "Ritual Dinner" set cd 6: Lydian
cooking pot, trefoil jug, cup, dish.

Fig. 147 Altar of Zeus Lydios on a coin of Elagabalus (A.D. 218–222) with image of Zeus under a
tree. Courtesy of B. Trell.

Fig. 148 Archaic image of Lydian Kore. Marble
capital from Roman gymnasium (S 58.50; P.H.:
0.235 m.).

Fig. 149 Goddess(?) with snakes. Archaic marble
votive (S 63.41). Restored by R. Jones.

Fig. 150 Ionic shrine of Cybele with goddess in front (S 63.51).

Fig. 151 Shrine of Cybele: drawing of right side showing priestesses and lions.

Fig. 152 Shrine of Cybele: drawing of left side showing priestesses, comasts, dancers.

Fig. 153 Fragment of a terracotta frieze with god or goddess grasping tails of winged lions or sphinxes (T 61.78; H: 0.11 m.).

Fig. 154 Lydian inscription (IN 71.1; max. P.H.: 0.39 m.).

Fig. 155 Corinthian flask (aryballos; P 68.75; H: 0.031 m.), ca. 600 B.C.

Fig. 156 Fragment of a vase with frieze of Lydian horsemen, found in NEW in 1914 and 1977.

Fig. 158 Die (dice) from Trench S, Artemis Precinct (T 58.5; 2.5 × 2.5 × 2.5 cm.).

Fig. 157 Inscription in an unknown language (so-called Synagogue inscription; IN 64.12).

Fig. 159 Stele of Atrastas, son of Sakardas, with inscription mentioning Artemis of Ephesus (H. of relief: 0.30 m.). Manisa Museum.

Fig. 160 Mythical scenes, reliefs on back of Cybele shrine (P 63.51).

Fig. 161 Pelops(?) as charioteer, relief from Cybele monument (S 63.51). Manisa Museum.

Fig. 162   Persian silver siglos (coin) found in Lydian Market (C 62.25).

Fig. 163   Gold plaques from a garment: walking and seated Persian sphinxes. Istanbul Museums. Courtesy of Princeton University, Research Photograph Collection.

Fig. 164   Unfinished bronze ibex from Lydian Market/HoB (M 62.57; H: 0.045 m.).

Fig. 165   Fragment of an Attic red-figure crater found in the Lydian Market (P 62.128; H: 0.06 m.).

Fig. 166 Dedication of the satrap Droaphernes in the thirty-ninth year of Artaxerxes II (367 B.C.) and ritual regulations. Roman copy, ca. A.D. 200 (IN 74.1).

Fig. 167 Sketch plan of Sardis with urban alignments of ancient structures.

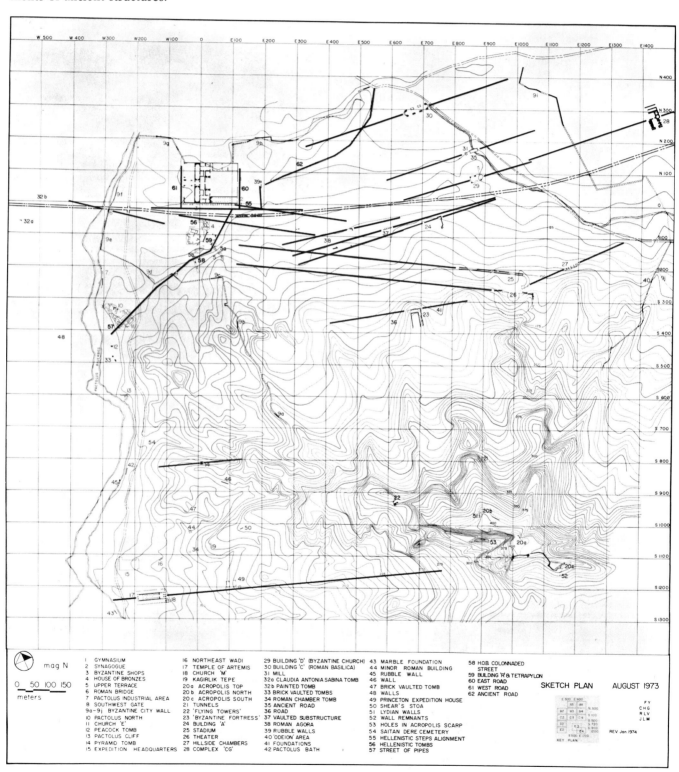

mag N

0 50 100 150
meters

1	GYMNASIUM	16	NORTHEAST WADI	29	BUILDING 'D' (BYZANTINE CHURCH)	43	MARBLE FOUNDATION	58	H.O.B. COLONNADED
2	SYNAGOGUE	17	TEMPLE OF ARTEMIS	30	BUILDING 'C' (ROMAN BASILICA)	44	MINOR ROMAN BUILDING		STREET
3	BYZANTINE SHOPS	18	CHURCH 'M'	31	MILL	45	RUBBLE WALL	59	BUILDING 'F' & TETRAPYLON
4	HOUSE OF BRONZES	19	KAGIRLIK TEPE	32a	CLAUDIA ANTONIA SABINA TOMB	46	WALL	60	EAST ROAD
5	UPPER TERRACE	20a	ACROPOLIS TOP	32b	PAINTED TOMB	47	BRICK VAULTED TOMB	61	WEST ROAD
6	ROMAN BRIDGE	20b	ACROPOLIS NORTH	33	BRICK VAULTED TOMBS	48	WALLS	62	ANCIENT ROAD
7	PACTOLUS INDUSTRIAL AREA	20c	ACROPOLIS SOUTH	34	ROMAN CHAMBER TOMB	49	PRINCETON EXPEDITION HOUSE		
8	SOUTHWEST GATE	21	TUNNELS	35	ANCIENT ROAD	50	SHEAR'S STOA		
9a-9j	BYZANTINE CITY WALL	22	'FLYING TOWERS'	36	ROAD	51	LYDIAN WALLS		
10	PACTOLUS NORTH	23	'BYZANTINE FORTRESS'	37	VAULTED SUBSTRUCTURE	52	WALL REMNANTS		
11	CHURCH 'E'	24	BUILDING 'A'	38	ROMAN AGORA	53	HOLES IN ACROPOLIS SCARP		
12	PEACOCK TOMB	25	STADIUM	39	RUBBLE WALLS	54	SAITAN DERE CEMETERY		
13	PACTOLUS CLIFF	26	THEATER	40	'ODEION' AREA	55	HELLENISTIC STEPS ALIGNMENT		
14	PYRAMID TOMB	27	HILLSIDE CHAMBERS	41	FOUNDATIONS	56	HELLENISTIC TOMBS		
15	EXPEDITION HEADQUARTERS	28	COMPLEX 'CG'	42	PACTOLUS BATH	57	STREET OF PIPES		

SKETCH PLAN   AUGUST 1973

FY
CHG
RLV
JLM

REV. Jan.1974

KEY PLAN

Fig. 168 Entrance to Hellenistic Tomb of the Lintel (1959), ca. 175 B.C.

Fig. 169 Block from a parastas of the Metroon with inscription of Antiochus III (IN 63.118; H: 0.295 m.).

Fig. 171 Grave stele of Matis, ca. 250 B.C. Manisa
Museum.

Fig. 170 Ash urn mentioning phyle Pelopis (IN
62.41; H: 0.075 m.).

Fig. 172   Theater, east parodos.

Fig. 173 Plan of theater and stadium.

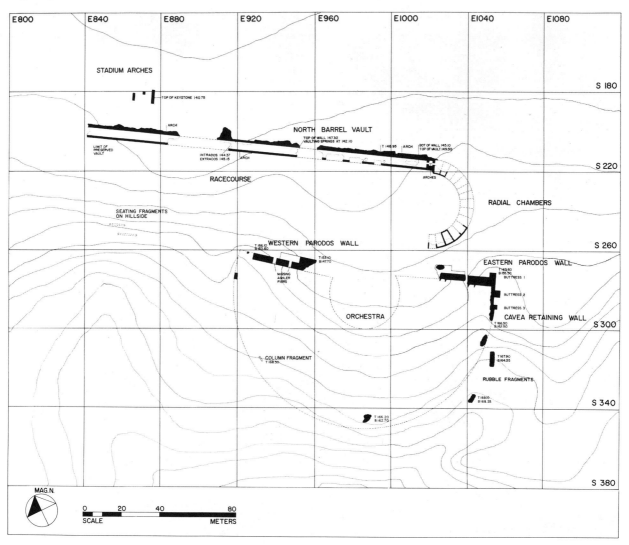

| E800 | E840 | E880 | E920 | E960 | E1000 | E1040 | E1080 |

STADIUM ARCHES

S 180

TOP OF KEYSTONE 140.75

ARCH

NORTH BARREL VAULT

LIMIT OF
PRESERVED
VAULT

TOP OF WALL 147.32
VAULTING SPRINGS AT 142.10

T 146.95   ARCH   BOT OF WALL 145.10
TOP OF VAULT 149.50

INTRADOS 144.37
EXTRADOS 145.15

ARCH

S 220

RACECOURSE

ARCHES

RADIAL CHAMBERS

SEATING FRAGMENTS
ON HILLSIDE

S 260

T 166.10   WESTERN PARODOS WALL
B 163.80

EASTERN PARODOS WALL

T 163.40
B147.70

T 165.60
B 155.50
BUTTRESS 1

MISSING
ASHLER
PIERS

BUTTRESS 2

BUTTRESS 3

ORCHESTRA

CAVEA RETAINING WALL

S 300

T 166.50
B 162.50

COLUMN FRAGMENT
T 166.30

T 167.90
B164.55

RUBBLE FRAGMENTS

T 169.10
B168.25

S 340

T 166.20
B162.70

S 380

MAG. N.

| 0 | 20 | 40 | | 80 |
SCALE   METERS

Fig. 175 Hellenistic acroteria found in Synagogue
and Church EA. Manisa Museum.

Fig. 176 Colossal head of Zeus (S 61.27; P.H.:
1.05–1.10 m.) from east cella of Artemis-Zeus
Temple.

Fig. 177 Base of image of Hera, dedicated by
Julia Lydia after the earthquake of A.D. 17 (IN
63.123; H: 0.33 m.).

Fig. 178   View of Artemis Temple after cleanup
of 1973, looking east across dividing wall into east
cella with east image base.

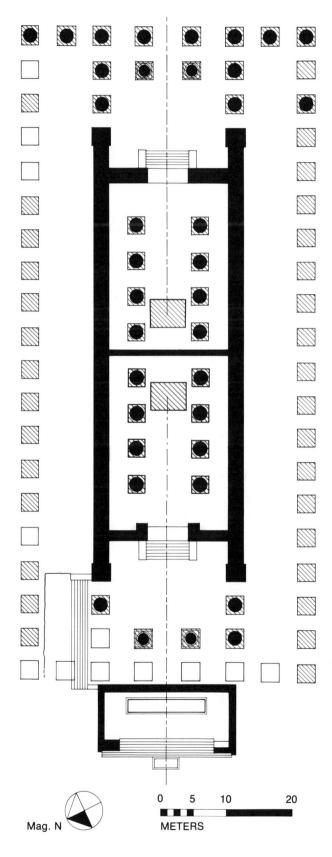

Mag. N

0 5 10 20

METERS

Fig. 179 Plan of Hellenistic Temple after division
in two parts.

Fig. 180 Hypothetical reconstruction of Altar LA 2 and west end of Temple after A.D. 17.

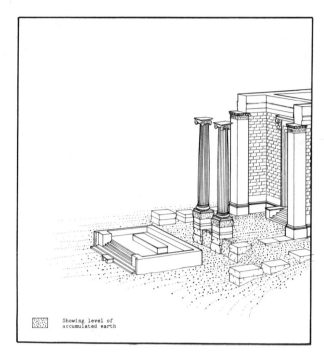

Showing level of
accumulated earth

Fig. 181 Plan of PN with Units XIX–XXI destroyed in 213 B.C.

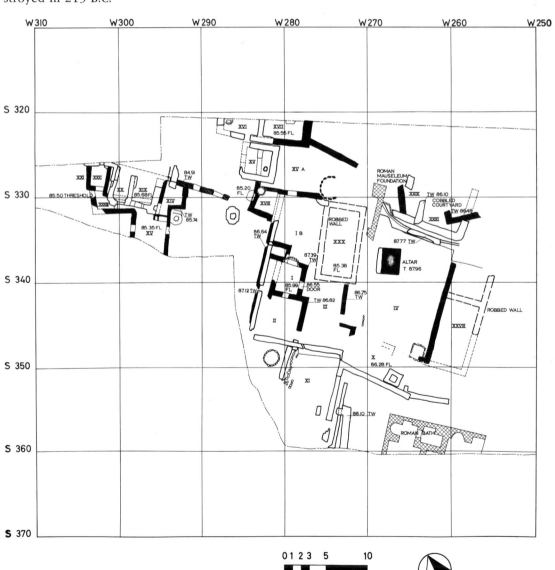

0 1 2 3 5   10

scale in meters   mag. N

Fig. 182　Clay alabastra from sarcophagus 61.3, Haci Oglan (P 61.23; average L: 0.196 m.).

Fig. 183　Hellenistic grave stele with mother, daughter, and son. First century B.C. (NoEx 71.1; max. P.H.: 0.58 m.).

Fig. 184　Doric column recut as late Hellenistic grave relief of a horseman-hero (NoEx 75.4). From Mersindere near Sardis.

Fig. 185　White-slip relief amphora in "Lagynos" technique with heads of Herakles and Omphale on shoulder. From Tomb of the Lintel (P 59.412; H. with lid: 0.40 m.).

Fig. 186   Plan of Hellenistic and Roman grave area at HoB, 1959.

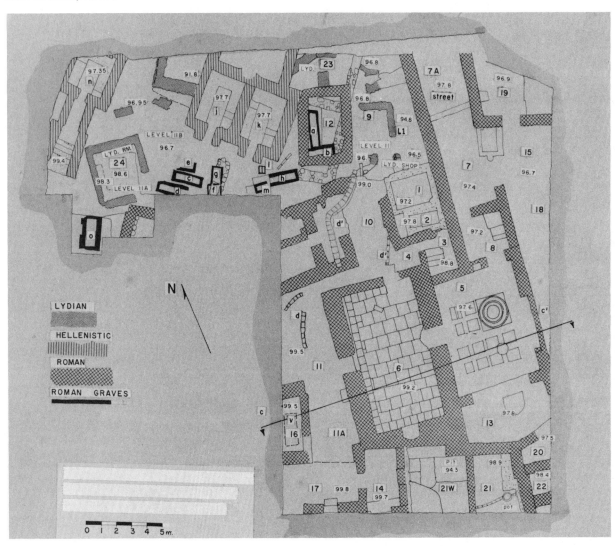

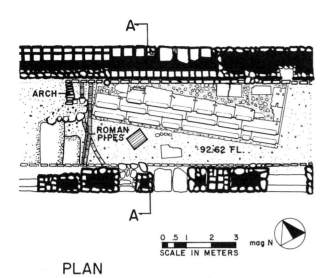

A⌐

ARCH

ROMAN
PIPES

92.62 FL.

A⌐

0 .5 1   2   3   mag N
SCALE IN METERS

PLAN

Fig. 187 Hellenistic mausoleum steps under south
wall of Synagogue.

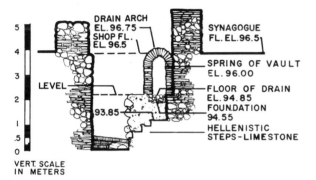

DRAIN ARCH
EL. 96.75
SHOP FL.
EL. 96.5

SYNAGOGUE
FL. EL. 96.5

SPRING OF VAULT
EL. 96.00

FLOOR OF DRAIN
EL. 94.85

LEVEL

93.85

FOUNDATION
94.55

HELLENISTIC
STEPS-LIMESTONE

5
4
3
2
1
.5
0

VERT. SCALE
IN METERS

SECTION AT A-A

Fig. 188 Vaulted late Hellenistic or Roman chamber tomb. Artemis Precinct, Tomb 2.

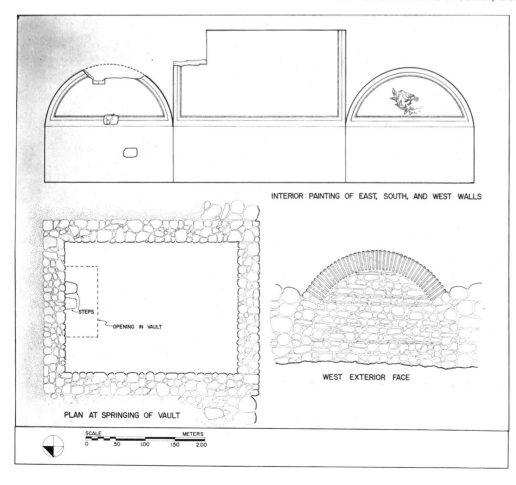

INTERIOR: PAINTING OF EAST, SOUTH, AND WEST WALLS

STEPS

OPENING IN VAULT

WEST EXTERIOR FACE

PLAN AT SPRINGING OF VAULT

SCALE   METERS
0   .50   1.00   1.50   2.00

Fig. 189 Urn with palmettes. Tomb "1" at HoB
(S 59.36; L: 0.49 m.; H. with lid: 0.325 m.).

Fig. 191 Hellenistic relief ware: bottom of bowl
with theater mask (P 60.51; diam. of base medallion: 0.04 m.).

Fig. 190 Handle with Silenic head (P 63.321; L:
0.057 m.).

Fig. 192   Hellenistic appliqué ware: erotic scene
(P 64.58; P.H.: 0.062 m.).

Fig. 193   Hellenistic relief ware mold: sphinx,
lovers, dancing Pan (P 59.475; H: 0.067 m.).

Fig. 194   Pottery from pre-213 B.C. floor at PN.
"Achaemenid" bowl (P 65.249; complete H: 0.05
m.).

Fig. 195 Pottery from pre-213 B.C. floor. Jug derived from local wavy-line ware (P 63.463; H: 0.028 m.).

Fig. 196 Eastern sigillata "B," bowl (P 67.114; H: 0.055 m.).

Fig. 197 Stamp of potter Mithres, first century B.C. (P 64.116; stamp: 0.8 × 0.4 cm.).

Fig. 198 Stamp of pottery owner Serenus of Puteoli on a bowl made in Sardis (P 60.150; stamp diam.: ~1.0 cm.).

Fig. 199 Small head of Zeus, late Hellenistic (S 70.1; H: ~ 0.15 m.).

Fig. 200 Hellenistic relief with Cybele or Tyche (NoEx 63.15; W: 0.034 m.; H: 0.237 m.).

Fig. 201 Coins of Sardis with Zeus Lydios and with Zeus Olympios plus head of Tyche. Courtesy of Société Française de Numismatique.

Fig. 202 Coin of Hadrian: inscribed bearded head of Zeus Lydios. Courtesy of Trustees of the British Museum.

Fig. 203 Selection of terracottas found at Sardis.

Fig. 204 Sardis, autonomous (133 B.C.), Augustus. Coin with Dionysus and panther. Courtesy of American Numismatic Society.

Fig. 205 Herakles (Hellenistic ruler?) herm (S 64.13; H: 0.65 m.).

Fig. 207 Restoration of Bath-Gymnasium complex looking southwest, with Synagogue and part of south colonnade of Main Avenue (A. R. Seager, 1971).

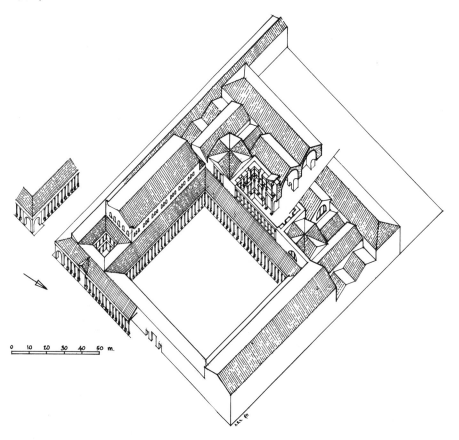

0 10 20 30 40 50 m.

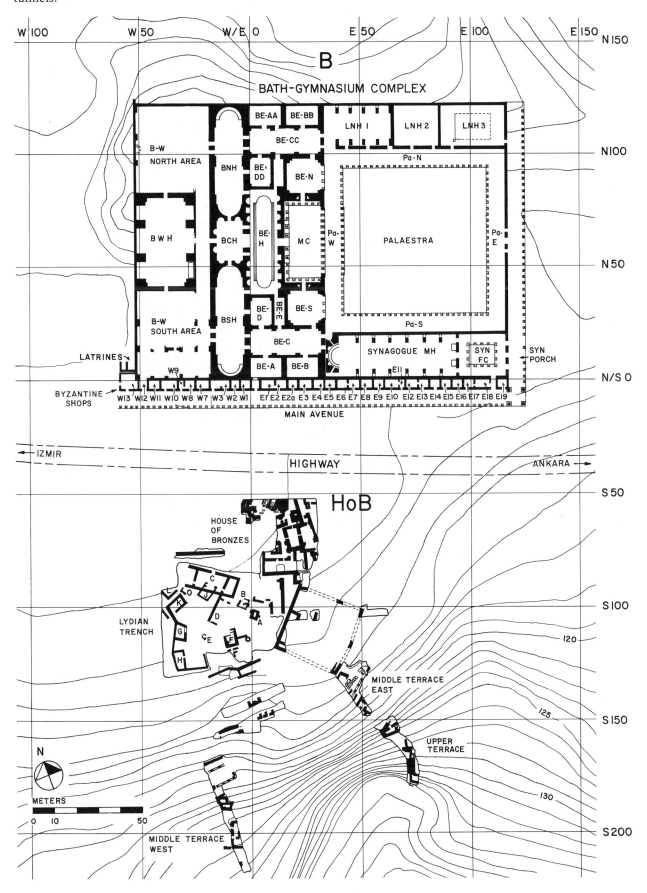

Fig. 206 Plan of the bath-gymnasium complex (B), House of Bronzes area (HoB), and terrace tunnels.

Fig. 208   Roman city wall, section 30 on Upper
Terrace (UT).

Fig. 209 Frieze with animal games, probably from
a Roman mausoleum, ca. A.D. 300 (NoEx 75.1; H:
0.62 m.).

Fig. 210 House of Bronzes, marble-paved room
and unexcavated Gymnasium and Synagogue in
background (1959).

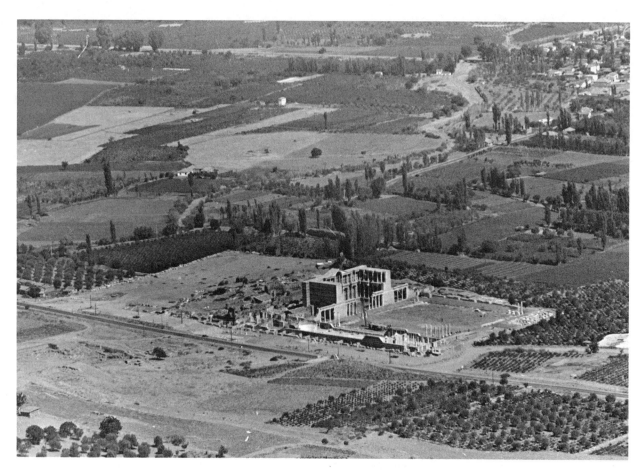

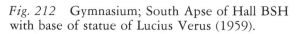

Fig. 211 Gymnasium and Synagogue after restoration (1973): view from Acropolis looking north.

Fig. 212 Gymnasium; South Apse of Hall BSH with base of statue of Lucius Verus (1959).

ΑΥΤΟΚΡΑΤΟΡΑΚΑΙΣΑΡΑΑΥΡΑΝΤΩΝΙ
ΝΟΝΟΥΗΡΟΝΣΕΒΑΣΤΟΝ Β ΝΕΩΚΟ
ΡΟΣΣΑΡΔΙΑΝΩΝΠΟΛΙΣ ΚΛ ΑΝΤΩ
ΛΕΠΙΔΟΣΑΝΕΘΗΚΕΝΑΡΧΙΕΡΕΥΣ
ΑΣΙΑΣΑΡΓΥΡΟΤΑΜΙΑΣΠΡΩΤΟΣΟΤΗ
ΠΕΡΙΤΟΓΥΜΝΑΣΙΟΝΠΟΛΙΤΕΙΑΣ
ΕΞΑΡΧΗΣΠΡΟΝΟΗΣΑΜΕΝΟΣ

Fig. 213   Inscription with dedication of statue of
Lucius Verus by Claudius Antonius Lepidus (IN
58.4).

Fig. 214   Corner of Central Hall (BCH) with circular, marble-revetted pool (basin).

Fig. 215 Latrine at southwest corner of Gymnasium and Byzantine Shops. Marble seats were on brackets (seen at left).

Fig. 216   Pool Hall (BEH, "West Hall"), looking south.

Fig. 217   West wall of Pool Hall (BEH, "West Hall") with reconstructed marble revetment pattern.

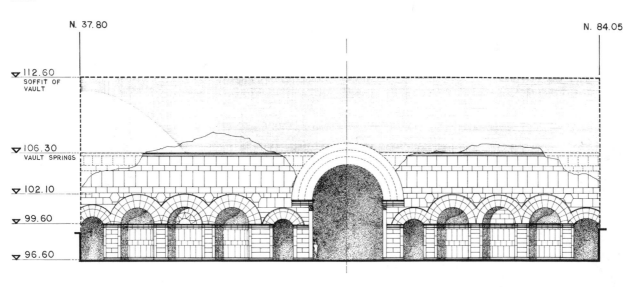

Fig. 218 Underground service tunnel north of
Pool Hall (BEH).

Fig. 219 Limekiln in gymnasium Room C, with
base of the Children of Kore at north wall.

Fig. 220 Looking along north side of Palaestra
with Hall LNH 1–3. (On right, mockup of entablature of second floor of screen colonnade.)

Fig. 221 Marble Court before restoration (1962),
looking north.

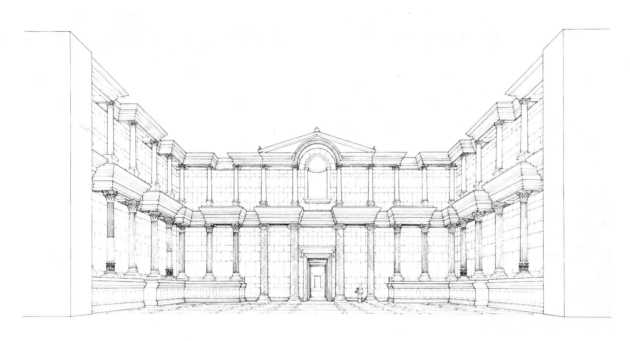

Fig. 222 Restoration drawing of Marble Court in
Severan Age, ca. A.D. 211 (D. DeLong, 1967).

Fig. 223 Marble Court as restored 1964–1973
(1972).

Fig. 224 Marble Court restored, looking toward
north wing.

Fig. 225 Setting the gate column (M. T. Ergene,
1964).

Fig. 226 Columns and entablature of pavilion
flanking the west gate during reconstruction
(1967).

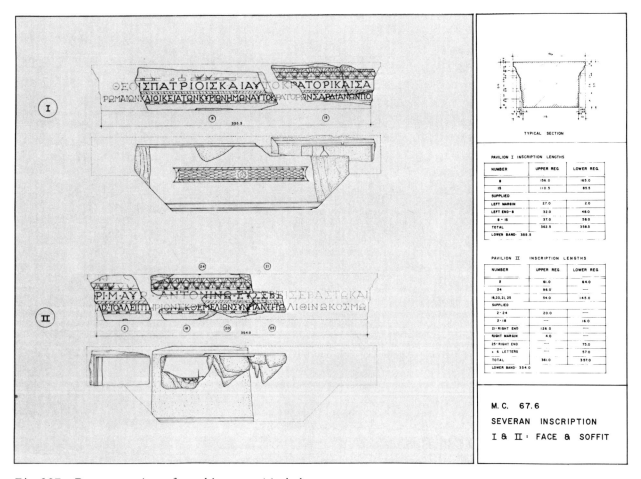

Fig. 227   Reconstruction of entablatures with dedicatory inscription of A.D. 211, pavilions I, II (D. DeLong, 1967).

Fig. 228 Marble Court walls. Reinforced concrete
frame concealed in the wall (M. T. Ergene).

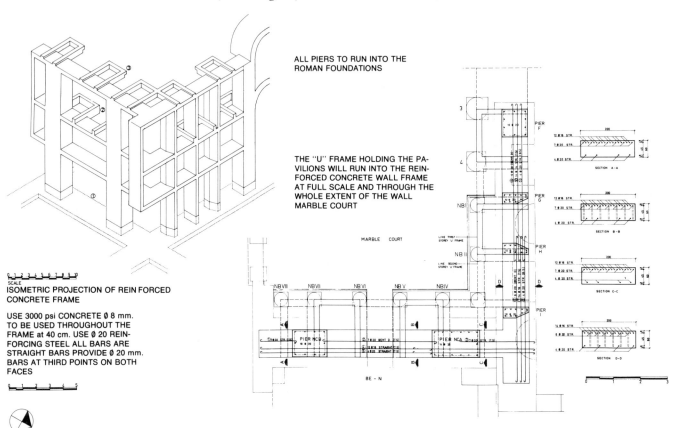

SCALE
ISOMETRIC PROJECTION OF REINFORCED
CONCRETE FRAME

USE 3000 psi CONCRETE Ø 8 mm.
TO BE USED THROUGHOUT THE
FRAME at 40 cm. USE Ø 20 REIN-
FORCING STEEL ALL BARS ARE
STRAIGHT BARS PROVIDE Ø 20 mm.
BARS AT THIRD POINTS ON BOTH
FACES

ALL PIERS TO RUN INTO THE
ROMAN FOUNDATIONS

THE "U" FRAME HOLDING THE PA-
VILIONS WILL RUN INTO THE REIN-
FORCED CONCRETE WALL FRAME
AT FULL SCALE AND THROUGH THE
WHOLE EXTENT OF THE WALL
MARBLE COURT

MARBLE COURT

SECTION A-A

SECTION B-B

SECTION C-C

SECTION D-D

Fig. 229 Marble Court: first story pavilion construction showing ancient part suspended from modern concrete balcony (M. C. Bolgil).

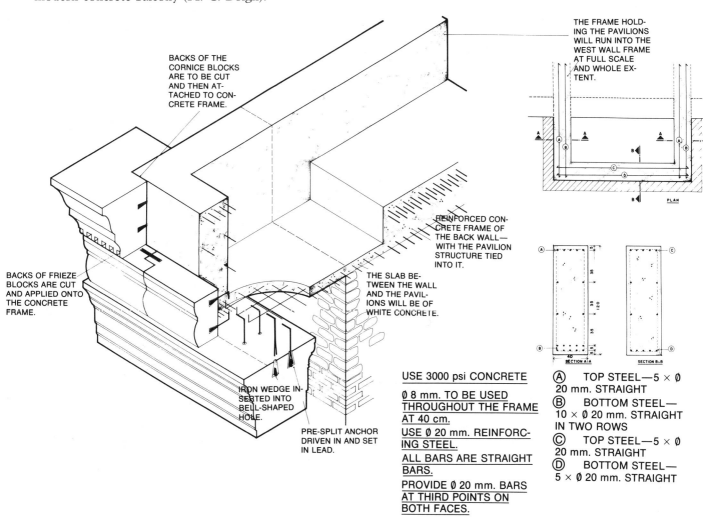

BACKS OF THE CORNICE BLOCKS ARE TO BE CUT AND THEN ATTACHED TO CONCRETE FRAME.

BACKS OF FRIEZE BLOCKS ARE CUT AND APPLIED ONTO THE CONCRETE FRAME.

IRON WEDGE INSERTED INTO BELL-SHAPED HOLE.

PRE-SPLIT ANCHOR DRIVEN IN AND SET IN LEAD.

REINFORCED CONCRETE FRAME OF THE BACK WALL— WITH THE PAVILION STRUCTURE TIED INTO IT.

THE SLAB BETWEEN THE WALL AND THE PAVILIONS WILL BE OF WHITE CONCRETE.

THE FRAME HOLDING THE PAVILIONS WILL RUN INTO THE WEST WALL FRAME AT FULL SCALE AND WHOLE EXTENT.

PLAN

SECTION A-A

SECTION B-B

USE 3000 psi CONCRETE

Ø 8 mm. TO BE USED THROUGHOUT THE FRAME AT 40 cm.

USE Ø 20 mm. REINFORCING STEEL.

ALL BARS ARE STRAIGHT BARS.

PROVIDE Ø 20 mm. BARS AT THIRD POINTS ON BOTH FACES.

(A) TOP STEEL—5 × Ø 20 mm. STRAIGHT
(B) BOTTOM STEEL— 10 × Ø 20 mm. STRAIGHT IN TWO ROWS
(C) TOP STEEL—5 × Ø 20 mm. STRAIGHT
(D) BOTTOM STEEL— 5 × Ø 20 mm. STRAIGHT

Fig. 230　Capital of screen colonnade with laughing satyr (S 59.78). Manisa Museum.

Fig. 231　Southern part of first story of screen colonnade with cast of laughing satyr capital being lifted into position (1970).

Fig. 232   Screen colonnade with cast of laughing
satyr in place (1972).

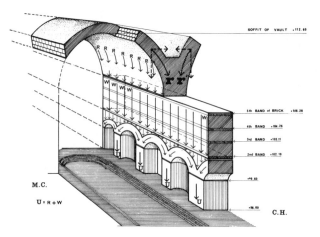

SOFFIT OF VAULT +112.60

5th BAND of BRICK +108.28
4th BAND +104.26
3rd BAND +103.11
2nd BAND +102.19
+99.60
+96.60

M.C.

U = R + W

C.H.

Fig. 233 Structural diagram of Pool Hall (BE-H, "West Hall").

Fig. 234 Isometric drawing of structural system of central part of bath-gymnasium.

Fig. 235 Late Antique (fifth century) floor of the Marble Court, looking east to Palaestra.

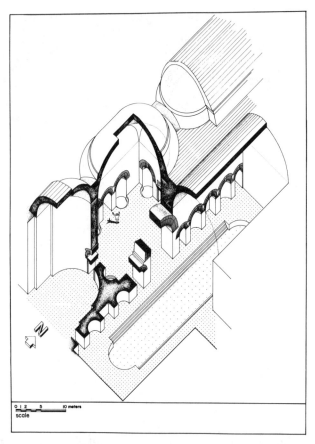

0 1 2   5   10 meters
scale

Fig. 236 East-west section across bath-gymnasium: Halls BCH, BE-H, Marble Court, west colonnade of Palaestra.

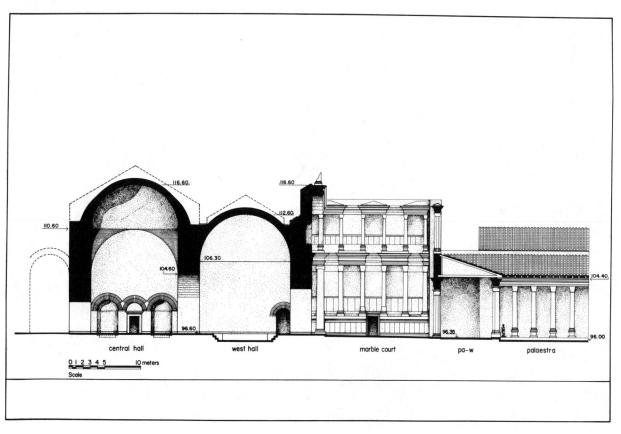

Fig. 238 Detail, head of bearded man (S 61.18; H: 0.30 m.).

Fig. 237 Marble Court: view of north side through Byzantine south entrance.

Fig. 239 South colonnade and Byzantine Shops
reconstruction: studies of different stages (F. K.
Yegul).

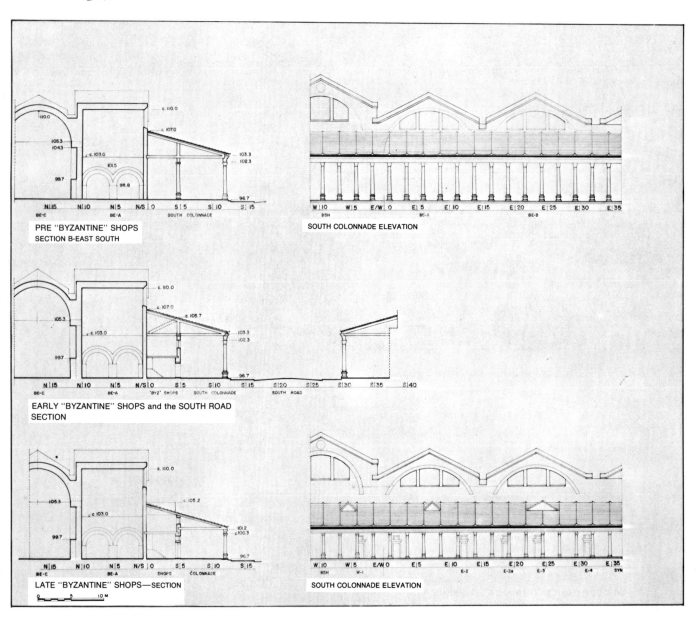

Fig. 240 Gymnasium complex with Byzantine
Shops, Synagogue, Marble Court, looking west.
Foreground, reused Lydian lion (1973).

Fig. 241 Byzantine Shops (E9–E11), north colonnade of Main Avenue, Main Avenue, stylobate of
south colonnade. Beyond the modern highway: the
House of Bronzes (1973).

Fig. 242 Shop of Jacob, elder (of the Synagogue; E14) as excavated in 1962. Note bronze vessels and storage jars in the corner and floor.

Fig. 243 Byzantine Shops E1–E2 (restaurants) after restoration (1973), looking toward north colonnade and Main Avenue. Serving window seen in first room.

Fig. 244 Terracotta flask (ampulla) with rabbits(?) eating green shoots issuing from the cross (P 68.165; P.H.: 0.24 m.). Manisa Museum.

Fig. 245 Suspension brass lamp in form of a lion holding a shell in his jaws. Shop E5 (M 67.4; L: 0.155 m.; H: 0.085 m.).

Fig. 247 Incomplete footed glass bowl (BS 1963; H: 3.0 cm.).

Fig. 246 Some of the 127 locks found in Hardware Shop E11.

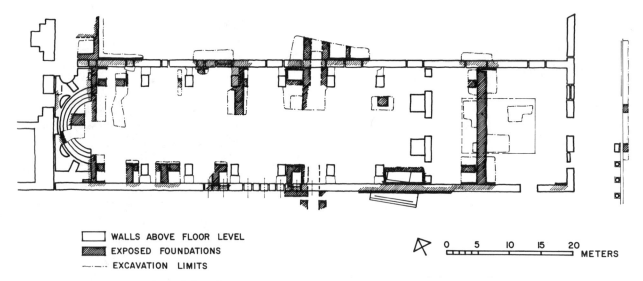

WALLS ABOVE FLOOR LEVEL
EXPOSED FOUNDATIONS
——·—· EXCAVATION LIMITS

0   5   10   15   20
METERS

Fig. 248   Synagogue: plan of foundations.

Fig. 249   Menorah (S 62.26) as found near south
shrine.

Fig. 250   Menorah incised on marble (S *62.26;* P.H.: 0.58 m.) found near south shrine.

Fig. 251   View of Synagogue Forecourt with Marble Court in background.

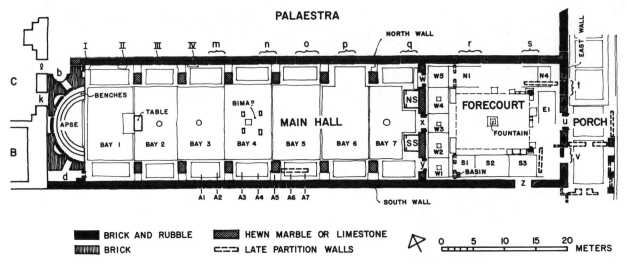

Fig. 252 Overall plan of Synagogue showing location of objects.

Fig. 253 Reconstruction drawing for the Synagogue (A. M. Shapiro; revised by A. R. Seager, 1966).

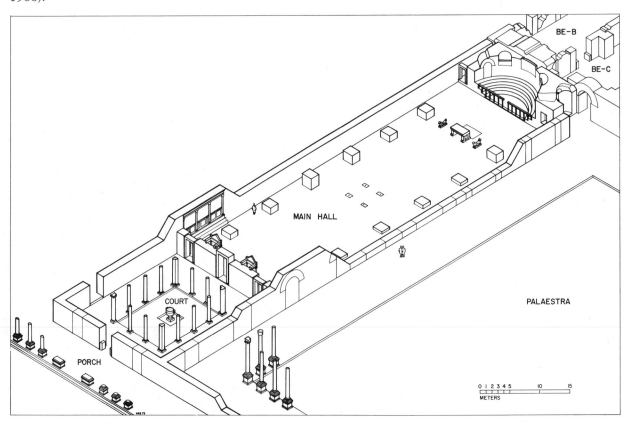

Fig. 254 West side of Forecourt with mosaic inscription (copy) of donor: "Aurelios Eulogios, God-Fearer (*Theosebes*) Redeemed His Vow (Pledge)."

Fig. 255 Northern part of apse and north wall during excavation (1963).

Fig. 256   Apse, lions, Eagle Table, Corinthian circular monument (SYN 62.20) after restoration (1973), looking west.

Fig. 257   Marble Eagle Table as restored (1972, A. Frantz).

Fig. 258 Synagogue Main Hall looking east
toward two shrines and entrance from Forecourt.

Fig. 259 Mosaic of Bay 3 with inscription of
Aurelios Alexandros. Restored drawing (L. J. Majewski).

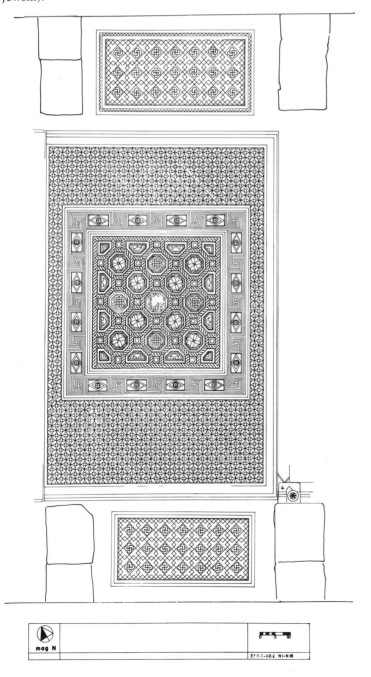

Fig. 260   Apse mosaic with donors' inscription and peacocks cut out in antiquity (during excavation, 1963).

Fig. 261   Original (top) and copy of apse mosaic (L. J. Majewski, 1972).

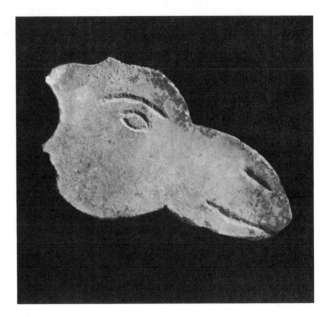

Fig. 262 Marble inlay: head of camel.

Fig. 263 Reconstruction of dado of marble revetment (1968).

Fig. 264 Skoutlosis fragments of two pilasters and panel (L. J. Majewski, 1966).

Fig. 265 Skoutlosis patterns arranged by J. Herrmann.

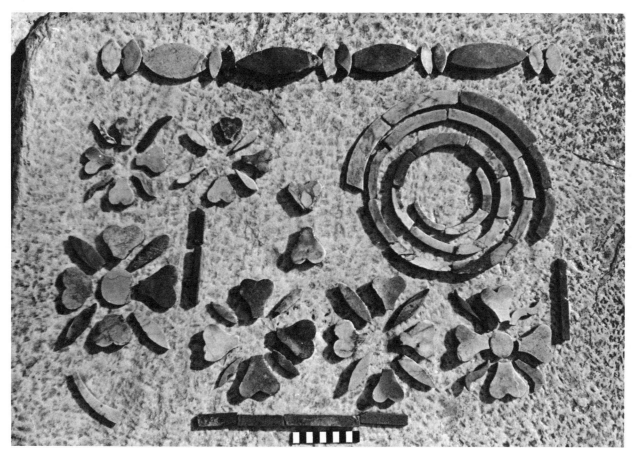

Fig. 266 Torah shrine and south wall with restored revetment panels.

Fig. 267   Bipod photograph of mosaic area with
the inscription of Samoe, priest and teacher of wisdom (*sophodidaskalos*) and the stone bases for a
structure (Bima?). Photograph J. Whittlesey.

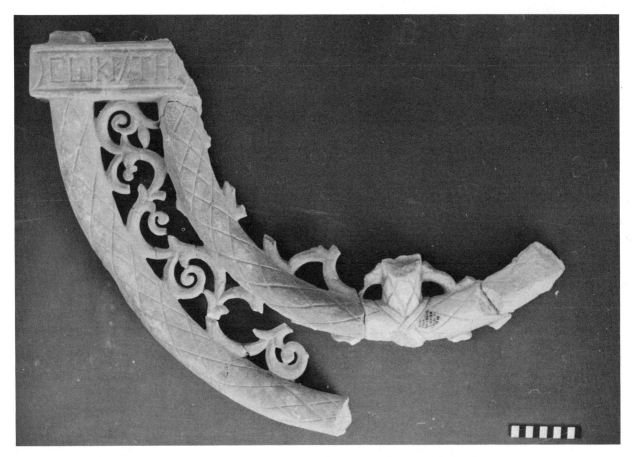

Fig. 268 Part of large marble menorah given by sculptor Socrates (IN 63.130; S 63.50; P.H.: 0.565 m.).

Fig. 269 Hebrew inscription: "Shalom" (IN 62.66; two pieces, W. of A: 0.12 m.; W. of B: 0.145 m.).

Fig. 270 Donors' inscription of Regina, her husband, and children: "From Bounties of Almighty God" (IN 62.37–38).

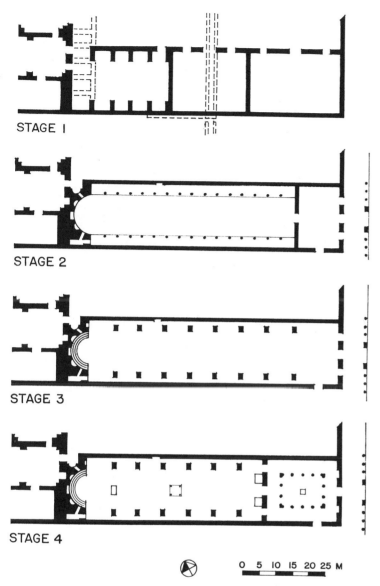

STAGE 1

STAGE 2

STAGE 3

STAGE 4

0 5 10 15 20 25 M

Fig. 271 Plan of four stages of Synagogue building (A. R. Seager).

Fig. 272 Base of Aurelius Basileides, a Roman Imperial official (IN 63.92; H: 0.44 m.).

Fig. 273 Glass weight with menorah (G 67.5; diam.: 0.017 m.).

Fig. 274 East wall of Main Hall with south shrine restored.

Fig. 275 *Nomophylakion,* "Place of Custody of the Law." Inscription of the donor Memnonios who gave the marble revetment (IN 63.124).

IN. 63.124

Fig. 276 "Find, Open, Read, Observe." Marble shield with admonition (about reading of Scripture?) (IN 63.77; H: 0.205 m.; W: 0.365 m.).

Fig. 277 Marble medallion from wall decoration of Main Hall invoking "Blessing upon the House (Synagogue)" (IN 63.43; H: 0.295 m.).

Fig. 278 Mosaic inscription of Count Paul (*Comes Paulus*).

Fig. 279 Cleaning reset mosaic in Bay 5 (L. J. Majewski, J. Sultanian, 1975).

Fig. 280 Synagogue after restoration (1973),
looking southeast. Lower left: corner of Palaestra;
lower right: Halls C and B of the gymnasium and
Main Avenue.

Fig. 281 Basin with crosses. Byzantine Shop W8.

Fig. 283   Bronze embers shovel with dolphins and cross (M 58.64; L: 0.136 m.). House of Bronzes.

Fig. 282   Red ware plate with Latin cross (P 67.2; diam. of plate: 0.13 m.). "Restaurant" Shop E1.

Fig. 284   Church M before restoration with inner and outer apse visible (1961).

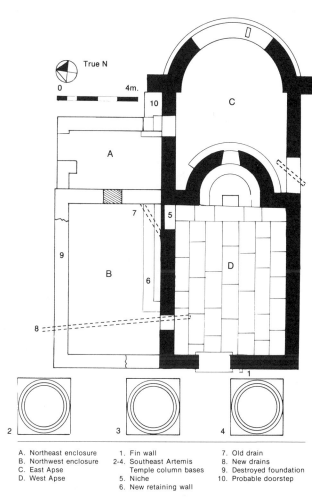

A. Northeast enclosure
B. Northwest enclosure
C. East Apse
D. West Apse

1. Fin wall
2-4. Southeast Artemis
Temple column bases
5. Niche
6. New retaining wall

7. Old drain
8. New drains
9. Destroyed foundation
10. Probable doorstep

Fig. 285 Church M after restoration (1973) with Artemis Temple, looking west.

Fig. 286 Church M: plan with adjacent units.

Fig. 287 Church D, looking southeast.

Fig. 288 Early Christian Basilica EA (large apse)
and Lascarid Church E, looking west.

Fig. 289 Early Christian Basilica EA with Church
E and graves. Field plan (1981).

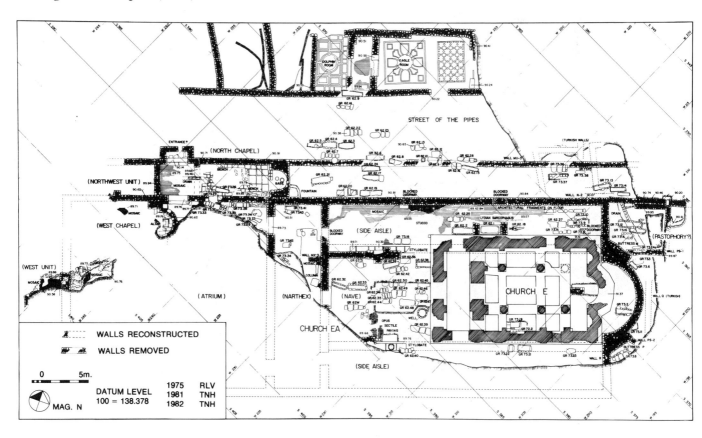

Fig. 290 Early Christian Church EA: mosaic in north aisle, looking east. On the right: podium of later Church E.

Fig. 291 Church E: pseudocrypt with most of marble floor removed. Grave 73.19 underneath.

Fig. 292   Glass bottle (G 72.1; H: 0.077 m.) from Grave 72.2.

Fig. 293   Marble closure slab inscribed *tos archi-diakon* (IN 73.11; H: 0.15 m.).

Fig. 294   Lascarid Church E: restored plan with quadratura diagram (H. Buchwald).

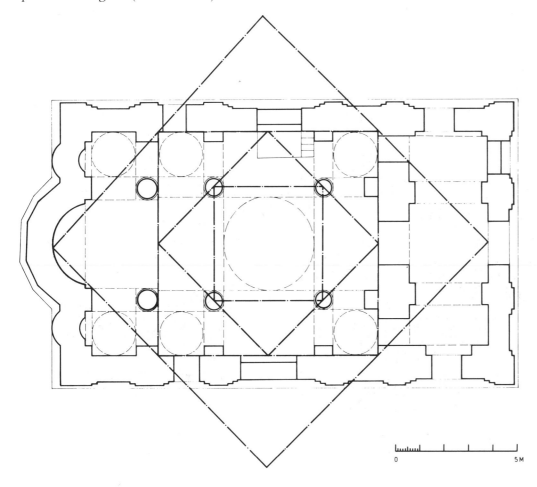

0   5 M

Fig. 295   Lascarid Church E: exterior of major
apse with brick frieze of quatrefoils (1972).

Fig. 296 Fresco from "Peacock Tomb": peacock,
small birds, rose basket. Manisa Museum.

Fig. 297 Tomb of Flavius Chrysanthios: fresco on
south wall with Christian invocation "God Help"
(Grave 76.1).

Fig. 299   Bronze ring with archangel from mass burial at Duman Tepe (M 66.1; diam. of ring: 0.025 m.). Sixth century.

Fig. 298   PN, mosaic suite, detail of "Eagle Mosaic" (eagle), ca. A.D. 400.

Index

Ancient authors are indexed here by name with the textual references in italics. Biblical references are indexed under New Testament and Old Testament.

Herodotus (*Continued*)
  1.94, 38, 55, 248n59
  3.48, 245n66
  5.49.5, 38
  5.99–102, 44
  5.100–101, 12, 34, 75
  7.32, 100
Hierapolis, Phrygia, 181
Hilarius, 194
Hittite
  archives, 24
  cremation cemetery, 22
  empire, 67, 68
  names, and Lydian, 24
  sherds and arrowhead, 22, 68
  survivals, 84
  see also Bogazköy
Hipponax, 89; *Masson fr. 42,* 57, 58
Homer, *Iliad 4.131–137,* 11,
  222n33; *4.141–145,* 80
Horse, 6, 85; *see also* Equids
Horseman, 6, 85, Figs. 142, 143,
  156
House of Bronzes (HoB)
  bronze-working at, 24, 105
  burn level, 28
  cemetery, 122, 205
  chamber tombs, 123, 208
  Christian: church official, 168; li-
    turgical objects, 192
  comparative stratigraphy of, 25
  construction, Lydian, 27, 30–31,
    74
  Cretan seals, 22
  destruction of, 122
  economic situation of, 28, 147
  flooding of, 20, 26
  glass, 24
  housing (Late Antique), 147
  iron, 24
  Iron Age, 27
  pithos burial, 26, 33
  pithos/cremation burial, 20–22,
    23
  Roman garden at, 143
  under Seleucid rule, 122
  shops, 81
  stone objects, 22
  under Persians, 101
House of Priest, 34, 36
  architecture, 72
  Lydian layout, 72
  Scythian bird found in, 95
  see also Pactolus North
Hunting, 6, 85; *see also* Boar
Hydrology, 4
Hypaipa
  Artaxerxes II's rule, 100
  Artemis-Anahita cult, 135
  games (Artemisia), 129
  Synagogue donor, 171
  textiles, 11

Ikiztepe, chamber tomb, 105
Imperial Arms Factory, 10, 11, 147,
  191; Chrysanthios, official of,
  205, 208

Imperial cult, 135, 145
  Artemis Temple, 120
  at Ephesus, 150
  Marble Court, 149–150, 155,
    194
  see also Ruler cult
Indere, graves at, 60, 63–64, 66
Industry at Sardis, 9–13
Inhumation, 19, 20, 62
  chamber tombs, 124
  rock-cut tombs, 59
Inscriptions, *see* Carian inscriptions;
  Greek inscriptions; Hebrew in-
  scriptions; Languages; Lydian
  inscriptions; Lydian-Aramaic
Iollas, priest of Roma, 114, 125,
  135, 137
Ionian Revolt of 499 B.C., 44, 52,
  68; *see also* Darius I
Iron, 9, 78
  in "Hardware Shops," 11, 24
  Lydian iron working, 78
  objects, 11, 24
  spearhead, 63
  tools, earliest, 212
Iron Age, *see* Early Iron Age
Iulia Severa, *see* Severa
Ivory, 11–12

Jacob (the Elder or Presbyter), 165,
  166; *see also* Byzantine Shops
Jerusalem, 166, 179
Jewish community, 140, 166, 174,
  182
  at Aphrodisias, 181
  of Asia, 180–182
  at Miletus, 180
  at Sardis, 156, 168, 176, 178–
    190
  see also Judaism; Rome; Synagogue
Josephus, *Antiquitates Judaicae,* 179
Judaism, 135–136, 178, 185–186;
  see also Jewish community; Synagogue
Julia Lydia, *see* Lydia
Justus, restorer of pagan temples,
  194

Kagirlik Tepe, cemetery, 144;
  painted chamber tomb, 207
Kaisersäle, see Imperial Cult; Marble
  Court
Kait (pre-Hittite goddess), 92
Kandytes, 105
Kaoueis, see Kaveś
Kapelos, 80
Karniyarik Tepe, *see* Gyges mound;
  Royal Mound
Kaveś, 84, 85
Kazar Tepe, *see* Miletus
Kelainai, 102; *see also* Apamea
  (Phrygia)
Keskinler, village, 13
Kestelli, tomb at, 54
Kilns, 9, 78, 110, 122–123, 151

Kimmerians, 6, 10, 29, 68, 80
  destruction by, 43, 238n5
  invasions by, 28, 41
  skeletal remains of victims of, 63
Kir Mutaf Tepe, 58; *see also* Bin
  Tepe
Klaros, oracle of Apollo, 94
Knucklebones, Lydian, 64, 90
Koraia/Aktia festival, 131
Kore, 52, 74, 92–93, 135, 155,
  265n20
  Artemis, 129, 265n20
  Children of, 92, 131, 147
  on Roman coins, 92
  see also Chrysanthina festival
Koros, 151
Kubaba, see Kuvana
Kuş Tepe, 61
Kuvana, 36, 65, 72, 74, 88, 91–92,
  95; *see also* Cybele
Kyriak(us) graffito with cross, 166

Lamps
  Hellenistic, Roman, 175–176
  Lydian, 79, Fig. 140
Land use, 5
Landslides, 1, 3, 43
Languages, in Sardis, 87
  unknown on inscription, 88–89
  see also Carian inscriptions; Hit-
    tite; Luvian; Lydian; Lydian-
    Aramaic
Laodice, Queen, 110, 113, 116, 134
  of Antiochus II, 119
  Artemis Temple, 120
Laodiceia, city, 181–182
Lascarid rule, 204; *see also* Church E
Late Bronze Age, Sardis, 20, 33,
  46, 212
  burial, 21–22
  hut, 33
  monochrome ware, 23
  pithos burial, 20, 33
  see also Bronze Age
Late Stone Age, 211–212; *see also*
  Neolithic
Lead, 8–9, 41
Leatherwork, 11
Leontioi, tribe, 184
Lepidus, Claudius Antonius, 145,
  148
Levs, god, 93, 132, Fig. 144; *see also*
  Zeus (Lydian)
Libation
  at burial, 64
  Croesus pouring, Fig. 126
Libonianus, Lucius Iulius, 144
Lime kilns, 13, 151; *see also* Kilns
Limestone, 3
Limyra, 103, 106
Lion, 6, 184
  and Cybele, 6, 37, 84, 95
  Hittite, 84
  of Meles, 45
Lion-Eagle monument, 50; *see also*
  Bakivalis; *Nannas*
Literacy, in Lydia, 88, 97